The Atlantic World

To Ron,
whose work, judicious
scholarship has served as a
model for me, but whose friendship and
corporate, I value even
more.
BEST, Dan

For Ron,
with best wishes,
Alison Games

The Atlantic World:
A History, 1400–1888

Douglas R. Egerton
Le Moyne College

Alison Games
Georgetown University

Jane G. Landers
Vanderbilt University

Kris Lane
College of William and Mary

Donald R. Wright
State University of New York at Cortland

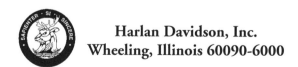

Harlan Davidson, Inc.
Wheeling, Illinois 60090-6000

Visit us on the World Wide Web at www.harlandavidson.com.

Library of Congress Cataloging-in-Publication Data

The Atlantic world : a history, 1400–1888 / Douglas R. Egerton ... [et al.].
    p. cm.
 ISBN-13: 978-0-88295-245-1 (alk. paper)
 1. History, Modern. 2. Civilization, Modern. 3. Atlantic Ocean—History. I.
Egerton, Douglas R.
 D210.A78 2007
 9 09'.09821—dc22

                                      2006030404

Cover photograph: A replica of Christopher Columbus's ship, *Niña*. Credit
AP Photo/*The Ledger Independent*, Terry Prather.
Cover design: Chris Calvetti, c2itgraphics.

Manufactured in the United States of America
09 08 07 1 2 3 MG

Table of Contents

Europe supported by Africa & America.

"Europe supported by Africa and America," from volume two of John Gabriel Stedman's Narrative of a Five Year Expedition *(London: 1796). Image courtesy of the Lilly Library, Indiana University, Bloomington.*

Introduction

Perhaps the best way to begin a history of the Atlantic world is to define Atlantic history. Generally, it is the study of the history of the people living in a geographic region: the four continents that surround the Atlantic Ocean. More specifically, it focuses on the societies transformed by the convergence of cultures following Christopher Columbus's momentous voyage in 1492. These societies are not necessarily places along the Atlantic Ocean itself—one thinks immediately, for example, of Peru, or the region surrounding the North American Great Lakes, or the rivers and valleys reaching deep into the interior of Africa. Indeed, places and people on the Pacific coast of the Americas became engaged in processes that originated in the Atlantic, just as Africans who lived hundreds of miles from the west coast found themselves ensnared in the Atlantic slave trade, even as new foods and drinks from the Americas were altering diets in Europe, Africa, and Asia. Many Native Americans who never laid eyes on a European or an African saw their lives changed radically by pathogens, animals, and plants that had arrived from across the ocean. Nor is Atlantic history limited to the literal points of contact—ports, traders, or migrants, for example—but rather it seeks to explain how conditions, experiences, and events in one place shaped and were shaped by conditions, experiences, and events in another place.

Admittedly, the Atlantic world is a geographic unit that many people in the past may never have conceptualized. What one today calls the Atlantic Ocean people living centuries ago perceived as several distinct seas. Similarly, the regions now labeled the North and South American continents are constructs of the modern mind. Well into the nineteenth century, no one had an accurate idea of what these landmasses looked like, or even whether they were connected to Asia. Therefore, the major components of Atlantic history—two of the four continents and the ocean itself—reflect the modern imposition of an analytic unit.

Nevertheless, this unit of analysis is valuable because it is explanatory. If people in the past often failed to see the larger geographic framework within which the events of their lives transpired, we historians—blessed and encumbered by hindsight—can appreciate the context. We know that the diseases that ravaged American populations came from thousands of miles away in

Europe and Africa; we know that the political opportunities indigenous people in strategic locations enjoyed derived from imperial rivalries elsewhere; we know that staple crops in modern Africa (peanuts, cassava) and in Europe (potatoes) were species unique to the Americas that had traveled across the ocean, just as it seems that a type of rice from West Africa, brought to the Americas on slave ships, was one of the ancestral plants of "Carolina gold," which brought great wealth to planters on the floodplains of South Carolina. By any number of measures, this world was linked. And it was linked in ways that often bore no relationship to the political boundaries that customarily shape the work most historians do. Atlantic history, then, is history without borders.

Students have an especially difficult time grasping this concept, and it is easy to see why. From the time they enter elementary school, most young people are taught that the history of their nation stands apart from, even above, the larger flow of global history, the latter considered a separate subject and one not typically encountered, if at all, until the college level. Unfortunately, not all professional historians have a much broader vision. Trained, as most of us are, to focus on a tiny portion of the globe over an equally narrow span of time, we easily fall victim to compartmentalized conceptions of the past—as well as to our professional need to stay current in our chosen, carefully bounded field. The result is that we frequently attempt to force transnational sagas into artificial political frameworks, or fail to see the broad connections that, ironically, far less educated people in earlier centuries instinctively understood. What possible meaning could national histories or political boundaries hold for an African captured well inland from the Atlantic, transported across the ocean in chains, then sold into slavery in Saint Domingue or South Carolina? Today most people who live in the Atlantic basin reflexively regard themselves as French or Brazilian or Canadian or American—a term, of course, that any resident of the Americas might embrace. But for a period characterized by constantly shifting populations, borders, and political loyalties, and at best a vague sense of nationalism, the study of the history of a single nation or people makes increasingly little sense.

Equally complicated is the question of time. If the beginning of Atlantic history—the point at which an Atlantic world forms—is relatively fixed in the fifteenth century, with the commencement of trade between Europe and west coastal Africa followed closely by Columbus's voyage to the Caribbean in 1492, the ending point is more fluid. The age of revolution and independence (through 1825) marks one possible ending, and the abolition of slavery in the Western Hemisphere (by 1888) marks another. We have elected to end this text with the abolition of slavery in the western Atlantic. Although this decision is an arbitrary one, the important trends in the nineteenth century reflected both the diminished coherence of the Atlantic as a self-contained unit of analysis and the nascent but unmistakable rise of global history.

Within the space of the four centuries considered herein, we adopted an Atlantic perspective to explore commonalities and convergences, seeking larger patterns derived from the new interactions of people around, within, and across the Atlantic. By no means, however, do we posit that the Atlantic ever formed a self-contained entity. It may be a coherent unit of analysis and understanding, but never was it a singular, uniform, or harmonious region. While people in the Atlantic world might have shared common ordeals that recurred over time in different places, marked variations always existed, so no single perspective, no single narrative on the Atlantic emerges. Recently the historian David Armitage identified three different types of Atlantic history: "circum-Atlantic history," which examines the Atlantic experience as a whole, and which is the main thrust of our book; "trans-Atlantic history," which emphasizes a comparative approach; and "cis-Atlantic history," which looks at a particular place within an Atlantic context. We offer one possible narrative within which to make sense of the interconnected Atlantic world over four centuries, but we appreciate that there are other stories one might tell.

There is also the question of what perspective to adopt. Such pioneering accounts as R. R. Palmer's classic 1959 study of *The Age of the Democratic Revolution* assumed a political viewpoint. In the early historical literature, actors such as Toussaint Louverture enjoyed the occasional cameo, but only when their sagas directly affected European or North American diplomacy. More recently, social historians analyzing Atlantic history have applied a bottom-up perspective, which pays special attention to common persons and assumes that their histories are every bit as crucial as are those of a king or a president in explaining the making of the modern world. Our approach embraces both perspectives. In the same way that we highlight connections between the many corners of the Atlantic world, we emphasize the endless interplay between classes, races, and genders. That is, this text explicitly recognizes the reality of power relations in all of their many forms, from that of king to peasant, master to slave, merchant to mariner, and man to woman. And while it is critical to stress how laboring people helped to create the societies described in this study, one should never forget that decisions made in London or Paris or Washington City or Bogotá not only affected the lives of millions of people in England or France or the United States or Colombia, but the lives of millions in Angola or Barbados or Quebec. As the wars of independence and revolution dragged on into the early nineteenth century, for example, coastal towns in the south of Britain and the north of France were nearly as plundered of young men and economically devastated as was any village in west Africa in the previous century, and no study should fail to take into account the men and women in power who chose to wage wars or create powerful commercial engines such as the Royal Africa Company or le Compagnie de Sénégal.

Regardless of the approach one takes to it, Atlantic history has come into its own. Although the existence of an Atlantic perspective dates from the middle of the twentieth century, the emergence of a cadre of scholars for whom Atlantic history offers a powerful explanatory tool is a distinguishing feature of the past two decades. These scholars tend overwhelmingly to represent particular fields: colonial history, the African diaspora, economic history, and increasingly British history. For colonial historians, well accustomed to juggling multiple perspectives and integrating European and American history, Atlantic perspectives come naturally. Historians of colonial North America have eagerly pursued an Atlantic context, which has helped them take early American history out from under the shadow of the new United States and its attendant nationalism. Greatly bolstered by the support of Harvard University's International Seminar on the History of the Atlantic World, under the direction of Bernard Bailyn, historians engaged in different aspects of Atlantic history find regular opportunities to present research in seminars, colloquia, and workshops. A new interdisciplinary journal, *Atlantic Studies*, provides another forum for research. Colleges and universities now advertise for positions in Atlantic history, offer lower- and upper-level courses in Atlantic history, and some institutions offer graduate students the opportunity to pursue degrees in Atlantic history. Yet despite the growing visibility of the field, no true survey of the Atlantic world existed. We collaborated on this book to remedy that deficiency by providing college-level students with an accessible, engaging, and thought-provoking narrative of the ways in which the people surrounding the Atlantic world found their lives transformed after 1400.

Although we do consider this book a survey text, by no means did we create a composite history, one in which we included the "greatest hits" from each region of the four different continents; rather, we tell a history of interactions. Our history of the Atlantic world contains many of the stories one will find in histories of its component places, but throughout we have highlighted the Atlantic contexts and repercussions of historical changes. The Reformation, for example, might get short shrift here compared to its coverage in a history of Europe, but our intent is not to detail the events of the period so much as to illustrate the connections between an event of historical importance in one part of the Atlantic world and changes unfolding in another. Therefore, an occurrence that might seem fundamental to the history of an individual nation might not even appear in our text—the Long Parliament, the Philadelphia Constitutional convention of 1787, the nineteenth-century Muslim jihads that created states across the interior of West Africa—because of our emphasis on connections. We also tried to incorporate the experiences of all Atlantic people, and in so doing purposely departed from a discussion of the region as a place divided between a *New* and an *Old* World, terms which in scholars' hands have tended to reflect a Eurocentric perspective: we argue here that every place around the Atlantic was transformed into something new by the exchanges that commenced in the fifteenth century. Nowhere was change modest or incremental, whether measured in diet or political power, mortality or access to new commodities. We have, by necessity and by deliberate choice, been selective, preferring to illustrate larger themes and trends through extended examples rather than trying to include everything relevant.

Method

In the course of our collaborative venture, we generally departed from the customary practice in multi-authored textbooks of assigning discrete chapters to individual authors. We individually drafted chapters or significant portions thereof, but then each one of us rewrote and reshaped the text in an effort to pool our different vantages on the Atlantic world. We ripped apart one early version of the book in order to reframe the entire project to bring into focus the interactions that interested us. We found in the course of our reading, writing, and collaboration that our different fields are separated by important historiographic traditions that make it difficult at times to see similarities and convergences. Historians of nineteenth-century Latin America, for example, think about liberalism, modernization, and state formation in ways unfamiliar to historians of North America. We also found that specialists in different fields use different terms to describe the same events and the same people. While it is easy to see such differences in the various names ascribed to conflicts (King William's War or the Nine Years' War), people (Pocahontas or Rebecca; Marina or Malintzin), or places (Derry or Londonderry; the Falklands or the Malvinas; Tenochtitlán or Mexico City; the Oil Rivers or the Niger Delta; Mahicanituk or Deer River or the Hudson River), the problem of terminology became more complex when we tried to figure out how best to describe entire categories of people. The Americanist's *hybrid*, for example, is the Africanist's *creole*. If North American Indian history has become a tale of tribes, with tribal affiliation the crux of modern Indian identity, in African history, tribalism is not a universally accepted category of analysis. Specialists in one region use *native* to describe indigenous people; elsewhere, that word is taboo. Canadians prefer *First Nations*; Americans waffle among *American Indian*, *Native American*, and *Amerindian*.

We found similarly profound problems of periodization. As we tried to view different events from multiple perspectives, we learned that characterizations of one place might not apply elsewhere. One place's age of revolution was another's age of imperial conquest; one nation's peace was another nation's enduring war as, for example, many British-allied North American Indian tribes found out in the wake of the Treaty of Paris of 1783, which was signed without their participation or consent. We have disagreed about the importance of nations, and we have argued about the relative importance of certain actors within the Atlantic. If we have learned and profited enormously from the process of collaboration, we also frequently had to compromise, to agree on a single language even if it jarred our professional sensibilities, to settle—finally—on one perspective or one narrative even if we could have argued forcefully and interminably for another.

The subjects we have included emphasize both our particular professional interests and an effort to let the text reflect what we see as some of the determinative constraints on people's lives. Three of us have an approach to the Atlantic centered on Africa, Africans, or people of African descent. With this perspective we hope to redress the conventional neglect of Africa and Africans in Atlantic histories generally focused on the differential of power in Europe and the colonization of the Americas. Two of us come from a perspective of colonial American history; one of us works in the history of a new nation. Atlantic history often has served as shorthand for a history of English America, which is largely an unintended consequence of the initiative colonial historians from all fields have expended in recent decades to generate a new style of transatlantic research and analysis. So while our own interests do shape this text, we were careful to emphasize other themes as well, including environmental and geographic constraints, disease environments, migration, adaptation, and power. Collectively we have taught students at every level, and of every ability; throughout we sought to make this book something that will be of value and interest to all of them.

Selected Readings

Armitage, David, and Michael J. Braddick, eds., *The British Atlantic World, 1500–1800* (New York: Palgrave Macmillan, 2002).

"The Atlantic World," *Organization of American Historians Magazine of History* 18, no. 3 (April, 2004).

Bailyn, Bernard, "The Idea of Atlantic History," *Itinerario* 20, no. 3: 19–44.

———, *Atlantic History: Concept and Contours* (Cambridge, MA: Harvard University Press, 2005).

Games, Alison, "Atlantic History: Definitions, Challenges, and Opportunities," *American Historical Review* 111 no. 3 (June 2006): 741–57.

Thornton, John, *Africa and Africans in the Making of the Atlantic World, 1400–1800*, 2nd ed. (Cambridge: Cambridge University Press, 1998).

*El Mina, the slave trading fortress of the Portuguese on the African Gold Coast. Detail from
the Catalan Atlas, 1502. Credit: The Granger Collection, New York.*

Chapter One

Conceptualizing the Atlantic World

> *Continents are local; ocean is world.*
> R. Buckminster Fuller

The year 1434 was not one of particular note around the world. In Europe, where populations had not fully recovered from nearly a century of bubonic plague, Italians were putting the finishing touches on the magnificent dome of the cathedral in Florence, Germans were tinkering with a way to print with movable type, and Christians in Istanbul were wondering how much longer they could hold out (it would be nineteen years) against the Ottoman Turks. In West Africa, desert-based raiders had seized Timbuktu from the Mali Empire, while across the continent, Coptic Christians in Ethiopia were hewing churches out of rock; to the south, stonemasons were topping off the ten-foot-high, mortar-free wall around Great Zimbabwe. In the Americas, the Iroquois Confederacy was forming in what is now upstate New York and southern Ontario, Aztecs in present-day Mexico were conquering Oaxaca, and farther south, in the Andes, Incas were readying military campaigns to make their empire grand and, they hoped, lasting.

But two events of 1434, transpiring halfway around the world from one another and centered not on land but at sea, held great importance for people of Europe, Africa, and the Americas. In the South China Sea, the mariner Zheng He, at the head of a massive fleet of the largest seagoing vessels the world had known, was nearing Canton on his return from a seventh voyage across the Indian Ocean, 7,000 miles in each direction. At the same time, Gil Eanes, the captain of a lone ship, departed the harbor of Lisbon, Portugal, headed for the northwest African coast, just a few hundred miles away. No Chinese sailor would retrace Zheng He's route for centuries to come, but many European sailors would follow in Eanes's wake—and soon.

The first half of the fifteenth century was a time of great sailing exploits. A new Ming emperor, Yong Le, first sponsored Zheng He's fleets beginning in 1405. On successive voyages over the next quarter century he sailed to Southeast Asia, India, the Persian Gulf, and East Africa. The Ming were eager to open trade connections and demonstrate the power and authority of imperial China. The typical fleet under Zheng He's command consisted of several hundred vessels carrying tens of thousands of soldiers. Many of his ships were nine-masted "treasure ships," 400 feet long and 160 feet wide, with four decks that could stow enormous amounts of cargo (including, on one return voyage, an East African giraffe and, on another, 300 Korean virgins). These voyages were the grandest ocean-going ventures up to their time, but they did not lead to long-term increase in maritime trade, expansion of Chinese political authority, or mingling of Chinese culture with that of Indians, Persians, or Africans. After Zheng He's seventh and longest venture, the state withdrew support for such activity and concentrated on its land-based empire, agriculture, and protection from Mongol raiders. The treasure ships stood bobbing in the Canton quay, pulling at their ropes like dogs straining at the leash, until broken up for other uses or rotting away.

At the same moment, thousands of miles away and entirely unknown to his Chinese counterparts—even to all but a handful of his fellow Europeans—the less-accomplished Portuguese mariner Gil Eanes was heading south and west in an armed barque of two masts, only 130 feet long and 45 feet wide, riding the wind and current along the coast of northwest Africa from his home base on the southwestern edge of Europe. Eanes may have feared the worst, for no one he knew had ever returned from a venture beyond Cape Bojador, an extension of the Sahara Desert that projects into the Atlantic Ocean two hundred miles south of the Canary Islands. Not many were eager to try. Violent waves lash the northern side of the cape, which is flanked by shallows and often blanketed in fog. Rumors abounded of the Great Green Sea that lay beyond and the desolate lands it washed. Gomes Eanes de Azurara, the royal chronicler of these voyages, summarized the talk among mariners: "That beyond this Cape there is no race of men nor place of inhabitants: nor is the land less sandy than the deserts of Libya, where there is no water, no tree, no green herb." Some of what the sailors said carried more truth: that beyond Bojador "the currents are so terrible that no ship having once passed the Cape, will ever be able to return." While no one knew exactly how many mariners had left Portugal over the years intending to round the cape and win lasting glory, everyone knew exactly how many had succeeded: none.

Gil Eanes changed that. With the moral and fiscal encouragement of his patron, the Infante Dom Henrique, brother of the king of Portugal, upon whom writers much later bestowed the misleading title "Henry the Navigator," Eanes raised his barque's sails to the north wind and pointed its bow toward the African coast. The prince told Eanes "To strain every nerve to pass that Cape," that he could not "find a peril so great that the hope of reward will not be greater." Perhaps it was thoughts of such a payoff that brought Eanes to screw up his courage and head so far into the unknown. In any case, he did so handily, doubling the cape after a mere two weeks at sea and, once past the previous physical and psychological barrier, lowering a boat into the water and stepping out on the African shore. He found no sign of human habitation, but he dug some herbs to take back to his patron. With this evidence of his success, Eanes turned toward home. Accomplishing the necessary tacking maneuvers against current and wind to head back toward Portugal took twice as long as did the voyage out, not to mention hard work, but joy must have swelled the hearts of Eanes and his small crew as they entered the Tagus River leading to Lisbon.

Atlantic Distance and Time

We tend not to consider the Atlantic Ocean much of a barrier in these days of jet travel, when a trip between London and New York lasts a few hours and North American college students think little of spending spring break in Spain or Italy. But for intercontinental travelers of not long ago, the Atlantic was a body of water to contend with. In January 1943, when United States president Franklin D. Roosevelt and British prime minister Winston Churchill met in Casablanca, Morocco, to plan allied efforts in World War II, Roosevelt's staff had to find the narrowest part of the ocean for crossing. Fuel capacity was limited in the airplanes of the day. Thus, Roosevelt's trip was an indirect and long one. The presidential party took a train from Washington, D.C., to Miami, Florida, where they boarded a seaplane for a flight to Trinidad and then to Belem, south of the Amazon River in Brazil. From there they made a 2,100-mile

Atlantic crossing. Nineteen hours after leaving Brazil the plane touched down in the estuary of West Africa's Gambia River, where Britain had a colony. The flight on to Casablanca was another 1,600 miles. Thus, the 3,600-mile direct "hop" across the Atlantic required more than 7,000 miles of traveling and ate up forty-six flying hours and twenty-six hours by rail.

But Roosevelt was lucky. Twenty-five years earlier President Woodrow Wilson had to cross the ocean by ship to attend the Versailles peace conference, outside Paris. Wilson plowed through the Atlantic in December 1918 aboard the steamship George Washington *to arrive in Brest, France, thirteen days after leaving Hoboken, New Jersey. And this would have seemed like flying to Benjamin Franklin, envoy of England's rebellious American colonies to France, who spent six weeks of 1776 under sail to reach his foreign post.*

Sailing ships passing the peak of Tenerife, Canary Islands, 1800s. Hand-colored woodcut. Copyright © North Wind/North Wind Picture Archives, GATL3A-00018.

In contrast to his Ming counterparts, Prince Henry could not act quickly enough to send more sailors down the route Eanes had charted. Some time in the 1440s a succession of Portuguese mariners guided their vessels to the vicinity of Cape Verde, the western tip of Africa, and then discovered that if they stood far out to sea and headed northwesterly toward the Azores, they eventually would catch the winds that blew faithfully out of the west toward Europe. This would quickly become the standard route home for voyages past what had been the point of no return. No single discovery was of greater importance for opening the Atlantic to European shipping. Hardly a generation later, Portuguese sailors passed the equator off the central African coast, and before the end of the century a Genoese sailor under Spanish sponsor-

Maps and Our Sense of Things

It is probably important to recognize how much our ideas of the size, shape, and importance of the world's lands and seas—and the people who inhabit and sail them—are influenced by the way we view them on maps. The world maps we see are projections onto flat paper of the global sphere, so they require distortion. Nearly all modern maps emphasize the inhabited landmasses rather than the uninhabited seas, so one does not get a proper notion that 71 percent of the earth's surface is water, and nearly all of that ocean. Our maps tend to have Africa and

Europe near their center, with Asia stretching out eastward and the Americas, across the bounded Atlantic, to the west. This projection shows the Pacific Ocean cut in two and thus fails to provide a proper understanding of the relative size of that body to other oceans. The Pacific has roughly twice the surface area of the Atlantic and is more than twice as wide at its maximum breadth. The Indian Ocean has 80 percent of the Atlantic's surface area and is equally as wide.

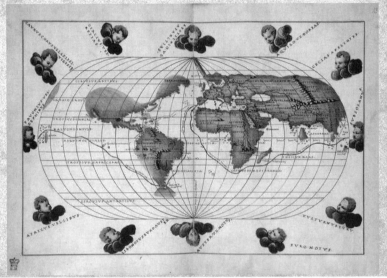

Global map from a Portolan atlas, circa 1545, showing routes of Magellan's circumnavigation and route from Potosí to Seville, with heads representing the winds on the border. Copyright © The British Library. Record: 2630, Shelfmark: Add. 18154, Page Folio: ff.12v-13.

ship crossed the Atlantic Ocean and returned with tales of what Europeans hailed as new lands filled with new people and potential wealth.

Eanes's voyage was a short one, but it was crucial for the transformation of the Atlantic from a barrier to a conduit for intercontinental contact. By the early sixteenth century, and with growing speed thereafter, the ocean that for thousands of years had separated the seeds and microbes, as well as the soils, people, plants, and animals, of the Americas from those of Africa and Europe became the means for passing back and forth these inert and living things, as well as ideas, religious beliefs, material goods, and political power. The voyage Eanes took in 1434, which must have seemed at the time to portend far less than that of Zheng He, stands symbolically for initiating contact among all four continents bordering the Atlantic Ocean. Indeed, one might think of Eanes's venture, a trip that took him less than a thousand miles from home, as the first step toward the creation of an Atlantic world that would come to affect the lives of millions of people to the present day.

The Atlantic and Its Continental Boundaries

Of course, Eanes and his mates saw only a tiny part of the ocean that stretches in the shape of a fat "S" between the frozen Arctic Ocean in the north and the ice floes of Antarctica in the south, lapping the western coasts of Europe and Africa and the eastern shores of North and South America in between. The Portuguese sailors had no way of knowing how much the Atlantic is a bundle of contrasts, or of sensing how much its size and shape, its winds and currents, and its accessibility and bounty would affect human history.

"It must have been something of a ditch when it all began," writes the late distinguished sailor and author Alan Villiers of the Atlantic. When it all began was less than 200 million years ago, when the bodies of land we know of as the Americas began to pull away from earth's singular landmass of the time, Pangaea. Thus began a long, slow, and continuing episode of what geologists call continental drift. But for the period of human activity, the last few million years, the Atlantic has been much more than a ditch. At its greatest east-west width, around 25 degrees north latitude, the ocean stretches 4,500 miles between West Africa and Mexico; at its narrowest, between Liberia and Brazil, it spans 1,800 miles. The average breadth of the ocean, 3,000 miles, is roughly the distance between New York and San Francisco.

The size of the Atlantic pales in comparison to that of the mammoth Pacific Ocean, and the Atlantic has only one-fifth more water than does the Indian Ocean. As mentioned, Zheng He traveled 7,000 miles as he traversed the South China Sea and Indian Ocean westward to Africa. Christopher Columbus's voyage almost sixty years later, from Spain to the Caribbean, was half that distance. The Atlantic is also a relatively shallow ocean, with an abundance of continental shelf extending well out from both its western and eastern shores. Where it does reach considerable depth in basins toward its middle, a long, generally north-south ridge juts up from the ocean floor. Lava welling up from this ridge annually increases the distance between Africa and South America and has even created a few volcanic islands—the Azores in the North Atlantic, for instance, and Tristan de Cunha in the South Atlantic. So in terms of relative breadth and depth, the Atlantic does not seem all that formidable.

But parts of the Atlantic remain fearsome to sailors, fishermen, and their loved ones even today. One need not try arguing the ocean's lesser relative features to residents of nations around the North Atlantic, from Norway and Scotland down past Cape St. Vincent, Europe's southwestern tip, or on down to the high-breaking surf along the western coast of Africa. The North Atlantic waters, writes Villiers, "do not 'wash' the coasts: they thrash them violently, turbulently, without end. From the Point of Sagres near St. Vincent to the North Cape of Norway, the wild challenge of Atlantic gales has screamed for a billion years, and the coastline that survives the onslaught is harsh and strewn with offshore rocks, over which the sea boils with fury."

Seafarers made progress more easily in kinder seas. Long before the great fifteenth-century Chinese voyages, Arabs, Persians, and Indians rode predictable monsoon winds back and forth across the Indian Ocean. The clear skies, calm seas, and steady wind made sailing these waters relatively easy, even in small and simply rigged ships. Such features made possible Indonesian settlement of Madagascar and patches of the East African coast centuries before the modern era. South Pacific waters were similarly benign. Long before Columbus, Polynesians in outrigger canoes voyaged across many thousands of miles in that ocean. Likewise the Mediterranean, an inland sea connecting to the Atlantic, made for easy travel in the days of Greeks, Carthaginians, and Romans, all of whom crisscrossed those waters in bulky and awkward galleys that would not have lasted minutes in an average North Atlantic gale.

What causes the North Atlantic to roil and crash while the South Atlantic keeps its relative calm and cool are prevailing winds and currents and the weather patterns that they help to spawn. As the Earth spins eastward it deflects the atmosphere and ocean waters in fairly constant patterns. This creates prevailing winds that sailors have counted on for centuries—the Westerlies of the North Atlantic, blowing from North America toward Europe, and the Southeast Trades in the South Atlantic, blowing south to north toward the equator and bending toward South America. North of the equator but below the Westerlies, lighter but still steady winds, the Northeast Trades, blow from Africa's hump toward Brazil and the Caribbean. In the vicinity of the equator lie the dreaded doldrums, bands of windless water that can bring vessels relying on the wind for propulsion to come to sit for days, in Samuel Taylor Coleridge's famous words,

> As idle as a painted ship
> Upon a painted ocean.

Atlantic currents follow similar patterns. The best-known current in the world may be the warm Gulf Stream, which flows steadily, sometimes at more than four knots, from Cuba and the Florida Keys northeastward along the southern coasts of the United States and thence across the North Atlantic toward western Europe. It is the Gulf Stream that keeps the waters around Iceland, Scotland, and Scandinavia free of heavy ice the year round, that renders the climate of much of northwestern Europe mild for its latitude, and that provides nutrients for fish in the Norwegian Sea. It is also the Gulf Stream that made sailing in certain directions from some locations nearly impossible—the Spaniard Juan Ponce de León, when trying to sail southward around Florida with a tail wind in 1513, actually found his vessel traveling backward because of the strong current. For ships sailing in other directions, as from the Chesapeake Bay in North America to England or France, the Gulf Stream was a great aid. Possibly more important still is the role this current, in its meeting with the cold waters of the Arctic Ocean, played in limiting contact between Europe and North America across the northern edge of the Atlantic. Handfuls of Norsemen nearly a thousand years ago used the succession of islands across the North Atlantic almost as stepping-stones—Britain to the Faroe Islands, to Iceland, to Greenland, to Labrador and Newfoundland—to cross between the two large landmasses. More sailors certainly would have followed had the course been less difficult to navigate and less dangerous throughout most of every year. The Arctic Ocean flows south past Greenland, toward Labrador, bringing icebergs and cold water. Sailing from the Gulf Stream into the Labrador Current, writes maritime historian Roger Morris, is like "opening the door of a refrigerator." When the cold waters of the Arctic meet the warm Gulf Stream, fog forms, and the combination of low visibility and floating chunks of ice—the size of houses or whole city blocks—kept many a wise sailor (though not the skipper of the steel-hulled and steam-powered *Titanic*) from taking that route. Seamen passed along such knowledge. Thus, Columbus, who may have sailed to Iceland in 1477, did not let the *Santa Maria* drift where it pleased as he left Spain in 1492. "With an assurance like that of a sleep-walker," writes Hans Konig in his critique of the "Columbus myth," Columbus headed southwest to the Canary Islands, where he knew he would find trade winds propelling him along a fog and ice-free passage to the west.

Other warm and cold currents had similar, if less-recognized, effects, which tempt one to credit winds and currents alone for the way parts of Atlantic history unfolded. It was the cool Canary Current that helped speed Portuguese ships south around Cape Verde and Africa's western bulge, though it was that same current and prevailing winds that made direct passage back home so difficult for so long; it was the Guinea Current that helped European slavers reach the coast of Central Africa, where they acquired millions of slaves, and it was the Benguela Current and the Southeast Trades that helped them sail with their human cargo to Brazil and Caribbean islands. Finally, it was currents and the confluences thereof that produced the great breeding grounds for fish that brought seafarers from distant lands to reap the ocean's bounty, most notably of codfish on Newfoundland's Grand Banks and sardines off Norway's North Cape.

If currents feeding the North Atlantic turned some regions into a fisherman's gold mine, those flowing south, below the Tropic of Capricorn, proved equally attractive to sealers and whalers. The English captain James Cook, when he sailed into the South Atlantic in 1775, found acres of seals basking on frigid islands and pods of whales cavorting in the food-filled waters. Whales give birth to their young in warmer latitudes, but they migrate south each summer to feed off krill, small fish, and crustaceans so numerous that they almost choke the cold waters of the South Atlantic. Industries would develop in the eighteenth century around the killing of these sea mammals, seals for hides and whales for blubber (oil) and bone, before modern restrictions on such activity led to their decline (if not, sadly, to their complete cessation).

Atlantic geography has shaped human history in other ways. Each of the four continents bordering the ocean has many large and small rivers and estuaries, some of which extend far inland. This natural network of waterways enabled communication and trade from coast to interior and back long before intercontinental contact. After contact, these waterways extended the zone of influence of people coming from some distance away to the Atlantic coast of each continent. Casual examination of the physical geography of the four continents suggests that Europe and North America might be more open to Atlantic influences than Africa and South America because, in the Northern Hemisphere, the coastlines are jagged and deeply indented, with seas, gulfs, and grand bays that provide ocean access to persons living well inland. The combination of the Mediterranean, North, and Baltic Seas gives entry by water to most European countries, all of North Africa, and several countries of Western Asia. The Caribbean Sea, Gulf of Mexico, Gulf of St. Lawrence, and Hudson's Bay allow seafarers to penetrate deeply into North America and to come within forty miles of the Pacific in Panama. Rivers flowing into these inland seas, gulfs, and bays enhance the penetration into North America and Europe.

But direct contact with the Atlantic or bodies of water connecting to it did not mean that West and West Central Africans and South Americans were isolated from the ocean; these extensive waterways drew landlocked regions in all four continents into the Atlantic system. Though the coastlines of tropical Africa and subequatorial South America are smooth in comparison to the more northerly Atlantic continents, major rivers flowing into the Atlantic helped transport people and things from deep in the continents to the ocean, and vice versa. Nearly all major West African rivers originate in the rain-washed Futa Jalon highlands of modern Guinea. Without inordinate portage, one could travel to the Atlantic by water from much of West Africa's interior—down the 1,600-mile Niger River, for example, or the shorter Senegal or Gambia Rivers. The Congo River and its tributaries also connected an enormous portion of West-Central Africa to the Atlantic. In South America the Magdalena, Orinoco, Amazon, and La Plata Rivers served the same function. The existence of river access to regions thousands of miles from the ocean enabled news of coastal events to travel far beyond the affected areas. Europeans, however, could not so easily exploit these river networks in the southern continents, hindered as they were by tropical diseases endemic to the regions or, in the case of Africa, by falls and rapids not far from the river mouths. Indigenous people kept control of river travel longer in Africa and South America than in North America. No matter who was in control of local waterways, however, once there emerged a genuinely Atlantic zone of communication, it extended far into each of the continents.

In addition to facilitating human communication, the riverine system of the North Atlantic makes it a drainage receptacle without rival. Though it comprises only about 15 percent of the world's ocean surface, the North Atlantic drains almost half the Earth's land surface—more than 25 million square miles, four times more land than drained by the much larger Pacific. One would suspect that these infusions of fresh water into the Atlantic, along with the connection of the ocean to both polar regions, would reduce the salt content of the Atlantic and render it colder than other oceans, but neither is the case. In fact, the Atlantic is the most saline and the warmest of all oceans—factors related to the large number of marginal seas adjoining it. The Mediterranean, for instance, warms waters flowing into it and exposes them to a dry atmosphere, causing evaporation of water (but not salt) before it passes through the Straits of Gibraltar and enters the Atlantic.

But the quality of the Atlantic that remained so important for human history for so long was its separation of the Americas from Africa and Europe. Europeans would label the sides of this east-west division (somewhat inaccurately and self-referentially, since all four continents were transformed in the wake of transoceanic contact) the Old World and the New World. For thousands of years this expanse of ocean made transatlantic contact so difficult that almost none took place beyond the realm of fishes. Sustained human contact would only be achieved in modern times. Such long separation enabled diversity to develop between cultures all around Atlantic shores. West Africans, American Indians, and Western Europeans—the primary groups who interacted in the Atlantic world in the period treated by this book—held many aspects of culture in common, though they tended to focus on one another's differences once they met. In the fifteenth century there were, indeed, important differences between and among the people of the Atlantic world, but the most important ones in terms of explaining how they encountered each other and interacted had little to do with the superficial differences of appearance or adornment or even social organization. Far more important in the long term were divergent notions of property, religion, political sovereignty, and the biological consequences of continental separation.

Atlantic People in 1450

Although Europeans, Africans, and Americans remarked on their great differences when they met, historians have been able to probe beyond the superficial differences that often shocked contemporaries. In fact, French or Spanish, Wolof or Yoruba, Aztec or Inca, all people faced similar problems in finding ways to survive and all came up with solutions that held much in common. Nearly everyone's existence in pre-Columbian times involved growing and harvesting crops, hunting game, fishing, and gathering food. Most people involved in agriculture lived in permanent or semipermanent settlements. Herders and hunter-gatherers were more mobile. People who had to transport their possessions with them as they moved tended to own few extraneous items, and their bands or clans tended to be small. Whatever their material base, virtually everyone around the Atlantic participated in trade. Most groups also had hierarchical social arrangements that gave some individuals authority over others; most shared a core of ideas about human beings' relationship to their environment and to other humans; and most had an idea of religion that vested creative, protective, and spiritual powers in commonly recognized objects or beings and which required active participation on the part of the individual to ensure the smooth continuities of the sacred realm.

What helped bring about many of the differences in people's lifeways were their varied environments and how they adapted to them. Environmental constraints and opportunities included, among other things, access to fresh water, arable land, and marine and mineral resources; the length of growing seasons; and the availability of game, wild fruits, nuts, herbs, and vegetables. People of the far north and far south faced extremely cold or wet weather, and hence had special needs for sturdy shelter, thick clothing, and abundant fuel for fires. Access to trade goods and seasonal movements of fish and animals similarly affected the size of some groups and their social organization. Settled agriculturalists had to reckon with insects, blights, frosts, warlike neighbors, and other uncertainties that threatened their security. In short, humans adapted to their environments in distinct and clever ways over the millennia, yielding a kaleidoscope of cultural differences. In many cases, these differences were more marked within environmentally distinct parts of the Americas, Europe, and Africa than among the continents as a whole.

These patterns of heterogeneity, whether caused by environmental challenges or something else, have not always been acknowledged. Until recently, racism, itself shaped partly by asymmetries of power and color produced in the Atlantic world, clouded otherwise rational minds, bringing with it, like excess baggage, an undue attachment to and admiration for European culture. Traditional racist, Eurocentric thinking allowed for diversity among Europeans, a phenomenon it lovingly traced into the distant past, but it denied such diversity to Africans and native Americans, who were more casually grouped together as if continental origins dictated a common culture. For many years the lingering effects of nineteenth- and twentieth-century European empires and the so-called scientific racism that accompanied and sustained European aggression framed scholarly analysis. The best minds recognized the cultural, linguistic, and historic differences between, say, Laps on the one hand and Greeks on the other, between Irish and Ionians, Portuguese and Poles, Catalonians and Celts, or among Finns, French, Flemish, and Franks. But diversity among sub-Saharan Africans—so easily lumped together as *black*—or among people native to the Americas—considered as *Indians* with equal ease—was something few scholars bothered to recognize. Most took the easy road and considered all non-Muslim Africans and Native Americans as generally alike unto themselves, with neither a history nor a culture worthy of respect or serious study.

Racialist approaches to culture died hard, despite the efforts of travelers and anthropologists beginning in the early twentieth century to attest to the varieties and complexities of human experience. The Oxford University professor of history Hugh Trevor-Roper expressed this sentiment as late as 1963 when he labeled the African past, before the arrival of Europeans, as "largely darkness, like the history of Pre-European, Pre-Columbian America." For Trevor-Roper, these histories involved "the unrewarding gyrations of barbarous tribes in picturesque but irrelevant corners of the globe." Of course, neither Africans nor Native Americans had a monopoly on gyrations that one might label "unrewarding," "barbarian," or "tribal." If one were inclined to seek the most glaring examples of unrewarding gyrations of barbarous tribes, the European-initiated Crusades might vie for top ranking. Though not without his own prejudices, Benjamin Franklin demonstrated a relativist sensibility almost two centuries before Trevor-Roper's infamous bleat: "Savages we call them," Franklin wrote, "because their Manners differ from ours, which we think the Perfection of Civility; they think the same of theirs."

In light of this long Eurocentric scholarly tradition, it may seem ironic to discover that the most homogeneous population in the Atlantic world consisted of precisely those European kingdoms that organized the first lasting

Atlantic ventures. If Europe as a whole was a place of striking diversity, that heterogeneity pales when compared with Africa or the Americas. Few European ethnic groups were part of the major westward migrations: the English, Portuguese, Spanish, French, and Dutch were dominant, although there were always smatterings of others. Compared to the people they met in Africa and the Americas, these Europeans possessed a striking cultural uniformity. They organized their political realms through the intertwined principles of primogeniture and hereditary monarchy. They shared a single faith. Secular members of society practiced (or at least preached) monogamy, whereas religious figures were enjoined to celibacy. Europeans came from a relatively compact, interconnected region. The nations engaged in Atlantic enterprises in modern times (England, France, the Netherlands, Spain, and Portugal) occupied a landmass that could be tucked easily inside Brazil and contained a population of 25–30 million in 1500. Thus *Europe* in this book generally refers only to a portion of Europe and a few kingdoms.

Europeans

It is an interesting exercise to lump together western Europeans and examine them in the mid-fifteenth century in the same way scholars have historically grouped Africans and Indians. The Europeans lived in colder climes on the whole, and this brought about different adaptations in terms of clothing and housing, but in other cultural aspects their lives held similarities. Most Europeans lived from agriculture, growing mainly wheat and barley. They differed in that they had the benefit of draft animals, big horses and oxen, to help them with the heaviest farm work, plowing, milling, and transporting grain. Their efforts had been abetted by the gradual development of a heavy, moldboard plow with sharp iron share and coffer that turned soil deeply and quickly. This innovation helped to trigger a steady rise in Europe's population, and then a recovery from the fourteenth-century Black Death that had carried off nearly one-third of all Europeans, many of its peasants in particular. Europeans supplemented their grain diet with fish, meat, dairy products, olive oil, and fruit.

European society tended to be grouped in hierarchies, with large landowners—the lords of the manor—being those with inherited wealth and status. Rulers of smaller or larger states came from this class. In addition to feudal dues they reaped from their own manor, those who ruled exacted fees from lesser lords of their realm, monies which in theory they used to organize defenses and construct public works. Catholic clergymen enjoyed an elevated status, free of rents and dues. They were respected for the services they provided, their higher levels of education, and their links to a wealthy and established church. Nearly everyone else belonged to a lower class, though as feudalism began to show cracks in its facade, as towns became more numerous in the thirteenth and fourteenth centuries, and merchants began to move about more, there was at least the remote possibility of someone from society's lower realms moving up. Military service, strategic marriage choices, and long-distance commerce were among the few means of social gain. Although the son of a lowly Genoese weaver, Christopher Columbus managed to transform himself into a worldly entrepreneur, marry the daughter of a Portuguese nobleman, and ultimately gain the title of Admiral of the Ocean Sea.

Energetic rulers in western Europe began to consolidate smaller kingdoms, and some monarchs entertained thoughts of empire. Still, few nations we know today existed in their modern form in the fifteenth century. Most were smaller, and what meager unity they enjoyed was achieved through marriages and wars. Many kingdoms, duchies, and city-states did not have a common language. Only after 1450 did the language that became modern French achieve more or less popular use, and most of the subjects of the kingdom spoke other languages and dialects, including Flemish, Breton, and Latin. The Iberian states had been fighting for centuries to push out the Moors—the North African Muslim invaders who had occupied much of the peninsula since the eighth century—and only thereafter (Portugal in the mid-1200s and Spain not until 1492) could their rulers seek political and economic expansion. The Crusades of the eleventh to thirteenth centuries were imperialistic efforts on the part of several European states to regain the Christian Holy Lands from Muslim control, and only the eventual military effectiveness of their Muslim enemies blunted the quest for empire east of the Mediterranean.

Hereditary privilege governed the distribution of wealth, power, and leadership within Europe. Families ruled kingdoms and city-states and passed on political power and material wealth to a single heir, generally the oldest son. This reliance on primogeniture rendered politics unstable: without a suitable heir, claimants to a throne could make cases based on kinship, and the need to secure an heir governed alliances. Children served as diplomatic pawns in marriage alliances, and civil wars erupted as kingdoms wrangled for control of dynastic succession. This pattern was not limited to the top of the hierarchy. In English law, primogeniture governed inheritance down to the meanest family, resulting in younger sons—those often denied inherited land or wealth—seeking new occupations, whether as artisans, farm laborers, soldiers, clerics, or civil servants. Roman law, the dominant legal system on the European continent, provided more equitable distribution in family estates, yet the parceling out of inheritance it entailed created similar frustrations for heirs of large families.

Over time, the dynasties that governed European kingdoms became interrelated. The result increased the incidence of such genetic conditions as hemophilia (a particular problem for nineteenth-century British royalty and their Russian royal cousins in the twentieth) and complicated European politics as cousins and siblings, aunts and nephews, came to each other's aid. The power given monarchs, moreover, meant that royal personalities and passions were important in shaping individual kingdoms. Thus, an avaricious, ambitious, pious, deranged, timid, or altruistic monarch could guide the future of his or her kingdom.

In mindset, Europeans were superstitious. They believed in horoscopes, fortunetellers, and omens, including such natural events as comets, and they based their actions and life's direction on such things. Still, the core of their worldview was shaped by the Roman Catholic Church, which dictated doctrine and commanded its acceptance. Roman Catholicism was one of the two main branches of Christianity in this period, the other being the Orthodox Church. The two had split in 1054, when the leader of each excommunicated the other. In the eastern Mediterranean, smaller Christian sects survived, including Druses and Coptics.

Despite their differences, Christians shared a single creed, avowing acceptance of a single god. Roman Catholics believed that this God had fathered a child whose mother remained a virgin at the time of the infant's birth. This child, Jesus, was a rabbi, a Jewish teacher in the eastern Mediterranean whose innovative doctrines came to be codified as part of a new faith. Three days after Jesus' execution, he was believed by his followers to have ascended from his cavernous grave into the sky (a place Christians identified as heaven) to join his father. This belief in the Resurrection was a fundamental tenet of the Church, and the day celebrating that event, Easter, was the most important day in the liturgical calendar, eclipsing in significance the date of Jesus' birth, Christmas. Believers commemorated Jesus's death in sacred rituals called masses in which they believed that the bread and wine sanctified in the rite were the literal presence of his body and blood. Salvation and eternal life were assured by doing God's will as interpreted by the head of the Church, the pope, and overseen by a hierarchy of priests, abbots, bishops, archbishops, and cardinals. Over the centuries the Roman Catholic Church had accumulated considerable wealth, especially in land, and its officials held power among secular leaders. Most people, upper-class lords as well as hewers of wood and drawers of water, tithed and obeyed unquestioningly in hope of achieving absolution of sins and life everlasting. The medieval church took an evangelistic turn: converting more people to save more souls was another way to take a giant step toward salvation. This evangelical zeal would serve as one motive for Europeans to sail away and encounter more people, thereby finding more souls to save.

Although the Europeans engaged in Atlantic endeavors came from two different language groups (Romance and Germanic), some of these populations (the Portuguese, Spanish, and French) spoke similar and often mutually intelligible languages within a common family, all derived from Latin. English shares many cognates with these romance languages. Moreover, all European elites were capable of communicating with each other in Latin; to be literate in this period meant to be literate in Latin, the language of government down to the local level. Latin was used in ecclesiastical, manorial, and borough records in England, for example, well into the seventeenth century. All Catholics worshipped in this language, associating it with things sacred. Even if the vast majority of people in western Europe remained illiterate—and most did not speak Latin in their daily lives—Latin served as the language of the liturgy, and Catholics dutifully repeated the creeds and the words of the holy service by rote. No other cluster of kingdoms or nations anywhere else around the Atlantic enjoyed such cultural homogeneity, such core agreement on fundamental ways of organizing religion and politics. But this widespread homogeneity never dictated harmonious relations. Europeans were often at war, both in civil and external conflicts. Even if Europeans were mostly

Christians, and thus identified themselves in opposition to the Muslim "infidel"—and to a lesser extent against local Jewish minority populations—they
discerned important ethnic and regional divisions among themselves.

It is impossible to generalize about "Africans" or "Americans" in a similar way (although the following discussion will attempt to identify such common characteristics as might have existed); differences outweighed commonalities in these three continents. A quick comparison to the languages of the
greater Atlantic reinforces the homogeneity of Europeans. "Linguistic scholars divide Indian languages, at the point where Europeans first arrived in
North America, into twelve linguistic stocks, each as distinct from the others
as Semitic languages are from Indo-European languages," writes the historian Gary B. Nash. "Within each of these twelve linguistic stocks, a great many
separate languages and dialects were spoken, each as different as English from
Russian. In all, about 2,000 languages were spoken by the native Americans—
a greater linguistic diversity than in any other part of the world." West Africa
had its own large language families. The Mande languages, for example, in-
terrelate much as the Romance languages do, and were spoken in the fifteenth century across as much of West Africa as were the Romance languages
in Europe. But Mande also comprised considerable linguistic and cultural
diversity, literally hundreds of separate languages, far exceeding the handful
of languages Europeans brought across the Atlantic.

Africans

Any broad discussion of the lives of western Africans prior to 1450 necessarily misrepresents reality. Individual and localized African societies differed
greatly. In addition to speaking many separate languages, the people of West
and West Central Africa practiced social customs that, in some extremes, were
as different from one another as they were from those of Europeans. Furthermore, as new anthropological studies are showing, African societies changed
as much over time as did any others. Any notion that they did not stems from
racial and cultural ideas that have clung tenaciously to the minds of European and North American scholars since the nineteenth century. Finally, evidence for African history between 500 and 1,000 years ago is not as abundant
as is that for European history of the same period, rendering the task of writing a regionally textured African background for Atlantic history particularly
daunting.

Although it is difficult to portray "Africans" uniformly, one can trace
certain shared cultural traits into the past. For example, most people identified primarily with family and descent groups. An extended family occupying
a section of a village was the group that lived and worked together. As in
many parts of the Americas, in Africa polygyny was widespread; men measured their wealth through the number of wives, children, and other dependents they could support and protect. Security lay in numbers of kinspeople,
sometimes distant, upon whom one's family could rely in times of need, and
in stores of food or animals on the hoof. Although large centers for trade
existed, particularly in some of the interior desert-side and river towns and
ports on the Atlantic coast, small villages were common throughout the whole

region. Villagers worked out a sense of community and cooperation that enabled them to gain the most security and pleasure from their varied situations.

The vast majority of these African men and women also relied on one of two basic modes of subsistence: pastoralism or agriculture. Herders kept cattle, sheep, goats, or camels in the drier lands farther from the equator and closer to the mid-latitude deserts, where rainfall was insufficient for growing crops. Farmers of the savannas north or south of the equatorial forests grew rice, millet, or sorghum; those of the more heavily wooded areas nearer the equator grew yams or harvested bananas, plantains, or palm products. (Such crops as maize in the savannas and manioc or cassava of the forests, which are among the most important food crops of Africans living today, are imports from the Americas and served no role in African diets before 1500.) Some of these distinctions are not so important when one considers that Senegalese millet farmers, Nigerian yam farmers, and Angolan sorghum growers used similar methods of cultivation, mostly variations of slash-and-burn, or that herders of the savannas often lived in symbiotic relationships with farmers, exchanging products from their animals (including dung for fuel and fertilizer) for foodstuffs for themselves and their herds and flocks.

Africans living primarily in small to middle-sized villages before 1450 often had identities with larger groupings of people. Modern maps that divide Africans into vast language families—Niger-Congo or Nilo-Saharan, for instance—do not give a complete picture of the linguistic diversity of sub-Saharan Africa. Many of the existent languages were spoken only by small groups, and some of the most widely spoken languages were divided into dialects that even fewer numbers of people spoke and understood. Certain times and places witnessed great political differences. In no sense of the word did Africans identify themselves as members of a *tribe* and thus take their places in a large sociopolitical realm of *tribal Africa*. Colonial officials, early anthropologists, museum curators, and makers of tribal maps—most of whom share a European ancestry—have created that false sense, and it is one that dies hard. Individual allegiances normally lay with the extended family and the village. Sometimes the allegiances carried more broadly, and nebulously, to a descent group or clan; sometimes they spread even further, especially when forced, to a larger political unit—a state or an empire. When Europeans first sailed south along the west coast of Africa, large political units existed at several locations inland from the Atlantic. The Songhai Empire, centered on the upper Niger River, is probably the best known of these, although it was simply one of the biggest and wealthiest of the large states that included Jolof, Kanem, Bornu, Benin, Lunda, Kongo, and Ndongo, and a host of smaller ones like the Hausa states of northern Nigeria or the Akan states of modern central Ghana. Songhai, on the edge of the desert, controlled commerce and held political authority over thousands of miles. Its focus was toward the Sahara rather than the Atlantic, its chief mode of commerce being transdesert trade in salt, figs, dates, hides, glassware, and ornamentals coming south in exchange for gold, kola nuts, and slaves, which the government oversaw and taxed. The extent of its control naturally varied with the productive potential of its outliers and the ability of its own military to stake claim to, and exact tribute from, those areas.

While the larger states are more easily identified, it is important to note that in many African regions local identity, customs, and language differences tempered a broad sense of unity. No doubt relations existed among people across political and language boundaries. Long-distance traders moved widely, religions and secret societies spread and provided a commonality in overlapping areas, and historical events united groups of Africans. Most frequently, however, people from West and West Central Africa retained a restricted definition of their own group. General outlooks tended to be local. "We" included the people of the lineage, the village, and the small political unit; except under special circumstances, "they" referred to everyone else.

Many of these Africans seemed to hold a common worldview. Most recognized a single, supreme being—a god, if you will, who created heaven, earth, and humans—but, like deists in early-modern Europe, they believed this deity to be removed from the daily happenings on earth, and thus Africans spent more time in worship of secondary divinities, with whom they felt more involved. The most common belief was that humans needed to stay on good terms with the deities to prosper—to find game on the hunt, to have animals produce offspring, to have crops grow full to harvest, to keep disease at a distance and enemies at bay. This they did through ritualistic worship. Ancestors sometimes served as intermediaries with the gods, and so to displease one's ancestors could be tantamount to displeasing an important deity. Human intermediaries divined the will of the ancestors and the gods, and they often prescribed the rituals necessary to keep harmonious relations with both. Such rituals typically involved offerings, sometimes libations or the sacrifice of an animal, with the hope that placating the offended deity would return goodness and harmony to life on earth.

Christianity was almost entirely unknown to West and West Central Africans before 1450, but such was not the case with Islam. As early as the tenth century, the trans-Saharan trade brought Islam, the religion of many of the Berber traders, to the commercial centers on the south side of the desert. Trade then spread the religion beyond the desert-port cities over the following centuries. This tended not to be a brand of Islam like the orthodox practices settled on by the learned followers of Muhammad, but a mixed variety that included the pre-Islamic religious practices of the sub-Saharan Africans, especially rituals that placated ancestors and lesser deities. Moreover, Islam did not spread rapidly in West Africa. The greatest period of conversion to Islam there did not occur until the nineteenth and twentieth centuries, in the wake of *jihads* (holy wars) and sometimes in resistance to European colonial policies. Still, Islam was present in the interior commercial centers of West Africa when Portuguese first landed on the coast with their militant, anti-Islamic version of Christianity.

Americans

Writers call Indians "native" to North and South America because they were the first human inhabitants of these continents, yet their ancestors, too, came

Transatlantic Voyages before 1492

For a long time individual historians have argued that Africans, hundreds of years before Columbus's initial passage, made one or more successful voyages to the Americas. Leo Weiner was the first to make this contention, in a remarkable, three-volume work titled, Africans and the Discovery of America *(Philadelphia, 1922); Ivan Van Sertima is among the more recent in* They Came before Columbus *(New York, 1976); and Jack D. Forbes in* Africans and Native Americans *(1993) presents "some tantalizing data which suggests contacts in both directions." To treat the issue briefly, one might venture that most interested historians find these authors' evidence—which includes linguistics, archaeology, and ancient Arabic writings—intriguing, but more spotty than one would like for substantiating such grand assertions of early transatlantic contacts. Perhaps small numbers of Africans crossed the tropical Atlantic and reached the Americas, but if so, their influence was localized and not of such long duration or historical significance as that of subsequent Europeans—or of Africans who would cross the ocean later as part of the Atlantic slave trade. Vikings sailed from northern Europe to Greenland and Newfoundland, but they, too, failed to leave influences that lasted beyond the local area and short term. Mythical accounts of Atlantic crossings have joined those stories verified through archeological evidence. The Irish priest St. Brendan and the Welsh prince Madoc were alleged to have crossed the Atlantic, and this helped Britons establish claims to the Americas that predated Iberian ones.*

Below: The Danish Viking ship, **Raven,** *at sea, showing oars and sails. Hand-colored woodcut. Copyright © North Wind/North Wind Picture Archives. EXPL3A-00238.*

from elsewhere, in this case Asia. Most of the ancestors of Americans crossed the Bering Strait during a glacial interval that exposed a land bridge linking present-day Alaska and Siberia. Precisely when the first migrants crossed and how many waves of migration ensued are matters of disagreement among scholars, but new discoveries continue to push back the accepted dates. What once was considered a steady movement of Asian hunters beginning 11,500 years ago is now thought more likely to have been several waves of immigration that probably began 20,000 years earlier and continued over the millennia until the land bridge disappeared, perhaps as few as 5,000 years ago. Such maritime people as the Inuit came later, and mostly remained in Arctic and sub-Arctic latitudes. Recent findings also indicate that early migrations from the Arctic to South America were not accomplished only by land. Dating of new archeological discoveries suggests that in order for people to have dispersed as rapidly as it seems they did, this diffusion must have happened by water along the Pacific coasts. This process left a scattered population similar in some physical characteristics, but with quickly emerging differences in language and culture. The land inhabited by the American Indians—from the Arctic Circle to Patagonia—was as varied as land on earth could get: it included enormous mountain chains, fertile plains, extensive woodlands, tropical forests, parched deserts, and lands forever covered in snow. Wherever they settled, human inhabitants of the Americas adapted their ways of living to their environment.

If Americans encountered Europeans from relatively few kingdoms with common cultural traits, Europeans encountered *all* Americans with *all* of their cultural divergence. The English explorer Martin Frobisher fought with Inuit kayakers near Baffin Island in 1577; Columbus met the agricultural Taíno in the Caribbean in 1492; Pedro Alvares Cabral bartered with the semisedentary Tupi of coastal Brazil in 1500; Hernando Cortés invaded the densely settled, hierarchical, urban, agricultural empire of the Aztecs in 1519.

The variety of ways in which Americans adapted to their environments, and how their civilizations had developed over time, was astounding. And Americans had not only adapted to their environments, they had altered them. Central Andean people, most subjects of the Inca Empire, managed to overcome the natural constraints of their environment through an ethos that supported reciprocal obligations among the clan, village, state, and god/ruler. Working communally, Andeans irrigated some of the world's driest deserts, terraced mountainsides, and developed such staple crops as potatoes and quinoa. They also domesticated llamas and alpacas for transport, meat, and wool, and elaborated rich textile and ceramic traditions. In the northern woodlands, semisedentary populations, who cleared and burned massive forests to facilitate agriculture, aided hunters by creating "edge" habitats that attracted game animals. One can easily see how cultures change in response to environmental conditions by looking at the people who lived along the Mississippi River during the Little Ice Age (c.1300–1850). We live today in an era of global warming, but six centuries ago people experienced a global cooling. When temperatures dropped, growing seasons shortened, particularly in temperate latitudes. As a result, cities along the Mississippi declined as agricultural yields fell. Political instability ensued, in part a result of the failure of religious leaders to control the natural environment. In the midst of this general crisis, people dispersed in search of more reliable sustenance.

Such steady shifts and adaptations, along with a lack of population data, make it difficult to estimate the number of people inhabiting the Americas in 1492. Most historians agree on a figure between 50 and 70 million, with more than half the total concentrated in Mesoamerica and the Andean highlands of South America. This means that only one-tenth of the total population lived north of the modern U.S.-Mexico border; the historian Daniel Richter estimates a population of 2 million east of the Mississippi in North America. One problem with the evidence is that newly arrived Europeans compiled the earliest population reports. These outsiders rarely spoke indigenous languages and most were not methodical in their estimates. Furthermore, virtually all judged Indian ways in accordance with European and Christian ideas of how humans ought to be living, and thus arrived at mostly unfavorable conclusions about native life.

We can nevertheless recognize some broad generalities about early Indian cultures. Perhaps most distinctive and historically significant were the foods Americans consumed. Over the millennia, Native Americans domesticated some of the world's most life-sustaining crops—maize, beans, potatoes, squash, and manioc. The movement of these crops to Europe, Africa, and Asia would alter the size of those continents' populations and their histories. Native American hunters were most successful in zones beyond sedentary agriculture—forests, deserts, and plains. Hunters of such migratory herd animals as the American bison (buffalo) adopted similarly migratory habits. Fish, netted from oceans, lakes, rivers, and streams, supplemented the diets of most Americans; in coastal regions, shellfish were vitally important. Common barnyard animals of today did not exist in the Americas. Only dogs were widespread, and many were even domesticated as a food source and for transportation. Animal domestication was most developed, however, in the Andes of South America, where the llama was rendered a useful pack animal and the alpaca a supplier of wool. The lowly guinea pig supplied meat for ritual occasions and fertilizer in the form of nitrogen-rich dung.

As with Africans and Europeans, the village was the common living unit, but cities developed where resources existed to support larger populations. Indeed, some of the biggest cities sixteenth-century Europeans ever saw were in the Americas. The Aztec capital, Tenochtitlán, was five times the size of Seville, Spain's largest city on the eve of Spanish conquest. Connecting people among villages were large clans whose members lived scattered over wider areas. Belligerent clans and confederations sometimes created large kingdoms with populations in the hundreds of thousands and even empires of millions. The array of resources and available technologies often dictated population density; in this regard, Native Americans were like Europeans and Africans.

Most Americans recognized an almighty force that created everything, gave and took away life, and controlled the earth's fecundity. Ritual life was rich and complex, with rites assigned to different events in the life cycle and organized to meet seasonal challenges. One could find shamans, or religious practitioners, in all Native American societies. Americans believed that shamans had the power to heal the sick and wounded and communicate with spirits and ancestors. In urban societies, more specialized priesthoods developed, some of which oversaw political, agricultural, hunting, and war ceremonies. Many Indians had personal dealings with the life force, sometimes enhancing their ability to perceive the will of the almighty through use of hallucinogens. Unlike Europeans, Americans did not depend on intermediaries for their own personal access to the sacred world. Almost all Indian groups embraced pantheistic views of the cosmos, with deities usually composed of elements of the human and natural worlds. Some persons associated predatory animals, including whales and sharks, with spiritual potency. Patron deities, such as the Inca sun god, Inti, were common, but attendant deities could be just as demanding. The Aztec ritual calendar required worshipers to propitiate numerous gods with special festivities and sacrifices, and the deities had distinct preferences. The rain god Tlaloc preferred that children be sacrificed to him. In some rituals, deity impersonators—people dressed as the god being venerated—were sacrificed after a period of living in godlike opulence. As was true with Christians, Jews, and Muslims, among the Aztecs, Incas, and Mayas a class of religious practitioners worked full time to fill complex ritual calendars and care for religious texts and objects. Sacred beliefs could be simultaneously local, embedded in ancestral ties and places of importance. The Maya of the Yucatan Peninsula, for example, maintained family altars and made pilgrimages to sinkholes, while Quechua-speaking Andean communities held sacred the mummified remains of ancestors. Mountains and springs were sites of pilgrimage and animal sacrifice. Like Catholics, Indians believed that divine forces could be found in inanimate objects, including stones, pieces of wood, and preserved human remains.

The most stratified Indian societies were urban, but all groups, regardless of complexity, assigned distinct roles to men and women. Different ideas about gender were reflected in political and sacred power (inseparable qualities to most American people). Among the Mexica of the Central Valley, war maintained the universe and the empire and structured gender roles. Male children were destined to be warriors whose ultimate role and supreme honor was to sacrifice themselves for the state. Upon the birth of a male child, happy relatives presented him with arrows and songs and buried his umbilical cord in a battlefield. At the age of six, boys entered military schools, and when they reached adulthood they joined prestigious military brotherhoods of the Jaguar, Eagle, or Coyote. Relatives also welcomed female children into the world with gifts and songs, but their umbilical cords were buried at the family hearth with a warning such as, "Thou wilt be in the heart of the home [and] go nowhere [or] thou wilt become fatigued [and] tire [for] thou art to provide water, to grind maize, to drudge." The supreme function of women was to reproduce new warriors, and only by dying in childbirth could women hope to go straight to paradise.

Everywhere, ideas about gender were linked to religious ideology and subsistence practices. The Incas claimed heavenly descent from the Creator god, Viracocha, and from Inti, the Sun, whose bride/sister was the moon. Inti emerged from Lake Titicaca, as did his children, the first Inca Manco and his sister/wife and their siblings. This foundational myth allowed women in the Inca world to occupy a parallel legitimacy and power that their counterparts in the Mexica world never enjoyed. Inca women traced their descent from women, inherited property from them, and maintained their own religious institutions. The status women enjoyed on earth was reflected in the makeup of the Inca cosmos by the power of the moon, Killa, even if Inti, the masculine deity represented by the sun, reigned supreme. In everyday terms, the Incas were like the Aztecs in that women and men occupied distinct but equally important spheres. Similarly, among the Iroquois of northeast North America and the Tupi of what became Brazil, a division of labor that gave women responsibility for agriculture while men roamed to hunt, trap, and fish left women in charge of village life.

Just as imperialism and trade were significant to Europeans and Africans in the pre-Columbian era, so they were with Americans. Both Aztecs and Incas were at the height of imperial expansion when the Spanish arrived in the sixteenth century. After conquests in the mid-fifteenth century, the Aztecs dominated Mesoamerica's trade and markets, collected tribute (which included persons to sacrifice on the altar at Tenochtitlán), and organized agricultural production in the core, highland districts. Inca conquests were equally recent. At roughly the time the Portuguese were exploring Africa's Atlantic coast, between the 1430s and the end of the century, the Incas, from their base of Cuzco in modern Peru, were conquering people as far away as modern Chile to the south and Ecuador to the north. By early in the sixteenth century the empire extended 2,000 miles up and down the Andes and contained more than 10 million people. Inca rule was proto-totalitarian, characterized by strict state control over trade, labor, and individual movement. If the Aztec empire had at its core an element of religious terror, the Inca state couched its demands on subject peoples in terms of traditional Andean reciprocity. Yet, whatever their motors or reasons for being, both empires, particularly after 1500, began to feel the strains of their extension. As in Songhai, Kongo, and Spain, the conquered subjects in Mesoamerica and South America resented imperial rule. By the time the Spanish arrived on the American mainland, rebellions at the fringes of the Aztec and Inca Empires were as unpredictable as brushfires. As a result, the European newcomers who sought to topple the empires found willing allies.

Markets were common to Indian groups, particularly those in areas of dense settlement, and trade in the form of reciprocal gift giving existed everywhere. Short-distance commerce in necessities (everything from ceramics to foodstuffs) was complemented by long-distance trade in luxuries (shells, exotic bird feathers, decoratively woven cloth). As in parts of Africa, salt and copper were among the few necessities traded across vast distances in the Americas. Both commodities, like feathers and certain animal skins, retained sacred connotations. Copper and gold currencies were found in the Andes, and in Mesoamerica cacao beans, or raw chocolate, took on this role. Long after the Spanish conquest, indigenous merchants in Mexico and Guatemala bought and sold items with cacao at a specified exchange rate, 400 beans to the peso. With the exception of the use of llamas in the Andes, virtually all transport was by human carriage. (In the absence of large domestic animals, wheeled vehicles were not developed beyond the realm of toys.)

Water transport technologies were more developed. Throughout the Caribbean dugout canoes plied a trade system that connected most of the islands with coastal regions. The Caribs and Taínos who met Columbus made some of the largest and most seaworthy canoes. (The word *canoe* is derived from the Taíno, or Arawak, term *canoa*.) Constructed from a large, hollowed log with built-up sides, these canoes could carry fifty people. Some canoes raised cotton or reed sails on several masts to harness Caribbean winds for propulsion. The Tupi of Brazil used large dugout canoes as well, but it was along South America's Pacific coast that people built the most complex ocean-going vessels of the Americas. Here, huge balsa rafts with rudders and square cotton sails plied trade routes extending from southern Peru to the southwest coast of Mexico. Meanwhile, large reed vessels with woven reed sails crossed the icy waters of Lake Titicaca, the world's highest navigable body of water, near the core of the Inca Empire. In North America, trade routes by land and the many waterways of the region crossed the continent. While Indians traded such bulk commodities as corn or fish, the greater distance that goods traveled, the higher their ritual and social value. Copper, mica, and beads made from shells were characteristic of long-range trade goods and served a spiritual function in gravesites and burial mounds.

Geographic Constraints and Cultural Divergences

Although the varieties of human experience in the Atlantic world resulted from local adaptations and cultural creativity rather than continental separation, that long separation did create unique disease environments that brought about differences among Atlantic people. The ocean's waters, winds and currents were not the only factors keeping human inhabitants of West and West Central Africa largely separated from other places. Crossing the earth's largest desert, the Sahara, required an effort similar to crossing an ocean. The earliest Arabs who crossed the Sahara in the eighth and ninth centuries considered camels their "ships of the desert" and referred to the first habitable stretch of land they reached on the Sahara's southern edge as the desert's "shore"— *sahel* in Arabic. People crossed the Sahara in both directions from Roman times or earlier. Inhabitants of West and West Central Africa were not at all isolated from contact with foreigners before the first Portuguese adventurers brought their vessels bobbing along the African coast and into rivers, but neither were they influenced greatly by persons and cultures from other continents. Thus they developed ways of life in their own fashion, as the relatively isolated Europeans had done until no more than a few centuries earlier.

No such barrier as the Atlantic Ocean or the Sahara Desert separated Europeans from people living in Asia or North Africa. As far back as the time of ancient Rome, an economic system extended from the British Isles and Iberian Peninsula in the west to Mesopotamia and Egypt in the east and included all lands bordering the Mediterranean Sea. Nor was this the end of it: Mesopotamia was in indirect commercial contact with China, India, Southeast Asia, and the East Coast of Africa. Even West Africa was connected to this network via irregular traders who crossed the Sahara. Over thousands of miles of dusty steppes, windblown waters, or sandy paths connecting oases, people passed goods and ideas back and forth in systematic fashion.

The decline of the Roman Empire after the fourth century led to the detachment of the western region from this commercial system, but lands lying east and south of continental Europe grew more important in it. The growth of Asian-African trade after the seventh century was tied to the expansion of Islam. After conquering most of the Middle East, North Africa, and the Iberian Peninsula, Muslim armies followed the central-Asian trade routes and swept down into northern India, where they established themselves as purveyors of the fineries of the East. By the ninth century, Arab and Persian sailors were in contact with East Africa, India, southeast Asia, and even China. The result was dramatic. The Muslim world, which now reached from northwest Africa to India, was part of a vast commercial complex that stretched to the Pacific Rim. East Asian goods flowed westward in unprecedented amounts; East African goods moved north and eastward. Just before the year 1000, Persian geographer al-Muqadassi listed items one could obtain in Oman, at the eastern tip of the Arabian Peninsula: he included an assortment of drugs and perfumes, saffron, teakwood, ivory, pearls, onyx, rubies, ebony, sugar, aloes, iron, lead, canes, earthenware, sandalwood, glass, and pepper. To finance this commercial expansion, Muslims needed gold. They found it south of the Sahara, in the alluvial deposits of Africa's western savannas. In gaining access to this precious metal in the eighth and ninth centuries, Muslim merchants established firmly the previously tenuous links that tied West Africa into the growing, intercontinental economic system. By the end of the first millennium, the commercial centers of this vast and thriving system were cities in the Middle East, India, coastal China, and Southeast Asia. At that time, most of Europe lay on the distant edge of this system, largely uninvolved with its transactions and detached from most cultural exchanges that accompanied them.

What finally led to European involvement in this vast, Asia-centered commercial enterprise—in ways that would affect the course of world history thereafter—were the Crusades, the Christian attempt to recapture the Holy Lands from Muslims that lasted for two centuries. Kicking off the Crusades was an appeal from the emperor of Byzantium in 1095 to Pope Urban II for help in combating the Seljuk Turks, who had defeated Eastern Christians in battle after battle. Urban II quickly set in motion the First Crusade with an appeal to Western Christians' religious zeal and their baser human instincts. "The possessions of the enemy will be yours, too," he announced, "since you will make spoil of his treasures." Eight more Crusades would follow over the next two centuries. The unhappy result for Christendom was considerable expenditure and little long-term religious or territorial return, for after the last Crusaders were expelled from Syrian shores in 1291, Muslims held more land than they did before Urban's summons. Under Sultan Mehmet II, the fast-emerging Ottoman Empire pressed on to take Constantinople in 1453, wresting it from a thousand years of Christian control. The Ottomans would eventually control most of North Africa, the Arabian Peninsula, and the Balkan region of eastern Europe. The Crusades and their aftermath made it evident to Europeans that avoiding land wars with Muslims would be good policy, and this played a role in focusing the attention of ambitious Europeans, who still desired access to the trade articles of the East, on sea routes or places where no Ottomans or anyone else with horses, swords, and organized armies stood in their way.

If Arab and African traders crossed the Sahara and Europeans were linked to the east by land routes, for the people of the Americas the Atlantic proved to be a genuine barrier, with profound consequences. Americans were isolated from most diseases that circulated in Europe, Asia, and Africa. Though still deadly, these diseases were endemic in most of Eurasia and Africa— that is, they recurred regularly in a given population. The list of so-called childhood diseases in Europe and Asia included smallpox, measles, mumps, chicken pox, rubella, diphtheria, and whooping cough. During their cyclical recurrence, the most virulent strains of these pathogens were such efficient killers of their hosts that they themselves disappeared. People who survived the less-virulent strains acquired immunity. Smallpox nevertheless remained deadly for Europeans and Africans, such that even in the eighteenth century the disease accounted for between 10 and 15 percent of all European deaths. In any given population, acquired immunity allowed those who had survived previous outbreaks to care for those who fell ill. Although Americans experienced intestinal parasites and other afflictions, they were never exposed to these virulent, frequently airborne illnesses. They were thus "virgin soil populations," people with no acquired immunity. When such groups encounter a disease such as smallpox, they tend to suffer catastrophic epidemics. More than any other factor, this epidemiological isolation shaped the ways in which Americans experienced European invasions. Following first contact, so many Native Americans died so quickly that some once-autonomous indigenous cultures ceased to exist altogether. The imperial Aztecs and Incas were as deeply affected as were small bands living in North America. These deaths occurred not because of the physical or cultural weakness of Native Americans (although some Europeans interpreted the deaths that way), but because of a temporary epidemiological vulnerability, the result of their long isolation from the diseases that regularly circulated throughout Eurasia and Africa.

Some Africans enjoyed a relative biological advantage as well, not because of geographic or biological isolation (which they did not experience because of trans-Saharan and Indian Ocean contacts), but because of regionally specific environmental features. The tropics are home to many diseases, from yaws to leprosy to various insidious parasites, which plague all inhabitants, longtime residents or newcomers. But in some places where such mosquito-born illnesses as malaria flourish, people who have lived in a region for generations enjoy an inherited relative immunity. This was the case in coastal regions of West Africa, where Europeans succumbed to malaria in such high numbers that it precluded their settlement there. Some people who live where malaria is endemic have sickle-cell trait, which is an inherited sickle-shaped hemoglobin gene. People with the gene have a better chance of surviving malaria when it is introduced to the bloodstream by mosquitoes, which is why this otherwise recessive and aberrant gene can endure in a given population. If a person inherits the trait from a single parent, the consequence is an acquired facility in dealing with malaria; if a person acquires the trait from both parents, the result is sickle-cell anemia, a condition that can cause a host of life-threatening side effects. Anyone without inherited immunity is likely to succumb to malaria on first encounter with the disease. Europeans who ventured to malarial regions caught the disease and often died from it and associated ailments. Not until after the mid-nineteenth century, when quinine came into widespread use as a malarial suppressant, were Europeans able to enter tropical Africa and have much of a say in things. In short, the diverse disease environments of the Atlantic world constrained Europeans in Africa (except for more salubrious regions such as South Africa) yet enabled their penetration of the Americas.

Atlantic people also differed fundamentally in their notions of property ownership and wealth. One can think of property ownership as a series of legal, cultural, and social fictions that serve a purpose in a society. Among Europeans, particularly those engaged in Atlantic enterprises, land was the most important form of property. Legal documents attest to the centrality of the possession of land and buildings: wealth could be measured in acres or similar spatial units. To this day the consequences of these legal traditions encourage people in most Atlantic regions to perceive land acquisition as one of the most stable ways to secure and increase their capital. So established is this concept that the modern United States federal government provides special financial benefits to those who purchase land.

European people and governments warred over the control of territory and associated resources, dependent on the idea that the victor could claim ownership of terrain and that others would recognize this right. Yet Europeans also believed that powerful men and institutions, such as municipal councils and religious orders, had the right to control the labor of others. For a number of centuries prior to the fifteenth, the feudal manor served as the basic social and economic institution that dominated the European landscape. By right of inheritance or pleasure of a ruler, aristocratic men owned tracts of land of varying size, upon which lived peasants and artisans. In return for protection from attack through the resources of the "land's lord," which consisted mainly of weaponry, military organization, and a defensive castle, the peasants owed the lord a specified number of days of service, some military and some in labor in the lord's fields. These peasant *serfs*, as they were called, were not the lord's slaves—they worked their own portions of the manor lands and had rights (albeit few) and obligations spelled out—but the term did derive from a Latin word for unfree labor, *servus*. Serfs were bound to live on the manor and most never ventured far from it, certainly not without the master's permission. If feudalism provided security, it also limited the freedom of the majority population of Europe.

West and West Central Africans, for their part, valued people, including dependents of varying degrees, over land. If Europeans "owned" land, used it to increase their wealth and power, and extracted labor and services from dependent people, Africans could "own" people, with the same consequences for prestige, wealth, and power. This ownership was embedded in ideas that Europeans dimly understood and in rigid and complex social hierarchies. It was common, for instance, for West African societies to consider artisans—metal workers, wood workers, leather workers, potters, and bards—as separate social entities from others, in a way fusing notions of social position and occupation. Men and women in these groups could not marry outside them, and their associations with others were limited to dealings necessary to conduct business or ritual functions. Members of the ruling class in many societies kept to themselves as well, so that it was more likely for a man of a ruling lineage of one ethnic group to marry a woman of a ruling lineage of another than to marry in a different social grouping within his own ethnic group. Of course, ruling elites in Europe acted similarly.

Slaves made up one of the social groupings of many of the pastoral and agrarian societies in Africa. Dependency, servility, and bondage in various forms were established social and economic institutions extending well into Africans' past. "Slavery was widespread in Atlantic Africa," observes the historian John Thornton, "because slaves were the only form of private, revenue-producing property recognized in African law." Land was owned communally and parceled out to families for their use according to need; need was based on the number of laborers the family could marshal to work the land. So to increase production, lineages had to acquire more laborers. On the one hand, they could do this by paying the bride price for sons to marry and then waiting for the offspring of the marriage to mature. This explains partly the widespread African proclivity to have large numbers of children. But this investment might never pay off because of high rates of infant and childhood mortality, and in any case it took years to rear productive offspring. On the other hand, lineage elders could invest in a slave, who could be put to work almost immediately for quick returns. Women slaves also could bear children, who eventually would add to the size of the labor force. Thus, writes Thornton, slavery was "possibly the most important avenue for private, reproducing wealth available to Africans."

Whereas slavery in Africa was characterized by the variety of roles slaves occupied, slavery as it developed in the western Atlantic came to be associated mainly with plantation labor because the vast majority of captives were sold to toil in agricultural settings. One role of African slaves that seems to have varied less than others was that given enslaved women, who made up the majority of slaves in some precolonial African societies. Female slaves often brought a higher price than male slaves, for the obvious reason that women produced useful offspring, but also because females tended in many ways to be the most productive members of society. Women also had the advantages of being more easily assimilated into a society and less likely to escape or act out violently. Besides gender differences, slaves associated with a family often did the same variety of tasks as other family members, though sometimes they specialized in a single craft, such as weaving. Over several generations, and increasingly with marriage and childbirth, slaves could become recognized members of the household, no longer liable for sale and movement. As in Roman times, slaves of royal lineages might serve in offices of state, as soldiers or administrators, and become particularly important in such matters. The difference was that slaves and their descendants were always outsiders, making them liable for exploitation by the insiders, the original family members. Although slaves' fortunes might rise with the wealth and position of the master's family, they could never shed their status as non-kin.

As in most places where slavery existed, African societies obtained slaves by more or less violent means. Warfare—including raids, banditry, and kidnapping—was the most common method. Even wars not fought to gain slaves often had that effect, for prisoners of war (who could have been put to death by their captors) were usually enslaved and sold or put to work to help defray the costs of the war. If ransom was impossible, victors could pursue other avenues of exploitation. Young boys could train as future soldiers; girls and women could become concubines; slaves of either sex could be given as gifts to religious persons or shrines. Generally, captives were not highly valued near their place of capture, in part because they were close to home and likely to escape. Wise captors moved prisoners rapidly and sold them away quickly. Even if the need for labor was strong nearby, it was often better to sell off local captives and buy slaves from some distance away. For these reasons African armies often had a following of merchants eager to buy prisoners at low prices and then march them off to distant markets where they would bring a better price. The trans-Saharan trade routes served as one such outlet, and this is why substantial numbers of West African slaves could be found in the medieval Mediterranean world. Less violent methods of enslaving involved condemnation through judicial or religious proceedings for civil crimes or supposed religious wrongdoing. West Africans did not put people in jail for long periods; instead they relied on physical punishment or enslavement.

African societies that regularly acquired slaves were also accustomed to trading them. The export of slaves from sub-Saharan Africa long predated the period covered by this book. Various groups across West Africa sold slaves into the trade that led to and across the Sahara to North Africa. The trans-Sahara slave trade out of sub-Saharan Africa in fact lasted much longer than the Atlantic trade, from before A.D. 700 to near the beginning of the twentieth century. The cross-desert route was dangerous, with supplies of food and especially water carefully calibrated to last between oases. In order to raise their value in the eastern Mediterranean, young boys were often castrated—the operation always painful and often lethal because of a high rate of infection. The trans-Saharan trade exported between 8 and 10 million slaves, primarily to Islamic buyers in the Mediterranean and Middle East. In terms of volume, the Atlantic slave trade did not surpass the trans-Saharan one until the seventeenth century.

Therefore, by no means was trading slaves something new for those living in West and West Central Africa when Europeans showed up on their coast. When the early Portuguese arrived with desirable commodities, Africans already had the social and economic institutions in place to provide slaves in exchange. Little would be different about trading slaves coastward instead of inland—just the shippers and their destination. Europeans arriving on African shores also adapted to these long-established patterns, bringing most of the same products that African traders expected to receive in exchange for slaves: cloth, decorative items, metalware, horses, weapons, and more. The principal novelty of the Atlantic slave trade was its scale. No other movement of slaves, at any time or place before or since, came close to the massive, forced migration of people out of West and West Central Africa to the Americas over the four centuries following 1450.

If notions of property held by Europeans and Africans shaped their commercial relations and dictated the largest migration in the pre-twentieth-century Atlantic world, American ideas about property proved no less consequential. It is a fiction that Native Americans did not recognize property ownership, although their concepts of it differed from those of the Europeans with whom they bartered and made treaties. In many areas of the Americas, ownership of land was corporate and focused on customary use rather than title or fixed boundaries. Bands shared widely recognized privileges to fish, plant, or hunt in particular regions. Disputes over access to resources could nevertheless be long running and serious. Although the indigenous name of the body of water in southern Massachusetts, Lake Chargoggaggoggmanchaugagoggchaubunagungamaug, does not translate as "you fish on your side, I'll fish on my side, and nobody fishes in the middle," as children in the region grow up believing, the name of the lake does point to the awareness of accesss rights to the resources of a property—in this case delineating the lake's role as a fishing place in a neutral boundary region.

In places where Europeans conquered Americans, they claimed control over people and land—the right of conquerors. But when Europeans sought to acquire legal title (as they understood it) through diplomacy and commercial exchange, the result was often a misunderstanding. The problems were perhaps most pronounced in North America, where Europeans encountered numerous semisedentary groups who identified property rights in terms of the use of a territory's natural resources—wood, animals, plants, fish—all of which were to be used only for consumption. Europeans thought they were securing ownership—sole dominion—of land that Indians believed they still owned corporately, thinking they were instead extending privileges of use. The difficulty was exacerbated by differences in political leadership. In areas where bands did not have a single powerful leader, no individual had the right to negotiate land held in common. These same kinds of issues would arise in Africa in the late nineteenth century, when Europeans would exact treaties with Africans and believe they thus received full right of ownership. In another, especially ironic, pattern, after despoiling native people of the Caribbean and finding themselves short of labor, the Spanish developed a legal system that set aside communal agricultural lands for Native American villagers. In some regions of Spanish America, such as Chiapas, Mexico, these rights are still hotly disputed.

Some American societies also recognized slavery, although once again the use of the term is problematic, given the limited vocabulary European observers had to describe the practices they saw. Native American societies often were stratified socially, although the degree of stratification and specialization varied enormously. In the hierarchical Aztec-Mexica world, a class of slaves made up the lowest stratum. Most of these slaves were war and drought survivors who sold themselves into slavery in exchange for food and protection (as Africans would do, too, when forced by necessity). In the woodlands of eastern North America, Indians took captives, some of whom occupied a status that later observers considered slavery because of the menial labor captives performed and the "social death" they experienced in captivity. Their position was certainly not enviable. Like the Tupi of coastal Brazil who so horrified the early Portuguese, Eastern woodland peoples often sacrificed select male captives, while "adopting" female ones into the domestic sphere. Captivity and various forms of dependency were ubiquitous from Canada to Tierra del Fuego, but no slave market comparable to those of Mediterranean Europe or West Africa ever developed anywhere in the pre-Columbian Americas.

If those of us living today had been able to look at the people of the Atlantic in 1450, we would be struck by the variety of cultures the region contained, and we would almost certainly recognize our inability to predict what might happen when these cultures converged. Why did some empires and kingdoms endure while others, even more populous and wealthy ones, crumble? Why did certain groups possessed of only the most basic technologies manage to avoid enslavement and annihilation by disease? It is only in hindsight that cultural variations in definitions of property, differing capacities to adapt to challenging environments, or the biological constraints of differential immunity to disease emerge as keys to understanding long-range trends. These differences shaped the ways in which the peoples of the Atlantic encountered each other after 1450 and they help us understand how environmental and geographic features (winds, water, deserts, mountains, currents, microbes, and insects) joined with the more visible elements of a culture (religious beliefs, political organization, domestic economy, subsistence activities, household structure and gender roles) to yield new and unanticipated cultural and political patterns.

Selected Readings

Adorno, Rolena, *Guaman Poma: Writing and Resistance in Colonial Peru* (Austin: University of Texas Press, 1988).

Austin Alchon, Suzanne, *A Pest in the Land: Native American Population History in Global Perspective* (Albuquerque: University of New Mexico Press, 2002).

Bacci, Massimo Livi, *The Population of Europe: A History*, Trans. by Cynthia De Nardi Ipsen and Carl Ipsen (Oxford: Blackwell, 1999).

Benson, Elizabeth P., ed., *The Sea in the Pre-Columbian World* (Washington, DC: Dumbarton Oaks Research Library and Collections, 1975).

Calloway, Colin G., *New Worlds for All: Indians, Europeans, and the Remaking of Early America* (Baltimore: Johns Hopkins University Press, 1997).

Clendinnen, Inga, *Aztecs: An Interpretation* (Cambridge, UK: Cambridge University Press, 1991).

Coe, Michael D., *Mexico From the Olmecs to the Aztecs* (London: Thames & Hudson, 1994).

Collinder, Per, *A History of Marine Navigation*, Trans. by Maurice Michael (New York: St. Martin's Press, 1955).

Cronon, William, *Changes in the Land: Indians, Colonists, and the Ecology of New England* (New York: Hill and Wang, 1983).

Durán, Fray Diego, *The History of the Indies of New Spain*, Trans. by Doris Heyden (Norman: University of Oklahoma Press, 1994).

Forbes, Jack D., *Africans and Native Americans: The Language of Race and the Evolution of Red-Black Peoples*, 2nd ed. (Urbana: University of Illinois Press, 1993).

Hopkins, Anthony, *An Economic History of West Africa* (London: Longman, 1973).

Josephy, Alvin M., Jr., *The Indian Heritage of America*, rev. ed. (Boston: Houghton Mifflin Company, 1991).

Krech, Shepard III, *The Ecological Indian: Myth and History* (New York: W. W. Norton & Company, 1999).

Morris, Roger, *Atlantic Seafaring: Ten Centuries of Exploration and Trade in the North Atlantic* (New York: McGraw-Hill, 1992).

Nash, Gary B., *Red, White, and Black: The Peoples of Early North America*, 4th ed. (Upper Saddle River, NJ: Prentice Hall, 2000).

Padden, R. C., *The Hummingbird and the Hawk: Conquest and Sovereignty in the Valley of Mexico, 1503–1541* (New York: Harper Colophon, 1970).

Reader, John, *Africa: A Biography of the Continent* (New York: Alfred A. Knopf, 1998).

Richter, Daniel K., *Facing East from Indian Country: A Native History of Early America* (Cambridge, MA: Harvard University Press, 2001).

Sahagún, Fray Bernardino de, *Florentine Codex: General History of Things of New Spain*, Trans. by Arthur J. O. Anderson and Charles E. Dibble (Salt Lake City: University of Utah Press, 1950–1982).

Silverblatt, Irene, *Moon, Sun, and Witches: Gender Ideologies and Class in Inca and Colonial Peru* (Princeton: Princeton University Press, 1987).

Stommel, Henry, *The Gulf Stream: A Physical and Dynamical Description*, 2nd ed. (Berkeley and Los Angeles: University of California Press, 1965).

Thornton, John, *Africa and Africans in the Making of the Atlantic World, 1400–1800*, 2nd ed. (Cambridge, MA: Cambridge University Press, 1998).

Townsend, Richard F., *The Aztecs* (London: Thames and Hudson, 2000).

Vansina, Jan, *Paths in the Rainforest: Toward a History of Political Tradition in Equatorial Africa* (Madison: University of Wisconsin Press, 1990).

Villiers, Alan, *Wild Ocean: The Story of the North Atlantic and the Men Who Sailed It*, rev. ed. (Washington, DC: National Geographic Society, 1973).

El Almirante Christoval Colon Descubre la Isla Española, ij haze poner una Cruz, etc.

"El Almirante Christoval Colon descubre la Isla Española," *by Pieter Balthazar Bouttats. Etching shows Christopher Columbus being greeted by native people upon his landing on the island of Hispaniola. In the background, soldiers plant a cross and native women flee from the arriving sailors. Spanish, 1728. Library of Congress Rare Book and Special Collections Division. LC-USZ62-8390.*

Chapter Two
The Roots of an Atlantic System, 1100–1492

Some [had] downcast heads and faces bathed in tears . . . ; others [were] moaning sorrowfully. Others struck their faces with their hands, and threw themselves flat upon the ground. Others uttered a wailing chant, after the fashion of the country. . . .
R. Gomes Eanes de Azurara, describing African slaves
at their sale, near Lisbon, Portugal, 1444

Ibn Jubayr, a Spanish Muslim, set out from Granada in 1183 to cross the Mediterranean lengthwise and then travel down to Mecca for the pilgrimage required by his faith. On his return in 1185, he passed through the seaport of Acre (modern day Acco) in the Kingdom of Jerusalem, thirty miles west of the Sea of Galilee. There was not much about Acre he found attractive. "It stinks," he wrote, "and it is filthy, being full of refuse and excrement." But such nastiness was not enough to keep people away. The streets of Acre were "choked by the press of men," Ibn Jubayr found, "so that it is hard to put foot to ground." What drew so many people—road- and battle-hardened Frankish Crusaders, Muslim pilgrims, Greek merchants, Italian sailors, Persian artisans, and a host of others from distant parts—to this city? The answer is a simple one: commodities.

In the last decades of the twelfth century, the ages-old, land-and-sea routes carrying trade between East Asia and the eastern Mediterranean had begun to converge on Acre. This meant that in addition to offering commodities familiar to Mediterranean folk, grain, wine, olive oil, fish, and vegetables, the city markets carried items that a western European would have considered exotic: silks and cottons, ivory and pearls, onyx and rubies, coffee and tea. One also could find spices, hundreds of the sweet and pungent "flavors of the East," most of which were either unknown or rare and expensive to provincial Europeans. As people ate and drank and felt the materials and ogled the jewels and sniffed the spices (which surely beat the noxious odors of the street) and interacted and even acquired one thing or another, they became an unwitting part of a process that would slowly connect (or actually *reconnect*) Europe to an economic system that stretched from Acre out over the land and sea horizons to distant parts of Asia.

One might wonder how this twelfth-century market in the heart of the Middle East figures prominently in a history of the Atlantic world that would

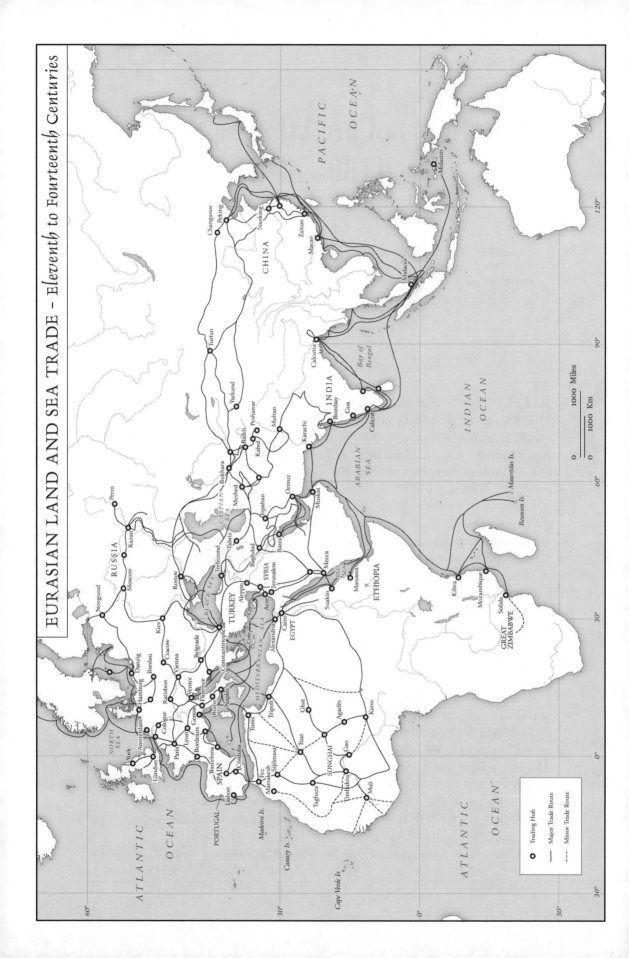

EURASIAN LAND AND SEA TRADE – *Eleventh to Fourteenth Centuries*

not fuse for another three centuries. The answer is because this story begins in the marketplace: pursuit of commodities largely shaped European commercial aggression in this period, which in turn encouraged maritime expansion and innovation. In the eastern Mediterranean, Europeans acquired a taste for spices and luxury commodities that prompted them to seek their own direct access to these goods without the expensive impediment of middlemen. Such acquisitiveness would take Europeans around the globe in search of luxury goods. Their craze for one spice in particular, sugar, stimulated the production of the crop throughout the Mediterranean and in the fertile islands of the eastern Atlantic. Among the institutions that Europeans developed in support of their commercial enterprises, none would have a greater effect on the course of Atlantic history and the lives of those involved than a plantation system using slave labor to produce staple crops, especially sugar, for a European market. But development of this system of agricultural production, which rested on slave labor, was only one of several parallel developments in this period, all of which would shape the Atlantic world in their convergence. With hindsight, one can identify from among the many historical changes of the period four trends that would mold the Atlantic world in subsequent centuries.

The intersection of southern Europeans' quest for commodities and the labor to help produce them brought about the annexation of Atlantic islands and generated trade south along the African coast for slaves and other commodities—most important gold to help finance their enterprises. In Africa, Europeans established themselves for the most part as traders, clinging tentatively to the western edge of the continent only with the consent of local rulers. This trade model subsequently accompanied many European ventures into the Atlantic. Northern Europeans sailed west into the North Atlantic, around Iceland and beyond, for coveted codfish. These multiple, parallel developments shaped the ways in which Europeans entered the Atlantic and guided exploration of the ocean. But if this is a story of trade, sugar, gold, codfish, and slaves, it is also one of dynastic consolidation and religious aggression. Noteworthy during this period was the belligerence of European Christians in their efforts to conquer Muslims outside of Europe, and the slow but steady routing of the perceived infidels from the previously multireligious Iberian Peninsula. At the same time, and similarly, Africans at various spots on the Atlantic coast were taxing trade and using religion to help them build states, some vast but all varied. An additional parallel action was the emergence across the Atlantic of two large American states, the Aztec and Inca Empires, both, like the Iberian and African kingdoms, shaped in their expansive impulses by belief systems and sacred imperatives. Some of these strands began to converge in this period. For example, the Christian kingdom of Spain, united in 1479 when the married cousins Isabella and Ferdinand ascended to the thrones of Castille and Aragon, respectively, sponsored the trade expedition of the Genoese merchant and mariner Christopher Columbus, himself experienced in the Portuguese world of trade. Other strands did not converge for another century. The different dynamics of expansion before 1492, both commercial and imperial, in Europe, Africa, and America shaped how people encountered one another—as subjects, conquer-

Spices of the East?

That Europeans had little accurate information on the origin of spices is evident in the thirteenth-century writings of one Joinville, who accompanied France's Louis IX (St. Louis) on a crusade in the Nile Delta: "Before the Nile enters Egypt the people spread their nets in the river at dusk. On the following morning they find in these nets the commodities which they sell by weight and which are brought to this country; namely, ginger, rhubarb, aloes, wood, and cinnamon. And it is said that these things come from the terrestrial paradise; the wind blows down the trees which are in paradise just as in the forests of this country the wind blows down the dead wood. The dead wood which falls into the river is sold to us by the merchants in this country."

Such ignorance was based on Europeans' heretofore narrow existence. Had they been regular travelers across the central-Asian Silk Road or the Indian Ocean, they would have known of the cloves and nutmeg of the Molucca Islands (the original "Spice Islands"), the cinnamon, licorice, and rhubarb of China; and the cardamom, turmeric, ginger, and peppercorns of India. In the geographically impaired minds of thirteenth- or fourteenth-century Europeans, the entire area beyond the eastern edge of the known Mediterranean and Red Seas was simply "The Indies." To get there and tap into the sources of the spices was one of the lures for western European expansion, south or west or east, whatever direction it took.

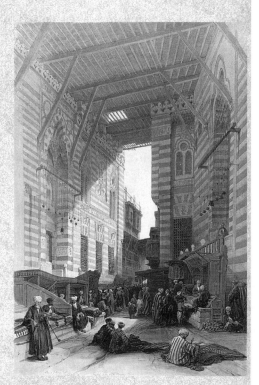

Bazaar in Cairo, 1838. Chalk lithograph after David Roberts. From: David Roberts and William Brockedon, "Egypt and Nubia," London (F.G. Moon) 1846-49. Courtesy: akg-images, London.

ors, preachers, allies, trading partners, or rivals—around the Atlantic world in the years after 1492.

Europeans and Sugar in the Mediterranean and Eastern Atlantic

The Crusader states—the feudal territories that Europeans carved out of land taken from Muslims along the eastern edge of the Mediterranean Sea—remained in Christian hands through most of the fifteenth century. These were the Biblical lands that "floweth with milk and honey," rich themselves in natural products and also serving for centuries as one of the western ends of the trade routes that brought luxuries from the East. Contact between the states and western Christendom was fairly constant. In addition to ferrying men and supplies for the armies, captains from southern European ports shipped east such bulky items as horses, lumber, and even siege machinery. On their return, these shippers brought back to Europe the high-value, low-bulk eastern luxuries, and the taste and desire for more of these niceties spread quickly. Some of the new products that western Europeans encountered spurred the sea-trade of Genoese and Venetian merchants and served as a foundation for the rise of markets and towns throughout the Italian Peninsula and into central and western Europe in the thirteenth and fourteenth centuries. Of all the new products Europeans craved, the eastern spices topped the list. Although salting and pickling were common practices, food preservation was more art than science in late medieval times. Many cooks thus found it desirable to disguise the taste of decaying and rotting food with spices.

One of the spices Crusaders encountered in the eastern trade was cane sugar. This was not a completely unknown commodity to Europeans, but it was scarce and extremely expensive—available only in pharmacies in the form of pills (which is probably the origin of many candies). Europeans used honey as their main sweetener, but it, too, was expensive and difficult to obtain in large quantities. In the Middle East sugar cane was abundant, and once imported to Europe it gained popularity with a speed that should surprise no one with a sweet tooth. One Crusader deemed sugar an "unsuspected and inestimable present from Heaven"; another proclaimed it "a most precious product, very necessary for the use and health of mankind."

From its original existence in the South Pacific, sugar cane and the production thereof had moved steadily west and northward. By the start of the second millennium, people cultivated sugar cane in the warm and moist regions east of the Mediterranean, primarily in and around India, whence it was transported to Acre and other ports by ship. Muslim traders monopolized this commerce. Europeans recognized that if they were going to get enough sugar to satisfy their cravings at a reasonable price, they would need to eliminate the intermediaries by finding a way to grow, refine, and transport it themselves. It was with this in mind that, early in the 1200s, enterprising Venetians learned techniques of growing and refining sugar cane and then started planting it on small plots in the Crusader states and larger ones on the sunbathed islands of the eastern Mediterranean. French and Italians soon took possession of much of Cyprus, then Crete, and then islands in the Aegean and Ionian Seas. On all of these islands, sugar production slowly took hold. Once Mongols invaded Syria in 1260, cutting off that source of supply, the Mediterranean islands became the major sugar producers for the European market.

European sugar growers quickly discovered that their medieval forms of land tenure and labor organization were adaptable, with some modification, to profit-oriented sugar production and export. The most productive agricultural unit throughout much of Europe remained the feudal manor, on which serfs grew what they needed to sustain themselves and, in return for protection, owed labor to their lords. But serfs maintained long-established daily and seasonal work patterns that served their own needs and inclinations rather than those of their lords, let alone those of some distant market. Raising sugar cane required more time-consuming and strenuous work than growing the grains that made up the bulk of European agriculture. And beyond the effort required in growing cane, extracting the sucrose-rich liquid from the stalks through crushing them in mills and then reducing the liquid to loaves or powder through boiling and purging was hot and mean work. Simply put, sugar making was a labor-intensive agricultural industry that required far more work, in more difficult conditions, than manor-bounds serfs were willing to perform. In lieu of technical innovations, landlords needed to effect an economy of scale—tracts far larger than the fields of the manor, devoted to growing cane—and a labor force that could be coerced to work seasonally through daylight hours in tasks that strained human capacity.

It was fortunate for sugar magnates that they lived in a region shaped by a culture of unfree labor. Mediterranean Christians still recognized the Roman legal status of chattel slavery, Muslims still approved of enslaving nonbelievers, and shippers maintained an active trade in people. For a time, captives from regional wars, including the Crusades, met the demand for labor on the sugar estates. Then, after the middle of the thirteenth century, Genoese colonizers penetrated the Black Sea, seized lands on the Crimean Peninsula and eastward, and tapped into a market of war prisoners among various Slavic groups. These people quickly became the most important work force in the burgeoning Mediterranean plantation economy—so important, in fact, that their name became synonymous with unfree labor, causing replacement of such Latin-based words as *servus, mancipium,* or *puer,* describing bondage in the Romance and Germanic languages, with words from the root *slav: esclave, esclavo, escravo, schiavo, sklave,* or *slave.*

Venetians on Cyprus may have been the first to recognize the efficacy of slave labor for sugar production and to establish what would become a colonial model for slave-based, market-oriented sugar production. New technical knowledge—which the early Crusaders had garnered from Muslim Syrians—capital, and shipping for the enterprise rested in the hands of Europeans, and nearly all production was for a European market. Owners sought labor, enslaved or otherwise coerced, from whatever source served best and cheapest. If this pool of labor consisted mainly of Slavs through the fourteenth century, it included at a later point—certainly after 1453, when Mehmed II captured Constantinople and the Turks closed the Black Sea to Italian ships—a variety of Mediterranean people and even some sub-Saharan Africans, the latter sold away from their homelands and transported across the desert or up the Red Sea to Mediterranean entrepots. As sugar production expanded westward across the Mediterranean to Aragon in Spain and the Portuguese Algarve in the fifteenth century, Venetians and Genoese continued to provide capital and expertise. The plantation model was easily expandable, if demand for sugar continued to grow and if, beyond the confines of the Mediterranean, new fertile lands, drenched in rainfall and sunshine, became available.

Europeans might have ventured earlier into the Atlantic, seeking contact with the commodities of West Africa and East Asia, had it not been for a series of economic and demographic setbacks. Of greatest consequence was the Black Death, the virulent bubonic plague, which between 1348 and 1400 killed one-third to one-half of the population of Europe.

It may seem ironic that Europeans' economic woes and disastrous encounters with the Black Death came about *because* of their participation in the economic system that stretched from the Mediterranean across Asia. Prosperity rested on connections and the efficient movement of goods across the network; when links broke down, the system declined. This is what happened with the onset of the flea- and rat-transmitted Black Death that spread across Eurasia after 1330, killing without discrimination. By the mid-1340s the disease reached ports on the Italian Peninsula, and it moved rapidly from there up the roads and trade paths through central and western Europe. So much death quickly dissolved political unity in central Asia, which had been provided since the early thirteenth century by Genghis Khan and his successors in the Mongol Empire. Without the order provided by the Khan's army, goods ceased moving smoothly across the trade routes that linked the Mediterranean to east Asia. The sea link to southeast Asia and China functioned sporadically, but following Zheng He's voyages between 1403 and 1430, the Ming rulers decided against further overseas ventures, and neither Arabs nor Indians could fill the Chinese void. This early-fifteenth-century "Fall of the East," according to the historian Janet Abu-Lughod, preceded any "Rise of the West."

Yet difficulties beyond the economic and epidemiological hindered Europe. Agricultural productivity declined after 1300, the result of climate change, land exhaustion, and technological stagnation. Europeans needed new sources of food, new fishing grounds, new stands of timber. Some historians argue, too, that European rulers had reached the limit of their ability to extract surplus production from their serfs, and that the serfs, or European peasants generally, were becoming dangerously disruptive to the existing order. French peasants rose in rebellion in 1358, looting and burning manor houses in what the chronicler Jean Froissant describes as "a marvelous tribulation"; in England, rebels led by artisan Wat Tyler followed suit in 1381. Related to these impediments was the ever-growing European need for precious metals to finance the eastern trade. Muslims continued to monopolize the largest supply of gold known then to Europeans, across the Sahara in West Africa. Some in Europe began to wonder if expansion away from the continent, into new lands where agents of European lords could produce cheap food, fuel, and new surpluses, might solve their problems. Such expansion could enable Europeans to outflank the Muslims and get direct access to the gold—and maybe even, farther along, the luxuries of the East. To some economically depressed Europeans of the fifteenth century, the best hope for economic and social salvation lay in expansion.

The search for another kind of salvation propelled Europeans into the Atlantic, too. European Christians had been fighting Muslims more than half a millennium. The fall of the last Crusader state, the kingdom of Jerusalem, in 1291 was a bitter pill for Western Christians to swallow, but it hardly signaled the end of their desire to take on the infidel. Rumors of a powerful Christian prince, Prester John, allegedly surrounded and beleaguered by Muslims out in the lands beyond (it was unclear precisely where, but Europeans looked everywhere they went for John's elusive kingdom), fueled a general European desire to find new fields upon which to resume the battle. A Christian missionary zeal that had been growing since the thirteenth century added strength to the religious motive for expansion. It was the duty of all good Christians, according to the doctrine of the Gospel, to convert nonbelievers wherever they may be found.

Actually, the thread of religious warfare ran deep among European Christians, nowhere more so than in Portugal and Spain, both long the home to culturally diverse and multireligious populations. Phoenicians, Greeks, and Carthaginians, attracted to Iberia by iron and coal, left early cultural imprints, and then six hundred years of Roman control established legacies in language, law, governing principles, a civic model, and concepts of imperial citizenship. Germanic groups invaded following the decline of Rome and helped spread Christianity in increasingly isolated kingdoms made up of feudal estates. The Muslim advance into Spain and Portugal after 711 left the so-called Moors in charge by mid-century, as Christians retreated into the northern mountains to ponder reconquest of the peninsula. From their capital at Córdoba in southern Spain, Muslim rulers formed what would become, in 929, an independent caliphate. Under the Muslims, urban life and trade in Spain rebounded, and wealth and luxury became hallmarks of Muslim rule. By the tenth century, Córdoba was the largest city in western Europe, with a population of as many as 100,000, and Muslim rulers took pride in the city's

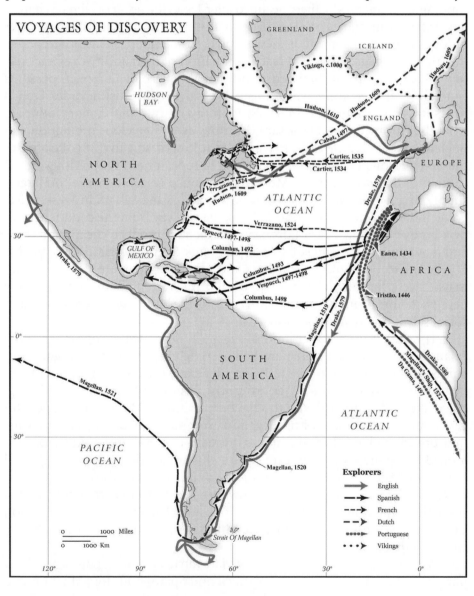

cleanliness and beauty, which so contrasted with the filth and stench of the pestilential cities of the rest of Europe. Into the centuries of the second millennium, Christians living in these cities and elsewhere in Europe looked on as Iberian Muslims preserved the knowledge of the Greeks in libraries, read texts of the world's finest minds on science and geography, and even maintained a tradition of religious toleration, protecting Jews and Christians as people of the Book.

For a long time Christians could only look on, but in the eleventh century Christian monarchs launched their first Crusade in Spain, and the fight for Iberia thereafter was a long one. As they began to win battles and slowly unify Spain, Christians maintained the religious tolerance they formerly enjoyed, requiring tribute from Muslim and Jewish vassals but allowing them to live in peace and practice their faiths privately. By the mid-thirteenth century, a Christian monarchy had won back Portugal and Spanish Christians were in control of much of Andalucia, as Muslims retreated to their great fortress, the Alhambra, in Granada, surrounded by beautiful gardens. It would take two more centuries before the Catholic monarchs, Isabella and Ferdinand, would finally win Muslim surrender, expel all Jews and Muslims who refused to embrace Christianity, and embark on the creation of an Atlantic empire.

So, as the fifteenth century dawned—as the worst devastation of the plague faded into the past and Europe's population and economy began to recover, and as the eastern realms of Asia were sending trade goods westward at irregular times, in insufficient amounts, and at high prices—a number of persons of means on the western side of Europe were wondering how they might get away from it all—literally—and find new lands to help bring about their economic, social, and spiritual recovery.

Into the Atlantic

Well positioned to lead this effort were the Portuguese. The notion persists that Portugal was always poor and backward, and that it was mainly the efforts of one Dom Henrique, or "Henry the Navigator," the younger brother of the Portuguese king, who, flush with funds from a religious order and possessed of a crusading and exploring spirit, brought Portuguese and Italian seamen to make the discoveries that opened the Atlantic and soon the world to European commerce and colonization. But there is much more to the story than Henry's will and sponsorship. Since the expulsion of the Moors in 1249, Portuguese seamen had been ranging wide in their quest for goods and markets—to Flanders and Ireland in the north and to the northwest African coast in the south. Supporting this quest after 1385 was a new dynasty of Portuguese rulers and a landed aristocracy eager to fight for glory, God, or loot. When it became clear by 1400 that Venice controlled the trade of the eastern Mediterranean and could prevent others from participating in it, Genoese and Florentines looked west and brought their sailing know-how, mercantile instincts, and banking practices to cities of coastal Spain and Portugal. All who made up the commercial community of fifteenth-century Lisbon hoped they could find a way to outflank Muslims and Venetians, those who still held the keys to the doors of African gold and Asian luxury goods.

Dependent on Wind
for Propulsion

Before the steam engine, sailing ships were the fastest mode of transportation, but they were slow by today's standards and dependent for motion on the wind. We take motion for granted; old-time sailors did not. Experiencing light winds when leaving to cross the Atlantic in 1492, Christopher Columbus remained in sight of the Canary Islands for two days after his departure. The nature of the wind takes up more space in captains' logs than any combination of other subjects.

Travelers less experienced with the vagaries of breeze had less tolerance. Henry Fielding, author of Tom Jones, *expressed his frustration in a journal of a 1754 voyage he took from London to Lisbon to improve his health. Eight days under sail had not gotten the vessel far out of the Thames River. On the evening of July 3 the ship's captain predicted "a prosperous wind in the morning." The next day, the disgruntled passenger wrote:*

"This morning, however, the captain seem'd resolved to fulfil his own predictions, whether the wind would or no; he accordingly weighed anchor, and, taking the advantage of the tide, when the wind was not very boisterous, he hoisted his sails and, as if his power had been no less absolute over Eolus than it was over Neptune, he forced the wind to blow him on in its own despite.

But as all men who have ever been at sea well know how weak such attempts are, and want no authorities or Scripture to prove, that the most absolute power of a captain of a ship is very contemptible in the wind's eye, so did it befall our noble commander, who having struggled with the wind three or four hours, was obliged to give over, and lost, in a few minutes, all that he had been so long in gaining; in short, we returned to our former station, and once more cast anchor in the neighborhood of Deal."

Henry Fielding, A Journal from this World to the Next and The Journal of a Voyage to Lisbon, *ed. by Ian A. Bell and Andrew Varney (Oxford: Oxford University Press, 1997), 159.*

But any such maneuvering was out of the question so long as the navigational wisdom and maritime technology available to European mariners limited their ability to return from voyages south along the west coast of Africa. Winds and currents were the problem. Northeasterlies blow steadily from Morocco to Cape Verde, Africa's westernmost point, and the Canary Current flows briskly in the same direction. Voyagers could leave Portugal and sail south along Africa's coast with relative ease, but beyond a certain point not far into the voyage, returning home became nearly impossible. Their vessels could not sail close enough to the wind to allow them to tack and make headway. Sailors needed greater knowledge of Atlantic winds and more maneuverable ships with different rigging. Without this knowledge and technology, they remained tethered to Europe.

Contrary to popular belief, Prince Henry did not single-handedly kick off a revolution in ship building and ocean navigation. Instead, he played a small but important role in advancing knowledge of ship construction, guidance, and mapmaking that others, mostly Arabs and Indians, had been working on for centuries. (Henry's motives were mixed and, reflecting his world of superstition, zeal, greed, and scientific inquiry, included, in addition to acting for Christianity and gaining wealth, fulfilling predictions in his horoscope for making "great and noble conquests" and uncovering "secrets previously hidden from men.") Italian sailors, in touch with mariners in Europe's northern seas and also aware of such Muslim maritime advances as the lateen (triangular) sail, added to efforts to build more maneuverable ships that could haul bulkier cargo. Equipped with new vessels called caravels, which sported mostly lateen sails to allow for tighter maneuvering, Portuguese sailors began venturing farther down Africa's northwest coast. To return, they had to make laborious tacks that took advantage of slight changes in wind direction, on and off shore, between morning and evening. It was in this fashion that they reached nearby islands as early as the 1330s.

The Azores, Madeiras, and Canary Islands, all within two weeks travel by sea from southern Portugal, were known to ancient Mediterranean sailors—Pliny had written of these "Fortunate Isles" in his first-century *Natural History*, noting they "abound in fruit and birds of every kind"—but they were lost again to Europeans until the fourteenth-century explorations. Only the Canaries were populated at the time—by the Guanche, whose ancestors came from the African mainland a thousand or more years before the arrival of Europeans. Each of these volcanic archipelagos has rich soil and some enjoy abundant rainfall, which renders them much better suited to cultivation than the arid islands of the Mediterranean. Temperatures in the Azores are cooler than in the Madeiras and Canaries, a fact that affected their history. While Portuguese settled the uninhabited Azores as soon as their king allowed it, in 1439, this nine-island group lying 900 miles west of Lisbon never paid off as more than a way station for voyagers returning from the Americas. The Madeiras (only two islands) and Canaries (seven separate islands) are the truly fortunate ones, having a sun-rich, Mediterranean climate well suited for growing grapes (the source of Madeira wine and Canary sack) or sugar cane.

The Portuguese came first to the Canary Islands, which they found particularly appealing because of their inhabitants. The Guanche had livestock, which could supply hides, tallow, and wool, and early visitors found they could extract orchil, a valued purple dye, from lichens found on the islands. But the Guanche themselves made colonization of the islands difficult. In the words of the French, who fought them first, the Guanche were "tall and formidable." The Mediterranean market for slaves was strong when Europeans arrived on the northeasternmost Canary Island in 1336, but less than a generation later the Black Death cut like a scythe through Europe's peasant population. So it was to capture humans for agricultural labor that some came to the Canaries, and over time the Guanche would fill that sad bill.

But the robust slave is also the robust defender, so the appropriation of the Canaries was neither easy nor swift. A succession of Europeans set about the task, but it would take nearly all of the fifteenth century to conquer the entire archipelago. French mercenaries fighting for Castile captured the lightly populated islands on the eastern edge of the Canary chain soon after 1400. Over the half-century following 1415, Portugal expended thousands of foot soldiers and hundreds of horsemen in efforts to take the larger, remaining islands, but they enjoyed more success in capturing Guanche slaves than in winning land. The Spanish were the most persistent in fighting to control the Canaries. In 1478, Isabella and Ferdinand sent Pedro de Vera to take Gran Canaria, the largest island; it took his hundreds of soldiers equipped with horses, cannon, crossbows, and lances nearly six years to do so. A Spanish

Ecological Imperialism

The historian Alfred W. Crosby recognizes the importance of weaponry, organization, and zeal in European conquests, but he believes "the success of European imperialism has a biological, an ecological, component." Europeans before 1900 colonized mostly temperate zones that held flora and fauna strikingly different from that of Europe. European colonizers brought with them their plants, animals, and disease-causing germs, and most of these thrived at the expense of native species. This gave the Europeans enormous advantage.

Porto Santo, one of the Madeira Islands, was the first to experience ecological devastation with European contact. A Portuguese settler on the island let loose a female rabbit and her offspring in the 1420s and, without any predators or disease organisms to limit the size of the population, within a matter of a few years rabbits ruled. "Our men could sow nothing that was not destroyed by them," wrote one of the first would-be settlers. The rabbits ate everything they could get their gnawing teeth into, driving native plants into extinction and with them native animals for want of food and shelter. "Wind and rain erosion followed," Crosby writes, "and then the empty econiches were occupied by weeds and animals from the continents. The Porto Santo of 1400 is as lost to us as is the world before the Noachian flood."

Other episodes of ecological imperialism are of consequence for Atlantic history and demography. These would include the introduction to natives of the Americas of smallpox, measles, diphtheria, trachoma, whooping cough, chicken pox, bubonic plague, malaria, typhoid fever, cholera, yellow fever, dengue fever, scarlet fever, amoebic dysentery, and influenza, bringing the weakening and decline of the population and greatly easing European conquest. The rapid growth in the Americas of populations of pigs, cattle, and horses—let alone rats and honeybees—affected native people, animals, and plants living on the continents and altered Atlantic history in myriad ways.

Alfred W. Crosby, Ecological Imperialism: The Biological Expansion of Europe, 900–1900 (Cambridge, UK: Cambridge University Press, 1986).

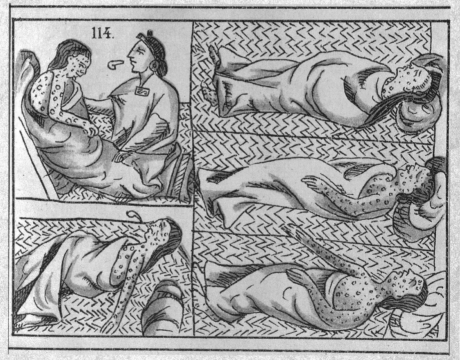

Aztecs suffering from smallpox. From B. de Sahagún, Historia de las cosas de Nueva Espana *(1569-75), pub. by F. del Paso y Troncoso, Book 12, Codex Florentino, Florence 1926/27, table 114. Photo: akg-images, London.*

force under Alonso de Lugo successfully invaded the smaller La Palma in September 1492—within days of Christopher Columbus's departure from neighboring Gomera, incidentally, for what he hoped would be a short hop over to Asia—but it would take Lugo three more years and two invasion forces comprising more than a thousand men to overcome the last Guanche hold-outs and solidify Spain's claim to the archipelago. The grit of the Spanish soldiers and the determination of their patrons, who appeared willing to throw endless resources into taking seven islands that promised meager returns, would have cast fear into the minds of the Americans Columbus encountered across 3,000 miles of ocean, had they but known.

What would have given Americans the greatest concern was the fate of the Guanche. In the conquest of the Canaries, perhaps 80,000 Guanche fell to a few thousand better-armed and organized Europeans. Assisting the conquerors was Guanche disunity, which enabled the Spanish to gain Guanche allies on one part of Tenerife Island, for example, to fight against those on the other side. But what ravaged the Guanche more than anything, according to the historian Alfred Crosby, was western Europeans' "portmanteau biota": "their extended family of plants, animals, and microlife—descendants, most of them, of organisms that humans had first domesticated or that had first adapted to living with humans in the heartlands of Old World civilization." The horse enhanced European military success, both in terms of fighting technique and psychology. Europeans' capture of cultivated land, burning off vegetation to enhance cultivation, and bringing new animals—cattle, horses, asses, chickens, goats, pigs, dogs, camels, rabbits, pigeons, partridges, and ducks—that devoured plants growing in unprotected fields reduced the Guanche food supply, forcing them to limit childbirth to avoid famine. Most important, Europeans introduced microbes that spread diseases: the Guanche had migrated from Africa so long before that, like Native Americans, they lacked acquired immunity to the Afro-Eurasian diseases the invaders brought with them. During the conquest of Tenerife in 1495, a Guanche woman who informed the Spanish of a pestilence, *modorra*, perhaps typhus, which had descended upon resisters holed up in the highlands, asked why they did not simply advance and occupy the land, writes the historian José de Viera y Clavijo, "for there was no one to fight, no one to fear—all being dead." The Guanche population, which probably exceeded 100,000 before European arrival, was gone by 1600. Dispossession of land meant loss of livelihood. Some survivors of the early wars and epidemics joined the Spanish and journeyed to Africa or America, many were enslaved to work in Madeira or Spain, but the largest number simply died without enough offspring to replace their numbers. By the mid-sixteenth century, Crosby writes, the "Guanches had become a paltry few, stumbling along the edge of doom, numbly observing their own extinction."

Some of the captured Guanche were taken to Portugal, where sugar plantations were thriving in the Algarve, and to Madeira. On this unpopulated island, plantation agriculture was taking hold at the very time the Guanche were coming under heightened attack. The original settlers of the island, which lies five hundred miles off the coast of modern Morocco, called it *Madeira*, meaning timber, because it was covered with trees—an impediment to those needing clear land for buildings, livestock, or vineyards. The island's earliest entrepreneurs in the 1420s began cutting the trees for export to timber-hungry Europe, but when the enterprise failed to clear land fast enough, hopeful inhabitants set the forests afire and kept the flames burning until they had reduced most of the indigenous trees to ash. This transformation of Madeira's environment allowed for experimentation with various nonnative animals and plants—cattle, pigs, honeybees, wheat, and grapes—to see if any would bring the kind of wealth the Portuguese wanted. None did. Sugar cane, however, sent from Sicily in 1425 by Prince Henry, promised great profit. In 1432 one of Henry's squires erected a water wheel and sugar mill near the town of Funchal, and the race to raise cane was on. In 1455, the Venetian Alvise Cadamosto reported, the "800 inhabitants of the south coast [of Madeira] make 400 cwt. of sugar 'of one boiling,' and will indeed soon make more and as much as anyone may wish to have." By the early 1470s Madeira was producing 200 tons of sugar and by the turn of the century, with 120 mills in operation, the island was exporting ten times that much sugar to locales as far away as England, Flanders, Genoa, Venice, and Greece.

The owners of Madeira's sugar plantations came from Portugal, mainly, but most of those who cleared the land, terraced the slopes, built the water courses for irrigation, grew the cane, or boiled it down into loaves came from elsewhere. Like all planters, Madeira's new landlords wanted workers who were plentiful, robust, long lived, and inexpensive. They did not have to venture far to find such individuals. First, they brought to the island a few Jews and Moors who still resided in Portugal, as well as some of the first Africans enslaved by Portuguese explorers as the latter headed down the African coast. Many more Madeiran slaves were Guanche, however, captured during the most aggressive period of warfare in the Canaries. So it was an ethnically and religiously mixed, unfree laboring corps that turned Madeira, over half a century, from an unpopulated woodland into the biggest sugar producer for the European market. Once cane took root in Madeira's fertile soils—owned and managed by Europeans with social as well as economic aspirations, and worked by men and women totally denied such aspirations—the mechanism that would carry European dominance, plantation agriculture, and a slave system to support both around the tropical and subtropical Atlantic fell into gear with a loud clunk that would echo on every continent bordering the ocean.

Sub-Saharan States and Empires

The desire for labor, in part to sustain this emerging plantation system, and hopes for direct access to markets for luxuries spurred Portuguese maritime ventures farther south along Africa's west coast. The Portuguese quickly realized that at various spots along that coast and for some distance inland were states and empires whose authority stretched across great distances and included large numbers of people. They could have barely known the half of it.

In 1324–25, not long before the Black Death reached Europe, the emperor Mansa Musa of the West African empire of Mali went on the *hajj* to Mecca, an event etched in the minds of many because he traveled there with so much gold—100 camel loads, some said—that he reduced the value of the metal in eastern Mediterranean markets. Mande-speaking people for centuries had controlled the south side of the trans-Sahara trade, and the wealth their ruling elites (like Musa of Mali) extracted from that trade and the people their armies conquered across a vast horizontal stretch of West Africa's interior was the talk of the Mediterranean world. North African travelers to Mali brought back stories of grand cities, at once centers of power, points of exchange, and loci of Islamic culture. It is no wonder that when a European Jew on Majorca produced the first reasonably accurate map of West Africa, in 1375, the dominant figure of the region below the Sahara was a seated African ruler, staff in one hand and gold nugget in the other.

Mali declined after the middle of the fourteenth century. That its ruling families never worked out a method for smooth succession took its toll on royal authority. Also, production in the goldfields, near the heartland of the empire on the upper Niger River, was waning and Mali's subjects may have suffered from the same plague that diminished European populations. West of the Niger River, states that formerly paid tribute to Mali broke away and formed independent political units. Between the lower Senegal and Gambia Rivers, several smaller entities united under Wolof rule to form the Jolof Empire, and farther south, below the middle Gambia, Mandinka elements continued to recognize the suzerainty of the Malian rulers, though such ties grew fragile.

To the north and farther inland, along several hundred miles of the Niger, where the river makes a grand bend toward the southeast as it heads toward its delta, 1,000 miles distant, Songhai-speaking people, adept farmers and boaters, separated early from Mali and slowly began to assume and extend political authority, first in cities along the river and then some distance beyond. Sunni Ali (r. 1464–92), ruler of the city-state of Gao, spent a lifetime gaining control of other commercial hubs along or near the middle Niger. Soon after Sunni Ali's death, one of his generals, Muhammad Touré, usurped power (taking the title *askiya*) and, further perfecting his predecessor's cavalry techniques, initiated wars of conquest that spread Songhai control 600 miles east and west and an equal distance north into the Sahara. Royal appointees replaced rulers of conquered territories, and tribute from these provinces flowed to the center of the empire. Touré walked a fine line between the traditional beliefs of the majority of his subjects, who kept spiritual ties to the lands of their birth, and the Islam of the urban centers of his realm, the latter ports of the trans-Saharan trade and vital to the wealth of the empire. Some of Touré's wars of conquest he termed *jihads*, and, like Mansa Musa, he went on pilgrimage to Mecca, returning with recognition as *caliph* (supreme ruler, successor to The Prophet) of the Western Sudan.

A revitalized trans-Saharan trade and an internal commerce in foodstuffs, both of which imperial authorities taxed, brought wealth to Songhai beyond the dreams of Portuguese sailors. A Moroccan from Fez, writing as Leo Africanus, visited Songhai in 1510 and 1511 and described the inhabitants of Timbuktu as "exceedingly rich . . . people of a gentle and cheerful disposition [who] spend a great part of the night in singing and dancing through all the streets of the city. They keep great store of men and women slaves." In Gao, Leo Africanus considered it "a wonder to see how much merchandise is brought here daily, and how costly and sumptuous everything is. Horses bought in Europe for ten ducats [a gold coin in European circulation] are sold again for forty and sometimes fifty ducats a piece. There is not any cloth in Europe so coarse, which will not here be sold for four ducats an ell."

In addition to the former Malian tributary state of Jolof, other territorial units existed along the Atlantic side of Africa at the time Songhai grew to maximum strength. Benin, west of the lower Niger River, for instance, following conquest of Yoruba and other neighbors, reached a height in power and influence early in the sixteenth century. Though nothing like Songhai in territorial control, Benin had a capital city, Edo, that later Dutch visitors described as "four miles broad," having thirty straight streets, forty yards across, that met at right angles and were lined with fine dwellings. Benin is best known for its sculptors, who created brass castings as fine as any ever made. Benin was a rare entity in being strong enough to stop the trading of slaves when its leaders felt that human commerce was harming the state. The Dutch geographer Olfert Dapper would relate, as late as the seventeenth century, that the ruler of Benin, the *oba*, could put into the field an army of 20,000 in a single day and follow soon with four times that many, making a total force roughly equal the population of Dapper's home of Amsterdam in the early decades of the century.

Farther south, the Kingdom of Kongo, which had expanded through the fifteenth century, held sway over a larger area. States had come into being in the vicinity of the lower Congo River early in the second millennium. Key to their existence was Pool Malebo, a twenty-mile-long by fifteen-mile-wide expansion of the river 200 miles in from the Atlantic. Above the pool, the Congo River is navigable for hundreds of miles and below it, an impassable cascade blocks river traffic. Goods passing up or down the river had to be portaged around the cascade, making it a trans-shipment point and a strategic spot in the control of trade. For some centuries, iron, copper ore, cloth (made from raffia or bark), ivory, and seashells were traded between the middle Kongo and the Atlantic coast. As with rulers of the Western Sudanic empires, Kongo chiefs and headmen, able to tax goods moving along the river and trade routes feeding into it, found the means to construct political power. In the second half of the fourteenth century, a group of clan chiefs, the Mwisikongo, who had been prospering from copper manufacturing, selected an outsider to organize and lead them, giving him the title *Manikongo*, ruler of Kongo. The manikongo and his successors would spread Kongo suzerainty until, by the late 1400s, the kingdom, actually a loose confederacy, was a polity of considerable size and strength.

The capital of Kongo, Mbanzakongo, had long been a commercial center, but it became a greater one as Kongo rulers extended control west, where raffia cloth was manufactured, and east to include Pool Malebo, providing access to goods coming from the river's central basin. They soon spread their authority to the Atlantic and then another 200 miles south, eventually taking

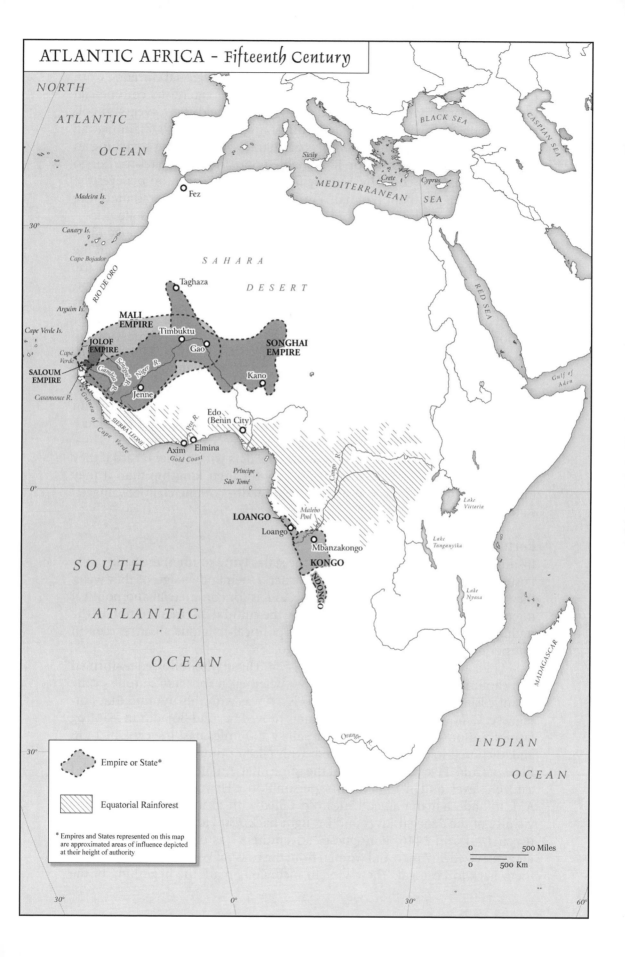

ATLANTIC AFRICA - Fifteenth Century

NORTH
ATLANTIC
OCEAN

Madeira Is.

30°

Canary Is.

Cape Bojador

SAHARA DESERT

Taghaza

Arguin Is.

Cape Verde Is.

MALI EMPIRE

Cape Verde

JOLOF EMPIRE

Timbuktu

Gao

SONGHAI EMPIRE

SALOUM EMPIRE

Senegal R.

Gambia R.

Niger R.

Kano

Casamance R.

Jenne

SIERRA LEONE

Pra R.

Edo (Benin City)

Axim Elmina

Gold Coast

Guinea of Cape Verde

RIO DE ORO

Fez

MEDITERRANEAN SEA

Sicily

Crete

Cyprus

BLACK SEA

CASPIAN SEA

RED SEA

Gulf of Aden

Príncipe

São Tomé

0°

Malebo Pool

LOANGO

Loango

Mbanzakongo

KONGO

NDONGO

Congo R.

Lake Victoria

Lake Tanganyika

Lake Nyasa

MADAGASCAR

SOUTH
ATLANTIC
OCEAN

Orange R.

INDIAN OCEAN

30°

Empire or State*

Equatorial Rainforest

* Empires and States represented on this map
are approximated areas of influence depicted
at their height of authority

0   500 Miles

0   500 Km

30°   0°   30°   60°

the island of Luanda, the source of *nzumbu* shells, the regional currency. Control of access to the currency helped Kongo further extend its commercial influence inland. By the late 1400s, Kongo rulers held sway over, and collected tribute from, dozens of states, from Loango in the north to Ndongo in the south, comprising some 400 miles of Atlantic coastline and stretching an equal distance into the interior. Reasonable population estimates for Kongo in 1500 are hard to come by, but the historian John Thornton believes the kingdom had a population of half a million in 1700, and this was after slave trading and attacks from rival armies had already weakened the state.

Despite the power they garnered from the trade of the lower Congo River and the Atlantic coast, the fifteenth-century rulers of Kongo lacked what the historian Anne Hilton terms a "strong legitimizing ideology." The basis of the manikongo's legitimacy was the support of heads of the major clans in central parts of the kingdom. The interests of the clan chiefs and the manikongo tended to coincide, so while it was not always difficult to gain and keep their support, that support was never a sure thing. Thus, through most of the kingdom's existence, Kongo rulers sought to broaden the basis of their legitimacy. They did so at times by establishing relationships through marriage to other powerful clans located some distance from the center. More frequently, they sought to enhance a legitimacy based on religion, working hard to gain the backing of local priests, who interpreted the will of the spirits of the land. The manikongos knew the priestly support they received was tenuous. Thus, those who ruled Kongo might look upon outsiders with higher regard if they came bearing some new form of legitimacy for their kingship than if they merely brought some new commodity to trade to the commercially advantaged state.

Portugal's "Guinea of Cape Verde"

Insufficiently aware of the strength of the states lying south of the Sahara, the Portuguese pressed ahead cautiously to extend their knowledge. As they went, they would slowly devise two different models for commercial and political interaction: a trade model, epitomized by the cultural interpenetration of the trading post, or factory, and a model of political-religious alliance, seen in this period only in the Kingdom of Kongo.

Gil Eanes passed Cape Bojador in 1434. Those who followed reaffirmed that capturing humans for sale as slaves, whether in southern Europe or the Atlantic islands, was a lucrative enterprise. It was with this in mind that Portuguese, Genoese, and Venetian mariners moved beyond Bojador in leapfrog fashion. Affonso Gonçalvez Baldaya sailed 300 miles past the cape in 1436 and anchored in an inlet he named, with false optimism, Rio d'Ouro—the River of Gold. Five years later, near the same inlet, Antam Gonçalvez captured a dozen slaves, and in 1444 the first person Prince Henry actually licensed for African trade, a man named Lançarote, sailed with six armed vessels into the vicinity of the Senegal River and brought back 230 kidnapped Africans. Between 1441 and 1446, Portuguese "adventurers," as these kidnappers were known, seized 927 men and women from the coast of West Africa and brought them back to Portugal. These violent incursions mark the beginning of the

Early Iberian Slavery

Even when slave trading was modest in numbers, the cultural impact of imported slaves could be significant. By the mid-fifteenth century, Portuguese traders were importing about 1,000 African slaves into Lisbon annually and after 1490 that number rose to 2,000 in some years. Some of those Africans filtered into southern Spain. A study of Seville's notarial archives in 1501–25 found that of 5,271 slaves recorded, almost 4,000 were listed as blacks or mulattoes. Muslims, white Christians, Jews, Guanches, and American Indians composed the remainder of those enslaved.

Just as not all slaves in Spain were African, not all Africans in Spain were slaves. Spanish slave law, codified in the thirteenth century, offered avenues out of slavery, and by the fifteenth century one could find a small but significant free black class in Spain's southern cities. While retaining much of their "national" culture, these free Africans claimed different corporate identities—as citizens in various municipalities and as members of parishes and religious brotherhoods. Such memberships awarded legal protections and privileges. Even as Portuguese slavers were collecting captives on the African coasts, free black mayorales (stewards) arbitrated disputes in black neighborhoods and defended their charges in courts, while black officials administered funds and responsibilities of black churches, hospitals, and welfare systems. Although those Africans seemed models of acculturation, they nevertheless preserved such visible cultural elements as language, music, dance, and ceremony, and probably many less visible social structures as well, because Spanish society never attempted to forbid it. Assimilationist policies and the relative cultural freedom Africans exercised may have worked for the

Iberians. Antonio Domínguez Ortiz compared early modern Seville to a chessboard with equal numbers of black and white pieces, but as far as we know, Africans never revolted in southern Spain or Portugal, nor staged any mass escapes, despite their proximity to Africa and their common employment as sailors. The medieval Spanish pattern of incorporating the converted outsiders, albeit never fully, shaped early modern Spanish society.

Moorish slave with a wine-skin in Castile, 1520–40, from the Trachtenbuch ("Das Trachtenbuch des Christoph Weiditz"). Plate XLVII in Authentic Everyday Dress of the Renaissance, Dover Books.

Atlantic slave trade, an unprecedented commerce in humans that would last four and one-half centuries and involve the transportation of millions of people from one side of the ocean to the other.

The Portuguese mariners soon learned a lesson that would hold up through all the years of this traffic in human beings: that there was a safer and more efficient way than kidnapping to obtain laborers from occupants of distant lands. Nuno Tristão, among the most fabled of the early Portuguese mariners, was the first one to find this out, and it cost him his life. His eight-foot bronze statue stands today along with those of Vasco da Gama and others, sword at the ready, stern visage glaring out at those idling through the high-ceilinged entry hall of Lisbon's Museu de Marinha. Tristão explored 700 miles of African coast south of Cape Bojador in the early 1440s. Other navigators had reached Cape Verde (the name they gave it denoting its green flora, as opposed to the drier, or "whiter," conditions higher off the coast of the Sahara) in modern Senegal. In 1446 Tristão sailed farther south, into the wide and seemingly welcoming mouth of the Gambia River. Not far up the river, he launched two boats from his caravel, with twelve armed men (including Tristão) in one and ten in the other. They rode the tide upriver in search of Africans they might capture, and in a short while they found some. But before they could act, an African potentate on the other bank of the river launched a dozen boats, each full of men armed with bows and poison arrows, and as soon as the bowmen reached lethal range, they shot at Tristão and his fellow invaders unmercifully. Only seven of the Europeans were lucky enough to survive and return to their larger vessel before limping home to spread the bad news. The next time Portuguese sailors entered the Gambia River or areas farther south, they came with hat in hand, and this approach served them better. Local rulers seemed inclined to welcome the commerce. Word trickled south that pale-skinned traders in the Senegal River were providing horses and iron bars, and African leaders quickly saw how their commercial interests might intertwine with those of their new trading partners. After recounting the tale of Tristão's death, the chronicler Azurara noted that henceforth, "deeds in those parts involved trade and mercantile dealings more than fortitude and exercise of arms."

And a policy of mercantile dealing was just what the Portuguese needed. They did not represent a large and powerful nation, and they were soon to be coming upon new lands with considerable commercial potential. So instead of coming to fight, Portuguese mariners moved on down the west coast of Africa with the idea of establishing trading outposts—*feitorias* (factories) as they were known—and integrating themselves into African commerce.

In 1448, Portuguese merchants built a fort on Arguim Island, off modern Mauritania, and outfitted it with provisions for passing vessels. Grain did not grow easily on the island or along the adjacent coast, but locally caught fish quickly became important for replenishing ships' supplies. Then, seven years later, Portuguese mariners sighted the Cape Verde archipelago, a dozen small, uninhabited islands lying 350 miles northwest of the cape, and it was soon apparent that the volcanic islands could serve as an advance base for trading with the coast. Prince Henry died in 1460, just as mariners he sponsored reached the coast of Sierra Leone. Two years later, Henry's cousin arranged for the first colonists to settle São Tiago, the largest of the Cape Verde Islands. To stimulate further settlement of the archipelago in 1466, Portugal's King Afonso V granted Cape Verde residents exclusive rights to trade along Africa's west coast. Quickly, the land lying along the coast between the Senegal River and Sierra Leone became, in Portuguese eyes, the "Guinea of Cape Verde." *Guinea* was the term the Portuguese used for all of Africa's west coast below the Sahara. They termed the northern part of the Guinea of Cape Verde "Senegambia" and the coast south of the Casamance River the "Southern Rivers." For the next century and a half, Portuguese and Cape Verdeans would operate out of a handful of the islands' ports to tie into the brisk trade of the coast and vast hinterland of this region.

That commerce showed real potential. From the earliest voyages, the Portuguese had learned of the great demand throughout Senegambia for horses. With the buildup of herds in Jolof in the mid-fifteenth century, followed by the growth of cavalries among smaller states across the savannas of West Africa, Portuguese traders had their hands full trying to meet the demand—especially since one caravel could carry no more than ten horses. In the beginning, they brought animals from home or purchased them along the coasts of Morocco and Mauritania, but after 1480 colonists began breeding horses on the Cape Verde Islands, and soon this became the major source for the Portuguese horse trade. The terms of trade were good. The earliest dealers received between nine and fourteen slaves per horse, which brought profits, once the slaves were sold on Madeira or in Portugal, of between 500 and 700 percent per voyage.

Of course, slaves were not all the Portuguese wanted, any more than horses were the only commodity Africans sought. In a visit with Gambia River merchants in 1455, the Portuguese learned of the availability of gold farther upriver. A seaman in the river later reported seeing merchants "come loaded with gold" and having learned that the "lord of all the mines," residing toward the east, "had before the door of his palace a mass of gold just as it was taken from the earth, so large that twenty men could scarcely move it, and [to which] the king always fastened his horse." Another seaman bartered for gold nearby, noting cheerfully that "they traded it cheaply, taking in exchange articles of little value in our eyes." Before long, others recognized profits available in transporting kola nuts northward from Sierra Leone. Yet Africans had other needs and wants besides kola. Caravels soon began bringing raw cotton and cotton cloth—much of it, after the 1470s, woven on the Cape Verde Islands, using African techniques and slaves to do the weaving—as well as iron (some of it manufactured elsewhere in Africa) and copperware to exchange along Senegambia's coast and riverbanks.

The Portuguese kept their mercantile antennae up to learn of products they could acquire in one place and sell elsewhere for a profit, and the list of these commodities, which they soon were carrying to and fro, grew long. Elephants still lumbered about the wooded savannas of West Africa in the fifteenth century, so ivory drew serious attention. So did the more mundane beeswax, used in candle making. Herders, most part of the Fulbe ethnic group, occasionally parted with hides; wood of some African trees proved useful in the manufacture of dyes, and salt that evaporated along Atlantic beaches could be bartered up the rivers. The Portuguese also became carriers of foodstuffs produced in Guinea. The population of the Cape Verdes needed grain and so did crews of coasting ships, so enterprising traders took up bartering for sorghum and millet along coastal Senegal. South of there, Africans were experienced rice growers. In fact, the implications of Atlantic mariners encountering Guinea Coast rice producers were great because, in addition to providing food for colonists of coastal rivers and nearby islands, the knowledge of the growers themselves eventually spread across the ocean and helped make some areas of the Americas thriving centers of slave-based rice production.

The trade in slaves remained important for Portuguese merchants in Upper Guinea, though through the fifteenth century the numbers of captives taken from the region remained small—in the hundreds per year, an initial trickle of what would become a torrent. This modest slave trade was initially conducted from ships, but not many years passed before a disgruntled Portuguese merchant here or a venturesome Cape Verdean trader there turned his back on royal authority and cast his lot on shore among the local population. In so doing, he established an important model of cultural interaction, embodied in the trade factory and its associated personnel and institutions, which would later be found around the Atlantic world. The kings of Portugal neither envisioned nor wanted European settlement among African populations, but the colonization of the Cape Verdes after 1460 started a process that would lead to a weakening of royal control and growth of unauthorized Portuguese residency among coastal populations. Portuguese living on the Cape Verde Islands imported slaves, many of them women from the coast of Africa, to perform a range of domestic tasks. In a short time, the inevitable unions between Portuguese men and African women brought about a sizable population of mixed parentage on the islands. These Luso-Africans, having the advantage of familiarity with both Portuguese and African cultures and languages, would be the primary facilitators of the trade of the Guinea of Cape Verde in the late fifteenth and sixteenth centuries.

The Portuguese kings may not have intended for their countrymen and Cape Verdeans to take up residence among coastal Africans—they called the settlers *lançados* (from *se-lançar*, to throw oneself, as if the men made decisions to cast themselves among Africans) or, later, *tangomaos*, connoting renegades—but African rulers, whose cultures were more inclusive and who were more experienced in cross-cultural dealings, expected nothing else. The lançados, not entirely familiar with local language and culture, had to adopt customs and norms of local residents. Simplifying this was an institutionalized landlord-stranger relationship that already existed among the coastal Africans. It allowed the new, foreign arrivals entry into the society and monitored the synthesis of Portuguese (or Cape Verdean) and African ways of living.

Evidence relating to the incorporation of early Europeans in coastal African societies is scarce, but some exists. The first lançados would have needed to make initial arrangements with local authorities. Rulers on the spot tended to sanction lançado settlement where such settlements would serve them best, often in villages attached to, or close by, existing commercial centers. Some societies had villages that were established specifically as settlements for "strangers," mostly traders from distant locales, coming to participate in the Portuguese-stimulated commerce growing along the waterside. The Gambia River village of Juffure, today known more than others because it was the African home of Kunta Kinte in Alex Haley's *Roots: The Saga of an African Family* (1976), is remembered locally as having been founded between 1495 and 1520 as a "stranger village" by members of an Islamic commercial and clerical lineage who moved to the Gambia from the middle Senegal River to trade. Local traditions suggest that the Muslim traders founded the village with the help of "some Portuguese," who already had their own town nearby. In any case, a symbiosis existed between enclaves of African, Portuguese, and Luso-African merchants. Early lançado-African settlements became points of contact between ruling families, African merchants, and Europeans coming to trade.

Naturally, the upper hand in these cross-cultural, commercial relationships remained with Africans. Europeans who came to trade did not have much power at their disposal. Some of the caravels mounted bombards, a kind of loud but generally ineffective mortar, and while Portuguese crossbowmen carried more effective weaponry, they always were badly outnumbered by African bowmen. Those of full or partial European descent who settled on African soil had to rely on local rulers to ensure conditions for safe passage of trade goods and for protection of their merchants. The Portuguese also came with more basic needs—water and food, most important. (One village that came into existence along the lower Gambia River in the fifteenth century was named Tubab Kolong, or "white man's well" in Mandinka.) The Portuguese also needed help with everything from navigating over shoals and sandbars to communicating with African rulers and traders. So after initial rough experiences, when they learned just how dependent they were, these early Europeans took on an accommodating manner, ready to do what they must to work out a mutually beneficial trading relationship. Although it would take centuries for their advantages to become broadly evident, the Portuguese trump cards were access to financial capital, long-distance sailing technologies, and commodities Africans wanted. Meanwhile, the settlers had to pay taxes to local lords.

Wherever an African leader might decide to settle a lançado, the latter needed to attach himself to a landlord, who would oversee his dealings with others. Besides help with essentials, the landlord represented and defended the stranger in disputes and in local councils. He vouched for the lançado when dealings required trust or credit and did what he could to ensure the stranger's commercial success. Over time, if the lançado was indeed successful, the landlord might help him find a spouse, one of his own daughters, perhaps, or another woman with good connections. All of this represented an institutional way of integrating useful foreigners into an African society.

Of course, African potentates did not allow outsiders to settle, and landlords did not aid these strangers, purely out of the goodness of their hearts. "Strangers make the village prosper" is a proverb in many West African languages, and people in many African societies seem to have had their own notions of trickle-down economics. As a lançado became successful he had something valuable to offer and an informal obligation to see that his landlord benefited from his success. This normally entailed the giving of gifts, with values commensurate to the stranger's level of success, and the payment of more regular fees and taxes to a ruling family.

In this fashion, lançado populations gained acceptance along the Upper Guinea coast. Much as Muslim traders had done across a desert-oriented western African trading complex in earlier centuries, the lançados developed their own identity, based not on their physical appearance—for soon they were not noticeably different from the Africans among whom they lived—but on cultural characteristics they shared and clung to tenaciously. They still called themselves "Portuguese" because they retained outward elements of a Portuguese background: they built and lived in square dwellings with lime-whitened walls; wore European-style clothing; possessed Catholic images, though many never had seen a cleric; kept Portuguese names; and considered themselves "white." Among other languages, lançados spoke Crioulo, a tongue with a Portuguese vocabulary but grammar and syntax from West African languages. Crioulo developed on the Cape Verde Islands and spread as a lingua franca for trade along the west coast of Africa and up its rivers. Finally, as many did throughout West Africa, the lançados identified with their profession: one way or another, they were engaged in trade. The longer they lived on African soil, the more these extended families looked and acted like their hosts.

Lower Guinea and the Kongo

Neither the death of Prince Henry nor the stimulus of trade in the Guinea of Cape Verde slowed the press of caravels heading south. In the 1460s, trade picked up below Sierra Leone, where Portuguese began acquiring "grains of paradise," an African species of pepper, malaguetta, they could sell in Europe to compete with Asian spices. Farther along, around Cape Palmas, they found ivory, though King Afonso V's stipulation that his Portuguese subjects could only sell ivory to him, at a fixed price, dampened profits. Still, the real bonanzas lay ahead: in 1470 two explorers spotted São Tomé, an island balanced on the equator and ideal for sugar production; two years later a caravel landed near the Pra River back up the coast, in trading distance of West Africa's most productive gold mines. All of the Portuguese crown's investments in ships, men, trade goods, supplies, equipment, and the merchants it had aided was about to pay off.

West African gold lay mostly in alluvial deposits distributed broadly rather than in underground veins, so there were no mother lodes or fabled mines to spark a mad rush—not that the Portuguese were strong enough to rush in and take over the goldfields, anyway. Early emissaries of the Portuguese crown ventured inland over several decades, visiting each of the gold-producing regions of West Africa and learning the hard way the cost paid by Europeans wanting to settle in these tropics: the death rate varied between 25 and 50 percent per year, mostly from malaria and dysentery. Coastal trade was the logical alternative. Gold was precious outside West Africa for its scarcity, and within—at least in part—for its cost in labor. It took so much work to obtain gold from scattered alluvial deposits that Africans did not bother with it during the rainy season, when growing a crop was a more cost-effective—and healthy—endeavor. To coordinate the trade along the newly coined "Gold Coast," the Portuguese crown ordered erection of a fort in 1482 at São Jorge da Mina, later shortened to El Mina ("The Mine"), and then to Elmina. The trade was strong enough that twenty years later they built another fort up the coast at Axim. Soon, Atlantic creole, or "Eurafrican," communities similar to those of the lançados of Upper Guinea grew in new towns surrounding the

Gold Coast forts. Portuguese merchants were eager to import whatever they could in exchange, but there were rules and restrictions. Pope Nicholas V banned the trade of weapons to Africans, a prohibition Portugal's kings respected in exchange for his granting them exclusive trading rights in Africa. Also, horses could not live long in the more forested, equatorial setting of Lower Guinea, where tsetse flies spread sleeping sickness (trypanosomiasis) among herds, so traders coming by water had to scramble to find goods to exchange for the gold they coveted.

It was to the good fortune of the traders—though clearly not to all involved—that the Akan-speaking people of the Gold Coast needed labor for agricultural and military pursuits, as well as for extracting gold. Before the Portuguese arrived at their waterside, local rulers had acquired slaves through trade from populated areas to their north, usually in exchange for gold. Now they could seek slaves from the Atlantic. As the Portuguese sailed eastward beyond Elmina and approached the Niger Delta, they encountered representatives of the Kingdom of Benin, who were eager to sell captives taken in recent conquests. In exchange for copper, iron, and cloth, the Portuguese acquired slaves from Benin and its neighbors along what they soon labeled the "Slave Coast" to exchange for gold from the Gold Coast. As early as the late 1480s, 8,000 ounces of African gold annually reached Portugal's royal treasury, and this amount rose to 22,500 ounces by 1496. Records of the number of slaves shipped to the Gold Coast were not kept so carefully, but it is clear that between 1500 and 1535 the Portuguese acquired more than 10,000 men, women, and children along the Slave Coast to enable the trade for gold at Elmina and Axim. Ironically, by reorienting as much as one-fifth of the gold trade to the Atlantic coast, away from the Sahara, the European traders played a role in the weakening of Songhai, which at that time was the largest state ever assembled in tropical Africa. In 1590 it would fall—not to Europeans, but to Moroccans from across the desert.

Slaves from Benin and elsewhere were important in building commercial wealth farther south, as well. Both São Tomé and Príncipe, islands lying between the Bight of Biafra and the equator, were lush and green, with good soil. With Madeira in mind, the Portuguese did not need to experiment to make the islands profitable. Following a failed private effort in the 1480s, Portugal's King João II granted land to would-be planters and sent out a party that included convicts and Jewish children (the latter torn from their parents as part of the crown's effort to rid the country of Jews) to begin clearing land and planting sugar. In this fashion, soon after 1500, São Tomé replaced Madeira as the largest supplier of sugar to Europe.

Slaves for the equatorial sugar islands' plantations came at first mostly from Benin, where the oba continued wars of expansion that yielded captives, but further Portuguese exploration opened new markets. In 1483, Diogo Cão reached the Congo River, where he encountered the Kongo Kingdom. From the beginning, the Portuguese saw wealthy and populous Kongo as a trade partner. The kingdom proved unusually receptive to Christianity, too. Religious culture there held similarities to Portuguese Catholicism in that royalty and commoners in both kingdoms looked to priests to interpret dreams and signs, and both people put great stock in the priestly interpretations. Moreover, Catholic Christianity, and especially the multitude of saints that Catholics revered, appeared to offer the rulers of Kongo a host of new spirits whom they could appropriate to solidify their legitimacy.

So in the last years of the fifteenth century, when Portugal's King Manuel I sent missionaries to Kongo to do the work of God (as he perceived it) and let traders do the bidding of Mammon, both found success. The former made quick work of converting the ruling elite of the state to Christianity (although Catholic priests had to accept some essential African customs), assisted, as they were, by a series of dreams and events that Kongo's rulers recognized (with some prompting) as signs of grace and salvation. After building a missionary town, São Salvador, next to the state's political and commercial center of Mbanzakongo, Portuguese priests converted prince Nzinga Mbemba in 1491. He would reign as King Afonso I when he took power in 1506.

For a time, Afonso was eager to serve both Portuguese interests and his own. A bona fide Christian (although the historian James H. Sweet recently has questioned the existence of such in Central Africa at the time), he sent young men from his kingdom to Portugal for training (one was made a bishop in 1518) and brought Western artisans, ideas, and fashions into his realm. But he used arms imported from the Portuguese (who ignored the Pope's ban on such commerce when they wished) to extend his control north and south along the Atlantic coast, and over the interior Congo basin beyond Pool Malembo. Among the products of the resulting warfare were captives that Afonso bartered away to the Portuguese, who wanted slaves for their offshore sugar plantations. It is possible to see in hindsight that this served for the ruler and many of his subjects as the beginning of the end of civilization as they had known it.

The North Atlantic

Portuguese maritime ventures and commercial ambitions had drawn Europeans south along the African coast (by 1488, around the Cape of Good Hope and then north into the Indian Ocean) and had taught Europeans and Africans the mutual advantages of expanded coastwise and intercontinental commerce. But the Portuguese were not the only Europeans active in Atlantic exploration, nor were Europe's demands limited to slaves, gold, ivory, and pepper. Besides being a waterway linking land-based trade, the Atlantic was a treasure trove of marine life. A separate and increasingly important strand of economic activity in Europe centered on the North Atlantic, where northwest Europeans engaged in commercial fishing off Iceland and Greenland. Although whales were increasingly sought for their oil, the prime commodity was cod, hardly as exotic as the spices Europeans craved from the east, nor as luxuriously tangible as Africa's gold and ivory, nor as brutalized as the human labor purchased to cultivate sugar on Atlantic islands. But cod was a product of enormous value nonetheless, more cherished by a hungry city dweller than the most intricately carved ivory, the heaviest gold ingot, or the tastiest sugar-laden morsel. In a period before refrigeration, food preservation was largely accomplished by pickling or dry salting. While salted meat eventually went

Food, Commerce, Consumption, and Catholicism

Catholic restrictions on food consumption both helped make a market for cod and aided the spread of sugar. The Catholic liturgical calendar contained fast days when believers were to abstain from sex and the consumption of flesh. Every Friday, the entire forty-day period of Lent, and other holidays comprised the days (almost half the year, altogether) when meat consumption was banned. Where did fish belong? Eating fish was permitted on fast days, and with its easy preservation, salted cod became associated with fast days. Thus, religious beliefs spawned a large market for Basques fishermen. As for sugar, such ethicists as Thomas Aquinas debated its nature. Was it food? Did believers violate the fast when they consumed it? Aquinas concluded that sugar had a medicinal value, and therefore was not food. Unencumbered by religious prohibition, conscientious Catholics could freely consume sugar. Thus the medieval church fueled consumption and generated markets of two commodities that shaped European involvement in the Atlantic world. Fishermen so aggressively harvested cod that the fisheries are nearing depletion, and enslaved agricultural workers produced sugar in conditions so extreme that countless numbers of them died to sate European appetites.

Slaves cutting sugar cane in Antigua, by William Clark. Published by Thomas Clay, London 1823. Copyright © The British Library. Record: c5673-01, Shelfmark: 1786.c.9, Page Folio: plate IV.

bad, dried cod proved exceptionally durable and easily reconstituted with water. Cod can be dried naturally in the open air or preserved longer through salting. It furthermore has a low fat content, and once dried becomes a hard, desiccated, and lightweight substance consisting almost entirely of protein—the energy bar of the medieval world. Highly portable and nutritious, cod could sustain mariners on long voyages or armies on the move. In times of commercial expansion and war, cod found a ready market, as it did among Catholics, banned from eating meat on fast days but allowed to partake of dried fish. Atlantic cod was heavily fished from an early date, which helps explain its scarcity today. Although Inuit and native Greenlanders had long fished for subsistence, Scandinavians were the first to exploit the North Atlantic commercially; the line of Viking settlement neatly followed the cold waters in which great schools of cod dwelled.

The Basques were the first to break the Viking monopoly; by 1000 they had established a thriving international trade in cod. Like other fishermen,

Basques did not reveal their fishing grounds, but the fact that they returned to Europe with salted cod, which required dry land for processing, suggested they had found an unknown North Atlantic landmass.

There was no such mystery about where the English fished for cod—in the waters off Iceland. Bristol, in southwest England, became an entrepot of the cod trade. When merchants there were cut off from Icelandic cod after 1475 by the powerful Hanseatic League, the result of a long-simmering commercial dispute, the English pursued their own fishing grounds. (If Italians and Portuguese wanted direct access to the spices of the east, Bristol merchants sought direct access to cod.) About this time, a merchant named John Jay funded a ship to search for a mythical Atlantic island known as "Hy-Brasil" in hopes of finding a new land base for cod drying and salting. Jay's ship returned with cod, but—in line with the tendency of all who fish toward secrecy—no report about where the catch had been found and salted. Bristol merchants soon funded John Cabot, a naturalized Venetian resident in England since the mid-1480s, to seek the fabled "Northwest Passage" to the spices of the East. With a crew of eighteen packed aboard the *Matthew*, Cabot probably made landfall on present-day Cape Breton Island. He almost certainly sailed along the coasts of Newfoundland and New England, which he believed, in a manner reminiscent of his contemporary, Columbus, to be the shores of northeastern Asia. A second and larger voyage in May 1498 gained no more intelligence. Instead of the Japanese islands he sought, Cabot had found the eastern coast of Greenland and weather so cold that his crews mutinied and forced him to turn south. That he returned with word of waters abounding in cod tells why others were not so easily dissuaded. When the explorer Jacques Cartier sailed to the same region almost four decades later, he staked his claim for France, despite the visible presence of Basque fishermen.

An Age of Territorial Expansion: The Empires of the Western Atlantic

When historians think of expansion in the fifteenth century, they often focus by habit on these well-known European enterprises, the aggressive quest for new commercial opportunities, the insertion of European merchants into African economies and polities, the transformation of Atlantic islands into specialized sugar enclaves, and the more furtive activities of fishermen. These were the prime agents in an older interpretation of world history, one centered on the rise of the "West," or the expanding political dominance of western Europeans around the globe. Viewed from an Atlantic perspective, however, the most impressive instances of fifteenth-century political and economic expansion came about either in Africa, with the rapid growth of the Songhai Empire, or on the American mainland: the near simultaneous rise of the Mexica (Aztec) Empire in southern Mexico and the Inca Empire in Peru. Each of these vast domains eclipsed any kingdom in Europe in size and population. In this period when European kingdoms were slowly consolidating power, Spain acquired its empire only by conquering the two great empires of the Americas, places of unimagined wealth and power. These indigenous empires controlled millions of subject people of varying ethnicities, and they extracted from them tribute in commodities and labor. Rulers flaunted the material treasures of conquest in imperial cities whose edifices dazzled the European invaders.

While Europe was slowly recovering from the population losses associated with the Black Death, and as Mansa Musa of Mali was dispensing trails of gold along the route of his hajj to Mecca, a group of city-states was rising around Lake Texcoco in the Central Valley of Mexico. The wealth and grandeur of those cities attracted a group of western nomads, who called themselves Mexica. Guided by their god of war and the sun, *Huitzilopochtli* (Hummingbird of the South), these people, referred to by some as "Aztecs" because they were thought to have come from a land called Aztlán, entered the valley in the mid-fourteenth century.

According to Mexica origin myths, a monstrous female creature named Cipactli swam in primordial seas devouring all before her until the gods Quetzalcóatl and Tezcatlipoca turned themselves into serpents and tore her apart. With Cipactli's destruction, Coatlicue appeared, but Coatlicue was another terror with intertwined snakes for a head. She wore a necklace of human hearts, hands, and skulls, and only human sacrifices would still her cries. Impregnated by a feather ball, Coatlicue gave virgin birth to the terrible Huitzilopochtli, the aforementioned Mexica god of war, who required blood sacrifice to renew the earth, and who guided his nomadic followers to their destiny in the Central Valley.

Over time, the Mexica were able to parlay their military skills into alliances with powerful kings and win a toehold in unwanted marshlands edging the lake. Adopting age-old techniques, they mastered the inhospitable terrain by dredging the rich muck and creating aquatic gardens, *chinampas*, on which they grew crops. Finally, the Mexica fulfilled their destiny, around 1325, by building Tenochtitlán on reclaimed land in the middle of Lake Texcoco, as Huizilopochtli directed. Over the next seventy-five years, the Mexica came to dominate the Central Valley, conquering other city-states, one by one, until by the late fifteenth century they reigned supreme. Having fought their way out of obscurity, the Mexica constructed a religious, ceremonial, social, political, and economic life centered on war.

From a fairly egalitarian society of kin-based groups called *calpulli*, with elected leaders, the Mexica developed elaborate social structures and a hierarchy featuring hereditary nobles, an idolized warrior elite, priests, commoners, a class of serf-like laborers bound to great noble estates, and slaves. At the top of the hierarchy stood the Mexica's ruler, who came to be considered divine. Still, every successive ruler had to reify his status in battle. Military expansion ensured tribute as well as a regular supply of honorably captured warriors to sacrifice to hungry gods like Huitzilopochtli. For peaceful interludes, when captives might be scarce, the Mexica devised the so-called Flowery Wars, theatrically staged conflicts among brilliantly garbed combatants. The Mexica's most important adversary in these events was Tlaxcala, a city-state located sixty miles to the east. Although the more powerful Mexica could have eliminated it, they preferred to permit Tlaxcala to survive in order to maintain a steady supply of captives for sacrifice. In a society that idealized war, even defeated and doomed warriors were treated with honor—right up to the moment the flint blades of Huitzilopochtli's priests cut open their chests to excise their still-beating hearts.

The cult of Huitzilopochtli encouraged the aggressive expansion of the Mexica Empire that eventually reached the Atlantic Gulf Coast and southeastward into Guatemala. Their far-flung subjects from 370 tribute-paying towns supported the conquerors with a variety of goods. Surviving lists compiled by efficient Aztec tax collectors and trader-diplomats detail which cities sent the cotton mantles, corn, wax, amber, jade beads, iridescent quetzal feathers, cacao beans, and jaguar pelts that poured into Tenochtitlán. Soon after the Spanish conquest, the priest and chronicler Diego de Duran puzzled over demands for certain odd and seemingly worthless payments in such currencies as centipedes, scorpions, and spiders. "The Aztecs were the Lords of All Creation," he wrote, "everything belonged to them [from] scallop shells [to] large and small sea snails, curious fish bones [and] stones from the sea, as well as turtle shells and pearls and amber which make more immediate economic sense to us." The historian Inga Clendinnen argues it was the ability to extract—the submission it signified—that was most important to the Mexica, but with the extracted wealth they also beautified their capital, erecting elaborate masonry temples and palaces, schools, aqueducts, canals, causeways, and bridges. The Aztec emperors filled zoos with exotic animals from all parts of the empire and created fragrant gardens and orchards in which to stroll. Looming above all this magnificence, in the center of the city, stood the Great Pyramid with its twin temples—one painted red for Huizilopochtli, the God of War, and the second blue for Tlaloc, the God of Rain. Nearby, wooden racks displayed the bleached skulls of the victims sacrificed to these deities. Just north of the capital was the great market city of Tlatelolco, Tenochtitlán's sister city, which the Mexica had finally chosen to subdue in 1473, and where sixty thousand buyers and sellers made daily exchanges of goods and services.

Well to the south of the Mexica, in the heart of the Americas' highest and longest mountain chain, a second American empire emerged, that of the Incas. Like their Aztec counterparts, and at roughly the same time, the Incas created a vast and powerful empire, theirs bounded by the Pacific coast and the great Amazon Basin to the east. Building upon the cultural groundwork of a series of older Andean city-states and regional empires and on agricultural and technological innovations that allowed them to maintain large populations in terrain not ideally suited for it, the Incas established military and administrative control over a vast resource base.

The Andean people managed to overcome the natural constraints of their environment through an ethos that supported reciprocal obligations among clan, village, state, and god/ruler. Working communally, Andeans irrigated deserts, terraced mountainsides, and exploited various altitude zones for farming and pasturage. They domesticated camelids (llamas and alpacas) for transport, meat, and wool, and elaborated rich textile, metalworking, and ceramic traditions. More impressive to the Spaniards were their ceremonial centers, such as the walled city of Chan-Chan that had a population of more than 50,000 by the tenth century, and such seemingly impossible megalithic struc-

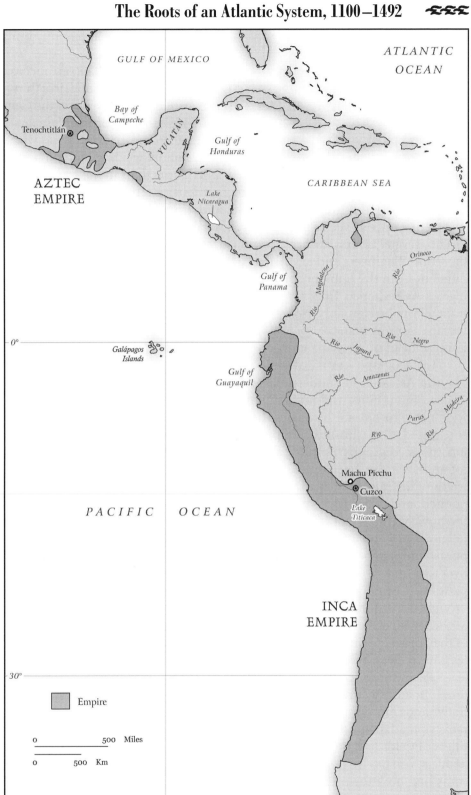

EMPIRES OF THE AMERICAS

tures as the so-called fortress of Saqsahuamán above Cuzco, apparently built in the fifteenth century.

In the mid-fourteenth century the Incas conquered Chan-Chan, on the coast, and established themselves as the greatest force in the Andean region. In a thirty-year span (1438–71), while the Mexica were consolidating power over the Central Valley of Mexico and Isabella and Ferdinand were making of Spain's separate kingdoms a prototype for the modern nation-state, Pachacuti Inca Yupanqui (the Earthshaker) conquered dozens of chiefdoms, rapidly yielding an empire that stretched from Colombia to Chile and included more than 10 million people.

Pachacuti transformed Cuzco into an imposing city of stone in the shape of a puma. Modern tourists still marvel at the massive stones fitted without mortar that once served as the walls of Inca palaces, temples, and villas. Machu Picchu, several hours downriver from Cuzco, remains one of the wonders of the world. Engineers and a work force of thousands built these structures, so different from the opulent splendor of Tenochtitlán but equally awe-inspiring. As he reshaped Cuzco, Pachacuti also promoted worship of the Sun, from whom he claimed descent, and like the Mexica emperors, he recast history to erase any grandeur predating the Incas and to make Cuzco appear the fountainhead of all civilization.

The geographic range of Pachacuti's empire, which encompassed deserts like the Atacama in modern-day Chile, tropical coastal lowlands, rugged Andean mountains, and Amazonian jungles, hosted great biodiversity and a wide range of natural resources. It also comprised human diversity. Only a core population within the empire was Inca—all the rest were conquered or incorporated groups. To rule their diverse subjects, the Incas adopted a carrot-and-stick strategy. Some groups allied voluntarily, rather than incur the wrath of the mighty Inca army; others, the Inca conquered. Into newly incorporated lands the Inca sent populations of *mitimaes* (loyal settlers) to teach the novices the lingua franca, Quechua, and instruct them in the social and religious precepts of the Inca. Other mitimaes were uprooted exiles being punished for rebellion. Certain ethnic groups in modern Ecuador and Bolivia were in fact relocated into each other's homeland during Inca times for political reasons, and their distinctiveness is still visible. Inca emperors also brought incorporated elites to Cuzco to undergo reeducation. Unlike the Mexica, who cared not that their subjects continued in their old ways as long as they provided annual tribute, the Inca sought to make all subjects Inca, at least in terms of recognizing the supremacy of the imperial cult.

Pachacuti organized his empire of more than eighty distinct provinces into four administrative quarters. Cuzco became the center of a vast administrative and communication network through which resources and people were redistributed. Required labor and military service drafts called *mitas* provided tillers of fields and builders of an empire-wide highway system, terraces, aqueducts, canals, irrigation systems, bridges, and warehouses. Although the Incas had no known writing system, they managed impressive amounts of data on troop movements and resources within the empire through *quipus*, elaborately knotted and color-coded string accounts. Some scholars now believe that quipus could also record non-numeric information, even poetry.

The need to support a form of ancestor worship drove the obsessive Inca expansion. As a descendant of Inti, the sun, each ruler was considered divine and when he died, the Incas mummified his remains, enshrined him, and made of him a sacred "living" object, a *malqui*. The Incas consulted malquis, presented them with food, and on feast days paraded them through the streets on litters. Because the sacred dead were in this sense still present and could not be usurped of their goods, subsequent rulers had to make their own fortunes through conquest.

Thus, Pachacuti's descendants continued to enlarge the Inca Empire. As Isabella and Ferdinand were subduing the Christian kingdoms of Spain, waging war against Muslims still occupying the southernmost Iberian Peninsula, and creating a centralized bureaucratic state, Pachacuti's son, Topa Yupanqui Inca (1471–93), expanded the empire from southern Ecuador to central Chile. Topa's son, Huayna Capac, was so often engaged in military expeditions that he was known as the absent lord. By 1511 Huayna Capac had extended the empire to the present-day Ecuador-Colombia border. Both the Inca and Aztec Empires were fully engaged in expansion at the time of Iberian territorial, maritime, and commercial expansion in the eastern Atlantic. Throughout good parts of the fifteenth-century Atlantic, then, militant expansion brought wealth, new subjects, and new enemies.

All kingdoms and empires in this period followed their own internal logic for expansion and conquest, whether dictated by sacred beliefs or by acquisitiveness or both. European expansion into the Atlantic was primarily commercial, but kingdoms gained in politico-religious and military power as rulers increased their wealth and converted subjects. As far as Iberians were concerned, the best subjects were dutiful servants and also good Christians. It was in this context of commercial expansion, social scrambling, and heightened religious sensibilities that Christopher Columbus came of age. The most-heralded story of the so-called discovery of the Americas by Europeans could well have been about cod in Newfoundland rather than gold in the Caribbean. The displaced Italians John Cabot and Christopher Columbus were contemporaries and competitors, simultaneously looking for backing for their maritime ventures. Cabot was likely in Barcelona in 1493, enduring the cheers for the recently returned Columbus. Hoping for similar acclaim, Cabot moved to Bristol in 1495. He, too, was received in glory when he returned to England, but his voyages occurred after those of Columbus, and Cabot disappeared with most of his fleet on his second voyage. As fate would have it, Columbus and Taíno gold trumped the humble but indispensable cod.

As we know, Queen Isabella and King Ferdinand of Spain supported Columbus's enterprise. The son of a Genoese weaver, Columbus was in his mid-thirties when he first approached the royal couple with a plan to beat the Portuguese to the Indies by sailing west across the Atlantic. He had experience at sea before marrying and living on Porto Santo, the smaller of the Madeira Islands, and he gained more on his voyage to the Portuguese trading post of Elmina. He may have had his ear cocked to pick up all the knowledge of navigation and sailing that he could, but he possessed nothing of the sort to rival the Portuguese, who continued to believe (correctly) that the route around Africa was the shorter path to the Indies. Columbus's mistake was in thinking that Asia was only 2,750 miles west of Europe, when it is four times that far. Dissuaded by his navigators, Portugal's King João II twice turned down Columbus's request for support for the westward voyage. Columbus persisted with Spain's Catholic monarchs, and finally, in their excitement after having taken the final step in the long *Reconquista* (Reconquest) of the Iberian Peninsula by vanquishing Muslim Granada, they agreed to provide three ships and crew. Money for the expedition was not on the crown's list of offerings, however, so it was ultimately Genoese bankers in Seville who helped foot the bill.

The details of Columbus's first transatlantic voyage, with three ships—two caravels and a larger nao—and ninety-some men, are widely known, though myth mixes with established fact in most accounts. Leaving the westernmost of the Canary Islands on September 6, Columbus steered mostly due west and, with almost ideal weather and the help of trade winds, arrived in the Bahamas thirty-six days later. Columbus and the captains of the other two vessels went ashore on the island to be named San Salvador where, among a group of the island's inhabitants and in a language they did not understand, Columbus proclaimed possession of the land for his royal sponsors. The commercial context of Columbus's aspirations and his voyage lend understanding to his initial reaction to the people he encountered on the island they called Guanahani. Given his geographic confusion, it is no surprise that Columbus considered the Taíno of these islands Indians. He described them as "well built, with good bodies and handsome features," having "the same color as Canary Islanders." He also evaluated them as trade partners, remarking on the objects adorning their bodies but expressing dismay at their poor value. But Columbus judged the people welcoming and eager to give all they had. Should commodities for profitable exchange become known here or nearby, the Taíno would likely prove cooperative trade partners. Perhaps keeping West Africa in mind, Columbus asked wherever he went where he could find gold, and if not gold, slaves. Columbus himself had lived on Madeira when captive Guanche, Portuguese, and African slaves were brought to plant and refine sugar for the European market. "Should your majesties command it," he wrote his patrons, "all the inhabitants could be taken away to Castile, or made slaves on the island. With fifty men we could subjugate them all and make them do whatever we want."

In the tropical Caribbean, Columbus saw only what his trade experience enabled him to see: likely trade partners or likely laborers. Encouraged by the favorable balance of trade and initial signs of friendship, Columbus and his men sailed on in search of the fabled wealth of the Orient described by Marco Polo, whose chronicles Columbus had carefully annotated. Reaching Cuba, Columbus sent emissaries to search out the Great Khan. Rodrigo de Xérez, a veteran of a Portuguese diplomatic mission to Africa, and Luis de Torres, a Jewish convert who spoke Hebrew, Chaldean, and "a little Arabic," carried letters of greeting from Isabella and Ferdinand with samples of the pepper and cinnamon they hoped would turn a profit. Finding neither Khan nor spices, the men returned to ship, but not before being treated to a reception and banquet at a village of 1,000 inhabitants. Nor did Columbus neglect the religious imperatives that shaped Spain's new unity. "I believe," he assured his patrons, "that they would easily be made Christians." In Columbus's venture, then, the several strands of European expansion converged.

But the Taíno were neither Asian spice traders nor gold- and captive-trading middlemen. As it turned out, they also were not immunologically prepared for the enslavement the Spanish ultimately settled on. Not surprisingly, the way in which Europeans, Africans, Incas, and Mexica pursued political and commercial power before 1492 shaped their encounters with one another in the decades that followed. For his part, Columbus's inability to understand such less-urbanized outliers as the Taíno and Caribs, the latter inhabitants of the Lesser Antilles, was to be repeated again and again, tens of thousands of times, in encounters in the next century. The core quest for commercial gain governed European expectations of all societies they met. Religious motives were nearly as strong, particularly for Iberians. Spanish and Portuguese insistence on Christian uniformity, in part a legacy of the Reconquest, governed expansionist impulses. At the same time, the nature of the state, whether Kongo's quest for legitimacy or the Aztec and Inca Empires' urgent need for expansion founded also on sacred imperatives, shaped European access to sites of indigenous wealth and power.

Selected Readings

Boxer, Charles R., *The Portuguese Seaborne Empire, 1415–1825* (New York: Alfred A. Knopf, 1975).

Clendinnen, Inga, *Aztecs: An Interpretation* (New York: Cambridge University Press, 1991).

Crosby, Alfred W., *Ecological Imperialism: The Biological Expansion of Europe, 900–1900* (Cambridge, UK: Cambridge University Press, 1986).

D'Altroy, Terence, *The Incas* (New York: Blackwell, 2003).

Deerr, Noel, *The History of Sugar,* 2 volumes (London: Chapman and Hall, 1949).

De Oliveira Marques, A. H., *History of Portugal, Volume I: From Lusitania to Empire* (New York: Columbia University Press, 1972).

Ehret, Christopher, *The Civilizations of Africa: A History to 1800* (Charlottesville: University Press of Virginia, 2002).

Fernández-Armesto, Felipe, *Before Columbus: Exploration and Colonization from the Mediterranean to the Atlantic, 1229–1492* (Philadelphia: University of Pennsylvania Press, 1987).

Fletcher, Richard, *Moorish Spain,* (Berkeley: University of California Press, 2d ed., 2006).

Hilton, Anne, *The Kingdom of Kongo* (Oxford: Clarendon Press, 1985).

Koning, Hans, *Columbus: His Enterprise: Exploding the Myth* (New York: Monthly Review Press, 1976).

Kurlansky, Mark, *Cod: A Biography of the Fish That Changed the World* (New York: Walker and Company, 1997).

Mintz, Sidney W., *Sweetness and Power: The Place of Sugar in Modern History* (New York: Viking, 1985).

Russell-Wood, A. J. R., *The Portuguese Empire: A World on the Move* (Baltimore: The Johns Hopkins University Press, 1998).

Sweet, James H., *Recreating Africa: Culture, Kinship, and Religion in the African-Portuguese World, 1441–1770* (Chapel Hill: University of North Carolina Press, 2003).

Verlinden, Charles, *Beginnings of Modern Colonization: Eleven Essays with an Introduction,* Trans. Yvonne Freccero (Ithaca: Cornell University Press, 1970).

Cortés communicates with Moctezuma through his interpreter, Malintzin, Colonial History of Latin America: Conquest of Mexico *by Hernando Cortez 1519–21. "Xaltelolco." Color lithograph after the Mexican hieroglyphics "Lienzo de Tlaxcala," 1519. Painting located in the Bibliothèque Nationale. Courtesy: akg-images, London.*

Chapter Three

Iberians in America, 1492–1550

Nothing but flowers and songs of sorrow
are left in Mexico and Tlatelolco where once we saw warriors and wise men
"Flowers and Songs of Sorrow," Cantares Mexicanos

As Queen Anacaona, flanked by her attendant servants, sailed along the western coast of Haiti in her elaborately painted canoe, she could not have imagined that the arrival of a strange new people from the east would soon destroy her flourishing world. The sister to one Taíno *cacique* (chief), Behechío, and wife to another, the Carib Caonabó, she outranked both men socially and controlled at least one hamlet of her own within her brother's territory. In addition, the queen—whom the Dominican friar Bartolomé de Las Casas later described as *palaciana* (very regal)—had warehouses filled with feathers, textiles, and wooden carvings like the anthropomorphic hardwood stools called *duhos* that were reserved for the exclusive use of chiefs. Anacaona enhanced her status by redistributing these tribute items during state visits to neighboring territories, feasts, and gift exchanges hosted in her own village. As her case illustrates, intermarriage created extended kinships and reinforced alliances among island caciques.

Using small vessels such as Anacaona's and larger seagoing canoes holding up to 150 people, the indigenous people of the Caribbean conducted long-distance interisland trade in spun cotton, parrots, feathers, spears, tobacco, and *cohoba* (a narcotic snuff). They had long since mastered the skill of processing cassava or manioc so that the flour made from the tuber nourished rather than poisoned them. They were also accomplished fishermen and hunters, their prey ranging from sharks to iguanas. Taíno artisans wove fine cotton cloth and carved stone and hardwood into utilitarian and luxury goods. They also knew metallurgy and crafted jewelry and decorative objects of gold and copper alloy. Taíno chiefdoms were based on elite intermarriage and matrilineal descent, reinforced by a complex religious system. A class of religious practitioners healed, predicted, and interpreted for worshipers in reverence of spirits called *zemis*, represented both in petroglyphic art and portable images. Taíno retold creation myths in word and song; on special occasions dancers performed on the large ball courts where men and women regularly competed in symbolically charged athletic contests, some of which were presided over by women of Anacaona's status. On the larger islands of Cuba,

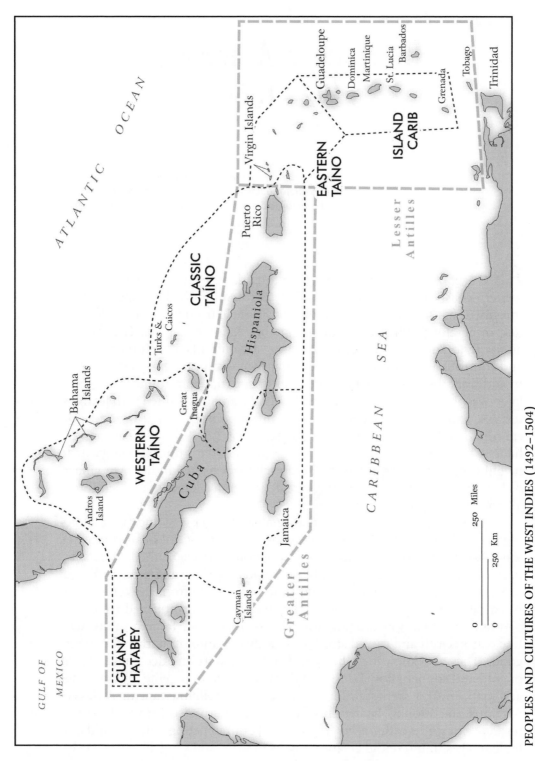

PEOPLES AND CULTURES OF THE WEST INDIES (1492–1504)
Adapted from Irving Rouse, The Tainos: Rise and Decline of the People Who Greeted Columbus (Yale University Press). Used by Permission.

Haiti (Hispaniola), and Boriquen (Puerto Rico) caciques commanded respect and tribute of large groups of subjects. How many persons they presided over on each island remains a topic of intense debate. Scholars are closer to agreement on a theory that Taíno society was undergoing profound change, becoming more socially and politically complex, when Columbus and his men arrived.

Captives

As Columbus sailed through the Caribbean, he took captives from among the people he encountered. Some assisted him in his explorations by serving as navigators, others he required to learn Spanish and serve as interpreters, and some he brought back to Europe. In the same way earlier explorers returned to Europe with exotic animals, plants, and other treasures, Columbus took these captives as human souvenirs to broadcast his success. Columbus paraded them about to further fund-raising efforts. From the late fifteenth century forward, indigenous Americans began crossing eastward across the Atlantic. Their names appear in baptismal and notarial records throughout Spain. In 1496 Columbus had two Taíno "servants," Cristobal and Pedro, baptized in the monastery of Santa María de Guadalupe. While Sir Walter Ralegh languished in the Tower of London after 1603, he enjoyed the company of at least two Indians from Guiana, some of a small number of Americans he had persuaded to come to England to study English. Other Indians, like the Taíno Diego Columbus, whom Columbus took to Spain from the Bahamas and who returned with him to Hispaniola, became culture brokers in the newly interconnected Atlantic world. This would become a common pattern among European explorers and invaders, and in this way many indigenous people reached Europe. By the sixteenth century, Europeans were gathering other exotic treasures in "cabinets of curiosity," which might contain weapons, adornments, human skin (the more heavily tattooed, the better), musical instruments, and sacred objects. Animals brought from the Americas fueled fanciful accounts of the wonders of foreign lands: two-headed beasts, one-breasted women, fish with legs. Plants were studied for their medicinal qualities and scientists reported their findings in published volumes. In Rouen, the capital city of Normandy, in 1550 an entire Brazilian village, complete with forest, was erected on the banks of the River Seine, populated by Tupinamba Indians whose numbers were increased by French sailors wearing Brazilian garb. The men staged a battle to entertain the royal court, all part of an effort to encourage the crown's support for activities in Brazil. In general, people in indigenous costumes, paraded about Europe as curiosities, were tangible proof of the authenticity of travel and the existence of new worlds.

Brazilian fête at Rouen (1551). Anonymous, French. Courtesy Newberry Library.

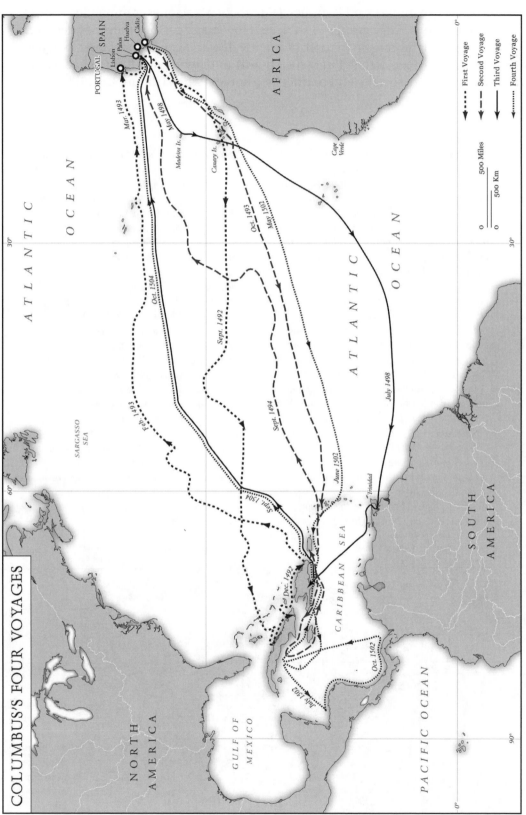

COLUMBUS'S FOUR VOYAGES

Adapted from W. D. Phillips, Jr., and C. R. Phillips, The Worlds of Christopher Columbus (Cambridge University Press, 1991). Reprinted with permission of Cambridge University Press.

The Spanish in the Caribbean

In many ways the Spanish path through the Caribbean resembled Portuguese movements along the west coast of Africa. In the course of his four voyages (1492–1504), Columbus leapfrogged through the Antilles, taking on wood, water, and food, distributing trade goods, and capturing individuals to serve as translators, all the while assessing the commercial possibilities of the islands. In early contacts with local people the Spaniards exchanged red caps, brass bells, green and yellow glass beads, keys, and even pieces of broken crockery for local items, including parrots and monkeys intended to entertain Columbus's royal sponsors.

But what most attracted the Spanish was the gold sparkling in their hosts' ears and noses, and they were determined to locate its source. They found it in the island they renamed Hispaniola. Even before Columbus had made landfall on that island, sailors from the *Pinta* had trekked into the interior and observed people mining gold. The inhabitants of the island were already wary of the Spaniards, whom they had heard had the habit of seizing people and sailing away with them. For ten days Columbus and his crew drifted along Hispaniola's northern coast but found only empty villages of considerable size. Only through intercession of kidnapped Bahamian guides did the Spaniards finally establish contact, once again by means of exchange. Once initiated, the pace of interactions among the Spaniards and the local populations of Hispaniola accelerated rapidly, to the point that the Spaniards were almost deluged with eager traders. Columbus reported that a few days before Christmas 1492, 120 canoes swarmed around the *Santa María* and the *Niña*. He estimated he received one thousand Taínos onboard and that five hundred more swam out to his ships.

But shortly afterward, disaster struck. Columbus's flagship, the *Santa María*, stuck fast then broke apart on a sandbar on Christmas Eve. The Spaniards' first ally, Chief Guacanagarí, saw that all the Spaniards' goods were safely unloaded "without the loss," Columbus marveled, "of so much as a needle." The chief reportedly wept at the Spaniards' misfortune. And still believing he had welcomed friends, Guacanagarí housed and fed the Spaniards and helped them build Fort Navidad from the timbers of the wrecked ship. Martín Alonzo Pinzón had sailed away some time before on the *Pinta* on his own unauthorized explorations, so only the *Niña* remained to carry home the rest of the Spaniards. Thirty-nine volunteers stayed behind at Fort Navidad when Columbus returned to Spain to report and claim his "discoveries."

Although filtered through interpreters and difficult to discern in other ways, it is worth trying to read Columbus's first logbooks and reports from the perspective of the unnamed Taínos, who, he claimed, so warmly greeted him. As critics like Peter Hulme, author of several books on the Island Caribs, point out, Columbus's dialogic exchanges were entirely fictional, since neither of the participants could understand the other's language. The first indigenous groups (those in the Bahamas) to see the Spaniards probably did wonder about them—about their different vessels, clothing, beards, and pigmentation. The anthropologist Samuel Wilson suggests the Taínos were "uncertain about where the foreigners should be treated in the indigenous system of social and political ranking: Were they equivalent to commoners, elites, or

gods?" It is possible the Taínos viewed the first Spaniards as semidivine beings, as Columbus claimed, but just as likely they considered them an unknown, potentially useful variety of trading partner—material-rich outsiders
to be hosted and given gifts. Either way, word of the arrival of exotic newcomers spread rapidly across greater Caribbean networks. Shortly after leaving the
Bahamas, Columbus passed a lone paddler, already transporting Castilian
coins to nearby Cuba.

As in Africa, Europeans in the Americas were at least initially dependent
on their hosts for sustenance, lodging, and, indeed, their lives. Columbus
may have modeled his early diplomacy on what he learned in Africa—where
Europeans seeking permission to trade rendered gifts and displays of friendship. Fort Navidad resembled the early Portuguese *feitorías* (factories) dotting
Africa's western coastline—a small trading post manned by a few Europeans
who remained there only at the pleasure of the local chief. These Spanish
equivalents of the lançados, however, fresh from victories against Muslims in
Granada, quickly overstepped the limits of Taíno hospitality.

Columbus's rescuer, Guacanagarí, controlled only one of the island's
five paramount chiefdoms, so learning the intricacies of island politics was
crucial to the survival of the few Spaniards whom Columbus had left behind.
Other chiefs like Anacaona's husband, Caonabó, controlled the island's main
gold fields in the Central Valley and led the fiercest resistance against what
would soon amount to a Spanish invasion. The Taínos, it turns out, were
hardly the naive, childlike creatures Columbus assumed he could bend to his
will and enslave. Just as Columbus and his crew had been assessing the labor-
and tribute-producing potential of the Caribbean people, the latter were also
sizing up the newcomers. After offering the generous welcomes tradition dictated, indigenous people of the Antilles soon discovered how demanding
and obnoxious Europeans could be. So before long, they determined to rid
themselves of them.

Sometime after Columbus sailed back to present parrots, cotton, and six
captured "Indians" to the Spanish court at Barcelona, warriors of Hispaniola
eliminated Fort Navidad. After the *Niña* had sailed away, the European men
began to abuse Taíno women and make excessive demands for tribute and
service. If Guacanagarí is to be believed, Anacaona's husband, Chief Caonabó,
descended on the fort with 3,000 warriors and killed every last inhabitant.
The Taínos may have considered these reprisals to have restored proper order.
Religious diviners probably prescribed the attack and people likely celebrated
the victory with dances, songs, and ball games. They could not have known
that Columbus would return the following year with seventeen ships carrying
1,200 men intent on permanent occupation. European women would arrive
later. The returning Spaniards found a burned shell of Fort Navidad and all
their compatriots dead, the eyeless corpses strewn about the ruins. Yet the
Spaniards apparently misunderstood the Taíno warning, for it did not dissuade them from repeating the same kinds of abuses that had triggered the
massacre.

One of Columbus's sailors boastfully described his shipboard rape of a
Carib woman, whom he beat into submission after her resistance. His letter
concluded, "Finally we came to an agreement in such a manner that I can tell

you that she seemed to have been brought up in a school of harlots." In analyzing what he terms the "sexual conceits of European conquerors," the historian Jonathan C. Brown emphasizes the gendered nature of these early contacts among people who misunderstood each others' cultural norms. The balance of power almost always lay with the European men, particularly in situations of captivity, and many European artistic renderings of the fascinating people of the new lands focus on the nakedness of the women. America "herself" came to be represented as a supine woman, ready for the taking.

Despite this inauspicious beginning, the settlers Columbus transported unloaded their animals, seeds, and supplies and began building the first European town in the Americas, near Guacanagarí's village on Hispaniola's northern coast. Archaeologists who excavated the site found bones of European pigs and rats, and digs at nearby La Isabella turned up remnants of Columbus's

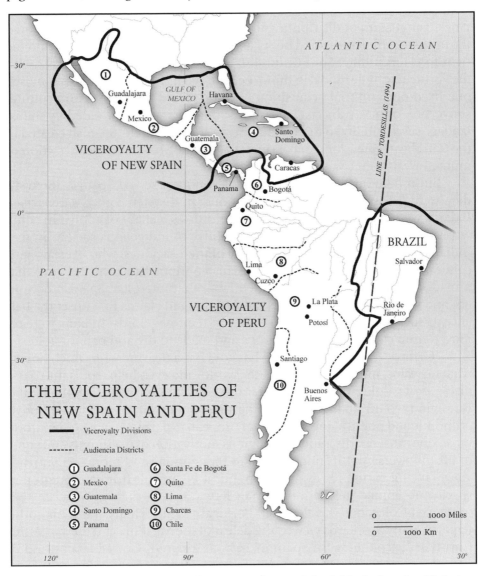

Adapted from Mark A. Burkholder and Lyman L. Johnson, Colonial Latin America *(Oxford University Press 2003). By permission of Oxford University Press, Inc.*

walled strong house, a church, a 113-foot-long storehouse, a hospital, and a Christian cemetery (the last of which saw much traffic). The archaeologists also found chain mail, cannon balls, crucifixes, and beads of mercury that Spaniards used to process the gold that would cost many Taíno lives.

With a force of 1,200, including farmers and artisans, along with some livestock, Columbus signaled a departure from the Portuguese-style trade model. When the Spanish could not obtain through barter enough gold to satisfy their ambitions, they turned to coercion and displacement. Now they drew on another Iberian model, not a dependence on local traders that spawned a hybrid commercial culture in coastal West Africa, but the military model of the Reconquest. When the Catholic Spanish conquered territories held by Moors, they sought to establish permanent control over lands and vanquished inhabitants. Christian settlers moved quickly to occupy these newly acquired territories, and they absorbed conquered subjects as laborers or tributaries. The custom of distributing the spoils of conquered regions motivated the invaders: soldiers secured booty and took control of people, land, and the right to claim tribute. So if Columbus reached the Caribbean in 1492 with the Portuguese trade model in mind, he returned in 1493 in a Spanish mindset, one fixed on territorial acquisition and the forced integration and cultural conversion of new subjects. He and his followers would be aided by the islanders' susceptibility to foreign disease. In short order the Spanish created in the Caribbean a new kind of conquest society, one based on the extraction of mineral wealth.

But if patterns established in the Reconquest served Spanish interests, they were devastating to local populations. In a system called *encomienda*, Indians were distributed to Spanish overlords as a share of spoils. In some respects the system was not wholly disruptive of indigenous society, in that Indians remained under the sovereignty of their caciques, who oversaw agricultural surpluses and labor. The Indians continued to own the land that provided their sustenance. It was their labor that interested Spanish occupiers, and it was the labor demands rather than land claims that upset the balance. Under the pretext of serf-like duty to their new lords, Indians were removed from cultivation of food crops and made to dig and pan for gold.

"O, most excellent gold! Who has gold has a treasure with which he gets what he wants, imposes his will on the world, and even helps souls into paradise," wrote Columbus. In his eyes, the gold he delivered to Isabella and Ferdinand would finance the Christian reconquest of Jerusalem. Although economic and political incentives for European expansion were perhaps foremost, one must not discount the religious motivation of Columbus and some of his followers. All this might seem, to modern-day and more secular readers, a fanciful excuse for exploitation, but it is difficult from a modern perspective to appreciate the millenarian fervor and medieval mysticism that motivated Columbus—as they had Portugal's Prince Henry—and his counterparts. Many Spaniards viewed the defeat of the Muslims and the successful Christian "Reconquest" of Spain in 1492 as a sign of God's blessing and of their divine mission. They also deemed providential the "discovery" of unknown and potentially lucrative territories across the Atlantic. The Spanish

Man's Best Friend? War Dogs and the Spanish Conquest of America

Along with germs, plants, and large livestock, Spanish settlers brought many dogs with them across the Atlantic. Household pets were still the preserve of nobles in contemporary Europe, so the breeds imported to the early Americas were intended for practical uses, such as hunting, herding, and defense. Throughout colonial times, settlers used dogs as sentinels, trail scouts, shepherds, and retrievers. Native American domestic dogs, though quick to raise the alarm when outsiders drew near, were generally small and not bred for defensive or helper traits. In Mexico, hairless breeds were raised for food.

As early Spanish conflicts with Native Americans ballooned into wars of conquest and enslavement, European dogs were immediately put to use for more offensive purposes, mostly as frontline attackers. Dozens of conquest chronicles mention the greyhound (lebrel or alano), used first to aid deer hunters but now turned loose upon native enemies. The Spanish liked greyhounds because they did not require large amounts of food or water, and their long legs allowed them to keep up with horses. Some sadistic conquistadors used packs of greyhounds to hunt Indians in the forest, a blood sport known as the montería infernal.

Another breed frequently mentioned by chroniclers is the Spanish mastiff (mastín), which was bred for war. These were the true dogs of conquest, and they had already gained a fearsome reputation in the Italian Wars of the 1490s. This dog's modern descendants have survived only on the Canary Islands, and the breed, the Presa Canario, is considered one of the largest, fiercest, and strongest of domestic canines. Conquistadors used mastiffs to attack and intimidate Native Americans, in some cases pitting captured warriors against the largest and meanest dog in staged fights to the death.

The conquistadors were often as fond of their dogs as they were of their trusted horses, giving them honorific names such as Leoncico (Little Lion), Marquesillo (Little Marquis), Capitán (Captain), and Turco (Turk). Others were named for famous knights and warriors, such as Hector and Amadís. Many wore protective collars and even armor, and some were buried with honors. The Dominican priest and official Defender of the Indians, Bartolomé de Las Casas, denounced the Spanish use of dogs against natives. A more positive approach is represented by St. Martin de Porres, a lay brother famous for caring for injured and abandoned dogs. As a former slave, he was the perfect inverse image of conquistador cruelty.

John G. Varner and Jeannette Johnson Varner, Dogs of the Conquest (Norman: University of Oklahoma Press, 1983).

Vasco Núñez de Balboa (1475–1519), Spanish explorer, ordering Indians to be torn to pieces by dogs. Copper engraving, sixteenth century. Credit: The Granger Collection, New York.

chronicler Francisco López de Gómara wrote, "The greatest event since the creation of the world, excluding the incarnation and death of the one who created it, is the discovery of the Indies." Having recovered their portion of the European mainland for Christendom, Spaniards hoped to evangelize the Americas in preparation for the final recovery of the Holy Lands from the Turks. With this worldview, Columbus interpreted many of the events of his voyages as God's will, and from his first voyage onward signed his correspondence *XpoFERENS*, or Christ-bearer ("Xpo" being the Greek abbreviation of "Cristo"). In 1498, when he sailed along the northern coast of South America, Columbus mistook the great Orinoco River for the River Jordan and the mines of Panama for those of King Solomon. He even claimed he had found the Garden of Eden itself. His was a Biblical landscape and, quoting the Book of John (10:16), he believed that he was fulfilling Biblical prophecy in having discovered "other sheep I have who are not of this fold."

Fresh from the victory against Muslim Granada and having just "purified" Spain by expelling Jews who refused to convert to Catholicism, Queen Isabella took seriously her religious obligation to evangelize the previously unknown people Columbus had found. The Spanish-born Pope, Rodrigo de Borgia, conveniently awarded the "New World" to Spain on the basis of that service. Portugal quickly protested this papal grant and negotiated a new division: the 1494 Treaty of Tordesillas, which granted Portugal rights to all lands east of a north-south line slicing through the Atlantic 370 leagues west of the Cape Verde Islands. As an exception, the Canaries were left to Spain. This arbitrary cartographic decision made in Europe would later allow Portugal to claim not only its footholds in Africa and Asia, but also Brazil.

While Iberian diplomats cavalierly divided the world and those European kingdoms left out of the bargaining scrambled to find new routes to "the Indies," settlers of La Isabella on Hispaniola struggled with the harsh realities and disappointments of their new home. Gold and food were scarce, disease and death were ever-present. Weakened by famine and the work of building a new settlement, Spaniards and Taínos began to die of some unnamed epidemic in 1494. All came to regard La Isabella as cursed.

The Taínos, whom Spaniards coerced into strenuous labor, paid the heaviest physical toll, but the occupiers suffered too. Not only was manual labor in a tropical environment more strenuous than most were used to, it was also an affront to status-obsessed Spaniards to have to work with their hands. Although Spain's monarchs awarded Columbus the magnificent titles of Admiral of the Ocean Sea, Viceroy, and Governor, many of his better-born subjects resented the pretensions of this son of a Genoese weaver to Castilian nobility. Columbus faced his first mutiny only one month after having founded La Isabella and quickly hanged the rebels. Within a year some of the most disaffected Spaniards commandeered ships and returned to court to complain of Columbus's failures as an administrator. Bitter and deadly internal disputes became a recurring theme in Spanish settlements in the Americas, as occupiers fought over access to the riches they found.

To guarantee continued royal support, Columbus had to deliver on his promises of riches. Hispaniola's gold deposits lay inland in the territories of the chiefs suspected of destroying Fort Navidad, so Columbus organized a military expedition into the interior designed to force hostile caciques into submission. In line with European military operations of the time, Columbus's entourage featured armored knights on horseback, fierce war dogs—huge mastiffs and greyhounds trained to maim and kill and far different from the small dogs the Taínos kept—blaring trumpets, and fluttering banners with triumphant Christian crosses held aloft.

The Taínos understood Columbus's threatening message and reacted with violence or flight whenever they could. Over the next year Columbus and his lieutenants spread terror through the interior, killing and enslaving. Columbus released some captives, distributed others to his army, and having little else to show for the effort and investment in his "Enterprise of the Indies," sent almost six hundred enslaved Taínos to Spain. He wrote the monarchs that if "one could sell 4,000 slaves that would bring at least 20 millions," adding comfort with the claim that the high mortality of these Indian slaves would be reduced over time, as it had been with slaves in other parts of the growing empire. Almost two hundred of the unfortunate Taínos succumbed to disease in the middle of the Atlantic and were tossed overboard. Isabella, a pious Catholic, was shocked. On the advice of her confessor, Juan Rodríguez de Fonseca, she insisted that Indians were "free and not subject to servitude." As subjects of Spain, the Taínos, Isabella believed, should work, but, like Spanish commoners, they should be paid wages for their labor. She ordered the surviving Taínos returned to Hispaniola.

Still determined to find the Great Khan and considering the Taínos "pacified," Columbus set sail on his third voyage and reconnoitered what we know today as Trinidad and Venezuela. But his departure was ill timed: in 1497 fourteen Taíno caciques of the Central Valley put aside earlier differences and coordinated an even greater rebellion. The fighting was bloody on both sides. Spaniards used their weapons and war dogs to terrible effect and the Taínos retaliated by strangling and decapitating captured Spaniards. Under command of Columbus's brother, Bartolomé, the Spaniards adopted a scorched-earth strategy, burning every village and all the manioc mounds they came across. They also burned alive Indians they suspected of withholding information. Survivors fled to remote mountain hideouts or escaped by sea to Cuba with the Hispaniola-born Taíno chief Hatuey, ready to join unsuccessful resistance against the Spanish conquest of that island.

Now Columbus attempted to create in Hispaniola something resembling a Spanish world. After abandoning the trading post model, Spanish conquerors pursued a town-based pattern of colonization. Where towns already existed, the Spanish occupied them; where there were no towns, they established them. On Hispaniola, Columbus laid out town sites, administered Castilian law codified in the thirteenth century as the *Siete Partidas*, and awarded the first settlers land and encomiendas as rewards for their services. He delivered to the Spanish crown the standard one-fifth of all wealth he appropriated in Hispaniola, and he hoped also to collect the tenth he had been promised in his original patent.

Finally fed up with the Columbus family's inability to govern in the Caribbean, in 1502 the Spanish crown established royal authority under a new governor, Nicolás de Ovando. Unfortunately, this appointment ensured

Pero Vaz de Caminha's Letter to the King of Portugal

Historians and literary scholars have closely examined Columbus's earliest reports of Caribbean contact, but they have paid much less attention to the first Portuguese encounter with Brazil. Soon after touching on the central coast of this vast landmass in late April 1500, a scribe on the Cabral mission to India, Pero Vaz de Caminha, composed a letter to the king of Portugal to report on the situation and potential of this "new" land, originally thought to be an island. Like Columbus, Vaz de Caminha was fascinated by the lush tropical vegetation and the unabashed nudity of the indigenous people, and was anxious to see signs of gold. Also like Columbus, the Portuguese under Cabral felt compelled to name the land in their own fashion, calling it "The Island of the Holy Cross." They assumed they beheld a landscape and people in need of Christianizing. Like Columbus, Vaz de Caminha reported on a sequence of mute, awkward, and sometimes humorous exchanges of caps, beads, and other items for local featherwork, live animals, and weapons. What differs most starkly, perhaps, is how Vaz de Caminha openly admitted in his letter to the monarch that Portuguese desires likely clouded communications with native peoples. "We interpreted it in this way because we wished to," he said of a Tupi man's gesturing to the land after touching the captain's gold collar. Whereas Columbus wrote as if communication were never a problem, and as if local desires perfectly matched his own, Vaz de Caminha conveyed an almost modern self-consciousness and relativism. That some of his shipmates would desert their captain and his noble mission to live among the Tupi seemed worthy of only passing comment. Vaz de Caminha died in battle in India soon after the encounter with Brazil, but his letter survives as testament to the variety of European contact experiences in the early Atlantic world. Perhaps Columbus's delusions of grandeur were not typical after all.

the continuation of violent occupation: Ovando had fought Muslims and would subdue Hispaniola as well. His rule finally established royal authority and saw to administration of Spanish law, taking the first census and collecting royal taxes. Settlement began in earnest. Ovando's administration marked the beginning of a Spanish pattern of replacing conquerors with bureaucrats as they sought to organize new territories.

In Seville, de Fonseca, Isabella's confessor, established the centralized commercial bureaucracy that became the powerful House of Trade, charged after 1502 with administering emigration to and commerce with the Americas. This centralization became a distinguishing feature of Spanish rule overseas, as no other European power developed such a layered colonial bureaucracy. As Isabella took back control of the new land from the admiral to whom she had promised it in perpetuity, she provided more royal support for the venture. Ovando arrived in Hispaniola with a fleet of thirty ships bearing 2,500 settlers, a virtual ark of large domestic animals, and sugar-cane cuttings. Knowing he needed land to develop livestock herds and agricultural lands to feed settlers, Ovando launched the final Indian wars in Hispaniola. After his forces slaughtered hundreds of peaceful Taínos in the southeast, Ovando attacked the western kingdom of Queen Anacaona, whose hospitality he repaid by executing her.

The Portuguese in Brazil

This murder of a powerful indigenous leader signaled the completion of Spain's shift away from the trade model of the coast of Africa; yet that model persisted in other parts of the Americas. As the Spanish worked out new dynamics of cultural interaction in the Caribbean, transplanting the coercive colonization of the Reconquest and grafting it onto Taíno society, the Portuguese continued to adhere to the trade-factory model. Different indigenous economies and diverse environments dictated this path, and the Portuguese, moreover, were diverted by the lure of Asia and realistic about the limited resources of their small kingdom. Thus, when Spain and Portugal divided the known world in 1494, Portugal did not immediately act on western Atlantic possibilities.

As Columbus was seeking a new western route to the Indies, the Portuguese were pursuing routes around Africa to the east. King João II sent three vessels under Bartolomeu Dias to take up the quest for a route around the southern tip of Africa—if indeed it had a southern tip, as so many wanted to believe—and Dias, somewhat by accident (since his expedition got caught up in a storm that blew his ships around the Cape of Good Hope and a short distance along Africa's southeast side), found the way by early in 1488. After rounding the Cape, the Portuguese established factories on the East African coast, with more violence than was customary on the Atlantic side because Muslim traders dominated ports there. Vasco da Gama reached India in 1498, and there the Portuguese carved out new trading factories at Calicut and "Golden" Goa. (One critic observed that "the Portuguese entered into India with the sword in one hand and the Crucifix in the other; finding much gold, they laid the Crucifix aside to fill their pockets.") Filling his ships with pepper, ginger, cloves, cinnamon, mace, and nutmeg, as well as gems and textiles, da Gama generated a 700 percent profit for the king and the private investors who helped finance his voyage. The small kingdom of Portugal, with a population of 1 million in 1500, quickly established a far-flung network of trading factories beyond Africa and India: throughout Indonesia, the Spice Islands, and the Malay Peninsula, to China and Japan. As one scholar put it, "the Portuguese prevailed upon the sea, not the land."

It was in this context of Asian trade that the Portuguese stumbled onto Brazil. On his way to repeating da Gama's voyage to India, Pedro Alvares Cabral and his substantial fleet were blown off course by the Southwesterlies, bringing him ashore near modern Porto Seguro, Brazil. Through his secretary, Pero Vaz de Caminha, Cabral dutifully reported this "discovery" to the king in 1500. Caminha wrote a brief survey of the land and its resources, noting lush vegetation and agricultural possibilities, but no mineral wealth or large, urban-dwelling indigenous populations to divert Portugal's eastward gaze. Though Caminha's letter bears comparison with Columbus's early logs, it is noteworthy that the Portuguese did not rush to enslave indigenous Brazilians, preferring instead to follow the trade model they plied in Africa. Nevertheless, several unhappy cabin boys, like self-selected lançados, jumped ship to live among the local population.

The Spanish had encountered in Caribbean islands large sedentary chiefdoms, perhaps beginning urbanization. The indigenous people of coastal Brazil, most speakers of Tupi languages, were similar. They farmed manioc and maize, lived in fairly large villages, and paddled long distances in dugout canoes. Scholars estimate their population at the time of Portuguese arrival at

2.4–4 million. Some Tupi were more like the so-called Caribs of the eastern Caribbean, in that they occasionally migrated over long distances for religious reasons and were almost constantly at war. Close to the coast, many Tupi dwelled in settlements of as many as 800 people, mixing intensive agriculture with gathering of forest and marine resources. Manioc, the Tupi staff of life, was planted, harvested, and processed exclusively by women. They stored food surpluses in the form of toasted manioc flour (*farinha*), still at the core of Brazilian cuisine. Equally important was women's production and control of manioc beer. Men devoted much of their time to the study of warfare: a man's status depended on his ability to kill enemies and acquire captives, who were sometimes subjected to ritual sacrifice and cannibalism. This culture of endemic rivalry and warfare proved useful to the Portuguese and later the French, both of whom allied with indigenous groups and encouraged interregional conflict when it furthered their goals.

The Portuguese could not readily identify any valuable resources of the region, with a single exception, brazilwood, which produces a red dye after processing and thus joined the body of dye products Europeans coveted. The Portuguese offered mirrors, cloth, axes, and iron to persuade the Tupi to cut and load brazilwood onto their ships. Since wood chopping was a traditionally male activity, Portuguese demands barely altered the social organization of Tupi households. For the next quarter century, Portuguese ships stopped only occasionally on the Brazilian coast to trade for brazilwood and drop off criminals or troublemakers. The Portuguese outcasts eventually formed families with indigenous women and served as cultural brokers and founders of early settlements. The children of these unions, whom the Portuguese called *mamelucos* or *mestiços*, like many other mixed offspring in the Atlantic world, proved important as cultural mediators between European and indigenous cultures.

The Portuguese encountered two difficulties with this casual trade, however. The first involved supply: the Tupi chose not to harvest as much brazilwood as the Portuguese desired, partly because of their limited demand for European trade goods. Semisedentary people prefer not to carry much with them, and thus what nonperishable items the Portuguese brought quickly saturated the market. The Portuguese fared better by using barter to persuade Tupi allies to trade captured enemies as slaves, resulting in raids farther and farther inland. It was advantageous for the Portuguese that Indian custom in war was to take captives alive (originally for sacrifice). But the new slave trade changed these captives from participants in rituals into commodities, *negros da terra*. The culture of barter turned into a culture of slavery. Portuguese labor needs became more severe after 1526, when sugar made its own migration from the eastern Portuguese Atlantic to the west. Sugar cultivation put new pressures on indigenous societies. Planters sought labor, which Indians eluded by simply fleeing. Men, who had willingly chopped brazilwood, refused to engage in sugar cultivation, since their culture prescribed agricultural labor as women's work. As in the Spanish Caribbean, high mortality from strenuous labor, poor nutrition, and Afro-Eurasian diseases characterized the new plantations.

The second challenge the Portuguese faced came from European rivals, particularly the French. France never recognized the Treaty of Tordesillas and claimed to have discovered Brazil. Since 1503, French ships had been stopping along the lengthy coast of Brazil for brazilwood and to raid Portuguese ships and settlements. Needing to respond to such harassment, but unable to afford a major state-sponsored settlement of the vast colony, Portugal relied on medieval precedents also used in Madeira, the Azores, and the Cape Verde Islands to encourage wealthy proprietors to settle and defend huge hereditary land grants at their own cost, in effect privatizing colonization. One such donatary captain, as these men were called, Martim Afonso de Sousa, expelled French "usurpers" in 1532 and established Brazil's first successful settlement and municipality at São Vicente, not far from modern São Paulo. The only other successful Brazilian captaincy was that of Duarte Coelho, who, with profits earned in the India trade, established sugar plantations in Pernambuco in northeastern Brazil. Despite significant private investments, Indian wars, French raids, and shortages of capital and labor plagued these early Brazilian settlements. Finally, spurred by ongoing French threats, the Portuguese crown decided in 1549 to assume the task of settling Brazil. A crown-appointed governor presided from the new capital of Salvador da Ba-

American Food Crops in Eurasia

Of course, the so-called Columbian exchange worked in both directions: Europeans encountered an array of unfamiliar, nutritious plants in the Western Hemisphere, many of which they took back to the eastern Atlantic, where they transformed Eurasian diets, even populations. Among the most important American crops were maize, potatoes, tomatoes, peanuts, manioc, cacao, and an assortment of peppers and squashes. Maize and potatoes produced more calories per acre than traditional Eurasian crops such as rye and could thus sustain far more people: the introduction of some of these crops to Europe and Africa spurred population growth and transformed traditional cuisines. Although at first Europeans held unusual ideas about American foods, believing potatoes and tomatoes (in Italian pomodoros, *or "apples of love") to be aphrodisiacs, they soon made the crops staples in their diet on both sides of the Atlantic. Food has always been invested with cultural meaning. Although Spaniards reluctantly learned to eat tortillas and breads made of corn and manioc flour, they still preferred wheat, and associated wheat bread with civilized living. Despite high costs and other difficulties, Europeans would continue to attach higher social value to European foods and drinks than to ones derived from Indian or African cuisines.*

The Potato Tribe: Tobacco; tomato; potato flower; capsicum/pepper; and other related plants from the potato family (Solanaceae). "Illustrations of the Natural Orders of Plants," by Elizabeth Twining, London 1849-55. Copyright © The British Library. Record: brg57837, Shelfmark: 1823.d.10

hia, in the northeastern sugar zone. The task of converting the Tupi and other native Brazilians was entrusted to the fledgling Jesuit order, and the first six missionaries arrived in 1549. By 1570, the Portuguese had expelled French settlers near Rio de Janeiro, "pacified" a number of coastal Indians after serious and protracted resistance, and imported Portuguese colonists and African slaves to support sugar cultivation for export to Europe.

Spanish Mainland Expeditions

Portugal's gradual occupation of coastal Brazil roughly coincided with Spanish conquests throughout the American mainland. Although they found gold in the Greater Antilles soon after Columbus's arrival, Spaniards' quest for mineral wealth would only be satisfied on the mainland. The first bonanza would be in Aztec Mexico, beyond the lands of the bellicose Maya of the Yucatán Peninsula. When Columbus first contacted the Maya, his men captured traders in an ocean-going canoe off the island of Cozumel. The cargo included embroidered textiles, wooden war clubs edged with obsidian blades, copper knives and hatchets, vegetables, and cacao beans. The Spaniards could not have known the beans were the currency of the region, noting only that when they spilled from their containers, the Maya scrambled to gather them "as if they were their eyes." This encounter seemed proof to the Spaniards that greater riches remained to be discovered.

Cuba's conqueror turned governor, Diego de Velásquez, was the first to finance and send expeditions searching for this suspected wealth. In 1517 Francisco Hernández de Córdoba sailed westward from Cuba with three ships and 110 men. On the northern coast of the Yucatán he encountered luxuriously dressed people living in cities with pyramid-shaped temples and elaborate stone architecture unlike anything seen on the Caribbean islands. So impressed were the Spaniards with the Maya city of Ecab that they dubbed it "Gran Cairo." But the seagoing Maya already had heard about Spanish tendencies to raid and enslave, and they were prepared. At each of three landings the Spaniards made to explore or fill water casks, Maya warriors and priests with blood-clotted hair whistled and taunted before attacking, killing more than half the interlopers and badly wounding Córdoba. The survivors sailed to Florida for their water, but received similar treatment there. Shortly thereafter they limped back to Cuba, where Córdoba died of his wounds. The seeming Indian victory would prove costly for them, for the Spaniards left behind an invisible, but deadly, ally—smallpox.

As would soon become evident, the widespread death of indigenous peoples from smallpox, measles, influenza, and a host of other Eurasian and African diseases was probably the single-most important factor in enabling Iberian and other European conquests in the Americas. When the first Europeans entered the Americas, they began a process akin to a biological rejoining of the tectonic plates. Once this happened, long-separated animals (in addition to humans), plants, and microbes mixed and mingled. For residents of the Americas at the time and their immediate descendants, the results were disastrous. But for persons across the Atlantic and for later inhabitants of the Americas, the blessings of this "Columbian exchange," as historian Alfred W. Crosby termed the process, continue to flow.

The post-1492 invasion of plants, animals, and microbes was at least as stunning for the natives of the Americas as it had been for the Guanche on the Canaries more than a century earlier. (The plants introduced by the Europeans were more of an annoyance at first—ragweed and different grasses fueled allergies; it would take longer for such Eurasian grains as wheat, oats, and barley to become staples in many American diets.) Enough big, new animals crossed the ocean to trigger a virtual zoological revolution: loosed on the American landscape were small numbers of horses, cattle, pigs, goats, sheep, asses, chickens, cats, and pests. But with few or no natural predators and an abundance of sustenance, the animals multiplied faster than anyone could have foreseen. Herds of wild horses soon raced over the grasslands of Hispaniola, Jamaica, and Venezuela, and rooting pigs—the feral variety eventually grew to immense size and featured fearsome tusks—roamed the forests of Florida. Meanwhile, Spanish cattle "took to the meadows of the Antilles like Adam and Eve returning to Eden," writes Crosby, and "[w]hen the Europeans set them loose in the grasslands of northern Mexico and the [South American] pampa, the cattle propagated into scores upon scores of millions." Before long the descendants of the recent arrivals were displacing local species, disrupting human land use and agricultural patterns, and destroying indigenous food crops that had never before been fenced.

But far more devastating in the Americas over the short run than the rapidly reproducing animals were the pathogens that came with Europeans and Africans to the Americas. Although the exact numbers of native Americans who succumbed to these diseases—first around the Caribbean and then wherever Europeans and Africans went—is impossible to calculate, most scholars estimate that within a hundred years of contact, nearly 90 percent of the Americas' "contact population" of 50–70 million persons perished. At least some people of the Americas before 1492 suffered from syphilis, tuberculosis, and intestinal illnesses but had never been exposed to the more devastating endemic Eurasian diseases—mumps, measles, rubella, whooping cough, influenza, typhus, chicken pox, and most ruinous of all, smallpox. Later, such mosquito-born diseases as yellow fever, malaria, and dengue fever joined the former to severely limit lowland tropical populations, particularly non-African ones.

The first known epidemic of smallpox swept through Hispaniola's already weakened population in 1518–19, and thereafter the agents who spread the dread disease were often not even on the scene. The smallpox virus spread in advance of actual contact, reducing indigenous populations to remnants before any Europeans reached them. "Any Indian who received news of the Spaniards," Crosby notes about smallpox, "could also have easily received the infection." Indigenous chronicles and art depict the recurrent tragedy. In a scene that could have been written about the Black Death, *The Annals of the Cakchiquels* describe a plague that devastated the Maya in 1519:

> Oh, my sons! First they became ill of a cough, they suffered from nosebleeds, and illness of the bladder. It was truly terrible, the number of dead there were in that period. . . . Great was the stench of the dead. All our fathers and grandfathers succumbed, half of the

> people fled to the fields. The dogs and the vultures devoured their bodies . . . the people were overcome by intense cold and fever, blood came out of their noses, then came a cough growing worse and worse, the neck was twisted, and small and large sores broke out on them. . . . Truly it was impossible to count the number of men, women, and children who died this year.

The same epidemic spread among the Aztecs. Although the Spanish were most interested in conquering living, tribute-paying, and laboring subjects, they ended up overcoming and ruling over mostly weakened and diminishing populations. This was truest in the densely settled Mesoamerican and Andean highlands.

As it turned out, more than disease underlay the Spanish conquest of the Aztecs. The Aztec-Mexica Empire was under great stress when the Spanish arrived. Like most Mesoamerican cultures, the Mexica regarded time as cyclical, such that events repeated themselves and could be foretold. (European Christians also held cyclical, if not exactly repeatable, ideas of time—the Christian calendar was organized around annual cycles and the most important millenarian ideas in Christianity, such as the second coming of the Messiah, were dependent on the acceptance of cyclical time—but Christians also treated time in a linear fashion, juggling both simultaneously, but allotting different explanatory weight to each.) Trained Mexica priests read the heavens and calculated time to see how intersections of a 365-day solar calendar and a sacred calendar of 260 days might align. Believing that the world might end with the close of each fifty-two year cycle, they destroyed temples, extinguished holy fires, and sacrificed human victims in acts of purification and placation. If these observances pleased deities, especially the war god Huitzilopochtli, the sun would rise again—and it always did. But all catastrophes—frosts, earthquakes, volcanic eruptions, losses in battle—had to be explained and might signify that the gods were unhappy. A series of disastrous droughts in the early sixteenth century had produced crop failures, famine, and discontent in Mexico. Hoping for relief, Moctezuma II escalated the pace of sacrifice, but to no avail. In the midst of this uncertainty, imperial enemies like the Tlaxcalans of the modern Puebla region were keen to find allies.

While the Mexica were trying to assuage their gods—and suppress rebellion among their tribute states—Cuba's governor, Diego Velásquez, had second thoughts about letting his ambitious secretary lead a third expedition to Mexico. But determined to make his own destiny, Hernando Cortés defied Velásquez and sailed off with a fleet of eleven ships and 550 men, including many indigenous Cubans and several African slaves, whom the Mexica would later describe as "soiled gods." Two priests also went along to administer sacraments to the members of the expedition. Missionaries would follow.

Following the route of his predecessors, Cortés reached Cozumel, where the island's hospitable ruler, Ah Naum Pat, surprised the Spaniards with the gift of Gerónimo de Aguilar, who had been shipwrecked and enslaved by the Maya in 1511. As was his Christian duty, Cortés tried also to recover a second Spanish survivor, only to get the startling news that Gonzalo Guerrero preferred to stay among the Maya. Before leaving Cozumel, Cortés felt compelled to destroy temple "idols" and replace them with a Christian cross and an image of the Virgin Mary. This pattern of iconoclastic replacement, of violently superimposing Christian symbols upon indigenous ones, and later of building Spanish cities atop indigenous metropolises, characterized Spanish colonization. The assembled Maya could not disguise their dismay at Cortés's violation of their sacred spaces and warned that the Spaniards would come to harm. This prophecy of misfortune came true at Tabasco, on the Gulf Coast of Mexico's Isthmus of Tehuantepec, where residents attacked the Spaniards as they landed in thick mangrove swamps. Although the Spanish historian Francisco López de Gómara reported that the Apostles Peter and Paul saved that day, old soldier and eyewitness Bernal Díaz credited the victory to Spanish horsemen. Cortés must have agreed. Realizing the psychological advantage he might gain, Cortés staged a beach-side theatre with charging horses and cannon-fire to "shock and awe" the defeated Tabascans.

Presumably impressed, or perhaps simply mystified, local leaders appeased Cortés's retinue with presents of indigenous women, one of whom

Tenochtitlán

Spaniards had never seen anything like this city. Even those who had been to Istanbul or Cairo did not have words to describe the sight. Bernal Díaz, a soldier who chronicles Cortés's conquest of Mexico, tried:
"When we saw all those cities and villages built in the water, and other great towns on dry land, and the straight and level causeway leading to Mexico, we were astounded. These great towns and pyramids and buildings rising from the water, all made of stone, like an enchanted vision from the tale of Amadís. Indeed, some of our soldiers asked whether it was not all a dream. . . . I stood there looking at it and thought that never in the world would there be discovered other lands such as these, for at that time there was no Peru, nor any thoughts of it. Of all these wonders that I then beheld today all is overthrown and lost, nothing left standing."

Bernal Díaz del Castillo, The True History of the Conquest of New Spain.

Tenochtitlán (Mexico City). "Great Tenochtitlán/The Market." Detail from Diego Rivera's mural of market day in the Aztec capital. The Great Temple can be seen in the background. Credit: The Granger Collection, New York.

would play a major role in the conquest of the Aztec-Mexica empire. Traded away by her impoverished mother, according to Spanish sources, the Nahuatl-speaking Malintzin had learned the Yucatec dialect of Maya spoken by her masters. When he saw that she could communicate with Gerónimo de Aguilar, Cortés recognized Malintzin's value to his expedition. Christened Doña Marina, Malintzin became a vital source of military and cultural intelligence; Cortés would later write, "next to God, I owe all to her." With Marina and Aguilar, Cortés had lucked upon linguistic bridges that would help him conquer Mexico. Marina bore Cortés a son before marrying another ranking conquistador, but this apparently did not diminish her status in either indigenous or Spanish eyes. In early postconquest art, she was nearly always depicted at the center of the frame, wearing fine garments and emitting "speech scrolls" characteristic of leaders and nobles. Long after the conquest, Bernal Díaz remarked on Malintzin's intelligence and "manly" courage.

THE EARLY CARIBBEAN AND THE ROUTE OF CORTÉS

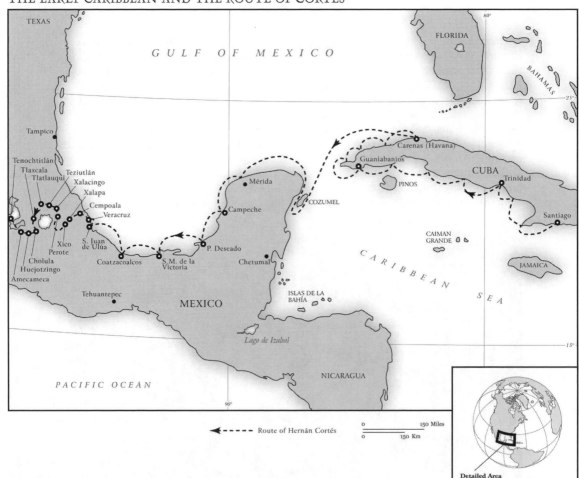

Adapted from Anthony Pagden, trans., Hernán Cortés, Letters from Mexico (Yale University Press, 1986). Used by permission.

On the Gulf Coast, Cortés founded a town, which he named Veracruz. Adhering to Castilian convention, his highest-ranking followers constituted a new town council and elected Cortés to govern. With this notarized act, Cortés claimed autonomy from his former patron, Velásquez, hoping to convince the crown he was not a rebel, but a proper Christian founder of towns and standard-bearer for Spain. With regard to the Aztecs, Cortés arrested Moctezuma's tax collectors, who happened to be nearby, thereby gaining the allegiance of the tributaries of the city of Cempoala. Hoping further to secure his position and the king's pardon, Cortés sent his pilot, Alaminos, back to Spain with treasure and explanatory letters to the emperor, Charles V. In them he extolled the potential wealth to be extracted from this newly discovered kingdom and described the people thereof as dressing and building in the "Moorish fashion." Comparisons to the elaborate architecture Muslims had created over the centuries in southern Spain were a compliment to the sophistication of the Mexica culture, yet they also cleverly prefigured a justified conquest. Cortés hoped the king would be intrigued and forgive him for striking out on his own, but he knew that his claim to leadership remained tenuous. So, fearful of mutiny, he burned the remaining ships to prevent the return to Cuba of any malcontents.

From Veracruz, Cortés began his march inland in 1519. If the expedition's leader and Bernal Díaz are to be believed, at Tlaxcala, high in the interior near modern Puebla, the small band of Spaniards fought for four days against thousands of Tlaxcalan warriors. Thanks in part to their disciplined efforts in keeping together horsemen and footsoldiers amidst chaotic fighting, and due to differences in their approach to armed engagement, the Spaniards prevailed and at the same time picked up their most important military allies. The Tlaxcalans hated the exploitative Aztecs and found in the Spaniards, who had proved strong enough to defeat them, a convenient mechanism for revenge.

If military battle between Spaniards and Aztecs was inevitable, a clash of cultures hastened the fight. Debate swirls around the timing of Cortés's arrival in Mexico and how the emperor Moctezuma interpreted it. The year 1519 corresponded to the year One Reed in the Aztec calendar—when, prophecies allegedly said, the ancient Toltecs' feathered serpent god/ruler Quetzalcoatl was due to return to reclaim his rightful throne. Spanish accounts later alleged that indecision over how to act in such circumstances immobilized the Aztec ruler. But this was likely a postconquest indigenous explanation for Mexica defeat. In fact, Moctezuma seems to have taken logical steps to determine what he could about the invaders. He sent envoys and artists to the coast to gather intelligence and produce portraits of the foreigners, and these minions recorded and drew what they observed in terms the emperor would understand. Ships were "mountains on the sea," horses were "deer [but] tall as the roof of a house," the Spaniards were "white as if made of lime [with] beards long and yellow though some have black." Their "tireless" war dogs were "enormous [with] their eyes burning yellow [and] flash fire and shoot off sparks." Cortés instructed his men to fire a cannon at a tree to terrify the Mexica witnesses, and some accounts have them fainting dead away. Yet they managed to report accurately on this weapon: "a ball of stone comes out of its entrails . . . shooting sparks and raining fire [with] the smoke with a pestilent odor—like that of rotten mud." The Mexica emissaries also offered what they considered a tempting bribe: gifts of blood-covered food in return for a quick Spanish exit. More disgusted than dissuaded, Cortés insisted on a personal meeting with the emperor. Moctezuma next tried deceit, the deploying of a double to convince the Spaniards to turn back, not knowing the invaders had burned their ships and bet their lives on winning.

As the Mexica were trying to divine all signs before them, so too were the Spaniards. Cortés's self-serving letters to Charles V stressed his mastery of events and contrasted his diplomacy with the incomprehension of the people he met. Modern scholars dismiss his claims to superiority, crediting instead the different notions the two groups held of the purpose and conduct of warfare for the eventual Mexica defeat. At the holy city of Cholula, Doña Marina warned the Spaniards of an impending attack, prompting Cortés to launch a preemptive strike during an Aztec banquet honoring the war god Huitzilopochtli, which resulted in the Spaniards' killing and dismembering as many as 6,000 of their hosts. The shock might have been similar if Mexica warriors had burst into Seville's great cathedral and cut down the celebrants at Holy Week mass. As at Cozumel, Cortés destroyed "idols" and whitewashed the temples of Cempoala. Before heading farther inland, he tried to persuade blood-matted priests to become keepers of Catholic shrines.

Once the Spaniards trekked across the high pass between the snow-covered volcanoes Iztaccihuatl and Popocatepetl, they looked down upon the unimagined wonders of the aquatic city of Tenochtitlán. When one reads Bernal Díaz's eloquent description of this first sighting, it is not hard to understand how he and his fellow Spaniards came to consider themselves champions of some medieval epic—Christian princes fighting against diabolic forces for the true faith. Cortés encouraged his men in that belief, and in many ways they aspired to live their assigned roles. Díaz recalled their force included only about four hundred men, but that estimate, meant to underscore the bravery of the outnumbered Spaniards, failed to acknowledge that many thousand Tlaxcalan allies swelled their ranks.

On November 8, 1519, Cortés met Moctezuma on the broad causeway that connected Tenochtitlán to the mainland. Throngs of Mexica crowded the causeway to see the spectacle. Greeting the Spaniards as foreign dignitaries, the elaborately dressed emperor gave Cortés shell necklaces strung with golden shrimp, other gold jewelry, iridescent quetzal feathers, and embroidered cloths. In his analysis of these events, historian James Lockhart writes of a "Double Mistaken Identity," arguing that because the Europeans and the Mexica were in many basic respects similar—people who lived sedentary lives based upon intensive agriculture, ruled by dynasties, with highly developed religious systems and social hierarchies—each was able to maintain cherished cultural principles long after contact. Thus, in this first exchange, the Spaniards believed they were being offered golden tribute as conqueror/gods, while the Mexica believed they were awing the foreigners with royal largesse.

In a display of generosity, Moctezuma housed the Spaniards in his own palaces and personally guided them through his magnificent city. Díaz described in detail the aviary, the teeming marketplace of Tlatelolco, and color-ful temples. But after several days of such beneficence, the Spaniards revealed their true intentions by violently seizing and making a hostage of their host. Not wanting to see their emperor harmed, and lacking an alternative leader, the Aztecs stood paralyzed. Next, the Spaniards looted Moctezuma's treasure house of all the gold they could gather and melt into ingots. In his letters to the king, Cortés claimed Moctezuma swore loyalty to Spain and agreed to his own house arrest, but Díaz reported that the emperor's advisors, who still visited him daily, urged him to resist. Cortés depicted the Spaniards as in control, but they were actually vulnerable, vastly outnumbered, sick, and iso-lated from their Tlaxcalan allies, who were housed elsewhere in the city. To make matters worse for Cortés, the governor of Cuba had sent a punitive expedition to arrest him for treason. That force of almost 1,000 men and eighteen ships reached Veracruz in May 1520, and its commander, Pánfilo de Narváez, sent messages to Moctezuma denouncing Cortés as an outlaw. Just as the conquistador had exploited indigenous enmities, Moctezuma now hoped to take advantage of division among the Spaniards.

Cortés rushed back to the coast with horsemen to face his challengers and left his lieutenant, Pedro de Alvarado, and a small force of 120 men in the Aztec capital. In a fierce night battle that cost Narváez an eye, Cortés con-firmed his authority and added almost 1,000 additional men to his forces. He would need them, for in Tenochtitlán the outnumbered and jumpy Span-iards under Alvarado confused celebrations for the war god Huitzilopochtli with preparations for battle. Mexica poets described how the Spaniards "ran in among the dancers, forcing their way to where the drums were played." The soldiers "attacked the man who was drumming and cut off his arms. Then they cut off his head and it rolled across the floor." The Spaniards "at-tacked all the celebrants, stabbing them, spearing them, striking them with their swords." A few tried to flee, "but their intestines dragged as they ran; they seemed to tangle their feet in their own entrails. No matter how they tried to save themselves, they could find no escape."

The citizenry rose up in fury at this unprovoked attack, so surprising the Spaniards that they were said to have "staggered as if drunk." They seized Alvarado and his men, who sat for almost a month inside their luxurious prison. Had Cortés not managed to reenter Tenochtitlán undetected one night, they would probably have starved. The fiction of Spanish control could no longer be sustained, and Cortés had to get his men out of the city. The Span-iards fought for four days to escape, and at some point Moctezuma was killed. Spanish accounts insist his own people stoned him to death as he appeared on the palace roof to try to calm the mobs. Indigenous accounts accuse the Spaniards of stabbing Moctezuma once he was no longer useful to them. They also claim the Spaniards murdered Moctezuma's heirs before abandon-ing the royal quarters.

During what Spanish accounts call *La Noche Triste* (the Night of Sor-row)—after protracted hand-to-hand combat—Cortés and his men escaped the city via the broad Tacuba causeway. "The canal was soon choked with the bodies of men and horses," Mexica sources recalled; "they filled the gap in the causeways with their own drowned bodies. Those who followed crossed to the other side by walking on the corpses." Between 150 and 400 Spaniards (and between 2,000 and 4,000 Tlaxcalan allies) died in the rout—some drowning under the weight of the loot they were trying to take with them. The victorious Mexica lined up the Spaniards' bodies for display, "white as the buds of the maguey," poets recalled, a reference to the large cactus from which sacred *pulque* (a kind of local beer with the consistency of mucus) was made. Although the Spaniards were the victors in one follow-up battle near the pyramids of Teotihuacan, it remains a mystery why the more numerous Mexica did not simply eliminate the Spaniards when they could have.

With the Spaniards evicted, the Mexica began to restore their world in Tenochtitlán. A council of elders elected one of Moctezuma's brothers, Cuitlahuac, to succeed him, perhaps because he had warned against trusting the Spaniards. Yet, prescient as he was, Cuitlahuac could not have imagined the extent of the danger the Spaniards still represented. In September 1520, smallpox hit Tenochtitlán, having already done its damage in Hispaniola and among the Maya. Postconquest codices depict Mexica lying helpless on their beds, covered with pustules. Cuitlahuac himself succumbed to the epidemic and was succeeded by a nephew, Cuauhtémoc. Meanwhile, Cortés and his men regrouped in Tlaxcala. As if to underscore their determination to stay and formalize their claims, the Spaniards established a second city, Segura de la Frontera, and plotted their next campaign. Humiliated but not defeated, Cortés ordered his men to build a small navy of twelve brigantines, with which he hoped to avoid the causeways on his way back into Tenochtitlán. With cannon mounted on the new ships, he went back to reclaim an empire.

Historians have long debated the relative advantage European technology gave the Spaniards and whether it sealed their victory. William Prescott wrote in the 1840s, "the Aztec monarchy fell by the hands of its own subjects under the direction of European Sagacity and science," and added that it was "a fall not to be lamented." Prescott did not read Náhuatl, and he wrote his conquest narrative when the United States was claiming Manifest Destiny to justify its seizure of half of Mexico. It is true that Spanish crossbows, steel-edged weapons, harquebuses, horses, and mastiffs were deadly and more effective than Mexica projectiles designed to wound, rather than kill, opponents destined for sacrifice. But modern scholars consider technology only a partial explanation for the Mexica defeat, along with epidemic disease and the internal divisions within the empire.

Nor does the depiction of a lethargic, depressed, or cowed emperor who handed his people over to a false god hold currency. In fact, despite Moctezuma's failures and their weakened state, the Mexica fought fiercely to defend their city, refusing Cortés's repeated pleas to surrender. Compensating for the Spaniards' technology, Aztec warriors learned to zigzag or fall flat when the cannons roared, and even to decapitate charging horses with their obsidian-edged swords. They adapted their warfare to the lake-surrounded city by breaking down bridges and ripping up paved streets. And like Cortés, they employed theatre, surprise, and psychological warfare to instill fear in their enemies. During the battle for Tenochtitlán the Mexica executed fifty-three Spanish captives in front of their comrades and displayed their heads and the heads of four horses on skull racks. They "harvested" even more Tlaxcalan warriors for sacrifice.

Over the next three months, ferocious battles and a complete cutoff of the city reduced the Mexica to eating grass, but they still refused to surrender. Both sides fought with determination, drawing on traditions, religion, and comradeship to rally sagging spirits and calling for assistance from St. James or Huitzilopochtli. In the end, the Spanish chose to raze the beautiful city they had so proudly, and prematurely, offered to the Spanish king. Postconquest accounts say that at the end of the long siege, a "flame" like a "copper wind" spun over the lake where the Emperor Cuauhtémoc was finally captured. He asked for an honorable death, but the Spaniards' obsession with "legitimacy" required a noble ruler through which to rule. Like Spanish religious gestures, political conquest was enacted through decapitation and replacement.

Spanish Expansion into South America

Once Spaniards learned of the fabulous wealth of Mexico, the search in the Americas for "another Mexico" was on. Several expeditions set out from the Isthmus of Panama; two adventurers who headed south from there were Francisco Pizarro and Diego de Almagro. Like Cortés himself, they came from the impoverished Estremadura region of southwestern Spain, and these regional connections bound them. They had also become comrades while fighting for slaves and searching for gold in the backlands of the Indies. Undaunted by failed missions in the late 1520s, Pizarro and Almagro encountered and captured indigenous trading vessels loaded with rich goods off the coast of the outlying Inca city of Túmbez, on the present-day border between Ecuador and Peru. Realizing they had finally come upon a society with the mineral wealth they coveted, Pizarro headed for Spain to petition King Charles (the grandson of Ferdinand and Isabella) for a charter to explore and conquer the region and secure titles for himself and his companions. He also took with him several indigenous boys who spoke Quechua to train as interpreters. Charles named Pizarro governor of Peru and gave Almagro the much lesser title, governor of Túmbez. In 1532, their third expedition sailed for Túmbez, only to find the once-impressive city destroyed by civil war in the wake of the death of Huayna Capac, the Inca ruler who had extended his empire as far north as present-day Colombia. Huayna Capac likely succumbed in 1527 to an invader microbe that preceded its hosts to the Andes by almost a decade. Deadly pathogens had already traveled from Hispaniola to Panama, and hence South America, by 1514. From 1514 through the 1520s, disease swept through Panama and southward into Peru. Deaths in Quito alone perhaps reached 200,000, and by the time the Spanish arrived in highland Peru in 1532 an Andean population of more than 10 million may have fallen to fewer than 2 million. As workers died, agricultural and other production dropped, famine hit, and armies curtailed conquests.

Of his many sons, Huayna Capac had chosen Huascar, who ruled in the imperial city of Cuzco, as his successor. But another of the Inca's favorite sons, Atawallpa, headed armies that ruled Quito in the north; with these resources Atawallpa challenged Huascar in 1527. For three years it was unclear who would win the fraternal contest, and this split created a crisis of legitimacy. Backed by the Inca nobility in Cuzco, Huascar seized Atawallpa, but Atawallpa's army freed him and, in turn, seized Huascar. Atawallpa's troops then staged a campaign against Cuzco.

When Pizarro's third expedition finally arrived on the Peru coast in late 1532, the Inca Empire was reeling from epidemic disease and civil war. The victorious Atawallpa was relaxing at the hot springs of Cajamarca with his army of 40,000 camped in the surrounding hillsides when Pizarro led his 168 men, 60 of them mounted, into the Andes in search of fortune. Fresh from victories and uncertain of the Spaniards' motives, Atawallpa failed to recognize the danger the small group posed and perhaps could not have imagined that such a pitiful handful of foreigners would dare lay hands on him. Like Cortés, Pizarro had picked up indigenous interpreters along the coast in earlier reconnaissance voyages, and they conveyed to the emperor Pizarro's suggestion that they engage in war exercises in the city. Atawallpa acquiesced.

In a scene recalling Moctezuma's meeting with Cortés, a procession of richly dressed musicians and courtiers carried Atawallpa into the square on a gold and silver litter lined with macaw feathers. Throngs of curious Inca subjects witnessed the scene as a Spanish priest and an Indian interpreter explained the Spanish presence and their claims to ultimate religious and political authority over the Inca Empire. Versions of the encounter differ over who understood what, but the Spaniards claimed that Atawallpa rejected the priest's Christian message, striking down the mute volume from his hand. Following this supposed blasphemy, Pizarro seized the surprised Inca and made him his prisoner as Spanish horsemen charged into the courtyard from hiding places, attacking the litter bearers and assembled observers and looting as they went. Considering this at worst a temporary setback, Atawallpa directed his followers to kill the remote Huascar and collect rooms full of treasure for his ransom. But fearing Atawallpa too much to release him as they had promised, after allegedly receiving eleven tons of gold and thirteen of silver, the Spaniards gave Atawallpa a last-minute baptism and garroted him in 1533.

In less than a year, and without a fight, the Spaniards had made themselves hugely rich, but they still stood on the fringes of the Inca Empire, so they headed for the capital of Cuzco. For a semblance of legitimacy they designated another of Huayna Capac's sons, Tupac Huallpa, as their puppet. When he died on the southward march, the Spaniards replaced him with yet another son, Manco Capac. Control of ranking native lords was already a core feature of Spanish rule in the Americas; in this case, it was essential to survival. Despite the misfortunes of their ruler, Atawallpa's armies fought four battles to keep the enemy from reaching their capital, but still it advanced.

Excitement surrounding the delivery by Pizarro's younger brother Hernando of the obligatory royal fifth of Atawallpa's ransom to King Charles prompted new waves of adventurers to sail for Panama, hoping also to make it rich in Peru. While some of Pizarro's closest associates did make fortunes, Diego de Almagro's 150-man crew felt shortchanged again. After squabbling, Pizarro designated Almagro acting governor of Cuzco, and in 1535, Francisco went to the coast to establish a maritime base on the Rimac River, formally called La Ciudad de los Reyes, later shortened to Lima.

Still dissatisfied, Almagro led an expedition southward to Chile in search of the fortunes and glory that had so far eluded him. With Almagro went Manco Inca's brother Paullu, a high priest, and thousands of Inca porters. The expedition had to cross snow-covered mountain passes in the southern Andes, where in March 1536 several thousand Indians and 170 horses froze to death. Farther south nomadic Mapuche warriors attacked the survivors. After enduring two years of hardships and failing to find rich civilizations to plunder, Almagro's diminished forces straggled back through the Atacama Desert toward Cuzco, even more embittered than when they had left.

Almost as soon as Almagro had departed Cuzco, the second Inca puppet, Manco Capac, led a rebellion. For ten months in 1536 the Incas laid siege to Cuzco, but thanks in large part to their own massive stoneworks, now in the hands of the invaders, they failed to finish off the remaining Spaniards. A rare casualty was one of Pizarro's younger brothers, killed by a stone when he removed his helmet. Now Manco Capac marched to the coast intending to besiege Lima. In line with previous uses of terror, the Spaniards captured Manco's wife, shot her full of arrows, and sent her riddled corpse floating downriver in a basket. For a people who regarded deceased rulers as divine and feasted and entertained their mummies, this disrespectful treatment of a *qoya* (female ruler) must have been shocking. Capac retreated with his army to the rugged mountains northwest of Cuzco and formed an independent Inca state at Vilcabamba. He and his sons ruled this remote refuge for the next thirty-five years, during which time the Spaniards battled one another rather than the remaining Incas.

This civil war among Spaniards in Peru exaggerated a tendency evident from the first settlement at Hispaniola when Columbus faced opposition from his men. Division among the conquerors was pervasive, and each conquest revealed new fissures. That of Peru exposed bitterness and envy between Almagro, Pizarro, and their respective factions. For several years the so-called *almagristas* and *pizarristas* fought over spoils, during the course of which both Pizarro and Almagro were assassinated. When the crown stepped in and threatened to end the encomienda system, another of Pizarro's younger brothers, Gonzalo, led a rebellion in hopes of establishing an independent state. Peru's first viceroy was killed in battle outside Quito in 1546. The bloody struggle did not end until the crown sent an envoy willing to pardon enough of the rebels to undermine their forces. Gonzalo Pizarro and his captains, including Francisco de Carvajal, the pathological killer known as the "demon of the Andes," finally surrendered and were executed, but twenty-five years of war in Peru had cost the lives of several Inca rulers, four Pizarro brothers, Almagro and his son, the viceroy, and thousands more who had been swept up in the almost incessant fighting.

Peace was slow in coming to Peru, but in 1569 an energetic and ruthless viceroy, Francisco de Toledo, arrived to establish a centralized bureaucracy. Using pardons, presents, and punishments, he secured royal control of the turbulent viceroyalty. Having subdued the Spanish subjects, Toledo waged war against the last Inca ruler, Túpac Amaru, executing him in Cuzco's main plaza in 1572. Although the Inca kingdom was no more, Peru was far from conquered, for the same indigenous groups who had bedeviled Inca overlords now harassed the Spaniards on the fringes of the empire.

Establishing Spanish Rule

As events in Peru indicate, securing Spanish rule in the Americas was a protracted process, one exacerbated by indigenous resistance and Spanish rivalries. Nevertheless, the Spanish established a pattern of occupation in the Valley of Mexico that would be copied elsewhere. There, the once glittering Tenochtitlán, symbol of the mighty Aztec-Mexica Empire, lay in rubble, and the Spaniards reworked the landscape to conform to their idealized model of a Spanish city. As the English, Dutch, and French would later do in their American colonies, the Spanish christened the territory they conquered in Mesoamerica "New Spain." They forced the defeated Mexica to raze buildings and incorporate the cut stones into new ones. Soon, Catholic churches and grand Spanish homes stood on sites where Aztec temples and palaces once towered over the valley floor. Spanish conquerors, priests, merchants, and bureaucrats occupied the core of the newly dubbed "Mexico City," while Indian subjects were assigned to peripheral barrios, removed from the mechanisms of power but close enough to provide labor. The restructuring of the city served to reinforce the change of regimes and underscore Spanish political and cultural authority. Although the Indians were segregated into suburban communities, the Spanish did not isolate themselves. Instead, they lived surrounded by the Indians and relied on their daily service in their own households.

To strengthen their claims and facilitate control over their vastly more numerous subjects, the Spaniards integrated themselves into the remnant Indian dynasties and existing political, economic, and social networks. Although conquest often resulted in the rape and violation of indigenous women, the postconquest situation offered some women opportunities for gain. In both the Andes and Mexico, this was most true in the marketplace, which soon became a female space. In the early years of Spanish colonization, many market women sought sponsorship from Spanish men, sometimes bearing their children. Some indigenous noblewomen married conquistadors and founded prominent *mestizo* (mixed) families. The Spanish had pursued sexual alliances from the first settlements, and early evidence indicates the eagerness of Spanish fathers to incorporate their mestizo children into the Iberian polity. As early as 1498, Francisco de Roldán, who had mutinied in Hispaniola and retreated to regions still under Taíno control, authored a document demanding that he and his men be allowed to return to Spain with their Indian concubines and children, and that these children be recognized as free Spanish subjects. Roldán's dream drowned with him when he tried to return to argue his case in Spain, but notarial documents record at least a handful of mestizo children born in Hispaniola whose fathers sent them to Spain for Christian educations. The mothers of these children usually were left behind, but throughout Spanish America many indigenous women and mestizo children successfully used the court system to secure titles to land, encomiendas, and other sources of rents.

In Mexico and Peru, this strategy of enhancing Spanish power through marital alliance pervaded for the first generation of conquerors. Before dying, Moctezuma had allegedly entrusted his children to Cortés, thereby establishing at least a fictive kinship between them. Several of these children died on the Tacuba causeway during the Night of Sorrow, but one royal daughter had a long and fascinating postconquest history. Sometime after the Spaniards first fled Tenochtitlán, Isabel Moctezuma married her uncle, Cuitlahuac. When Cuitlahuac succumbed to smallpox, Isabel married Cuauhtémoc, with whom she was captured by Cortés. Although Cortés eventually tortured and killed Cuauhtémoc in a remote Honduran jungle, Isabel survived to be married off to a Spanish husband. When that husband died, Cortés impregnated Isabel before marrying her to a second Spanish husband, who died within two years. He also granted her perpetual encomiendas in Tacuba. Thus, by the age of twenty-one, Isabel Moctezuma found herself four times a widow and a wealthy woman commanding the tribute and fealty of large numbers of indigenous laborers. She also enjoyed the status of a woman of honor. The first Bishop of New Spain, Juan de Zumárraga, baptized Doña Isabel's children, and her daughters were later admitted to Mexico City's most elite convent, La Concepción, where admission requirements included *calidad* (good family lines), legitimacy, literacy, and a 4,000–5,000 peso dowry, a vast sum in those days. Like other indigenous elites, Isabel, and subsequently her children, pursued claims against the Spanish crown through its own legal system. After fifty years of litigation, King Philip II settled with the Moctezumas, confirming their perpetual encomiendas (despite abolishing many others), and in return the Moctezumas renounced their claims on New Spain.

Throughout Peru and even New Granada, as Colombia was then known, the daughters of Atawallpa, Huayna Capac, and other Incas married conquistadors in a pattern similar to that which unfolded in early Mexico. Although these women were treated initially as war prizes, several of them managed to convert their youth and numerous offspring into lasting dynasties. Conquistador husbands had a tendency to get themselves killed, particularly in the violence and frontier rambling typical of early Peru, leaving behind indigenous widows. Fortunately, Spanish inheritance law favored them and did not discriminate in any racial way. In the centuries after conquest, the most durable of the indigenous Andean dynasties came to dominate several sectors of Cuzco.

The Spanish exploited existing imperial structures of the conquered Aztecs and Incas to impose themselves on their new subjects. Of course, they shared the hierarchical vision of these empires, and they created their own bureaucratic hierarchy, with the crown overseeing viceroys, one for each of the two main territories in New Spain and Peru, and smaller administrative units within the purview of each viceroy. They continued the Aztec custom of requiring tribute from subjects, and in Peru they required draft labor. But the Spanish also made fundamental changes: Indians were forced to engage in new productive activities to yield the tribute items the Spanish demanded— gold, wool, and even dye-producing insects. Some of the products were new to Europeans, but the real novelty lay in the mercantilist system of trade and marketing. Most disruptive, perhaps, was the Spanish requirement for scattered farming people to live in concentrated, more-or-less Spanish-style villages. This concentration of people served Spanish administrative, religious, and economic demands, but it also sped the spread of disease and left terrain open for Spanish farmers and cattle ranchers. Of course, this was part of the purpose. A system of indirect rule found Spanish encomenderos and officials selecting native lords or chiefs to serve as intermediaries, collecting tribute and assigning workers to labor drafts in mines, fields, houses, and public works projects. The system borrowed from traditional structures of authority, but was in many ways new.

As they built Spanish-style cities and established Spanish law, the Catholic Spaniards of early modern times also sought, by whatever means necessary, to convert their new subjects. After 1492, Spain was officially a Christian kingdom, with all non-Christian subjects expelled. Roman Catholicism was crucial to Spanish identity, and the conversion of Indian subjects would facilitate their integration into the Spanish polity. Within several years of Columbus's first landing on Hispaniola, representatives of the Franciscan, Dominican, and Jeronymite orders arrived, followed later by the Mercedarians, all intent on advancing their gospel and speeding the recovery of Jerusalem. One Jeronymite, the Catalan Ramón Pané, lived for two years among the Taínos of Hispaniola, studying their language and customs and recording their origin stories and beliefs, becoming, some argue, the first ethnographer of the Americas. Among Taíno customs the Spaniards found especially offensive were constant bathing and urinating on and burying Christian icons, as they earlier had done with their own *zemis* to ensure good harvests.

Cortés had demonstrated an almost foolhardy determination to convert the Mexica, and as soon as he completed his conquest, he asked the crown to send him Franciscan missionaries. This order had recently undergone reform in Spain, believing that a notorious laxity within the missionary orders threatened the faith every bit as much as Muslim gains in the Holy Lands. They eagerly responded to the call to Christianize New Spain: twelve Franciscan "Apostles" walked barefoot from Veracruz to Mexico City in 1524. The group included the linguists and collectors of indigenous lore Fray Torribio de Benavente (also known as Motolinía), Bernardino de Sahagún, and Diego Durán, each of whom used Indian codices and informants to write about indigenous culture and history. Although intellectually curious and painstaking in their research, these men ultimately hoped to change rather than preserve native lifeways. The Dominicans, who had led the fight for indigenous rights in Hispaniola, arrived in New Spain the following year, and in 1529 Juan de Zumárraga (formerly of the Franciscan order) came to establish the secular, or diocesan, church in New Spain.

Zumárraga was New Spain's first bishop (and later its first archbishop), but he also held the title "Protector of Indians." Encouraged by the Indians' early willingness to kneel, imitate signs, pray, and sing, as well as by their enthusiasm for ritual, the early Franciscans exulted at mass baptisms of their new charges. The friars recognized the Mexica's love of theatrical displays and staged dramas—such as "The Conquest of Jerusalem"—to attract audiences and promote conversions. In these pieces, Indian actors played both Moors and Spanish conquerors, and black actors raced on horseback across stage sets, killing wild animals in fake jungles. Cortés even acted in one of these plays. Judging from crowd reaction, the spiritual conquest seemed to be a success. But as in Europe and elsewhere that Christianity spread, eradicating deeply held beliefs in the Americas was more difficult than it initially seemed. The perfunctory nature of early Mexico's mass baptisms never squelched indigenous beliefs, and the worship of old gods and use of old rituals persevered. Discovering that some of his flock still worshiped their old deities, Zumárraga initiated an inquisition, roughly following rules established by the Spanish Holy Office, to determine the extent of the "heresy."

One such "heretic" was the indigenous prophet Martin Ocelotl, who had predicted the fall of Tenochtitlán. The accuracy of his predictions had enhanced his reputation among Nahuatl-speakers in Mexico's Central Valley. Ocelotl became wealthy as a clandestine priest and healer, but he also worked as a farmer and moneylender in Texcoco. Like many former Aztec subjects, he bowed to many new requirements imposed by the conquerors and was baptized at the age of twenty-nine. But also like other indigenous subjects, Ocelotl continued to honor old ways. Discovered and denounced by a Franciscan friar, Ocelotl was ordered to choose one of his many wives to marry and forswear the others. His public renunciation of "extra" wives and his Catholic marriage were to serve as models for other Indians. But Ocelotl's "reform" proved temporary, and before long he was prophesying again, warning followers of a drought and giving them digging sticks with which to plant agave and prickly pear cactus. He also predicted the end of the Spanish world and return of a previous age, all of which was enough to bring his case to the attention of the first viceroy of New Spain (Great Mexico, its capital Mexico City), Antonio de Mendoza. Although the prosecutor sought his death, Ocelotl's denials and contradictory evidence allowed him to escape with a sentence of exile. After his public trial, Ocelotl was put on a ship bound for Seville, which sank mid-ocean.

Even so, the trial records show that Ocelotl, like Isabel Moctezuma and other influential Mexica, was able to retain wealth and status after the conquest. Ocelotl's estate consisted of houses and fourteen acres of land in four towns, along with orchards, gold dust, coins, cotton cloth, blankets, jewels, 400 bushels of maize, furniture, tools, four women slaves, religious objects (fans and plums), gourds, tortoise shell mixers for making cocoa, two pairs of painted shoes, dyes, belts, drums, liquid amber, and censers for incense. Oceltotl's early indiscretions paled in comparison with the supposed discovery of noble Mexicas' ongoing worship of war god Huitzilopochtli, whom the Spanish called "Huichilobos." After investigation, in 1539 Zumárraga burned at the stake the alleged leader of this heresy, Don Carlos of Texcoco.

Shortly thereafter, a great Maya leader, Nachi Cocom, led a revolt against Spaniards in the Yucatán. Angered by heavy-handed Spanish demands for tribute and their penchant for desecrating indigenous religious sites, Cocom crafted an alliance of six Maya provinces in a synchronized uprising, launched on a day that signified "death" and "end" on the Maya calendar in 1546. After bloody fighting, the Spaniards prevailed in the so-called Great Maya Revolt, but surviving Maya waged a long guerrilla war. It would take the Spaniards more than twenty years to gain control of the northern portion of this rela-

The Legend of El Dorado

One might be tempted to think the Spanish met with more successes than failures in their transatlantic colonial enterprises. Certainly, they enjoyed spectacular successes. But for most Spaniards who came to the Americas in the wake of Cortés and Pizarro, there would be no golden kingdoms. Legends abounded, however, and they continued to draw hordes of would-be conquistadors into rugged lands, in some cases long after the end of the sixteenth century. One of the most persistent of these legends regarded El Dorado, or "the Gilded One," a chief said to cover himself with resin and then be dusted with raw gold before an annual ritual bath in a sacred lake. Many versions of this legend circulated in the sixteenth century, primarily in New Granada and Venezuela, but also in Ecuador, Peru, and the Guyanas. Sir Walter Ralegh was one foreign believer and promoter of the legend, but he had gleaned most of his information from deluded Spanish prisoners in search of the same thing. El Dorado expeditions were organized from a number of Atlantic ports as well as highland cities, and nearly all such undertakings proved disastrous for everyone involved. African slaves and drafted Indian porters died by the hundreds and even thousands from overwork, disease, and starvation, prompting authorities to limit the size of the perennial treasure hunts so as not to depopulate entire regions. Spanish merchants kept quiet, however, as they made a killing selling guns and supplies to wave after wave of fortune seekers.

Perhaps the most famous El Dorado expedition was the one led by the Navarrese nobleman Pedro de Ursúa, which set out for the lower Huallaga River valley of northern Peru, and then the great Amazon itself, in 1560. Along for the voyage was a minor Basque officer and failed conquistador named Lope de Aguirre. Aguirre would soon lead a mutiny that deposed, then hanged, Ursúa deep in the Amazon jungle, and later proclaimed independence from Spain and openly insulted King Philip II. Aguirre and his band of followers managed to survive a murderous, half-starved trip down the Amazon, and upon reaching the Atlantic they sailed to the coast of Venezuela. Aguirre soon clashed with colonial officials on the island of Margarita, still declaring himself a rebel, now bent on taking over Mexico and Peru. Increasingly isolated as his terrorized followers left to seek amnesty, Aguirre was finally surrounded and killed outside the Venezuelan town of Barquisimeto. Debate over Aguirre's possible insanity continues, but whatever the judgment, he still symbolizes the dark side of the El Dorado legend. He was hardly the only one felled by El Dorado fever. Indeed, from colonial times to the present, entrepreneurs and adventurers have continued to engage in mad quests for this fabled treasure, going so far as to drain a number of Colombia's highland lakes. Other tales of lost Indian treasure continue to inspire seekers of fortune.

The Gilding of El Dorado. Attendants puff gold dust on the mythical king's body through a tube while his lords carouse in a hammock. Engraving, 1727. Credit: The Granger Collection, New York.

tively impoverished peninsula, and Maya resistance continued for more than 150 years in the southern reaches of the Yucatán. As one Maya witness recounted, "They did not wish to join with the foreigners; they did not desire Christianity." Before the Spaniards, "everything was complete [and] good [with] no sin [and] no illness [for] humanity was orderly."

Another rebellion in Peru followed this pattern, with religion providing a language and means of opposition. Native beliefs endured everywhere in the new Spanish territories, and some of them encouraged resistance. In the 1560s, Indians in the central Andes participated in a movement called *Taki Onqoy* (dancing sickness), which peaked in 1565. The movement centered on messages from Andean gods, who predicted an alliance and uprising of indigenous deities that would defeat the Christian god and visit the Spanish with sickness and misfortune. Everywhere, Indians turned back to their gods and *huacas* (sacred objects) and rejected Catholicism, but 1565 came and went with no calamitous transformation. Spanish missionaries were slower to establish themselves in the Andes than in Mexico, which in part explains the limited documentation of the Taki Onqoy uprising, but once they did they began to persecute native people for their persistent non-Christian beliefs, particularly in Lima's hinterland.

It was clear that early optimism about a quick and easy conversion of native Americans had been unwarranted, and Spaniards began to evince a more cynical and hostile view of them. Many already believed in Aristotle's "natural law," which considered some people natural lords and others natural slaves. As Spanish authorities became increasingly aware of continuing resistance, they began to give up the idea of a peaceful incorporation of an innocent mass of new subjects. Instead, they created a dual republic—one for Spaniards and one for Indians—separate and unequal. Indigenous rulers retained limited authority over their own subjects as long as they behaved, swore loyalty to Spain, practiced the Catholic faith, and handed over tribute and personal service when required. But all native people remained subject to the laws and authority of Spain, which trumped their own.

Spain's Advancing Frontiers

As they secured and consolidated their rule by building cities, establishing bureaucracies, securing elite wives, and converting Indians to Christianity, the Spanish engaged in continued explorations, most of them motivated by the quest for wealth. They launched expeditions north and south from many vantage points. From Hispaniola, the Florentine merchant Amerigo Vespucci reached the southern mainland in 1500, and his report, sent to Florence in 1503 and published as *Mundus Novus* (New World), was soon translated into eight languages and printed in sixty editions. (A German mapmaker who read the popular work named the new continent America in Vespucci's honor.) A litany of Spanish conquests followed, conducted by some of the most brutal and battle-hardened veterans of Hispaniola. Juan Ponce de León conquered Puerto Rico in 1508, Juan de Esquivel occupied Jamaica in 1509, Diego Velásquez defeated his old enemy Hatuey in Cuba in 1511, and, from Puerto Rico, Ponce de León reached La Florida in 1513, allowing Spain to claim sovereignty over the Atlantic coast of North America from the Florida Keys to

Newfoundland. In 1509 Alonso de Ojeda took up the conquest of Colombia's Gulf of Urabá and, to the northwest, Diego de Nicuesa tackled Nicaragua. In these cases, the Indians won the day and Spanish survivors regrouped along the north coast of Panama. From here, Vasco Núñez de Balboa crossed the isthmus to become the first European to see the Pacific Ocean in 1513. In 1517 and 1518 Diego de Velásquez commissioned expeditions from Cuba that touched Yucatán. The following year, Ferdinand Magellan sailed west through the straits at the southern tip of South America into the Pacific Ocean; although he did not survive the voyage, one of his ships circumnavigated the globe and returned to Spain three years later.

Other forays carried the Spanish north. In 1515 Lucas Vásquez de Ayllón conducted slave raids up the coast of modern-day South Carolina. Ayllón later attempted the first full-scale settlement on La Florida's Atlantic coast at San Miguel de Gualdape, a site believed to have been located near present-day Sapelo Sound in Georgia. Ayllón's expedition included six hundred Spanish men, women, and children, as well as the first known contingent of African slaves brought into what is now the United States. Africans, enslaved and free, embedded as they were in Iberian life, accompanied Spaniards in their forays into the Caribbean and were a part of all Spanish conquests. Disease, starvation, and his own death undermined Ayllón's enterprise; disaffected settlers mutinied and took control of the failing colony. Then, with the approach of winter—a problem the Spanish had not faced in the tropics—some slaves set fire to the mutineers' compound, an act that raised questions about the Africans' political alignments. At the same moment the Guale Indians rose against the Spaniards, completing the destruction of the settlement in 1526. The escaped slaves took up residence among the Guale, becoming maroons (or runaways) as many of their counterparts were already doing in Hispaniola, Puerto Rico, Jamaica, Cuba, Panama, and Mexico, while the other survivors of Ayllón's failed colony straggled back to Hispaniola.

Because Mexico and Peru were the wealthiest and most populous regions of Spain's Atlantic empire, they became viceroyalties and absorbed most of the crown's interest in the Americas. But Spanish officials also devoted resources to extending their mainland empire beyond its already far-flung frontiers. In 1541, the year of his brother Francisco's murder, Gonzalo Pizarro led an expedition from Quito to the Amazon River in search of the fabled El Dorado, where an indigenous king supposedly dusted his body with gold. Pizarro's entourage included 220 Spaniards, 4,000 Indians, 200 horses, 2,000 hogs, and almost as many dogs and llamas, but once in the Amazon the expedition quickly disintegrated. Pizarro was forced to send a foraging party to search for food. Francisco de Orellana and sixty men, including the monk Gaspar de Carvajal, who later wrote about the ordeal, eventually drifted down the Napo River and into the world's greatest river drainage, following its course to the Atlantic. Always resourceful, the party rigged sails at the mouth of the Amazon and finally reached a Spanish settlement on the Caribbean coast of South America in 1542. Pizarro's force ultimately limped back to Peru, with nothing to show for their travails. Lured onward by hope of another Mexico or fables of golden men and golden cities, Spanish adventurers like the Basque rebel Lope de Aguirre spent their lives (or ended them) in the peripheral areas of Spanish America, far removed from the glitter of Mexico City and Lima. Exploitation of most of these remote frontiers did not yield another Peru or Mexico, but all had geopolitical value to Spain.

From 1539 to 1540, an expedition led by Hernándo De Soto trekked through eleven of the current southeastern United States. Archaeologists to-day track its progress through mass burials of Indians, with gaping rents in skulls and bones caused by Spanish broadswords, and European goods traded or discarded along the way. At De Soto's winter camp in Tallahassee, Florida, archaeologists have found coins, weapons, pig bones, and chain mail dumped by the overburdened Spaniards. Before dying of fever, De Soto explored Arkansas and "discovered" the Mississippi River, in which his men buried him before heading southward in hopes of rescue. Meanwhile, financed by the viceroy of New Spain and guided by Estévan, the black survivor of the Narváez expedition, De Soto's contemporary, Francisco Vásquez de Coronado, led an exploration northward from Mexico City into the deserts of present-day New Mexico and Arizona. Although Coronado's expedition never found the fabled Seven Cities of Cíbola, his companions became the first Europeans to see the Grand Canyon and other natural wonders of what is now the United States before being driven back by the Zuni Indians, who allegedly killed Estévan.

Early Spanish expeditions to the River Plate district of South America were slightly more successful, but only after disasters. In 1535, a crown-sponsored fleet under Adelantado Pedro de Mendoza set out to conquer and settle lands beyond Buenos Aires, in what today is Paraguay and eastern Bolivia. As with Ayllón in La Florida, Mendoza's expedition succumbed to indigenous attacks and Spanish infighting. Subsequent, smaller, privately sponsored expeditions succeeded in establishing such cities as Asunción and Santa Cruz de la Sierra, both of which retained a frontier character throughout colonial times. This vast region, the Paraná-Paraguay River basin, would eventually become the heart of Jesuit mission territory in South America.

In all these expeditions Spaniards possessed the land, named and marked it with notarized ceremonies, and placed claims on maps as they accumulated geographic knowledge. Their pattern of movement was self-consciously Roman. If they managed to conquer a region, they immediately began to try to hold and populate it. La Florida, which French Protestant refugees threatened briefly, was violently retaken by Pedro Menéndez de Avilés in 1565. A generation later, in 1598, Juan de Oñate settled New Mexico, a place truly at the outer edge of the Spanish American world. Like Cortés before them, these Spaniards tried to remake their settlements in the image of Spain, establishing *pueblos* (towns), *presidios* (military posts), and missions and instituting Spanish law and the Catholic religion. On both fronts of Spanish expansion, regular orders, especially Franciscans, tried pacific conversions and congregated local Indians in mission villages for tribute, labor, and religious instruction. They gloried in their initial successes, and by the mid-seventeenth century a chain of Franciscan missions ran along the Atlantic coast from St.

Augustine to present-day South Carolina and west through the Florida Pan-handle. Despite the churchmen's best intentions and efforts, Indians rebelled and attacked Spanish settlements, winning themselves ferocious punishment. The combination of missions and military outposts was typical of Spanish frontier life and would become more prominent in years to come.

Iberian settlements in the Americas in the first sixty years of contact demonstrated connections with patterns already established across the Atlantic— trading posts, sugar plantations, the religiously charged culture of the Reconquest—but they also revealed the innovations that indigenous economies dictated and the catastrophic mortality that accompanied European invasions. By 1565, Spain had two centers of power and dozens of satellite settlements in cities on the mainland and islands around the Caribbean. When the Taíno and Caribs showed little to trade aside from gold, and because they did not by custom mine it in amounts the Spanish required, the conquerors responded with permanent settlements, and the introduction of slavery, livestock, and sugar production. On the mainland, the Spanish grafted themselves atop existing imperial structures, and thus required political dominance to secure power. The Portuguese, with a much smaller population base to govern satellite holdings, had turned more slowly toward a policy of state-sponsored colonization. The relatively scattered Indian population and Tupi reluctance to meet Portuguese requirements for brazilwood shaped colonial dynamics there as well, departing from the trade model familiar to their countrymen around the globe. As all of these Ibero-American innovations were underway, Spain's transatlantic settlements began producing mineral wealth of such value that European rivals took notice and turned their attention to the profits they, too, might glean from the Americas.

Selected Readings

Alchon, Suzanne Austin, *A Pest in the Land: New World Disease Epidemics in a Global Perspective* (Albuquerque: University of New Mexico Press, 2002).

Benítez-Rojo, Antonio, *Sea of Lentils* (Amherst: University of Massachusetts Press, 1992).

Christopher Columbus: The Four Voyages, Ed. & Trans. by J. M. Cohen (London: Penguin Books, 1969).

Clendinnen, Inga, *Ambivalent Conquests: Maya and Spaniard in Yucatán, 1517–1570* (Cambridge, UK: Cambridge University Press, 1987).

———, *Aztecs: An Interpretation* (Cambridge, UK: Cambridge University Press, 1991).

Crosby, Alfred W., *The Columbian Exchange: Biological and Cultural Consequences of 1492* (Westport: Greenwood Press, 1972).

Hassig, Ross, *Mexico and the Spanish Conquest* (London: Longman Group, 1994).

Hemming, John, *Red Gold: The Conquest of the Brazilian Indians* (London: Macmillan London, 1978).

Hulme, Peter, *Colonial Encounters: Europe and the Native Caribbean, 1492–1797* (London: Methuen, 1986).

Lockhart, James, *The Nahuas after the Conquest* (Stanford: Stanford University Press, 1992).

Metcalf, Alida, *Go-Betweens in Early Colonial Brazil* (Austin: University of Texas Press, 2005).

Moya Pons, Frank, *The Dominican Republic: A National History* (New Rochelle: Hispaniola Books, 1995).

Powers, Karen V., *Women of the Conquest* (Albuquerque: University of New Mexico Press, 2005).

Restall, Matthew, *Seven Myths of the Spanish Conquest* (Oxford: Oxford University Press, 2003).

Rouse, Irving, *The Taínos: Rise & Decline of the People Who Greeted Columbus* (New Haven: Yale University Press, 1992).

Sauer, Carl O., *The Early Spanish Main* (Berkeley: University of California Press, 1966).

Stern, Steve, *Peru's Indian Peoples and the Challenge of Spanish Conquest: Huamanga to 1640* (Madison: University of Wisconsin Press, 1982).

Townsend, Camilla, *Malintzin's Choice: An Indian Woman in the Conquest of Mexico* (Albuquerque: University of New Mexico Press, 2006).

Weber, David J., *The Spanish Frontier in North America* (New Haven: Yale University Press, 1992).

Whitehead, Neil, ed., *Wolves from the Sea* (Leiden: KITLV Press, 1992).

A romanticized view of the Dutch in South Africa. The landing of Jan van Riebeeck at Table Bay, South Africa in 1652. Credit: The Granger Collection, New York.

Chapter Four

European Rivalries
and Atlantic Repercussions,
1500–1650

*There met our armies in their proud array. Both furnished well, both full of hope
and fear, Both menacing alike with daring shows. . . . Both raising dreadful
clamors to the sky.*
Thomas Kyd, *The Spanish Tragedy*

Francisco Manuel of Seville, Spain, was only seven years old in the
last decades of the sixteenth century when he started a career that would daunt
many an older man. Seville was a city that had grown in step with the American trade. Already the biggest city in Castile, it expanded into one of the largest in Europe after being designated the official departure point for the Indies
fleet. Well inland in Andalusia on the river Guadalquivir, Seville bustled with
port activity, and when the fleet was in, mariners crowded the inns and savored the entertainments. The orphaned Francisco Manuel was one of the
many casualties of port life, a "lost boy." But his fortune took a good turn
when a shipbuilder took him in and set him to work, sending him first on a
long voyage to northern mainland South America, and then on a second to
New Spain in Central America. Many children suffered abuse aboard ship;
some elected to stay in the Indies rather than return to their families in Spain
because of the violence inflicted on them at sea. But Francisco Manuel persevered and prospered.

Francisco Manuel traveled on the galleons of the Spanish fleet that, laden
with silver and other American treasures, trumpeted Spain's wealth. The galleons were great, three-masted ships of an average 500-ton burden, rigged
with a mix of square and lateen sails. Once the conquistadors had plundered
the premade treasures of the Aztec-Mexica, Incas, and others, they turned to
production of gold, silver, and precious stones. Gold existed in western Mexico,
Panama, Venezuela, and parts of the Andes. Richest of all was New Granada,
today's Colombia, which boasted the world's largest emerald deposits, and
neighboring Venezuela, with rich pearl beds. In the 1530s and 1540s, Spanish prospectors fanned out from Mexico City and located massive silver deposits in Pachuca, Taxco, Guanajuato, and Zacatecas. In Bolivia, the old Inca
mines of Porco were soon displaced by the richest silver deposit of all, the
Cerro Rico (Rich Hill) of Potosí. At the base of the mountain was the Villa

Imperial de Potosí, by Francisco Manuel's time one of the largest cities in the world. A word still synonymous with great wealth in the Spanish language, *Potosí* was discovered by two native Andean llama drivers in 1545. The Spanish initially smelted silver in furnaces fueled by wood, charcoal, and, in highland Bolivia, llama dung, but a major technical innovation came about in 1554, when a merchant from Seville established a mercury amalgamation process at Mexican mines. The method spread to Potosí in the early 1570s, and everywhere it was practiced it generated an unprecedented boom in silver production. Although amalgamation required less fuel than smelting, mercury—produced in Spain and Peruvian mines—is a deadly substance and it posed great health risks to the Indian draft laborers and African slaves forced to work with it. However high the social, economic, and environmental costs of its production, American silver soon flowed across the Atlantic in a regular stream, altering the economy of Spain, Europe, and ultimately the world in the process.

To protect their ships from corsairs, as early as 1525 Madrid required the galleons to travel in a convoy. By 1561, the Spanish instituted a fleet system: twice each year, in January and August, merchant ships sailed with armed escorts from Spain. The return fleets left from Cartagena, on the South American coast, and from Veracruz in New Spain, and rendezvoused at Havana, in the city's large natural harbor. From there, the ships caught the Gulf Stream and prevailing winds and returned to Spain via the Azores, a trip of two to three months. The voyages were timed to avoid hurricane season, but unexpected delays led to the destruction of several ships and even whole fleets off the Florida coast. Pirates and privateers captured straggling vessels from time to time, but with relatively few exceptions, the fleets made it home. The mineral wealth they carried transformed Spain's differential of power in Europe. When the Spanish crown granted permission for explorations and conquests in the Americas, it demanded one-fifth of all profits derived through such expeditions. Rooted in the Reconquest tradition of the division of spoils, this *Quinto Real* (Royal Fifth) went directly into the monarch's coffers and offered the Spanish crown a ready, flexible source of funds. With this wealth, the Spanish were able to wage war on a scale not previously imagined. Wars are expensive in general, requiring provisions for soldiers and, in this era without standing national armies, salaries to hire mercenaries. Firearms, horses, carts, and ships added to the costs. Financed not so much by American silver itself but by loans taken out against future yields, Spain launched wars all over Europe. For Spain's neighbors, targeting the fleet and undermining Iberian holdings in America emerged as important strategies in challenging Spanish dominance. But Spain's wars, many of which proved to be stalemates punctuated by occasional victories (as in the Netherlands) were so costly that in spite of all the incoming treasure, the crown went bankrupt on several occasions in the sixteenth century.

By 1570, Spanish strongholds dotted the western Atlantic, from north Florida to Buenos Aires. Portuguese Brazil was on its way to becoming the world's most valuable sugar colony; its capital, Salvador, was well protected. Iberians were the envy of Europe thanks to their American riches, and after 1580, when Philip II annexed Portugal, the Spanish seemed unbeatable. Spanish power in America made it imprudent for other Europeans to launch settlements carelessly. Only a few naturally defensible sites could withstand Spanish hostility, and even these required regular provisioning and naval reinforcement. Thus Spain's European rivals found themselves in the fringe regions of the Americas. It is only in this context of international rivalries and the intransigence of Spanish resistance to territorial incursion that we can understand the uninviting location of some the earliest northern European colonial settlements.

Spain's dominance dictated where and how other Europeans were drawn to the Americas and Africa, but the impulses behind these Atlantic interventions were complex. European dynastic politics, a result of the attachment to hereditary monarchy, played a role, as did new religious animosities in the wake of the Protestant Reformation. Northern European rivals, first the French, then the English and the Dutch, pursued a range of strategies in their efforts to thwart Spanish power in the western Atlantic and Africa. None emulated the accomplishments of the Spanish, however much they tried. Even at the turn of the seventeenth century, as Spain's power waned, its rivals had established little more than trading posts and small, precarious settlements in the Americas, and then only in those regions deemed undesirable by the Spanish and only with the cooperation of indigenous populations. Northern Europeans, particularly the Dutch, were most successful when they focused their intervention on commercial and maritime opportunities, not settlement. No French, English, or Dutch settlement anywhere in the western Atlantic through the 1620s boasted more than a few hundred Europeans in residence, and these few settlements tended to be characterized either by the culture of the trade factory or the culture of piracy.

A Fractured Unity

In the early modern era, no firm separation existed between religious and political worlds: upheaval in one meant upheaval in the other. Until 1517, western Europeans shared a single religion, Catholicism. All acknowledged the power of the pope and shared a common form and language of worship (although regional variations and vestiges of pre-Catholic practices continued). Opposition to the church often took the form of attacks on the clergy, represented in the satirical writings of such men as Erasmus. But church reform took a new direction when Martin Luther, an Augustinian friar, challenged papal authority when he nailed his *Ninety-Five Theses* to the church door in Wittenberg (Germany) on All Saints' Eve, October 31, 1517. Luther attacked a range of church customs, including simony, the practice of buying and selling church offices, and the sale of indulgences, which granted purchasers remission from punishment in hell or a lingering torment in purgatory. He rejected the belief that model behavior could secure salvation. Luther also advocated making religion less mysterious to the mass of worshipers, most of whom were illiterate. He believed the word of God should be available to all, not simply held in the hands of priests and theologians. He translated the Bible into the vernacular (German in his own case), but he inspired others to do the same for French, English, Dutch, and all the languages of Europe.

Because his criticism of the Church ultimately required separation from it, Luther inadvertently launched a religious revolution. Luther inspired men in other countries, including John Calvin in Geneva, whose followers (known as Calvinists) believed in predestination, the notion that people could do nothing to effect their own salvation, as it was predetermined by God. This was a stark doctrine that could drive believers to feelings of despair and inadequacy—and to frantic introspection as they sought clues that God had chosen them as among the elect. God had his plan, and people could never hope to know His will. Some followers carried this logic to an extreme position, arguing that if all were predestined, then it did not matter how people con-

DIVISION OF RELIGION
circa 1560

ducted themselves on earth. "Heretics" of this persuasion generally suffered grisly torments for the error of their ways.

Calvinism soon spread beyond Geneva. The people known as Puritans in England were Calvinists, as were the Huguenots in France. Puritans have gotten bad press over the years. Twentieth-century social critic H. L. Mencken famously derided them as dour killjoys, people who worried that someone, somewhere, might be having a good time. In fact, Puritans pursued the same sensory pleasures as their non-Puritan neighbors. What most concerned them, however, were their Lord and the world that awaited them, not the earthly pleasures that surrounded them, and they sought to minimize distractions from a person's focus on her own salvation.

All Protestants launched church reforms, some radical, some moderate, but Protestant beliefs and practices lacked uniformity. Protestants reconfigured churches, moving the altar, eliminating images, ridding the sacraments of mystery and distance, putting all worship in the vernacular, and encouraging literacy so people could read and interpret the Bible for themselves. During mass, Catholic priests stood with their backs to a distant congregation, speaking in Latin, a language few knew. Protestants spun the minister around, moved him closer to the worshipers, and emphasized persuasive interpretations of scripture and not mysterious rituals and esoteric knowledge. Some Protestants stripped the minister of priestly vestments and banned the incense and bells used in Catholic masses. Calvinists rejected all saints, although Lutherans and some Anglicans continued to revere them. Some Protestants rejected church hierarchies, dispensing with bishops and synods, and all Protestants de-emphasized the importance of saints and of Mary, the mother of Jesus, insisting that people focus on the Lord, not on intermediaries.

Most radically, Protestants rejected the celibate priesthood. They dismantled convents and monasteries, among the wealthiest and most powerful landholding institutions of the time, and enjoined priests to seek wives: the former monk Luther married a former nun, Katharina von Bora, whom he had helped escape from a convent. Protestants also sought to strip the church of what they deemed extraneous influences that might distract individuals from worship. In some places, that conviction translated into the act of destroying all "idolatrous" decorative elements, decapitating the statues of saints and hurling stones through stained glass windows. A visitor would know after taking one step inside a church what type of worship was practiced therein. For some Protestants, reform included banning instrumental accompaniment to sacred music. Religious reform could even lead to social revolution (both radical and conservative), as believers carried their vision into secular realms, including gender roles, household organization, state polity, and relationships between church and state. In a time when worldviews centered on religious beliefs, Protestantism gave individuals the chance—indeed, the obligation—to make the world anew. Catholics would respond with reforms of their own, some also aimed at heightening individual responsibility.

Until the middle of the sixteenth century, both Protestant and Catholic reformation lay in the hands of men who maintained political control over the process. Luther himself rejected the efforts by the men and women of the Peasants' Revolt (1524–26) to take control of their own faith, siding instead with their rulers. Henry VIII (r. 1509–47) who had originally opposed Martin Luther and earned the title of Defender of the Faith, soon led England's break from Rome and in 1534 had Parliament declare him head of the new (Anglican) Church of England. Elsewhere, warring leaders found in this new age of religious divisions sudden openings for political gain. In some places, pragmatic sovereigns sought to steer a middle path between warring factions. Most successful in this effort was Henry's daughter, Elizabeth I (r. 1558–1603) of England, whose subjects ranged across the Protestant spectrum, some seeking to maintain elements of Catholic ritual (including the liturgy and the veneration of saints) and others seeking a rigid and uncompromising Calvinist reformation.

These different Protestant sects, each of which called for its own version of reform, shattered the religious unity Western Europe had known for centuries. Although concentrated in the north, Protestants emerged throughout the Catholic European world. Of those kingdoms involved directly with the Atlantic, England became Protestant by will of the sovereign, the northern provinces of the Low Countries were Calvinist, and France remained divided between Huguenot and Catholic. But these characterizations cannot begin to convey the complexity and animosity of the sixteenth century. Henry VIII's sickly son Edward (r. 1547–53) was an ardent Protestant, but he died young and was succeeded by his sister Mary, the devoutly Catholic daughter of Henry and Catherine of Aragon, a Spanish princess. Elizabeth, an ardent Protestant, took the throne in 1558. The people of England were thus obliged to shift religious practices with each new sovereign, four different ones with different religious persuasions in the space of two decades. The official religious situation in France was similarly volatile. Henri IV abruptly abandoned Protestantism (he referred to his "perilous leap" from Calvinism to Catholicism) in 1593 in order to secure the throne and fend off rival claimants (including Philip II of Spain). When Protestant rulers made themselves the head of new national churches (as Henry, Edward, and Elizabeth did in England), they put Catholic subjects in the untenable position of being traitors by virtue of their continued attachment to the pope and their rejection of the political authority of their own sovereign.

Brutality characterized the civil and international wars unleashed by early modern religious division. Those judged "heretics" by their enemies were tortured and burned alive. Massacres accompanied civil wars in a political climate in which opponents demonized each other and fervent religious positions made compromise impossible. Political drawings from the period show Catholics and Protestants eating children and the pope as the Antichrist, leading Protestant lambs to slaughter. One of the best-known massacres transpired on St. Bartholomew's Day in France in August of 1572, when Catholics in Paris hacked to death three thousand Huguenots (men, women, and children) before the murderous rampage spread to the rest of the country. Just back from a stay in Brazil, the Protestant Jean de Léry wrote that fellow Frenchmen, not the Tupi, were the real barbarians. The rivalries of the age destroyed vestiges of empathy: the pope, told of the carnage, rewarded the messenger for the happy tidings.

Luther's critiques and the Reformation they sparked provoked a response within the Catholic Church called the Catholic Reformation or Counter Reformation. Reformers gathered at Trent, in northern Italy, for meetings that lasted between 1545 and 1563 and tackled a range of church issues. Those who participated in the Council of Trent particularly sought a clarification of church doctrine and reformation of the most egregious abuses of officials and priests. (Like Protestants, Catholics spared time to focus on music during services: the great Italian composer Palestrina was told by the Council to make his polyphonic music less busy so that listeners could hear every word.)

The reenergized Catholic Church would affect events throughout the Atlantic world and beyond. In 1537 Ignatius Loyola founded a new religious order within the Catholic Church. This was an age of religious innovation, and Loyola, a native of the Spanish Basque country and a veteran of the Italian Wars, shared the initiative of Luther and Calvin, whom he would have identified as his most bitter rivals. Loyola and his followers swore absolute obedience to the pope, and in good military fashion called themselves the Company of Jesus. By 1540, Loyola had ten fellow "Christian soldiers"; by 1556, there were 1,000, and by 1624, 16,000. The Society of Jesus or Jesuit Order, as it came to be known, rapidly grew into one of the most important forces in Catholic renewal. Rather than retreat into a cloistered, monastic life, as most orders did, Jesuits embraced the world. Theirs was not a community organized around a communal liturgical life, but a more individually oriented one with a mission of preaching and educating in public places and foreign lands: the schools and universities they founded continue to function as distinguished centers of higher learning. Where Catholicism seemed to be in disunion and retreat, Jesuits reinvigorated it, and where it was unknown, they introduced it. Jesuits spanned the world, becoming a mobile, global force.

Jesuits also immersed themselves in politics. In France, they wrote pamphlets urging the assassination of two French monarchs, one whom they believed to be an insufficiently ardent Catholic (Henri III), and the other a Protestant (Henri IV). In early 1580 Pope Gregory XIII renewed Pius V's 1570 bull of excommunication, *Regnans in Excelsis*, against the Protestant English queen, Elizabeth I, enjoining her subjects not to recognize her rights as sovereign and absolving them from sin for acts—including murder—they might undertake in removing her. That summer, Jesuits from the continent quietly began arriving in disguise in England, where the island's Catholic minority protected and sheltered them. In the modern era, this sort of international political subversion, secret cells of religious zealots bent on assassination and overthrow of foreign governments, would be regarded as international terrorism. Protestants responded by planting spies in Spain and Portugal and launching violent attacks on merchant ships and in overseas colonies.

As the Catholic Church girded for attack and pursued reformation from within, the Jesuits stand out as one of its few innovations; for the most part, conservatism and retreat still held firm in church thinking. The Papal *Index of Forbidden Books* included some of the great humanist works of Renaissance

Figure 4.2 Philip II's Wars

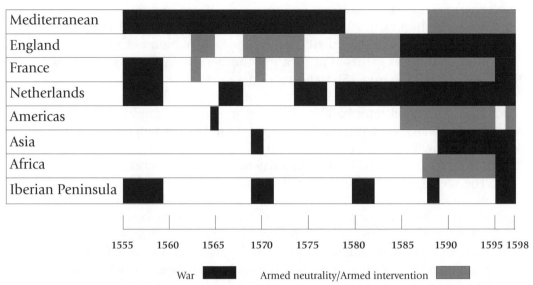

Philip's monarchy enjoyed peace for only six months: between February and September 1577, when hostilities ceased in both the Netherlands and the Mediterranean. Thereafter, although the king never went to war with the Turks again, conflict returned to the Netherlands (lasting until 1609) and began with England (1585–1603), involving attacks on Spain, the Atlantic Islands, the Americas, and the High Seas. After 1509, Philip became increasingly involved in the French Religious Wars until the peace of Vervins in 1598. Meanwhile, overseas, the Portuguese outposts in Africa and South Asia engaged in various hostilities: first against their local enemies, above all in Ceylon, and then against the Dutch. From **The Grand Strategy of Philip II** *(New Haven, CT: Yale University Press, 1998) by Geoffrey Parker. Copyright Geoffrey Parker.*

Europe (including the writings of Erasmus, a Catholic advocate of religious toleration), and the Inquisition was charged with rooting out heresy. Nowhere was this retreat more evident than in Spain, where Christian unity expressed through Catholicism had been part of national identity since the fifteenth-century expulsion of Muslims and Jews. Spain's King Philip II, scion of the Austrian House of Habsburg, styled himself as the protector of Catholicism. Deeply religious, he followed personal convictions into European politics at great cost to his empire. After he moved to repress two Spanish Protestant groups in 1559 and 1560, burning alive the heretics, Protestantism disappeared from the peninsula. In 1558, Philip II banned all foreign books, and a year later he ordered home all Spaniards studying abroad. Spain retreated from the cosmopolitan intellectual world of the rest of Europe, but not its political world. Determined to protect and expand Catholicism, Philip II immersed Spain in expensive wars on the continent and in the Mediterranean.

This was a time when the personality of a monarch could shape a kingdom's future, and Philip II was among the most powerful monarchs in the world. Born in 1527, the eldest child of Charles V (the Holy Roman Emperor, King of Aragon, Castile, Naples, and Sicily) and Isabel of Portugal, Philip grew up long and lean with dark, piercing eyes and a thin beard he trimmed so that it drooped into two pointed tufts just below an even thinner mustache. (According to Dutch critics, his style of facial hair gave the devilish impression of two horns jutting from his chin.) His holdings and influence were vast. When Philip acceded to the Spanish throne in 1556, he already governed the duchy of Milan (conferred upon him at age thirteen), the kingdoms of Naples and Sicily, and the seventeen provinces of the Dutch Netherlands. With Charles's abdication, Philip also inherited Spain's vast empire in the Americas. As the husband of Mary Tudor, elder daughter of England's King Henry VIII, Philip held little official prerogative in England beyond their shared titles of queen and king. The marriage contract stipulated that he conform to English law and custom and admit no foreigners to office in England. Yet Philip's influence on Mary's rigid Catholicism was unmistakable.

Philip's most notable success against religious adversaries came in 1571, when the greatest Mediterranean naval battle of the sixteenth century, waged in Greece's Gulf of Lepanto, halted Ottoman westward expansion. But Philip proved less successful in his interventions in western Europe, and his passion to defend Catholicism bankrupted the royal treasury. Philip's German, Italian, and Belgian bankers grew reluctant to extend him credit despite the promise of more American treasure, and following his death in 1598, his successors faced almost constant economic crisis. Deficit spending was not yet a refined art, and in Spain's case, no amount of American treasure could offset it. From Europe's great power, Spain began to fade by the turn of the seventeenth century. Although still the richest and largest empire in the Atlantic world, a position it would hold for another century, Spain fell increasingly on the defensive. The rebellion of the Low Countries, Spain's most protracted and expensive conflict in the early modern period, exemplifies a larger pattern of Spanish overextension, inflexible, shortsighted policy, and ultimate failure. Even before Philip took the throne, a resolute opposition to Spanish control had coalesced around William of Nassau (known as William the Silent due to his taciturn nature), the Prince of Orange, in 1559 the *stadhouder* (chief magistrate or governor) of Holland, Zeeland, and Utrecht.

Dutch-Spanish antagonism only intensified after 1556. Unlike his father, who had been raised in the Netherlands, Philip spoke neither Dutch nor Flemish, disliked the people and their culture, with the exception of their architecture, and visited his holdings there only once after Charles's death. For many Dutch and Belgian Protestants, the moment of truth arrived when Philip decided to reorganize the Catholic Church in the Low Countries. By increasing the number of bishops therein from four to eighteen, and by nominating the clergymen himself, Philip made clear that he intended to enforce the decrees of the recently concluded and uncompromising Council of Trent.

The delegates at Trent had completed their labors in 1563; three years later, in August, Calvinists in Antwerp rose in revolt. The year 1566 ushered in high grain prices, and it was no coincidence that the first rebels against Habsburg rule came from the poorest classes, or that they launched the assault against ostentatious displays of Catholic wealth. Inspired by market preachers, crowds swept into the Cathedral of Notre Dame (named after its Parisian counterpart), smashing altars and statues, slashing paintings, and tearing ancient, hand-lettered manuscripts from their bindings. Before the multitudes were finished, thirty more churches lay sacked. Similar riots erupted to the north in Ghent and Brussels before spilling into the provinces of Holland and Zeeland; in western Flanders alone, mobs pillaged some 400 churches. Along the Atlantic coast, Dutch corsairs, the famous "sea beggars," raided Spanish ships.

From 1566 on, Philip maintained a substantial army in the Netherlands. The Duke of Alba headed a legion of 65,000 men that laid siege to the fortified towns of the region. Befitting his continental authority, Philip raised a continental army. Spanish and Italian soldiers marched north along the "Spanish Road" from Genoa to Lorraine, while German-speaking mercenaries tramped west from the Tyrol. With good reason, Alba bragged that his army

The Day of the Dead

Among the Catholics of Europe, Easter was the most important holy day of the year, but in Mesoamerica, a different religious day emerged: All Souls' Day (November 2), which followed All Saints' Day. All Souls' Day was supposed to be dedicated to praying for all of the souls in purgatory, a place where Catholics believed that the souls of the dead awaited until they had served sufficient penance for entry into heaven. For people of Mesoamerica, who envisioned a continuum between the living and the dead rather than the stark division posited by Christians, the dead were a real part of everyday life. Mesoamerican families maintained their own shrines and altars and tended to the wishes of their deceased relatives. Indeed, these were among people's most sacred religious obligations, and they believed that each year, the souls of the dead returned to visit the living. New converts in Central America easily incorporated the

Christian holy day into their customary ritual observance. The Aztecs already had feasts of the dead, and one alert priest, Diego Duran, openly worried about the similarity. All Souls' Day, or the Day of the Dead in Mexico, emerged as the most important religious day in the Catholic calendar. All-night vigils at cemeteries, in which favorite foods and gifts are offered to the deceased, take place on All Souls' Eve. (All Hallows' Eve, or Halloween, the eve of All Saints Day, has its own traditional observances in many cultures, similarly featuring sweets and icons of the dead). The enthusiasm people of the Americas demonstrated for Catholicism may have reflected genuine intellectual and spiritual interest, but the new faith also enabled people to continue former practices within a Christian idiom. It was essential that the dead be honored by the living, and Catholicism happened to provide the mechanism to do so.

Detail of a modern-day Dia de los Muertos (Day of the Dead) altar, 2005. Photo credit: Michael Hennig.

was the finest force in the Western world. Military superiority came at a high price, however. Despite heavy taxes imposed on the conquered towns, most of the funding came from Spain and foreign creditors, which meant that military resources were dependent on wealth from America. For the next decade, Philip yearly supplied Alba's forces with the equivalent of England's total royal revenue, a fiscal policy that drained his kingdom of hard currency, even as silver continued to pour in from Peru and Mexico. Between 1580 and 1620, Spanish ships carried home roughly ten thousand tons of bullion and coin, which trebled the existing European supply of silver. Even so, these vast amounts of hard money proved too little. Alba's men fought for gold as much as for Spain, and by 1572 his soldiers commonly mutinied over lack of pay. Their revolts spurred local resistance and crippled Philip's hopes of a quick victory.

To fuel their opposition to the Habsburgs, Dutch insurgents drew on stories of Spanish depredations in the Americas. Even if Europeans were not sure where America was or how its inhabitants might be assimilated into their Biblical view of the world (were they the lost tribe?), news of the new world reached European shores as surely as did the Spanish treasure that altered European power dynamics. Between 1524 and 1572, 109 books were published about the people of the Americas. Particularly influential were accounts of the Dominican Bartolomé de las Casas and the Jesuit José de Acosta.

Along with accounts of the people, animals, and plants of the Americas, these priests also reported on their success in harvesting souls. During the so-called golden age of the Catholic Church in America, between 1520 and 1570 (which coincided with the first battles of religious reformation in Europe), priests converted thousands of people weekly. One weary Franciscan got calluses on his hands and sunburn on his tonsured head after baptizing 5,000 people in a single day; his arms ached from holding the jar of holy water. Indians' enthusiasm for Catholicism often masked continued attachment to pre-Columbian gods and rites, but Protestant European observers had little sense of the complexity of this dynamic, as indeed priests in the Americas were perplexed or deceived by the endurance of indigenous practices.

This process of selective assimilation, or syncretism, was hardly new. As had been true of so many converted people in the late Roman Empire and medieval Europe, Catholic converts in the Americas did not accept their new faith in its entirety. Priests' hasty and rudimentary catechisms often gave the so-called neophytes a superficial understanding of Christian practices. Indians chose what parts to accept and what to reject, and they altered the meaning of rituals and holy days in the Christian calendar. To new, zealous European Protestants, Indian conversions to Catholicism smacked of alliances with the Antichrist. European competitors thus added to their desire to thwart Spanish power in Europe a zeal to turn these fragile new Christians away from Catholicism and toward their own faith. Northern European Protestants who ventured into the Atlantic world would cast themselves as rescuers of Native Americans, and later also of African slaves, whom the Spanish and Portuguese had more or less forcibly converted to Catholicism. The contest for souls continued on both sides of the Atlantic, even if Protestants could not get direct access to regions of Spanish settlement and mass conversion. For a time, this remained but a war of words.

At the core of the debate were the writings of Bartolomé de las Casas. He had been a Spanish colonist, an encomendero on Santo Domingo before giving up his commended laborers, becoming a Dominican priest, and emerging as the most ardent defender of indigenous Americans. In this role, Las Casas petitioned his friend, King Charles V, to protect America's native population, and he made public the horrors they endured under Spanish rule. He immortalized the catastrophic decline of Taíno populations in *A Short Account of the Devastation of the Indies*, an indictment not only of Spaniards' cruelty but also of the encomienda. Las Casas's tale of torture, slaughter, and inhumanity was first published (in Spanish) in Seville in 1552, then (in Dutch) in Antwerp (then under Habsburg rule) in 1578. The timing is important. Las Casas's work languished initially in Spain (for obvious reasons) and might have vanished from view were it not for its Dutch resurrection. The Antwerp edition drew international attention, albeit posthumously, to Las Casas within Europe. A French edition followed in 1579, with Latin and German versions emerging soon thereafter and an English version by 1583. Vivid illustrations of Spanish acts of cruelty in the Americas heightened the power of the prose. With the spread of literacy that followed the Reformation, the publication and translation of Las Casas's writings fueled the interest of Protestant Europe in American enterprises. Although his aim had been to reform Spanish imperial policy by depicting the worst acts of his countrymen, Las Casas inadvertently provided another language for expressing the political and dynastic rivalries of Europe, a religious language that enabled Protestants to cast themselves as rescuers of indigenous people oppressed by Spanish tyrants and forced to convert to a religion that Protestants had come to view with horror.

As a Spaniard criticizing Spanish atrocities, Las Casas in his *Short Account* had a special effect on the Netherlands. Numerous tracts depicting Spanish atrocities in the Americas were already circulating in the 1560s. The Dutch rebels, in particular, deployed the printing press in their battle against the Spanish, drawing on accounts from America to depict a tyrannical power abusing its subjects. Las Casas served the Dutch well. Before 1578, they spoke vaguely of Spanish abuses in the Americas, but in the late 1570s they cited Las Casas, an inside whistle-blower, to illustrate the perfidious nature of Habsburg rule. Dutch rebels devised a single narrative that united innocent victims of the Indies and the Netherlands.

Reading and hearing reports of the Indies and watching the devastation of the Netherlands with growing alarm was England's new queen, Elizabeth Tudor. The Low Countries provided the chief market for the woolens that drove the English economy and provided the crown customs revenues. English Protestants, who had refused to accept Philip during his sojourn in their country, feared Alba's standing army across the channel. For his part, Philip feared the influence of a Protestant monarch in London as much as he feared England's economic ties to his Low Countries. Whenever Philip demanded to know why Alba enjoyed so little success, the excuse was the same. "The only remedy for the disorders of the Netherlands," the duke explained, "is that England should be ruled by someone devoted to your Majesty."

For a host of reasons, Philip was not likely to restore England to the Catholic fold. Mary Tudor's brief reign, which saw her burn Protestants as heretics, had served to make Catholicism ever more disreputable among the English people, and the Catholic Church viewed Elizabeth I, the child of Henry VIII's Protestant wife Anne Boleyn, as a bastard and, as such, legally unfit to be queen. In the context of this international turmoil and domestic and dynastic insecurity came Queen Elizabeth's single success in colonization exploits. This success—from the local perspective a tragedy that still rankles—was England's renewed conquest and colonization of Ireland. This imperial project resolved long-standing problems of regional control but also drew on Spanish models. Although Ireland's conquest would seem far removed from the colonizing and extractive activities of the western Atlantic, it was in fact inspired by them, was carried out by some of their champions, and was similarly shaped by rivalries on the European continent.

Elizabeth inherited Ireland when she assumed the English throne in 1558. In 1565, the Catholic Irish rose in rebellion. The English in turn pursued a bloody conquest fueled by religious antagonism and cultural differences. The Irish economy was driven more by stock raising than agriculture. In part for this reason, some English found Gaelic culture inexplicable. Fynes Moryson, who worked as an English official in Ireland, marveled at the people he saw there. "Barbarous" he called the Irish, for their diet, their recreation, their lack of beer, their manner of sleeping. "These wild Irish," he concluded, "are not much unlike to wild beasts." With the perspective of an invader faced with resistance, the English deplored the Irish as idle and obstinate for preferring their own ways to those of their conquerors. "They blaspheme, they murder, commit whoredome," snarled one Protestant, "hold no wedlocke, ravish [and] steal."

Among those who heartily endorsed the queen's tough new course was Sir Humphrey Gilbert, an English soldier and adventurer and a royal official in Ireland. At the time, Gilbert was already hatching plans to confront Catholic power on both sides of the Atlantic. Although he was regarded as something of a humanist in England, Gilbert despised the Irish: "He thought his dogs' ears too good to hear the speech of [even] the greatest nobleman amongst them." In crushing Irish rebels, Gilbert's army slaughtered women, spiked severed heads on poles, and burned crops to induce famine. In hopes of better identifying the enemy and instilling in the colonized the requisite sense of cultural inferiority, Parliament decreed "every Irishman shall be forbidden to wear English apparel" upon "pain of death."

What distinguished this conquest was not its violence, which was typical of the age, but its use of mass settlement from the home country to bring the Irish into submission. In this, the Spanish example in the Canaries and the Americas inspired the English. When Sir Henry Sidney, who had spent time in Spain and knew its colonization model, proposed the plan to Eliza-

Enclosure

The slow transformation of England, and soon thereafter much of western Europe, from a manorial society into a mercantile capitalist nation-state was hastened by the process of enclosure, in which lands long held in common were consolidated into compact properties and enclosed, or fenced with stone walls or hedges. Although most of Parliament's laws on the subject—formally entitled Enclosure Acts, for Waste, Common Lands, and Open Fields—were passed between 1750 and 1840, a few acts pertaining to the draining and enclosure of marshes appeared on the statute books as early as the sixteenth century, typically by decree. Private enclosure acts, that is, laws that pertained to specific areas, became more common in the next century and mushroomed in the eighteenth century, until Parliament finally turned to general acts after 1801.

In England, the driving force was the emergence of woolen manufacturers (which helps explain Elizabeth's military support for her textile customers in the Low Countries). The growing need for wool was a powerful inducement for the gentry to increase their revenues by raising sheep, rather than by renting land to peasant tenants with customary long-term leases, especially in an age of inflation. In addition, landlords amassed sizeable acreage by taking over common lands traditionally used by all villagers, consolidating scattered farms into compact properties, and converting arable land into pastures. Since sheep raising required fewer workers, landlords evicted tenants, whose families may have worked the same plot for generations. These large numbers of evicted tenants became known as the "masterless men"; despite the gendered nature of the term, entire families flocked toward towns in search of employment, which inspired writers like Hakluyt to suggest colonizing them in America. As a popular adage complained, "enclosures make fat beasts and lean poor people," but it was never clear whether the fat beasts were the sheep or the landlords.

Sheep pasture enclosed by stone walls, North Yorkshire Moors at Malham, England.
© Photographer: Linda & Colin Mckie Agency: Dreamstime.com.

beth, she worried that such an approach might hinder reconciliation between the English and Irish. Yet she resolved to try it, so tens of thousands of English people (100,000 by 1641) migrated to Ireland. The hope was that pockets of English settlers might inspire the Irish to emulate English habits, which the English flattered themselves to be a vast improvement on Irish mores.

In a reprise of the strategic concerns that compelled the Spanish to expel the Jews and Moriscos from the Iberian Peninsula and predatory Europeans from American footholds, the English thought it necessary to secure their tenure over Ireland because of the continental religious situation. A reasonable fear of Spanish intrusion into Catholic Ireland enhanced the strategic importance of the Emerald Isle. By quietly supporting the Irish rebels—similar, in an ironic twist, to Elizabeth's aid to the Dutch—Philip forced England to invest far more money and men in a colonial system than even an optimist like Gilbert would have found prudent. By the time that Hugh O'Neill, the Earl of Tyrone, surrendered his sword in 1596, the English crown had expended £2,410,000 in crushing the Irish revolt.

But even as Elizabeth navigated the dynastic entanglements and religious antagonisms of Europe's incestuous monarchies and rebellion in her Irish kingdom, she struggled with England's economic and demographic strains. Money to be made by exporting wool to the Low Countries led many nobles, who were rich in land but poor in cash, to evict their tenants and enclose their estates into sheep pastures. With little arable land available for rent, the dispossessed farmers—known as the "masterless men"—wandered toward provincial towns and seaports in search of employment. Following feudal custom, such migration was deemed vagrancy and was illegal: wanderers could be punished if the state desired. In the wake of this migration, London quadrupled in size during the sixteenth century, from 40,000 to 200,000, many of the latter number impoverished and starving. Dispossession alone did not fuel urban growth, underemployment, and poverty: the entire kingdom experienced population growth. Between 1580 and 1640, the English population rose by 40 percent, leading some observers to conclude that the island nation was overpopulated and on the verge of social anarchy.

Taking Quarrels out of Europe

As Europeans took their quarrels into and across the Atlantic, politics and religion intersected with economics. Many historians now use the term *mercantilism* with some caution, but in the sixteenth and seventeenth centuries, European political leaders accepted what the historian Richard Dunn characterizes as "the psychology of limited wealth," a philosophy that had repercussions for overseas ventures. In broadest terms, European states believed in aggressive state intervention in economic activity for the public good. Governments offered price supports for such necessities as grain and granted monopolies to protect domestic manufacturers and trading companies from foreign as well as internal competition. Of course, state intervention in economic affairs furthered political power. In mercantilist thinking, bullion (hard mineral wealth) was key: states sought to secure as much as they could by conquest, as in the case of Spain, or by maintaining a favorable balance of trade. States also pursued self-sufficiency, which spurred overseas colonization and trade. The theory required close policing of commercial exchanges, though this was always a utopian ideal, with smuggling so rampant it may have accounted for as much as 50 percent of economic activity in the sixteenth- and seventeenth-century Caribbean. No state embodied the theory perfectly, but these guiding principles shaped much of the overseas activity of

European states, Catholic and Protestant alike, as they sought to gain power through economic means. If state intervention in the economy is familiar to modern readers, other aspects of this economic philosophy might seem more alien. Domestic consumption, for example, was frowned upon, as it was equated with squandering accumulated wealth: frugality, even hoarding, better suited mercantilist thinking.

One English clergyman showed how concerns over economic turmoil at home and weakened national power might be united in ambitions for colonization abroad. In a state paper drafted for Elizabeth, Richard Hakluyt, who from his youth had been fascinated by geography, argued that a commercial presence in the Western Hemisphere could provide a twofold remedy for England's woes. In his *A Particular Discourse concerning Western Discoveries,* Hakluyt recommended permanent colonies stationed at "the mouths of the great navigable rivers" along the North American coast, to function as trading posts with the indigenous populations. English woolens not finding buyers in the Netherlands could be traded with the natives. The southernmost colonies might not only produce tropical products for use in the home island, which would reduce reliance on the Asian trade, but they could also serve as privateering bases from which to attack Spanish shipping in the Caribbean. Best yet, from Hakluyt's perspective, the colonies would provide a new start for the homeless men who had been enclosed off their tenant farms. Even as London swarmed "with valiant youthes rusting and hurtfull by lacke of employement," the Americas housed equally valiant Indians groaning under the Catholic whip. The resources of America would pull up England, even as colonies of (piratical) yeomen and Indians would join forces to pull down Spain.

As Hakluyt's vision indicates, Spain's rivals had long refused to accept the exclusive jurisdiction over the Americas that Pope Alexander VI had given Ferdinand and Isabella following Columbus's initial voyage. That Alexander was a Spaniard helped to make the deal suspect outside the Iberian Peninsula; newly Protestant kingdoms felt no obligation to respect a papal decree. Nonetheless, Spanish power dictated a cautious pragmatism to colonial efforts of its rivals. Those who risked settlement in the midst of territory claimed by Spain learned quickly how perilous this action might be. Europeans thus pursued two strategies in their challenges to Spain in the sixteenth-century western Atlantic: they tried to plant settlements where the Spanish had little interest; and they tried to horn in on and steal outright from Spain's thriving colonial commerce.

It is important not to think of these probes and forays as efforts geared toward full-blown colonization. The subsequent history of European involvement in the North American mainland and the Caribbean tends to make most students of history assume that colonization—the large-scale resettlement by Europeans—was always the main goal of European enterprises; admittedly, men like Hakluyt did think in such terms. But a glimpse at the many failed expeditions of the sixteenth century reminds us that northern Europeans, like Columbus in his day, pursued a variety of Atlantic strategies. Many of the short-lived settlements of the period were merely trading posts, which experience showed to be an inexpensive and speedy path to profits. Some were intended only as bases for maritime ventures. No other European nation rivaled Spain's success in securing and holding territory, nor was that a goal of most settlement in this period, which was more simply oriented toward using indigenous economies to further trading goals and sabotaging Spanish wealth through theft and contraband trade. Among northern Europeans it was not at all clear—yet—that the massive transfer of Europeans and Africans to the Americas would prove a viable way for investors to exploit the resources of the Americas. It would be some time before the northern European nation-states would effectively mimic, and then alter to meet different needs and environments, the established Iberian models of transatlantic colonization.

The Western Atlantic: Entrepreneurs, Pirates, and Trading Posts

The French were the first to learn how difficult colonial enterprises in America could be. King Francis I purportedly asked to see the will that made Spain's monarchs Adam's sole heirs as outlined in the papal bull. "The sun," he allegedly insisted, "shines on me just as it does on them." He resolved that one way to thwart Spanish power in Europe was to challenge it in America. To that end, he sponsored efforts to gain American ground for France. Emulating Henry VII of England, who had commissioned the Genoese captain John Cabot to explore the North American coastline in 1497–98, in 1522 Francis sponsored the Florentine Giovanni de Verrazano on an expedition to survey the Atlantic coastline between modern-day Georgia and Maine in a quest for the fabled Northwest Passage (a direct water pathway that did not, of course, exist, but an idea that never fully died until Lewis and Clark reached the Pacific). Fearing Indians and unknown animals, Verrazano never ventured far inland. Ten years later, the Frenchman Jacques Cartier sailed up the St. Lawrence estuary in hopes of discovering the same elusive passage. He returned to Europe with nothing but what his critics dubbed "false gold," probably copper or iron pyrites. The costly failure also soured relations with the indigenous population. Cartier offered the people he met hardtack and red wine, which led to the not unreasonable belief that Europeans ate wood and drank blood.

With little discernible profit from these northern ventures, the French tried again farther south, but attempts to put trading posts or small settlements on the southern coast of the Americas, or to discover rich empires that rivaled those of the Aztecs or Incas, fared little better. In 1531, a French consortium established a settlement on Brazilian soil. Its leader, Jean Duperet, landed with 120 men, who began to plant cotton and, with the aid of Tupinamba men (a Tupi-speaking tribe), harvest brazilwood. (The colonists also discovered that wealthy Parisians paid six ducats for each monkey they could capture.) The Tupinamba were relieved to find new allies in their struggles with the Portuguese, who were making increased demands on indigenous labor. And this disenchantment would grow stronger in subsequent decades, as the Portuguese made a greater commitment to sugar cultivation. Groups of Tupinamba who migrated away from regions of Portuguese settlement often wandered into territories later claimed and briefly occupied by the French and later the Dutch. For the most part, these European interlopers found willing indigenous allies, at least at first. For other reasons, the first French settlement in Brazil was not to be; within a year of landing, a Portuguese squadron laid siege to Duperet's wooden fort. Captain Pero Lopes de Sousa promised the French quarter should they surrender, but instead had their commander and twenty others hanged. According to one report, two Frenchmen were bartered to local Indians, allegedly to be eaten, and the rest were imprisoned in Portugal. Only eleven of the failed colonists eventually made their way back to Paris.

A second attempt to establish a French colony in the southern Atlantic came in 1555, when the Calvinist noble Nicolas Durand proposed a Brazilian colony that could serve as an asylum for Protestants. Durand set sail with three ships and 600 men, many of them impoverished Catholics, and landed on Governador Island in Guanabara Bay, near what would become Rio de Janeiro. The commander of the new fort, Nicolas de Villegagnon, enforced discipline with the lash and pillory and made the non-Calvinist seamen bristle with his edict that they marry the Indian women with whom they slept. In its discipline and in its infighting, the settlement adhered to the trading-post model first used by the Portuguese. The French placed boys in Tupinamba villages to learn the local language. To Durand's chagrin, some Frenchmen readily assimilated to Indian ways, "eating, drinking, dancing, and singing with them," he noted, wearing no clothes and adorning their bodies in red and black paint and feathers. Such was life in tropical "France Antarctique," as the settlement was called. A Portuguese Jesuit remarked that the only thing missing to make the French Brazilians fully Tupinamba was a diet of human flesh. The exasperated Durand required his subjects to wear a heavy monastic costume that was punishment in and of itself in the tropical climate. In a final attempt to achieve harmony, he reconverted to his earlier Catholicism and demanded that the startled "heretics" under his command do likewise. Most Calvinists refused and set sail for France, and in 1559 a dejected Durand did likewise.

Frenchmen continued to live and trade in the region, protected by the Tupinamba until 1567, when the Portuguese routed the last surviving settlers and founded Rio de Janeiro to prevent a return. The French attempted no further settlement in Brazil until the early seventeenth century, when, near the mouth of the Amazon, indigenous support of French colonists again proved insufficient in the face of Portuguese hostility. This third Brazilian effort, however, offered one twist that placed the scheme fully within the religious climate of its time. In the 1612–15 settlement, the French attempted to convert local Tupi-speakers (whom the French labeled Tupinamba, as if they were their former allies) to Christianity. (For a century the French had pursued a policy of *not* converting the Tupinamba.) Organized by French Catholic nobility and energized by a contingent of Capuchin monks (the Capuchin order being newly established in the late sixteenth century as part of Catholic reformation), the settlement was intended to promote Catholicism in France during a period of Catholic renewal. As part of the propaganda, six Tupi villagers sailed to France, where they were baptized in a public ceremony and toured around, attracting crowds in Rouen and Paris. The episode serves as a reminder that European politics were never separate from American enterprises, even with regard to the smallest, least permanent settlements.

Pirates

Piracy became an important strategy of European nation states, the rules of which could make a relatively inexpensive investment in hopes of great return while passing the physical risk off to ambitious and avaricious mariners and soldiers. But piracy also became an individual strategy for personal advancement. After 1650 piracy receded as a state-sponsored practice, but the activity endured into the eighteenth century, a period historian Marcus Rediker dubs piracy's "golden age." By then, piracy had become the preserve neither of nations nor merchants, but of "the outcasts of all nations," as one English official allowed. Some were refugees from the harsh discipline typical of naval vessels or merchant ships; others were runaway servants and slaves. For many, piracy offered an alternative to the regimented life, one with distinct codes of conduct. It offered others opportunities for revenge on those who had brutalized them. Each ship had its own articles, which the pirates signed, allocating authority and arranging for the distribution of plunder. In contrast to the draconian discipline governing merchant or naval vessels, pirates selected their captain and he served at their pleasure. Although people look less fondly on modern-day pirates, who continue to raid ships, kill crews and passengers, and steal cargo, piracy remains heavily romanticized and commercialized, with tourist sights and Disney theme-park rides and films centered on this colorful and violent aspect of Atlantic history.

Below: Captain William Kidd (1645?–1701), English pirate. Captain Kidd welcoming visitors on board his ship in a New York harbor. After a painting by Jean Leon Gerome Ferris. Credit: The Granger Collection, New York.

France's final effort in this phase of exploratory settlement transpired in Florida, and the choice of location indicated the second strand of northern European strategy: piracy and plunder in the direct pursuit of Spanish wealth. One way to challenge Spanish power in Europe was to steal the American wealth that funded its bellicose activities. Theft, at least, was how Spain characterized the activities; rival states tended to view them differently. When pirates received state support, usually in the form of letters of marque and reprisal, they were considered *corsairs*, or later *privateers*. The corsairs and their sponsors drew on old medieval North Atlantic and Mediterranean customs (essentially the rule of "an eye for an eye") that served in lieu of maritime courts in otherwise lawless seas. (Soon after Columbus's great "discovery," French corsairs applied the custom of state-sanctioned reprisal to meet new, international political ends by robbing him in the Canaries.) Throughout the early modern period, the captains of privately armed and outfitted French, Dutch, and English vessels were granted licenses to plunder Spanish shipping indiscriminately in alleged reprisal for equivalent Spanish acts of aggression on land.

The line between corsairing in the name of a prince or monarch and piracy, or theft for personal gain, was always thin, yet the importance of piracy as an extension of warfare can be seen through its national chronology. The story of pirates was largely a French one between 1500 and 1559, when France and Spain were most consistently at war; largely English from 1560 to 1600, in Elizabeth's reign; and mostly Dutch from 1600 to 1648, when the Spanish began to lose steam in the Netherlands. In the later seventeenth century, use of piracy for geopolitical purposes retreated, and the men who remained as pirates in the western Atlantic were more often than not free agents, lining their own pockets with stolen goods and having no national agenda. As a result of their increasingly indiscrete attacks, as well as their socially presumptuous behavior, every imperial power aggressively pursued these thieves beginning about 1680. By 1730, this state suppression almost entirely eradicated Atlantic piracy. It would resurge from time to time, however, particularly when war otherwise occupied imperial navies. And privateering remained standard practice throughout the period covered by this book.

While piracy was a peril familiar to all mariners, it only became a central state strategy in the European struggles of the sixteenth and seventeenth centuries, when sea links to rich overseas colonies became essential. In the midst of their efforts to plant settlements in Brazil, the French—Protestant and Catholic alike—turned to the riches of the Spanish Caribbean, raiding ships and settlements on the islands and mainland from Santo Domingo to Santa Marta. The names of pirates like Jacques de Sores and Jambe de Bois ("Peg-leg") resounded throughout the Spanish colonies. Their attacks on these largely unfortified settlements were terrifying and destructive, and the fear that they would ally with Indians and African slaves was real.

The great lure for pirates, if ultimately a sort of Holy Grail, was the convoy of Spanish galleons making its regular journey from the Americas to Spain. In 1572, the English pirate and contraband slave trader Francis Drake managed to nab a portion of the fleet's riches by land. Each year, heavily laden mule trains carried Peruvian silver across the Isthmus of Panama to the Caribbean port town of Nombre de Dios. There, in alliance with slaves escaped from Spanish masters (called *cimarrones*) and a group of French Huguenot pirates, Drake attacked the mule train and came away with a small fortune in silver and gold. Drake's African allies employed his Protestant fervor to attack Spanish religious symbols, thus striking at the heart of their ex-masters' culture. Shouting "I, English; pure Lutheran," the cimarrones fought side by side with Englishmen as they engaged in petty piracy along the Panamanian coast.

In 1577, Drake sailed again from England and returned three years later, after having circumnavigated the globe, with £800,000 in Spanish treasure.

The shareholders—all English overseas ventures were funded by investors, a roster that included Queen Elizabeth—realized a 4,700 percent profit. (The queen's share was £160,000.) This gain was allegedly at Philip II's expense, but in fact Drake stole nearly all of the treasure from private citizens, some of whom he kidnapped and held for ransom. Madrid's ambassador to England demanded Drake's head as a thief, but Elizabeth instead knighted her favorite pirate aboard his ship, the *Golden Hind*, and ordered it moored on the Thames as a symbol of Protestant heroism. Drake's success seduced a host of English raiders to try their luck in the Spanish Caribbean, particularly after England declared war on Spain in 1585, and they remained active there until England and Spain reached a peace in 1604, at which point *corsairs* became *pirates* again.

For Spain's enemies, the wealth of the Indies was irresistible. Both the French and English planned North American settlements as part of their privateering strategy in the sixteenth century, the French in Florida and the English in what is now North Carolina, both locations selected by their proximity to Spanish settlements and the route of the fleet. From its earliest days, Florida was threatened by piracy growing out of depressed European economies and the religious and political dissent sweeping the Continent. The waters near Puerto Rico were soon said to be "as full of French as Rochelle," and French and English pirates attacked Spanish ships and settlements with impunity. Since treasure fleets were hard pickings, most raiders became rich on *rescate*, the practice of holding persons or towns for ransom. Others traded contraband slaves to Spanish colonists willing to break the royal monopoly. Like a mix between modern organized crime and paramilitary activity, early modern piracy represented the dark side of mercantilism. Its florescence in the age of Spanish treasure fleets was also a reminder that the Atlantic Ocean was still as lawless as the wildest frontier.

To facilitate these raids, French rivals in 1562 established a mainland settlement near modern Jacksonville, Florida; they christened the fort they built Caroline. The settlers, all Protestants, were not interested in emulating the local Timucua Indians by settling down to farm and fish. Instead, they envisioned the settlement in the context of plunder. The location gave the French access to the Spanish homebound fleet; the colonists hoped to survive on booty taken from their Catholic enemies. Compelled to respond, the Spanish destroyed Fort Caroline, executing 111 settlers, and erected forts in places otherwise unlikely for European settlement, stretching up to the Chesapeake Bay. Piratical activity continued in the region nonetheless, carried out primarily by the English. When Spain's ambassador to England complained about the violence, Elizabeth articulated her position: "The Spaniards by their hard dealing with the English, whom they had prohibited commerce, contrary to the laws of nations, had drawn their mischief upon themselves."

The story of the failed English settlement at Roanoke, in modern-day North Carolina, reveals the complex international forces that governed the selection of sites and the timing of settlement. Sir Walter Ralegh, the principal advocate of a settlement in the region, was an ardent enthusiast for Atlantic ventures: in later years he sought El Dorado, in the English telling a city—rather than an Indian cacique—in Guyana. But in the 1580s, Ralegh focused on Roanoke, the first English settlement on the North American mainland. Ralegh's backers shared the goals of the ill-fated French at Fort Caroline: they believed Roanoke could provide a good base for corsairs like Drake and other so-called sea dogs. Like Fort Caroline, Roanoke was destroyed by Spanish aggression, not directly and not on site, but by the diversion in European waters of the supply ships the colony so desperately needed. But the story of Roanoke also illustrates a defining feature of northern European ventures in North America: Indians in coastal regions had acquired long experience with Europeans—in the wake of fishing ventures and casual trade along the coast— and the European habit of kidnapping indigenous people and taking them to Europe. The Taíno might have been unfamiliar with and trusting of Europeans when they washed ashore in the Caribbean in 1492, but such was not the case for indigenous people on the northern mainland a half century later.

Philip II again showed that he would regard any foreign settlement along this stretch of North American coast not as a mere annoyance, but as cause for war. In the Netherlands, Don Juan of Austria, Philip's bastard half-brother and hero of the naval victory at Lepanto, began to hatch a master plan that could solve Philip's mass of Atlantic problems. Formed in consultation with Rome, Don Juan's plan proposed vastly increased forces to destroy the Dutch rebellion, and then use of the Low Country ports to stage an invasion of England. After Spanish troops captured London, the Catholic Mary Stuart, the deposed queen of Scotland, was to be recognized as queen; Don Juan even considered the possibility of taking Mary as his bride. Either way, with the "heretic" Elizabeth dead, all of Philip's troubles, at least with regard to the Dutch and English, would vanish. English support of the Dutch resistance would be cut off, and both Drake's privateering and Ralegh's American settlements would fizzle out. Massive action in Atlantic Europe would thus resolve the recurrent problem of intrusions into Spanish territory in the Americas. When Philip seized the Portuguese throne in 1580, he also appropriated his neighbor's impressive fleet and many prosperous colonies and outposts. Always powerful, Philip was now the richest monarch ever in western history. "It will be hard to withstand the king of Spain now," Elizabeth fretted.

Making it harder still was the act, in July 1584, of the apprentice of a Catholic cabinetmaker who, in striking a blow for his God, shot William of Orange at Delft in the world's first handgun assassination. Most of Elizabeth's subjects believed Philip lay behind the assassination, and they rightly feared that their queen was next on the list. The unexpected death of the leader of Dutch resistance nearly put an end to that revolt and left Elizabeth as the sole royal advocate of Protestants in the Atlantic basin. By mid-August 1585, the Duke of Parma's soldiers encircled Antwerp, and Elizabeth could no longer avoid open conflict with Philip. The queen dispatched a small army under her incompetent favorite, Robert Dudley, which, despite its poor leadership, began to turn the tide against Parma.

With the cold war in Europe turning hot, it made sense to hurry Ralegh's plans for settlement in North America. In the long run, a colony still farther south might provide the sorts of commodities—fruits, dyes, oils, and sugar— that English consumers were forced to acquire through expensive trade with foreigners. But for now, Elizabeth wished for a base close enough to Philip's Caribbean colonies to aid her swelling numbers of corsairs. Every treasure ship that someone like Drake could capture was one less shipment of silver that Philip could use to finance his war in the Netherlands. Ralegh chose a tenuous location, a barrier island off the North Carolina coast inhabited by the Roanoke Indians. In keeping with their reading of Las Casas and their economic aspirations, the English hoped to convert the Indians into images of themselves through benevolence and trade. Ralegh made clear that his men were not to mistreat the natives, whose assistance they desperately needed. Under threat of penalty, Englishmen were not to strike the Roanokes, enter their towns without permission, or sexually violate Roanoke women. The Spanish crown—also inspired by Las Casas—had long since passed virtually identical laws (sometimes harshly enforced) governing the behavior of Spaniards living near Native American villages.

In the initial English reconnaissance of the site in 1584, two Roanoke Indians, Manteo and Wanchese, were persuaded to return to England, where they lived at Ralegh's London residence and studied English, while Thomas Hariot, their tutor, learned Algonquin. Both men returned to their home in 1585, with Ralegh's second expedition to the region; this comprised some 600 men, including one painter, John White, and Thomas Hariot, all inauspiciously under the command of a veteran of the Irish wars, Richard Grenville. Interestingly, Manteo assisted the English in their settlement, while Wanchese opposed their presence in his homeland. The English imposed on Roanoke hospitality, depleting limited supplies of food, and pursued violent and abusive tactics in trying to get their way. The settlement was resupplied with what would be a final deposit of 114 colonists in May of 1587. These weary travelers found prior English settlements collapsed, and no sign of the earlier English visitors who had been left behind. Even the Indians had moved to the mainland, with only Manteo and his people (the Croatoan Indians, who lived on Croatoan Island) ready to offer any support. Without Manteo (who apparently converted to Christianity in this period) this English settlement would have failed immediately. Instead, it limped along and in 1587 the governor, John White, sailed back to England for supplies.

But European power politics delayed Roanoke's resupply, for by then Queen Elizabeth's spies in Spain were aware of Philip's plan to invade England, depose her, and elevate her Catholic cousin Mary Stuart to her place, thereby ending once and for all Protestant interference in the Netherlands and the Americas. Now, Elizabeth and her advisors realized, something had to be done about Mary. With her dead, English Catholics would have no champion and Philip II would have no figurehead to crown. And so, with Elizabeth's reluctant consent, Mary was executed in February of 1587. In a sad coda to the affair, Mary's lap dog, which she had concealed for comfort beneath her petticoats, marched out and bravely attempted to guard her severed head. Having no desire to create relics by which Catholics might remember their queen, Mary's executioners burned the chopping block and vigorously scrubbed the bloodstained dog, a small Skye terrier. According to Catholic writers, the grieving pet refused to eat and died shortly after his mistress.

Protestants saw the matter differently, insisting the foolish animal was simply scrubbed to death.

If Mary's death complicated Philip's scheme to restore England to the old faith, it also made him more determined to separate the Protestant Jezebel from her throne. So with the endorsement of Pope Sixtus, Philip prepared to invade by way of the English Channel. Bearing crosses on their sails and flying banners depicting the Holy Virgin, a fleet of 130 ships—the Spanish Armada—heaved north in the fall of 1588. Thirty thousand men, speaking six languages and armed with 2,431 cannon, prepared to administer the vengeance of Rome. Only the commander appeared vaguely concerned that his twenty great galleons, the core of his fleet, were medieval relics—more floating fortresses than maneuverable ships suitable for navigating the notoriously rough waters of the Channel. Soon after the parties engaged, the English and their Dutch allies sent eight blazing fire ships into the center of the Spanish Armada. Scattering into the sea, the lumbering galleons fell prey to the faster, more maneuverable English ships. The wooden walls of the galleons, four feet thick, became a death trap of exploding timbers. In all, less than half of Philip's Armada limped back to Spain. When news of the disaster reached the Escorial, Philip barely paused in his work. "Even kings," he warned a monk, "must submit to being used by God's will without knowing what it is."

And so it happened that English supply ships, freed of the Spanish threat in the Channel, finally prepared to return to Roanoke. On August 17, 1590, the *Hopewell* and the *Moonlight* anchored off the island. The next morning, John White and a party of men landed on the spot the governor had abandoned three years before. They found fresh footprints on the beach, but the colonists were nowhere in sight. Grass and weeds grew in the fields, and pumpkin vines climbed the walls of ruined houses. White found his "books torn from the covers," his "Maps rotten and spoiled with rain," and his suit of armor lying rusted in a corner. The search party discovered none of the agreed upon distress signals; only two hints. The letters CRO had been carved on a tree in "faire Romane letters," and on a post by the entrance to a house the word CROATOAN was carved "in fayre Capitall letters." Evidently, the colonists planned to quit Roanoke for Manteo's home at Croatoan Island. When White explored the region, however, he found no survivors. Historians' best guess is that the English inhabitants moved (as they had planned) to the mainland to find food and intermarried with people there. The Outer Banks tribes were later destroyed in 1607 by Powhatan, a chief from the Chesapeake region embarked on his own territorial expansion. White never discovered the fate of his subjects, or of his granddaughter Virginia Dare, trumpeted as the first English child born in the Americas, but more accurately the first child born of an English woman in the Americas: English men had no doubt fathered many children over the decades of coastal encounters with Americans in the western Atlantic.

North Atlantic Settlements

Through the sixteenth century, Spanish wealth and power continued to shape northern European settlement efforts. Although interlopers made inroads in the Caribbean after 1600, in the sixteenth century they had stumbled in main-

The Fur Trade

A European craze for felt hats made with beaver pelts fueled the North American fur trade in the late sixteenth and seventeenth centuries. By the sixteenth century, the European beaver had been hunted to extinction in much of western Europe, and only the new American source of beavers sustained this fashion trend. The fur trade gave American trading partners, who, thanks to long experience were expert beaver hunters, access to guns and a range of useful trade goods. As one Indian explained to a missionary in the 1630s, a beaver "makes kettles, hatchets, swords, knives, bread; and, in short, it makes everything." The demand for beaver altered indigenous hunting practices. Men focused their hunt on beaver to the exclusion of other game, and they extended both their hunting season and territory. Competition and violence among hunters increased in beaver-rich areas. Individuals with access to beaver (and thus trade goods) enhanced their power and prestige and sometimes disrupted traditional community hierarchies. The beaver hunt also had environmental consequences. As early as the 1640s, beaver were likely hunted to virtual, although temporary, extinction (the beaver is a resilient animal) in some regions of the East Coast, including New England, New York, and Pennsylvania. The loss of beaver dams and the ponds they formed altered habitats for other creatures (including ring-necked ducks, muskrats, otters, mink, raccoon, deer, bear, and foxes), increased soil erosion, and left behind meadows ideal for new European settlers and their agricultural practices. And beavers were not the only animals facing a threat from European fashion trends. Moose, mink, fox, raccoon, otter, elk, deer, and bear were all hunted beyond subsistence levels for natives. By 1723 one Jesuit reported that the Indians of Maine had no game left at all.

Castor de 26. pouces de longueur entre tête et queuë.

An early illustration of an American beaver from Baron de Lahontan, Nouveaux Voyages Dans L'Amerique, published in 1704. Courtesy Newberry Library.

land ventures in North and South America. The best chance for Spain's rivals to plant a permanent post lay in territory so uninviting that the Spanish would not begrudge their presence.

Canada had not seemed promising as a commercial opportunity when Cartier reconnoitered the St. Lawrence River in 1532, but after several failed efforts to plant settlements in American soil, the French looked again to North America's northern interior. French Canada was far enough from the Spanish to interest them little. Samuel de Champlain, a French geographer and explorer, led a party down the St. Lawrence in 1608, and he established a trading post in Quebec. Like almost every successful European invader before him, Champlain benefited from indigenous alliances. He reached a region where the Montagnais, Maliseet, Algonquin, Huron, and Micmac lived in alliance against their traditional enemies, the Iroquois, who for reasons historians do not understand had temporarily moved away in 1608. These were tribes of several thousand members who migrated seasonally, exploiting the resources of their territory's microclimates, taking advantage of hunting, fishing, farming, and foraging. (The exception were Hurons, who farmed maize annually and lived in fortified villages.) The French established alliances, too, offering assistance in war in return for furs, which they could sell profitably in France. In 1609, the French proved their value in this alliance, when Champlain fired his musket at three Mohawk chiefs, killing two of them. (The Mohawk were one of the five tribes of the Iroquois Confederacy). Although the Indians fought wearing armor, it was wooden armor designed to deflect arrows, not lead balls propelled from guns.

In part due to limited agricultural potential, the small French settlements in Canada adhered to the trading-post model. No more than 400 Europeans, mostly men, lived there by 1643. They remained dependent on Indians for provisions and for the furs that garnered profits for investors across the Atlantic. As was true in Brazil, where the Portuguese and French sought to extract the commodities they needed through barter, the French in Canada did not intend to alter indigenous economies. European men became hunters and adopted indigenous skills and mores to survive. They formed sexual and romantic alliances with indigenous women, both for companionship and to further their trade aspirations, despite the disapproval of the few priests who accompanied French administrators to Canada. In Africa, Europeans who operated trading posts had to accommodate African preferences; in the Americas the effects of infectious diseases and the commercial value placed on animals combined to have more drastic consequences, often undermining indigenous economies, practices, and culture.

Like the French, the English had also turned north in their effort to find a safe place for settlement, but they sought not a trading post but a sanctuary for impoverished English men and women who might gain a fresh start in colonial undertakings. Newfoundland, a large protrusion into the raw and windy North Atlantic off Canada's eastern coast, would seem a forbidding place for colonial settlement, but it was its relative isolation that made it appear viable as a colonial site for people seeking to be left alone. Sir Humphrey Gilbert shared Richard Hakluyt's view that the answer to England's entangled demographic and religious dilemmas lay in America. In a 1577 essay, bluntly titled *A Discourse How Her Majesty May Annoy the King of Spain*, Gilbert proposed that a fleet of ships seize control of the Newfoundland coasts due west of Land's End, England's westernmost tip. The next year, Elizabeth obliged Gilbert and his brother, Walter Ralegh, with a patent to explore and colonize American shores. Philip II refused to countenance this assault on his territorial rights, of course, and when Spanish patrols found Gilbert's ships off the African coast (where they had sailed first in search of slaves), Philip's mariners dispersed the fleet and forced it back to England.

Soldier-entrepreneurs like Gilbert were not easily dissuaded, however. Gilbert's brave new world was not merely for those who "live idly at home" and could now "be set on worke" in America. Although formerly a soldier who had slaughtered Catholics in France and Ireland, Gilbert now hoped disgruntled English Catholics might join his second expedition to Newfoundland. In his vision, wealthy Catholics would join with ambitious younger sons of the landed gentry and American "savages" to produce a prosperous colony. Most of all, Gilbert's corporation was designed to turn a tidy profit for himself and the thirty-nine other stockholders of the venture. He sailed for Newfoundland in 1583. The small settlement, located near present-day St. John's, was the first English town in the Americas. But the relentlessly punishing weather of the forbidding coast proved too much even for colonists accustomed to English dampness. Agreeing to return home with mutinous colonists (yet still hoping, somehow, to acquire more settlers), Gilbert's nine-ton frigate went down with all hands in a storm. (Persons on an accompanying, larger vessel reported that they last saw Gilbert sitting in the stern, calmly reading a copy of Thomas More's *Utopia*).

If permanent settlements proved difficult and uninviting in the northwest Atlantic, Europeans nonetheless employed a variety of commercial and extractive strategies. Evaluation of European activities in the Atlantic in terms of numbers of people taking part shows that, at least for a time, the quest for cod, which every year attracted thousands of mariners, remained dominant. The writer Mark Kurlansky refers to this age of fishing enthusiasm as the "cod rush." The fishing ground lay in the Banks off Newfoundland, New England, Nova Scotia, and Labrador. Although Portugal claimed the Banks by virtue of the Pope's grant in 1494, other Europeans disregarded this injunction. The French were the early leaders in North Atlantic cod fishing in the first half of the sixteenth century, and then, spurred by economic growth in much of Europe, fishing activity surged in the second half of the century. Anthony Parkhurst, an English merchant and explorer, visited the Banks in 1578 and tallied the vessels he saw there: 150 French ships, 100 Spanish, 50 English (who were at the time transferring their activities from the Iceland fisheries to Newfoundland), and 50 Portuguese. By 1600, the Spanish and Portuguese had lost their dominant position in the American fisheries: Spain needed the ships and manpower for military and naval ventures elsewhere and had the cash to purchase cod thanks to the American mining bonanza. Some may have appreciated the irony that the Protestant English and Dutch ended up supplying Iberian Catholics with the fish their religion demanded.

Cod fishing was a seasonal venture: the fleets arrived in Newfoundland in the spring, and fishermen established spots on land for drying. They fished all summer and sailed back to Europe before the North Atlantic became too stormy and icy for safe passage. (Not until the English settled land farther to the south, in the region of Cape Cod, did cod fishing become a year-round enterprise.) The fisheries were an international meeting ground, and they had their own cosmopolitan culture, reflected in communal ideas about property and land use. French, Portuguese, English, and Spanish fishermen devised a method for sharing the shore. When the ships arrived, the captain and crew of each one staked claim to a space on the beach and erected sheds for drying fish. A customary first-come, first-served policy prevented investment in permanent structures, since no one had assurance that he would be able to claim the same site in the following year. The shared-space policy similarly guided political leadership in a given season. The first three captains to arrive became the leading officers of the temporary community and adjudicated disputes. Here, then, was an unusual instance of international cooperation and communal use of resources in an Atlantic world generally characterized by violent disputes over terrain, power, and resources.

Undermining Spain: Africa and Commerce

Commercial strategies were similarly successful in thwarting Iberian strength in Africa. The unhappy fate of French colonies in lands the pope granted to Spain or Portugal made clear the dangers of openly confronting the most powerful monarch in the Atlantic world. So, instead, English, and later Dutch, mariners looked to southeastern waters. The Portuguese had rights to western Africa thanks to the likes of Dias and da Gama, but the long coastline from Fez to the Cape of Good Hope was too vast for the Portuguese to patrol. In 1551, Captain Thomas Wyndham of the London-based ship *Lion* entered into what England dubbed "the Barbary trade," although how far south he reached remains unclear. Wyndham returned with a hold full of trade goods, and three years later another merchant, William Towrson, returned to London with five African slaves. Although Towrson never bothered to explain how he acquired the captives, he almost certainly bought them to serve as translators. They were to be kept in England "till they could speake the language," he wrote, so they might "be a helpe to Englishmen" engaged in the coastal trade. Hakluyt later met Towrson's five companions—among the first Africans held by the English—and reported that although they had come to enjoy "our meates and drinkes," they thought less of "the colde and moyst aire." What they thought of their captivity Hakluyt failed to record. The English who ventured to Africa south of the Sahara were struck by the appearance of the people they met there. "These people are all blacke," marveled Captain John Hawkins, an early English slaver and a cousin of Sir Francis Drake, "without any apparell, saving before their privities." Robert Baker, whose narrative poem recounted his two voyages to African shores in 1562 and 1563, was cruder yet: "Their Captaine comes to me as naked as my naile, Not having witte or honestie to cover once his taile."

These Africans' lack of what the English (overdressed for the climate) might deem proper apparel did not deter Hawkins from joining a growing number of northern Europeans in horning in on Portugal's near monopoly on African coastal trading. (In 1557 the Portuguese governor of Elmina on the Gold Coast complained to his king of the foreign ships, bringing traders who "glut the whole coast with many goods of all kinds.") Hawkins was likely the first Englishman to participate in the transatlantic slave trade. Between 1562 and 1568, he and his cousin Francis Drake, having gotten wind that "Negroes were very good merchandise in Hispaniola," headed three journeys to Guinea in search of such cargo. Providing financial backing were government officials and successful so-called adventurers, among them Queen Elizabeth. On each occasion, Hawkins visited the Guinea of Cape Verde, between the Gambia River and Sierra Leone, obtaining slaves in the several hundreds and then taking them to Spanish ports in the Caribbean where, through ruses and threats, he contravened Spanish law prohibiting colonists to conduct trade with other foreign nationals and unloaded the captives at a profit.

Hawkins appears to have seized many, perhaps most, of the slaves he traded from Portuguese vessels readying to set sail for the Cape Verde Islands. Others he captured in raids on shore. As with the first Portuguese more than a century earlier, and much to their dismay, mariners like Hawkins discovered that the Africans they derided as ill-clad heathen were formidable soldiers and sophisticated traders. West African merchants, as Portuguese traders had learned, had little interest in bartering either their commodities or their captives for useless trinkets and gadgets. According to Towrson, perhaps the most experienced of the "Guinie" captains, African businessmen demanded iron bars, tin basins and pots, and most especially "linen cloth." Men like Towrson regarded Africa not so much as an export market, but as a place to obtain such compact, high-value imports as gold, ivory, and malaguetta pepper.

Not only did Africans drive a hard bargain, but political conditions in Europe kept the English trade small during its early years. The Treaty of Tordesillas and the still formidable Portuguese navy prohibited England from establishing a permanent settlement on the African coast. Without a secure base, traders like Towrson had to sail the length of West Africa and then back to England or across the Atlantic, hoping to pick up whatever trade might be available. Without forts and factors, any arrangements they made with African merchants were temporary, since they could not be counted on to return at regular intervals or fulfill their agreements. Even with so extensive a coastline, good harbors were few in Atlantic Africa, and those that existed already served as ports for Portuguese vessels. English mariners had to lie offshore and wait for African traders to approach them in small boats, a situation that placed English traders at a disadvantage.

The Rise of the Dutch

These early English forays into trade along the African coast did little to undermine Iberian power in the southern Atlantic. Instead, it was the Dutch whose commercial and maritime strategies edged out the Spanish and Portuguese in the region as well as in strategic locations in the western Atlantic. In the early seventeenth century, Dutch traders, whose main interest lay in breaking the Portuguese monopoly on the East Asian spice trade (as evidenced by the Dutch formation of an East India Company in 1602), lacked an overseas base for trade and plunder. They had only a tiny outpost on the Portuguese-dominated Gold Coast, one vulnerable to attack from land and sea. But with new infusions of arms, sailors, and capital provided by the East India Company, Dutch ships began prowling the Iberian Atlantic.

Eager to find Atlantic venues to attack their Habsburg occupiers, the Dutch were active in the Caribbean and had joined the French in smuggling goods in Brazil as early as the 1580s. By then they were already processing raw sugar and brazilwood in Holland. The North Atlantic salt-fish trade, long a staple of Dutch commerce, also spurred incursions into the Caribbean. Cut off from Portuguese salt supplies after 1585, the Dutch sailed to Venezuela, where massive deposits of salt lay along an abandoned stretch of coast. These salt-mining incursions provoked brutal Spanish reprisals. Partly in response, the Dutch turned to armed raids on Spanish ships and settlements, plundering port towns for all the wealth they could find. Despite a brief truce between 1609 and 1621, the Dutch soon eclipsed the English as the most successful raiders in the first age of Atlantic piracy.

No corsair attack was more spectacular than Piet Heyn's capture of the Spanish silver fleet off Cuba in 1628. So entrenched is Heyn's accomplishment in historical memory that Dutch soccer fans sing a song about him to this day. Heyn had at his disposal a fleet of 32 ships, and 3,500 men. The Spanish fleet that year was small, only 15 ships. When the Spanish commander, Juan de Benavides, espied Heyn, he tried to hide his vessels in Matanzas Bay, east of Havana, but some of the ships foundered and Heyn's men seized them all. The Dutchman returned home with a cargo worth almost 8 million pesos, not just in silver but in other colonial products, including silks and dyes. Crewmen of the fleet rioted in the streets of Amsterdam for a portion of the booty as the West India Company shared its biggest dividends ever, a gain of 75 percent in one fell swoop. Meanwhile, Benavides was jailed and later executed in Seville for alleged cowardice.

In the wake of Heyn's attack, the Spanish invested heavily in improving fleet security, spending as much as 1.4 million pesos for one roundtrip voyage in 1632–33. The transatlantic fleet played an urgent role in the finances of the kingdom, and any diminution of the annual income enabled Spain's increasingly able rivals, the Dutch, French, and English, to seize Spanish possessions overseas. As the historian Carla Rahn Phillips argues, Spain's status as the dominant political power in sixteenth-century Europe was linked to its position as the continent's major shipping power. The security of the fleet was paramount.

As the carrying trade in sugar with northeast Brazil expanded around 1600, Dutch merchants began to think it time to capitalize on their strengths, along with Portugal's—and Spain's—weaknesses. In 1612, Dutch merchants fortified Fort Nassau on the Gold Coast, and five years later Dutch nationals negotiated with Lebou fishermen of coastal Senegal to allow them to occupy Bir, an island sheltered under the neck of Cape Verde. Two decades later, they built a fort and trading center there, renaming the island Gorée.

The Gorée and Gold Coast settlements helped whet the Dutch appetite for transatlantic trade, particularly the profits to be had from transporting slaves and sugar. In 1621, Dutch investors had founded the West India Company. The merchant oligarchs of the Calvinist Netherlands, having finally succeeded in removing Habsburg power from their portion of the Low Countries (Belgium remained a Spanish province), employed a private, semicapitalist model of commercial organization that contrasted with the more state-interventionist style of the Spanish and Portuguese. Indeed, Amsterdam investors went well beyond their London counterparts in granting the great trading companies nearly sovereign political authority. It helped that the main investors were top figures in Dutch government, but, nevertheless, both the East and West India Companies enjoyed the right to build and maintain fleets and arm regiments of soldiers. Thus was armed the great corsair Piet Heyn. The stockholders could even negotiate treaties and govern colonies. Given this free rein throughout the Atlantic basin, the West India Company expected good profits for its shareholders, and for most of the seventeenth century it met expectations; stockholders typically received an annual dividend on their principal of 18 percent.

The West India Company's prompt construction of nearly a dozen warships showed how aggressively the Dutch sought profits in the greater Atlantic. As far as Amsterdam merchants were concerned, any land claimed but not physically occupied, even by the Protestant English, was fair game. Like their

Portuguese counterparts, Dutch merchants remained less interested in lands to settle than in fortified outposts from which to trade. The mix of a maritime trading culture and relatively small home population was broadly similar. Typical of Dutch trade ventures was the island of Manhattan. The French example in Canada suggested the relative safety from Spanish assault of northerly settlement. Even before the formation of the West India Company, and in the midst of a truce with Spain, in June 1613, Captain Thijs Volchertz Mossel sailed the *Jonge Tobias* into a harbor along what the Dutch called the Hudson River. As a way of staking a claim, the captain left behind a single crewman, an evidently free African calling himself Jan Rodrigues. Like many of the first Africans brought to mainland North America, his name suggests more than passing experience with the Portuguese. Well-stocked (or fortified, perhaps) with knives and hatchets, a sword, and a musket, Rodrigues set about learning the local language so he might act as an interpreter. Other Dutch mariners who arrived later found that Rodrigues, a Dutch version of the lançado, had married a Rockaway woman, who bore him several children. For the next few years, Rodrigues remained the sole nonindigenous resident of the island. With the formation of the West India Company in 1621, the Dutch returned to the Hudson River in force. Soldiers constructed Fort New Amsterdam, and from its docks young merchants obtained furs and fish for the home market. Four years later, a contingent of Walloon pietists settled near the fort, where they grew maize and wheat and tended livestock.

The successful settlement along the Hudson pointed to a shift in the fortunes of northern European forays in the western Atlantic beginning in the 1620s. The proceeds from Piet Heyn's haul in 1628, for example, financed the Dutch settlement and, more important, fortification, of the Caribbean island of Curaçao in 1634. Situated so close to the Spanish Main, the new Dutch colony became an entrepot in the smuggling trade, in which tobacco and slaves proved to be as lucrative as gold and silver. Heyn's success also invigorated the Dutch West India Company's efforts to annex Brazil, and in 1630 a company-sponsored fleet seized Pernambuco, in northeastern Brazil. The Dutch would hold the region until 1654.

Although in the spirit of Las Casas, the Dutch had initially been ambivalent about—and occasionally opposed to—slavery, they soon changed their minds. Holding the world's greatest sugar-producing lands was next to useless if one did not have access to labor, and slavery, as the Portuguese had shown, seemed the most effective solution. So the West India Company renewed its efforts to gain necessary toeholds along the west coast of Africa. In 1633 the company took a Portuguese fort on Arguim Island off the arid Mauritanian coast, and between 1637 and 1642 it captured Elmina, which Portugal had possessed since building the fort in 1481, and Axim, both on the Gold Coast. At the same time, company officials continued efforts to spread sugar-cane production to the Dutch-held islands in the Caribbean. The company cared less about who owned the land and more about the fact that sugar production would mean demand for slaves and carrying sugar to Europe, both Dutch specialties. By 1650, with possessions to support their Atlantic trade dotting the African and American coasts and several Caribbean islands, the Dutch had edged out the Spanish and Portuguese as commercial masters of the Atlantic. But soon they, too, would be eclipsed, first by France, then England, as competition grew fierce.

By mid-century French smugglers and buccaneers had converted the western portion of Hispaniola into a French colony, and other Caribbean islands soon lay in French hands, most important Martinique and Guadeloupe, all havens for pirates and contraband traders. In 1655 the English took Jamaica (they already had settlements on Nevis, Antigua, Barbados, and St. Kitts) following a failed raid on Hispaniola, thereby establishing an economic and military base from which to attack Spain in the Caribbean. It was from Jamaica that the famed buccaneer and privateer Henry Morgan sailed, and it was to this island that he retired to set up life as a gentleman after his raiding days had ended. Piracy thus shaped settlement efforts, and a number of pirates became planters. Although the post-Heyn buccaneers never managed to seize a treasure fleet, the growing number of incursions and territorial concessions revealed Spain's diminished power by the second quarter of the seventeenth century.

So as it turns out, the orphaned child Francisco Manuel found employment on the Spanish fleet in the last years of the sixteenth century, just as—despite its undisputed possession of the largest and richest land empire in the world—Spain's age of Atlantic glory began to fade into memory. Manuel's personal successes were embedded in a larger narrative of Spanish decline. Philip II had driven his kingdom to bankruptcy in his religious, dynastic, and imperial ventures. The loss of the Armada ran to nearly 10 million ducats. (Philip never tabulated the human cost.) The disaster in the English Channel meant the war in the Netherlands would continue, and this drained another 2 million ducats annually, not counting the 3 million Philip sent annually to buy French neutrality. More than slaves and Indians underwrote these expenditures: Spanish peasants gave up more than half of their income in taxes, church tithes, and feudal dues. In 1589, the *Cortes*—Philip's weak national legislative body—created a new tax, the *millones*, which squeezed another 8 million ducats out of the populace, and even this was not enough. To run his empire, Philip had to borrow so heavily from the likes of the Fuggers and Welsers of Augsburg that the interest alone came to consume half the crown's income. Much of the money went to soldiers in Italy and the Netherlands; the result was a crippling outflow of hard currency.

Philip labored to rebuild his fleet, but the failure of the Armada doomed his scheme to impose his will on western Europe, the Mediterranean, and the Americas. By 1598, his treasury was bankrupt, a condition that would repeatedly visit Spain throughout the seventeenth century. Among the long-term consequences of this belligerent foreign policy fueled by American silver was that Spain's formerly diversified economy became distorted. Inflation and ready cash diminished investment in agriculture and textile production. Spain became an importer of products it formerly had produced while the countryside became increasingly impoverished. Despite promises to God that he would fight on, Philip began to scale back efforts in the Netherlands. The proud king never admitted defeat, nor did his son and successor, Philip III. But in 1609 the new monarch agreed to a truce and final withdrawal, which was tantamount to recognizing the independence of the United Provinces.

War returned to the Netherlands when the truce ended in 1621, but by then, the Dutch dominated the seas and the greater part of Atlantic trade. Stories of the Americas tend to emphasize colonization as the main European emphasis, but an Atlantic perspective reveals the centrality of commercial and maritime enterprises—trade and plunder. In the century and a half after Columbus, more Europeans were involved in trade and the fisheries than were settled in the Americas. With the exception of Spanish elites in Mexico and Peru, Europeans derived greater success through maritime ventures than on land. Following the Portuguese model, Dutch emphasis on maritime and commercial enterprise and their commitment to trade factories in the Atlantic and, indeed, around the globe, fueled their emergence as a new Atlantic power. But that trend would change in the ensuing decades, as other Europeans reinforced their interest in the Americas with large-scale migration. A story of piracy and trading posts would become one of bulk commodities for mass consumption and the expansion of forced labor.

Selected Readings

Andrews, Kenneth R., *Trade, Plunder, and Settlement: Maritime Enterprise and the Genesis of the British Empire, 1480–1630* (Cambridge, UK: Cambridge University Press, 1984).

Davies, K. G., *The North Atlantic World in the Seventeenth Century* (St. Paul: University of Minnesota Press, 1974).

Dunn, Richard S., *The Age of Religious Wars* (New York: W. W. Norton, 1970).

Haigh, Christopher, *English Reformations: Religion, Politics, and Society under the Tudors* (New York: Oxford University Press, 1993).

Kamen, Henry, *Philip of Spain* (New Haven: Yale University Press, 1997).

Kupperman, Karen Ordahl, *Roanoke: The Abandoned Colony* (New York: Rowman and Littlefield, 1984).

Kurlansky, Mark, *Cod: A Biography of the Fish that Changed the World* (New York: Walker and Company, 1997).

Lane, Kris E., *Pillaging the Empire: Piracy in the Americas 1500–1750* (Armonk: M.E. Sharpe, 1998).

McLaren, Anne, "Gender, Religion, and Early Modern Nationalism: Elizabeth I, Mary Queen of Scots, and the Genesis of English Anti-Catholicism," *American Historical Review* 107 (June 2002): 739–767.

Pérez-Mallaína, Pablo E., *Spain's Men of the Sea: Daily Life on the Indies Fleets in the Sixteenth Century*, Trans. by Carla Rahn Phillips (The Baltimore: Johns Hopkins University Press, 1998).

Phillips, Carla Rahn, *Six Galleons for the King of Spain: Imperial Defense in the Early Seventeenth Century* (Baltimore: The Johns Hopkins University Press, 1986).

Postma, Johannes and Victor Enthoven, eds., *Riches From Atlantic Commerce: Dutch Transatlantic Trade and Shipping, 1585–1817* (Leiden: Brill, 2003).

Quinn, David Beers, *Set Fair for Roanoke: Voyages and Colonies, 1584–1606* (Chapel Hill: University of North Carolina Press, 1985).

Randall, Adrian, and Andrew Charlesworth, eds., *Moral Economy and Popular Protest: Crowds,Conflict, and Authority* (New York: St. Martin's Press, 2000).

Rediker, Marcus, *Villains of All Nations: Atlantic Pirates in the Golden Age* (Boston: Beacon Press, 2004).

Schmidt, Benjamin, *Innocence Abroad: The Dutch Imagination and the New World, 1570–1670* (New York: Cambridge University Press, 2001).

Steele, Ian K., *Warpaths: Invasions of North America* (New York: Oxford University Press, 1994).

Vaughan, Alden T., "Sir Walter Ralegh's Indian Interpreters, 1584–1618, *William and Mary Quarterly* 59 (April 2002): 346–76.

"The Crowning of Powhatan, 1608," by John Gadsby Chapman. The border reads "(1608) Jamestown," "Engraved for Graham's Magazine *from an original picture Painted for Henry Gilliant Esqr." Mid-Manhattan Picture Collection, The New York Public Library.*

Chapter Five

Labor, Migration, and Settlement: Europeans and Indians, 1500–1800

> *Without [indigenous labor], the republic could not be preserved,*
> *since the Spaniards do not work, nor is it fitting they should.*
> Juan de Matienzo, sixteenth-century Peruvian jurist

"**I** have been," recalled the indentured servant William Moraley in 1743, "the Tennis-ball of Fortune." Barbara Rolfe would have identified with his feelings of powerlessness—although as a Calvinist she might have characterized divine providence, not fortune, as the guiding power force in her life. In a time when young men dominated European migration to America, Rolfe, who traveled to New England from England in 1635 at the age of twenty, was an anomaly. Her father, George, had approached the ship captain Thomas Babb about his intractable daughter, whom he could not persuade to pursue "a civil and orderly course of life." Barbara repeatedly disobeyed him, so he feared for his reputation if she remained in England. The new English colonies in North America offered a solution. Contemporary misogynist ballads, including "A Net for a Night-Raven, Or, A Trap for a Scold," and "The Woman Outwitted," recount similar decisions made by husbands to rid themselves of their wives. In an era when patriarchal control seemingly defined domestic order, men without such authority deplored assertive women as "scolds" and sometimes sought external solutions to troubles within their households. For five pounds sterling, Babb agreed to transport Barbara to New England and find a family to hire her as a servant once she arrived. But Barbara was "so evil" during the journey that by the time the ship reached Boston, no one there would take her in. Babb shipped her north to Maine in hopes of finding a place for her there, and Barbara then vanished from our view. If unusual in her gender, she was typical in her disappearance from historical records soon after having reached mainland North America.

Economic cycles, population growth and collapse, declining opportunities for employment and marriage, domestic discord, death of a parent, custom, war, invasion, deception: all helped define the constraints within which people found themselves laboring for others. Moraley and Rolfe, both English, were part of the largest cohort of European migrants who ventured to the Americas, and as servants they represented the majority of that popula-

149

tion flow. The Atlantic world depended on bound labor, so Indian, European, and African migrant streams were all linked and dictated by the demand for labor. The quest for profit motivated all European incursions into the Americas. Although Europeans stumbled onto the new lands as part of expanding trade explorations, they soon turned to activities other than commerce. Most of these enterprises, including many not oriented toward transatlantic markets, depended on coerced labor for pragmatic and cultural reasons. No sane person would volunteer to perform the backbreaking work of silver mining or endure the punishing heat of tropical sugar plantations. If these tasks were to be done, force would be necessary. Migration and labor were thus linked to the commodities and minerals of the Atlantic and the consumer tastes and commercial demands that encouraged their production. Along with precious metals, pearls, and gemstones came the core cash crops: sugar, tobacco, indigo, rice, cotton, and coffee. Even in such regions as the pampas of the River Plate district of South America, which became huge exporters of beef and hides, the *gauchos* (cowboys) who produced the commodities were most often coerced.

Indian Labor Systems

Given the primitive state of technology throughout the early modern Atlantic world, the majority of tasks, from washing clothes to harvesting grain, had to be done manually. Even where animal, hydraulic, or wind power aided farmers, subsistence agriculture alone consumed an extraordinary amount of time and effort. And in the Americas, Europeans hoped not only to subsist but to prosper, that is, to accumulate capital rapidly through the production and export of cash crops and minerals. To this end, mobilizing Indian workers became a priority. Columbus made no idle comment when he observed of the Taíno, "they should be good servants." Europeans demanded labor from indigenous people in various ways. Soon after arriving in the Caribbean, the Spanish devised the system of encomienda, which, in theory, marshaled labor through village leaders. The crown allocated shares of Indians—technically limited rights to their labor and agricultural surpluses—to Spanish invaders, and successful conquistadors soon came to expect encomiendas as their rightful share of the spoils. In the Caribbean, these demands were highly disruptive: Indians were compelled to abandon subsistence agriculture or fishing and mine gold in the mountain interior. Spanish encomenderos on Hispaniola demanded that their subjects deliver a tribute of three ounces of gold dust every three months, a huge amount considering excavation and panning were performed exclusively by hand. Even the Spaniards could not subsist on gold alone, however, and as they forced more Taínos to the mines, and as disease diminished Taíno ranks, fewer and fewer laborers were left to plant and harvest the manioc on which all the inhabitants of the island depended. Despairing, Taínos began to commit suicide in great numbers, and women aborted and killed their children rather than raise them under Spanish rule. On the mainland, where indigenous groups lived in dense agricultural settlements, the encomienda more closely matched existing tribute and rotational labor structures.

In theory, encomenderos were obliged to tend to "their" Indians' needs, protecting them from predatory neighbors, providing adequate clothing and shelter, and paying a priest to oversee their induction into the Catholic faith. Some took their duties to heart. Andrés Chacón told his brother from Peru in 1570 that he planned to bequeath his Indians enough of his estate to liberate them from tribute burdens, "so that whoever enjoys the tributes will not mistreat the Indians to get his revenue." It was true, he acknowledged, that many thought his estate should go to his family, but Chacón believed he owed something to the Indians, "these children," who had served him for more than thirty years. "It is," he explained, "a debt of life, and if I did not repay it I would go to hell." Few were so scrupulous, however; a number of Chacón's contemporaries were tried and convicted of what today would be judged gross human rights violations. The burdens of encomienda, combined with the devastation caused by invading pathogens and microbes, compelled the crown to revisit the allocation of Indian labor and the demands placed on indigenous people and economies. In this enterprise, the crown faced pressure from men who had emerged as advocates for the Indians and from the legalistic and moral philosophies that undergirded and justified the Spanish conquest.

Beyond encomienda was out-and-out slavery. Despite Queen Isabella's early condemnation of Indian slavery, even she came to accept the time-honored concept of "just war," which permitted the enslavement of anyone who forcefully rejected Spanish dominion (and by extension, Christianity). Spaniards derived their notion of just war from the writings of Aristotle and St. Augustine. In the Indies particularly, Spanish settlers saw themselves as a natural aristocracy, destined to govern those weaker and less perfect. Other justifications for enslaving Indians included their "unnatural" practices of cannibalism and sodomy. After long debates, in 1510 the legalistic Spaniards created a document, the Requirement, which conquerors were to read to all whom they encountered in the Americas. The document gave a brief account of Biblical creation and the establishment of the Roman Catholic Church and claimed the new territory for Spain. It declared the Spaniards would not compel conversion, but would require their newly conquered subjects to recognize Spain's sovereignty and the right of missionaries to preach. Punishment for failure to comply was severe: "I will make war everywhere and however I can, and I will subject you to the yoke and obedience of the Church and His Majesty, and I will take your wives and children, and I will make them slaves," the Requirement warned. "I will take your goods, and I will do all the evil and damages that a lord may do to vassals who do not obey or receive him." The document ended with what sounds today like a liability waiver: "And I solemnly declare that the deaths and damages received from such will be your fault and not that of his Majesty, nor mine, nor of the gentlemen who came with me." Of course, the intended audience could not have understood the pronouncement, almost always delivered in Spanish, often immediately before combat over the beating of drums.

Only a few Spanish priests decried the hypocrisy, and some such men became aggressive defenders of the Indians. West of Santo Domingo, in the goldfields, the Spaniards constructed their second fortified settlement, Concepción de la Vega, to defend a bustling town, a Franciscan monastery, and gold-smelting works. The red brick ruins of Concepción's great medieval church still rise amidst the rainforest that is slowly enveloping it, and today Dominican peasants hang their laundry on its broken walls. It is hard to imagine that the most important critique of the European exploitation of the Americas was launched in this forgotten structure. But in 1511 the fiery Dominican friar Antonio Montesinos stood in his pulpit and condemned to damnation all Spaniards who mistreated their commended Indians. "Are these not men? Do they not have rational souls?" he thundered. "Are you not required to love them as yourselves?" He told the listeners, who included the dignitaries of the island, that they had no more hope of salvation than Turks and Moors who rejected the faith of Jesus.

Many of the insulted Spaniards stormed out of Montesinos's church, but one chastened auditor was slowly moved to action. Bartolomé de las Casas had reached Santo Domingo in 1502 and soon thereafter received an encomienda. By 1510 he was also a secular priest, but this status little affected his daily life. He heard Montesinos's sermon without immediate reaction; indeed, he went to Cuba and took part in its conquest, as full of massacres and brutality as any. But Christian scripture finally moved Las Casas to a change of heart. After reading Ecclesiastes 34:21–22, he decided there was no justification for Spanish invasion, occupation, and enslavement in the Indies. With Montesinos, he returned to Spain as an advocate for those he had once enslaved and an ardent defender of their humanity. In Valladolid, he debated the royal historian and noted scholar Juan Ginés de Sepúlveda over whether it was legal to wage war in order to subject and then convert the Indians. While Ginés de Sepúlveda, who had not been to the Indies, argued that Native Americans were "barbarous and inhumane" and by natural law should be enslaved, Las Casas responded "[W]hat man of sound mind will approve a war against men who are harmless, ignorant, gentle, temperate, unarmed and destitute of every human defense? For the results of such a war are very surely the loss of the souls who perish without knowing God and without the support of the sacraments, and, for the survivors, hatred and loathing of the Christian religion."

Las Casas later immortalized the catastrophic decline of Taíno populations in *A Brief Account of the Devastation of the Indies*, blaming not only Spaniards' cruelty but also the institution of encomienda. To relieve the fast-disappearing Indians, Las Casas advised that Spaniards import African slaves, a suggestion he later came to regret. While Spaniards were certainly capable of individual and group actions of brutality, no other Europeans in the Americas so agonized over the legal, religious, and moral implications and justifications of colonization. Nor did any imperial government in the Americas produce more legislation attempting to ameliorate ill treatment of native subjects, accept the concept of natural lords among them, or so long recognize and protect their legal claims to communal landholdings.

In the wake of these frank and heated discussions came two reforms. First, the crown promulgated the New Laws of 1542, which initiated administrative reforms but also prohibited the enslavement of the Indians. At first, the crown ordered an end to the encomienda, but this provoked such violent civil war in Peru that Charles V was forced to concede. The encomienda would survive, but it could only be inherited for one generation. After this, Indian tributes would be rendered as a head tax to the crown, and a royal magistrate would allot Indian laborers for temporary work projects. Later, in 1573, in an act that would alter the pattern of conquest in areas where the Spanish presence remained weak, the crown issued ordinances that eliminated use of the term *conquest* in favor of *pacification*. Alleged Indian rebels, like invading pirates, were to be summarily "punished." In part for broader strategic reasons, this legislation effectively allowed the encomienda to survive for centuries in fringe areas of Spanish America.

With Indian slavery prohibited, the Spanish turned instead to repartimiento (in Central America) and mita (in South America). These were temporary labor drafts, a practice the Spanish used during the conquest and occupation and which predated conquest. The Inca relied on the mita system to construct temples, bridges, and canals. It was easier to move people over roads through the Andes than goods, so labor service became the primary way of satisfying imperial demands. Under the Spanish, the mita and repartimiento required communities to provide male laborers, 18–50 years old, for a fixed period, generally two to four months. The workers received modest wages, which they could apply to the tribute they were required to pay. With the demise of the more feudal encomienda, Indians increasingly were required to pay tribute in cash, which meant they had to find ways to obtain wages.

Repartimiento appeared by the 1550s in New Spain, and over the next few decades the mita was established in South America. The labor Indians performed varied depending on their location. Those near mineral deposits were allotted to private mine owners for work as miners and ore carriers. Indians also worked in domestic service, commercial agriculture, stock raising, textile production, church building, and a host of other tasks. Many projects were ostensibly for the public good. Draft laborers constructed the city of Santa Fe, New Mexico, and coerced Indians built the immense stone fort at St. Augustine, Florida, after English pirates destroyed the old wooden structure, a project requiring fifteen years of hauling, cutting, and placing stone.

The English Dominican Thomas Gage, who visited Guatemala in the early seventeenth century, remarked that while the Indians he met there were not slaves, "their lives are as full of bitterness as is the life of a slave." Spaniards distributed laborers according to their needs, and Indian towns had to have people ready for deployment on any contingency. The Indians Gage saw received modest wages (three cents per week), but colonial labor demands so disrupted their households that even men working near home were not allowed to stay with their families during their service. To add insult to injury, they were subjected to degrading corporal punishment.

Because Gage wrote to persuade the English to invade Spanish territories, he sought to depict the suffering Indians as natural allies. Nonetheless he captured accurately the exploitation of the labor drafts. Even though repartimiento and mita were intended to protect Indians from the worst abuses, the social impact of forced migration in communities where people defined themselves and maintained their link to the sacred world through their proximity to ancestral shrines was profound. Indians who worked in the Mexican and Peruvian silver mines often lived far from their spiritual centers. In addition, lengthy separations from family encouraged many *mitayos* (mita workers) in the Andes to bring their families along with them to work sites. Many of these relations soon found themselves compelled to work for the Spanish as well, in order to meet tribute demands, and Indian women were vulnerable to sexual assaults from Spanish officials and colonists. Working-class children were also exploited in numerous support tasks in mines, cane mills, sweatshops, and elite households. As Gage traveled in Guatemala, he observed that there were always laborers available "in a slavish bondage" to meet the needs of any traveler, who could demand porters in any number to tote goods to his destination. Indian bearers strapped heavy chests to their backs with ropes; by journey's end, their foreheads bled from the pressure of the bonds. Gage also described the mechanisms used to cheat workers after such service. Travelers would "pick some quarrel" with their exhausted porters, and at best refuse to pay; at worst they beat their bearer. As the historian David Weber put it, on the Spanish frontier laborers were "unpaid, underpaid, paid in overvalued merchandise, unfed, underfed, kept for longer periods of time than regulations permitted, and pressed into the personal service of individuals who confused their own good with the public weal." When it came to protecting Indians, law and practice were two separate things.

Some of the work Indians were compelled to do was deadly. Mining was particularly dangerous, especially when deposits were followed underground. Many Andean mines were located at high altitudes, where the air was cold and thin. Miners labored underground, chipping out and lugging by hand ore from hundreds of feet below the mountain surface, emerging exhausted and sweaty into the cold air. Respiratory illnesses among miners were common, as were severe injuries from falls and cave-ins. The mercury mines at Huancavelica, Peru, posed particularly hazardous conditions, as workers suffered from mercury poisoning and choked on mercury dust in the poorly ventilated tunnels. Mercury poisoning sickened and ultimately killed many of those who endured mita service; sufferers became moody and excitable, depressed and agitated; they experienced hallucinations and memory loss. Mita labor, for all the enormous hardships and sacrifices it entailed, did not even guarantee laborers enough of a wage to cover their cash tribute burden.

Of course, as with every aspect of the history of the western Atlantic, the story of Indian labor is embedded in a larger one of Indian demography, characterized by a precipitous, unprecedented sixteenth-century collapse. In the Caribbean, the Taíno population was nearly eradicated before Columbus died in 1506. On the South American mainland, large and densely settled precontact populations dwindled quickly, meaning there would be progressively fewer Indians to serve Spanish labor needs. Waves of infectious diseases ravaged the mainland, with two or three "epidemic series," or cycles, occurring between the 1540s and 1600. Measles followed smallpox, and then came typhus and plague and mumps and measles again—and on the cycle went. Some people recovering from one illness were hit in their weakened condition by another. The population of Mesoamerica bottomed out in 1622 at 750,000, down from a preconquest high of nearly 25 million. The Andean population seems to have reached its nadir a century later, after a massive epidemic in 1717–18. By 1750, the Andean population, once numbering more than 10 million, had recovered to 650,000. If disease facilitated the Spaniards' ability to subjugate a vast continent, it also generated a labor crisis. The Peruvian encomendero Andrés Chacón wrote his brother in 1570 that only 200 remained of the 2,000 Indians once living on his estate. As a natural consequence of forced laborers' mass death, wage labor appeared, and it came to replace repartimiento and mita in many places by the seventeenth century. Naturally, Spaniards continued to prefer bonded labor, so first in the Caribbean and later on the mainland they turned to enslaved Africans to replace the diminished and, in some places, vanished American population. As would soon prove true in other American colonies, the value of Spanish exports was high enough to subsidize the forced, transatlantic migration of millions of Africans.

Other Europeans in the Americas pursued different strategies to persuade indigenous people to work—always in a context of Indian populations diminished by catastrophic epidemics. None of these other Europeans found the kind of settled, bureaucratic states the Spanish conquered, but they devised ways to meet their labor demands that were consistent with the economies they encountered. The Portuguese established the pattern early in Brazil in the sixteenth century, when they sought to barter with the coastal Indians to persuade them to harvest brazilwood and haul the logs to the coast for shipment overseas.

In the mid-sixteenth century, the Portuguese began raiding settlements in Brazil, stealing people into slavery, often under the guise of "just war." The Indians of Brazil found advocates among religious men, as had the Indians of Spanish America. But unlike the Spanish monarchs, Portugal's rulers paid relatively little attention to evangelization. They left that work to the Jesuits, the first of whom arrived in 1549. Led by Manuel da Nóbrega and José de Anchieta, Jesuits established schools for Indians in protected mission villages called *aldeias*, "all for the love of their souls." Among the first aldeias was São Paulo de Piritininga, which later became Brazil's largest metropolis. In some cases the Jesuits transformed nomadic Gê-speaking hunter-gatherers into industrious agricultural laborers and stock raisers. Like the Franciscans, Dominicans, and Augustinians in Mexico, they sought to turn Indians into European peasants. Indians were not allowed to become priests themselves.

Although the Portuguese crown forbade Indian slavery as early as 1570, the law proved unenforceable, with loopholes that enabled people to enslave those Indians they claimed to have rescued from ritual execution and cannibalism. Moreover, the Portuguese continued to have the right to enslave Indians who committed acts of violence against colonists, and by the 1680s, some Portuguese *bandeirantes* (backwoodsmen) operating in the vicinity of Brazil's northern Atlantic coast were permitted to barter for slaves from Indian leaders who had legitimately acquired them in war. Jesuits accompanied a number of these slave exchanges to ensure compliance with the law. In fact, the law held the ironic requirement that all slaves carry certificates, drafted and signed by Jesuits, assuring their legitimate enslavement. One Indian slave, a woman named Francisca, petitioned authorities for her freedom in 1739 on the basis that she had been illegally enslaved. Her ordeal illustrates the many flaws in the Portuguese legal and moral code governing the Indian slave trade. Francisca had been taken in an illegal expedition, and was sold without the proper papers. After twenty years of service as a household slave, she sought her freedom, collecting her own witnesses (primarily other Indians, both free and enslaved). Her owner responded in kind, bringing his own witnesses to the proceedings, almost all of whom were white and literate. Although a justice ruled in Francisca's favor, his decision was overturned by the Council of Missions, a body of religious leaders with jurisdiction over Indians, who dismissed Francisca's witnesses as unreliable. Her fate sealed, Francisca was ordered to return to her mistress. The fact that Francisca's owner fought so tenaciously to keep her as a slave is explained in part by Brazil's growing labor demands. Indian slavery would persist in Brazil, particularly in backcountry regions, despite the massive introduction of African slaves.

Virtually all Europeans enslaved Indians in the course of their colonial projects. The French did in Canada and Louisiana, their mainland holdings in North America, although never on a large scale. The English relied on an Indian slave trade as well, primarily in the southeastern part of the North American continent. Although the English did not share the bureaucratic and legalistic culture of the Spanish, they nonetheless debated the circumstances under which a person could be enslaved. At the time of American settlement, the English were in fact new to slavery in anything other than penal form. In contrast to the Iberian Peninsula, where numerous Africans lived as slaves prior to Columbus's voyages, in early modern England slavery was unknown. Furthermore, with the writings of Las Casas in their minds, the English in the years around 1600, like their Dutch neighbors, wished to cast themselves as rescuers of native people otherwise oppressed by Spanish Catholics. Slavery would seem inconsistent with these goals. Nonetheless, whenever profit was to be had, the English, like so many others, conveniently lost their scruples.

In fact, the English enslaved Indians as casually and expediently as any Europeans, although until the 1680s it was mostly sworn enemies they relegated to slavery. Since in most places in the Americas the English, like the French, were few in number at first, and highly dependent on Native American trade goods and alliances for survival, they always faced practical constraints to the development of large-scale enslavement. The circumstances that permitted slavery in English North America, then, were more or less the same "just wars" that Iberians used to rationalize their actions. That, at least, was the justification for the enslavement of alleged rebels after the Pequot War in 1637, in which an English-Mohegan-Narragansett alliance fought the Pequots in southeastern New England. A similar fate was assigned to surviving members of a pan-Indian alliance led by Metacom, a Wampanoag leader, after his defeat in 1676. In both cases, Native American children served in

INDIAN TRIBES OF NORTH AMERICA IN THE SEVENTEENTH CENTURY

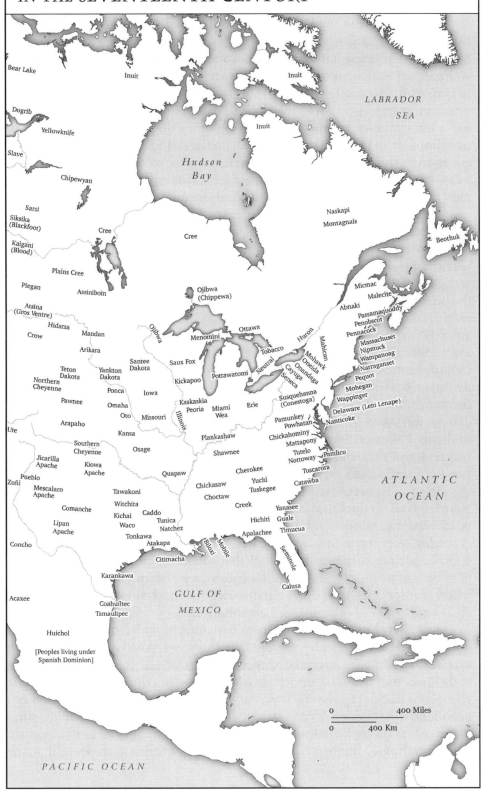

Bear Lake

Inuit

Inuit

LABRADOR SEA

Dogrib

Yellowknife

Inuit

Slave

Hudson Bay

Chipewyan

Naskapi

Montagnais

Beothuk

Sarsi

Siksika (Blackfoot)

Cree

Cree

Kaigani (Blood)

Plains Cree

Micmac

Piegan

Assiniboin

Malecite

Atsina (Gros Ventre)

Ojibwa (Chippewa)

Abnaki

Passamaquoddy

Penobscot

Hidatsa

Pennacock

Crow

Mandan

Ojibwa

Menomini

Ottawa

Huron

Massachuset

Nipmuck

Arikara

Tobacco

Mohawk

Mahican

Wampanoag

Teton Dakota

Yankton Dakota

Santee Dakota

Saux Fox

Neutral

Oneida

Onondaga

Narraganset

Northern Cheyenne

Kickapoo

Pottawatomi

Cayuga

Seneca

Pequot

Mohegan

Pawnee

Ponca

Iowa

Erie

Susquehanna (Conestoga)

Wappinger

Omaha

Kaskaskia

Peoria

Miami

Wea

Delaware (Leni Lenape)

Oto

Missouri

Illinois

Pamunkey

Powhatan

Nanticoke

Ute

Arapaho

Kansa

Plankashaw

Chickahominy

Southern Cheyenne

Osage

Shawnee

Mattapony

Tutelo

Nottoway

Pamlico

Jicarilla Apache

Kiowa Apache

Quapaw

Cherokee

Tuscarora

Pueblo

Zuñi

Mescalaro Apache

Tawakoni

Chickasaw

Yuchi

Tuskegee

Catawba

ATLANTIC OCEAN

Comanche

Witchita

Choctaw

Creek

Lipan Apache

Kichai

Waco

Caddo

Tunica

Natchez

Hichiti

Yanasee

Guale

Concho

Tonkawa

Atakapa

Apalachee

Timucua

Karankawa

Citimacha

Biloxi

Mobile

Seminole

Acaxee

Coahuiltec

Tamaulipec

GULF OF MEXICO

Calusa

Huíchol

[Peoples living under Spanish Dominion]

0   400 Miles

0   400 Km

PACIFIC OCEAN

English households, while their parents (those not executed) were sold to other colonies. In Virginia, the English similarly took up Indian slavery after a 1622 attack that killed one-third of the colonists. Whereas before, according to one document, the English hands were "tied with gentlenesse and faire usage," now they were "set at liberty by the treacherous violence of the Sauvages." The English treated their European enemies in similar ways in the aftermath of war, but already there were important distinctions when it came to Native Americans. In the Greco-Roman legal tradition, which most Europeans followed, victors had the right to execute the defeated, or to enslave them if they preferred (the Latin term *servi* meaning spared). In the wake of rebellions in Ireland and uprisings in England and Scotland, defeated enemies were shipped overseas as laborers, turning soldiers into slaves. What was different was that this was slavery for a finite period, a penal sentence rather than an inherited, permanent condition.

Even in war, colonists deliberated the best course for dealing with Indian captives. In some circumstances, enslavement and exile posed dangers. During Metacom's War in 1676, John Winthrop, Jr., the governor of Connecticut, opposed selling captives to Barbados, lest Metacom's soldiers retaliate against English captives or in case selling captives so far away might hinder the possibility of peace. Yet Winthrop's enterprising sons, Wait and Fitz, had no such qualms and were deeply involved in the postwar slave trade. Thus, at an early stage of European settlement among them, North American Indians found themselves scattered around the Atlantic. On Barbados, they joined Indians from South America and Africans from that continent's Atlantic rim. By the mid-seventeenth century, English households in the western Atlantic contained bound laborers of all sorts, including indentured Europeans, Indian servants and slaves, and African slaves. In Bermuda, the estate inventory of Richard Norwood in 1676 listed his human property as including several African slaves, "one old indian woman," and one child described as an "indian negrow girle." Mixed captives gave rise to mixed populations, slave and free.

In contrast to this ad hoc approach to enslavement in the wake of war in New England, in the Carolinas, an elaborate slave trade developed at the end of the seventeenth century. Here the English departed from the practice of enslaving only those Indians ensnared in "just wars." More like the Portuguese bandeirantes in Brazil, the English took advantage of conventional practices of warfare among the Carolina tribes they encountered. Indeed, everywhere Europeans went in the Atlantic world, indigenous practices shaped economies and opportunities for exploitation.

English colonists migrating from Barbados began settling the Carolinas in 1663, and they quickly encountered Indians accustomed to taking war captives. The Indians executed some prisoners of war in communal rituals and others they adopted into their own tribe, sometimes into a status that Europeans likened to slavery. It was not a complicated matter—as it had not been for the Portuguese a century earlier in Brazil—to persuade Indian allies to make war on their habitual enemies and sell the captives to the English, who then shipped them to the West Indies and elsewhere as slaves. Still, many of these laborers were kept in the colony: one 1708 estimate put the population of the Carolina colony at 5,300 whites, 2,900 Africans, and 1,400 Indian slaves. The wars soon moved inland, engrossing more tribes, with raids as far south as Spanish Florida and well into the interior. Captives were marched to the coast and shipped overseas, most frequently to Barbados, where demand for plantation labor was insatiable and where many of Carolina's settlers had commercial and familial ties. When imperial wars overlapped these local conflagrations, English colonists joined their indigenous allies to make war on the Indians in Spanish Florida. The Carolina slave trade did not cease until a final convulsion of warfare in 1715–16, by which date thousands of Indians had been sold and the local indigenous economy had been devastated. The historian Alan Gallay has estimated that between 24,000 and 51,000 southern Indians were sold in the British slave trade between 1670 and 1715.

If the lack of acquired immunities rendered indigenous populations unreliable for European labor demands, particularly in the first generations after contact, Indians also resisted forced service. Many slipped away into forests or swamps where Europeans could or would not follow them. For this reason, Europeans often transported slaves far from their homes. Some Indian groups, in turn, relocated to avoid war and enslavement. So while some tribes, eager to engage in trade and procure commodities they desired not only for practical use but for social prestige, moved toward Europeans, other tribes fled from Europeans and their demands, especially those who lived in regions embroiled in slave raids. Some Tupi-speakers in Brazil were engaged in such a movement north, away from Portuguese settlement in the middle of the sixteenth century, when they found themselves moving toward the French, who proved to be useful allies. Four thousand Indian refugees migrated away from areas lost by the Dutch to the Portuguese after the Dutch surrender of Pernambuco in 1654. Having been allies of the Dutch, they had reason to fear reprisals. In sum, across the first three centuries of colonial rule and throughout the Americas, Indian populations were in steady motion as forced laborers and refugees.

Migration within America offered Indians one strategy for avoiding or engaging Europeans. Migration across the Atlantic offered another for a much smaller but politically significant Indian population. In the mid-seventeenth century, Tupi-speakers in northeastern Brazil greeted the Dutch army (a force that included Scots, Italian, and German-speaking mercenaries) as a potential ally against the Portuguese and their policies of forced labor and migration. One Tupi group, the Potiguars, asked the Dutch to take them to Holland so they could escape for good, and so they commenced a long journey, reversing the trip that had brought so many Europeans to Brazil. This small group lived for several years in the Low Countries, where they learned Dutch. One Potiguar leader, Anthonio Paraupaba, used the linguistic and cultural skills he learned to secure political power back in Brazil. In the wake of the Portuguese revolt that ended Dutch rule in Brazil, Paraupaba returned to Holland to gain continued Dutch support in their struggles with the Portuguese. Many of the Dutch-allied Tupi had converted to Protestantism, and they migrated into the Brazilian mountains to form a refugee community.

Indians also engaged in overt resistance, especially in places where labor was institutionalized as part of European occupation. Excessive work demands by ranchers, planters, mining overseers, and even churchmen triggered revolts, but so did such culturally inappropriate requirements as forcing local leaders to bear burdens, humiliating punishments (like head-shaving), priestly intervention, and attempts to end polygamy and drinking parties. Spanish meddling in native political life, especially attempts to alter succession patterns, also created conflict. In southeastern North America, revolts against Spanish rule included those of the Guale in 1645, the Apalachee in 1647, and the Apalachicola in 1675 and 1681. This was a region dominated by Franciscan missions, not plantation agriculture or mining. In the west, various groups of Pueblo revolted against their Spanish overlords in 1632, 1639–40, 1644, 1647 and 1650.

The largest and most successful indigenous rebellion against the Spanish in North America occurred in 1680. Spaniards' new labor and tribute demands not only brought physical hardships but also disrupted peaceful trade between the settled Pueblos and more nomadic Athabaskan groups to their north. Distracted by labor demands, the Pueblo no longer could produce surplus crops to trade with such gathering and hunting groups as the Jicarilla Apache of northernmost New Mexico, so previous trading partners began taking what they wanted through force. Drought and famine exacerbated the dwindling food supply and increased frontier tensions, while thefts of Pueblo animals by Navajo and Apache raiders further stressed Pueblo groups. If labor was not the revolt's sole cause, it nonetheless created the starvation and warfare that signaled to the Pueblo that their world was awry and that good order needed to be restored to the cosmos. Finally, the Pueblos' despair drove them to a unified nativist revolt in 1680 that was reminiscent of the Great Maya Revolt of 1546. Coordinated by an indigenous religious leader, Popé, whom the Spaniards had whipped and humiliated for alleged witchcraft, 17,000 Pueblos speaking six different languages and spread across twenty-four towns rose in rebellion. Within weeks they had killed more than four hundred Spaniards and destroyed farms and settlements. The rebels also murdered twenty-one of the twenty-three Spanish missionaries living among them and directed anger toward religious symbols such as statues, bells, crosses, and holy oils.

Although the rebels turned their hostility at these emblems of Spanish culture, they also focused on labor, insisting that the Spanish deliver their wives and children from enslavement. One Pueblo leader, Juan, made the demand emphatic, asking for return of all Indians in Spanish control. He even exhibited pan-Indian unity in his feelings toward slavery: deliver as well, he insisted, enslaved Apaches, "inasmuch as some Apaches who were among them [the Pueblo] were asking for them." Once driven from New Mexico in this fashion, the surviving Spaniards and loyal Pueblo refugees retreated south and set up a government in exile in El Paso, and they did not attempt to return to New Mexico for more than a decade. The Pueblo revolt made visible

Table 5.2   *European Migrants to the Americas, 1500–1800*

Country of Origin	Number	Date
Spain	680,000	1500–1760
Portugal	570,000	1500–1760
Britain[1]	722,000	1607–1780
France	51,000	1608–1760
"Germany"[2]	100,000	1683–1783
Total Europeans	2,123,000	1500–1783

SOURCE: *This table reproduces Table 1.1 in Ida Altman and James Horn, eds.,* To Make America *(Berkeley, 1991), 31, with additions to the Spanish and Portuguese figures from Stephen Haber, ed.,* How Latin America Fell Behind *(Stanford, 1997), 264.*
1. *Includes between 190,000 and 25,000 Scots and Irish.*
2. *Southwestern Germany and the German-speaking cantons of Switzerland and Alsace Lorraine.*

Indians' fury toward those who stole their labor. Such violent resistance, coupled with demographic collapse, signaled the long-term inadequacy of Indian labor as the sole means of extracting wealth from the Americas.

European Laborers and Migrants

Although Indians made up the majority of coerced laborers in Spanish America, they were hardly the only ones in the early modern Atlantic world. In English, French, and Dutch colonies of North America and the Caribbean, indentured Europeans produced plantation crops in the first decades of settlement, performing the same tasks as enslaved indigenous people and Africans. The product of northern European population growth, enclosure, and other factors converging by the early seventeenth century, these indentured men and women joined tens of thousands of free Europeans who traveled to the Americas and Africa to establish settlements and seek opportunities for social and commercial gain. For those in charge of overseas colonies and plantations, labor remained the main issue at hand. Indeed, one can best grasp European migration within this period by understanding the centrality of labor to the exploitation of the Atlantic's resources.

The numbers in Table 5.2 provide only a starting point, illustrating the extent of European transatlantic migration and the people involved. They do not include one of the largest populations of transatlantic travelers: fishermen who worked seasonally in the Newfoundland cod fisheries. (No formal estimate exists for this population, but, as mentioned in Chapter Four, hundreds of ships carried thousands of men annually to the Banks.) Among European migrants before 1783, Britons predominated, closely followed by Spaniards. Due to a far more open immigration policy than that pursued by the Iberians, British holdings in the Americas ultimately attracted a unique mix of colonial subjects. (In 1707, the kingdoms of England and Scotland united, and historians tend to use *British*, rather than *English*.) German-speaking migrants headed primarily for British American destinations. It is worth remembering, too, that British numerical dominance in transatlantic migration does not tell much about the relative power, wealth, or size of settler populations.

The Spanish and Portuguese held larger and richer territories than their competitors. Furthermore, the former began migrating to the Americas much earlier than other Europeans, giving rise to large creole and mestizo populations that had little need for continued inputs of immigrant labor or capital. Nor, for that matter, did the volume of transatlantic migration reflect the size of home populations: France was the most populous Atlantic power, but it sent relatively few people to its western Atlantic holdings. Colonial domination was not necessarily a function of migration. If anything, high rates of European migration could reflect colonial weakness and troubles at home.

The Portuguese, Dutch, and French comprised the smallest European migrant streams. Reliance on other populations—European, Indian, African—characterized the Atlantic ventures of these nations. The Portuguese settled primarily in Brazil and the French in settlements on the American mainland—in Canada, the Mississippi River valley, and Louisiana—in addition to the island colonies of Saint Domingue (the western portion of Hispaniola, which the French first occupied in the 1640s with formal recognition in 1697 in the Treaty of Ryswick), Martinique, and Guadeloupe. The Dutch were dependent on other nationalities to help populate their far-flung holdings. In their small numbers overseas they generally proved unable and unwilling to impose linguistic and cultural domination—the one exception being in the Cape region of southern Africa. Spanish migration, strong in the first 140 years of conquest and settlement, started to decline in 1625. Official control over migration also declined in this period, rendering statistics less reliable. Spanish migration to the Americas initially was characterized by young men, who still tend to dominate world migration flows, although within decades of the conquest women and children joined in migrating west. The historian James Lockhart characterized the first years of Spanish migration as a flow of nephews. Men wrote home from the Americas seeking young men as dependents, overseers, and commercial factors. One encomendero wrote from Peru, "what I would need here is what there is too much of there, which is a boy among those nephews of mine, to ride about on horseback inspecting my properties." This appeal emphasizes the kinship connections that shaped European migration and the recurring importance of young men as necessary "fresh blood" in the larger colonial project. Spanish men were assured that opportunity awaited those who worked hard. Early Spanish migrants came primarily from the provinces of Estremadura and Andalusia, with many originating in the Andalusian capital of Seville. The dominance of these two southern regions serves as a reminder that migration from any single European nation did not necessarily represent a cross section of that society. Conversely, while most Spanish migrants settled in Mexico, many others went south to Venezuela, New Granada, Peru, and the world's fastest growing mining town, Potosí. The Caribbean islands were soon relegated to the role of stepping-stones.

Unlike English migrants, most of whom arrived in the western Atlantic as agricultural laborers, the Spanish settled generally in urban areas. Because Spanish colonialism centered on extracting agricultural surpluses and labor from large indigenous populations, Spaniards tended to settle in preexisting Indian towns and cities. When they built new cities, they sought to recreate

Spanish urban life as they remembered it. The port of Santo Domingo, on Hispaniola's southern coast, exemplifies the pattern. It boasted many European "firsts" in the hemisphere: the first monastery, first hospital, first cathedral, first court of appeals, and first university. Even had the English wished to emulate Spanish colonialism a century later in North America, they could not have, because they found no large population centers and no silver and gold to finance building projects. By the turn of the seventeenth century, the Spanish population in America was able to reproduce itself, and thus the pace of transatlantic migration from Iberia dwindled, only to pick up again in the eighteenth century.

Migrants to the English colonies in the western Atlantic, as many as 700,000 altogether, came from all of Britain and Ireland. They poured into the eastern seaboard of North America and ventured to the islands of the Caribbean, especially Jamaica and Barbados. Dominated by agricultural laborers and artisans, these migrants also contained family groups who settled mostly in the more northerly British colonies. In some instances, entire communities migrated together; the British, Spanish, and German-speaking migrants in particular demonstrate this pattern of "chain" migration. The town of Dorchester, Massachusetts, was only one of many settled by neighbors and kin who traveled in successive waves from England, recreating, in some cases, their English world in new settings overseas.

The historian Ida Altman documents similar chain migrations between the towns of Brihuega, Spain, and Puebla, Mexico. Beginning in the mid-sixteenth century, these towns grew interdependent, with some residents voyaging back across the Atlantic to join kinfolk and much sending home of money to support family members and church organizations. Altman traces the clustered movement of Andalusians into other parts of Spanish America as well, and the historian Juan Javier Pescador has found similar ties between Basque Spain and various American communities. Many historians have noted similar concentrations of *paisanos*, or country-folk, maintaining "Old Country" ties throughout Spanish America and Brazil.

Of course, the numbers alone mask other crucial features of migration—the dominance of young men, for example. Especially in the seventeenth-century northern European colonies, a need for labor drove migration, and most laborers were young, able-bodied men. In their earliest years, colonies welcomed populations that were as high as 95 percent male. This was the case for European populations in the English Caribbean in the 1630s, and women composed only 20 percent of seventeenth-century migrants to the Chesapeake. Both male and female servants traveled across the Atlantic in a dependent status, answering a seemingly insatiable need for laborers to produce the tobacco, cotton, indigo, or sugar that promised to provide profits to landowners and investors. Most northern European migrants were unfree. They traveled as bound laborers (indentured servants or *engagés*) from England and France, and as redemptioners from the Holy Roman Empire. Redemptioners were usually German-speaking Protestants traveling as families, who were unable to fund their own voyage, particularly after they endured the expensive trek from central Europe to major Atlantic ports. The

British welcomed these religious refugees into their colonies; Catholic empires did not. When they reached American ports, the redemptioners sought a sponsor who could "redeem" them by paying a ship's master the cost of the voyage. If they failed, they were bound out as servants, required to work until they had covered the cost of the journey.

Indentured servants and engagés, predominantly young and male, agreed to serve for anywhere from 4–8 years in America in return for their passage, which was otherwise priced beyond their reach, and then for freedom dues that varied among colonies. Although apprenticeship and other forms of non-slave, contract labor were common throughout the Iberian world, transatlantic indenture was an innovation designed specifically to meet English, Dutch, and French labor needs in the Americas, combining features of agricultural workers' one-year contracts and multiyear apprenticeships designed to teach boys a skilled trade. Freedom dues might include the promise of land or agricultural equipment to start a new life as a farmer, or a bushel of corn or new set of clothes. Servants' ability to extract the promised dues from masters always depended on the willingness of courts (composed of masters) to support their claims. Many servants acquired indentured status reluctantly. One study of late-seventeenth-century London finds that people might wait in the metropolis a full year, first seeking employment, before resigning themselves to failure and, out of desperation, boarding ships for the colonies as servants. The colonies offered only one of many options for the poor, hungry, and desperate.

Some migrants were seduced on board ships with promises; others were tricked or kidnapped outright. (The term *Barbadosed* was coined to describe illegal methods of procuring servants in the same way that *Shanghaied* later described a similar fate.) Young John Wise was apparently duped in such a circumstance. In 1635, he joined other unemployed men who made their way to London in a period of economic stagnation and population growth, seeking "better fortune" only to end up on a ship bound for Barbados. But Wise was luckier than most. His cousin came chasing after him and appealed for his release to the Commissioners for the Admiralty and Navy. He was but "a country lad," the cousin protested, who "was deceived and most violently brought on board." Those not so duped often made decisions under the influence of alcohol. William Moraley signed his indenture for Pennsylvania only after being flattered by a broker and plied with beer. The former servant John Hammond urged young men to secure written contracts, and such promotional literature as *A Relation of Maryland* (London, 1635) provided a boilerplate that interested individuals might follow. As too many servants discovered, mere verbal assurance of adequate care typically "signifie[d] nothing."

On arrival in the Americas, servants were sold to anyone needing laborers. The *Tristram and Jeane* sailed to Virginia in 1637, stopping at points along riverbanks and selling servants for between 500 and 600 pounds of tobacco each. Buyers tallied servants as commodities, making marks in ledgers to signify but one of their capital assets. The Virginian John Baddam's inventory in 1652 listed his ten hogs, one maidservant, and eight old books. Much like

African and Indian slaves, alongside whom they often worked, indentured Europeans were bought and sold at the will of their masters. Many resented the apparent equivalence. Thomas Best wrote his brother from Virginia in 1623, fuming that his master had "sold mee for 150 pounds like a damned slave."

Treatment of indentured servants varied. Abuse cases that appeared in court invariably entailed testimony of violence, coercion, and exploitation. Masters and mistresses of sadistic inclinations found easy targets in their servants. Cheap and easily replaced in the first part of the seventeenth century, servants endured rough treatment. A maidservant of Ralph Hunt in Virginia was so brutally kicked, whipped, and clubbed with a tobacco stick the day before she went into labor that the stillborn baby bore bruises from the attack. The servant John Thomas complained to the Barbados council about his masters, Francis Leaven and Samuel Hodgkins, who suspended him by his hands and placed lighted matches between his fingers, putting Thomas at risk of losing his right hand. In this singular instance, the tortured servant found rare justice, receiving 5,000 pounds of raw cotton as compensation along with his freedom and medical treatment. His masters were imprisoned.

Servants resisted ill treatment in a variety of ways: they ran away, refused to work, and went to court to complain about their treatment. In New England, a court allowed Twiford West to serve a different master, but made him agree to serve an extra year for this largesse. Running away brought its own risks for those caught and punished by courts comprised of masters. Augustine Addison ran away from his master in Virginia in 1658 and was gone for fifteen weeks. He was punished by having his term of service extended by nearly a year. Servants even plotted rebellions against their owners. Some servants in Barbados in the 1640s, overcome by "the intolerable burdens they labour'd under," resolved to cut their masters' throats and declare themselves free and rulers of the colony. Unfortunately for them, another servant revealed the plot to his master, and in the ensuing punishment eighteen of the ringleaders were put to death as an example to the rest.

In their flight from service, runaways sought whatever sanctuary they could, some among Indians. Others ran away to rival colonies or to the buccaneers, renegades who materialized first in the uninhabited fringes of the Caribbean to become free-lance pirates. Runaway slaves often joined fleeing servants. Tortuga, Hispaniola, and Jamaica were well known for their pirate populations. Jamaica's Port Royal, where pirates such as the supposed ex-indentured servant Henry Morgan (he denied the claim) congregated to spend their wages, was a hard-drinking, hard-playing town where vice and crime, funded mostly by stolen Spanish silver, ran rampant in the seventeenth century.

The high number of laboring migrants pouring into the northern European colonies of the western Atlantic in no way predicted the size of colonial populations—this thanks to disease environments, natural increase, and patterns of repeat migration. Return migration was a defining feature of transatlantic movement. Indeed, many migrants left for the Americas with the hope of returning home. At times of diminished economic opportunity in England,

Promotional Literature

Potential immigrants were enticed overseas through formal promotional literature. Today we would consider these texts as advertising campaigns and, as good consumers, read them skeptically. Early migrants were less wary. Promoters tugged at national and religious ties. John White, who advocated settlement in New England, assured readers of his pamphlet that God was not happy when his people used only one portion of the earth. Everywhere in the Americas, promoters assured curious migrants, the climate was salubrious, temperate, and indistinguishable from that of England. They generalized about Newfoundland and Bermuda that, in such remote and varied places, the sick would be cured. The climate of New England, another promoter added, could restore health to the infirm and cure digestion problems. Aggressive writers used negative advertising, too. In his pamphlet for New England, William Wood disparaged Virginia's weather, with its "extreame hot Summers" and myriad diseases. In addition to their competitors, promoters had to combat word of mouth. Returning travelers and mariners returned with more accurate reports about colonial destinations and opportunities therein. After Opechancanough's attack on Virginia in 1622, the

Virginia Company had to contend with all manner of bad press, including a ballad about the ordeal that killed one-third of all colonists. In response, the Virginia Company investors warned migrants away from the "sulphurious breath of every base ballad monger." Investors also hired agents to travel and recruit colonists. When seeking people to settle Pennsylvania, William Penn had agents in Ireland and the Holy Roman Empire. The motive was always profit: investors in new settlements needed people to work the land, pay them rent, and produce marketable goods.

NOVA BRITANNIA.

OFFERING MOST

Excellent fruites by Planting in
VIRGINIA.

Exciting all such as be well affected
to further the same.

LONDON
Printed for SAMVEL MACHAM, and are to be sold at
his Shop in Pauls Church-yard, at the
Signe of the Bul-head.
1609.

Title-page of Nova Britannia, *a pamphlet issued in 1609 by the Virginia Company in London to win support for their enterprise in America. Credit: The Granger Collection, New York.*

young people had to delay marriage until they found the means to sustain themselves. In these circumstances, migration and temporary servitude offered the prospect of the material prosperity with which one might start a household. Other migrants came west with greater resources but still regarded migration to colonial America as the springboard to European prosperity and status. James Dering traveled to Barbados in the 1630s with credit sufficient to obtain land and laborers. He hoped to make enough with a tobacco crop to repay his debts, turn a profit, and take his earnings home to England. Only a poor crop kept him on the island. In this attitude, he resembled men involved in the early settlement of the Spanish Indies, who also dreamed of returning home to flaunt their prosperity. Nicolás de Guevara went to Peru in 1581 and settled in Potosí, where he made his living from mining. He planned to return to Spain after almost twenty years away, if, he told his family, he could secure enough wealth from his ore. Those men who did make it back to their hometowns with extravagant wealth from American enterprises were called *peruleros*, or "Peru-men." They inspired others to emulate them, sparking new cycles of migration from the same regions.

Europeans moved back and forth across the ocean in numbers that seem surprising when considering the discomfort and danger of early transatlantic travel. Some took part in numerous, and longer, overseas ventures, of which their American tours were only one part. The Galician captain Alvaro de Mendaña and his wealthy wife Isabel Barreto not only crossed the Atlantic but sailed to the Solomon Islands in the 1590s. England, Portugal, Spain, France, and the Netherlands all had extensive global commercial activities, and subjects of varied wealth and status—including many slaves—circulated among these holdings. Captain John Smith was a mercenary in Europe and a slave in the Ottoman Empire before he turned up in Virginia, and he remained only briefly in Jamestown before returning to England. Another Virginia governor, Thomas Dale, was also a soldier in Europe before he spent a few short years in Virginia. After that, the East India Company hired him for his military prowess, and he died serving in the Indian Ocean. Political events lured home others. England's civil wars, which erupted in the 1640s and 1650s, encouraged some to leave England but drew others back. Puritans especially reacted, feeling it necessary to take part in remaking England in accordance with God's plan. As many as 15 percent of English New Englanders may have returned to England during this period. In sum, it is important to keep in mind that many, perhaps most, of those who traveled across the Atlantic never intended a permanent stay, even if that is what they ended up doing.

With some important exceptions, colonial populations were not closely related to the number of a country's migrants, largely because mortality rates were so high. The Dutch, for example, settled regions with adverse disease environments, making it necessary to replace constantly the European population with gullible or desperate newcomers. Such was life in early Suriname and Curaçao. The historians Peter Emmer and Wim Klooster estimate that in any given year, 4,000–5,000 Europeans resided in Dutch settlements in the western Atlantic, with perhaps 600 Europeans living permanently in Dutch factories in Africa. In order to replace the annual losses from mortality, these settlements required 2,400 newcomers each year. The Dutch tendency to occupy high-mortality locations rendered the Atlantic world an effective drain on the Dutch population, not, as was ultimately true for other nations, a source of population growth. The majority of seventeenth-century English migrants also went to places where they died quickly: through the century, Maryland and Virginia greeted newcomers with a 40 percent chance of death in the first year of arrival; gravediggers in Barbados buried one-third of the island's inhabitants after a 1647 yellow fever epidemic, which ushered into the Caribbean a new, deadly age of mosquito-born illnesses. Even in the more bug-free highlands of Mexico and the Andes, colonial inhabitants endured dysentery from poor sanitation and a host of other ills. In North America, only the cooler regions north of the Chesapeake—New France, New England, the mid-Atlantic—were healthy enough that northern Europeans there improved on European life expectancies and produced large families and population growth.

Governments regulated migration to the extent they could. If states perceived population loss as a threat to national power, then overseas migration suffered. In the early seventeenth century, a growing English population led promoters to propose colonies as solutions to overpopulation, underemployment, and poverty. But in the 1770s, British landlords who worried about losing their rent-paying tenants pressed the government to restrict migration. Despite its enormous population compared to other European kingdoms, France's government was hesitant to encourage large-scale overseas migration. With such contradictory pressures operating, some states relied on foreigners to settle specific territories. The Spanish, who generally restricted foreign emigration, leased the conquest and settlement of backcountry Venezuela and northern New Granada to German banking families in Augsburg. The descendants of Nicolás de Federmann and other German conquistadors were soon absorbed into the local elite. Despite restrictions, Italian, Portuguese, Greek, Flemish, and even Irish settlers found their way to the Spanish Indies; colonial officials left most of them alone as long as they proved themselves good Catholics and married locally. Much later, the English recruited European Protestants to settle American lands (including the 100,000 German-speaking migrants noted in Table 5.2, while the Dutch relied on a range of settlers, and the Swedes, in their experiment with colonization in New Sweden (in present-day Delaware), relied on Dutch and other nationals. The government of chronically underpopulated Portugal did little to sponsor migration of any kind, and in fact tried to slow it following the discovery of gold in Brazil just before 1700. Thus a range of factors shaped the flow of migrants overseas, including perceptions of population growth or decline and state attitudes toward population as a source of national power.

Settlements

European migrants established five categories of settlements around the Atlantic world: urban centers (including mining towns), trading posts, missionary villages (more or less), plantations (centered on agricultural export), and dispersed, family-centered productive units. The last encompassed economic activities ranging from subsistence and commercial farming to fishing to iron smelting to the export of naval stores—in other words, extractive economies requiring intensive use of available natural resources. (The term *plantation* can be confusing, since the English referred to all their settlements in this period as plantations. They considered all of Ulster, Munster, and New England *plantations*, and the men who led them as *planters*.) Indigenous economies and environmental constraints dictated all settlement types. Where Europeans sought commodities they could acquire without profound disruption of local societies, where indigenous people were militarily powerful, or where disease environments hindered European settlement, the trading-post model prevailed. Where warfare or disease more easily displaced indigenous people, and where arable land promised good farming (or mineral deposits beckoned), more-invasive settlement types emerged. In fringe regions, mixed-type settlements appeared, as happened with the interdependent missions and presidios, or military outposts, of northern New Spain and the River Plate district.

The Dutch and French followed the trading-post model in North America. With the French to the north, along the St. Lawrence River, the Dutch established their own posts along the Hudson, with Fort Orange/Beverwijck (modern Albany) the main settlement for trading furs. The French had sided with an Algonquian-speaking alliance, initially shutting out the Iroquois to trade goods. When the Dutch showed up in Fort Orange, the Iroquois found in them their own access to goods. Once both the Iroquois Confederacy and their traditional Algonquian enemies acquired guns, indigenous wars became more deadly. As chiefs sought revenge for their dead, these conflicts had longer-lasting, sometimes devastating repercussions. But as long as Europeans sought deerskins and beaver pelts, they tried to disrupt indigenous practices as little as possible, so as not to prevent or discourage the Indians from hunting. But whatever the Europeans' intentions, trade was always disruptive in this world, one in which disease and new material goods complicated cultural resilience and response.

In spite of their seemingly simple, profit-making aims, those who ran trading posts often became entangled in regional politics. Diplomatic and commercial relations in nearly all early modern trading posts, in Africa and the Americas, were more complex than any short narrative can portray. Indigenous groups identified commercial or military opportunities in European alliances. Such was the case in southern New England, where English and Dutch traded with different tribes. From their location between the two European outposts, the Pequots became principal trading partners of the Dutch, as the English allied with Narragansets and Mohegans. As conflict increased, the Pequots in 1637 constructed a fortified, pallisaded village, only to have 500 Indians and 80 allied English warriors set it on fire. As the blaze spread, English attackers cut down anybody who fled, violating the Narragansett stipulation that no harm should come to noncombatants. "Mach it, Mach it" (enough, enough), shouted one Narraganset, but to no avail. By afternoon, the invaders killed hundreds of Pequots and enslaved the survivors; English casualties numbered two dead and twenty-seven wounded, leaving the English free to cultivate the land made available by Pequot annihilation.

Of course, Atlantic settlements changed over time. A mere trading post could become a permanent settlement; a rich mining town might be abandoned once its deposits played out. In North America, New Netherland evolved from a fur-trading post into a self-sufficient colony that exported foodstuffs to the Caribbean. Available resources and the interplay between European and indigenous goals determined the direction settlements took. The best example of this transition is the Dutch colony in southern Africa. The colony the Dutch East India Company established at the southern tip of Africa in 1652 was as different from other European Atlantic settlements as it was removed in distance from its mother country. In its Dutch population, it was an anomaly among Dutch settlements as well. Seventeenth-century southern Africa offered no commodities of sufficient value to persuade many migrants to make the voyage from Europe. From a European perspective, the Cape of Good Hope had one lone advantage: it was situated halfway to East Asia's Spice Islands. The spice trade, topped up with such other Asian commodities as silk, cotton cloth, tea, porcelain, opium, coffee, carpets, and pearls, commanded Portuguese attention from the time of da Gama's validation of the cape route into the Indian Ocean in the late 1490s. When, after a century, Portugal's lack of manpower and dwindling wealth left its Afro-Asian maritime empire vulnerable, merchant-shippers from the Dutch Republic readily moved in. Within half a century of receiving its charter in 1602, the Dutch East India Company was working out of a headquarters in Batavia, on the island of Java, employing 48,000 sailors to sail 6,000 ships that regularly plied the Asian trade. Every year by 1650, grand fleets of some of the largest ships that ever had sailed from European ports were rounding southern Africa, coming and going between the Netherlands and the East Indies.

The six-month voyage between Dutch and Indonesian ports-of-call took its toll on crews. When fresh supplies and potable water ran low, sailors suffered from maladies that rendered them useless for their duties long before the voyage ended. The principal threat was from scurvy, a generalized breakdown of body tissue caused by nutritional deficiencies, particularly a lack of Vitamin C. Early symptoms include malaise, joint pain, and shortness of breath. Gradually, scurvy victims' teeth loosen, making it difficult to eat; they suffer from internal hemorrhages; their hair cannot grow and in its place lesions appear. Jaundice and convulsions come next. Left untreated, scurvy is fatal. Given this horror, it is no surprise to learn of Dutch relief when survivors of early-seventeenth-century shipwrecks near the Cape of Good Hope reported finding indigenous people willing to exchange fresh meat, fruit, and vegetables. Company directors responded by establishing an outpost near the cape to serve as a refreshment station for its ships sailing to and from the East Indies. Jan van Riebeeck was the company man placed in charge. In 1652, he directed his ship into Table Bay, twenty-five miles up the Atlantic coast from the cape, and went about a business he described to company directors in self-aggrandizing terms:

> On a parched, poor soil without a dwelling place, and only some light material to build a fort, work had to be started with about ninety persons just from a sea voyage, and suffering from scurvy. They were as raw as the whole world had ever seen. I had to work myself as engineer, digger, gardener, farmer, carpenter, mason, smith, etc., so that after ten months the Company's return fleet, which remained between six and seven weeks, was abundantly supplied with refreshments, including cattle obtained from the natives.

Of course, these "natives" of southwestern Africa had no way of knowing that the sharp-nosed, light-skinned men offering iron, copper, and tobacco for their puniest cattle would end up destroying their pastoral way of life and turn their surviving descendants into a dependent, laboring class. So it went in these days of new and widening global contacts.

The company recognized quickly that, rather than keep large numbers of employees on its payroll, it would be better from a business standpoint to release settlers from employment and allow them to acquire land, produce what the company needed (fruits, vegetables, grains, and cattle), and sell these commodities to the company at low, fixed prices. To this end, van Riebeeck released nine "free burghers" from their contracts and established them on twenty-acre parcels in 1657, a process the company continued. Over the decades to come, the East India Company transported more Dutch and some German and French settlers—the latter Huguenots fleeing after Louis XIV's revocation of the Edict of Nantes—to the fledgling settlement. The settler population of the Cape Colony in 1700 numbered 1,200 men, women, and children, nearly all of whom by this time were independent of the company.

These settlers, who identified themselves as "Christians" or "Europeans" to differentiate themselves from all others in their surroundings, soon aspired to do more than farm for the benefit of the company. Some remained close to the original community, known as Cape Town, working at skilled trades or as shopkeepers to service the ships and crews that put in at Table Bay. A greater number of settlers opted to focus on the land stretching north and east from the cape, concentrating primarily on stock raising, an enterprise that required tracts of pastureland far beyond anything the company had envisioned. Eventually, "Christian" families came to consider it the birthright of all good sons, upon reaching manhood, to receive their own farmstead of some 6,000 acres, an area frequently determined by walking a horse from a fixed point for one-half hour in each of the four points of the compass. In this fashion, over the generations, the European population of southern Africa moved into and occupied land extending several hundred miles away from Cape Town. The more the population grew and moved, the more they came into their new identity: as *trekboers*—Dutch for migrating farmers. A favorable disease environment permitted population growth: southern Africa was one of the few parts of the continent in which European settlement was not thwarted by deadly pathogens.

Of course, the company, settlers, and everyone else knew that the land they were moving into was occupied. It had long been the home, as well as the pasturage for the cattle and sheep, of an indigenous, seminomadic, pastoralist people, the Khoikhoi. (The early Portuguese, in a way of mocking Khoikhoi speech, which included labial and velar "clicks," gave them the name "Hottentots.") Khoikhoi at the cape did not object to the presence of the earliest settlers, who brought useful metal objects and body decorations and seemed happy to exchange them for mediocre cattle, but the honeymoon period of this relationship did not last long. Once free burghers began occupying Khoikhoi land, the latter resisted. The first of a quarter-century of battles commenced in 1659. The Khoikhoi had occasional successes in these engagements, but always, in time, the united settlers triumphed because of their superior arms and their ability to exploit divisions among the Khoikhoi, who lived in relatively small and often competitive groups.

That the trekboers' indigenous enemies—who also included the still less-politically stratified or organized hunting-and-gathering people known to the Portuguese as "Bushmen" and to the Khoikhoi as San—were all different in physical type and darker in complexion than the European settlers, and that the trekboer victories came at a predictable and steady pace, made it easy for the newcomers to develop assumptions of racial superiority. This fit nicely into the design of their Calvinism, which, as mentioned, considered some individuals preordained by God as worthy of salvation and others damned from the start to perdition. In the narrow vision of the light-skinned intruders, *they* obviously were God's elect, and He was on their side as they took possession of what seemed to be the promised land from their dark, different, heathen enemies. It is no surprise that these descendants of Dutch farmers developed an affinity for the Old Testament and an imagined identity with Abraham, Isaac, and other great Hebrews of old.

When the settlers won victories over the Khoikhoi, they seized their cattle and treated captives with a brutality often reserved for lower animals. On the bad end of such treatment, Khoikhoi watched their society disintegrate with startling speed. Many saw few options besides turning themselves over in service to the trekboers as herders of cattle and sheep. When a homeward-bound Dutch ship brought smallpox to the Cape Colony in 1713, the disease swept through the immunity-impaired Khoikhoi population and all but destroyed what remained of it. Those few who survived faced a future that appeared similar to that of the slaves in their midst, persons who tended cattle, hewed wood, and drew water for the white population of the colony.

The slaves had been another introduction of the Dutch East India Company. When the Cape Colony was founded, the Dutch were the most competitive slave traders in the Atlantic. The Dutch colonists who arrived at Table Bay envisioned a society like those surrounding other company settlements, particularly in East Asia, where slaves performed most manual tasks. So it was at the request of the settlers (though without opposition from its directors) that the company, in 1658, unloaded West African slaves, to be followed over the years by more enslaved people from as far away as India and Indonesia, and as close as Madagascar and Mozambique. By 1700 the colony had more slaves than settlers. The company itself owned and kept slaves in Cape Town, where they performed public works. Cape Town burghers also owned slaves, using some as domestics and allowing others to become skilled artisans, but it was out on the ranches, extending farther east by the year, where slaves performed the essential work of the pastoral economy. Their owners assumed positions of manager, patriarch, and master—literally—of all they surveyed.

What thus had evolved at the southwestern tip of Africa was a slave- and race-based society, but one unlike its counterparts along the western edge of the Atlantic. Extending north from Brazil, through the Caribbean islands, and into the North American mainland there emerged a vastly larger slave-based plantation economy in which, by the turn of the eighteenth century, the laborers, at the lowest rung of all economic and social ladders, were almost exclusively Africans or persons of African descent. At the same time, on the eastern shores of the ocean and near its southern extreme, was the Cape Colony, which featured no plantations, no exports, no grand concentration of unfree laborers on any single plot of land, and a slave population as diverse as any on the globe. Yet in spite of the remarkable ethnic, linguistic, and religious diversity of the Cape Colony, the relatively small portion of its population that held power was drawing lines around race as sharp as any that would come to exist in the Americas.

Plantations

In the western Atlantic, the English were the first to establish plantation colonies that relied almost exclusively on European labor. The rapid growth and diffusion of this plantation model helps explain why so many people migrated to British colonies, particularly in the seventeenth century. Ironically, the English did not initially travel overseas with a commitment to plantation agriculture. In North America, they sought to trade, to co-opt local indigenous headmen as allies against competitors, and to find gold. Their failure at these ventures in most places led to the formation of more or less independent agricultural settlements, often at odds with indigenous people. The mainland colony of Virginia offers a good case study of this shift in interest.

The Virginia Company was a privately financed joint-stock corporation, as were all English overseas ventures. Nonetheless, King James I (r. 1603–25), son of Mary, Queen of Scots, and Henry Stuart, Lord Darnley, granted the charter permitting the attempted settlement on American lands and remained an interested party. As with companies formed in the previous century, the London bourgeoisie—merchants, bankers, adventurers—held the majority of shares, but stock was cheap enough to allow artisans and shopkeepers to purchase a share or two. Thomas Hobbes, then a nineteen-year-old Oxford tutor to the future Earl of Devonshire, was a shareholder, as was the playwright William Shakespeare. Although the directors of the Company reported to a Royal Council on Trade, Virginia was, like all trading companies of the time, essentially a private, capitalist venture subject to little governmental oversight. The English established their settlement on a peninsula they called Jamestown Island, located some fifty miles from the coast and thus safely distant from the Spanish ships they feared.

Ideas for the settlement lay in the culture of the trading post. Instructions for its leaders enjoined them to seek mines, particularly gold mines, and a water route to the South Seas, or Pacific Ocean. Settlement leaders placed young boys with Indian tribes to learn local languages and become interpreters. There was even a marriage alliance between the Englishman John Rolfe and the daughter of the most powerful leader in the region, Powhatan, which typified the way political bonds were created throughout the early modern Atlantic world. But when the settlers failed to uncover rich mineral resources, the colony floundered. The investors had hoped, secondarily, that the settlers might make their wealth through tribute exacted from Indian subjects, in imitation of the Spanish, but that goal, too, proved unrealistic. In despera-

Who was Pocahontas?

The child Pocahontas remains an enduring icon of American popular culture. Like Squanto, another famous Indian of the period, she is the protagonist of a Hollywood feature film. But a gap exists between public perception and what little historians know about Pocahontas. John Smith, the first European to describe her, met her when she was ten years old and was so struck by her appearance, "wit, and spirit," that he thought none equaled her. Her father, Powhatan, was the most powerful leader in the Chesapeake. To the English, whose gender norms and cultural assumptions placed little value on girls, Pocahontas seemed like a "tomboy," but her outgoing demeanor, initiative, and importance spoke of the high regard her own culture held for her. Pocahontas allegedly rescued Smith from execution, but there is no evidence of this, aside from Smith's description of it, not in his first accounts but later, after Pocahontas traveled to England. It seems likely that Smith hoped to benefit from the attention she received during her visit. In 1610, the chronicler William Strachey reported, Pocahontas married a Powhatan man, but the marriage was short-lived. In 1613, when she was sixteen, the English kidnapped and held her for several months, during which she converted to Christianity and started to wear the formal and confining clothes of an Englishwoman. Isolated from her family in these months, she also met—and, reports suggest, fell in love with—the Englishman and widower John Rolfe, who was twenty-eight. The couple married in Jamestown in 1614 in a ceremony attended by two brothers and an uncle, but not her father. Her marriage, dubbed the "Peace of Pocahontas," ended the state of warfare between the English and Powhatan. (Just as European and African

Pocahontas, after 1616 engraving by Simon van de Passe. Print Collection, Miriam A. & Ira D. Wallach Division of Art, Prints, and Photographs, The New York Public Library, Astor, Lenox and Tilden Foundations.

monarchs married for diplomatic purposes, Powhatan took numerous wives; after bearing children, wife and child returned to their village, so that he might expand his political influence there.) With Rolfe, Pocahontas (now Rebecca) traveled to England in 1616, bringing along her son, Thomas. In England, Pocahontas posed for the famous portrait that is our only image of her. Soon thereafter, she fell ill, too sick to return with the fleet to Virginia in the spring of 1617. She died in England, far from her Chesapeake home.

tion, the colonists turned to nearby Algonquians for food, but even then disease from Jamestown's stagnant water supply had begun to fell settlers. By the fall of 1609, the arrival of more immigrants brought the colony's population to nearly 350, but only 60 cadaverous settlers survived that harsh winter. Gentlemen boiled their shirt ruffles to extract the starch for porridge, while the rest of the inhabitants were reduced to eating acorns and roots. One ravenous Englishman killed his pregnant wife, chopped her into pieces, and salted her for food. Less murderous men dug up corpses and cooked them into a stew "with roots and herbs."

Two things, nevertheless, helped this colony hang on where others had failed: embrace of the drug trade, in this case tobacco cultivation for export, and regular infusions of personnel. Rolfe—whose wife Rebecca was previously known as Matoaka or Pocahontas—discovered that tobacco transplanted to Virginia from the Orinoco River basin in South America grew well in the area and found a ready market in England. King James denounced the product as a "noxious weed," although he was not above trying to turn a tidy profit for the crown by taxing its importation. Within three years of Rolfe's first cargo, Virginia planters shipped 50,000 pounds of tobacco to English wharves. For shareholders, who at last saw a return on their investment, this highly addictive and virtually uncontrolled substance was the gold their employees had never found. The cultivation of tobacco soon exhausted the soil, however, driving plantations inland along Virginia's waterways and creating an almost insatiable demand for more land—and more labor. Tobacco production in this period was highly labor intensive: seedlings needed to be tended with care, and workers had to inspect plants every day to remove parasites.

Trading posts, while disruptive, intruded only marginally on indigenous people's lands and lifeways; plantations caused upheaval. As planters moved farther up the newly christened James River, it became clear to the Powhatans that the settlers posed a danger to their control of the Chesapeake. When Pocahontas went to England in 1616, she was accompanied by an entourage of Powhatan Indians, including Uttamatomakin, who was there at Powhatan's request to learn more about the English. Uttamatomakin proved invaluable in shaping Indian diplomacy. He returned home after his voyage and spoke against the English: he was particularly repelled by the religious intolerance of the English and their ideas about the exclusive worship of a single deity. There is a story—apocryphal, it seems, and exactly the kind of condescending anecdote that the English liked to invent about Indians—that Uttamatomakin tried to count the English he encountered, in order to deliver an accurate reckoning to Powhatan. The story tells us that he tried to notch a stick for each person he met, but that he quickly gave up at the vast numbers. The larger point—Powhatan's desire for accurate information about the English— nonetheless remains important. The report of such a populous kingdom, capable of replenishing any diminution of the colony's population through disease, would have been vital information that helped guide Indian strategies. Uttamatomakin's news confirmed a fear the Powhatans had from the very earliest appearance of the English: how many were there? John Smith's *Map of Virginia*, first published in 1612, included an Indian sentence translated into English that conveyed this concern: "In how many daies will there come hether any more English ships?"

The 1622 attack on the scattered English settlement and some 1,000 settlers launched by Opechancanough (Powhatan's successor) permanently transformed Indian and English relations, clarifying and solidifying growing cultural divergences. One-third of the colonists were killed. The military logic of the attack—its selective and partial nature, in which Opechancanough left two-thirds of the colonists alive when he probably could have killed them all—was governed by indigenous strategies and goals. But the great success of the attack, and perhaps some of the instigation for it, derived also from the imperative for cultural understanding in this transformed world, more

What's In a Name?

When they claimed the right of conquerors and renamed the places they saw, Europeans evoked the Christian world's first man, Adam, who named the plants, birds, and animals in the Garden of Eden. The new names represented political and cultural choices and often reflected the power dynamics of conquest: they tended to echo places from home or broadcast the claim of a first-time European observer. In Connecticut, the English victors over the Pequot Indians changed the town of Pequot to New London and the Pequot River to the Thames. The Spanish christened as Hispaniola the island the Taíno called Haiti. (In 1804, former slaves reclaimed the original name for their new republic on the western part of the island.) The Aztec Empire became the viceroyalty of New Spain; the Aztec capital of Tenochtitlán was renamed Mexico City. Sweden's colonial settlement was New Sweden; the Dutch had New Amsterdam (twice) and New Netherland; the Scots tried Nova Scotia; and French territory in the Americas was New France. There were also New England and New Britain, New Orleans and New York, New Jersey and New Hampshire. Monarchs received their due in Virginia (named for the virgin queen, Elizabeth I), Williamsburg and Willemstadt, Jamestown and Charles Town, Maryland and Louisiana. Catholics used names of saints in Santo Domingo and San Salvador. Yet, for whatever reason, indigenous names endured in Cuzco, Oaxaca, and Massachusetts.

Redraft of the "Castello Plan, New Amsterdam, 1660," drawn by John Wolcott Adams, 1916. Collection of the New York Historical Society, call number NS4 M32.3.15, negative number 57812.

urgent, perhaps, for Powhatans than for the English. Despite English fears of Indians, and a commensurate desire to separate themselves from them, Indians lived among the English on their plantations. The Indians had become dependent on convenient English goods and were forced to conform to English methods of exchange in order to get them. Some Indians worked for the English, learning English in the process, in order to be able to procure desired European trade goods. Proximity and familiarity facilitated the ferocity of the Powhatan attack.

But the attack also liberated the English from feigning friendship with the Powhatan. To be sure, it posed a public relations problem for the Virginia Company, but imaginative interpreters explained the advantages of the attack. One writer proclaimed in 1622 that the massacre would actually end up being good for the plantation because now the English were "set at liberty [presumably to kill all Indian groups who stood in the way of their commercial development] by the treacherous violence of the Sauvages." The Spanish precedent came to the fore: drive the Indians on their enemies, the author urged, as the Spanish had exploited fights among Indians. He credited these internal divisions for giving the Spanish two kingdoms, those of Peru and Mexico, and hoped the English would find similar success.

The number of Indians shrank as the vengeful English burned their fields and destroyed their crops. Long before Opechancanough's capture and murder in 1645, Powhatan power had been crushed. Under the peace agreement, land north of the York River was set aside for the survivors, making it the first Indian reservation in English North America. As a reminder of who had won the war, as well as why it had been fought, the English kept native prisoners as slaves for their fields. But in these and later years, indentured English men always outnumbered the Indian slaves who toiled beside them. Only the constant infusion of new arrivals, made possible by economic hardship and population growth in England, enabled Virginia to survive.

This model of the plantation staffed by European laborers to produce a cash crop for transatlantic shipment was soon carried to other English settlements in the Atlantic basin. Barbados, St. Kitts, and Jamaica, in the Caribbean and New England, Chesapeake, and the Low Country on the Atlantic coast of the North American mainland: by the end of the seventeenth century, the English had turned all of these regions into places of intense cultivation by European planters, midsize farmers, and forced laborers. If not everyone embraced plantation production—inhabitants of a few coastal communities sought profits from the sea—all were committed to intensive and exhaustive use of the land, a pattern that displaced indigenous people whose land-use patterns the English derided as wasteful. European arguments about land use derived from what they referred to as natural law: English promoters argued that land belonged to those who transformed it in a way that produced harvests, profits, or rents. If the people who occupied a territory did not exploit its full generative potential, or, as the minister and poet John Donne put it, "so as the Land may bring forth her increase for the use of men," they did not deserve to hold it. Such arguments were crucial in legitimating the transition from a small trading post to a colony that required vast amounts of land.

The Spanish and Portuguese had been developing Atlantic plantations for more than a century before the English began such enterprises. It was the profitability of the Iberian model that inspired London (and, about the same time, Amsterdam) stockholders. The Iberians' most lucrative plantations in the era of Jamestown were dedicated to the production of sugar and tobacco. The developers of northeastern Brazil and islands and mainland patches around the Caribbean had groped through pragmatic labor and land-holding structures that resembled those the English followed later. What differed most was the massive English, and later French and Dutch, use of indentured European workers instead of enslaved or otherwise bound Native Americans as a bridge to African slavery.

Inspired by success in Virginia, the English spread the European-staffed plantation model to the Caribbean. Because of the rapid spread of the smoking habit in Europe, early English investors in the Caribbean focused on to-bacco. Captain Thomas Warner, who established the colony of St. Kitts in 1624, first scoured the Amazon River basin in search of suitable land for planting. Dissatisfied with the terrain north of the river and displeased with the Portuguese settlements south of the river's mouth, Warner returned to England by way of the Caribbean. After landing on the Leeward Islands, Warner pronounced St. Kitts "a very convenient place for the planting of tobaccoes, which was ever a rich commodetie." In 1627, English adventurers founded a second island colony on Barbados. From the point of view of London merchants, Barbados was a smarter proposition than St. Kitts, as it lacked a native population to be eradicated and was remote enough from the Spanish Caribbean not to excite the anger of Madrid.

All of this changed by the 1640s, as Barbadian planters introduced sugar cane into their fields. Inspired by the vast sums that cane produced in Brazil, English planters began, as one investor put it, "a great change on this island of late from the worse to the better, praised be God." Soon the island's great planters found themselves the owners of estates worth four times the largest Chesapeake tobacco plantation, and for decades Barbados remained the most populous and prosperous of England's Atlantic colonies. The wealth sugar generated was soon invested in a more permanent and reliable labor force: African slaves. The English thus joined what to that point had been an Iberian Atlantic triangle.

The shift to sugar shoved more than small farmers off the island. By making the finite soil itself so valuable, the sugar industry effectively halted production of cereal crops and livestock. Barbados quickly went from being self-sufficient to an importer of foodstuffs. Virginia grew some of those commodities next to tobacco, but not in sufficient amounts to feed the islands' growing African population. Luck again was with English investors, for by the 1640s, as many as 20,000 Calvinists had relocated to New England. These "Puritans" had fled Stuart England to avoid its "multitude of irreligious, lascivious and popish affected persons," and they sold their grains, fish, and lumber to help prop up the fledgling slave society in Barbados. As Massachusetts governor John Winthrop approvingly noted in 1647, the English Caribbean "had rather buy food at very dear rates than produce it by labor, so infinite is the profit of sugar works."

Family Settlement and Religious Migrations

English activity in New England in the 1630s points to yet another model of European settlement: the transatlantic family enterprise. This model existed mostly in places poorly suited to export-commodity production, yet suitable for a range of agricultural activities and livestock raising. Both plantations and family farms profoundly disrupted indigenous economies, and in all regions of such settlements, Europeans benefited from the diseases so destructive of indigenous life. In the wake of a 1633–34 smallpox epidemic in southern New England, the region's Indians suffered catastrophic losses. Governor Winthrop struggled to assist Indian communities devastated by smallpox, but, nonetheless, took such deaths in stride, interpreting the "emptying" of the land as God's hand in support of English settlement.

Although most northern European transatlantic migrants experienced childhood deprivation, indenture, and premature death, focus on this pattern should not obscure the important opportunities that migration offered, particularly religious freedom. Without exception, profit-seeking investors organized all colonial ventures, but some of these had strong religious sensibilities and sought like-minded people to settle and generate profits from their Atlantic holdings. Lord Baltimore, who envisioned Maryland as a place where beleaguered English Catholics might be able to worship freely, made it possible for such a man as the urbane Charles Egerton (who had converted to Catholicism for the woman he loved) to flourish in a new setting after being denied offices and status in England. The Quaker William Penn, tired of the discrimination and oppression his radical sect endured in England because of its egalitarian, antinomian, and pacifist sensibilities, hoped that his colony of Pennsylvania would offer oppressed Protestants from all over Europe a haven in which to enjoy liberty of conscience. Through multilingual recruitment, Penn gathered Mennonites, Schwenkfelders, Church of the Brethren, Huguenots, Lutherans, Reformed, Quakers, and a smattering of small sectarian movements into his wide embrace. People of all these sects and others found their way to America to seize the opportunity to pursue their faith. Those who wished could distance themselves from neighbors, pursuing, if they desired, a communal or celibate life to accommodate their consciences.

These refugees were often parts of larger diasporas, or at least scatterings of human populations. In 1685, the French government revoked the Edict of Nantes, which had guaranteed Protestants the right to worship freely. The revocation of the Edict instantly produced more than 100,000 Huguenot refugees. Just as a small group joined the Dutch in southern Africa, a few thousand others made their way to the Americas. So did German-speaking migrants from the Holy Roman Empire, though they comprised only 10 percent of the larger German diaspora, most of whose members journeyed east, into central Europe and Russia.

Jews also moved west into the Atlantic as part of broader migrations into the Mediterranean, north and coastal West Africa, and Europe after the 1492 expulsions from the Iberian Peninsula. Some "New Christians" (Jews forced to convert but sometimes continuing to practice Judaism in secret) found their way to Spanish America, resulting in the establishment of Inquisition tribunals in Lima (1570), Mexico City (1571), and Cartagena de Indias (1610) to monitor beliefs and punish alleged heretics. The less-consistent Portuguese Inquisition never established a permanent tribunal in Brazil. Many Jews who still wished to practice their faith found a short-lived haven in Dutch Brazil, and they established the first synagogue in the western Atlantic in Recife. Portuguese takeover of that area prompted another diaspora, this time to old and New Amsterdam, Dutch Guyana, or Suriname, and a few British colonies—the cities of Kingston, Savannah, Charleston, and Newport all had Jewish populations. Most Jewish migrants from Brazil made their way to Curaçao, where they comprised one-third of the island's white population.

Holy Women

European gender roles primarily confined women to the domestic sphere and limited their legal identity and autonomy. Most European women who ventured to the Americas did so in the context of family migrations or as indentured servants under the authority of a master. Even the unpredictability of new overseas settlements offered only limited opportunities for women who might wish to challenge gender norms. An important exception to this pattern was religious women. Along with the thousands of Catholic men who ventured to the Americas and Africa to convert people to Christianity were hundreds of women similarly bent on achieving their own salvation through missionary work. The first such women reached Canada in 1639. They created institutions including hospitals (where they could care for the Americans ravaged by unfamiliar diseases in successive epidemics, saving the souls of their patients while tending to their bodies) and convents that provided education to indigenous women and children. One such migrant was an Ursuline nun, Marie Guyart de l'Incarnation, a widow who left her son in France to establish a convent in Quebec. She was joined there by other French women, and together they arranged to have religious edifices erected in Quebec and Montreal, all while pursuing their own religious vocations, talking with God, having visions, and hoping to achieve the sainthood of the models they emulated. Those women who sought the "martyrdom" of male counterparts (particularly the Jesuits who were the vanguard of Catholic missionary efforts in New France) were thwarted by the inability of women to evangelize among indigenous people in the region and to risk their lives in the process, but they nonetheless pursued lives of physical hardship, flagellating themselves and enduring pain and discomfort with the stoicism of martyrs (of whom they had only read) or of the Native Americans around them, whose courage in the face of pain was famous and much admired and who offered real, tangible examples of the legendary bravery of the saints.

A romantic depiction of the arrival of the Ursulines and the Sisters of Charity in New France, painted by Sister Marie-de-Jésus in 1928. In 1639, Marie de l'Incarnation left the Ursulines of Tours in order to found an Ursuline order in New France. The convent that she established was an integral part of expanding French territory, educating young girls, and anchoring the nascent community around their teachings. © Musée des Ursulines de Québec. Photo: François Lachapelle, 1980.PMA:J99.1626.

These religious migrants tended to move in family groups, with one notable exception: priests and nuns who traveled to the Americas and some regions of Africa to minister to Catholic settlers and engage in missionary enterprises. The cultural impact of these missionary men and women was out of proportion to their numbers. At their best, they served as fearless advocates for indigenous people, even if their efforts signaled disdain for the practices they sought to replace with Christian beliefs. Like the tireless Las Casas, they lobbied kings and bureaucrats for better treatment for their charges, and, hoping to protect them from the worst abuses of the colonial system, sought to provide havens for them through their missions. Little did they realize that gathering Indians into missions would facilitate the spread of disease.

Missions were a feature of nearly every European colonial enterprise at one time or another, but nowhere were they more developed, and historically more consequential, than in Spanish America. Priests of several religious orders made their way across the Atlantic from the time of Columbus forward, and most of the orders established monasteries and schools in the fast-growing colonial capitals. From these bases, which thrived on a mix of private and royal support, the Franciscans, Dominicans, Jesuits, and others sent European and locally born priests into both nearby Indian villages and distant conquest frontiers; a few administered sacraments to newly arrived African slaves, and some even ventured into maroon (runaway) communities. In many cases, priests advanced well beyond the limits of Spanish political control in hopes of converting what they regarded as undefiled native peoples. Some millenarian priests, like the Dominican Las Casas, envisioned themselves as creators and guardians of Eden-like American utopias. Many such men were killed as a result of misunderstandings and abuses, but these "martyrs of the True Faith," as their brethren in Lima, Mexico City, Bogotá, and elsewhere memorialized them, only served to inspire others. By the turn of the eighteenth century, hundreds of Catholic missions dotted the frontiers of Spanish America, from the deserts of Arizona to the jungles of Amazonia.

Mission life, while hardly utopian by modern standards, was not without some attractions for native people. The priests offered desirable trade goods from time to time and, more important, could help protect vulnerable groups against a wide range of enemies, including hostile tribes and secular Spaniards. The extent to which Catholic conversion actually succeeded in terms of what the priests intended remains a subject of considerable debate, but virtually everywhere the erosion of native belief structures ran deep. All missions punished native shamanic and divining practices, for example, and some devalued native languages as well as chiefly customs like polygyny. The missionaries did not let up, and in fact advanced and expanded through most of the eighteenth century, transforming life for more and more nonsedentary and semisedentary people. The expulsion of the Jesuit order from Spanish America in 1767 deeply affected the vast mission system of Greater Paraguay, but in other areas, such as northern Mexico, the American Southwest, and Alta and Baja California, other missionary orders such as the Franciscans expanded to fill the void.

Parts of the Americas (those in Dutch and British control) clearly offered people of conscience opportunities for free worship, yet, oddly, the story of religious freedom has been grossly distorted in the history of the United States by those who give credit for the nation's allegedly immaculate birth to the most intolerant population of all. One of the these populations held up as the seed of American exceptionalism was the tiny group of migrants later known as Pilgrims. These dourly dressed and pious migrants were English Calvinists and separatists who had fled the unacceptable practices (in their eyes) of the Church of England to settle in Leiden, in the Netherlands. When they left Leiden, they abandoned a place where they had complete religious freedom to move to one where they could sharply curtail any such liberty. In Leiden, the separatists' children grew up in a climate of religious openness. They learned Dutch and saw competing forms of worship, including variants of Protestantism and Judaism. Such religious toleration, in part born of Spanish oppression, was not restricted to the Netherlands proper, but existed in many Dutch settlements overseas. But for these pious English refugees, such freedom of choice was intolerable and likely to infect their children. So off they sailed to a place where theirs would be the only established faith—with no alternatives. Self-exile was a means of expressing religious freedom, but settled life in the colonies would be otherwise: believers could practice their faith and none other; nonbelievers were forced away, excommunicated, and banished if they followed their own interpretation of the Bible. The Puritans in Massachusetts in the 1650s banished some dissidents and executed others, most notably Quakers. More like Iberian Catholicism in the heyday of the Inquisition, such religious intolerance could hardly compare with the liberty offered by the Dutch or that available in other English settlements.

English family migrations and the larger migration of young laborers caused the rapid occupation and exploitation of the North American mainland and the Caribbean islands. By the end of the seventeenth century, the English, French, and Spanish had claimed the eastern seaboard and substantial portions of interior North America. The English were strongest in the northeast and mid-Atlantic, the Spanish through the southern portion of the continent, and the French snaked their way along the Mississippi River and into holdings in the Great Lakes and St. Lawrence. Europeans similarly divvied up the Caribbean islands: England claimed Bermuda and the Bahamas, Jamaica, Barbados, Antigua and Barbuda, and St. Kitts; France claimed Guadeloupe, Martinique, and western Hispaniola (Saint Domingue). The Spanish clung to Cuba, Puerto Rico, and eastern Hispaniola. That all but a handful of depopulated islands were already occupied and exploited by indigenous people did not deter the Europeans. In the first two centuries of their invasion in the Americas, Europeans answered their need for labor primarily by making slaves and serfs of Indians and indentured servants of poor and luckless Europeans. But the demographic collapse of indigenous populations, inadequate numbers of European laborers to meet growing production demands, and shifting views of race, environment, and culture turned European interest in labor to enslaved Africans. The forced migration of Africans—which we now refer to as the African Diaspora—across the Atlantic quickly dwarfed the much smaller flow of Europeans, bound and free.

Selected Readings

Altman, Ida, and James Horn, eds., *'To Make America': European Emigration in the Early Modern Period* (Berkeley: University of California Press, 1991).

Armitage, David, and Michael J. Braddick, eds., *The British Atlantic World, 1500–1800* (New York: Palgrave Macmillan, 2002).

Bailyn, Bernard, *The Peopling of British North America* (New York: Knopf, 1986).

Brooks, James F., *Captives and Cousins: Slavery, Kinship, and Community in the Southwest Borderlands* (Chapel Hill: University of North Carolina Press, 2002).

Calloway, Colin, *New Worlds for All: Indians, Europeans, and the Remaking of Early America* (Baltimore: The Johns Hopkins University Press, 1997).

Canny, Nicholas, ed., *Europeans on the Move: Studies on European Migration, 1500–1800* (Oxford: Oxford University Press, 1994).

Chiappelli, Fredi, ed., *First Images of the New World* (Berkeley: University of California Press, 1976).

Cook, Noble David, *Born to Die: Disease and New World Conquest, 1492–1650* (Cambridge, UK: Cambridge University Press, 1998).

Elphick, Richard, and Herman Giliomee, *The Shaping of South African Society, 1652-1840*, 2nd ed. (Middletown: Wesleyan University Press, 1989).

Gage, Thomas, *Travels in the New World* (Norman: University of Oklahoma Press, 1958).

Gallay, Alan, *The Indian Slave Trade: The Rise of the English Empire in the American South, 1670–1717* (New Haven: Yale University Press, 2002).

Games, Alison, *Migration and the Origins of the English Atlantic World* (Cambridge, MA: Harvard University Press, 1999).

Giliomee, Herman, *The Afrikaners* (Charlottesville: University Press of Virginia, 2003).

Hanke, Lewis, *The Spanish Struggle for Justice in the Conquest of the Americas* (Boston: Little, Brown, 1965).

Hemming, John, *Red Gold: The Conquest of the Brazilian Indians* (Cambridge, MA: Harvard University Press, 1978).

Klooster, Wim, and Alfred Padula, eds., *The Atlantic World: Essays on Slavery, Migration, and Imagination* (Upper Saddle River: Pearson Prentice-Hall, 2004).

Las Casas, Bartolomé de, *A Short Account of the Destruction of the Indies* (New York: Penguin, 1992).

Ligon, Richard, *A True and Exact History of the Island of Barbadoes* (London, 1673).

Lockhart, James, and Enrique Otte, eds., *Letters and People of the Spanish Indies, Sixteenth Century* (New York: Cambridge University Press, 1976).

McAlister, Lyle N., *Spain and Portugal in the New World, 1492–1700* (Minneapolis: University of Minnesota Press, 1984).

Meuwese, Mark, "A Comparative Study of Intercultural Mediators in Dutch Brazil and New Netherland, 1600–1664," Ph.D. Diss. (University of Notre Dame, 2004).

Moraley, William, *The Infortunate: The Voyage and Adventures of William Moraley, an Indentured Servant*, Susan E. Klepp and Billy G. Smith, eds. (University Park: Pennsylvania State University Press, 1992).

Rountree, Helen C., ed., *Powhatan Foreign Relations, 1500–1722* (Charlottesville: University Press of Virginia, 1993).

Schwaller, John Frederick, *Church and Clergy in Sixteenth Century Mexico* (Albuquerque: University of New Mexico Press, 1987).

Stern, Steve J., *Peru's Indian Peoples and the Challenge of Spanish Conquest: Huamanga to 1640* (Madison: University of Wisconsin Press, 1982).

Sweet, David G., and Gary B., Nash, eds., *Struggle and Survival in Colonial America* (Berkeley: University of California Press, 1981).

Townsend, Camilla, *Pocahontas and the Powhatan Dilemma* (New York: Hill and Wang, 2004).

Weber, David J., *The Spanish Frontier in North America* (New Haven: Yale University Press, 1992).

Bringing African captives to slave ships on the west coast of Africa, 1700s, hand-colored halftone. Copyright © North Wind/North Wind Picture Archives. SOCI3A-00173.

Chapter Six

The Transatlantic Slave Trade and Slavery in the Americas, 1580–1780

> [W]e took our leave from [the king]. And in exchange for
> the present we had offered, he gave us a Negro and an ox.
>
> François de Paris, aboard the French brig *Conquis*,
> in the Gambia River, May 2, 1682

The morning of January 19, 1975, found Al Haji Seku Momodou Darbo seated on the veranda of his house in Diabugu Tenda, one of the many wharftowns along the middle Gambia River, this one 210 miles up from where the river empties into the Atlantic Ocean just south of Cape Verde, Africa's westernmost extension. The large Darbo clan was one of the oldest *jula*, or merchant families, of Senegambia and Al Haji Seku was its oldest living member. He had been a traveling trader through most of his life, but at the age of eighty-three he was content to sit on the shaded porch through the heat of the day and allow younger family members to provide for him. As remains typical of Africans living some distance from urban outposts of modernity, Darbo knew a lot about his family's past. On no end of occasions throughout his life he had sat around a nighttime fire, listening to his elders pass along stories their elders had told them about *chosan*, loosely translated as "old things," or *history*. Some of the tales went *foolaw, foolaw*—way back. Darbo remembered many of them.

The distant ancestors of this branch of Gambia's Darbo family had been slave traders. From their homes along the middle and upper river, they had ventured off toward *Tilebo* (the East), in the direction of the upper Niger, to obtain captives, often prisoners from one or another episode of warfare. Once in possession of a number of slaves, they turned around and marched back down to the lower Gambia, where they could exchange the slaves for, in Darbo's mental shorthand, "cloth, wine, and tobacco." Normally, the captive Africans would end up on board a vessel bound for the Americas. If Darbo's memory and the tales he recalled hearing are accurate, this was a carefully organized business: merchants of the time had broad connections through marriage with rulers of states and prominent families living at spots along the line of march, and these strategically located people helped provide for the caravan on its way to market. At the village of Juffure, the main point of Afri-

The Slave Trade and Numbers

Through the 1960s, authoritative texts cited figures of between 15 and 20 million for the number of African slaves transported across the Atlantic. In 1969, the historian Philip D. Curtin exposed the lack of evidence for such statements—showing how one accepted line of authority spiraled back to a guess made by an American lobbying for the Mexican government on the eve of the American Civil War—and offered estimates of his own based on an admittedly inexhaustive survey of published literature. Calling his work "an intermediate level of synthesis" and "a point of departure that will be modified in time as new research produces new data," Curtin estimated that a total of 9,396,100 slaves landed in the Americas, with a death rate in passage of 16 percent, meaning that some number not far beyond 11 million departed Africa on slave ships. These figures caused a furor among some historians, at least one of whom, Joseph Inikori, implied that by lowering the numbers Curtin was suggesting that the slave trade was somehow less evil in its nature. Yet Curtin's lower numbers have held up well under long and careful scrutiny. New evidence has brought the acceptance of only slightly higher figures, as statements in this text indicate.

"Insurrection on Board a Slave Ship," by L. Walton, London, 1851. © The Trustees of the British Library. Record: c3071-06, Shelfmark: 4765.e.13, Page Folio: 116.

cans' interaction with Europeans in the lower river, twenty-five miles up from its mouth, a branch of the Darbo clan had settled and risen to prominence. Slave trading there was handled by the extended family: the folks in Juffure dealt with Europeans and Eurafricans, made sure operations were on the up-and-up with the local ruling elite, found ways to put slaves to work growing provisions if there were no ships in the river or if prices were not what the merchants wanted, and arranged for large manned canoes to convey the traveling traders and the goods they acquired back up the river toward home.

Darbo was one of the few persons in The Gambia—and, in fact, in much of West Africa—who did not mind talking about his ancestors' dealings in buying, transporting, and selling human beings two or three centuries earlier.

It was something done in many places, not only Africa, he noted, and "those were different times." Most other Gambians are more circumspect, however. Although Juffure now has a small museum of the slave trade that attempts to portray an accurate story—the initial curator having read Hugh Thomas's 1997 book, *The Slave Trade*—no one living in the village, including Darbo family members, tells much of anything beyond Alex Haley's version of how young men like Kunta Kinte were nabbed by slave catchers, while the helpless villagers, who never had seen a white person, accepted the loss stoically.

Darbo's ancestors had been agents on one end of an Atlantic economic system that lasted four centuries and brought millions of Africans to live and labor in the Americas. It was a massive operation by any accounting. In the first three centuries of sustained transatlantic connections—that is, until about 1820—vastly more Africans crossed the Atlantic to populate North and South America than did Europeans. Altogether, it is now reckoned that approximately 12 million captive men, women, and children departed Africa between 1450 and 1880 for various Atlantic-based venues. With a mortality rate of between 12 and 15 percent for the Atlantic crossing alone, this means that between 10.5 and 11 million Africans arrived at their destination, which more than 98 percent of the time was a port in the Americas. In terms of specific destinations, Brazil was the end of the voyage for 40 percent of captives in the Atlantic slave trade; the islands of the West Indies, including Barbados, Saint Domingue, and many others, of 37 percent; and Spanish America at least another 16 percent. It may surprise many readers that only a little less than 6 percent of enslaved Africans came directly to lands that would become the United States. Why so many men, women, and children were brought from so far away—western tropical Africa—to work throughout the Americas remains a subject of intense debate. But it is clear that once Europeans found ways to profit from the American landscape, particularly in large-scale agriculture and gold and silver mining, they would go to almost any lengths to find workers. When indigenous and European hands proved inadequate to the tasks at hand, Africa seemed to offer the logical solution.

Appetites for Sugar—and Labor

Having come from a culture that equated the good life with exemption from manual labor and unlimited access to fine food, drink, textiles, and other luxuries, Europeans in the Americas from the time of Columbus were as interested in finding workers as they were in finding gold and spices. Indeed, Columbus was no more inclined toward Native American genocide than Cortés, Champlain, or John Smith. Indians were assumed the most obvious means to wealth accumulation and good living, either through enslavement, serfdom, or rotational service. Yet native populations throughout the Americas, however large and seemingly stable at first contact, were rapidly diminished through overwork, forced migration, and worst of all, epidemic disease. The deadly combination of mercantilist assumptions and a virgin-soil disease environment quickly snuffed out the lives of millions of Indians, and with them, their conquerors' dreams of using their labor to gain riches. Iberians were the first to fill the gap in lowland mines and sugar-cane fields with African slaves. It was a costly alternative that northern Europeans would be slow to imitate, but which they would come to prefer.

Demographic conditions in Europe were relevant to this process, as population trends and sudden shifts heightened American labor shortages. Europe's population had recovered steadily, if slowly, from the fourteenth-century bubonic plague. A return of the disease, coupled with the Thirty Years' War—a costly struggle that originated as a civil war between Catholics and Protestants in the Holy Roman Empire and became an international conflict—set back any natural rise in population growth in the first half of the seventeenth century. But the population began inching up again around 1650, and this was just at the time when northern Europeans in particular were taking a liking to new hot drinks: coffee, tea, and chocolate. The first London coffeehouse opened its doors in 1652, tea was slowly becoming standard for late afternoon consumption among the fashionable in England, *café au lâit* was gaining a cult-like following in Paris, people in Holland were developing their own love affair with chocolate, and the most popular way to consume each of these drinks was laced with sugar. At about the same time, mill owners found that the molasses residue from the sugar-boiling process, after mixing with water, fermenting, and distilling, made a tasty and potent drink, which the English called Kill Devil (for obvious reasons) or rumbullion— later shortened to rum. Early European planters considered rum a useful palliative for the aches and illnesses associated with the tropics. Ships on call at Caribbean islands laid in stores of rum to maintain the health of their crews —so they claimed, anyway—or assuage the monotony of the long voyage home. This hastened the appearance of rum in English and French grog shops and its rapid popularity in the drinking circles of these nations. By the 1730s, the Royal Navy was doling out a half-pint of rum as a daily tonic for its crews, and by the start of the next century, no lesser sage than Lord Byron would proclaim, "There's nought no doubt so much the spirit calms as rum and true religion." By then, some were thinking that religion's place was rightly relegated to one day per week, while rum's was gladly given the other six.

The story of sugar and slavery in the Americas must be traced back at least to sixteenth-century Brazil, however, when Portuguese planters first looked to Africa to solve their labor problems. Indigenous slaves continued to fell the trees, plant the cane, cut and grind the stalks, and tend the proliferating animal- and water-driven mills of coastal Brazil well into the seventeenth century. But despite raids and ransoming expeditions penetrating farther and farther into the interior of the continent, Portuguese sugar exporters could not satisfy their labor needs. Men from Portugal could not fill the bill, because, for reasons noted, Portuguese immigrants to Brazil were few and those who came immediately aspired to the position of landowning cane farmers, or *lavradores de cana*, not cane cutters. Such work, hard enough without the added health problems posed by a tropical environment, was already deeply associated with slavery. Even if Portuguese immigrants—as hardy as any European peasants, to be sure—could survive the tasks, they could not bear the humiliation. Part of the culture of race-based hierarchies, European refusal to work alongside slaves would be a recurring pattern in the Atlantic world for as long as slavery lasted in it.

So it was to the good fortune of Portuguese planters in late-sixteenth-century Brazil that their countrymen, almost straight east across the ocean along the coasts of West Central Africa, were busy fighting a war with the *ngola* (ruler) of Ndongo to gain rights to the island of Luanda, two hundred miles south of the mouth of the Congo. It was their aim to establish a fortified trading outpost that could tap the coastwise and interior trade of that region, and when they won the war, they did so. Thus by 1590, Luanda was the headquarters of Portuguese commerce along the central African Atlantic coast. From this base, the Portuguese would have access to what a Jesuit described as "all the slaves one might want," for a cost of "practically nothing." Enslaved Africans began to appear in Brazilian cane fields around 1540, but only with the opening of Angola did the Portuguese trade in transatlantic captives balloon. By 1600, 15,000 African slaves made up nearly three-quarters of the labor force of Brazil's sugar mills; the last patch of African soil many of these people saw was Luanda.

Starting with this early transition from indigenous to African labor in Brazil, funded largely by Europe's seemingly insatiable demand for sugar, one can trace a veritable sugar revolution in the tropical Americas. Altered in some of its details and phases, but leading to a similar end—vast plantations staffed by hundreds of enslaved Africans—the sugar complex developed in Brazil spread northward into the Caribbean, to Barbados, Suriname, Jamaica, the Bahamas, and Louisiana.

Throughout Spanish America, meanwhile, the sugar plantation worked by African slaves had been a fact of life since shortly after Columbus's time. In Mexico, Hernando Cortés used a large portion of the booty won from conquest to establish a large, African-slave-staffed sugar estate in the hot lowlands outside Mexico City. Sugar plantations also were established in the steamy valleys between the Andean cordilleras right after conquest, and by 1650 coastal Peru, including the viceregal capital of Lima, counted an African and African-descended majority numbering in the tens of thousands. For Spanish planters with silver and gold to invest, African slavery and sugar production seemed a match made in heaven. For the slaves, of course, it was a match made in hell. The only work considered worse was gold mining. It is worth noting that Spanish American sugar production was initially oriented toward export to Spain, but the proliferation of large and wealthy internal markets, such as Potosí and Mexico City, meant most American-grown sugar stayed in the colonies. Only in later years would Cuba break the mold.

Unlike the Portuguese, northern Europeans had no local source for sugar. For them, sugar was always a transatlantic crop and, like tobacco, a highly lucrative, if not exactly addictive, one. In the course of the seventeenth century, the French and English gained possession of most of the "sugar islands" of the Caribbean, but the Dutch were the early force behind the explosive growth of sugar (and African slavery) in the region. With the West India Company (established in 1597, reconstituted in 1621), the Dutch hoped to edge out Portugal and Spain as major controllers and benefactors of the Atlantic

The Atlantic Slave Trade and History

The Atlantic slave trade is one of the most poorly understood aspects of world history, partly because of the evidence available for its study: few Africans left records of their experience and those European participants who did eventually thought of the enslaved men and women as units of labor rather than as human beings. (Better evidence exists now: since 1999 one can purchase a CD-Rom containing evidence of 27,000 Atlantic slaving voyages between 1562 and 1867, about half of all such voyages undertaken.) Another reason for the misunderstanding has to do with ideology during the modern period of historical study. During the late-nineteenth-century period that saw Europe conquer and begin ruling Africa, most European and American historians who considered the prior centuries of slave trading did so in light of the widely held view that Europeans were bringing the benefits of "civilization" to Africans. From this perspective, the commerce in humans was part of a necessary process of breaking Africans away from their "backward" ways. Then, following World War I, with imperialism held in a different light, historians tended to see Africans as the hapless objects of a long barrage of European aggression, the opening of which was the slave trade. Based more on notions of how critics thought things must have worked than on evidence, and not countered by more grounded scholarship until the 1970s and later, this study created myths about the nature of the slave trade that have died hard in a world fractured by race and trying to come to terms with cultural diversity.

trade in all its forms, and to this end the company waged war against the Iberians through much of the first half of the seventeenth century. At the time when they controlled sugar-producing regions of northeastern Brazil (1630–54), the Dutch were carrying thousands of slaves to Bahia and Pernambuco and introducing the plantation model for sugar production—popular by this time on both sides of the Atlantic—to various islands and at least one mainland portion of the Caribbean. In addition to providing slaves for the plantations, the Dutch proved eager to bring management expertise, technical proficiency, and even Italian-made machines for milling the cane, and they always were ready to carry the sugar produced on the islands back to Amsterdam or Antwerp.

Sugar production following the indenture model then spread to the French Antilles and several islands under English control. On Barbados, where colonists had struggled to turn a profit growing tobacco since English settlement of the island in 1627, a surge of sugar production occurred between 1640 and 1660. Dutch planters and shippers encouraged the English in their switch to sugar, knowing that even without civil war raging in England, Dutch carriers would be involved in providing laborers and hauling English sugar. For their part, English planters were quick to recognize the economy of slave production from the Brazilian model, and they made the transition from white indentured laborers to enslaved Africans with considerable speed. Between 1640 and 1650, Barbadian planters imported nearly 19,000 enslaved Africans, and the value of the land on the island increased tenfold over the first seven years of that decade. Jamaica would have a similar experience after 1650. By mid-century, the sugar revolution across the American tropics was in full swing.

Key to the profitability of the sugar economy was the relative abundance of African men and women, purchasable as slaves off ships coming from Africa's Atlantic coast. An English planter on Jamaica in 1690, for instance, could venture to Kingston and buy at the port a healthy, young African man for about £20. In only one year on the plantation, this man's labor would yield 600 lbs. of raw sugar, the value of which would be £20, the slave's original cost to the planter. Barring accidents, ill health, or rebellion, everything after this was pure gain.

The rapid expansion of such a profitable enterprise naturally meant a corresponding rise in the number of slaves crossing the Atlantic. Between 1626 and 1650, slightly more than 180,000 African men, women, and children arrived in the Americas as slaves (averaging just over 7,000 annually), but between 1651 and 1675 that number jumped to nearly 370,000 (an average of almost 15,000 per year), and the figures would continue to rise through almost all of the next century. More than 90 percent of all the captive Africans who arrived on American shores did so between 1650 and 1850. In the lone decade of the 1780s, European-financed and captained vessels brought three-quarters of a million captive Africans across the ocean, or some 75,000 every year. Slave labor, once expensive, had become relatively cheap.

From this peak period in the late eighteenth century—which coincided almost exactly with the beginning of the French Revolution, the coming into existence of the United States of America, and the outbreak of the Haitian Revolution—the Atlantic slave trade would start a slow, century-long decline, which remained gradual until Cuba ended slavery, and thus slave importing, in 1866. The decline was thereafter much more rapid. The abolition of slavery in Brazil in 1888 marked the end of transatlantic slave trading.

Slavery and slave trading were ancient institutions, and they were found in much of the Atlantic world from the time of the first Iberian forays south along the African coast or west to the Americas; still, few people living in the age of Columbus and Cabral could have imagined how massive both would become as a result of the sugar revolution. Eventually, the transoceanic slave trade would be the largest forced movement of human beings in history and the largest intercontinental migration, forced or otherwise, to occur before the turn of the twentieth century.

Captives and Trade Goods in Africa

By the time labor demands were becoming acute in the Americas, Europeans operating in the Atlantic trade knew two important things about Africans living along the continent's west coast. One was that they—like so many others around the world at the time—accepted slavery as a social institution and actively traded in captive humans; the other was that they were astute and experienced merchants, whom Europeans could not dominate or easily overcome. These facts would shape the Atlantic slave trade throughout its long duration.

West Africans in the fifteenth century drew from long commercial experience. Their ancestors had been trading everything from foodstuffs to metals, luxuries to stimulants—including captive men and women—across short and long distances for more than a millennium. By the fifteenth century, the western coast of Africa was one edge of a commercial network of considerable scope and sophistication. Long-distance trading was an occupational specialty that Africans held in high regard, more so than among contemporary Europeans. Sub-Saharan Africa's Atlantic hinterland contained a grid of trade routes dotted regularly with commercial settlements and markets. These formed a social network as well that permitted traders to travel among communities where they could employ local associates as their aids and agents. For hundreds of years before the coastwise trade in slaves, itinerant merchants had funneled gold, kola nuts, and slaves to the cities of the Sahel, the last "ports" encountered before crossing the Sahara. In return they had carried goods from North Africa, including salt, metal and glassware, figs and dates, back from the southern edge of the desert to locales across the western savannas and into the coastal forests. Likewise, Central Africans had traded copper, hides, and ivory toward the coast for palm cloth, palm oil, and salt.

European traders quickly learned that they could not force their commercial will on coastal Africans. It is simply wrong to think that, through most of the years of slave trading, the foreigners possessed sufficient technology or other skills to dominate militarily the Africans they met. That would come much later, with the development of advanced firearm technology, the repeating rifle and maxim gun in particular, in the last third of the nineteenth century, when the Atlantic slave trade was coming to an end. The early Portuguese, Dutch, English, and French had to deal with Africans on African terms rather than their own: when Europeans settled, they recognized clearly the necessity of abiding by local rules and customs; when they traded, they paid duties or fees (and respect) to local rulers and spent far more time carrying African goods from one part of the coast to another, to their own benefit and that of African traders and rulers, than often is recognized; if they sold European manufactured goods to Africans, they also purchased African manufactures; and on the few occasions before the nineteenth century when they fought and defeated any sizeable group of Africans, it was nearly always because the Europeans had allied with other Africans in the effort.

As one would expect, Europeans seeking slaves went to the places along the three thousand miles of Africa's populated Atlantic coast where captive men and women were most readily available and least expensive. Such locations moved over time, largely because the level of warfare existing in a natural hinterland of the coast or, later, regions some distance from the coast but connected thereto by road or water, changed with local political conditions, and this factor, more than others, determined slave supply. When demand for slaves was strongest in the trans-Sahara trade leading to North African markets, as it had been for centuries before Europeans came into direct contact with coastal West Africa, captives tended to flow in that direction. But once the sugar plantations in Brazil and the West Indies brought a skyrocketing demand for labor across the Atlantic, prices for slaves on the coast became higher and pulled the captives westward toward the ocean, eventually from farther and farther inland.

Thus, slave trading was particularly heavy along the Upper Guinea Coast through the sixteenth century, when fighting accompanied the disintegration of the Jolof Empire between the Senegal and Gambia Rivers and the west-

Warfare and Slave Trading: Chicken or Egg?

Students of African slave trading disagree over the causes of the wars that generated slaves for the Atlantic market. Some argue that the great majority of wars in the hinterland of West Africa had the same kinds of causes that wars did elsewhere—they were civil wars, or wars over succession, or wars between small states over disputed territory, or related to the political expansion of large states fighting to become empires. Others believe that the enormous demand for slaves along parts of Africa's Atlantic coast—the Slave Coast, the Bight of Biafra, and Angola, for example—prompted powerful Africans to instigate wars with the end of obtaining captives for sale, and that proceeds from slave trading then helped build armies to fight more wars and capture more slaves in an upward spiral. Most recently, the arguments have merged into suggestions that most African leaders who engaged in warfare had political (or political-economic) ends in mind. But the victors in wars sold their captives to enhance their power and status, and they took prisoners with that in mind. Moreover, where warfare and slave trading occurred most regularly, social order and discipline were casualties, leading to greater banditry and slave raiding for the purpose of individual or small-group gain through the selling of captives. When wars occurred, according to an expression current in the eighteenth-century Gold Coast, the victors "ate the country," and, then as now, one cannot fail to see elements of greed in the appetites of winners generally.

Portuguese soldier. Brass figure from Benin, Nigeria, Seventeenth century. © The Trustees of the British Museum.

ward expansion of Mande-speaking people among coastal societies of modern-day Guinea, Sierra Leone, and Liberia. Trading grew heavier in the seventeenth and eighteenth centuries along the Gold and Slave Coasts, with warfare associated with the rise or fall of Benin, Oyo, Dahomey, and Asante, and with fighting among commercially oriented city-states among Igbo-speaking people of the Niger Delta and areas to the east. It was the fate of Africans living inland of the Congo River and in lands to its south, in modern Angola, that a combination of African warfare and Portuguese-encouraged slave raiding kept the flow of slaves into the Atlantic from that region at a high level through most of the period of the slave trade.

Of course, if Europeans had not possessed, or had lacked the ability to acquire, items that Africans wanted, there would have been no trade. That European voyagers were in contact with regions of the world where people produced items of high value to Africans was a factor in the rise and duration of the Atlantic slave trade. African demands varied greatly according to time and place, but some items found a fairly constant market. In the most general terms, slaving vessels—both the captains and ships were often referred to as "slavers"—from one or another European port were floating hardware and dry goods stores, with spirits in the cellar. According to John Atkins, a surgeon in the British navy in the 1720s, slavers traded "crystals, oranges, corals, and brass mounted cutlasses" on the Windward Coast, "brass pans" along the Gold Coast, and "copper and iron bars at Callabar," although "arms, gunpowder, cottons, and English spirits [whiskey] are everywhere called for."

One or another form of cash was always an important element in Atlantic trading, too. Best known of the monies used was that which predominated along the Gold and Slave Coasts and in the Bights of Benin and Biafra: cowrie shells. The Portuguese originally obtained these small shells from islands in the Indian Ocean, using them as ballast for returning ships even before realizing their value among certain African societies. Cowries (the word derives from the Hindi *kauri*) made their entry into West African commerce early in the sixteenth century, and many thousands of tons of them were imported (with the Dutch and British East India Companies displacing the Portuguese as the main suppliers) over the next four centuries. Other currencies used in different coastal regions and at other times included gold, cloth, copper or brass bracelets (commonly called *manillas*), and iron bars.

The elites of coastal West Africa expected European suppliers to provide them with most standard staple and luxury goods traded in markets around the world between the sixteenth and nineteenth centuries. Key were items of apparel and personal adornment (making up probably half of all of Atlantic Africa's imports through the slave-trade years), metals and metalware (another third), spirits (brandy, rum, wine), tobacco and smoking apparatus, horses, firearms, shot, and gunpowder. (The slaver *Cleopatra*, sailing out of Newport, Rhode Island, in the early 1770s carried "two hundred and thirty-four hogsheads [of] New England rum," which came to roughly 14,742 gallons.) A variety of goods always was crucial for Europeans desiring the best prices for captive Africans. An inventory by Dutch traders in 1728 revealed

In Exchange for Slaves

A list of items exchanged for 180 slaves in the Gambia River, 1740–41:

1,178 silver coins
37 lbs. of cowrie shells
150 pieces (660 lbs.) of linen
63 pieces (324 lbs.) of Indian textile
30 pieces (286 lbs.) of Manchester textile
219 yards (219 lbs.) of woolen cloth
398 lbs. of fringe
4,391 lbs. of glass beads
66 lbs. of carnelian beads
60,700 stones (288 lbs.) of crystal
430 iron bars @ 10 lbs. apiece
102 brass pans @ 9 lbs. apiece

662 lbs. of pewter ware
2 copper rods @ 1 lb. apiece
164 guns
1,140 lbs. of gunpowder
450 gunflints
35 lbs. of lead balls
92 cutlasses
71 pairs of pistols
119 gallons of rum
2,556 lbs. of salt
47 reams of paper

Source: British Public Record Office, Kew, Surrey, T 70/573 and T 70/575.

218 types of merchandise stored at Elmina Castle on the Gold Coast for use in acquiring slaves.

For a time, when slave trading grew brisk and huge profits beckoned, several European governments got involved and, following examples of the English and Dutch companies of the Indies, granted monopolies to private, joint-stock companies for conducting slave trading using the factory model. The idea that underlay these ventures was that the large profits the companies would make would offset the startup costs and expenses necessitated by maintaining fortified outposts on Africa's Atlantic coast. The Dutch West India Company (from 1623), the English Company of Royal Adventurers (1663) and Royal African Company (1672), and the French Compagnie du Sénégal (1673) were such monopoly companies, and they had mixed success through the seventeenth century. After several decades, however, it became clear to most European governments that the state-sanctioned companies were having trouble holding their own in the face of competition from their illegal countrymen and foreigners (called "interlopers" by the English), who seemed always around, blatantly ignoring the rules and trading with Africans out of gunshot of company forts. So with a few exceptions, the royal charters expired or were completely ignored, and by the eighteenth century independent shippers went back to dominating the slave trade, as they had since the first forays of the Portuguese. In this period of rapid growth, however, competition grew fierce.

Particularly fierce was competition for the Spanish *asiento* (or contract). Created in 1513 by King Ferdinand in response to the seemingly insatiable demand for African slaves in his American colonies, the monarchy assigned trade contracts to the highest bidder among Portuguese, Genoese, Dutch, French, and English suppliers. But during the negotiations leading up to the 1713 Treaty of Utrecht, which ended the War of Spanish Succession—known as Queen Anne's War in North America—Britain demanded the exclusive right to supply Africans to all Spanish colonies as a spoil of war. As a result, England dominated the Atlantic trade in humans for most of the eighteenth century, carrying, on average, twenty thousand captives west across the Atlantic each year. Of course, this human cargo arrived in many ports outside Spanish America as well.

One would hope it is no longer necessary to denounce the hoary myth that Jews dominated the Atlantic slave trade, but the fact remains that *The Secret Relationship Between Blacks and Jews*, published by the Nation of Islam in 1991, continues to circulate on college campuses, where some read and believe its assertions. Although it is true that a number of the financiers behind the trade in seventeenth-century Lisbon were converted Jews or their descendants, many of these *conversos* were bona fide Catholics, and so were Jewish only by the racial blood definitions of the Nazis. As the historian David Brion Davis has observed, "for every Jew involved in the Atlantic slave system there were scores or even hundreds of Catholics and Protestants." Indeed, the real crime, from a modern perspective, should be how socially acceptable the trade was. Among those who invested in England were James, Duke of York (the future King James II), who poured £2,000 into slaving ventures, and a young professor at Oxford, John Locke, the philosopher of natural rights. Investors in the trade in France, the Netherlands, and other parts of Europe were equally prominent in their societies, and members of political elite groups in Africa increased their wealth and enhanced their personal positions through participation in, or taxing of, the trade of humans.

Though monopoly companies did not survive, the factory model established by the Portuguese did, and European governments saw it to their own and their countrymen's advantage to maintain and staff African coastal forts with small garrisons. These operated like early forms of consulates: officials running the forts looked out for national interests as best they could, giving gifts to influential people in nearby communities, gathering commercial intelligence, and making sure the wheels of commerce were sufficiently greased for traders from home. Keeping a viable staff in these forts—in a region where malaria, dysentery, and other tropical maladies brought quick death to many Europeans on their initial African tour—was never easy but deemed essential. Only along the Gold Coast did more than small numbers of slaves pass through these forts, it not being sensible for Europeans to acquire slaves long before their embarkation and have the obligation of controlling and feeding them until a ship arrived. On Gorée Island, five miles off modern-day Dakar in the Atlantic, there is a *maison des esclaves* with a "door of no return," where an entrepreneurial local guide tells visitors of the "millions [sic]" of slaves who were kept in chains in the dungeon of the "slave house" and passed through the notorious door. In recent years presidents of the United States have visited the site and spoken about the horrors of the Atlantic slave trade, but the fact is that few captive men and women ever awaited departure for an Atlantic crossing on the island. Goreé had neither fresh water nor a source of food, which made maintaining its small population difficult enough without the regular addition of large groups of captives.

Of course, along the more than 3,000 miles of coastline where slaves were available, and over the roughly four centuries of Atlantic-oriented slave trading, commercial methods varied. Indeed, variety in trading practices unfolded along any given stretch of coast. Thus, generalizing about these practices is difficult. In Senegambia, slave-ship captains arrived, paid customs and dues to local officials, and then took their chances on African traders bringing slaves to coastal ports or river towns for exchange. Captains in the Gambia often sent small vessels some distance upriver, staffed largely by "linguisters" and boatmen hired from local rulers, to seek slaves brought in "coffles" from the interior. The Scottish explorer Mungo Park, who traveled with a seventy-three-person coffle (thirty-five enslaved men and women, thirty-eight freepersons and their domestic servants) across the hinterland of the Gambia in 1797, described how the captives moved: "They are commonly secured, by putting the right leg of one, and the left of another, into the same pair of fetters. By supporting the fetters with a string, they can walk, though very slowly. Every four slaves are likewise fastened together by their necks, with a strong rope of twisted thongs; and in the night an additional pair of fetters is put on their hands, and sometimes a light iron chain passed round their necks." One enslaved woman in the coffle, too weak to continue the march and having been stung badly by a swarm of bees, was simply left "on the road, where undoubtedly she soon perished, and was probably devoured by wild animals."

Down the coast in Sierra Leone, independent European and mixed-race traders set up enterprises like the one run by an Irishman, Nicholas Owen. "[I]f any of the blacks comes I buy their commodities at as cheap a rate as I can," Owen admitted, "which enables me to trade aboard the ships once or twice a month, which just keeps me from sinking in the principal stock." On three separate voyages in the 1750s, slaver-turned-evangelical-Christian John Newton spent six to eight months sailing up and down the Sierra Leone coast, purchasing men and women in twos and threes from individual traders like Owen. Exchanges along the Gold Coast could be more formal and organized, with operations conducted through such English, Dutch, or Danish forts as Cape Coast Castle, Elmina, or Christiansborg. Along the Slave Coast (of modern-day Benin and western Nigeria), experienced African rulers did not allow Europeans to construct strong fortifications, so slavers tended to anchor their vessels in lagoons and trade directly from their ships. Robert Harms's analysis of the journal kept by a Frenchman, Robert Durand, on a voyage of the French slaver *Diligent* in 1731 may give the best idea of how European captains acquired captives along this stretch of coast. It took three months of haggling, with most of the Europeans involved getting sick at one point or another, to acquire 256 slaves.

The African Kingdom of Benin, inland on the Bight of Biafra, was in European eyes a fickle slave-trading state, seldom willing to allow export of enough captives to meet European demand, and notoriously unhealthy. "Beware and take care of the Bight of Benin," went the old coaster's shanty, "Only one comes out for forty goes in." At lower parts of the Niger River delta and beyond, in the Bight of Biafra, European shippers entrusted trade goods to African heads of commercial organizations (referred to as "canoe houses"), who would then organize ventures up the rivers to exchange the goods for slaves and return with them. Over time, such commerce developed standard customs and institutions, among which was a system of pawning, or leaving family members with the shippers as surety for the return of those entrusted with the goods. At the southern extreme of the slave-trading region of Africa's Atlantic coast, at the ports of Luanda and Benguela, a Luso-African group of merchants purchased slaves from mulatto traders, who had ventured into the interior with goods and brought back captives in coffles of one hundred or more, and kept them penned until the arrival of slaving vessels. Demand was frequently sufficient that merchants did not need to hold the slaves for long. In fact, as demand increased through the eighteenth century, competition among slavers seeking cargos grew especially keen. A vessel seeking slaves at a port along the Loango Coast north of the Congo River in 1742 found fourteen other European ships at the same place, doing the same thing, and it took four months to purchase 362 captives for the transatlantic voyage.

The Middle Passage

The heart of the Atlantic slave trade, the transportation by ship of the millions of captive men, women, and children from the shores of western sub-Saharan Africa to islands or mainland areas of North or South America, often referred to as "The Middle Passage," is difficult to describe and assess because of the lack of appropriate evidence available for its study. Because of the circumstances of the voyages, practically every scrap of firsthand information relating to the subject comes from the captors rather than the captives. (The most remarkable aspect of first-mate Durand's journal of his 1731 transatlantic slaving voyage, sixty-six days in the middle passage, is how frequently in daily entries he mentions the 256 captive Africans on board: twice, only to record deaths, once only with a skull and crossbones drawn in the margin.) Moreover, much of what exists beyond raw statistical data comes from the post-1780 period, when efforts to outlaw slave trading were gaining strength in some intellectual and political circles. Persons testifying on the trade before British Parliament, say, or writing a pamphlet on the subject, did so with an end in mind: either to emphasize the horrible circumstances of the slaves during transit—and this was easy to do, since by most reasonable, modern standards, those circumstances were deplorable—or, less frequently, to show that, if for no other than economic reasons, the human cargo was dealt with as humanely as possible. Statistics allow one to surmise about conditions on the typical voyage, but numbers offer no insight into the human condition of those most intimately involved—the men, women, and children loaded on board along some choppy stretch of African coastline and hauled in for sale at a steamy American port. These millions of people simply have no voice whatsoever.

One can argue reasonably that the health of the slaves was of importance to ships' captains, because these men tended to be paid on a formula related to the number of slaves arriving at an American port in fit, saleable condition. But captains, and even more so the crew members on slavers, who had the most direct dealings with the enslaved persons on board, were often callous, violent people, and purposeful cruelty entered into the circumstances on board more frequently than profit-motivated owners may have wished. And even when masters' intentions for treatment of slaves, from whatever motives, were the best, the general ignorance of proper measures to sustain human health and ward off disease through the centuries of Atlantic slave trading meant that human well-being lay at risk through the length of the voyage for all concerned. Finally, factors largely out of the control of captain and crew had the greatest effect on slave health and mortality between Africa and the Americas.

The typical shipload of Africans differed from the makeup of other vessels crossing the Atlantic at the same time in more ways than in the forced movement and captivity of the human cargo. It has long been a misconception that adult male Africans composed the overwhelming majority of forced migrants who crossed the Atlantic to the Americas. The historian David Eltis's painstaking comparisons illustrate that, in fact, European indentured laborers were predominantly adult men, but African migration was characterized by a comparatively even sex ratio and a higher percentage of children. Men dominated (sometimes in high percentages) all indentured migrant labor flows, ranging from 75 to 90 percent for French, Irish, and English laborers before 1775. In contrast, men comprised 59 percent of African migrants to the Caribbean between 1663 and 1700, and that percentage increased only to 63 in the eighteenth century. Moreover, among coerced migrants (enslaved and indentured) as a whole, more children were found aboard slave ships than aboard European migrant ships. In other words, enslaved Africans more fully resembled in their demographic characteristics the small minority of Europeans who traveled in family groups than they did the flow of bound European labor. That the cargo of the typical slaver was made up overwhelmingly of adolescents and young adults—these being persons not at all likely to die over a period of one or two months under normal circumstances—makes the average slave mortality rate during the middle passage in the eighteenth century, of 12 to 15 percent of the slaves on board, all the more shameful.

Captive Africans did not necessarily board a slave vessel all at once, in one large group. Instead, slavers frequently gathered their cargoes in small groups, meaning that some captive people were on board for weeks prior to leaving the African coast. At boarding, slaves commonly were stripped of their clothing, washed down, and shaved, all for reasons relating to health, according to masters of the vessels. So long as the craft was close to land, slaves on board were shackled to another slave or several others. Once at sea, only men tended to remain in iron shackles, the women being considered less of a threat to rebel, as well as easier prey. Captain Newton, the future clergyman, was surely unusual for clapping a seaman into irons for raping a woman "in view of the whole quarter deck." More typical was the South Carolinian Joseph Hawkins, who noted that "the officers" on his ship "all provided themselves with three or four wives each."

It almost can go unsaid that Africans crossing the Atlantic in slave ships had little space. The diagram reproduced in so many authoritative treatments of the subject, that of the late-eighteenth-century English slaver *Brookes*, which shows men and women packed onto lower decks like sardines in a can, lacking room to stand upright, is typical at least of the theory that undergirded the loading of captives: get as many on board as possible. Yet even this diagram is questionable as solid historical evidence, given that it was drawn from a description of the *Brookes*, a 297-ton vessel capable of carrying 609 slaves, written by an officer in the Royal Navy and sent to the abolitionist Thomas Clarkson, who commissioned the drawing of how the slaves would be fitted on decks at night for the express use as anti–slave trade propaganda. It is more accurate that each enslaved African was normally allotted between five and seven square feet of deck space, less than half that accorded contemporary European convicts, emigrants, or soldiers being taken across oceans for their varied purposes. Decks on slave ships were usually four or five feet high. A man sold off a slaver in Charles Town, South Carolina, remembered, "It was more than a week after I left the ship before I could straighten my limbs."

Partly because of the cramped space, slaves were brought up onto the top deck and kept there through much of the day when weather permitted. Men frequently were put to work with the more difficult tasks of ships under sail—hauling lines, turning the windlass, pumping—or with scraping, scrubbing, and perfuming the decks, especially in the slave quarters, below. Crews were directed to encourage slaves to move about. Ship owners often paid for the addition of a musician to the crew, so that accordion, bagpipe, or hurdy-gurdy music and drumming could bring the slaves to dance. It was topside where slaves ate their meals, commonly twice daily, morning and evening. Food varied so much on voyages that it is hard to generalize about what the enslaved men and women ate during the middle passage, except to say that it was on the low side of what we now consider a sufficient daily caloric intake. Besides such foods brought from Europe as beans, oats, and wheat flour (for biscuits), the fare depended on which part of the African coast captains had purchased food: yams, manioc, plantains, bananas, and coconuts were standard for those coming from the more forested regions from the Slave Coast to the Congo River; millet, rice, and maize were the staples from the savannah regions north and south of there. Peppers, palm oil, or small amounts of salted meat or fish might be added occasionally to the soups and stews that slaves ate from common tubs. Such meals might not have been particularly appetizing to the hungry captives, especially those who were seasick, but they tended not to differ greatly from what Africans ate on the continent. Fresh water was more of a problem. Each person normally received one pint of water with a meal, which, even when augmented by liquid in the food, was insufficient to meet bodily requirements, especially for those exposed to the heat above and below decks, and suffering, as many frequently were, from diarrhea. Dehydration thus was among the most important factors in slave mortality during the middle passage, though it was not recognized as such. Unaware of what is known today about the importance of hydration, crews looked at the sunken eyes, physical weakness, emaciation, apathy, loss of appetite, and delirium—all manifestations of water and electrolyte loss—that slaves often exhibited before death on board and judged them willful acts or symptoms of psychological conditions: "fixed melancholy" to the English, *bonzo* to the Portuguese.

Days on deck were one thing; nights below another. Slaves were supposed to sleep, the men still shackled to one another, on platforms or decks made of wood planking. This would be difficult under the best of conditions, but on a rocking and pitching ship on the ocean, it must have been nearly impossible. Heat built up below decks during the day and then was slow to dissipate after sundown. Hatches and air foils were designed to direct air to the lower decks, but they were inadequate, particularly with the large numbers of humans below. The French slave trader Jean Barbot, considering the heat and lack of oxygen on a ship's lower decks, wrote that surgeons visiting among the slaves would "faint away and the candles would not burn." On top of this misery, the vast element of captive humanity still had to attend to bodily needs. Tubs were located around lower decks for slaves who needed to relieve themselves, but reaching the tubs, especially when shackled to another person, was not always worth the effort. Diarrhea and vomiting from illness or common seasickness compounded the problem. Thus, from the first day of the voyage to the last, filth and stench were constant companions. Crews made slaves spend time daily scraping decks, swabbing, and fumigating with heated vinegar, but it was a futile effort over the long run, and bilges ran particularly foul. A port physician in eighteenth-century Charles Town,

South Carolina, who was normally the first person to board a slaver upon its arrival from the Atlantic crossing, encountered "Filth, putrid Air, putrid Dysenteries," so much so, he noted, that "it is a wonder any escaped with Life."

Probably too much has been made of slave-ship owners' theories about how densely to fill their vessels with slaves, as if there were discrete "tight-packing" and "loose-packing" schools of thought. Did some owners believe that by acquiring fewer slaves for the transatlantic passage and thus allowing individuals more space aboard ship they would have more slaves survive and arrive healthier, bringing higher prices? Perhaps some reasoned thusly, but probably not many, such ideas tending to arise more from abolitionists' arguments or modern-day scholars' tendency to back up statistical evidence with logical reasoning. General ideas prevailed about the appropriate "slave-per-tonnage" ratios, but the size of a ship's human cargo frequently was determined by how easy or difficult it was to purchase slaves at decent prices over how long a stay on the Guinea Coast. Waiting time in the tropics cost money and posed a danger to the health of the crew. Historians of the trade do not themselves agree about the effects of tight or loose packing on health or death rates of slaves: data from the largely Portuguese trade between Angola and Brazil suggest that higher shipboard density did lead to greater mortality, but when English slave traders steadily increased the density of captives on board through the eighteenth century, probably because of rising prices for slaves in the Americas, average mortality rates fell.

Other factors intervened, of course. What affected mortality most during the middle passage was time at sea, which varied according to miles of ocean to cross—Sierra Leone to northeastern Brazil is about 2,000 miles, Angola to the Chesapeake Bay, 6,000—and ship speed, which was related to winds and the configuration of the individual vessel. Captains planned for six to eight weeks in the crossing and often took double the amount of food and water needed for such a voyage, but food could spoil and water become contaminated, leading to "the bloody flux," dysentery, which only heightened needs for potable water and accounted for the shipboard deaths of a great number of slaves. Statistically speaking, another important factor in slave mortality was the slave's point of origin along the African coast. Curiously, persons purchased in the Bight of Biafra, east of the Niger Delta, had the highest mortality rates, whereas those from the Loango coast, 500 miles to the south, experienced the lowest. This probably relates to the individual's health at the time of sale and embarkation, and several uncontrollable factors affected this: circumstances and length of conveyance to the coast, regional droughts and famines, or strength of demand on the coast, which prompted Africans to sell weaker persons when demand raised prices.

Actually, slave mortality in the middle passage declined after about 1750. This was the case partly because ships of newer design were faster and could carry more water and catch more rainwater. Medical advances, primitive though they may have been, also improved the health of those experiencing the Atlantic crossing. The realization after the 1750s that citrus-fruit consumption prevented scurvy was a big step forward for all people on ocean voyages; so was the new technique of producing fresh water through the boiling and evaporation of salt water. And that slave prices went up steadily must have made persons in charge of human cargoes try all the more to see that as many as possible arrived in saleable condition.

Despite the drop in mortality rates after mid-century, slaving still involved considerable financial risk, and no responsible captain sailed west out of Africa's slave harbors without first obtaining insurance. If most of the Africans arriving in the Americas landed to the south of Philadelphia, most of the merchants and bankers who offered policies on them resided in the urban centers to its north, particularly in Boston and Newport. Typical of the captains who insured their cargo at a rate of 8 percent was Bermuda-based Joseph Vesey, the owner of the future abolitionist Denmark Vesey. Because the captain's ship, *Prospect*, carried a $20,000 bond from a Boston firm, that meant that the human cargo below its decks was probably appraised at $250,000. Typical also of those who insured such ships were the four brothers in Rhode Island—merchants, industrialists, and bankers—who in 1765 formed the firm of Nicholas Brown and Company. Although some of the brothers found the practice morally dubious, John Brown insured a number of slaving voyages. Some of his profits went to subsidize Rhode Island College, for which he served as treasurer; today the ancient grandfather clock in University Hall— in what is now known as Brown University—was donated by Esek Hopkins, whose slave ship, *Sally*, the Brown brothers financed.

When dealing in numbers in the hundreds of thousands or millions, it is easy to lose sight of the terrible costs in individual human lives of the Atlantic slave trade. The historian Joseph Miller has tried to add meaning to the large numbers for one of the most active segments of the trade —that between Angola and Brazil. Of 100 Africans seized in the Angolan interior (and who knows how many men, women, and children died during the episodes involved in their capture), Miller estimates that some 36, on average, would perish during their six-month movement to the coast, leaving 64. Because more would die waiting at the coast, where they were held until ships came to claim them, only 57 of the original 100 captives would finally board ships headed to Brazil, and 51 of these would survive to be unloaded at the wharves. Beyond these estimates, more would perish during an acclimatization process over their first year, leaving perhaps 40 of the original 100 persons alive and working in Brazil less than two years after their capture in Africa.

Slavery in the Americas

Those who assume the United States has always been at the center of world historical trends are invariably surprised to discover that approximately 94 percent of the Africans sold into the Americas went to colonies outside British North America. In large part, this was because sugar did not grow in temperate latitudes. The Spanish were the first to capitalize on the quick adaptation of sugar cane to the American tropics: early settlers on Hispaniola copied the plantation model from Madeira, the Canaries, São Tomé, and Príncipe that relied on Genoese and Catalán capital and technology and indigenous and African labor. Spaniards also established sugar plantations along the coast of the Gulf of Mexico. Mostly because of the expansion of sugar production there and in parts of the Mexican interior, an average of 2,000 slaves were shipped annually to the port of Veracruz between 1580 and 1650. The first shipment of African slaves to arrive in Virginia had been on their way to Veracruz when Dutch corsairs seized the Portuguese vessel carrying them in 1619.

But the Atlantic sugar colony that would transform the lives of the greatest number of African slaves—some 4 to 5 million, or 40 percent of all Africans transported to the Americas—was Portuguese Brazil. By the early seventeenth century, Brazil had more African slaves than any other American society, and slavery lasted longer there than anywhere else in the hemisphere. Graced with large quantities of flat land and good soil close to rivers and millstreams, and with access by sea to Africa and Europe, Brazil had the geographic features to make it a plantation success. Ripe cane and refined sugar were heavy and hence expensive to haul overland. Near Bahia was the *recôncavo*, a large, sheltered, Chesapeake Bay–like watershed that abounded in navigable estuaries and contained some of the best-situated cane land in the Atlantic. Here, slaves worked more than 4,000 square miles of cane fields—roughly the size of the island of Jamaica. And this was but one of Brazil's several sugar zones; Pernambuco, to the north, was even larger and more productive. For more than three and a half centuries, captive, African-born men and women poured into Brazil, rendering it more African than any other American colony.

By the mid-sixteenth century, Portuguese planters had created sugar estates in northeastern Brazil worked by Africans imported from the Guinea of Cape Verde. With the union of the Spanish and Portuguese crowns in 1580, the Portuguese Company of Cacheu began to introduce more slaves from Angola and the Kingdom of Kongo into Brazil. From 1570 to 1600, Angola was the home of approximately 50,000 slaves sent to Brazil. Contractors for this trade were in some senses tax farmers who collected rent-like duties on each slave. Brazilian contractors obtained licenses stating the number of slaves they could import, where they were to be obtained, and the tax per slave. Factors in Angola certified the cargoes, their destination, and the tax collected there. Finally, port authorities in Brazil took the Angolan registration, inventoried the slaves, and then collected duties on all individuals embarked, even if many had died en route. Although a tightly controlled system in theory, this mercantilist, state model of trade was frequently bent and stretched to make room for profit. The value of slaves on the western side of the Atlantic was high from the beginning and grew higher, making the slave trade a ripe plum for contrabandists, pirates, and corrupt officials.

Most of Brazil's slaves worked growing, cutting, and processing sugar cane, but the largest sugar mills, some of them run by the Jesuits, were nearly self-sufficient units requiring many skilled and semiskilled laborers as well. Captive Africans served as the estates' coopers, smiths, carpenters, cattle drivers, hunters, fishermen, and even master sugar makers. Some Brazilian sugar plantations resembled feudal estates in that they carried on in relative isolation, far from urban institutions and crown authority. But Brazilian planters were hardly detached from the Atlantic world, and they constantly adjusted their enterprise in response to changing commercial tides, diversified their investments, and kept track of profits and expenditures like good businesspersons. There was plenty of room for technical innovation, such as the three-roller mill invented around 1610, and for smaller entrepreneurs, usually farmers with only a few slaves, to work their way up to the status of mill owner. Still, the Brazilian sugar industry retained many feudal-like social aspects. It was only natural for the *senhores de engenho* (masters of the mills and plantations), living as they did in remote locations, to assume powers normally granted to courts and magistrates. Although some planters supported priests on the estates to minister to their families and educate their children, they made no serious effort to convert rural slaves. Law enforcement and crown oversight were generally lacking, meaning Brazilian slaves enjoyed almost none of the protections available (at least theoretically) to slaves on Spanish estates. On the flip side, Africans in Brazil had more space to carve out and develop an autonomous culture than those living under Spanish rule.

Following Portuguese reconquest of Pernambuco in 1654, expelled Dutch planters transferred capital, sugar technology, and many of their slaves to the Caribbean, where the English had already established a sugar colony in Barbados. In 1655 the English seized Jamaica from the Spanish after a failed attack on Hispaniola and shifted the economy of the thinly populated and mountainous island from ranching to sugar. The French followed by seizing the western half of Hispaniola, a land grab later legitimated by the Treaty of Madrid in 1670. Waves of pirate attacks had largely depopulated the region. Ironically, like Jamaica, it would soon become one of the Caribbean's most significant pirate bases. As sugar plantations spread across the western plains of the island originally called Haiti, the newly dubbed Saint Domingue became rapidly more African—and more prosperous.

Landowners in Cuba eventually entered the sugar race, too, and by the mid-eighteenth century they had developed plantations around Havana and Matanzas. But the sugar economy of Cuba leaped forward when the English captured Havana in 1762, during the Seven Years' War. Taking full advantage of the situation, English slavers began to clog Havana harbor. The Cuban historian Manuel Moreno Fraginals estimated that British traders introduced as many slaves into Cuba in the eleven months before returning the island to Spain in the 1763 Treaty of Paris as the Spaniards, at their previous rates, would have in twelve to fifteen years. Wealthy and powerful scions of Havana like Ricardo O'Farill y O'Daly, the holder of the slave import monopoly for the English South Sea Company, established huge sugar estates in Matanzas, and a new port opened the province to international trade and capitalists investing in sugar and coffee estates, slave trading, and merchant houses. There, as elsewhere, highly profitable industries had a way of dissolving religious and national borders, and of bridging even the most profound political differences. In Cuba, the success of the African-slave-supported sugar regime produced yet another anomaly: while the rest of Spanish America rebelled in the 1810s and 1820s, the island, like Puerto Rico, remained "faithful" to Spain until the end of the nineteenth century.

All of this success came at a high cost. Mortality rates on the middle passage were only slightly higher than on sugar plantations. One Cuban insurance company, striving to create precise actuarial tables, concluded that plantation deaths exceeded births. Workers on coffee estates fared better, and urban slaves who labored on Havana's docks lived longer still. The insurer

Confusing Slavery with Cotton

To students of history in the United States, slavery appears so inextricably linked with cotton production—undoubtedly because it was the question of "King Cotton's" expansion into the western territories of the United States that sparked the Civil War—that few can imagine that slaves performed any other type of labor. This holds true for both the generators of popular culture as well as political historians of the antebellum period. In Roots, Alex Haley's highly fictionalized account of his family's history (made into a television "miniseries" in the 1970s), the protagonist Kunta Kinte harvests cotton in colonial Maryland in the 1670s, long before it was feasible to grow and export cotton almost anywhere in North America. Similarly, in Clifford Mason's 1968 play Gabriel, an even more fanciful account of the Virginia slave conspiracy of 1800, the artisan Gabriel, who resided on a tobacco and wheat plantation just outside of Richmond, where he often hired out

his time as a blacksmith, is dropped into a generic cotton setting. The opening stage directions read: "As the curtain rises, slaves are seen picking cotton."

More seriously, classic accounts of the political battles of the 1850s by historians Allan Nevins and David Potter imply that the partisan bickering over the Kansas-Nebraska Act and the southwestern territories was pointless, since cotton expansion had already reached its natural limits. But this argument assumes that enslaved workers could do nothing more than pick cotton. White southerners knew better. The Confederate constitution recognized and protected slavery in the western territories, which the C.S.A claimed; and during the Civil War, President Jefferson Davis received a dispatch from his southwestern field commander, who insisted that seizing California would add "the most valuable agriculture and grazing lands, and the richest mineral region in the world."

"In a Cotton Field," romaniticized illustration by Horace Bradley for Harper's weekly, *1887 Aug. 20, p. 592. Courtesy of the Library of Congress, LC-USZ62-115201.*

estimated slave mortality on sugar plantations at 8 percent, while the death toll "in the towns, on coffee properties, and other farms [was] much less." It is a small wonder that slaveholders on the British mainland used the threat of sale to the Caribbean as a method of controlling unruly bondpersons. As Cuban planters often said, "sugar is made with blood."

If most of the Africans sold into the Americas toiled in sugar fields, enslaved workers also performed every imaginable sort of labor. Modern residents of the United States conflate cotton with slavery and wrongly assume that Africans and their descendants harvested little else, but only in the last fifty years of the existence of the institution in North America did slavery move into the Gulf South states and undergo a switch from tobacco and rice production to cotton. Particularly in port cities from New York to Port-au-Prince, slaves worked the docks, loaded ships, and carted goods. Many served their masters in a domestic capacity. Trained as manservants (like Mark Twain's fictional Valet de Chambre), cooks, butlers, coachmen, valets, and grooms, African slaves labored inside their owners' homes. Others had been purchased in Africa because they possessed a particular artisanal skill or were trained in the Americas as artisans. In Charles Town, South Carolina, more than half of all white artisans retained at least a single bondman as an apprentice. In select trades, the percentage was even higher. Sixty percent of urban carpenters in South Carolina held slaves, and some carpenters ran their entire businesses using gangs of bond carpenters; a full 25 percent of carpenters possessed more than ten bond artisans, whom they employed in small groups at construction sites.

In Rio de Janeiro, the capital of Brazil after 1763 and on its way to becoming one of the largest cities of the western Atlantic, slavery pervaded virtually every aspect of urban life. Slaves worked the docks and shipyards, built churches and government buildings, carted sewage, and fed and clothed their masters. In fact, slaves or ex-slaves did most of the manual labor. By 1821, 40,376 of Rio's 86,323 permanent residents were enslaved. As punishing as slavery was, freedom in Brazil, as in much of Spanish America, was made more accessible by the common practice of hiring out. Particularly in bustling Atlantic ports like Rio, where workers were always in demand, slaves were generally considered sources of steady rents rather than unlimited profits, and thus many set out daily to hire themselves out for a variety of tasks. Masters demanded a set sum called a *jornal*, what amounted to the slave's daily wages, but anything earned beyond this, usually from self-hire on weekends and feast days, could be applied to a slave's self-purchase account. Religious confraternities run by former slaves served at times as savings-and-loan institutions for those wishing to purchase themselves or their loved ones. Many slaves worked extra hours not to purchase themselves, but rather their children. As the historian Zephyr Frank and others have shown, some, upon acquiring freedom, also acquired slaves, a reminder of how normalized slavery had become in this part of the Atlantic world.

Elsewhere in the Americas, legal structures intended to hold people in bondage grew more rigid. Not surprisingly, these laws, or codes, varied over time and place and were shaped by such variables as religion and the percentage in a given population of enslaved to free persons. In the French colonies, slavery was regulated by the *Code Noir*, promulgated by King Louis XIV in 1685 and modified by his successors. Like the laws of other Catholic nations, the French code mandated religious instruction for slaves and, in theory, named church and state as guarantors of slaves' meager rights. The palace of Versailles, however, was far removed from the sugar plantations of the French Caribbean, and as in most slave societies, the gulf between royal edict and practice was wide. The Code enjoined masters from torturing or mutilating their human property, yet it granted them the privilege of hanging their slaves in chains while beating them with rods and whips. Moreover, since the edict denied slaves the right to appear in court as plaintiffs or defendants, or to seek reparations for excessive beatings in criminal courts, such fine legal distinctions were undoubtedly lost on most enslaved Africans in French colonies.

In part because of their long and intimate relationship with slavery, the Portuguese and Spanish responded differently to the situation. By the seventeenth century, Portugal's slave codes were drawn from the *Ordenações Filipinas*, a huge corpus of laws and edicts issued by Philip I and Philip II for all Portuguese holdings under Spanish control, and later confirmed by the Portuguese King João in 1643. The ordinances remained in force even after Brazil achieved independence in 1822. As in Spanish America, where similar laws remained in effect until 1789, owners were allowed to dispense only "moderate punishments," the same, in fact, that a master could administer to a free servant or a father to a wayward son. Subsequent amendments hinted that these vague prohibitions were often ignored. In 1824, Brazilian legislators forbade branding with a hot iron, and six years later banned whipping in excess of fifty lashes. By comparison, some evidence indicates that in Spanish colonies, the few rights granted to slaves were taken more seriously. Spanish law in *Las Siete Partidas* allowed bondmen direct access to courts, thus recognizing that slaves had a legal personality. These legal rights were expanded rather than curtailed in a new 1789 code, and many slaves took advantage of them to sue for forced sale under a clause banning cruel and unusual punishment. As was true of Native Americans under Spanish rule, royal courts were required to provide free legal representation for slaves, and a surprising number of these public defenders won their cases.

In contrast to the Spanish and Portuguese, whose familiarity with slavery in Iberia facilitated the expansion of the institution and a legal system to support it, and to the French, who had a centralized system and a single code that encompassed all overseas holdings, the English did not have laws in place to administer an institution of chattel slavery. This is not to say the English were unfamiliar with slavery, although they tended to think of it more in its Mediterranean context, wherein Christians were captured by Muslim pirates and sold into slavery in North African ports. Tales of Englishmen in captivity were mainstays of popular literature in England, and one well-known Englishman in America, Captain John Smith, had endured this fate in the Ottoman Empire. But in order to regulate African laborers and hold them and their descendants in perpetuity as slaves, the English had to develop new laws, and in doing so they drew on their growing knowledge of African laborers. They initially employed slavery in the Caribbean, with Providence Island becoming the first English colony to contain a slave majority in the 1630s. So rebellious were the slaves of nearby Tortuga—eventually a favorite base of both French and English buccaneers—that the English inhabitants actually abandoned the island in 1635. To control slaves the English passed laws requiring them to reside in English households, and in 1638 the Providence Island Company ordered that for every one African there should be two English people. Slowly the English drafted laws, first on Barbados, whose Slave

Act of 1661 was the first comprehensive British slave code, then on the mainland, to which Barbadian migrants transported their laws and experience. By 1662, the Virginia House of Burgesses determined that children inherited the legal status of their mothers, thus ensuring the inheritability of slave status. Jamaica (1664 and 1696), South Carolina (1691), and Antigua (1697) followed suit with codes of their own, as did all subsequent colonies that contained slaves. In this respect, the English colonies of the western Atlantic devised laws without parallel in England and contributed to an important legal divergence in the English Atlantic world, one that facilitated abolition by judicial decree in England in Justice Mansfield's famous *Somerset* decision of 1772, which pointed to the absence of laws that supported slavery in the British Isles.

Maroon Settlements and Slave Revolts

Of course, slaves, too, made choices—and history. As colonies in the western Atlantic changed from societies with slaves in their midst into full-blown slave societies, Africans began to resist their bondage in greater numbers and with greater organization. Captives never passively accepted their enslavement, and the emergence of plantation economies unintentionally provided them with the numbers they needed to rebel in groups. Initially, slave revolts exhibited a restorationist quality, to the extent that African insurgents aimed not so much at overturning the institution of slavery—a system they were sufficiently familiar with—but at withdrawing from slave societies and creating small worlds at the margins similar to the ones they had left in Africa. By escaping into the American hinterland to create *maroon* colonies (from the Spanish, and possibly Taíno, term *cimarrón*, or runaway), rebels did not directly challenge the emerging slave systems as much as they plagued individual planters and mine owners. As early as the mid-sixteenth century, maroon communities in present-day Mexico, Panama, Colombia, Venezuela, and Ecuador grew populous enough—or inhabited such naturally defensible terrain—to defy the Europeans and force colonial administrators to recognize their freedom and autonomy.

Not surprisingly, the scattered nature of sugar estates in Brazil, together with a densely forested mountain range abutting the coast that could provide a refuge for runaways, made the Portuguese colony the home of the most impressive maroon communities in the Americas. The most famous, Palmares, formed by 1603 in the Alagoas backcountry of Pernambuco, existed for almost a century. The leader of a military expedition sent to destroy the community in 1645 reported that Macaco, the main village, was fortified by a double palisade and its intervening trench filled with pointed stakes. Inside the village walls stood a large council building, 220 houses, a church, and four forges arrayed along a broad street, six feet wide and a half-mile long. By the 1670s, Palmares comprised more than a dozen village sites that stretched ninety miles. Its leader, Ganga Zumba, ruled by election over as many as 20,000 people. Ganga Zumba developed an elaborate court and a large army, among whose war captains were some of his sons. His brother, mother, and nephews governed associated villages, making his almost an African dynasty in exile.

Palmares survived repeated assaults until, finally, in 1694, an army of more than 6,000 Indians, slaves, and hired mercenaries, the *bandeirantes*, destroyed it. But the fall of Palmares hardly signaled the end of the struggle: survivors scattered through the forests to form new maroon sites, and slave resistance remained a leitmotif running through the history of colonial Brazil.

Most other maroon communities in Portuguese Brazil, called *quilombos* or *mocambos*, were smaller. One of the first to be crushed was at São Vicente, where authorities captured six Africans, eight Indian men, nineteen Indian women, and twenty-one children called *caborés* (persons of African and Indian parentage). Although runaways in the English mainland colonies tended to be single young men, as the population of the São Vicente colony indicates, women often made up a considerable proportion of Brazil's maroon groups. Many were not fugitives from the sugar estates, but indigenous women from nearby tribes whose numbers disease had depleted or who had been displaced by plantation expansion. Several of the communities elected black women as their leaders *rainhas* (queens). Later, the discovery of gold and diamonds in *Minas Gerais* ("General Mines" in Portuguese) just before 1700 turned this vast interior region into a veritable hotbed of quilombos. Descendants of maroons in this and other parts of Brazil have recently gained official recognition, and with it certain property rights. In Spanish America, the largest maroon settlements of the seventeenth and eighteenth centuries emerged in the gold-producing regions of interior New Granada (in what is now Colombia), and in the hills, forests, and swamplands around the slave port of Cartagena. As in Minas Gerais, access to gold and other valuable minerals in New Granada allowed some runaways to bargain for their freedom in ways not possible in the sugar colonies.

The hills high above the sugar fields on the Caribbean islands also offered runaways an inviting refuge. Here, however, what the French called *petit marronage* was more common than *grand marronage* like Palmares. Only rarely did mountain colonies in the French islands number more than one hundred, since stealing food while remaining safely hidden became more difficult once the settlement grew too large. Yet in one instance, on Martinique in 1665, a maroon colony grew nearly as large as Palmares. Fugitives led by the runaway Francisque Fabulé (who had taken his master's name) established a colony that briefly became home to nearly five hundred escaped slaves. Finding it easier to negotiate with Fabulé than send an army into the hills, the colony's council agreed to free the settlement's leaders and not to punish any maroons who chose to return quietly to their labors. For a time, Fabulé worked as a domestic in the governor's household. But after seducing a domestic slave, Fabulé convinced her to steal what she could, stab her master, and join him in the mountains. This time the council sent soldiers after him, and he spent the rest of his life in the galleys.

Away from the sugar fields, where the percentage of Africans to European colonists was lower—as well as in places where the percentage of African Americans to Africans was higher—resistance to enslavement took different forms. On the English mainland, where Indians were just as inclined to return or enslave runaways as they were to adopt them as tribal members, flight was the most common form of resistance. Skilled artisans, and especially those who had been in the colonies long enough to learn a smattering of English, were the ones most likely to flee their bondage. Judging from the runaway slave advertisements that littered colonial newspapers, men tended to run off more than did enslaved women, whose lack of marketable skills or ties to children served to chain them to their masters' homes. Carpenters, "fishing Negroes," and boatmen were particularly inclined to make good on their escape, since growing cities and the maritime world required their skills and allowed them to disappear into urban sanctuaries. In a time when slavery was legal in all corners of the English empire, there was no bastion of freedom to run to—as there would be in the nineteenth-century United States, once slavery ended in the northern states—but these fugitives often headed for towns where they could get lost among the handful of free blacks and working-class whites who made up the substratum of society. Escaping blacks ran away alone, many to rejoin relatives, and they relied on their skills and cunning to find employment and build new lives.

Poisoning was another common way in which slaves retaliated against their masters and even against other enslaved people. Like arson, poison is an ideal crime for the weak and powerless, since it requires no physical strength, only proximity to the target. In British America, women in particular were believed by authorities to be responsible for poisoning their masters' food. In Antigua, during one forty-year period, courts put twelve women to trial for the crime of poisoning; women amounted to 6 percent of the slaves executed in that colony in the four decades before 1763. A study of Virginia reveals similar numbers: between 1740 and 1785, more blacks in the colony (and the new state) stood trial for poisoning than for any other crime besides theft. Among those executed in Virginia was Eve, who in 1745 mixed poison into her master's milk. The court found her guilty and inflicted upon her the unusual form of execution typically reserved for traitors: "that she be carried upon a Hurdle to the place of Execution and there to be Burnt."

In Brazil, Portuguese and creoles understood poisoning in terms of witchcraft, which was how Catholics redefined some African religious practices when they appeared among enslaved communities in the western Atlantic. Herbs and potions used correctly, for example, were believed to protect a slave from an owner's wrath, as some slaves in Minas Gerais hoped when they used scrapings from their master's shoe in rituals. But religious rituals could also be performed with the aim of injuring owners and their families. Manuel Rodrigues de Senna, a slaveholder in Recife in Brazil, suffered from an unexplained illness that abated only when a priest performed an exorcism. Senna suspected his slaves of bewitching him and plotting to poison him, and the cook confirmed his fears by admitting that she had put potions in his food. Masters often feared that their slaves plotted to poison them, but in this case Senna came to believe as well in the supernatural powers of his slaves.

Far more dangerous than poisoning, but much less common, were full-scale revolts. Collective slave rebellions were most likely to occur in time of war, when Europeans and colonists were divided against themselves. Yet even where geography proved inhospitable to successful flight, large-scale conspira-

COLONIAL BRAZIL
Adapted from Leslie Bethel, ed.,
**The Cambridge History of Latin
America** *(Cambridge University
Press). Reprinted with permission
of Cambridge University Press.*

cies remained closer to mass escape attempts than revolutionary activity, a pattern that changed little through the mid-eighteenth century. At the very end of what settlers in British North America dubbed Queen Anne's War, blacks rose in New York City. On the morning of April 1, 1712, two dozen slaves, led by a core of Gold Coast Africans (who may have shared an identity as Coromantee) set fire to the home of a prominent New Yorker and then shot and stabbed whites who rushed to extinguish the flames. Altogether the rebellion took the lives of eight whites, with about a dozen more wounded. New York authorities retaliated by executing eighteen slaves through a variety of tortures, from burning at the stake to hanging in chains to "breaking on the wheel." Among those executed were slaves who belonged to merchants, two butchers, several mariners, a barber, a widow, and at least two persons sold into New York from Spanish colonies. The sole female insurgent, Abigail, was pregnant and was spared after she "pled her belly."

In Virginia, the colony with the largest number of blacks on the British mainland, rebellion reached its peak in 1730, when "the Negroes in several parts of the Country" plotted to "obtain their freedom." In what would become a common theme in popular revolts around the Atlantic basin, Virginia bondmen came to believe that a far-off authority—in this case King George II—had issued an edict demanding the freedom of those who converted to Christianity, but that local masters had suppressed the order. By the first decades of the eighteenth century, several generations of blacks had been born into the colony, time enough for a significant percentage of them to convert.

Virginia planters imported large numbers of Africans during these decades, of course, but nearly half were "black Christians of the Congo." According to the historian Anthony Parent, a good many "of these captives took pride in their Christian heritage and comprehended the rumored emancipation of 1730 in religious terms."

Although enslaved Africans never required a particular grievance or religious inspiration to rebel—as the historian Herbert Aptheker once bluntly put it, the cause of slave revolts was slavery—neither were slaves any less rational or suicidal than anyone else, and they organized for their liberty only when circumstances were propitious. The Virginia conspiracy matured during harvest season, when white farmers were so fatigued that they frequently failed to patrol the plantation districts. One can also easily see the hand of the Atlantic world in the events of 1730. When several hundred slaves assembled near Norfolk to choose "Officers to Command them," their tactics replicated the Kongolese military model of waging war, which included the election of officers and divisions into martial units. The rebels "did a great deal of Mischief" but were quickly suppressed by white authorities and their Pasquotank allies, who hunted down the fugitives. Vengeful whites hanged "four and twenty of these Negroes" in the woods, and authorities later tried and executed five of the "most Suspected" leaders.

White colonials described the "many outrages" such rebels committed against their owners, but in colonies with heavily armed white majorities, sporadic uprisings hardly endangered slavery as a system of labor. Consequently, Euro-Americans continued to import more enslaved workers, and Africans and their American-born children continued to resist at the point of a sword. In 1739, the number of runaways in Jamaica "made the Island tremble," and one year later, maroons in Suriname battled Dutch settlers. Then, in 1741, slaves in New York City—in alliance with Irish immigrants, who frequented the city's waterside taverns—again began to plan an escape, this time to French Canada. The historian Graham Russell Hodges detects "a powerful proletarian republicanism" in the plot, since some of the conspirators were aware of a general black rebelliousness then existing around the western Atlantic. Conspirators like Caesar Varick and his common-law wife, "Irish Peg" Kerry, consorted with slaves like Will, a veteran of conspiracies in Danish St. John and Antigua. As before, arson was the conspirators' favored tool. Fire destroyed New York's Fort George and several homes before whites in power uncovered the plot. Even a stream of executions through the summer did little to quell black rebellion. In January 1742, the lieutenant governor reported "cabals of negroes" burning homes and farms just outside the city, and the discovery of another conspiracy in South Carolina led to more hangings in Charles Town. Only the brief European truce of 1748, following the War of the Austrian Succession (known as King George's War in British North America), momentarily silenced the cycle of slave rebellions.

None of this should imply that enslaved people in the Americas lived in a constant state of overt rebellion—it was more often a slow boil. Aware of the odds against successful escape, and even more aware of the state and private machinery designed to hold them in bondage, black men and women instead resisted their enslavement as best they could. Historians draw a distinction between rebellions—like the plots in New York City in 1712 and 1741—and more common acts of daily resistance. From feigning sickness to breaking tools, from working as slowly as possible to "outlaying" (hiding on the outskirts of their master's plantation for a day or two), Africans and their descendants found ways to assert their humanity in the face of oppressive labor systems. Such private forms of resistance might earn the slave a few stripes of the whip, and certainly perceptive masters understood that quiet obstructionism was itself a type of confrontation. "[T]he Majority [of slaves] are of plotting disposition," slaveholder Benjamin Franklin complained to a European correspondent, "dark, sullen, malicious, revengeful and cruel in the highest Degree." But if malingering or mistreating the master's livestock were relatively safe forms of resistance and allowed angry bondmen to avoid the gallows, kicking a cow or breaking a hoe was hardly going to put an end to slavery in the Western Hemisphere.

As with the maroon activity of enslaved Africans, neither the solitary acts of poisoning nor the collective rebellions north of Spanish Florida were truly revolutionary, in that they did not effectively challenge the established social order. Instead, as these colonies evolved (or regressed) from societies with slaves to slave societies, most captives sought merely to flee their enslavement or restore lost traditions by escaping into the forests of the American hinterland. Only in Atlantic seaports, where news and gossip changed hands like cargo, did slaves like Caesar Varick begin to perceive themselves as part of a larger, and possibly revolutionary, movement—and the result of this realization was to be burned alive at the stake.

All of this changed with the age of revolution. By the time creole elites began to assert their autonomy from European monarchs, the bond servants of these same men, inspired by religious leaders from Richard Allen to Dutty Boukman, and by soldiers from Gabriel to Henri Christophe, abandoned their restorationist visions in exchange for demands of political inclusion and civil rights. Those demands, together with the emergence of the industrial order in much of the northern Atlantic, helped end the international traffic in human beings. But no commerce of such magnitude ends quickly; the last verified disembarking of Africans in Cuba took place in January 1870, when nine hundred captives were sold into Jibacoa. Several smaller boats may have found their way past British patrols over the course of the decade. In 1907, at a time when Theodore Roosevelt was president of the United States, an aged African woman named María la Conguita told a Cuban journalist that she had been sold into Cuba in 1878. If true, she may well have been the last African slave sold in the Americas.

Selected Readings

Barry, Boubacar, *Senegambia and the Atlantic Slave Trade* (Cambridge, UK: Cambridge University Press, 1998).

Berlin, Ira, *Many Thousands Gone: The First Two Centuries of Slavery in North America* (Cambridge, MA: Harvard University Press, 1998).

Blackburn, Robin, *The Making of New World Slavery, from the Baroque to the Modern, 1492–1800* (London: Verso, 1997).

Davis, David Brion, *In the Image of God: Religion, Moral Values, and Our Heritage of Slavery* (New Haven: Yale University Press, 2001).

DeCorse, Christopher, *West Africa During the Atlantic Slave Trade: Archaeological Perspectives* (New York: Continuum International Publishing Group, 2002).

Eltis, David, *The Rise of African Slavery in the Americas* (Cambridge, MA: Cambridge University Press, 2000).

Frank, Zehpyr L., *Dutra's World: Wealth and Family in Nineteenth-Century Rio de Janeiro* (Albuquerque: University of New Mexico Press, 2004).

Genovese, Eugene D., *From Rebellion to Revolution: Afro-American Slave Revolts in the Making of the Modern World* (Baton Rouge: Louisiana State University Press, 1979).

Harms, Robert, *The Diligent: A Voyage through the Worlds of the Slave Trade* (New York: Basic Books, 2002).

Hodges, Graham Russell, *Root and Branch: African Americans in New York and East Jersey, 1613–1863* (Chapel Hill: University of North Carolina Press, 1999).

Karash, Mary, Slave Life in Rio de Janeiro, 1808–1850 (Princeton: Princeton University Press, 1987).

Law, Robin C., *The Slave Coast of West Africa, 1550–1750: The Impact of the Atlantic Slave Trade on an African Society* (Oxford: Oxford University Press, 1991).

McMillen, James A., *The Final Victims: Foreign Slave Trade to North America, 1783–1810* (Columbus: University of South Carolina Press, 2004).

Miller, Joseph C., *Way of Death: Merchant Capitalism and the Atlantic Slave Trade, 1780–1830* (Madison: University of Wisconsin Press, 1988).

Parent, Anthony S., *Foul Means: The Formation of a Slave Society in Virginia, 1660–1740* (Chapel Hill: University of North Carolina Press, 2003).

Schwartz, Stuart, ed., *Tropical Babylons: Sugar and the Making of the Atlantic World, 1450–1680* (Chapel Hill: University of North Carolina Press, 2004).

Sweet, James H., *Recreating Africa: Culture, Kinship, and Religion in the African-Portuguese World, 1441–1770* (Chapel Hill: University of North Carolina Press, 2003).

Thomas, Hugh, *The Slave Trade: The Story of the Atlantic Slave Trade, 1440–1870* (New York: Simon & Schuster, 1997).

"Un cavalier, et une dame beuvant du chocolat *(Cavalier and Lady Drinking Chocolate),*"
by N. Bonnart. The maid is preparing the drink by rolling a dasher to make it foamy.
Photograph credit: The Pierpont Morgan Library, New York.

Chapter Seven
Trade in the Atlantic World, 1580–1780

Money is like muck, not good except it be spread.
Francis Bacon, *Of Seditions and Troubles*, 1601

In the last quarter of the sixteenth century, Bernardo de Vargas Machuca served in Spain's American colonies, first as a soldier and then as an estate manager and a district official. On his return to Spain—like many people who traveled to the Americas, he sailed for home after a stint overseas—he settled down to write of his experiences. He challenged the assertions of the missionary Las Casas regarding excessive Spanish cruelty in one text and also composed several military treatises. In one of his works, Vargas Machuca offered a manual on how to subdue rebellious, nonsedentary Indians and incorporate them into colonial society. Inculcating good market behavior was a principal concern of his. "Being barbarous people," he complained, desert- and forest-dwelling Indians grew only the minimum of crops needed for their use, thus "wasting" any potential surplus. In his view, "They should be encouraged to produce goods for sale, especially goods in demand" in Spanish towns. Indian mine workers and African domestic servants might need cotton cloth, for example, or maize. To facilitate the Indians' transition to a commercial mentality, he urged colonial officials to organize a weekly market, where Indians could trade freely, exchanging the products of one district for the bounty of another. Such market days could bring together Indians and Spaniards, thus assisting in the process of "hispanicization." All parties might be satisfied and, Vargas Machuca observed, the Indians would have more money with which to pay tribute to their Spanish overlords. In essence, Vargas Machuca proposed a repeat in fringe areas of Spanish America of what had happened after conquest in the core regions of Mexico and Peru.

Vargas Machuca's recommendations serve as a reminder that economic gain—through monopolistic control of production, exchange, and consumption—underlay European transatlantic expansion. Spain's rulers initially hoped that religious conversion would be the most effective means of making Indians like Europeans, but it was arguably market exchange that proved most transformative. Many Indians learned quickly the new rules, and across sixteenth-century Mexico and Peru indigenous traders grew so numerous and even wealthy that Spanish officials tried to suppress them. At the unconquered fringes, as Vargas Machuca suggested, inducements to trade might transform even the most resistant Indians, many of them hunters and gatherers, into dependent, colonial subjects. On many frontiers, this proved true. The historian David Weber points out that in northern New Spain, markets and exposure to the Atlantic economy did more than missions to alter indigenous practices. In the newly interconnected Atlantic world, trade required not only new spaces but new habits, as people became consumers and decided how and what to purchase. These exchanges were rarely symmetrical, yet people everywhere made choices about how to incorporate new goods into their lives.

Above all, the Atlantic world was one of commodities: goods enticed Europeans first to Africa and then across the Atlantic to the Americas, and they created the demand for labor that led European investors to transport 12 million Africans and 2 million Europeans in the same time span across the Atlantic. Trade and consumer demand changed lives around the Atlantic basin, transforming sleepy provincial capitals into metropolitan giants, creating cities where none had existed, altering what people ate and drank and even the customs by which they did so, and enabling outsiders to acquire political and cultural power. In Africa, where people became commodities, the impact of the Atlantic trade was profound, but also surprisingly varied.

Urban and Regional Transformations

Even as they altered social and political circumstances, new commodities and their exchange changed the physical landscape. Trade required places where merchants and consumers could meet to exchange either goods or, through letters of credit, the promise of goods. But alteration of the physical landscape went beyond the emergence of things such as fairs, trading posts, and bourses. Expanding Atlantic trade fueled the growth of existing cities and led to the emergence of new ones, while vagaries in trade caused the eclipse of others. Cities that were regional or international powerhouses in earlier centuries but have since receded include Ipswich, Massachusetts, Newport, Rhode Island, Port Royal, Jamaica, Charles Town, South Carolina, Porto Bello, Panama, Salvador, Brazil, and Cacheu, Guinea Bissau.

Urban growth was not inherently dependent on Atlantic trade. Historically, migration has driven urban expansion, particularly in times of population growth and economic pressure, when able-bodied young people move from rural areas to provincial towns and cities. Mortality rates were generally so high in early modern cities that their growth hinged on continued in-migration. This was because cities, like new colonies, had unique disease environments. Newcomers endured a period of urban "seasoning" in the same way that new migrants to American and African colonies and factories did, and just as newcomers to colonies tended to die earlier than those who stayed in the nation of their origin, the same held true for new arrivals from the countryside to cities. Predominantly young males between the ages of ten and thirty, migrants were the most likely to succumb when epidemics hit, and consequently urban populations constantly needed replenishing. In 1625, for example, 35,000 people died from a London outbreak of the plague, but within two years, rural migrants had replaced the loss in population. And like colonies, cities had high rates of childhood mortality. In the worst periods in seventeenth-century London, deaths outnumbered births by 65 percent. When cities grew in this period of poor sanitation and high incidence of disease, they did so because people moved to them in numbers sufficient to offset the deaths. The pattern was particularly evident in London, which grew from 40,000 people in 1500 to 900,000 in 1801. Other British cities grew in the same period, particularly between 1750 and 1800, when Glasgow, Liverpool, and Manchester tripled in size. Some cities grew because they became national capitals; others grew because they were centers of regional, Atlantic, or global trade.

While regional demographic circumstances and economic strains in part determined urban growth in Europe, the Atlantic economy also shaped patterns of urban transformation. When young people ventured to cities to find employment, port towns were often the most promising destinations, and growing seaports attracted even more newcomers. Most of the towns that experienced dramatic expansion between 1500 and 1850 were those drawn into the Atlantic economy.

In Europe, Atlantic contact elevated some previously secondary cities to commercial prominence, while it demoted others. In nearly all cases, however, the chronology of a city's transformation was linked to Atlantic trade and specific commodities: as these commodities came in and out of fashion, cities' fortunes waxed and waned. Among the first European cities the new Atlantic orientation transformed was Seville, which is actually not located on Atlantic shores, but some fifty-five miles up the Guadalquivir River. In the early fifteenth century, Seville was a provincial city of 40,000 people, the largest in Castile. In 1503, the Spanish crown established the House of Trade in Seville, and in less than a century the population of the city soared to nearly 150,000, largely because of the economic activity surrounding its hosting of Spain's transatlantic fleet. The size of what had become a crowded city, along with the poor sanitation habits of the time, meant that such potentially deadly communicable diseases as smallpox and measles became endemic, and they were readily spread by sailors coming in and going out on ships plying trade in the Indies. Diseases that may have originated in the Americas, such as syphilis, soon appeared in Seville as well.

The selection of Seville as the fleet's official port of departure—a good choice in terms of defense and provisioning, but inconvenient in other ways—transformed the city into one of Europe's great metropolitan centers. Seville had convenient access to the various agro-pastoral products of Spain's interior—wine, vinegar, and olive oil; salted cod and dried beef; cider and hardtack; chickpeas and rice—so ships were provisioned in Seville and later Cádiz with food to last the voyage and winter layover. In her analysis of six seventeenth-century Spanish galleons, the historian Carla Rahn Phillips finds that a typical Atlantic-bound vessel carried wine to last 191.4 days, and enough beans, chickpeas, and rice to sustain 500 men for 273 days.

Supplying ships for long voyages was hardly a challenge limited to a few European cities and their agricultural hinterlands. As early as the sixteenth century, African farmers living near the Atlantic responded to new demands for foodstuffs. Slave ships needed large amounts of food for the transatlantic voyage (one rule of thumb being one ton of food for every ten captives on board). Some of this food, in the form of dried beans, flour, salted beef, or oil, came from Europe, but because of the long time spent along the African coast acquiring slaves and the desirability of fresh products, captains purchased much food in Africa. The master of the French slaver *Diligent*, which crossed the ocean with 256 slaves in 1731, purchased millet (to mix with fava beans brought from France) as he acquired captives along the coast. On the islands of Príncipe and São Tomé, his last stop before crossing the ocean, he purchased chickens, goats, ducks, geese, lemons, bananas, and figs of unknown quantity, along with a thousand plantains, 1,700 coconuts, 192 bushels of manioc flour, and 4 bushels of peas. Near major ports of call, export industries eventually developed to supply slavers' needs. Ironically, villages of slaves often did most of the work of production. Migrants from the hinterland, pushed by famine in their homelands or pulled by their desire for imported commodities, moved toward busy coastal areas to take up farming there.

The expansion of port towns had unanticipated repercussions. King Ferdinand's choice of Seville altered the city, but it also forced changes in nautical technology: the sandbar at the mouth of the river kept out the biggest ships, so shipbuilders worked to develop smaller, lighter-draft vessels that could sail over the bar and upriver to the city. Seville bustled with the activity related to the fleet, with passengers waiting for their ships, suppliers bringing goods to replenish holds, and artisans working to repair and maintain hulls, sails, and rigging. The Spanish historian Pablo E. Pérez-Mallaína describes old Seville as a "human stewpot." Yet constraints of the shallow river eventually restricted the city's growth. The great lumbering ships of the fleet got caught on the river bottom, so passengers and cargo had to travel downriver on barges before being taken on board gradually as they neared open sea.

Urban prosperity also became associated with specialized trades. In Britain, Liverpool became a center of the eighteenth-century slave trade, while Glasgow, home to the Tobacco Lords, was built on smoke. Other colonial products, such as sugar, reached Europe in semiprocessed form, and those places that established refineries for further processing experienced similar growth. Such was the case for London, Glasgow, and Bristol. If Seville's growth was propelled by the Indies fleet, cod drove the growth of the French port of La Rochelle. In the commercial world of sixteenth-century Europe, goods were customarily transported on rivers. La Rochelle, situated on the coast, occupied a second tier status as a port. But in the sixteenth century, the city emerged as Europe's main base for the Newfoundland cod fisheries. Out of a total of 128 voyages to Newfoundland in a fifty-year span, more than half originated from La Rochelle. Bilbao and San Sebastian, shipbuilding centers in the Basque country of northern Spain, also grew, prompted by the cod industry and the demands of the Spanish fleet (southern Spain was always short of suitable timber). Basque ironworks in the provinces of Biscaya and Guipúzcoa produced anchors, pulleys, rendering pails, harpoon points, and other nautical and fishing equipment. (This was a perilous age for ocean travel, and the regular shipwrecks alone generated a steady market for new vessels.) But the importance of cities in the Atlantic trade was dynamic. La Rochelle and the other southern Atlantic French ports, including Bordeaux and Bayonne, abandoned the cod trade after the sixteenth century, and two northern ports, Saint-Mâlo (in Brittany) and Grenville (in Normandy), took their place. Together, these two ports accounted for 58 percent of the green (i.e., fresh) cod and 92 percent of the dry cod imported to Europe in the eighteenth century.

Atlantic commerce altered African livelihoods, as well. Before the integration of the Atlantic, the commercial, political, and cultural focus of many West African societies was inland, toward the progressively dry savannas leading toward the Sahara Desert. Across that vast body of dry earth and scrub, rock, and sand, North African merchants for centuries had used pack camels to carry commodities to the populated regions south of the Sahara: the desert

Down the Road to Underdevelopment

Historians do not agree on the role Europeans played historically in the underdevelopment of Africa. Many have sided with writers of the 1960s and 1970s, Basil Davidson and Walter Rodney among the most prominent, in arguing that Europeans, stronger militarily and economically, forced Africans into giving up valuable raw materials and slaves in exchange for European manufactured goods, thereby starting Africans down the path toward greater and more generalized dependency. More recently, John Thornton has disagreed. Africans had more control over what they traded than the earlier historians believed, he argues; they made commercial decisions they considered in their best interests, their manufacturing could compete with that of pre-industrial Europe, and not for a long time did Europeans call the shots along the African coast in the Atlantic trade.

"[T]rade remained competitive" along Africa's Atlantic shores, Thornton summarizes, "probably favoring no particular national or regional actors —and certainly not Europeans at the expense of Africans."

Basil Davidson, Black Mother: The Years of the Atlantic Slave Trade *(1961); Walter Rodney,* How Europe Underdeveloped Africa *(1972); John Thornton,* Africa and Africans in the Making of the Atlantic World, 1400–1800, *2nd ed. (1998).*

Below: A recent street scene in Latrikunda, the Republic of the Gambia, ranked 155 of 177 nations in the United Nations Human Development Index (2005). Photo by Doris Wright, 2003.

was their conduit of trade. It was these merchants, nearly all of whom were Muslims by the ninth or tenth century, who brought with them related religious and cultural influences that spread steadily across the grasslands of West Africa, and it was control of the south side of this trans-Sahara trade that provided the economic wherewithal for the rise of West African empires— Ghana, Mali, Songhai, Kanem, and Bornu. When Portuguese mariners first arrived on the Atlantic coast, few Africans living far inland paid them much mind, their interests in the ocean being mainly in fishing and local trade. For most West Africans in the thirteenth, fourteenth, or fifteenth centuries, all blessings, in the form of commodities, with a cultural overlay, flowed from the desert.

Farther south, below the Niger Delta, toward the Congo River and beyond, economy, polity, and culture before the rise of Atlantic slaving involved less-distant influences. Individuals or families tended to come to power as guardians of ancestral land and its spirits or shrines, especially rainmaking shrines. Ensuring harvests, protecting against external attack, and securing trade routes enhanced authority, which meant increased tribute payments and, under the right circumstances, growth of the political unit. Kingdoms of various sizes and shapes thus existed near the coast and at some distance inland when Europeans came exploring.

The rise of a brisk Atlantic trade, which progressed unevenly in spatial terms over two centuries, altered these conditions. In some places it began an almost immediate transformation of commercial and cultural refocus toward the Atlantic coast and led to rapid political and social change. In others, widespread change would await the rise of the enormous demand for human laborers on plantations in the Americas and the growth of the transatlantic slave trade in the middle of the seventeenth century. In West Africa, trans-Saharan trade did not cease with the start of Atlantic trading, and, indeed, Islamic culture and traditions continued to spread in an east-to-west belt below the desert. But the Atlantic trade eventually brought new focus to West Africans' commercial interests and new access to commodities and cultural influences. It is probably no mere coincidence that, following Songhai's defeat by a Moroccan force in 1591, no vast empire rose to fill the political void between the upper Niger and the Atlantic coast to the west. By this time, there was simply less trade to control moving toward the desert and more to command people's attention coming from the Atlantic. Similarly, the sharp rise in Atlantic trading in the vicinity of the Congo River brought new traders, new merchandise, new influences, and new rules for cultural interaction that altered power balances and human relationships, initiated the fall of old states and the rise of new ones, and brought a trickling in of new religious and cultural elements that changed the ways people spoke, thought, and acted.

In economic terms, it is equally important to examine what Atlantic trading did not do. African economies in the slave-trading zone were overwhelmingly agricultural before the Atlantic commerce in humans began, and they were overwhelmingly agricultural four centuries thereafter. In certain areas the farming economy changed because of Atlantic trading, becoming more productive because of the introduction of new crops. Once large numbers of

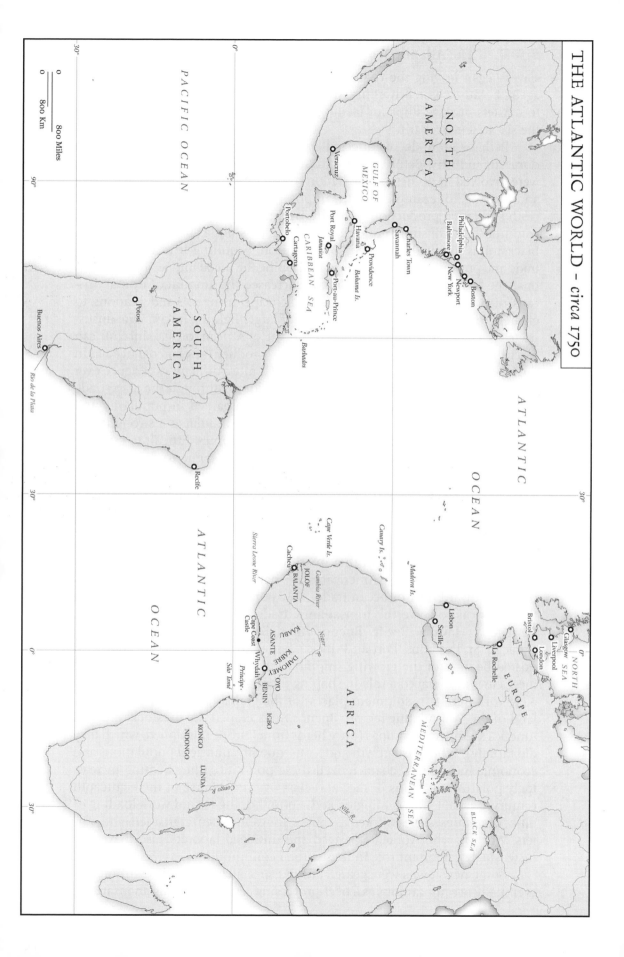

THE ATLANTIC WORLD – *circa 1750*

NORTH AMERICA

SOUTH AMERICA

AFRICA

EUROPE

PACIFIC OCEAN

ATLANTIC OCEAN

ATLANTIC OCEAN

GULF OF MEXICO

CARIBBEAN SEA

MEDITERRANEAN SEA

BLACK SEA

NORTH SEA

0   800 Miles
0   800 Km

Veracruz
Portobelo
Cartagena
Port Royal
Jamaica
Havana
Providence
Bahama Is.
Port-au-Prince
Barbados
Savannah
Charles Town
Philadelphia
Baltimore
New York
Newport
Boston
Potosí
Buenos Aires
Río de la Plata
Recife

Cape Verde Is.
Canary Is.
Madeira Is.
Sierra Leone River
Cacheu
JOLOF
BALANTA
Gambia River
KAABU
ASANTE
Cape Coast Castle
Whydah
DAHOMEY
KABRE
OYO
BENIN
São Tomé
Príncipe
IGBO
Niger R.
KONGO
NDONGO
LUNDA
Congo R.
Nile R.

Lisbon
Seville
La Rochelle
Bristol
Glasgow
Liverpool
London

30°
0°
90°
0°
30°
30°
0°
30°
30°
0°

slaves began leaving the coast for a transatlantic voyage, farming changed again, because coastal-dwelling African farmers began producing food to sell to masters of slave ships for feeding the humans in the ships' holds during the six- to ten-week trip.

Perhaps more deeply affected by the new economic relationships was domestic industry. Before the rise of Atlantic trading, most African societies were involved in domestic production of one or another type: iron smelting and weaving, for example. Did the importation of iron bars and new types of cloth stifle such production generally, or did domestic industries adapt and continue? As with similar questions, there is no simple answer. West African blacksmiths gradually stopped smelting iron, acquiring it instead through trade and putting their energies into fashioning the metal into tools and weapons. The heavy iron imports may have increased the amount of iron at Africans' disposal and led, through more and cheaper iron tools and weapons, to greater crop production and the arming of larger fighting forces. One unsuspected result of importing iron was the saving of African forests, since African blacksmiths no longer needed to fell trees to produce the charcoal needed in the smelting process. Weavers may have had a more difficult experience over the long run. Africans continued to operate looms through the slave-trade centuries (as they do today), but imported cloth gained in popularity and met much of the mass demand that could have stimulated a strong indigenous textile industry. As in all such matters, it becomes difficult to estimate what would have occurred had imported cloth not come to dominate the market—because it did. On the effect of the slave trade on domestic industries generally, there is a growing consensus that only in particular, coastal locales did a stifling of African manufacturing occur, and the slave trade actually stimulated some domestic industry.

If Africa and Europe experienced a general reorientation and elaboration of economic activity, in the Americas cities appeared where none had existed. The largest Native American states had landlocked capitals, not cities oriented toward river or ocean trade. New ports thus sprang up throughout the Americas to serve the transatlantic trade. Veracruz, Nombre de Díos, Cartagena, Havana, Recife, Buenos Aires, Baltimore, Newport, Kingston, Curaçao, St. Eustatius, Port-au-Prince, Charles Town (today Charleston): all existed because of the growing shipment of goods. And the hinterlands of these cities also played a role in shaping them. Baltimore, Philadelphia, and New York were transshipment places for the grains raised in the rich farmland of the mid-Atlantic region. Buenos Aires tapped the livestock of South America's temperate pampas (once herds from Europe multiplied, which they did rapidly). When fast growth and, consequently, transient populations and economic inequalities characterized these port cities, they became increasingly polarized in terms of race and class over the course of the eighteenth century. Casual laborers mingled at the port, hoping to find work loading or unloading ships; slaves worked as sailors, longshoremen, craftsmen, and porters. Women, who worked as waged and unwaged laborers, also played an increasingly important role in these urban communities.

Some new towns were geared around specialized activities. Although it eventually became famous as a beef-processing center supplying an insatiable

European market, Buenos Aires first became wealthy as a center of contraband trade. After peace was established between Spain and the Netherlands in 1648, Dutch ships choked the River Plate estuary to trade slaves and luxury goods to Spanish merchants traveling inland to the rich silver mines of Potosí. Likewise, despite Spain's longstanding ban on trade with foreigners and recurrent conflict between the home governments following Portugal's rebellion against Spanish authority in 1640, Brazilian traders flooded Buenos Aires with sugar, hides, tallow, and other commodities they could exchange for Peruvian silver. This South Atlantic "back door" to Spanish America's mineral wealth remained open until the Spanish crown at last decided to make the trade of Buenos Aires official through redistricting in 1776. From that date forward, Buenos Aires was a viceregal capital, and Potosí fell under its jurisdiction. Spain monitored and taxed the formerly illegal trade.

Some specialized activities of new Atlantic towns, distant as they were from a European metropole, went beyond contraband in their lawlessness. The commercial buildings and residences of Port Royal, Jamaica, a cosmopolitan spot inhabited by as many pirates and prostitutes as soldiers, merchants, and artisans, were crowded onto a narrow spit of land, forcing houses to reach up, not out. To accommodate the town's many lawbreakers, authorities constructed two courthouses and two prisons, and they kept a dunking stool and cage on hand to punish and restrain malefactors. Ashore, the buccaneers spent their stolen loot on gambling, drinking, and sex. The town boasted a beer garden, taverns, pits for cockfighting, and music houses (a delightful euphemism for a whorehouse). When this diverse entertainment proved inadequate, rowdy pirates generated their own: one account maintained that Port Royal's buccaneers liked to buy wine or beer, place the barrel in the street, and compel passersby (with a persuasive pistol) to take a swig. The English writer Ned Ward mocked Jamaica as "the Dunghill of the Universe"; another observer dubbed Port Royal the "Sodom of the Indies." Apparently the deities agreed. Soon after an earthquake in 1692, the city plunged into the ocean, visiting gruesome punishment on the townsfolk, hundreds of whom drowned in their houses as Port Royal was sucked beneath the waves.

But in an age of rich commodities packed aboard underprotected wooden ships, it took more than a single earthquake to eliminate piracy. In 1733, buccaneers found a new base when the English philanthropist James Ogelthorpe, who had procured a royal charter for the Georgia Colony in 1732, began to lay out plans for a town atop a walled bluff overlooking the Savannah River. Oglethorpe envisioned his colony as a refuge for British debtors (as well as a buffer against the Spanish), but Savannah's location, sixteen miles upriver from the Atlantic, was a perfect haven for smugglers. With the outbreak of the War of Jenkins' Ear in 1739, the line between English privateer and independent pirate, always a fine one near Spanish colonies, became hazier still. Within decades, inns and taverns crowded the bluff—a 1743 law that banned strong spirits in the colony did not extend to beer or wine—many of them home to seamen of various nationalities and flexible state loyalties. The Mariner's Inn, built in 1753 (and which still stands), was an indication of how quickly the demands of illicit trade could alter the philanthropic intentions of a town. The novelist Robert Louis Stevenson even had his fictitious Captain Flint die in an upstairs room at the inn, but not before passing the map of Treasure Island to his faithful mate, Billy Bones.

In the same way, Georgia's initial ban on slavery (with the idea that hard work and faithful husbandry would be the proper tonic for heading the debtors and prisoners brought to settle the colony down the road toward nobler pursuits) was quickly overturned as the colony grew. Yet the counterpart of gloomy Ellis Island in the eighteenth century was not Savannah, but rather the port city eighty-five miles to its north. Charles Town was the slave mart of the age for British mainland North America; at least one-quarter, maybe more, of all Africans imported into the English mainland colonies before 1775, and a much larger proportion once the United States came into being, passed through South Carolina. If Glasgow was built on tobacco, Charleston was financed through the trade in Africans. The import duty levied on slaves during the 1730s—£50 Carolina currency for every man, woman, or child over the age of ten—funded nearly half of the colony's operating revenues. Eighteen major firms and countless smaller companies raised the necessary capital, hired the ships and captains, imported the human merchandise, and re-sold cargoes along the coast from North Carolina to Georgia. Although city authorities required slavers to quarantine the enslaved Africans on nearby Sullivan's Island, merchants averaged twelve days between ship's arrival and final sale. The fortunes to be made did not come without a cost, however; Africans sometimes mutinied within sight of land, and dead bodies thrown from slave ships often washed into Charles Town harbor. Visitors found the sight ghastly, but locals learned to ignore the problem, except when the bobbing corpses became so numerous that "nobody [could] eat any fish."

The way a commodity became important and lucrative steered regional development. Sugar moved slowly but steadily around the Atlantic world, compelling environmental transformations wherever workers cleared forests for cane fields. The nature of cod fishing and whaling meant these activities would have more profound long-term consequences in the ocean ecosystem than on land. Other commodities that spurred transatlantic commerce appeared overnight: the discovery of silver, gold, or diamonds generated "rushes," frenzied migrations of men and women eager to seize their share of what they believed to be a resource of finite availability. If silver mining remained Spain's most profitable American industry through colonial times, Portugal seized upon major discoveries of gold and diamonds in Brazil.

In 1693 slave-hunting bandeirantes discovered gold in Brazil's south-central highlands. What followed was America's first great gold rush, an event with consequences in Europe, Africa, and the Americas. In Brazil itself, the discoveries drew thousands of people, enslaved and free, from the already depressed sugar areas of the northeast. Many more came from Portugal, the east Atlantic islands, and western Africa. The outflow of residents, most of them young men, caused Portuguese officials to worry about the collapse of the home country's economy. The slave trade received an enormous boost as well, such that the mining district soon became a kind of neo-Africa. Discovery of diamonds in the Brazilian backcountry in the 1720s only enhanced the treasure fever, and with it the desire to dodge all manner of crown taxes and controls. As a result of this drastic demographic and economic reorientation, imperial interest and administrative control shifted permanently southward. Portugal created new captaincies, or administrative units, in Minas Gerais and São Paulo and sent officials to set up mints and collect the quinto, or royal fifth, in the boomtown and regional capital of Vila Rica do Ouro Preto. Further discoveries of gold to the west in Goiás and Mato Grosso, though not as rich, also led to the creation of new towns and the expansion of Portuguese bureaucracy. Reflecting the importance of this newly vital region, in 1763 Portugal moved Brazil's viceregal capital from Salvador to Rio de Janeiro.

The discovery of gold in Brazil transformed the whole colony. Miners found gold in a sparsely inhabited area, with few indigenous people to coerce to work. Those they did encounter, such as the so-called Botocudo, did not welcome the newcomers and made life on the mining frontier precarious. The Portuguese response, long established in the sugar districts, was to populate the region with enslaved Africans. The mines and miners required extensive support systems: merchants with iron tools and dry goods, mule trains capable of long marches, and planters to raise food crops and livestock. Such market towns and Atlantic ports as Parati and Rio gained sudden importance and opulence, which, almost naturally, brought French and Anglo-American pirates, forcing the Portuguese to reorganize defenses. By 1720, Minas Gerais was home to more than 35,000 African slaves, many of them internal migrants and nearly all of them men. The movement of slaves to Minas Gerais in fact created a labor shortage in other regions, particularly Bahia, Pernambuco, and Rio. Not until the gold and diamond industries began their slow decline after about 1750 were enough plantation workers available to meet the demands of coastal tobacco and sugar planters. Neighboring São Paulo and the more southern pampas of Rio Grande do Sul, by contrast, became rich agricultural and livestock regions as a result of their commercial links to the mines. By 1775, 300,000 people (20 percent of Brazil's population), African and European, lived in what until the turn of the century had been a barely inhabited zone. As the Minas Gerais economy became more diversified with the expansion of livestock ranches and plantations, its population continued to grow even after the decline of the mines. Its next revival would come with the arrival there of coffee. Yet another consequence of the gold rush was to transform the natural environment through the turning over of hundreds of square miles of mineral-bearing soils and the massive cutting of the Atlantic forest, up to the era of the gold rush second only to the Amazon basin in extent and biodiversity.

Portuguese officials might have greeted the new wealth with unbridled delight, but the lawlessness and allegedly immoral character of the region tempered their pleasure. Brazil's governor-general Dom João de Lencastre wrote from Salvador in 1701 to disparage the people attracted to the boom: those "leading a licentious and unchristian life" were already turning Minas Gerais into a haven for criminals and wanderers. Monastic religious orders, especially the Jesuits, were forbidden from the region since it was believed, probably rightly, as the Spanish example proved, that they would absorb too much gold. Like most boom districts, Minas Gerais was settled so quickly that the

Atlantic Drugs and Popular Music

In the modern era, fans of popular music are accustomed to tunes dedicated to controlled substances, whether alcohol or other drugs. Not that long ago, artists outwitted vigilant censors—The Beatles' "Lucy in the Sky with Diamonds," popular forty years ago, was allegedly a "secret" ode to the hallucinogenic drug LSD—but today, lyricists and performers have few compunctions about heralding their devotion openly. In the wake of initial transatlantic contact, some Atlantic commodities, particularly those unfamiliar to European consumers, were first appreciated for their alleged medicinal value. Europeans had to learn how to consume these stimulating plants and to handle the possible effects thereof. In the early seventeenth century, as tobacco traveled the Atlantic and gained more popularity in Europe, its alleged medicinal benefits helped consumers overcome the complaints of critics who reviled the plant. (To be sure, the reverse is true today, and none would defend tobacco for its curative powers). One English song, "Come, Sirrah Jack, Ho," celebrated the effects of tobacco. Thomas Weelkes, an English composer of religious and secular songs in the early seventeenth century, wrote this three-part song (called a madrigal) about the marvels of tobacco. He evoked an old English country dance (the Trenchmore) to convey the dizzying effect of the strong, unprocessed, tobacco with its powerful nicotine punch, which made the user, in Weelkes's words, "giddy." He marveled at its medicinal

Image depicting the use of coffee and tobacco in a negative way. From Two Broadsides against Tobacco (London, 1672). Image used by permission of the Folger Shakespeare Library.

value: it purged the user of all pains. As for those who condemned its use, Weelkes dismissed them as people who did not know good tobacco when they saw it, and who failed to appreciate the "sweet of Trinidado," the preferred strain in the seventeenth century.

government found itself forever playing catchup in trying to erect regulatory and bureaucratic agencies. As a result, the crown had trouble collecting its quintos from the miners. The government's portion of Brazilian gold and diamonds remained substantial, but insufficient to bring economic development to Portugal. Instead, in part by diplomatic agreement under the 1703 Methuen Treaty, Lisbon became a de facto English dependency. It would take a turnaround in Portuguese policy, enacted after 1750 by prime minister Marquis de Pombal, to undue the damage.

The Cultures of Consumption

If the story of these changes in the Atlantic world seems driven largely by commodities, it is because the commodities themselves reflected consumer tastes and preferences. In early centuries, some of the most dramatic shifts for the people of the Atlantic came from the shock of contact and conquest, most particularly from the pathogens and microbes that accompanied European invaders. But commodities, too, changed people's lives, profoundly altering diets and consumption patterns. Tobacco is a case in point. It was a controversial product when it first appeared in Europe, and Spanish priests quickly forbade smoking in church. In early seventeenth-century England, James I condemned tobacco as a "noxious weed." Because this weed could be grown in northern Europe (and it was, in the Netherlands), it was not an ideal crop from a mercantilist standpoint. Nonetheless, soaring demand soon turned it into a popular colonial crop, and tobacco prices remained high in its first decades of cultivation in the Americas. By the 1730s, merchants imported 50 million pounds of tobacco into England each year, and only forty years later, 100 million pounds reached the kingdom. In its early years, tobacco was an expensive luxury, so only a decline in price—which its cultivation in America effected—could enable the crop to gain in popularity.

Like most drugs, tobacco soon spawned elaborate paraphernalia and rituals of consumption. Its proper use required a degree of learning. Indigenous Americans had long used tobacco in religious rituals, and Europeans could see early engravings of American inhabitants that demonstrated the sacred importance of the plant. Europeans initially heralded tobacco's medicinal qualities: in an era when people believed it was important for the body's humors to remain in balance, tobacco, which packed a particularly strong kick in its unprocessed form, was believed to cleanse the body of its bad humors—consumers literally broke out into sweats from the strength of the nicotine. Earlier experiments had treated tobacco as if it were tea or even hashish, to be consumed in a water pipe, and one seventeenth-century song refers forlornly to having had no tobacco to drink that day. But people slowly learned how to smoke tobacco in a pipe, as at least some Native Americans did. Soon, pipe smoking became so common that by the end of the seventeenth century, "every plowman," one English observer reported, "has his pipe." Tobacco was popular in Africa, too, among a population that had long treasured chewing the addictive and stimulating kola nut. Introduced initially in Senegambia and the Gold Coast in the sixteenth century, American tobacco spread eastward and northward with kola traders as well as hand-to-hand. It took no more than half a century for its use to become fairly widespread across West and West Central Africa and beyond. As with other goods, tobacco use generated its own ancillary market. The archaeologist Christopher R. DeCorse reports recovery of more than 4,000 pipe fragments from excavations in and around Elmina on the Gold Coast. Some of the pipes date to the seventeenth century; most are of Dutch manufacture, but some are from England and some locally made. In Brazil and Spanish America, African slaves soon were demanding tobacco as an essential ration. Since it staved off hunger, their masters were generally happy to oblige.

Other new products initially considered luxuries also became staples. Sugar and beverages associated with it illustrate the trend. The Atlantic world introduced new drinking opportunities and new social rituals around those drinks. Sugar made bitter drinks more appealing. Combined with sugar, tea (an Asian commodity) became so popular that it actually reduced beer consumption in England, something that to that time only gin had accomplished.

Before Starbucks

"Up and to the office; and at noon to the Coffee-house": so wrote the celebrated English diarist Samuel Pepys in January 1664. The coffeehouse was a place where men (these were rigidly gendered spaces) gathered to discuss politics, business, and the day's news. In port towns, coffeehouses provided up-to-the-minute information on the arrivals and departures of ships, and with each arrival came fresh gossip and news from abroad. A gentleman's magazine described coffeehouses in 1711 as a place to "transact Affairs or enjoy Conversation." Pepys delighted in the company, characterizing one companion as "one of the most rational men that I ever heard speak." Men did not consume only coffee at a coffeehouse; they also smoked tobacco and drank tea and chocolate, both, like coffee, flavored with sugar to counteract their natural bitterness. At the same time that coffeehouses depended on the most violent and degrading aspects of Atlantic plantation production, with sugar cultivation the deadliest labor a slave could be forced to perform, they emerged as places of fashion, where men of European culture defined themselves as gentlemen through their clothing, demeanor, diet, conversation, and manners. In this way, bourgeois gentility depended on violence and exploitation, and consumer preferences furthered the exploitation of millions. The coffee house, a place for gentlemen to enjoy a "calm and ordinary life," was a product of Atlantic commodities and the consumer culture they spawned.

Christopher L. Doyle, "Caffeine Culture Before Starbucks: Shared Interests, Outlooks, and Addictions in Eighteenth-Century Atlantic World Coffeehouses," OAH Magazine of History 18, No. 3 (April 2004): 33–37.

Early London Coffee house, c. 1705. Anonymous artist. © The Trustees of the British Museum.

Since drinking water had to be boiled anyway (this in an era of open aqueducts and the general use of rivers as sewers and dumps), tea was a rare, safe alternative to alcohol.

Other Atlantic commodities generated their own distinctive drinks with special rituals of consumption and social meaning. Chocolate was another exotic American product new to Europeans. The cacao tree was indigenous to Central America, where local people valued the contents of its mango-size seedpods. The Aztecs demanded cacao beans as tribute, and chocolate (from the Náhuatl *xocóatl*) had important ritual uses that contributed to its elevated status. Columbus's fourth voyage in 1502 marked the first European encounter with the substance. Although the Spanish saw readily that the Maya and other Indians cherished chocolate and appreciated the high status accorded the beverage and its consumers, Europeans were slow to acquire a taste for it. One Italian traveler remarked that the drink was fit only for pigs. Those Europeans who lived most closely among Indians—once Indians instructed them in how to prepare and consume it—soon came to appreciate chocolate's unique texture and bitterness.

Contrary to popular belief, chocolate was originally not dependent on sugar for its popularity. Some Mesoamerican Indians used honey to sweeten the drink, but most Maya and Aztec elites preferred it bitter. Froth was essential. Europeans kept the froth, but almost universally added sugar (thus furthering that crop's marketing possibilities). Europeans further doctored their chocolate by adding cinnamon, then a luxury spice available only through Portuguese and Dutch merchants in Ceylon (known since 1972 as Sri Lanka). Europeans mimicked ritualistic Mesoamerican meanings of chocolate. As in pre-Columbian times, it was associated with aristocratic life (some households in Europe designated a separate chocolate room). And chocolate maintained in Europe an older preconquest association with romantic love. Indians used chocolate in marriage negotiations, and today that historical meaning lingers each time chocolate is exchanged as a symbol of love.

Like chocolate and tea, coffee became popular among Europeans in the later seventeenth century in large part because of the availability of sugar to temper its bitterness. Originally from Abyssinia (modern-day Ethiopia) and called *Kaveh*, the Arabic word for wine, coffee was eventually transplanted to the tropical highlands of the western Atlantic, first to the French colony of Saint Domingue, then to Brazil, New Granada (Colombia), and Jamaica. Both coffee and chocolate were consumed in coffeehouses, the antecedents to modern cafés, patterned after the coffee houses of Cairo, Istanbul, and other Islamic cities where alcoholic beverages were generally condemned. Coffee houses appeared in most major European cities by the 1650s, and they became generally popular on both sides of the Atlantic by the 1720s. As in the Ottoman world, they were sites of relaxation, business, and political agitation. And as in the Islamic case, men who gathered in coffeehouses also enjoyed tobacco; indeed, wherever it appeared, the coffeehouse was a celebration of Atlantic commodities and vices.

Europeans, Indians, and Africans all adopted and integrated the Atlantic's new, mood-altering substances into existing social rituals, and in some cases expanded and elaborated rituals to celebrate new commodities. By following alcohol around the Atlantic, one can see such a complex process at work. Liquor was yet another element in the Columbian exchange, but the impact of new spirits was varied because in many parts of the Atlantic, Indian and African populations had prior experience with fermented drinks or substances with a similar physiological affect on consumers.

In coastal West Africa, where fermented palm wine had long been a favorite intoxicant, newly imported rum, brandy, grape wine, and gin came into steady demand. European traders included spirits in customs payments, recognizing that "cordial water" served as high-grade oil for the wheels of commerce. "Without brandy there is no trade," complained the Royal African

Company's factor in the Gambia River in 1680. (Of course, one is never sure if agents prodded officials back in Europe to send more alcohol for the Africans they dealt with or themselves, inhabiting a distant outpost and wanting more drink to help them through the long hours of inactivity). Over the last quarter of the eighteenth century, as British and French traders had their attentions drawn to revolutionary and military matters in other colonies or at home, New England and Caribbean traders worked the African trade and brought copious quantities of rum. Non-Muslim ruling families were great consumers of brandy and rum, not only because they possessed the wealth to procure the expensive drink, but because many worshipped in traditional faiths that involved ceremonial libations for the spirits (and the practitioners). In what may have been the case in a number of societies in Atlantic Africa, the availability in Senegambia of strong spirits from the Atlantic trade played a role in the growing militancy and predatory nature of rulers and their entourages. By the mid-eighteenth century, the regular drinking of strong spirits was part of the lifestyle of ruling warrior elites like the *ceddo* in Senegal. The arrogant, often drunken and unpredictable ceddo made life hard for European traders, and by the early-nineteenth century they were making it hard for their own subjects. Only Muslim lineages and those unable to afford a tankard of "bumbo" now and then remained outside what seems to have been a growing culture of alcohol, but even some of these extended families were at times caught up in the alcoholic swirl. Francis Moore, an English writer stationed at James Fort in the Gambia River in the early 1730s (and a settler of Georgia with James Oglethorpe in the last years of that decade), described how the "King of Barsally" (the *bur*, or ruler of Saloum, a state with a capital on the Saloum River, north of the Gambia) broke into Royal African Company stores to get at brandy, which he drank until he was inebriated. "The king, as well as all his attendants, are of the Mahometan religion," Moore noted, "notwithstanding their being such drunkards; and this monster, when he is sober, even prays."

In Central America before the Spanish arrived, the Mexica had consumed pulque, a beverage made by fermenting the juice of the maguey plant. As with other elements of Mexica society, strict codes governed the consumption of pulque. The Mexica nobility consumed it regularly and savored it on ritual occasions. But under Spanish occupation, mores underlying restrictions on consumption eroded. No longer limited to religious rituals, pulque drinking spread into the social realm. Moreover, pulque became commodified in ways that deviated from its prior sacred status. In fact, by the eighteenth century, pulque production was one of New Spain's most profitable industries, lucrative for producers and the government, which taxed producers and shippers and licensed sales.

Spaniards and Native Americans continued to view and experience drinking differently, and they defined "moderation" from divergent perspectives. For the Spanish, moderation entailed the regular consumption of modest amounts of wine, and later brandy: in other words, moderation was roughly the amount of alcohol one consumed on a more-or-less daily basis. For Indians, moderation was associated with the appropriate occasion on which to drink oneself into a drunken state. An intoxicated person whom the Spanish derided as violating norms of moderation might have been viewed by Indians in Peru or Mexico as a temperate drinker. The Portuguese would have similar differences of opinion with the native peoples of coastal Brazil and the Amazon.

The impact of new alcoholic beverages was more dramatic in North America, where, for the most part, fermented drinks were unknown. Some North American Indians used hallucinogenic substances in their ritual life but did not have access to alcohol. Some substances were in the form of beverages, such as the "black drink" consumed in the southeastern United States, which contained caffeine and an emetic that violently flushed the system. The goal of consumption (and the ensuing purging and sickness) was to achieve ritual purity. John Smith observed such a ritual purging when he visited the Chesapeake Bay in 1608. The Indians there drank the juice of a root until they made themselves so sick that it took days to recover. Nonetheless, the speed with which Indians adapted alcohol to their own ritual uses, and the agreement on the importance of alcohol for drunkenness, reflects the ease with which alcohol meshed with precontact practices.

North American Indians integrated alcohol into their world in ways consistent with cultural practice but that seemed anomalous and destructive to outside observers (and even some participants). As in Africa, potent alcoholic beverages entered Indian communities through commerce that was central to European-Indian contact in North America from the first coastal trade. The English shared Vargas Machuca's sentiment that trade fostered Europeanization, which in this case involved a fondness for heavy drinking. The alcohol trade also helped tie together Britain's mainland alcohol trade with its Caribbean sugar-and-slaves nexus of misery. The Portuguese acted similarly in trading large quantities of *cachaça*, or rum, to Africa for slaves. There, as in North America, offerings of alcohol were central to diplomatic relations. But for North American indigenous communities, the costs of the alcohol trade were more disruptive. Communities customarily admired for their good order were suddenly marred by violence. Productive life was also altered by reorientation of internal economies toward external trade. In reaction, many Indians turned to temperance by the early eighteenth century.

Indians consumed alcohol in culturally specific ways that showed the choices they made about how alcohol, like other trade commodities, fit into their lives. Indians drank alcohol specifically to get drunk, and they did so in patterns that the historian Peter C. Mancall has delineated. They integrated alcohol into preexisting mourning and hospitality rituals, and they drank to gain the power they believed drunkenness offered (agreeing, apparently, with a French traveler in Montreal who reported, "A drunken man is a sacred person.") Whereas English men and women drank much of the time but not to get drunk, Indians drank at special occasions for the purpose of achieving complete inebriation. Each culture defined drinking differently, and the Indians did not see their own use of alcohol as "abuse," as one might characterize

Eating Goober Peas

Confederate soldiers during the American Civil War, who munched on "goobers" (peanuts)— sometimes for want of sufficient biscuit and jerky—and sang satirically, "Goodness how delicious, eating goober peas," had no idea how the song spoke to Atlantic history. The peanut was a South American crop that sixteenth-century Portuguese sailors introduced to the lower Congo River. Men and women living there named it nguba. When slaves from the Congo were transported to the Caribbean in the seventeenth century, they brought with them their taste for peanuts, their knowledge of how to grow them, and their name for them. When peanuts from British Caribbean colonies passed on to Britain's colonies on the southern North American mainland—probably, again, in the hands of captives—the slightly altered form of nguba, "goober," came with them and entered into the English spoken there. Probably not a single member of some Georgia militia knew, as they sang and munched "goober peas," that they were using a word derived from a once-native language of some of the slaves they were fighting to keep in bondage.

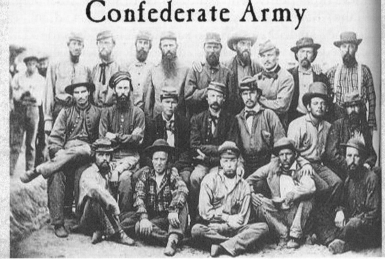

Confederate Army

A group of the Confederate States Army, newly formed and poorly outfitted, 1861. This is a somewhat rare image in that Confederate photographers were not as frequently employed as those of the Union due to scarcity of funds.

it today. (It is probably important to note here that no modern scientific evidence supports the popular theory that modern North American Indians have a genetic predisposition to alcoholism.)

In their choices about consumption, however, whether of alcohol or of less harmful trade goods, Indians always operated in a context of demographic adversity. They drank to excess in a world in which entire communities vanished in the wake of epidemics; they buried their dead with all of their treasured new trade goods in the desperate hope that such a gift might encourage the supernatural world to lift from them the burden of death and sickness. They chose how to assimilate and to adapt and use new commodities, but few of these goods helped Indians to weather the challenges of conquest in ways that, in hindsight, seem effective.

New edibles and consumables were also important in Africa. Over the long run, American maize and manioc (known as cassava in Africa) improved the quantity of food African farmers could produce. These American crops eventually may have been a factor in stimulating population growth across the continent. Maize would come to supplement millet, sorghum, and rice as a food crop in the savannas, successful in part because it had greater resistance to drought and shucks protected the ears from birds; the root crop cassava would join the African yam as a staple for coastal forest dwellers.

Peanuts, thought to originate in Peru, were introduced to West and Central Africa in the sixteenth century, but peanut production failed to spread as quickly as that of tobacco because Africans were slow to develop a taste for them. Africans in equestrian regions sometimes grew peanuts not for the legume, which is affixed to the roots of the plants and must be dug up, dried, and opened for eating, but for the value of the greens as fodder. Not until the first half of the nineteenth century, with the slave trade declining and Africans seeking new products to trade to Europeans, did peanut growing for export flourish in upper Guinea and northern Nigeria.

Beyond food and drink, Africans and Native Americans from first contact were ardent consumers of European metal goods. This may help explain why students often assume that European weaponry was superior to African or American armaments. In fact, indigenous Africans and American Indians did not always esteem European arms, and in many instances guns did not have the transformative impact we have been conditioned to presume. European harquebuses and muskets, especially in the sixteenth and early seventeenth centuries, required substantial maintenance and rarely worked according to design. Matchlock muskets, furthermore, were extremely heavy, often requiring a sort of crutch to support them while aiming and firing. And without a blacksmith at hand, guns of any kind quickly fell into disrepair. They rusted in damp climates, wore out, and occasionally exploded in the faces of their operators. Firing matchlock guns also required dry gunpowder, always problematic in wet or humid climates, and access to a steady flame to be fired, so they were often thwarted as impractical. When fired at night, the flash of the musket revealed the location of the shooter, a great aid to ready and less visible archers. Similarly, guns were noisy, revealing a shooter's whereabouts and hindering any subsequent element of surprise or the chance of a second shot at fleeing game. And even when they did hit game, musket balls could tear large holes in an animal's pelt or leave otherwise edible meat filled with shards of lead. For these and other reasons, muskets were not always useful to indigenous people, especially those who sought to hunt or fight at night, with stealth, and in inclement or even normally humid weather.

Because of these deficiencies, in North America traps, clubs, and bows and arrows remained popular for hunting. In South America, the Native Americans Vargas Machuca encountered, and others, continued to use poisoned darts shot from blowguns in animal and man hunting. More useful to hunters were the edges that they could put on arrows, hatchets, and war clubs with metals gained from the Europeans. These tips made weapons—and wars—more deadly, and thus help to explain the urgency with which some Indian tribes who were otherwise shut out of the Atlantic trade might seek a connection to it. Outside Chile, new muskets began to replace modified Indian weapons only in the 1620s, and even then, the natives regarded them as of secondary importance. During the March 22, 1622, attack on Jamestown, Opechancanough's forces carried a few muskets, but primarily relied upon hatchets and clubs to "beat out [the settlers'] braines."

Metals and metalware also made up a significant portion of African imports. "Without iron and alcohol one cannot live there, much less trade," wrote the French chaplain on Gorée Island, Abbé Demanet, after a trip to the Gambia River in 1764. African blacksmiths pounded iron into farm implements, weapons, utensils, chains, and gongs. In some regions of the Upper Guinea Coast, so much iron entered from the Atlantic that the "bar," based on a standardized piece of flat wrought iron common in the lower Rhine and early brought to West Africa by the Dutch, became the standard unit of currency. The ability to obtain good quality, inexpensive iron benefited farmers and soldiers. Moreover, as more metal containers—copper basins, brass pans, and pewter ware—became available, one suspects that the women's traditional art of pot making declined. In any case, metal tools and utensils made their way into the lives of wealthier people.

Weapons of one sort or another also were important items of European trade to West and West Central Africa. Swords and cutlasses were major imports throughout the slave-trade era, particularly in savanna regions where men on horseback used them. Firearms are a different story, and as with the Americas, their use and effect on bringing change to African societies has been misunderstood. Some even have postulated a gun-slave cycle, whereby rulers sold slaves to obtain firearms, with which they armed more fighters to obtain more slaves, to obtain more guns, and so forth. This model, however, misrepresents the efficacy of guns in the African environment.

For reasons noted, in the sixteenth, seventeenth, and eighteenth centuries, firearms seldom tipped the balance in African battles. (This was not true in every case, of course. Cannon could knock holes in fortifications, enabling entry of soldiers for hand-to-hand fighting; guns fired down from ships at canoes naturally were effective; and large forces armed with guns, firing in volleys, sometimes carried the day.) In some African societies before the nineteenth century, use of firearms in battle was considered cowardly. Not that African leaders did not purchase guns for military use—some did indeed, and in such armies as those of Asante or Dahomey, firearms eventually would play a role. But the role firearms played was seldom a decisive one, especially in capturing slaves, and most authorities discount the theory of an upward spiral of slave traders acquiring guns to bring in more slaves. It was just more complicated than that.

So why so much importing of firearms, gunpowder, and shot? The answer is that guns became useful to Africans for other things than warfare: hunting, keeping wild animals away from crops and livestock, and noise making during celebrations and ceremonial functions (rulers at Atlantic ports returned salutes from arriving vessels). Guns also served as symbols of royal prestige and power, since in many instances only the wealthiest of ruling lineages could afford to keep guns in any number. So before 1800, firearms affected Africans in surprising ways: they enhanced personal safety and crop production and provided another way for the wealthy and powerful to display their status—as a form of conspicuous consumption.

The commodities of the Atlantic trade as a whole, however, significantly altered the material basis of people's lives along the Atlantic rim and for a considerable distance inland. In Atlantic Africa, trading provided societies access to material goods they otherwise would not have had or could have afforded. One of the enduring misconceptions of African history is that Europeans traded worthless goods and trinkets to Africans for the heart of their most productive manpower. In fact, Europeans provided precisely what Africans wanted in exchange for slaves: generally speaking, a variety of goods.

With the growth of Atlantic trading, dress and personal decoration more than ever became how West Africans displayed their wealth, indicated their status, or expressed their tastes. Clothing, jewelry, and beads served this function, and the Atlantic trade supplied all three. Africans had access to these items long before the time of Atlantic trading, of course, but the varieties and styles that became available from Europeans caught African fancies the way new styles of jeans or flip-flops with particular markings (at outrageous prices) hold appeal today across all social rankings. Beads—perhaps the ultimate cheap-bauble import in the eyes of critics of African traders—stand as a good example. Africans were wearing beads when the first Europeans arrived along the Atlantic coast, but eventually Europeans were able to bring multicolored glass beads from France, Holland, and the Holy Roman Empire, along with crystal, pearls, coral, and semiprecious stones from more-distant places. All of these provided new possibilities for wealthy Africans to express themselves through personal decoration. Some of the beads purchased in Venice or Amsterdam were inexpensive, but others were not. Popular carnelians that came from Bombay, coral, and crystal were dear wherever they were purchased.

To some extent, cloth served a different purpose. Africans wove cloth from cotton, supple palm fiber, or, in places, bark. Even when Europeans brought cloth from elsewhere, many Africans continued to prefer their own. But as English and French traders got easier access to the finely woven, brightly colored Indian textiles that were passing through Liverpool or Marseilles, and as Indian imports gained elite status among African consumers, Europeans coming for slaves began to import more cloth. Northern European producers also imitated Indian cottons (though most Africans continued to prefer the real thing), and they made fine woolens and linens and such useful clothing as kerchiefs, hats, and caps. Cloth and clothing imports thus rose steadily after the seventeenth century.

All of this enabled Africans—not only the wealthiest, but increasingly segments of societies with little or no connection to slave trading—to adorn themselves more fully and colorfully. With greater frequency, people dressed with more clothing, draping linens and woolens around cotton garments, and wrapped themselves in more layers on chilly nights. Brightly colored wraps covered the heads of prominent women in public; men wore long gowns with wraps and often hats or caps; cotton sheets covered things appropriately kept from sight—corpses at funerals, brides at weddings. Among Muslims, religious men had an easier time dressing like their North African models, in long, loose-fitting gowns. Across a broadening expanse of western Africa, persons who possessed power and authority were increasingly easy to spot.

Yet in Africa, importing quantities of personal decorations and cloth had a social effect beyond the aspect of wearing one's wealth. In some areas, cloth was a currency used in social exchange: men wishing to marry needed cloth for bridewealth, material goods to provide to the family of the prospective bride. This compensated the woman's family for its loss of a productive member—the amount was related to the economic, social, or political position of the bride's family—and it symbolized the mutual obligations each family had to its in-laws. Cloth, and to a lesser extent items of adornment, all easily-stored goods that retained their value, became standard payments for bridewealth. The more and better cloth and beads one had, the more wives one could marry from larger and stronger families from a wider region. And the more of such marriage ties one had, the stronger and more prosperous were the outsiders upon whom one could rely in times of need—famine, especially, or physical threat. This trend came at a time when, because of the disproportionate relative numbers of women to men in the wake of the slave trade, polygyny was gaining wider acceptance. African men realized what men were coming to accept at the same time in England and France, colonial Virginia, and Spanish America: that a fast way to get ahead in society was to marry women from the wealthiest and most influential regional families. The interfamilial ties thus created became the essence of security, and the Atlantic trade helped provide the wealth and goods for prosperous families to create and maintain such relationships. Political and social stability across West and West Central Africa was based even more on the mutuality of interests of the region's leading lineages.

Europeans and colonists of European descent in the Americas used their wealth from Atlantic trade in the same way—to improve and display their status. New wealth was particularly important in a political world in which people believed that rich and powerful men were the rightful political leaders; this assumption made for volatile politics. Commerce being an uncertain venture, men made fortunes and lost them overnight with the loss of a single vessel at sea. Waiting for one's ship to come in was hardly a metaphor—it was the hope on which one's future rested. When the ship failed to appear, with its goods and passengers lost, merchants' fortunes could be destroyed unless they had diversified their holdings. Likewise, families shot to prominence when their fortunes soared. With profits from sugar, Jamaica and Barbados magnates established themselves comfortably in England. Young men with new fortunes from trade could launch themselves into Parliament, demonstrating a social mobility once considered beyond the realm of possibility.

Colonial merchants who flourished in the Atlantic trade turned their wealth to personal advantage. In eighteenth-century New England, men could buy the social position that would have eluded them a century before, when genealogy and church membership were the principal markers of stature. But the "nouveau riche" like the French merchant Peter Faneuil of Boston could buy the clothes, house, and goods that delineated his status. This process was replicated around the Anglo-Atlantic world in the eighteenth century. Men used profits from tobacco, sugar, slaves, rice, rum, pitch, tar, flour, and other essential trade items in the Atlantic economy to buy exalted status for themselves. To the extent that these new ruling classes consisted of rough and common parvenus, elite goods were important, for one was a gentleman if one looked and acted the part.

The historian David Hancock's study of a cluster of eighteenth-century merchants called the "associates" details this process. These were men whose success in trade enabled them to move from being "restless outsiders" into the heart of British politics and society. They owned Caribbean estates and profited off sugar, rum, and slaves. James Grant alone held eight Jamaica plantations and invested heavily in the slave trade. The merchants in the beginning owned counting houses, which they also used as dwellings, but as they prospered, they acquired fashionable townhouses and country estates. Real estate enabled men to participate in politics: in England, if a man owned freehold land valued at more than forty shillings per year, he could select members of Parliament. So the associates remodeled their houses to be barometers of genteel taste and filled them with treasures, allowing their refined taste in art to reflect their character.

Alone among the people of the Atlantic, indigenous North Americans used new commodities not for personal aggrandizement but in ways consistent with custom. This pattern reflected the control Indians often exerted on trade. Europeans learned in Brazil and on the North American coast that the barter economy had limits and that Indians did not have an insatiable need or desire for European products. This was true especially for those who lived in seasonally migratory households, people obliged to transport their possessions from place to place. Some new goods were certainly useful: metal buckets, fabric, or knives eased customary tasks. Consider, for example, the challenge of making fire. The historian Daniel K. Richter has pointed both to the availability of axes, which made it easier to obtain firewood, and "strike-a-lights," flint and steel gizmos that obviated the need to transport a live coal in a treated shell in order to start a fresh fire.

As with most others, for Native Americans new trade goods similarly opened new aesthetic possibilities. Needles and thread, combined with new glass beads and other decorative items, led to a creative and cultural flowering in beadwork. Hair combs among the Northern Iroquois, once objects with no more than five teeth, were transformed with new tools and crafts material into fine-toothed combs with elaborate patterns and designs. Many functional trade goods acquired ritual significance in Native American societies, reversing in some respects the process by which such ritual and animate beings as beavers or deer became commodities. Archaeologists have found American burial sites that contain trade goods, carefully arranged to accompany the dead. The collections of trade goods in Narragansett graves may indicate that these Americans hoped to make ever-larger gifts to the supernatural realm in a time of terrifying disease. The commodities did not enable individuals to rise to prominence in seventeenth-century Native North American societies that cherished the reciprocity of gift giving, condemned hoarding, and valued most those who could give away their goods. Instead, tribes might benefit if they had access to traders and could acquire valuable goods, but the benefits tended to be corporate, not individualist, in contrast to patterns elsewhere in the Atlantic. Across the Americas, precontact mores endured so long as the native inhabitants did.

In Mesoamerica and the Andes, native people adopted elements of European dress, including lace, hemp sandals, and types of jewelry. At the same time they retained ponchos and wraparound skirts. The resulting *trajes* (uniforms), which identified a person according to town residence and status, have survived to degrees throughout highland Spanish America. Some of these composite outfits became even more complex during such feast days as that of Corpus Christi, when descendants of the Incas displayed their heraldry on European-style floats that passed through the streets of Cuzco and other cities. People there expressed native idioms in Chinese silk, Dutch linen, and French lace.

Over the course of the eighteenth century, American Indians became more enmeshed in what historians have characterized as an "Empire of Goods." Now Indians' list of necessities and conveniences expanded: it included dyes for face paint, tools, clothing for men and women, tobacco, weapons, and alcohol. But most evident in their use of these goods was continuity with Indian customs. The goods they procured were manufactured for their tastes: "duffels," or heavy woolen cloth, was produced specifically for the North American market. (Manufacturers also produced special cloth for enslaved people around the Atlantic, but the consumer choice was governed by a master's stinginess, not a slave's preferences; Africans preferred cottons to woolens in their tropical climate.) Indian preferences dictated the size, shape, and color of glass beads, and they preferred lighter brass kettles than those made for the Euro-American market. In general, Indians preferred more portable and less expensive goods, and in these demands, according to Richter, they "stretched European technological capabilities to their limits." And Indians were not only consumers, but producers in the Atlantic trade, providing furs and sometimes slaves. With the exception of the destructive trade in alcohol, North American Indian societies were not dramatically transformed by commodities, nor did they use them to alter their individual position within their communities in the same way that people in Europe, Africa, and Euro-America tended to do.

Transformations in Africa in the Wake of the Slave Trade

Europeans and Africans alike used wares and wealth acquired from the Atlantic to gain political power and prestige, but the impact of Atlantic trades on Africa was yet more complicated and pronounced, and of great importance and interest to scholars because Africa was engaged in Atlantic trade in two interrelated ways. African merchants bought and sold wares, as merchants did around the world, exporting some commodities and importing others. But Africa was also absorbed in the enormous, intercontinental slave trade, in which the commodities were not simply trade goods but human beings, ultimately millions of them. The connection of the Americas with Atlantic Africa and the growing influences of Atlantic trading, particularly slave trading, brought changes to African societies and planted seeds that would grow, almost literally in some cases, into greater changes in the future. Over the more than four centuries of its existence, and especially over the two centuries of the heaviest exporting of slaves (between 1650 and 1850), the Atlantic slave trade played an important role—though not the most decisive role in every case—in altering the foundations of human life in West and West Central Africa.

In terms of demographic change, did the Atlantic slave trade depopulate large parts of Atlantic Africa and, for this reason alone, have deep effects on African societies? As with the question of whether the slave trade crippled African economies, the answer is complex, since we do not know many of the factors involved: the size of African populations before the rise of Atlantic trading; the effects of new food crops from the Americas on population size; changing levels of fertility and mortality related to drought, famine, and epidemic; and more. Basing estimates on a sophisticated model, the historian Patrick Manning has concluded that the Atlantic slave trade simply slowed population growth in West African societies prior to the eighteenth century, but that between about 1730 and 1850 the trade actually reduced the population, and that the size of the reduction, while uneven, was considerable in some societies. Manning also postulates that the growth of the slave trade increased the proportion of slaves to free persons in Atlantic African societies,

Using Oral Traditions to Understand Africa's Past

Evidence for activities occurring half a millennium ago in West African societies comes partly from oral data—stories told by family elders and griots, a generic term for African bards. Most of these societies had no written language before the twentieth century, but they passed on memories of historical events orally, around fires on a nightly basis and on more formal occasions, often sponsored by rulers or wealthy families

with a stake in the way the story was told. These tales, heard and recorded in more recent times, probably telescope into a short period events that occurred over a longer time—because oral traditionists do not have sufficient ways of describing processes of change—but like traditional stories everywhere, they often contain a core of truth, and these fit into the pattern of events taking place throughout the region.

Below: "Le Griot, le maitre de la parole" ("The Griot, the Master of the World"), painting by Pascal MPeck, 2004. © *Pascal MPeck, www.pascalmpeck.com.*

perhaps to a ratio of one to six, meaning that by 1800 as many slaves existed in West and West Central Africa as did in the Americas.

One demographic turn that seems to have had particular societal effects along Africa's Atlantic rim involved the creation of a sexual imbalance, with women outnumbering men five to four by the late eighteenth century. In the much older trans-Saharan slave trade, men and women were sold and moved across the desert in roughly equal numbers, women being in demand in North African and Mediterranean markets as much as were men, but such was not the case with the Atlantic slave trade. Men were favored on American plantations, as planters held to the notion that men could accomplish more work under the controlled circumstances of plantation labor, so prices for male slaves were generally higher in the Atlantic trade. In Atlantic regions of Africa, the opposite circumstance was true: women were judged more valuable for their ability to produce offspring (a quality not in particular favor on early American plantations, it being more economical to purchase an adult slave than to rear one from birth into the productive age of early adolescence) and their equal or greater productivity in agricultural pursuits. Women thus commanded higher prices in African markets for the internal trade rather than for the Atlantic trade. For these reasons, twice as many men as women were sold across the Atlantic, while female slaves tended to accumulate in Africa.

This demographic imbalance became a factor in the creation of certain social arrangements that, when observed by European social scientists toward the end of the nineteenth century, were assumed to be "traditional"— that is, the way Africans had lived for centuries. Among these arrangements were polygyny, with the wealthiest of men sometimes having dozens or scores of wives, a circumstance that must have been demeaning to women generally and not likely to move marriage toward an institution of benevolence; female dominance of important productive enterprises (potting, for example); and a disproportionately important role for women in agricultural production.

As slaving increased through the eighteenth century, African societies adjusted in order to find ways to survive. Populations moved to defensible areas, residents erected defensive stockades around the perimeters of their villages, and persons curtailed movement alone or in small groups. Manning believes that heightened slave trading polarized the ideologies of captors and captives. The former, who profited from slave trading, valued "hierarchy, centralization, and the glorification of wealth," while populations in danger of enslavement practiced "self-sufficiency, an egalitarian opposition to authority, and a willingness to live without great accumulations of wealth." It would take a great many years of struggle after the end of slave trading for African societies to reconcile these differences in values.

Scholars have paid greater attention to the effects of the Atlantic slave trade on African political structures and social institutions. It is increasingly clear that throughout the eighteenth and the first half of the nineteenth century, when the mechanisms of slaving in Atlantic Africa were reaching far inland to funnel thousands of captives per year toward the coast, the Atlantic slave trade was the defining institution for West and West Central Africans, the slavers and the enslaved alike, as well as all those who, by grace of the gods or natural forces, did not fall fully into either group.

Unfortunately, generalizations about the political effects of Atlantic trading are rarely useful. Slave trading played a role in the development of large states in some regions where the commerce was particularly heavy (Asante on the Gold Coast or Dahomey on the Slave Coast, for example), but in other areas increased slave trading was a factor in the demise of large and once-powerful African states (such as Jolof in Senegambia, Oyo inland from the Bight of Benin, and Kongo to the south). To confound matters further, in such places as Igboland, east of the Niger Delta, the trade seemed to prevent extensive political consolidation in favor of numerous small, competitive political units. Moreover, one cannot make grand regional generalizations because the political effects of the Atlantic trade changed over space and time. By the nineteenth century, the demise of the trade was itself politically disruptive. About the only truly broad, relevant, political generalization one can make is that wherever it existed the slave trade stirred the political pot. The stew turned out differently in different places because of the great variety of ingredients. A handful of examples from different periods and parts of Africa's Atlantic coast show how the effects varied.

In Senegambia, the area of westernmost Africa between and on either side of the Senegal and Gambia Rivers, Atlantic trading grew rapidly with Portuguese contact. Merchants based on the Portuguese Cape Verde Islands sought gold up the Gambia River in the 1460s and began bringing salt, kola nuts, raw cotton, and woven cloth for exchange. They quickly found other products in demand in Africa: iron and horses.

A steadier and more plentiful supply of iron meant, among other things, an ability to arm a larger fighting force for defense, raiding, and conquest. Horses were another matter. Travelers crossing the Sahara brought horses to West Africa's savannas as long ago as the third century BCE, but because of difficulties with breeding and their expense, horses remained more an item of prestige, to be paraded by wealthy rulers, than of utility. This began to change not long before Portuguese arrival, when African horsemen adopted the Arab stirrup, which enabled mounted warriors to use their legs and upper bodies to thrust spears and thus rendered the cavalry soldier a more formidable element of warfare. The Jolof state quickly built its cavalry force to more than 8,000, while smaller states struggled to keep pace.

This sale occurred at a time when the Mali Empire was in decline. Taking advantage of Mali's weakness, a new group of Fulbe cavalry-warriors gained control of the Senegal River valley in the first years of the sixteenth century and cut off Jolof from its desert-side supply of horses, facilitating a rapid decline of Jolof authority. With horses from the Portuguese and the western-most Sahel, Jolof's Atlantic tributaries achieved independence. Other tributary and peripheral regions of Mali began to break away as well.

At the same time, political realignments were occurring between the south bank of the Gambia and the Futa Jalon highlands. With access to horses from Portuguese traders, lineage-based groups began breaking from Mali and join-

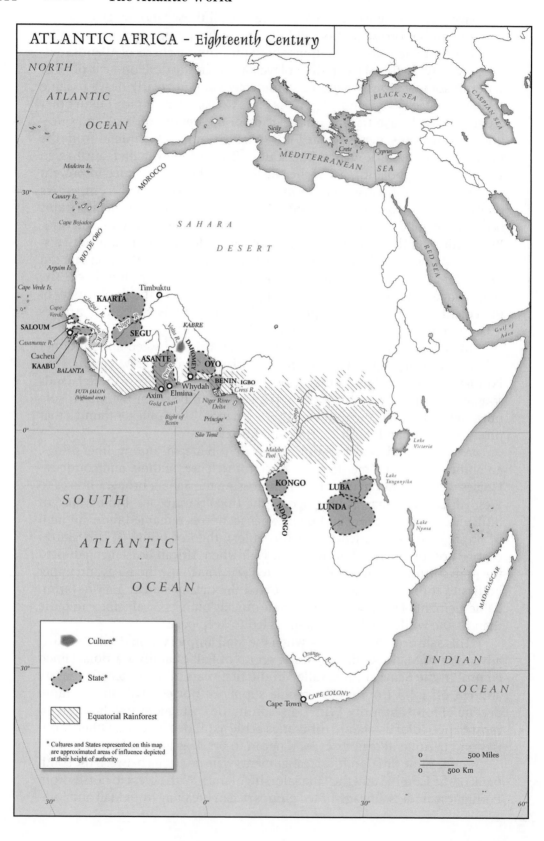

ATLANTIC AFRICA – Eighteenth Century

NORTH

ATLANTIC

OCEAN

BLACK SEA

CASPIAN SEA

Sicily

MEDITERRANEAN SEA

Crete

Cyprus

Madeira Is.

MOROCCO

30°

Canary Is.

Cape Bojador

SAHARA

DESERT

RED SEA

RIO DE ORO

Arguim Is.

Cape Verde Is.

KAARTA

Timbuktu

Cape
Verde

SALOUM

KABRE

Senegal R.

Gambia R.

Niger R.

SEGU

Volta R.

Gulf of
Aden

Casamance R.

Cacheu

KAABU

BALANTA

DAHOMEY

ASANTE

OYO

BENIN

IGBO

Whydah

Cross R.

FUTA JALON
(highland area)

Axim

Elmina

Niger River
Delta

Gold Coast

Bight of
Benin

Príncipe

São Tomé

Lake
Victoria

Malebo
Pool

Congo R.

0°

SOUTH

KONGO

LUBA

Lake
Tanganyika

NDONGO

LUNDA

ATLANTIC

Lake
Nyasa

MADAGASCAR

OCEAN

INDIAN

30°

Orange R.

OCEAN

Culture*

CAPE COLONY

Cape Town

State*

Equatorial Rainforest

* Cultures and States represented on this map
are approximated areas of influence depicted
at their height of authority

0   500 Miles

0   500 Km

30°

0°

30°

60°

ing their separate, small political units to form a larger state called Kaabu. The ruling lineages of the new state encouraged their young male members to find areas of their own where they could command cavalry forces and rule. Because there were too many potential princes to achieve this in Kaabu itself, ambitious Mandinka warriors did what adventurers had tended to do far into the past: they cast about for regions where they might take or share political control. Prime targets for Mandinka conquest were those where there was sufficient production and trade to maintain the elite lifestyle and expensive cavalry. One such place, the region around the lower and middle Gambia and Saloum Rivers, was located at the end of a major artery for trade into the interior, and its population produced agricultural goods and salt. Also, enclaves of Mande and Portuguese merchants were already paying for the right to participate in the commerce of the region, and Portuguese ships were bringing horses, iron, cloth, and other useful martial and luxury commodities. By the mid-sixteenth century, when stability had returned to the region, political units resembled, in many ways, small models of the old Mali Empire. In nearly every case, these small and middle-sized states held onto authority until falling to European forces at the end of the nineteenth century, more than half a century after the Atlantic slave trade had ended in those parts.

Unlike in Senegambia, along the Gold and Slave Coasts and in the Bight of Benin, the slave trade brought a general trend toward political consolidation and large-state building. In its broadest sense, it affected the rise of several political entities: Asante, Oyo, Dahomey, and Benin.

Akan-speaking lineage groups had organized to control the gold and kola trade already spreading northward from the hinterland of the region the Portuguese would call the Gold Coast. Slaves were part of this: they mined gold, harvested kola, and grew crops. Slave-owning lineages gradually organized with others engaged in the same enterprises in order to defend more effectively their holdings and bring stability to the trade. The appearance of the Portuguese on the coast toward the end of the fifteenth century offered a market for their gold and a source of labor for their business. The growing trade and wealth led to further organization, into state-like systems. A number of such small states came into being through the sixteenth century. Until demand from the Atlantic grew, however, the focus of these states' production and trade remained northward—the routes toward markets connecting to the trans-Sahara trade.

As coastwise trade grew throughout the seventeenth century, several small, inland kingdoms consolidated under the leadership of a dynamic figure, Osei Tutu (r. 1680–1717), and soon the confederation known as Asante conquered a broad region around the Volta River basin. With weapons obtained from representatives of European commercial interests, who operated forts along the Gold Coast and were eager to be in his good graces, Osei Tutu further broadened his control in the interior. This new Asante Empire marshaled the northward trade in kola nuts and slaves as well as delivery of captives from the hinterland to European merchant groups on the coast. By the middle of the eighteenth century, Asante armies were ranging wide to hold the empire together, take more captives, and collect tribute, usually in slaves.

European Views of Sixteenth-Century Benin

Historians do not have written descriptions of many African cities in existence five centuries ago, but they do of Benin. Early Europeans who visited Benin were aware they were looking upon something old and grand, and they wrote about what they saw. At the height of its importance in the sixteenth century, Benin City sat behind protective walls and stretched eight miles across, with broad avenues and intersecting streets connecting the city's neat houses. The ruler lived in an elaborate palace with a court more lavish than that of Portugal's king. Ever interested in diet following an ocean voyage, European visitors found wealthy Benin residents feasting on stews made of yam, beef, mutton, and chicken; poorer people mixed their yam with dried fish, bananas, and beans; and others took advantage of the "great quantity of provisions, ready dressed, which the king sends into the town for the use of the poor." Perhaps most noteworthy was Benin's artwork: fine bronze, brass, and copper heads honored former rulers; elaborate copper plaques commemorated great past deeds. Some European visitors eventually commissioned Benin artists to depict themselves on copper plaques and in ivory carvings.

View of Benin City and a procession from "Description de l'Afrique, Avec des cartes & des figures en taille-douce. Traduite du flamand," by Olfert Dapper, produced in Amsterdam, 1686. © The British Library. Record: c5053-03, Shelfmark: 457.e.4, Page Folio: plates 308–309.

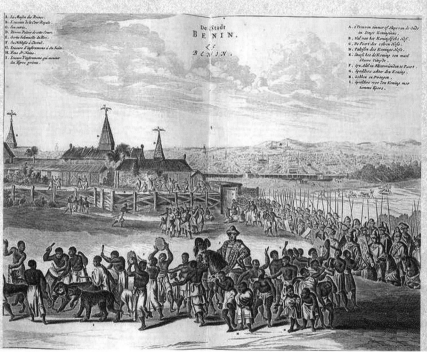

The stories of Oyo and Dahomey are similar. One of several Yoruba states that had come into being in the thirteenth and fourteenth centuries in what is now western Nigeria, Oyo found that, through wealth gained from trade, it could acquire horses from drier regions to the north. Over time, its cavalry forces defeated rivals and, by the beginning of the seventeenth century, Oyo was in a position to expand westward, north of the forests, should that prove beneficial. It would do just that once demand for slaves along the Atlantic picked up in the 1640s and 1650s. Controlling trade in several directions, Oyo grew wealthy through the eighteenth century. The state's capital had 100,000 inhabitants and spread over twenty square miles.

Like Asante, Dahomey was a latecomer, forming as a small interior kingdom in the 1620s and expanding south, overcoming coastal kingdoms to gain direct access to the Atlantic trade a century later. Through the port of Whydah, Dahomey officials controlled trade with Europeans along the Slave Coast. Wars between Oyo and Dahomey produced slaves in the thousands and commensurate wealth for the states' rulers as they traded captives toward the Atlantic. Oyo's mid-eighteenth-century ruler lived in a palace covering nearly a square mile. At the same time, Dahomey's King Agaja was sending unsolicited gifts of slaves to England's King George I with a letter offering forty times as many and informing his fellow monarch that he (Agaja) could acquire what he wanted without regard to price, "even to a thousand slaves for any single thing."

Benin's history was different. Located seventy miles west of the Niger River and fifty miles in from the Atlantic, Benin was a city-state on the rise when the Portuguese encountered it at the end of the fifteenth century. Benin armies were then overcoming other towns as they expanded east toward the Niger and west toward the lagoon of Lagos, so it was an ideal time for Benin's leader, the *oba*, to sell captives from the wars to the Portuguese (permitting the latter to take the slaves to the Gold Coast to trade for gold). Once Benin's military expansion came to a halt, early in the sixteenth century, however, its rulers stopped exchanging slaves entirely and turned to trading ivory, pepper, and cotton cloth—which the Portuguese also traded along the length of the Guinea Coast and which, being a prized commodity, raised the status of the Benin women who wove the cloth. Not for another century and more would Benin sell slaves into the Atlantic trade.

If consolidation and state building were the norm from the Gold Coast to Benin, something less grand was happening east of the Niger River. There, in the sixteenth to eighteenth centuries, among the mainly Igbo-speaking population, clansmen in small, often competing groups of towns had for some time cooperated to speed along trade in cloth, iron, ivory, salt, and fish. Once European demand grew along the coast, the towns became more competitive, some relying on spiritual authority to enhance their means to obtain and trade slaves. Best known of these is the group of lineages and towns that came to be known as Aro, who exploited an oracle named Arochukwu near the Cross River to obtain captives, bring order, and further trade. In time, Europeans would entrust goods to merchants representing expanded Igbo lineages, and the latter would load the goods in canoes, head up the maze of rivers, and return in weeks or months with slaves. Political organization never reached beyond the level of groupings of towns and clans.

The changing situation in the region of the Congo and Angola was more complex still. The kingdom of Kongo enhanced its considerable power in the lower Congo through the early sixteenth century by trading slaves, obtained in frontier wars, to the Portuguese, but its regional importance diminished once the Portuguese focused more on the Ndongo kingdom, to the south, in 1576. Kongo had a resurgence in the seventeenth century, however, as Portuguese and Afro-Portuguese merchants tied the region more systematically into the Atlantic trade.

Once Portugal established a small colony at Luanda, it began extending its influence inland in search of organized states that could use military forces to provide slaves. This created a frontier of violence and commercial state creation that moved steadily into the interior through the eighteenth century. The Ndongo kingdom was involved in the early years; its remarkable Queen Nzinga, in a forty-five-year reign that lasted until 1663, used strength gained through trading slaves and her own guile and ability to overtake neighboring Matamba and create one of the most significant slave-trading states of its time. Farther inland, the militant Kasanje state became a greater supplier of slaves late in the seventeenth century. The growing tendency was for Portuguese, Afro-Portuguese, and African merchants to depart coastal enclaves and head for one or another interior trading center, where they would exchange goods for slaves and bring them back to the coast. As demand increased, slaving markets developed farther away from the Atlantic, bringing the political-economic slaving system to stretch far inland. By the end of the eighteenth century, slaves from the Lunda people living between 700 and 1,000 miles inland reached Portuguese-controlled ports on the Angola coast.

But the rise and fall of political structures of varying size does not tell the entire story of the effects of the slave trade on African people, culture, and

Black Rice

It is common to draw attention to all of the food crops that entered African societies from the Americas following the integration of the Atlantic world—everything from maize and cassava to peppers and peanuts. Less frequently does anyone consider how the African crops brought westward across the ocean affected the lives of people in the Americas. In a recent book, Black Rice: The African Origins of Rice Cultivation in the Americas (Cambridge: Harvard University Press, 2001), the geographer Judith Carney shows how techniques for growing West African rice, Oryza glaberrima, which Africans living along the floodplains of the upper Niger River domesticated two thousand years ago, were transferred to an area in the Americas stretching from South Carolina in the north to Brazil and New Granada in the south. West African upland and estuarine rice-growing techniques were introduced by skilled Africans, many of them women, and wedded with Asian sativa rice, which Europeans collected in their journeys to the Far East. Slaves relied on African knowledge systems to produce rice in the Americas, in some places—like South Carolina—to the great financial benefit of their masters. Carney takes the story full circle with the re-introduction into Sierra Leone in the nineteenth century of "Carolina gold," the rice that made South Carolina planters wealthy, by free persons returning to West Africa and Christian missionaries. Ironically, the Africans

who grew this rice called it "Méréki," a corruption of the word America.

A Charleston, South Carolina, broadside ad, 1852. Broadsides and certificates, Manuscripts, Archives and Rare Books Division, Schomburg Center for Research in Black Culture, The New York Public Library, Astor, Lenox and Tilden Foundations.

society, or maybe even most of it. Students of African cultural history are beginning to recognize the broad and deep effects that slave trading, raiding, and related wars had on people in stateless societies, who lived across the hinterland of the 3,000 miles of sub-Saharan Atlantic coastline. Activities related to the Atlantic economy, of which slaving came to be a vital part, seem to have been the most formative factors in people's lives—certainly by the eighteenth century and in some places much earlier. Evidence of this is harder to come by because the Europeans, who left most of the records useful for reconstructing the history of the region, dealt chiefly with individuals representing the more-powerful societies and often paid no attention to the circumstances of those less involved in the conduct of coastwise commerce or outside positions of political authority. New studies, however, make one point particularly clearly: the dominant motive in the lives of generations of Africans was simply to find a way to survive the conditions of their existence—conditions made grueling by the centuries-long enslavement, sale, and movement of men, women, and children in the direction of the Atlantic Ocean to meet the demand for slaves in the Americas.

A study by the historian Walter Hawthorne of politically decentralized farmers living in the coastal area of what today is Guinea-Bissau offers an example of how a culture of slave raiding turned peaceful societies into militant groups and altered the most fundamental aspects of people's lives. The Balanta ethnic group lived on the western edge of the large, slave-producing state of Kaabu. Kaabu's leaders regularly sent armies among such coastal dwellers as the Balanta to obtain slaves. Beginning around the mid-sixteenth century, Balanta families began to relocate their households from the drier, upland regions where they had lived for generations to harder-to-reach marshy areas nearer the coast. In the new location they concentrated houses of a new design (that made abducting family members more difficult) in fortified villages. Over time, a number of Balanta became slave raiders themselves, some for the less-noble reason of enriching themselves with cloth, adornments, alcohol, or tobacco, which were obtainable in exchange for slaves, but others for the reason, viewed as more legitimate, of obtaining slaves to exchange for iron and iron-tipped weapons that would enable them to defend themselves against other slave raiders. "They produced captives by convicting those deemed socially deviant and criminal to sale," writes Hawthorne, "and by organizing young men into raiding parties who struck distant strangers. As a result, one of the cruel ironies of the slave trade in Guinea-Bissau was that in order to obtain the iron necessary to defend themselves, coastal people captured and sold those in their midst."

In typical fashion, the Balanta connected themselves to the Atlantic market through kinship: foreign merchants seeking slaves and having access to imports married Balanta women, who became, in Hawthorne's words, "the nexus of coastal-Atlantic exchange." Eventually, age groups of young men, whom Balanta elders sent to raid distant communities for slaves in the early years, turned their attention to growing rice, which they could exchange for slaves. Thus, Hawthorne concludes, "Balanta communities were generally able to defend themselves against threatening raiders and to provide food for growing numbers of people. By the nineteenth century, Balanta were producing increasing volumes of paddy rice for both domestic consumption and export and their populations were among the densest on the Upper Guinea Coast. The slave trade did not, then, devastate communities in the Guinea-Bissau area. It presented great challenges to them. Coastal people met these by planting rice and harvesting slaves."

Another example of the effects widespread slave gathering had on people's ways of life involves a group known as Kabre, found today in northern Togo. Several centuries ago a number of noncentralized groups of people similar to the Balanta, living in farming communities and growing cereals, occupied the rich plains east of the Volta River, a few hundred miles from the Atlantic. These people faced a growing crisis in the seventeenth and eighteenth centuries as demand for slaves on the Gold and Slave Coasts brought armed raiders into the area. With insecurity growing, the farmers sought refuge in harder-to-reach areas—mountainous regions or the banks of rivers—where they could more easily defend themselves. The ancestors of today's Kabre took to the mountains during this period, so anyone wishing to raid their villages would have to ascend steep and easily defensible slopes. This mountainous refuge became the home of many formerly disparate peoples, where they were forced to live in densely packed villages. Eventually, these refugees began speaking a common language, practicing common customs, and recognizing a common identity—as Kabre.

The density of their living circumstances led them to develop intensive cultivation of the hillsides (permanent cropping, terraced fields, manure fertilizing, continual weeding) and complex cultural manifestations (kinship ties, commodity exchanges, housing patterns, spiritual interventions, and more). They also became participants in an economy based on periodic markets, which owed their origin to the commercial networks that the traffic in slaves fostered and the cowrie-shell currency facilitated. According to the anthropologist Charles Piot, the existence of today's Kabre and much of their way of life "was produced by the ravages and pressures of slaving" less than 300 years ago. He calls the period of intensive slaving "a defining moment in the larger history of the Volta basin" and notes the irony that European anthropologists in their initial study of the Kabre and neighboring people, late in the nineteenth century, labeled these groups and their cultures "traditional," as if they had existed back into distant times in the same form, somehow untouched by history.

On the other side of the coin, those who profited from capturing and selling slaves organized and led such centralized states as Asante, Dahomey, Oyo, and Ndongo. Many Africans joined these groups or paid them tribute to avoid becoming their victims. Less-centralized groups like the Balanta and Kabre were those who made decisions and took steps in efforts to enhance their security and keep from becoming enslaved. The circumstances of the slave-trading years determined much of their way of life. And, of course, further millions of Africans were neither part of centralized polities nor successful in their attempts to find security. They were the ones who died in warfare, perished in movement to the coast or across the ocean, or added to the growing African presence in North or South America or, to a lesser extent, Europe.

Human interaction with Atlantic commodities shaped history, often in ways that such men as the Spanish soldier Vargas Machuca could not have predicted. The variety of responses to trade, the cautious and deliberate assimilation of new commodities and new habits, and the new orientation of people toward the Atlantic reflect the increased integration of the Atlantic world and the effects of that world on the most mundane habits, from drinking tea in London to placing a lightweight brass kettle over an open flame in northern New York. They also remind us of the importance of consumer demand (fickle as it was) as much as supply in the shaping of the Atlantic's economic history. Commodities generated profits for those who looked to the Atlantic for their prosperity and status, but they also enabled people to make choices and express their tastes and preferences, furthering integration by encouraging distant producers to fabricate special goods for remote markets. This process similarly contributed to the distinctive ways in which inhabitants of the Atlantic world experienced the region and to the unexpected cultural innovations that came to characterize it.

Selected Readings

Akyeampong, Emmanuel, *Drink, Power, and Cultural Change: A Social History of Alcohol in Ghana, c. 1800 to Recent Times* (Portsmouth, NH: Heinemann, 1996).

Alpern, Stanley B., "What Africans Got for Their Slaves: A Master List of European Trade Goods," *History in Africa: A Journal of Method* 22 (1995): 5–43.

Bergad, Laird W., Fe Iglesias García, and María del Carmen Barcia, *The Cuban Slave Market, 1790–1880* (New York: Cambridge University Press, 1995).

Blackburn, Robin, *The Making of New World Slavery: From the Baroque to the Modern, 1492–1800* (London: Verso, 1997).

Curto, José C., *Enslaving Spirits: The Portuguese-Brazilian Alcohol Trade at Luanda and Its Hinterland, 1550–1830*, Atlantic World Series (Leiden: Brill, 2004).

Dean, Warren, *With Broadax and Firebrand: The Destruction of the Brazilian Atlantic Forest* (Berkeley: University of California Press, 1997).

Dunn, Richard S., *Sugar and Slaves: The Rise of the Planter Class in the English West Indies, 1624–1713* (Chapel Hill: University of North Carolina Press, 1972).

Eltis, David, *The Rise of African Slavery in the Americas* (New York: Cambridge University Press, 2000).

Hancock, David, *Citizens of the World: London Merchants and the Integration of the British Atlantic Community, 1735–1785* (New York: Cambridge University Press, 1995).

Hawthorne, Walter, *Planting Rice; Harvesting Slaves: Transformations along the Guinea-Bissau Coast, 1400–1900* (Portsmouth, NH: Heinemann, 2004).

Higgins, Kathleen J., *"Licentious Liberty" in a Brazilian Gold-Mining Region: Slavery, Gender, and Social Control in Eighteenth-Century Sabará, Minas Gerais* (University Park: Pennsylvania State University Press, 1999).

Hunter, Phyllis Whitman, *Purchasing Identity in the Atlantic World: Massachusetts Merchants, 1670–1780* (Ithaca: Cornell University Press, 2001).

Kea, Ray A., *Settlements, Trade, and Politics in the Seventeenth-Century Gold Coast* (Baltimore: The Johns Hopkins University Press, 1982).

Langfur, Hal, *The Forbidden Lands: Colonial Identity, Frontier Violence, and the Persistence of Brazil's Eastern Indians, 1750–1830* (Stanford: Stanford University Press, 2006).

Law, Robin, *The Horse in West Africa: The Role of the Horse in the Societies of Precolonial West Africa* (Oxford: Oxford University Press, 1980).

———, *Ouidah: The Social History of a West African Slaving Port* (Athens: Ohio University Press, 2005).

Mancall, Peter C., *Deadly Medicine: Indians and Alcohol in Early America* (Ithaca: Cornell University Press, 1995).

Manning, Patrick, *Slavery and African Life: Occidental, Oriental, and African Slave Trades* (New York: Cambridge University Press, 1990).

Mintz, Sidney, *Sweetness and Power: The Place of Sugar in Modern History* (New York: Viking, 1985).

Northrup, David, *Trade without Rulers: Pre-Colonial Economic Development in South-Eastern Nigeria* (Oxford: Clarendon Press, 1978).

Norton, Mary, "Conquests of Chocolate," *OAH Magazine of History* 18, no. 3 (April, 2004): 14–17.

Parry, John H., and Robert G. Keith, eds., *New Iberian World,* Five volumes (New York: Times Books, 1984).

Phillips, Carla Rahn, *Six Galleons for the King of Spain: Imperial Defense in the Early Seventeenth Century* (Baltimore: The Johns Hopkins University Press, 1986).

Piot, Charles, *Remotely Global: Village Modernity in West Africa* (Chicago: The University of Chicago Press, 1999).

Richter, Daniel K., *Facing East from Indian Country: A Native History of Early America* (Cambridge, MA: Harvard University Press, 2001).

Ryder, Alan F. C., *Benin and the Europeans, 1485–1897* (London: Longmans, 1969).

Schwartz, Stuart B., *Sugar Plantations in the Formation of Brazilian Society* (New York: Cambridge University Press, 1985).

Taylor, William, *Drinking, Homicide, and Rebellion in Colonial Mexican Villages* (Stanford: Stanford University Press, 1979).

Vargas Machuca, Bernardo de, *The Indian Militia and Description of the Indies,* Kris Lane, ed., Tim Johnson, trans. (Durham: Duke University Press, 2007).

LE DINER.

Slavery in Brazil. Enslaved Africans attending a Brazilian plantation owner and his wife at dinner. Colored lithograph, French, c. 1835. Credit: The Granger Collection, New York.

Chapter Eight

Racial and Cultural Mixture in the Atlantic World, 1450–1830

*No lover worth a lady's while would waste his time and breath
in all that speech making. If our people were to make love in
that way our race would be extinct in two generations.*
Mohawk leader Thayendanegea, also known as
Joseph Brant, on a London production of *Romeo and Juliet*

Tucked inside the sheltering claw of the Cape Verde peninsula, at the westernmost point of Africa and near the northern limit of the continent's 3,000-mile-long Atlantic trading zone, Rufisque was a coastal entrepot where Europeans traded for slaves and hides under the watchful eye of royal officials of the Wolof state of Cayor. By the mid-1600s the village had a population of 1,500 and a cosmopolitan air. Resident Luso-Africans, who considered themselves "Portuguese" and "white" (though indistinguishable from the village's "African" inhabitants), were intermediaries in the trade, which they carried out in a creole Portuguese language, but which local Africans could also negotiate in vulgar forms of French and Dutch. In the 1660s and 1670s, the resident commercial agent of Cayor's ruler was a "white" woman, Senhora Catarina. Her two adolescent daughters, described as "between white and black," frequently served bananas and pineapples to merchants visiting Rufisque from Amsterdam or Paris. Down the way from the house of Senhora Catarina was that of "Portuguese" resident Senhor Dom João, who regaled European traders with regional cuisine and palm wine. Visiting priests looked askance at Catholic Dom João, not because he was married to an African woman, with whom he had children, but because he was married to *several* of them. "[T]his man was devout, having always a large Rosary in his hands, & several Images of our Saviour, of the Virgin, & of the Saints, around his bed," wrote the Frenchman Sieur Du Bois in 1669, "[so he] could not be ignorant that he offended God in having so many wives."

Visiting Rufisque in 1681, the French slave trader Jean Barbot rendered a panoramic sketch of the village, as seen from the road, which remains an appealing scene. In it, people are fishing with poles and nets, children cavort with their dog on the sandy beach, and a two-masted European ship and an African-styled vessel with a single sail move off shore with the wind. Sixty buildings are in the sketch, mostly round dwellings with conical, thatched roofs sitting inside compound walls, but a few are rectangular structures "in the fashion of the Portuguese," some fenced like African compounds and some sitting exposed. In Barbot's drawing, Senhora Catarina's residence stands out, not because of its structure—it being, like most, an African-type dwelling—but because it shows a large cross over the main gate of the compound. Barbot remembered Senhora Catarina as "a woman of high standing, a black lady of a good presence, and a very jovial temper," but he was put off by the meal she served: couscous on wooden platters with "stinking boiled beef" and only tepid water to drink. Barbot expected, at the least, a decent French wine.

Sixteen hundred miles down the African coast from Rufisque and half a century later, the circumstance was similar—with a touch of the absurd. The territorial governor in the Kingdom of Whydah with whom European slave traders dealt, "Captain Assou," was a practical joker. When a French merchant dining at Assou's home found himself in need of a toilet, Assou directed him behind the house to a particular privy. Within minutes, the trader came running back, pants in hand, fleeing a serpent he had found coiled in a corner. Assou's brother was head of a local religious group that recognized the serpent as sacred, and Assou found humor in introducing Europeans to "our sacred animal."

Assou was a man of several worlds. He followed the local religion, holding up well in theological discussions with French missionaries, practiced polygyny, and derived authority from the kinship ties that multiple marriages provided. One of his daughters married a French soldier, who had joined the army of the King of Dahomey. Such relationships helped Assou play English, French, and Dahomean interests against one another to his advantage. But rare was the European who visited Whydah in the 1720s and 1730s and failed to take advantage of Assou's "grandeur and generosity" or notice his "polite French manners." Dinner at Assou's two-story house involved drinking wines from Bordeaux and Madeira, eating multiple-course servings of stews and patés with silver forks and knives (accompanied by French bread declared the equal of any in Paris), and enjoying desserts of curds, nuts, and fruits. Each course was set at a table covered by beautiful cloths in a room with tapestry-draped walls. An evening's entertainment consisted of performances by a trumpet player and a dance troupe. At times, the diner at Assou's, whether a captain from Bordeaux or a mate from Liverpool, must have forgotten that he was seated in a house on Africa's "Slave Coast."

The Atlantic's New People

Catarina and Assou were not unique or even unusual, but rather typical inhabitants of the river and ocean ports of Africa in the era of Atlantic trading. Like Kongo's King Afonso centuries earlier, these cosmopolitan coast dwellers were consciously oriented toward the Atlantic: their dress, language, diet, and customs reflected their willingness to adopt new habits in order to further their interests. Such cultural go-betweens, common throughout the Atlantic world from an early date, were only a few hundred among millions who found their ways of life transformed by four centuries of transatlantic trade, conquest, biological exchange, and migration.

Despite attempts to create a "New" Spain—or France, Holland, Sweden, or England—in the Americas, the linking of the Atlantic world resulted in the creation of numerous mixed and creole, or locally born, populations with distinct, often non-European cultural characteristics. People with skin tones and features that did not match established European categories soon challenged the very idea of racial difference. A key question was this: if people from all parts of the Atlantic world could produce fertile children, how could they be of different races? Such suppositions of sterility were behind the Luso-Hispanic term *mulato*, derived from *mula*, or "mule." In a different vein, the Portuguese called the first *mestiço*, or mixed, Euro-indigenous inhabitants of Brazil *mamelucos*, or "Mamluks," a reference to certain Egyptian subjects of the Ottoman Empire. As this label suggests, racial and cultural fusion had long been occurring in the Mediterranean, but the rate and scale of blending paled in comparison with the larger and more diverse Atlantic. How did colonial Atlantic contexts give rise to local identities, languages, and other cultural expressions, and how did these change over time? How different was this process in places where immigrant populations predominated, versus sites like Rufisque, where local populations won out? In slave societies in the Americas, how different was life among mostly locally born slaves as opposed to populations dominated by incoming Africans of varying ethnicities? With regard to this last question, historians and others have noted that children who were born into slavery and grew up speaking the language of their natal territory had a markedly different experience—in almost every sense, including work assignments—from that of their first-generation parents. To follow another vein, African American Christianity in North America emerged in a region where creole, or locally born, slaves predominated, muting the most obvious African influences. African American Christianity in Brazil, Haiti, and Jamaica, on the other hand, emerged in contexts dominated by African-born enslaved populations, producing a distinctly African hybrid. Creole elites also developed cultures distinct from those imported by their European ancestors. They adapted to new climates and disease regimes, transformed landscapes, and commanded new social hierarchies based increasingly on color or race. Many elites who concentrated in American cities formed their own universities, printed their own books and pamphlets, and supported a mostly creole clergy.

In areas not dominated by Europeans or their descendants, indigenous, mixed, and even European go-betweens, or brokers, emerged. Malintzin in Mexico was one such person, aiding Cortés in his conquests, and in Brazil Portuguese castaways who married into native Tupi families played a similar role. All moved freely between cultures and helped mediate the moments when societies with no shared language met and clashed. In order to survive, and sometimes to seize an opportunity, such people had to be culturally flexible and multilingual. They understood diverse tongues and different systems of thought and belief. More important, they were able to translate these differences, explaining the seemingly strange habits of each side to the other. From the standpoint of relatively weak states, the ability of such cultural brokers to elucidate different perspectives put them in positions of considerable sensitivity and value.

Many more inhabitants of the Atlantic rim had new worlds thrust upon them. Millions of Africans were forced unwillingly into new societies; indigenous peoples found their societies transformed around them, and were compelled to adapt or migrate to survive. Efforts to retain customary practices were strenuous, even for elite Europeans, and rarely successful. Throughout the developing Atlantic world, people of all colors and cultures faced new pressures and demands on their linguistic abilities, control over their bodies and sex lives, access to material goods, and their political roles and religious beliefs. Innovative fusion was a natural result of the intensification of Atlantic ties, but the results were hardly predictable: the new commodities and new foods discussed in the previous chapter were only two indicators of the trend. In other words, to answer the question of what it meant for people to live within this new Atlantic world, it is worthwhile to emphasize the degree to which cultural transformation accompanied every aspect of political and commercial interaction. Not only did old cultural forms come under new pressure, but new populations emerged, and these were categorized in racial hierarchies in the Americas that almost always reflected western Atlantic power relations.

Africa's Coastal Cosmopolitans

At the nodes of European-African and European-Indian contact, first along the Atlantic coast and then farther inland, cosmopolitan individuals emerged who pursued and facilitated the contacts, some of whom lived embedded in cultures wholly oriented toward Atlantic exchanges. The pattern was established first in the trading posts of West and West Central Africa, where Europeans and Africans sought out one another for trade and alliance. The shape these societies took was unpredictable, because people made different kinds of choices about the extent to which they wanted to adapt to foreign ways. Some migrants sought to evoke a lost past through leisure activities. Take, for example, Africa's first (as far as we know) golf course, built in the eighteenth century. It existed on Bance Island, an English trading post in the Sierra Leone River estuary, owned by a group of London merchants. The course was modest, only two holes separated by a few hundred yards. Accompanied by a European visitor who described the scene, British players "hit the links" using clubs made from wood from Central America. The golfers dressed in suitable attire—all-white cotton shirts and trousers—and their attendant caddies wore tartan loincloths. When they finished their exertions, the gentlemen retired indoors to savor a dinner that included ape and boar, and to refresh the palate afterwards with Virginia tobacco and Madeira wine. Here was a scene shaped by commodities of the Atlantic (the woods, wine, and tobacco), fabrics of India (the source of the tartan loincloths), game meats from Africa, and the recreational habits of Britain (the golf game). In this instance, the traders preferred to surround themselves with familiar habits and luxuries. But their blending of commodities, customs, and companions reflected cultural innovation and intermingling, a process with common elements whether it took place up a river on the Guinea Coast, inside or outside a Dutch fort on the Gold Coast, at a point of contact on the Niger Delta, at a fair distance inland in Portuguese-dominated Angola, or across the Atlantic in America.

Languages were also transplanted and transformed. Trading requires communicating, and with remarkable speed coastal Africans and alien Europeans developed ways of understanding one another, initially using pidgin forms of Portuguese. The pidgins became more developed and complex, and thus moved toward what we know as creole languages, as Portuguese (and a few Europeans from other locales) took up residence on Atlantic islands off West Africa or on the mainland itself, and as more Europeans brought sub-Saharan Africans to European cities (mostly as slaves). This early creole consisted of a vocabulary that was largely Portuguese, but had a grammatical structure more akin to patterns in African coastal languages. As early as 1491, King Afonso of Kongo used this language in letters to Portuguese royalty. European playwrights such as Christopher Marlowe and Thomas Kyd included African characters speaking this creole in early-sixteenth-century theatrical productions, and it became the language of everyday discourse on the Cape Verde Islands and São Tomé. By 1500, a common, Portuguese-based creole was the trade language of Africa's Atlantic coast. European visitors referred to the language as "Portuguese," but in the words of one visitor to Lower Guinea, it was a "very corrupt and perverted Portuguese."

Over time, as merchants from other parts of Europe began frequenting Africa's coast, new creole languages developed, especially around permanent European outposts. By the seventeenth century, people living near Cape Verde were speaking "French," the king of an African state at Cape Mount could communicate in "French" and his wife in "Dutch," and Africans living along the Gold Coast were speaking "English," "French," or "Dutch." The Portuguese creole remained the common trade language in regions with no long-term contact with a single European nation.

Linguistic change was only a marker for broader mixing that led to the gradual transformation of existing cultures and the emergence of new ones. Because people integrated more easily than did their ideas, other cultural aspects, worldviews, and religious practices tended not to change with the same ease and speed. Most African societies—where kinship was the basis for social organization, group security, and personal identity—had institutionalized ways of integrating foreigners into local social structures. Along the Upper Guinea Coast, a more or less formalized landlord-stranger relationship enabled visiting outsiders to establish relationships of reciprocity with local kin groups that could lead, in time, to marriage into the family and permanent integration. Elsewhere, people could be attached to kin groups as dependents—the English language had little beyond the word *slave* to stand for the varying levels and types of dependency—from which status they or their descendants could be incorporated more fully into the community. In such fashion, European settlers and more frequently the offspring of European men and African women (because settlers from outside the tropics were unlikely to live long) became fully functioning members of local societies while retaining and spreading elements of the culture of their foreign ancestry. Such amalgamated cultures were most evident where European "renegades," in defiance of their governments' displeasure and the unhealthy African disease environment, had taken up residence along the Atlantic coast. In settlements on islands off Africa's westernmost edge (like the Cape Verdes or São Tomé), or around coastal enclaves where Europeans had long-established factories

Trader Solidarity

The Englishman Richard Jobson visited the Gambia River in 1620. Hoping to find mountains of gold inland, Jobson sailed the river to the head of navigation and then paddled for eleven days, ending up more than 250 miles from the Atlantic. At this distant point he met an African merchant named Bokar Sano and the two men bonded, not over a common language (English and Serahule) or religion (Anglican and Muslim), but over their being merchants trading away from home. Jobson describes Sano's appeal to trader solidarity for beneficial terms for his private exchanges:
"In our time of trading together, if it were his owne goods he bartered for, he would tell us, this is for my selfe, and you must deale better with me, then either with the Kings of the Country or any others, because I am as you are, a Julietto, which signifies a Merchant, that goes from place to place, neither do I, as the Kings of our Country do which is to eate, and drinke, and lye still at home among their women, but I seeke abroad as you doe, and therefore am nearer unto you."

Richard Jobson, The Golden Trade, or a Discovery of the River Gambia *(London, 1623), 106.*

Wolof merchant. "Marchand Wolof" *from* Esquisses Senegalaises, *1853, by P. D. Boliat. General Research Division, The New York Public Library, Astor, Lenox and Tilden Foundations.*

(Elmina on the Gold Coast or Whydah on the Slave Coast), communities that dealt almost constantly with Europeans formed. But the area of cosmopolitanism spread beyond the enclave settlements to a considerably wider hinterland. By the seventeenth century, along parts of sub-Saharan Africa's Atlantic coast and, in places, to one hundred miles or more inland, the ways people lived showed a blending of cultures.

Because Europeans deemed religion second in importance only to commerce—and because Europeans kept most of the records available for understanding Africa's Atlantic-coastal cultures in the sixteenth and seventeenth centuries—we know more about the mixing of religions than other aspects of African/European cultural blending. A merging of religions among coastal societies was easier than one might suspect, because African religious practices of the time were similar in some ways to those of European Christians. The historian John Thornton points out how both African and Christian religions were based on the philosophical interpretation of revelations: Europeans turned these interpretations into an orthodoxy, whereas Africans did not. But Europeans of the time continued to believe that within the broad doctrine of the church, revelation from a variety of sources, including worldly diviners, geomancers, and astrologers on the one hand, and unworldly saints and spirits on the other, offered valid understandings and wisdom on how to proceed in daily matters. (One should not forget that Prince Henry, sponsor of the early Portuguese exploration of Africa's Atlantic coast, was motivated throughout his adult life by his horoscope.) Religious merging among European and western African cultures involved a meshing of similar worldviews and a sharing of accepted revelations. "The way in which the revelations interacted and were validated," writes Thornton, "determined the nature of the resulting religion: African Christianity."

To be sure, the nature of this resulting religion among the Atlantic Africans differed. The sixteenth-century religion of the coastal population of the Upper Guinea coast was an amalgam of African, Christian, and Jewish practices. Jews and "New Christians" made up part of the early settler population of the region. The Jesuit Balthasar Barreira in 1606 encountered "a village of 100 Portuguese who follow the laws of Moses" on the coast of Senegal— some of these people had come directly from Portugal and others had arrived with Dutch merchants from Amsterdam, after having fled northward to escape the Inquisition. The Jewish character of the religion diminished over the decades following Barreira's visit, and Christian elements rapidly became Africanized. In the absence of regular visits from priests and thus regular access to the sacraments, these "Portuguese" incorporated African rituals in their worship. Barreira complained about "Christian Blacks" in Sierra Leone, who "by contact with the heathen had so forgotten the obligations of our holy faith that either they possessed *chinas* [shrines typically worshiped by Africans] themselves or they allowed their slaves to do so and they had dealings with these chinas and made them offerings." Ibn Battuta, the great traveler from Tangier, had offered similar complaints about West African Muslims he met after crossing the Sahara four centuries earlier.

This is not to suggest that all Atlantic-oriented people on the African coast found Christianity attractive. In parts of Upper Guinea, Muslims were entrenched long before the arrival of Christians, and in Senegambia, as agents of commerce connecting West Africans to the Sahara-based trade, Muslims were already making their influence felt with local political authorities. One of the early Portuguese to sail into the Gambia River, Diogo Gomez, in 1458, found a Muslim holy man in residence with the ruler of territory near the mouth of the river—Gomez touted his version of a victory over the royal advisor in a theological discussion—and Muslims were thoroughly involved with trade a good distance up the river. But even in places where Islam had not already spread, Christianity before the arrival of dedicated missionaries did not hold great appeal. Along the Gold Coast, where European contact was continual since the late fifteenth century, there was never much semblance of Christianity outside the European forts. Down the coast at Whydah, people who ate French bread and danced the minuet regarded the local snake as sacred, as mentioned, but had little use for the Catholic catechism. When French chaplains pestered Assou, Whydah's early-eighteenth-century leader, to convert (or, at least, to give Catholicism a greater role in his religious practice), Assou argued that the Catholic idea that communion bread and wine becomes the body and blood of Christ "fills me with horror and contradicts all sense of reason." "Why" he asked, "should one eat one's god?" He concluded, "I find nothing in that belief except impiety, folly, superstition, and cruelty, for which we (whom you label as pagans and idolaters) would never be capable."

Even farther south, around the Congo River and coastal Angola, a more Catholic form of African Christianity spread inland. Thornton suggests that the Africans sold into England's Jamestown, Virginia, settlement in 1619, who were initially captured more than one hundred miles inland from the African coast, may already have been Christians. Christian "Portuguese" from São Tomé had been living in a chain of settlements stretching through the kingdoms of Kongo and Ndongo, south of the Congo River, for many years before a Portuguese-led military campaign into Ndongo in 1618 or early 1619 produced the captives bound, indirectly, for Jamestown.

But much besides religion characterized Africa's coastal trade cultures. European-style clothing spread from coastal outposts until it became commonplace in some areas and influenced African perceptions of style. Even those indigenous Africans preferring to wear simple loin cloths and wraps in the warm climates might fashion them from imported cloth, perhaps donning a cap with the outfit. Near Cape Mount in Sierra Leone, local traders of the mid-eighteenth century, known as "big men," wore European-style clothing when they wanted to look their best. Two competitive big men of the Sierra Leone coast, known to Europeans as Captain Martin and King William, settled a two-year disagreement with a treaty that included the stipulation that "Captain Martin was not to wear shoes or stockings, as was his habit when he went out to Europeans' ships [since] that honour was to be left to King William alone." "Honourable" dress among the more religious of Atlantic creoles might include large crucifixes draped around the neck (which, in an ironic circumstance in Senegambia, tended to dangle over long gowns favored by Muslims), while others eventually broadened their taste to include discarded military uniforms, breeches, or even hot and uncomfortable wigs and bustles.

The diet in these Atlantic-oriented entrepots was eclectic as well. As at Assou's table in Whydah, the fanciest meals might include several courses of soup, meats, fruits, nuts, desserts, and choices of wines and liquors. The historian George Brooks reports that prominent Luso-African traders of Upper Guinea ate meals that included "citrus fruits, poultry, and pigs from Portugal; pineapples, chiles, and peanuts from South America; and bananas, mangoes, and paddy rice from South Asia." And groups such as the Luso Africans must have been factors in the dissemination of plants, trees, and domestic animals from around the Atlantic world and beyond among broad elements of West African societies. Archaeological studies from coastal Ghana show, however, that even people living nearest to the trading forts did not follow European trends toward eating off plates with individual portions. Around Elmina, methods of food preparation and consumption have remained largely unchanged over the past five hundred years.

Senhora Catarina of Rufisque was typical of women living between Cape Verde and Sierra Leone, who parlayed family and marital ties into positions of prominence on the African side of the Atlantic trade. On an inspection trip in 1686 for the French concessionary company in Senegal, Michel Jajolet de la Courbe encountered Signora Belinguere residing at Juffure, a day's sail up the Gambia River. She was the daughter of the local ruler, who had been married to several Luso-African traders and had, through her father's rights by custom, inherited her husbands' property when they died. Signora Belinguere was literate in French, Portuguese, and English, and she lived in a "Portuguese house," which was square—rather than round, as were typical African dwellings in the area—with white-washed walls, a vestibule, and interior rooms. She had a network of sources that provided her with commercial intelligence, and she could secure credit for African and European traders. La Courbe admired Signora Belinguere's "noble manner and refined tongue," but he was wary of what he perceived as her feminine wiles. "She is beautiful, large, and well-built, though a bit past her prime, and she is the shoal upon which a number of whites from several nations have been shipwrecked," he wrote. "After having made her a present of some coral and amber, I withdrew from this place like Ulysses from the house of Circe."

As he continued, La Courbe met others who were products of one of West Africa's oldest Atlantic hybrid cultures. Across the Gambia and up a good-sized creek, he met the "king of Geregia," a "small and robust man; he had on a Portuguese cap and an African robe; in his hand he carried a Spanish style sword upon which he leaned." The ruler welcomed La Courbe's gift of "a little iron and some schnapps." Asked into the king's "house built in the Portuguese style," La Courbe found lunch waiting. "He joined us to eat," writes the Frenchman, "as did his wife, which showed me that, in this place [thirty miles up a West African River and another twenty miles up a tributary creek] they have begun to take on English manners."

Cultural Transformations in the Western Atlantic

Assou and Catarina would have found much they recognized in Isabel Montour of North America. Her father, Louis Montour, the son of a French man and an Algonquin woman, worked as an interpreter and fur trader. Isabel, who appears consistently in records with the honorific "Madame," followed in this family tradition. As a child she was taken captive and adopted by the Iroquois, which added to her linguistic knowledge: she was fluent in French and English and at least three indigenous languages (Oneida, Mohawk, and Delaware). By the early eighteenth century, working as an interpreter in Albany and Philadelphia, Madame Montour had emerged as an important figure in diplomatic negotiations among Europeans and Indians in northeastern North America. Colonial and imperial officials recognized her insight into Indian affairs and sought her advice: her son Andrew continued the family tradition.

Records of diplomatic meetings in North America are replete with such people. Yet a glimpse at these interpreters in the Americas, who often lived between cultures, reveals significant differences from their African counterparts. The historian Jan Parmenter suggests that Montour's mixed-race heritage might have put her in the position of outsider, thus inclining her toward dealings with other outsiders. This would be consistent with the patterns of the first contacts Europeans made with Indians, which generally placed multilingual, cross-cultural persons in a central position.

Often these cultural intermediaries were people already dislodged from their home communities. Unlike their African counterparts, they did not seek European trade in a context of cultural or familial strength, but as people on the margins of society trying to make a living as best they could. Malintzin, who accompanied Cortés as his interpreter as the conquistador made his way from Veracruz to Tenochtitlán, had been traded away by her parents to the Gulf coast Maya. Squanto, who facilitated the survival of the first English to reach New England in 1620, had been taken captive by Europeans in 1614 and transported to Málaga, Spain, and then, somehow, found his way to England, whence he was able to get himself home to Cape Cod. At the end of his transatlantic journeys he discovered that he was the sole survivor of his tribe, the Patuxet, who in his absence had been ravaged by an epidemic. Europeans—and presumably Squanto—were shocked at the gruesome evidence: the sight of unburied dead, their bones scattered about, made one observer remark, "it seemed to me a new found Golgotha." Unable to reconstitute his society or his political power, Squanto found a temporary haven among the English at Plymouth, who were filling the political void of the region in the wake of the epidemic's upheaval. For Squanto, home was already transformed, devoid of family and familiar ritual, a place where only the people with whom he shared a language and culture were his traditional enemies, the Pokanoket. Like Isabel Montour or Malintzin, Squanto became a cultural mediator as a result of a mix of tragic personal circumstances, resourceful adaptation to a new cultural context, and aspirations for future political power.

In the Americas, more than any other part of the Atlantic world, new social and sexual relations emerged and new mixed-race populations resulted. These relationships, however, reflected the power dynamics of colonial societies everywhere, with European men claiming rights to American and African women's sexuality as well as to the material riches of a conquered or enslaved society. Indigenous and enslaved women occasionally derived benefits from these alliances, especially for their children. Sexual power was almost always a two-edged sword. Cross-cultural unions also could further political and diplomatic goals. European traders in Africa sought alliances with prominent families through marriage or informal sexual unions. The first Spanish conquistadors likewise secured their power and legitimacy in conquered territory in America through alliances with noblewomen. The process began on Hispaniola and was soon carried to the mainland. Isabel Moctezuma, the daughter of Moctezuma II, was treated as a sort of lady-in-waiting by Cortés, who presented her to a loyal fellow Spaniard for marriage following the conquest of Mexico. Many female descendants of Inca royalty faced similar prospects in greater Peru, maintaining titles for many generations.

Mixed-race households in the Americas were similar to those formed along the African coast. Spaniards usually insisted that their wives and children adopt Catholicism, speak Castilian Spanish, and otherwise become acculturated to Spanish customs. But Kathleen Deagan and other archeologists have found that although early Spanish American homes displayed elite European imports in the domestic sphere—in kitchens for example—indigenous and African utensils and cooking methods persisted. Brazil's early mixed-race households were even more indigenous and African in terms of utensils, foods, and even language, for Portuguese settlement there was generally less dense and slow to develop. But in many parts of the Americas, marriage alliances continued to be essential to diplomacy into the eighteenth century. John Rolfe's marriage to Pocahontas in Virginia in 1614 offered a tantalizing possibility that the English might follow the example of Spanish conquerors and Indian elite women, but, ultimately, English sexual alliances with indigenous women tended to be informal, and more than occasionally violent and coercive.

Many sexual unions grew out of expediency. In trading cultures, men were able to form immediate alliances with trading partners and political leaders through marriage. Elsewhere, men pursued informal unions for sexual gratification and access to indigenous survival skills and labor. The English traders of the Hudson's Bay Company, founded in 1670, discovered that they lacked the skills to survive in the challenging woodland environment. Specifically, they needed moccasins in order to hunt successfully, and moccasins wore out quickly, so they required a reliable and abundant supply. In England or in regions of English settlement, these men would have patronized male cobblers and shoemakers for the footwear they needed, but in any case, English-style shoes and boots were inadequate for woodland travel. Among the Indians of the Hudson Bay region, women traditionally made moccasins, so English traders quickly formed pragmatic alliances with them. From this pragmatic beginning, however, grew many affectionate relationships; if these

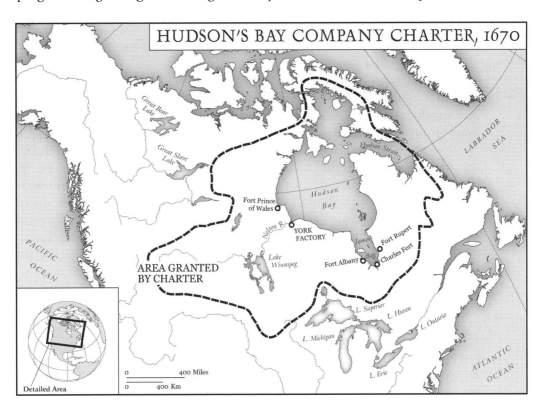

HUDSON'S BAY COMPANY CHARTER, 1670

were not legal marriages, they were certainly respected by common law. Still, traders often terminated these unions: English men viewed their Canadian residence as temporary, and when they retired home to England, they left behind wives and children in North America.

The *métis* (mixed) daughters of these liaisons at Hudson Bay were married to English Company clerks there, displacing the Indian women of the first generation, but they, too, were displaced, this time by English women. In the same way, when Spanish women began to migrate to the Americas in greater numbers, Spanish men turned from Indian or *mestiza* (mixed) women to European women. After conquest, color would gradually displace noble origins as the key signifier of female status.

It is difficult to find a comfortable language to describe these relationships, as many were forced on indigenous women by powerful men. So far as records indicate, Isabel Moctezuma had little choice when Cortés dictated her future. Everywhere, winners treated conquered women as spoils of battle and tended to share them. As for Pocahontas, contemporary sources suggest that she was in love with John Rolfe, but English men generated these documents. Pocahontas agreed to marry Rolfe in a context of captivity. The English kidnapped her, she converted to Christianity, she embraced English culture and fashion, and she took a new name, Rebecca. We cannot know how she regarded this union: as a reprieve, as a way of creating a new family as she lived in limbo, or as a romantic union. Rolfe himself was careful to temper the affection with which he wrote of Pocahontas. Unlike most Iberian men in the Americas and Africa at the time, the Englishman was troubled by the cultural intermixture his wedding would produce. And yet, there he was, "in love with one whose education hath bin rude, her manners barbarous, her generation accursed, and so discrepant in all nurtriture from my selfe." And so they married, and had a son, Thomas Rolfe.

When exploring cultural change in the western Atlantic, then, it is important to remember the different contexts within which people encountered one another and integrated new cultures. In Africa, where Europeans were numerically insignificant and culturally weak (albeit economically strong in certain locales), those Africans and Europeans who altered their habits did so voluntarily, usually for pragmatic reasons. Across the Atlantic, a different dynamic was in place for some populations, although one does see a continuation of the pattern of voluntary engagement. For Europeans and Africans in the western Atlantic, one needs to consider the extent to which people could retain their cultural practices against the compound shocks of enslavement, extended stays in holding areas, the middle passage, and finally resettlement among strangers. A variety of factors dictated the likelihood of cultural survival, including the demography of migration to a given region, rates of survival in different work regimes, and the interest of imperial governments in regulating people's behavior.

European and African Ethnicities in the Western Atlantic

As people met, traded, conquered, and had sex in various regions of the Atlantic world, new social identities, ethnicities, and nationalities came into being. Whatever the precise circumstances, experiences with others helped people define most clearly who *they* were. Terms of differentiation at first derived from such traditional categories as language, customs, and religious beliefs, but soon included newer ideas based on color, degrees of nudity, eating habits, and conceptions of property and price. At the same time that forced or voluntary migrants were trying to hold on to familiar cultural practices, residence in the western Atlantic demanded cultural flexibility.

The extent to which any immigrants retained their traditional cultures was largely a matter of demography. Europeans from nations that already wielded political power in the Americas had an advantage in transplanting core features of their homelands. English, French, Spanish, and Portuguese legal systems, for instance, followed familiar practices, even if at first many lawyers lacked books. And if the transmission of local government was incomplete, it was at least functional. Everywhere the church provided a cultural glue that linked European migrants in the western Atlantic to the different ecclesiastical polities of the eastern Atlantic, whether Catholic or Protestant, even for dissenters. Catholic priests in Spanish America were bound by decisions made in Rome; Anglican and Lutheran ministers were similarly tied to their governing bodies in Europe. But at the same time, no European culture could transplant itself in its entirety. One fundamental impediment was the average age and sex ratio of new migrant populations. Most colonial societies in the Americas retained the demographic peculiarities of migrant societies (young and male, with no natural increase, dependent on migration to sustain population) beyond the first decades of settlement.

Caribbean islands, Brazil, and the Carolinas remained migrant societies for Europeans and Africans throughout this period. High mortality, low fertility, male majorities, and stunted family formation characterized these western Atlantic societies more than others. Such features shaped the ability of newcomers to transfer and reproduce cultural forms. Newly arrived men and women typically did not live long enough to teach their children more than a few core traditions. The young men dominating seventeenth-century European migration, especially those who comprised 95 percent of the 1630s migration to the English Caribbean, could replicate only those aspects of English culture with which they were familiar. In such other places as New England and New Granada, European-born people and their descendants could reproduce themselves and maintain links to their mother countries. Some of those places where settlers were able to reproduce themselves nonetheless remained migrant societies because of the continued influx of newcomers. These included the so-called "middle colonies" of British North America—New York, New Jersey, and Pennsylvania—and the highland valleys and desert coasts of Spanish America, which were relatively healthy places to live. Families in these places were able to sustain themselves; parents lived long enough to rear their children in their own traditions. At the same time, these regions remained attractive to newcomers. Pennsylvania continued to receive tens of thousands of migrants who reinforced European customs, thus ensuring the continued use of German, for example, more than a century after the first German-speaking migrants appeared in the colony.

Yet even those regions could not fully replicate European cultures. The inhabitants of early New England provide a useful example. This region was settled quickly by a single wave of migration in the 1630s. The migrants, 20,000 of them, shared religious convictions (mostly puritans) and a common ethnicity (English, although they came from different regions of England). Families dominated this migration, almost reproducing the age and sex structures of England itself. In addition, the migrants had sufficient resources to keep their families together, if they so chose, although the custom was to farm out adolescent children as servants and apprentices in other households. Of all the migrants in the Atlantic world, the English in New England were best positioned to transplant English culture wholesale if they sought to do so. In some ways they did, building houses in the styles to which they were accustomed and planting fields as they had learned in England. They spoke English only, although not by law, and they often settled among neighbors, friends, and kin, frequently following their English ministers across the Atlantic to America.

But in other ways these pious migrants had no desire to replicate the world they had left. They preferred to base their laws on Biblical traditions, not only English common law. They deliberately rejected the structure of the Church of England, omitting bishops, synods, ecclesiastical courts, and an array of festivals and holidays (from secular observances of a May Day to sacred holidays like Christmas). They sought to rebuild their transformed, almost utopian English world around a new church based on congregational organization. Each town selected its ministers, which in turn led to decentralized worship of varied forms. This new religious climate transformed people, too. Schisms proliferated, as colonists disagreed on how to express what they viewed as god's will. Families deviated from conventional practices in naming children, for example. In England, the Munnings had christened their children Mary, Anna, and Michelaliel, but in New England they switched to hortatory names, popular among puritans, and christened their New-England born children Takeheed, Hopestill, and Return. The Preston family reached New England with six children: Elizabeth, Sarah, Mary, John, Daniel, and Edward. In New Haven they christened four more children, now in a more prophetic mode: Jehiel, Hackaliah, Eliasaph, and Joseph. Like other traditions, naming practices changed in new environments and offer a glimpse at ways in which migrants deliberately departed from European customs.

In regions where Europeans from different kingdoms settled in proximity, historians find more evidence of local formulation, rather than pristine transplanting, of ethnic identity. In North America, German-speakers from discrete kingdoms and principalities in the Holy Roman Empire became known as "Germans," and the polyglot people of New Netherland, some of them Portuguese Jews, became "Dutch." The creation of ethnic identity was a complex process of interaction not only with other inhabitants of the colonies, but also with the exigencies of a new environment.

For Africans, many factors hindered cultural transmission. Cultural autonomy varied among the countries and colonies, from plantation to plantation, mine to mine, city to city. It once was a commonly held idea that the middle passage was so traumatic that no elements of African culture survived the Atlantic crossing, but historians have tempered this, and many argue that it is possible to discern the transmission of African ethnicities to the Americas. But delineating patterns of cultural transmission is a difficult task. Consider the problem of sources for African ethnicities. Historians are forced to rely on identifications recorded by non-African scribes in the Americas, geographic origin in Africa as reflected in ports of departure by slave ships, or a host of observed cultural and physical attributes as reported by non-African observers, often years after Atlantic slave trading had ended. Thanks to the recent compilation of a searchable slave trade database using a range of documents, historians can talk with more certainty about the number of slaves who left from a particular port, but it is more difficult to link a particular slave to a particular geographic place of origin. The slave trade also prompted certain patterns of internal migration within Africa, with captives often marched hundreds of miles from their place of origin to their point of departure.

Historians who examine a single plantation often find that enslaved populations were characterized by their ethnic variety: so Lorena Walsh discovered in her analysis of Carter's Grove plantation in Virginia. Trevor Burnard tracked slave purchases in eighteenth-century Jamaica and found that Africans were dispersed to different plantations on arrival. Burnard characterizes the lives of Jamaican slaves as one of "constant flux, disruption, and misery," and this characterization applies more broadly. The enslaved populations of the Brazilian and New Granadan gold mines were mixed in terms of regional origins, although in some places high concentrations of slaves from the Gold Coast and Calabar were evident by the early eighteenth century. Some mine owners along New Granada's Pacific coast complained that slaves from Calabar, although adept miners, were prone to rebel. In such circumstances, and considering the rigorous disease regime of this area, the vastly outnumbered Spanish elites had to negotiate with their slaves in order to keep the gold flowing.

A glimpse at the languages spoken in the Americas also points to the enormous complexity of the question of cultural transmission. Ethnic majorities did not necessarily impose their language in their place of settlement, as in the case of Montserrat, where despite an Irish (and Irish-speaking) majority, English remained the island's lingua franca. In late eighteenth-century Suriname, many slaves spoke an English-based creole, despite the fact that the colony had been English for no more than two decades and slaves always outnumbered planters, Dutch or English. Both examples reveal that language was connected to migration patterns, but that configurations of settlement mattered as well. In other places, however, migrants from one region had a profound linguistic impact. The languages of Kongo became the lingua franca in parts of eighteenth-century Saint Domingue because of the predominance there of slaves from the lower Congo River region.

Elsewhere, in places with no ethnic (and linguistic) majority, pidgins emerged, as in the case of Gullah and Geechee in the Sea Islands off the coasts of modern South Carolina, Georgia, and Florida. These languages share African grammatical features and a mixture of vocabulary from numerous languages. Speakers use English words, but Gullah also contains words with origins in the parts of Africa from which most coastal slaves came, Senegambia, Sierra Leone, and West Central Africa (Kongo and Angola). In some ways, these pidgins have survived. Today, Americans commonly use the verb to bad-mouth, a Gullah word that literally translates an African linguistic convention to use body parts to describe behavior. In another example, linguistic "islands" still exist in San Basilio del Palenque, outside Cartagena, Colombia, where escaped slaves lived in relative isolation from the surrounding Spanish population for several centuries.

It is clear that Africans transported with them a range of cultural attributes. The slave trade did not destroy vestiges of home cultures, as expressed through language, architecture, dress, hairstyles, worship, food, styles of warfare, gender, music, art, animal husbandry, and other practices. Moreover, because of high rates of mortality, most slave populations remained migrant populations, steadily replenished by newcomers from Africa. In Jamaica, mortality among those engaged in sugar production was so high that the eighteenth-century enslaved population was between 75 and 80 percent African born. Newcomers arrived with fresh knowledge of traditions—that might have already grown dim in an American mining district or plantation—or with news to rekindle a person's connection to home, or with skills in rituals or crafts to infuse a plantation with a heightened range of cultural expressions. That said, African cultural traditions were no more static than European ones, such that a person arriving to the Americas in 1750 would have had a different story to tell from one arriving from Angola a hundred years earlier. In a concrete example, especially in northeast Brazil, the arrival of Muslim slaves in the nineteenth century reflected deep cultural upheavals underway in West Africa.

In Cuba, Brazil, and Saint Domingue, where concentrations of Africans were especially high, slaves who shared a single ethnic or quasi-national origin banded together in their new homes, seeking each other out, often knowing only the African names each man or woman brought to America, not the new names bestowed on them by planters. In parts of New Granada, where the ratio of African men to women was not so unbalanced as in the plantation zones, couples originating from the same region were common. These ethnic or "home country" ties were important in enabling slaves to pursue one of the most deadly strategies of resistance: violent rebellion. In South Carolina in 1739, Saint Domingue in 1791, and Brazil in 1835, slaves from a common nation rose up against planters in organized rebellions. Typical was an incident in 1828, when Africans in Iguaupe, in the heart of Brazil's cane-growing northeast, suddenly rose in revolt. The ringleaders lived on the Engenho Novo plantation, but planters guessed that slaves on a number of estates setting fire to their masters' houses at virtually the same time indicated that a cadre of newly arrived Africans of the same region had devised the plan together. So fresh were these Africans to American soil that the plantation overseers had not yet learned their new Christian names, which made the task of detecting the guilty all the more difficult.

But subordinate subjects in colonial societies also learned how to work within the new legal and cultural structures imposed on them. If some used African ethnicity to organize rebellion or reconstruct communities, others turned to the dominant culture's language and values, manipulating masters with their own ideology. In 1774 in Massachusetts, a group of slaves drew on the political language of the colonial elite to insist, in a petition to the colony's governor and general court, on their own "natural right" to freedom. Appealing to contemporary notions of domesticity, they deplored their forced separation from "tender parents," their own children who were sold away, and their distance from "dearest friends." They played on the court's piety, too, explaining that their condition kept them from practicing Christianity. No law of the land upheld slavery, they argued. Familiar with appropriate forms of redress, they unsuccessfully requested that the legislature pass an act guaranteeing freedom for all adults and their children at the age of twenty-one.

A similar petition from late-eighteenth-century Brazil suggests that slaves there were equally familiar with European law and religious tendencies. The slaves of Engenho Santana did not ask for liberty, which in their context was unlikely to befall them, but for more freedom to fish, move about, and farm for subsistence. They even negotiated for freer access to the market and, appealing to their masters' alleged Christian charity, more reasonable work hours in the fields and mills of the plantation. Slaves in New Granada, meanwhile, used old and new Spanish laws, particularly after a 1789 reform, to petition successfully for changes of masters in cases of mistreatment and separation of marriage partners.

None of these incidents suggests mutually exclusive forms of cultural expression. What is apparent is the multiplicity of identities subject people around the Atlantic world relied on at different moments, manipulating their captors' language and beliefs to gain freedom, or celebrating with recreated, or revised rituals from home when in the company of compatriots. Slaves throughout the Atlantic world worked the systems in which they lived to mitigate the daily horrors and humiliations of their existence and create living circumstances that were as fulfilling as possible.

Indigenous Responses and Cultural Innovations

If Europeans and Africans had difficulty transmitting their cultures across the Atlantic, indigenous people experienced equally profound upheaval as a series of convulsions altered their worlds. Americans endured three stages of interaction with Europeans. First was demographic collapse due to epidemic diseases, which in places coincided with violent conquest and labor demands that further disorganized communities and families. Second, especially in North America, came trade, which many greeted eagerly but which brought with it gradual incorporation into the Atlantic market economy. And third, over the course of the seventeenth and eighteenth centuries, as the French, English, Portuguese, and Spanish expanded settlement, indigenous people had to adapt to the engrossment of their prime agricultural lands, diminution of territory once used for hunting, diminished access to customary resources, and appropriation of sacred sites for European occupation. Each phase led to cultural transformations, some more profound than others.

As noted, in the worst cases, losses in indigenous American populations from epidemic diseases, often accompanied by violent conquest, malnutrition, forced resettlement, and unfree labor regimes, topped 90 percent. Survival required flexibility and innovation. Many mobile hunter-gatherers and even some sedentary farming people could not sustain themselves in their former, corporate, or clan-oriented way. This was as true for the native inhabitants of southern Chile as for those of northern Canada. To survive, Native Americans at and beyond the frontier of European contact formed new bands comprising the remnants of a variety of groups. These "new peoples" then faced fresh challenges, often advancing or retreating in response to European aggression. European observers often misunderstood these processes of migration, resettlement, and cultural restructuring. The Catawba of southeastern North America, for example, have not inhabited the Carolina backcountry since time immemorial. Rather, they are the descendants of what historian James H. Merrell describes as "a kaleidoscopic array of migrations." A similar process of amalgamation and resettlement transpired in the Ohio Valley, where newly constituted communities had to negotiate cultural practices. What language would they speak? What customs might they follow for marriage, childrearing, courtship, or political deliberations? How, where, and what would they plant? Who would exercise political authority? Throughout the western Atlantic world, this cultural renovation and innovation transpired amid circumstances in which old practices eroded from memory, lost with the deaths of elders and religious practitioners. One early nineteenth-century observer noted the Catawbas had "forgotten their ancient rites, ceremonies, and manufactures." As refugees gathered and built new societies, they navigated a cultural world composed of conflicting visions and expectations.

The Iroquois of North America's eastern woodlands offer a case study of one confederacy's response to seventeenth-century colonizing pressures. The Iroquois weathered the century in a grueling cycle of war, replenishing members lost to violence with captive outsiders, including Europeans, whom they incorporated into clans depleted by disease and warfare. As in most Native American societies, captivity among the Iroquois was ritualized and connected to notions of death. Ideas of death, in fact, were one of the main reasons Iroquois went to war. They believed that each individual had special power and strength, and when a person died, the community lost that power. Complex rituals surrounding mourning the dead indicate the importance they attached to human life. People covered their faces with dirt, cut their hair, donned ragged clothes, turned their faces to the wall and refused to speak, and exempted themselves from the regular conventions of daily life. And if the griever's anguish was not assuaged after a period of mourning, he or she could request that their friends and kin undertake a mourning war. The purpose of such a war was to retrieve captives, and they were carried out with stealth and care, as any Iroquois death in battle would recommence the process. Once a captive was brought back, the grieving kin could decide the person's fate: adoption or excruciating death through torture. If adopted, the victim was given the deceased's name and assigned his or her status.

The European presence brought new variables that increased the number of deaths and thus fueled the need for more captives. First, of course, Europeans brought their pathogens, resulting in inexplicable population loss.

Second, Europeans enabled Indians to acquire more deadly weapons—brass tips for arrows, iron heads for war clubs, guns with large bullets—that made the traditional practice of war more deadly. Finally, the incentive to hunt more beaver or deer in order to trade pelts for more imported goods and cement the alliance of European trading partners pushed the Iroquois farther into others' territory, increasing conflict. So even without significant numbers of Europeans present in Iroquois country, the first decades of European trade and settlement in North America posed new challenges and caused more deaths.

That the drop in the Iroquois population was more gradual—from an estimated 10,000 in the 1640s, to 8,600 by the 1670s and to 7,000 by 1700—than that experienced by other tribes under similar circumstances is at least partly due to the Iroquois policy of war and adoption. Over the course of the seventeenth century, the Iroquois remained in a state of war, and by the 1660s, one observer noticed more foreigners than Iroquois in Iroquois country: by then, two-thirds of the population had been adopted from other tribes or European settlements. In an era when disease and warfare dismantled many tribes, the Iroquois were unusual in their resilience: preexisting beliefs survived European arrival and adopted captives absorbed Iroquois practices.

European and colonist incursions into Native American territories continued, of course: groups adapting to European rule in one place stood in contrast to others, who continued to live independently beyond the contact frontier. The process had echoes of a repeating history, although each group's circumstances differed in timing and intensity of contact. Some responses and adaptations worked for some groups but not others. Even rebellions took different forms, as not all of them were spawned by anger over material losses. So-called nativist revolts were a kind of religiously tinged rebellion most characteristic of the first decades following European conquest and displacement. In such uprisings, messianic figures with knowledge of the conquerors' culture tended to call on their followers to reject European ways in hopes of regenerating native society. Such revolts were generally appealing only to people not yet enmeshed in religious or commercial exchanges with the colonizers.

The Maya of sixteenth-century Yucatan initially embraced Franciscan missionaries, but once the outsiders' motives became clearer, the Maya launched a violent nativist revolt. In this instance, indigenous leaders, mostly elders whose power had been eroded under Spanish and Catholic rule, found themselves pitted against younger members whom the Franciscans had favored and even taught to read and write. The failure of the revolt was largely a result of this generational division. Despite general agreement about the unpleasant nature of Spanish rule, similar wheels of acculturation already had begun to turn in Andean communities. Thus, at about the same time, a Taki Onqoy revolt broke out in Peru, and, later, the so-called Santidade cult emerged among native people and runaway slaves in northeastern Brazil. While a violent revolt never blossomed, Santidade remained a kind of alternative religious movement that inspired rebellious acts and kept the Portuguese on guard. Indigenous groups subjected to Spanish and Portuguese rule rebelled throughout the seventeenth and eighteenth centuries, sometimes successfully, such as the aforementioned Pueblo Revolt in 1680 that drove the Spanish out of Mexico for more than a dozen years.

The pattern of nativist revolt was repeated in mainland North American territories claimed by the French, Dutch, and English. The Delaware prophet Neolin launched a nativist movement among Indians of the Ohio Valley in the 1760s. "Put off entirely from yourselves the customs which you have adopted," Neolin ordered, and "return to that former happy state, in which we lived in peace and plenty, before these strangers came to disturb us." But for many Indian populations, such wholesale rejection of Europeans and their commodities and culture made no sense. By the eighteenth century, it would have been peculiar to see tribes in the Iroquois Confederacy join such a movement as Neolin's, since they had been trading and allied with Europeans since the early seventeenth century, with the result a long-term, deeply embedded acculturation and accommodation to European culture. The Iroquois were unlikely to imagine a world free of European goods, which they found convenient and necessary, nor could they any longer envision one in which Indians and Europeans walked separate paths. Many had converted to Christianity, not just Catholicism, but also Anglicanism and Congregationalism.

In this context it is easier to understand the path hewn by Samson Occam, a Mohegan who grew up in Connecticut, where he was born in 1723. Occam's childhood was characterized by a mixture of adherence to tradition—he lived in the customary wigwam and his parents "lived a wandering life"—and adaptation to European settlement. English towns surrounded the Mohegan and acquisitive colonial neighbors sought their lands. Among the many intrusions of European life, including diplomatic alliances and trade commodities the Mohegan had known for a century, literacy and Christianity had made few inroads. Some English ministers had engaged in missionary work among New England Indians, and some tribes came to be identified as Christian, but the Mohegan had not been a part of this evangelical network. This trend reversed in the 1730s, when Occam and others converted during the wave of religious upheavals in the British Atlantic world known as the "Great Awakening." Occam and his mother became Christians, and Occam became a missionary to his people. Central to his enterprise was literacy, a skill that would enable people to read scriptures but which also permitted them to navigate the legal culture around them, helping them secure claims to land and inheritances. Occam went to study with Eleazer Wheelock, famous for taking Indian pupils at his school, and by 1749, after several years of instruction in English, Latin, Greek, Hebrew, and music, Occam was ready to teach Indian children. He then went to England to raise money for Wheelock's work, and while there he was a figure of considerable interest. Although hardly the first Indian to visit Britain, he was the first Indian Christian minister. In his ministry in North America, Occam preached as far from home as Iroquois land.

Individuals like Occam learned to navigate multiple worlds, operating within colonial society in ways that worked to personal and communal advantage. The *pulque* (cactus-beer) dealer Micaela Angela Carrillo pursued a similar path in mid-eighteenth-century New Spain. She passed her entire life

Praying Towns

In the 1640s, two English ministers launched missionary efforts among the Indians of New England. Thomas Mayhew was the first, on Martha's Vineyard off the coast of Massachusetts, and he was followed by John Eliot, who established the first of what came to be called "praying towns" at Natick in 1646. On Martha's Vineyard, the Wampanoag expressed little interest in Mayhew's gospel until the onset of two epidemics in 1643 and 1645, after which they turned to Christianity to seek solutions to the woes of their turbulent world. Yet they shaped their own Christianity, giving themselves Christian names but keeping their Indian ones and continuing to live in wigwams. On the mainland, John Eliot believed that only a complete cultural transformation could ensure a religious conversion. Like all Protestants, he prized literacy, so he translated the Bible into Massachusett by 1663 and taught Indians how to read. Although the Scriptural basis for such requirements was certainly shaky, Eliot demanded that Indians conform to puritan social, sexual, and gender norms. Thus he insisted that Indian men cut their hair short and that Indian women wear theirs tied up. He sought to end the informality of Indian sexual practices by requiring people to join monogamous marriages. Newly monogamous men cast off their second or third wives as well as the children from these unions. Eliot also pushed modesty on Indians, and by the 1650s converts at Natick placed partitions in their wigwams to give married couples privacy. Indians in praying towns were required to organize time around the cycles of their new religion, not around the old seasonal rituals linked to subsistence cycles: daily and weekly prayer, with (among puritans) no holy days. In short, conversion in puritan Massachusetts demanded a social revolution and, as Harold W. van Lonkhuyzen suggests, "sucked at the very marrow of Indian identity." As for the conversions, Christianity spread around the western Atlantic precisely as it had spread earlier in Europe: converts grafted together new and old practices.

Idealized depiction of John Eliot preaching to the Indians. Humanities and Social Sciences Library, Print Collection, Miriam & Ira D. Wallach Division of Art, Print and Photographs, The New York Public Library, Astor, Lenox and Tilden Foundations.

in an Indian village, Nuestra Señora de la Asunción de Amozoque, so she did not have the cosmopolitan career of other coastal traders and diplomats. But as the historian Edith Couturier details, Carrillo was comfortable in various cultural settings. Typical of Mexico's society, Amozoque's population of 3,000 was, according to a 1742 census, 15 percent Spanish, mestizo, and mulatto, with poor and exploited Indians making up the rest. Laws reinforced Indians' low status by prohibiting their bearing arms, wearing boots or shoes, or riding on horseback. By law, Indians throughout Spanish America were required to

Could Indians be Nuns?

In eighteenth-century Mexico City, a former viceroy made a donation to establish a Franciscan convent for upper-class Indian women. The creole elite were, however, appalled at this proposal, and they objected to the proposed convent, suggesting instead that the building might better be put to use to educate Indian girls in order to equip them to support themselves. Could Indian women be nuns? Did they have the right attributes? The controversy reveals the racialized assumptions European creoles possessed about Indians. Critics worried that Indian women might possess one important quality, humility, but lacked the commitment to chastity required of nuns. Indian women, unlike their European counterparts, could simply not be trusted to be celibate. Nuns, moreover, had to be racially pure: in New Spain, women who wished to be nuns had to present a certificate that asserted their blood was untainted by Indian, Muslim, or Jewish ancestry. Thus nuns in New Spain occupied a special sexual and racial status, one defined by its purity. The controversy was particularly intense in 1723–24 and it was in 1724 that a remarkable book was published in Mexico City, La gracia triunfante en la vida de Catharina Tegakovita, India iroquesa. This book told the story of Catherine Tekakwitha (1656–80), an Iroquois woman who moved with other Mohawks to a mission settlement established near Montreal by the Jesuits of New France. There, Tekakwitha's behavior following her conversion to Catholicism conformed ideally to saintly ordeals in her self-denial, fasting, mortifications, and adamant attachment to her new faith despite the great hostility of those around her. Particularly important in this narrative biography was her vow of chastity (which it is unlikely she actually took). Her story attracted considerable attention, and after her death in 1680 a cult rose around her in Canada among both Indians and French

Canadians. The story of her exemplary life was first published in Paris in 1717, and then translated into Spanish. It was the version that appeared in Mexico City in 1724—a politically deployed hagiography—that made the case emphatically that Indian women, sexually pure and of uncommon piety, were indeed well suited to a religious vocation. The doors of Corpus Christi opened to Indian postulants in 1724.

Allan Greer, "Iroquois Virgin: The Story of Catherine Tekakwitha in New France and New Spain," in Allan Greer and Jodi Bilinkoff, eds., Colonial Saints: Discovering the Holy in the Americas, 1500–1800 (New York: Routledge, 2003).

The earliest known portrait of Kateri (Catherine) Tekakwitha, painted by her friend Father Claude Chauchetière between 1682–93 after her death. The original is located in St. Francis Xavier in Montreal.

wear a sort of uniform (as were free people of color, women of African descent having to wear special headdresses and forbidden from wearing silks and calicoes). Elite Indians, generally those descended from conquest-era chieftains and sometimes conquistadors, had rights of Spaniards in dress, conveyance, and political power, however, and Carrillo was of such mixed parentage. She married a *cacique* (local leader) and they lived in the cultural middle ground between Indian and Spanish society. After her husband's death, Carrillo supported herself through pulque production, renting maguey plants, tapping them, and fermenting the sweet sap.

Details of Carrillo's religious and domestic world reveal her place between, and within, two cultures. While making a living from production and sale of an indigenous product, she belonged to four Spanish-style *cofradías*, a type of Catholic lay organization found throughout the Iberian world, each affiliated with a particular church and dedicated to the celebration of a particular saint. Carrillo's house was constructed in the Indian tradition, with several small, discrete buildings arranged within an adobe-walled yard. In what appears to have been a rare confluence of indigenous and Spanish inheritance patterns—widows having power in both traditions—Carrillo managed her family's estate following the death of her husband. She also followed the practice of partible inheritance, which meant that each of her children, regardless of age or sex, received an equal share of her holdings upon her death. This was a central tenet of Spanish law, but was also compatible with the egalitarian values of Indian villages. Through her will and estate inventory, Carrillo lets us see how people adhered to old customs and thrived in new circumstances.

Carrillo's story is further evidence that European, Indian, and African worlds intersected almost everywhere around the western Atlantic. The process of migration, settlement, and reproduction generated variety in the Americas: some regions had populations predominantly of European descent, others predominantly African, and still others indigenous. And throughout the western Atlantic emerged people of mixed heritage, who would be afforded different treatment in different imperial jurisdictions.

In cities and rural areas, on imperial frontiers, and at the impoverished margin of colonial societies—everywhere in the western Atlantic—Europeans, Indians, and Africans found themselves creating blended families, communities, and cultures. The Atlantic world was hardly a place where people's natural tendency was to care for others, so these new familial forms often reflected necessity. Nonetheless, it is possible to see instances of cooperation and the creative ways in which people whose families had been ripped apart by slavery or diminished through epidemic disease created new, hybrid communities.

The town of Gracia Real de Santa Teresa de Mose, established in 1738 by African slaves who escaped from English plantations and were granted religious sanctuary in Spanish Florida, was one such example. The cacique of Mose was an African-born Mandinka man, who upon conversion to Catholicism adopted the name Francisco Menéndez. He had been enslaved and transported from West Africa to Carolina. After fighting for three years in the Yamasee War, he spoke Yamasee and English in addition to his native Mandinka. In Florida he learned Spanish, in which he wrote beautifully. Other of the freed Africans at Mose came from Senegambia, Calabar, the Kongo, and Angola. Some had brought Indian wives with them from Carolina, and some of the second generation of Mose residents married free blacks and Spaniards from other parts of the Caribbean. Whatever their origins, because the residents had sworn "to shed their last drop of blood in defense of Spain and the True Faith" and had converted, they were considered loyal vassals and free subjects. The men formed themselves into a free militia, which

Menéndez commanded, and they and their families became valued home-steaders on Spain's northern frontier. They built a Catholic church at their palisaded settlement and thatched houses said to resemble those of the local Indians, with whom they interacted frequently, as they did with the Spanish town of St. Augustine, two miles south. Mose's settlers were actively engaged in the almost constant eighteenth-century contests between Spain and England, and its militia fought repeatedly to defend Spanish (and their own) interests. In 1740, Menéndez wrote the king, asking for appropriate rewards for his service, a petition which Florida's governor supported. The following year Menéndez and other Mose militiamen took to the seas as corsairs for Spain. After a tumultuous life, Menéndez ended his days in Cuba at some seventy years of age.

Free People of Color

Every slave society in the Americas experienced a steady growth of a small population of free people of mixed race. The term used commonly at the time, "people of color," might sound peculiar to modern ears, but it reflects what contemporaries viewed as an important attribute of this population—these people were not white, and often not black, but "brown," or "colored." The peculiar logic in most of the Atlantic world of an earlier day dictated that people of partial European descent should have more legal privileges than those entirely of African descent. Here and there, this "free colored" population could be statistically significant. In Spanish New Orleans in 1805, people of color represented 19 percent of the total population and 30.6 percent of the free population, and in Rio de Janeiro by 1849, free people of color made up about 5 percent of the *total* population, nearly 11,000 out of more than 200,000 people. Rio's enslaved population was an astounding 78,855 in that year, and many free people of color of means sought to own slaves themselves.

Slaves attained freedom in a number of ways. Military service was one route to liberty in the Dutch colony of Suriname, where runaway slaves were common. Slaves who took part in expeditions to retrieve runaways sometimes received their freedom, as did one African-born slave named Quassie. He served as a scout during the so-called "maroon wars" and in 1755, after twenty years of service, his master manumitted him in recognition of his services to the government. If Quassie's assistance in slave chasing strikes modern readers as a betrayal of other slaves, it is important to remember that Quassie and the runaways he pursued shared the same goal, their own deliverance from slavery, and probably less of a common identity in their race or circumstances than we might suspect.

Different paths existed toward freedom. In some jurisdictions, slaves could buy themselves. Spanish law required that slaves be given the right of *coartación* and enjoined masters to settle on a price or accept arbitration. Slaves in mining districts and urban areas had the greatest access to self-purchase, often raising necessary funds by hiring themselves out on feast days and Sundays, and self-purchase was common in several parts of Brazil. Such opportunities were not limited, however, to Spanish and Portuguese territories. Once free, men and women often turned to buying the freedom of their family members. Juan Bautista Hugón, a free black man in New Orleans, bought the freedom of three of his children and their mother before his death in 1792. Other free people of color were the children of free men and enslaved women, often manumitted by their fathers.

In one curious case, the slave Telemaque won the Charleston, South Carolina lottery in 1799 and used his proceeds to purchase his freedom and set himself up as a carpenter under the name Denmark Vesey. Already the resident of a culturally mixed household—as an enslaved manservant, the multilingual Telemaque had served a Bermudan-born sea captain and an East Indian mistress—Vesey took three wives over the course of his long life, all of whom bore him numerous children. By saving for years, Vesey was able to purchase the liberty of his last wife, Susan, but his children's masters refused to sell at any price. By early 1822, if not before, he began to plan an exodus of slaves out of Charleston harbor for Haiti. Although freed blacks walked such a precarious line in slave societies that most freemen were more inclined to report a servile conspiracy than create one, the aged Vesey was determined to do "what he could" for his children and "his fellow creatures." Among his chief lieutenants were the slaves Monday Gell, an Ibo, and Jack Pritchard, an East African–born spiritual leader believed to be impervious to harm. After the plot was revealed, thirty-five slaves and freedmen, including Denmark, swung from the Charleston gallows, while another thirty-five rebels—among them Denmark's son Sandy Vesey—were transported to Spanish Cuba and other parts of the Caribbean.

Susan Vesey survived the conspiracy, only to face a life of poverty in Charleston and Liberia. But as a freed woman, she was at least able to escape the predatory assaults of white men. By comparison, enslaved women often were hard-pressed to resist the sexual demands of their masters and overseers. Only in Spanish territories were sexual abusers of enslaved women prosecuted, albeit infrequently. The diary of the Jamaican overseer Thomas Thistlewood, written over the second half of the eighteenth century, details his casual expectation of sex from enslaved women. He evidently recorded every one of his encounters. August 21 found him "with Eve in the curing house," and two days later "with Mountain Lucy on my bed." He gave Lucy money and sugar. In between, he was with Phibbah, a woman with whom he maintained a sexual relationship for thirty years. Thistlewood roamed the plantation as a sexual predator, raping when he pleased, giving his victims small tokens or bits of money as if to suggest he was engaging in a commercial exchange, not one in which one party did not, in legal fact, own her own body and therefore could not own—or sell—her sexuality. Ironically, Thistlewood described an attempted rape more graphically, only this time he came to the rescue of a child named Coobah from a bookkeeper who had gagged her with a handkerchief and dragged her into the sugar mill's boiler room. Equally graphic descriptions of rape and prostitution come from the gold and diamond districts of eighteenth-century Brazil. One can make an argument that slave women were never able to consent to sexual relations with white men, yet some of the long-term relationships we know existed complicate this easy explanation to black and white, enslaved and free, female and male, liaisons.

The prospect of privileges for their children led some enslaved women to form attachments to white men. As Trevor Burnard puts it, "by 'whitening' her children, Phibbah had accentuated their advantages in life." Thistlewood freed his and Phibbah's son, John, when he was two years of age. At the age of five John began his formal education, and he was apprenticed to a carpenter and joined the "colored" militia when he reached his teens. He died at the age of twenty, so he was unable to achieve the status his education and background predicted. Had he lived, he may well have become established among Jamaica's "brown" elite, and he would have inherited the separate estates of his mother and father. Elsewhere, some white men invested considerable resources in their mixed-race children, paying for educations and ensuring their economic viability with property. In Saint Domingue, the free people of color inherited so much from their fathers that they became major holders of property. In 1789, free people of color comprised a mere 5.2 percent of the population but owned one-quarter of the slaves and real estate of the colony. The career of the Brazilian Francisca da Silva of Diamantina revealed the economic and social ascent possible for enslaved women and their free children. She began as a slave in the household of a Portuguese diamond contractor, but she ended her life in the first years of the nineteenth century as one of the wealthiest slave owners in the region. Several of her sons received an education in Portugal.

The single notable exception to acceptance of these interracial unions was in British North America, and it is perhaps best witnessed in the actions of Thomas Jefferson, the white creole revolutionary and third president of the United States, who had a long-term relationship with his deceased wife's half-sister, the slave Sally Hemings, herself a product of two generations of such unions and, in the terminology of the time, a *quadroon*. Jefferson's public disavowal of this liaison, and his white descendants' bitter rejection of it, stand in contrast to the conduct of planters in other parts of the Atlantic world.

Historians sometimes apply the word *privileged* to those bondpersons who managed to secure and retain freedom in slave societies, but this was a circumscribed privilege in which people were denied full legal equality and had to wrestle with assaults without an avenue of redress. It is easy to identify the successful free black elite: they owned estates and slaves, and through patronage and kinship networks had close links to white society. But the larger mass of free black persons passed their lives on the economic margin. Isabella, a free black woman in Suriname, knew all about these hurdles to full freedom. She confided to a minister in the 1730s that she found her life unbearable. At church, worshipers mocked her as a "black animal" and told her that black people did not go to heaven. No white man would marry her; such men would only treat her as a concubine.

Governments had mixed sentiments about free blacks like Isabella. In Spanish Louisiana, royal officials encouraged the growth of the free black population—as they had done in Florida—to resolve recurring labor shortages and fill midlevel positions, including transportation jobs that masters were reluctant to let slaves perform. Free people of color performed manual labor, repairing the levee that protected New Orleans from the river; fought

Brown Masters

No better illustration exists of the precise racialist distinctions drawn in American societies than the tendency of many free people of color to own slaves. The practice was particularly common in the Caribbean; in Saint Domingue, a significant minority of the gens de couleur—mulattoes and a few freed blacks—owned African slaves. In part because they walked a fine line in a world in which racial theorists like Thomas Jefferson regarded them as biological inferiors based on their percentage of African "blood," free slaveholders had to be diligent in expressing their fealty to the established social order. As one historian has noted of Saint Domingue, "the mulatto slaveholders, especially the females, often outdid the grands blancs in mistreating their slaves."

In the northern mainland, the practice was less common, although Charleston and New Orleans both had large populations of mixed-race slaveholders. By the early nineteenth century, fully 85 percent of those African Americans who owned slaves were mulattoes. As in New Orleans, free people of color typically married partners of the same phenotype. In 1790, in the ultimate expression of racial schism, "five free brown men" in Charleston founded the Brown Fellowship Society, a fraternal organization closed to Africans, whom they derisively dubbed "the backward race." In many slave societies, free mulattoes also earned the reputation as turncoats, which proved to be the case in Charleston in 1822 when three "brown men"—Peter Prioleau, George Wilson, and William Penceel—turned in Denmark Vesey and his followers.

Below: Freedwomen with slaves socializing in Barbados, late eighteenth century engravings. Credit: Rue des Archives/The Granger Collection, New York.

the fires that were the fear of all pre-modern cities; and captured runaway slaves. Free blacks were also bulwarks in hostilities against foreign invaders. But their racial classification and their connections to slaves through kinship, friendship, and the workplace made them potentially dangerous in the eyes of white leaders, who worried that free blacks might orchestrate or join slave rebellions. Soon after the region was settled in the early eighteenth century, free blacks were expelled from the mining camps of westernmost New Granada. As the proslavery writer E. C. Holland put it in 1822, in the wake of Vesey's thwarted rebellion, "the existence of Free Blacks among us [is] the greatest and most deplorable evil." Governments gave free people of color opportunities to identify with white society (and thus to invest in its security) by acquiring the status symbols associated with full freedom and participation. They were allowed to hold slaves, and they often did. But elsewhere, governments, particularly state governments in parts of the United States, moved to shut the door to freedom, forbidding owners to manumit slaves and requiring former slaves, once freed, to leave their homes upon attaining freedom. Freedom thus sometimes required a high price of permanent family separation, the very fate slaves feared when masters threatened to sell away family members. The trend in the United States was toward harsher treatment of free people of color than in most other parts of the Atlantic world, particularly Latin America. Rights to self-purchase, access to social advancement through skilled trades and military service, and legal protection against family separation were all standard in Brazil, New Granada, Cuba, Mexico, and Peru.

In the United States, more than anywhere else, laws governing work, dress, and living arrangements circumscribed the daily lives of free blacks. In South Carolina, Vesey had to purchase a license in order to conduct his business: his white neighbors faced no such requirement. Movement was also restricted; except for fishermen, freemen were not allowed to own boats. In addition, the city of Charleston placed a cap on daily wages. All free people of color had to pay a special annual tax simply because they were free, legislation intended in part to encourage free blacks to leave the state. After the 1822 conspiracy, the government passed further restrictions, forbidding free people to hire slaves and restricting conversation between visiting black mariners and the slaves who toiled the docks by requiring captains to incarcerate black sailors while in harbor. The Brazilian port cities of Salvador and Rio de Janeiro could not have provided a sharper contrast to Vesey's Charleston. Here, free black populations were so large, well-rooted, economically powerful, and diverse that one simply could not divide society along white-black lines. Brazilian authorities worried instead about jihad-inspired rebellions sparked by newly arrived Muslim slaves, many of whom were literate in Arabic.

Talk of "mixture," which began in the earliest phases of Atlantic integration, assumed some primordial sense of human difference based on physical features. Europeans would eventually categorize these differences in terms of *race*. This term was in fact rarely used before the eighteenth century, and it was most commonly applied by the anti-Semitic Spanish and Portuguese to refer disparagingly to people of Jewish descent. As will be seen, the concept of race developed differently throughout the Atlantic world and changed over time, but it was always connected to the possession, exercise, and maintenance of power. Children of various colors and cultures might have played together innocently in eighteenth-century Salvador, Mexico City, or Quebec, but when they became adults they would discover how their assigned racial identities defined their social roles and expanded or limited their options.

Their mixed-race children and proximity to Africans appear to have done little to alter the racial attitudes of white planters and overseers. Burnard's analysis of Thistlewood's diary reveals the racial attitudes of Caribbean planters. Like other white observers of his time before and since, Thistlewood thought little of Africans' intellectual ability, and he admired their physical courage only in the course of condemning their ability to feel pain and emotions. Typical of Euroamericans of the eighteenth century, Thistlewood was preoccupied with racial classification, always careful to record the appearance (and thus degree of racial mixture) of the people he encountered: "negro," "mulatto," "sambo," or "white," even when intruding these adjectives in his diary required awkward and inefficient language. In this he had much in common with Enlightenment thinkers like the Swedish botanist Carolus Linnaeus, whose 1758 *Systema Naturae* characterized *Homo Sapiens afer* (Africans) as cunning yet indolent, phlegmatic yet "ruled by caprice."

Not surprisingly, the most detailed—and tortuous—explication of racial categories and adaptation in a hybrid society came from the rationalist political philosopher Thomas Jefferson. In 1815 a brash young correspondent, Francis C. Gray, indelicately challenged Jefferson on the question of whether black Americans were held back by nature or by a racist environment. In reply, the sage of Monticello calmly turned to mathematics. Following several pages of calculations, he concluded that when a "quarteroon" and Caucasian (yet another imagined category of humanity) produced children, "their offspring . . . having less than $^1/_4$ pure negro blood, to wit $^1/_8$ only, is no longer a mulatto." This "third" introduction of white genes "clears the blood." Octoroons, in other words, being seven-eighths Caucasian, were effectively purged of African blood and would thus improve their biological ranking in the pre-Darwinian Great Chain of Being. The fact that Jefferson briefly used the example of a merino ram was surely designed, consciously or unconsciously, to disguise the fact that he was talking about Hemings and his own mixed-race children, who were octoroons. Should such a child "be emancipated," Jefferson added, switching back to human examples, "he becomes a free *white* man, and a citizen of the United States to all intents and purposes."

Although typically regarded as a disciple of the Enlightenment, Jefferson and his views foreshadowed the scientific racism of the late nineteenth century. Indeed, a mass of evidence from across the Americas points to a hardening of racial lines by the end of the eighteenth century, precisely when the slave trade expanded most rapidly. In Saint Domingue, by the 1780s new racial laws prevented people of mixed ancestry from identifying themselves as white. Some free colored families like the Trichets in Torbec Parish managed to avoid the racial labels—"quadroon," "mulatto," etc.—that others carried. Other laws reinforced the secondary status of free blacks and other free people of color. By 1782, it was illegal to call a person of color "sieur," and after 1769, free people of color were banned from commissioned positions within the Saint Domingue militia, a reform they protested to no avail.

Eighteenth-century Spanish visitors to the Americas expressed a fascination with racial mixture, evidenced by their fondness for so-called *casta* (race, breed, or caste) paintings. Usually sixteen in a series, although sometimes executed on one large panel, casta paintings demonstrated in a quasi-scientific, typological way the range of possible mixtures of Spanish American subject peoples. The earliest of these paintings appeared in the first decades of the eighteenth century, but the real heyday for casta painting was between 1760 and 1790. Each painting depicted a family group: a man, a woman, and the child they produced. The artists, some well known, lavished attention on domestic details, apparently intended as a commentary on the appropriateness or inadvisability of certain unions, as well as the class roles assigned to each. The paintings, almost all from Mexico, often evoke a conversation or

Sally Hemings and Thomas Jefferson

Published first in 1802 by the polemicist James Thomson Callender in the Richmond Recorder, the story that Jefferson had a decades-long sexual relationship with his enslaved sister-in-law, Sally Hemings, pursued the third president. Accepted by African Americans as a matter of course, doubted by most whites, and vehemently denied by the majority of white historians, the allegations remained unresolved for two centuries. Jefferson's white daughter Martha once confided to her son that her cousin Peter Carr was the father of Hemings's children, while Ellen Randolph Coolidge, one of the president's grandchildren, remembered being told that Peter's brother Samuel Carr had fathered all of her children.

Contradicting the white family's disunited front was the testimony, given late in life, of Madison Hemings, who claimed that his "mother became Mr. Jefferson's concubine." Israel Jefferson, another former Monticello slave, confirmed that claim and added that Hemings's father was John Wayles, Jefferson's father-in-law. Despite the fact that Jefferson was at home roughly nine months prior to the birth of all six of Hemings's children, few scholars gave much

credence to Madison's claim, and several writers, including Alf Mapp, tried to resolve the contradictions in the white family's testimony by suggesting that both of the Carr brothers fathered Hemings's "numerous progeny" (an uncharitable term he never applied to Martha Wayles Skelton Jefferson, who bore seven children for her two husbands).

What resolved the debate was the publication of DNA studies in 1998 that revealed a high probability that Jefferson fathered Hemings's youngest son, Eston Hemings. Since the study also ruled out the Carr brothers, a small band of self-proclaimed "Jefferson admirers" attempted to argue that the president's simple brother Randolph Jefferson was the father, but with little success. As the historian Joseph Ellis put it, "the scholarly consensus [regarding Jefferson's paternity] in the wake of the DNA evidence is beyond a reasonable doubt."

Peter Onuf and Jan Lewis, eds., Sally Hemings and Thomas Jefferson: History, Memory, and Civic Culture (Charlottesville: University Press of Virginia, 1999).

Thomas Jefferson (Library of Congress, LC-USZ62-3795) and a view of his home, Monticello (Library of Congress, LC-USZ62-122242).

exchange. Some display male and female artisans in their work, others show families relaxing or quarreling.

Each person in the panel is identified by a socio-racial classification: Spaniard, Indian, black, mestizo, morisco, mulatto, *china cambujo*, *Chamizo*, *loba* (the child of a mestizo and mulatto or an Indian and a black). Terms for almost all the so-called castas, even those at the allegedly higher levels, were derogatory, including *salta en el aire* (suspended in midair, or unfathomable). Yet the categories were not fixed or even consistent: that is, one painting might depict a mestiza and a mulatto producing a "wolf," while another labels such a person a morisco, or "Christianized Moor." The paintings provide a glimpse of ideas about race in the Spanish world, but mostly from the perspective of Spanish and creole elites; almost none of the terms besides *mestizo* and *mulatto* appear in colonial documents of the time—other than as fighting words. "Whitening" was nevertheless as much a Spanish-American obsession as it was Haitian or Virginian. After three generations, a mestizo or mulatto could "whiten" to become an "albino," while after a similar passage of time a person of distant African or Indian descent might be regarded as a "throwback" if his or her complexion proved darker than that of either parent.

The terminology devised for racial classification in parts of the Atlantic world reflected the ways in which race came to be a crucial category of identity (imposed in legal records if not accepted by people themselves). By the eighteenth century, color was most critical. To appreciate the shift in how people perceived themselves and those around them, one need only reflect on the major dichotomies of the period before 1492, when Europeans divided their known world into "Christians" and "infidels." When Europeans met the people of the Americas, they categorized them uniformly as "heathen," continuing the custom of allowing religious beliefs to define a population. But after first decades and then centuries of conquest, conversion, exchange, and sexual interaction, Europeans and their descendants who held power in the Americas devised new ways of classifying people—first by continental origin ("European" or "Indian") but subsequently based on perceived physical differences. Religious distinctions faded in importance, since many of those defined as "Indian," "mulatto," "mestizo," or "moreno" in fact shared the same religion as the dominant governing population.

Thus, *raza* (race) in the context of Atlantic colonization and the slave trade came to be associated mostly with color. Late in the Reconquista, Christian Iberians established a legally binding principle called "purity of blood," an alleged absence of Jewish or Muslim background in one's family tree. In order to hold public office or enter the priesthood or convents throughout the colonial period in the Americas, Africa, and East Atlantic Islands, Iberians had to produce a genealogy demonstrating descent from "Old Christians." Those born out of wedlock were similarly forbidden from high society, since they could not prove so-called blood purity. In the context of widespread colonial exploitation of Indians, Africans, and other people of color, children of mixed background were often assumed to be illegitimate, and therefore of dubious lineage. By the late seventeenth century, blood purity affidavits took on the weight of licenses.

Spanish American and Brazilian elites sometimes made these licenses provisions for marriage. In Spanish Florida, if there were opposition to a marriage or discrepancies in status between bride and groom, the intended couple had to obtain a special dispensation. One Spaniard sought to marry a woman of one-quarter African descent in 1795. He attested to his own "pure" Spanish origin and asked the governor to let him marry his fiancée, who was not only a "quadroon" but also illegitimate. He implored the licensing tribunal to declare her "free of the stain of a vile race as she was very light and no one would suspect her origins." The case was referred to an ecclesiastical court and the couple subsequently married.

The Bourbon monarchs of Spain began to sell certificates of whiteness, legitimacy, and purity of blood in the late eighteenth century to just about anyone who could pay. Colonial vanity and racial obsession was thus turned into a gold mine for a cash-strapped crown. In the end, for all the interest in defining people by race, there were always ways to circumvent derogatory categories and to redefine one's self.

The emergence, and in some places the hardening, of racial distinctions shaped but never fully determined the ways people understood their place in the world. Official and personal identities were often not the same thing: double consciousness was the rule. If the western Atlantic was a world of racial hierarchies, and racialized ideologies were a product of Atlantic exchanges, it also was a world of cultural and demographic variety: European or creole majorities were dominant in some places; African, Indian, or mixed-heritage majorities were dominant in others. The distribution of population circumscribed the political behavior of European and creole leaders. For example, Indian and enslaved African majorities hindered anti-imperial politi-

Table 8.2 Ethnic Composition in Some Western Atlantic Populations (by percentage)

	Europeans /creoles	Native American	castas	slaves (Africans /creoles)	free black "mulatto"
New Spain (1650)	9	86	5		
Mexico (1800)	18	61	21		
Peru (1795)	12.6	58.2	29.2		
Brazil (1800)	28	6*		38	28
United States (1776)	80			20	
Jamaica (1713)	11			89	
Jamaica (1730)	9.8			89	1.2
Jamaica (1788)	7.7			89	3.2
Saint Domingue (1787)	5.3			90	4.7

* in settled areas only

Sources: Richard S. Dunn, *Sugar and Slaves: The Rise of the Planter Class in the English West Indies, 1624–1713* (Chapel Hill: University of North Carolina Press, 1972); Burnard, *Mastery, Tyranny, and Desire*; Thomas O. Ott, *The Haitian Revolution, 1789–1804* (Knoxville: University of Tennessee Press, 1973); Thomas E. Skidmore, *Brazil: Five Centuries of Change* (New York: Oxford University Press, 1999); James Lockhart and Stuart B. Schwartz, *Early Latin America: A History of Spanish America and Brazil* (New York: Cambridge University Press, 1983).

cal activity on the part of colonial elites in the late eighteenth and early nine-teenth centuries. Anything similar to a democratic rebellion meant that they would lose everything, or so they feared.

Atop western Atlantic racial hierarchies stood Europeans and people of European descent (the creoles). Not all of these persons were wealthy or po-litically powerful, but they nonetheless enjoyed privileges of birth and status in a world ranked by color. Because those in the colonies with the greatest power, whether in Buenos Aires or Port-au-Prince, looked upon Europeans as their arbiters of fashion, elite colonial values and aesthetics tended to be de-rivative. Popular culture, full of indigenous and African influences, was often far more original, and (some elites admitted) stimulating. In music, particu-larly, mostly African-influenced mixtures of old and new forms and instru-mentation gave rise to enduring styles that would later be treated as national treasures: jazz, tango, cumbia, blues, son, and samba. Hybrid art styles, some created in clear rejection of European influences, blended freely almost any iconography or medium at hand. Elites almost universally looked on indig-enous, African, and mixed-race talent as second rate. Even creole artists and musicians from the upper classes were not esteemed. To secure local status and patronage, the likes of colonial painters Benjamin West and John Single-ton Copley studied in Britain.

Along Africa's Atlantic coast, some commercial families identified them-selves as "European" or "white" even when, by the judgment of most observ-ers, they were neither. Senhora Catarina was of this ilk, and she was but one member of a group of Luso-Africans found on both sides of the tropical At-lantic who clung to a "Portuguese" identity and manifested a "Portuguese" style. "Throughout the Gambia-Casamance-Bissau region during the seven-teenth- and early-eighteenth centuries," writes the architectural historian Pe-ter Mark, "wherever the presence of Luso-African traders provided a model, houses 'in the Portuguese style' were adopted by local rulers and merchants as symbols of social status and wealth." Mark found similar structures, only with raised ground floors, as the preferred dwellings in parts of seventeenth-century Brazil associated with Atlantic commerce. For many people of this population, what they considered good in terms of food, clothing, or social etiquette either had its roots in European manners and customs, or was per-ceived as European, regardless of its actual origins. "Portuguese" houses could have packed mud floors, mud-brick walls, and thatched roofs, but they re-mained symbols of status so long as they kept enough "European" elements—whitewash, square shape, vestibule—to be considered in the "Portuguese," rather than "native," style.

In the English colonies, men with wealth sought to establish themselves as English gentry. They constructed homes on British models, copying archi-tectural and decorative details down to the molding on the ceiling and the mantel above the fireplace. They even made efforts to recreate English archi-tecture and domestic furnishings in places where these efforts would produce profoundly uncomfortable dwellings and impractical items. While the Span-ish and French in the Caribbean constructed houses suited to a warm and humid climate, with wide windows to catch the trade winds and comfortable verandas for outdoor living, neighboring English sugar planters built traditional brick homes, complete with fireplaces and steep gables for shedding snow. Whatever the cost, the English wore the clothes and ate the food they deemed suitable for their station: planters of Barbados and Jamaica were thus overdressed in English fashions and ate heavy, meat-based diets. In contrast were the servants and slaves of these men, who were underdressed and underfed.

Facilitating the copycat efforts of the colonial elites were books detailing the decorative touches used in European estates: free and enslaved artisans from Boston to Minas Gerais copied these models. In some British colonies, creole elites established academies and colleges for the education of their sons (no such institutions existed for girls): Harvard in Massachusetts, William and Mary in Virginia, and Codrington College in Barbados were thus established in the seventeenth century. Spanish American universities were even older, dating from as early as the 1550s. But in some regions, planters preferred to have their sons educated in Europe. To give his son the best possible status and standing in colonial society, one Virginia tobacco planter, William Byrd, sent off the six-year-old child to England, where he remained in school until he returned to Virginia as an adult. Brazil's elites sent their sons to Coimbra, Évora, and later to military academies in Lisbon and elsewhere. Generally, metropolitan values formed the basis for colonial culture for creole elites except where religious sensibilities dictated otherwise.

But the populations of the western Atlantic, a mixture of European, African, and Indian, served as constant reminders to white creoles that they lived in a mostly non-European sphere. Since incoming European officials and migrants were quick to remind them of this fact, the elites often experienced anxiety about their status, and at different times in different places that anxiety would fuel a rising desire for national independence. The creole elite deviated from European models in the same way that Africans in the Americas struggled to establish new cultural forms amid the variety they brought and that Indians had to reconstitute their communities amid horrific external pressures. If Senhora Catarina, Captain Assou, and Isabel Montour were unusual in the extent of their engagement with people of other cultures and their ability to navigate different worlds, they nonetheless effectively symbolize the innovation and cultural fusion that defined the Atlantic world.

Selected Readings

Brooks, George E., *Eurafricans in Western Africa: Commerce, Social Status, Gender, and Religious Observance from the Sixteenth to the Eighteenth Century* (Athens: Ohio University Press, 2003).

Brown, Kathleen, *Good Wives, Nasty Wenches, and Anxious Patriarchs: Gender, Race, and Power in Colonial Virginia* (Chapel Hill: University of North Carolina Press, 1996).

Burnard, Trevor, *Mastery, Tyranny, and Desire: Thomas Thistlewood and His Slaves in the Anglo-Jamaican World* (Chapel Hill: University of North Carolina Press, 2004).

Cope, R. Douglas, *The Limits of Racial Domination: Mexico City, 1620–1720* (Madison: University of Wisconsin Press, 1992).

Deagan, Kathleen, and José María Cruxent, *Columbus's Outpost Among the Tainos: La Isabela* (New Haven: Yale University Press, 2003).

Egerton, Douglas R., *He Shall Go Out Free: The Lives of Denmark Vesey*, 2nd ed. (Lanham, MD: Rowman and Littlefield, 2004).

Frank, Zephyr, *Dutra's World: Wealth and Family in Nineteenth-Century Rio de Janeiro* (Albuquerque: University of New Mexico Press, 2004).

Hancock, David, *Citizens of the World: London Merchants and the Integration of the British Atlantic Community, 1735–1785* (Cambridge, UK: Cambridge University Press, 1995).

Katzew, Ilona, *Casta Painting: Images of Race in Eighteenth-Century Mexico* (New Haven: Yale University Press, 2004).

Landers, Jane G., ed., *Against the Odds: Free Blacks in the Slave Societies of the Americas* (London: Frank Cass, 1996).

Mark, Peter, *"Portuguese" Style and Luso-African Identity: Precolonial Senegambia, Sixteenth–Nineteenth Centuries* (Bloomington: Indiana University Press, 2002).

Metcalf, Alida, *Go-Betweens and the Colonization of Early Brazil, 1500–1600* (Austin: University of Texas Press, 2006).

Northrup, David, *Africa's Discovery of Europe, 1450–1850* (Oxford: Oxford University Press, 2002).

Richter, Daniel K., *The Ordeal of the Longhouse: The Peoples of the Iroquois League in the Era of European Colonization* (Chapel Hill: The University of North Carolina Press, 1992).

Szasz, Margaret Connell, ed., *Between Indian and White Worlds: The Cultural Broker* (Norman: University of Oklahoma Press, 1994).

Thornton, John, *The Kongolese Saint Anthony: Dona Beatriz Kimpa Vita and the Antonian Movement, 1684–1706* (Cambridge, UK: Cambridge University Press, 1998).

Van Lonkhuzen, Harold W., "A Reappraisal of the Praying Indians: Acculturation, Conversion, and Identity at Natick, Massachusetts, 1646–1730," *New England Quarterly* 63 (1990): 396–428.

B. West into.   *Grignion sculp*

The Indians giving a Talk to Colonel Bouquet in a Conference at a Council Fire, near his Camp on the Banks of Muskingum in North America, in Oct.r 1764.

The Henry Bouquet Peace Council, 1764. Colonel Henry Bouquet of the British Army in council with the Shawnee, Seneca, and Delaware Indian tribes on the banks of the Muskingum River (in present day Ohio), October 1764. Color English engraving, Benjamin West, 1766. Credit: The Granger Collection, New York.

Chapter Nine

The Atlantic Shrinks: War, Reform, and Resistance, 1689–1790

> *An empire founded by war must maintain itself by war.*
> Baron of Montesquieu,
> Considérations sur les Causes
> de la grandeur des Romains *(1736)*

Number *Four, New Hampshire, August, 1754:* In the span of a single night, Susanna Johnson's life came entirely unraveled. That evening, she hosted a party for her neighbors, and a few hours later, at sunrise, she started a forced march to Canada, a prisoner of the French and their Indian allies. The people who settled at Number Four, the hamlet later known as Charlestown in the English colony of New Hampshire, were a small and hardy contingent. Susanna Johnson remembered her first visit to the town at the age of fourteen, in 1744, when this was the northern frontier of English settlement in the Connecticut River valley. The availability of land in a region characterized by big families with numerous children had drawn townsfolk seeking their own plots for farming. Population growth put pressure on available land, and the result was regular dispersal to the edges of settlement, which happened to be a contested region where empires met. When the teenaged Johnson first visited Number Four, nine or ten new English families lived there in huts and socialized with each other and with Indians living nearby. Such was the practice at the time in New England, where Europeans and Indians lived in proximity, trading and speaking to each other with words cobbled together from each other's languages. It was, she recalled, "such a mixture on the frontiers of savages and settlers [that] the state of society cannot be easily described."

Johnson ended up staying in Number Four, marrying, and raising her children there. One summer night in August of 1754, the Johnsons hosted their neighbors in an evening's entertainment. Johnson offered her guests watermelon and a concoction called "flip," a warm beverage with a base of beer or ale, mixed with rum and an egg and sweetened with nutmeg and sugar. After the company left, one young man lingered to flirt with Johnson's teenaged sister, Miriam, making it a long night for the vigilant chaperone. All finally went to bed, but the Johnsons were woken at sunrise by the gentle knock on the door of a neighbor, ready for a day's work; then, suddenly, they realized their household had come under a harrowing attack by Indians. The Johnsons had been swept up in an extension of international rivalries. Abenaki Indians allied with the French had descended from Canada in a raiding party.

As was their custom, they attacked English settlements, destroying property and whisking away captives. Heavily pregnant with her fourth child, Johnson made the trek with her husband, sister, a neighbor, and three small children. The infant, christened Captive by her parents, was born just days into the journey north. The new mother rode the family horse, Scoggin, but after a few more days the food supply ran out and they were forced to shoot Scoggin. The Indians prepared a soup with his bones, flavored with the roots of the forest, and "each one partook of as much as his feelings would allow." Johnson continued in a weakened condition, carried on her husband's back in a make-shift sling, her survival uncertain. In one chilling moment, she fainted and one of her captors raised his hatchet to her head. "Do go," her terrified son Sylvanus screamed, "for they will kill you." Sister Miriam suffered lesser trials, but she endured the taunts of her young Indian captor, who pulled her hair and deliberately stepped on the hem of her inconveniently long dress, part of English women's fashion of the period. All the Johnsons faced uncertainty about their fate.

After their arrival at Crown Point, the family dispersed. Indians adopted six-year-old Sylvanus and a French woman in Montreal adopted one daughter. The rest of the family spent several years in a Montreal prison. It took a long time for Johnson to reassemble her family. After five years, her daughter, also named Susanna, was redeemed from her Canadian home, but she spoke only French. Sylvanus returned from his Indian family after four years, but he spoke only Abenaki and a little broken French. "My family," Johnson reported, became "a mixture of nations."

Kingdom of Timbo, West Africa, 1788: A day of this year was as life-altering for Abd al-Rahman Ibrahima as was the one thirty-four years earlier for Susanna Johnson. Ibrahima was twenty-six and head of a force sent to fight a rival group blocking Timbo's trade with the Atlantic coast, several hundred miles away, when he blundered into an ambush. Ibrahima's last memory of himself as a Muslim warrior was of seeing an enemy swinging a gun barrel toward his head, feeling the crack, and then having his world spin away.

Ibrahima was born in 1762, eight years after Johnson's capture and one year before the end of the Seven Years' War; he was reared through decades that saw fighting on every populated continent (between Russians and Turks, Boers and native South Africans, Chinese and Burmese, Swedes and Danes, and the British and their colonial subjects in India and North America, for example). But Islamic learning rather than soldiery captured Ibrahima's interests through his early teens: he spent five years studying in distant Timbuktu before returning home in 1779 to assume a post in his father's army. Ibrahima's father was the ruler of Timbo, an Islamic kingdom in the Futa Jalon highlands of what is now the nation of Guinea. Ibrahima merely "followed the horsemen," he later remembered, until reaching maturity; then he became a successful cavalryman and, as princes do, ascended quickly in rank. Perhaps it was inexperience that caused Ibrahima to lead his group into the ambush. In any event, after being clubbed in the head, he was dragged away, stripped of his clothes, tied up, and led off. "They made me go barefoot one hundred miles," he later wrote, "and led my horse before me." "They" were the slave traders, to whom his captors had sold him, and the one hundred miles was only part of the way north that led finally to the middle reaches of the Gambia River, where a slaver not long out of London loaded Ibrahima and 160 other captives on board and then headed for the Americas. Within a matter of months he would be sold to a tobacco farmer in Natchez, on the Mississippi River, 175 miles north of New Orleans, in territory belonging to the fledgling United States of America.

Eighteenth-Century Atlantic Warfare and Its Consequences

Susanna Johnson and Abd al-Rahman Ibrahima shared the misfortune of finding themselves embroiled in wars whose origins were not perfectly clear and, in some cases, lay thousands of miles away, but for many living along the edges of the Atlantic basin, such was life in the eighteenth century. From the beginning, war had defined the Atlantic world. Violence accompanied territorial expansion whether it was Europeans in the Americas, Mande or Yoruba in West Africa, or Trekboers in southern Africa, and warfare continued as a defining feature of territorial expansion and displacement of indigenous people throughout the eighteenth century and beyond. But imperial wars originating mainly on the eastern side of the ocean increasingly embroiled the people of the Americas in the eighteenth century. In Europe, the century opened in the aftermath of King William's War, known also as the War of the League of Augsburg and the Nine Years' War (1688–97). The War of Spanish Succession (1702–13), called Queen Anne's War in the English colonies, soon followed. Europe enjoyed peace for almost three decades until the eruption of the Anglo-Spanish War (1739–44), also known as the War of Jenkins' Ear, King George's War (1744–48), and the War of Austrian Succession (1741–48). Hostilities also broke out between Spain and Portugal following the 1750 Treaty of Madrid, but worse yet was the global conflict known in North America as the French and Indian War (1754–63) and more broadly as the Seven Years' War (1756–63). (The French called it the English War; Prussians the Petticoat War; Austrians the War for Silesia; and French Canadians the War of Conquest.) But even this momentous conflict did not end the ordeals Atlantic people faced on land and sea: wars broke out again in the 1770s and 1790s. The multiple names of these increasingly sophisticated, deadly, and wide-ranging conflicts for Atlantic domination reflect the multiplicity of viewpoints and goals of their participants.

If Europeans outdid others in naming wars, they held no corner on imperial struggles. Over the same period, an equal amount of conflict occurred in sub-Saharan Africa. In areas once part of the Songhai Empire, near the great bend of the Niger River, such centers of regional authority as Jenne, Gao, and Timbuktu fought, sometimes successfully, to beat back incursions by the desert Tuareg, militant merchants intent on siphoning off local trade. Farther south, resurgent elements of the old Mali Empire sought militarily to regain past glory, while such newer empires as Kaabu in Senegambia, Ashanti inland from the Gold Coast, Oyo on the Slave Coast, and Luba around the headwaters of the Congo River waged war to extend territorial control. Though none of these states' varying modes of warfare and expansion could be classified as typical, the circumstances involving Oyo may serve as an example for the others.

At the start of the sixteenth century the small state of Oyo, consisting mainly of Yoruba-speaking people, began using wealth gained from production of cloth and iron and regional trade to obtain horses from tsetse fly–free areas to its north, over time developing an effective cavalry. Through the seventeenth century, Yoruba conquered neighboring people until, by 1650, its head, the *alafin*, ruled over a territory that rivaled in size (if one can make comparisons between areas of such different political authority) the British colonies on the North American mainland. Oyo continued to expand in the eighteenth century, waging wars to conquer Dahomey in the 1720s and 1740s and, partly through trading captives, became more involved with European traders along the Atlantic coast to the south. At its height, shortly after the middle of the eighteenth century, Oyo received tribute from 6,600 towns and villages.

Smaller states fought, too, with a regularity that kept full the paths of refugees and captives heading away from conflicts, the latter often toward sale in the Atlantic or trans-Saharan trades. The state of Segu, for example, began in the seventeenth century as a Bambara-speaking group raiding traders along the upper Niger River, but by the eighteenth century Segu had a strong army under an energetic leader, Mamari Kulibali, who controlled the Niger between Bamako and Timbuktu. Rival Bambara-speakers, driven from Segu during Kulibali's conquests, created the state of Kaarta away from the river, between Segu and the upper Senegal, and wars between Segu and Kaarta, followed by fighting over succession and revolts of military units and slaves, made the state of war in the region almost continuous.

The eighteenth century also was a period of religious and colonial wars in Africa. Some of West Africa's earliest Islamic revolutions began in this century, spawning wars that were harbingers of later, grander struggles waged by devout Muslims, not so much against non-Muslims as against nominal followers of The Prophet who had strayed from the path of righteousness. In the area of the upper Senegal River and the Futa Jalon highlands, the specter of Islamic jihad entered into the political realm. Also, at the southern tip of the continent, beginning in the 1770s, poorly organized Trekboers in the Dutch Cape Colony fought with indigenous, Bantu-speaking people over rights to land, cattle, and water. If one includes the desires of rulers to generate captives to sell as slaves, then the African wars had as many causes as did those around the rest of the Atlantic world, and their results were no less telling for migration or the change the migrants brought to their new homes across the ocean.

In the wake of these wars, territories and populations got reshuffled. Historians tend to stress more that Africa's eighteenth-century wars generated captives for sale into the Atlantic trade—nearly three times more Africans were taken across the Atlantic in the eighteenth century than in the 200 years prior to 1700—than that treaties following European conflicts launched waves of immigrant refugees. European wars certainly prompted people to move away from areas engulfed in violence, while the redistribution of territory that followed these wars spurred transatlantic migration. Many of the same places of strategic or economic importance—the Caribbean, New England, southeastern North America—bore the brunt of these swaps.

Examples of refugees coming from wars and their subsequent peace agreements are found in all parts of the Atlantic. The 1750 Treaty of Madrid between Spain and Portugal, which required redrawing the border between Brazil and Spain's River Plate district, was one of several disruptions suffered by the Guaraní Indians. For the 30,000 Guaraní inhabiting seven Spanish Jesuit missions east of the River Uruguay who suddenly found themselves in Portuguese territory, this international agreement—in which they had had no say—brought profound shock. Additional wars between 1754 and 1756 led to the resettlement of Guaraní refugees to distant parts of Paraguay, Argentina, Brazil, and Uruguay. Some Guaraní men joined African slaves to become *gauchos*, or cowboys, of the southern pampas, while others retreated into the backcountry to avoid the entanglements of life and labor in the Spanish and Portuguese colonial worlds. (Contrary to some popular representations, the Guaraní were literate—and fully clothed—agriculturalists who participated in the production and marketing of yerba maté, a local tea that never appealed to Europeans but was widely consumed in South America.)

When the British claimed Florida from Spain in 1763 (under the terms of the Peace of Paris that ended the Seven Years' War), they were eager to have the colony's tax-paying subjects remain, but many Spanish Floridians, particularly the numerous free people of color, found Spanish law more sympathetic to their intermediate position in the colonial racial hierarchy. So Florida's Spanish population, free and enslaved, evacuated to Cuba, which Spain retook from Britain as part of the same treaty. The reverse was the case in 1783, when Spain retrieved Florida: race was less an issue and British settlers stayed. For that matter, race was not an issue in most African wars, though the conflicts produced captives who, when taken on forced migrations to the western Atlantic, entered worlds where race was the major factor determining ways of life and opportunities.

As they multiplied in frequency, scope, and expense throughout the eighteenth century, wars defined and transformed the Atlantic world. With colonial populations drawn into imperial and European conflicts, wars reinforced Atlantic connections. Sometimes they offered new opportunities to subordinate or enslaved people, who managed to navigate their way through the imperial rivalries and their captors' conflicting desires. Some Atlantic wars required Europeans to court Indian allies (though not in the case of the Guaraní) and treat colonial subjects carefully, but they also could place civilian populations in great peril. Eventually they broke the banks of European governments, resulting in imperial reform. Intended to heighten control over colonial possessions and raise money in the form of new and expanded taxes, these reforms had divergent effects. Although they reconfigured western Atlantic holdings in ways that made colonies more efficient in responding to

European demands, the reforms also sparked resistance movements that exposed weaknesses of imperial rule. In one case, these reforms led to rupture in the form of an independence movement.

Total War

Historians of the modern era speak of the emergence of "total war," that is, the entry of an entire society into martial affairs. By the eighteenth century, the age of ad hoc militias and mercenaries, staged confrontations, and other traditional forms of warfare was passing. Total war entailed the use of professional armies and navies, high technology, and no sparing of civilian populations from war's rigors. For those civilians living in eighteenth-century Atlantic war zones, whose cattle and homes, clothing and kettles, even brothers and sisters were the focus of attacks, total war seems an apt description.

Warfare never affected Atlantic regions equally. Where competing powers claimed territory in close proximity, the hazards of conflict were protracted. The Brazilian outpost of Colônia do Sacramento, a fort across the River Plate from Buenos Aires and a territory disputed by Spain and Portugal, was one such place. Similar circumstances prevailed in parts of sub-Saharan Africa, where natural phenomena added to the backdrop for wars. Cyclical periods of drought or plagues of locusts made food scarce, prompting fighting among neighbors for survival. The ongoing desiccations of West Africa between the mid-seventeenth and mid-nineteenth centuries forced such groups as the Fulbe, primarily cattle herders, to move south and disrupt settled populations in what was farming country. Some Fulbe were among West Africa's first and most devout Muslims, and eventually their ideas of the proper nature of things would clash with those of other Africans, many of them farmers, whose notions of religion remained tied to their ancestors and the homeland spirits with whom their ancestors communicated. The drying of the land gradually lowered brush levels and pushed southward the habitat of the tsetse fly, a transmitter of trypanosomiasis, especially deadly to livestock. This enabled more Africans in authority to acquire horses and use cavalry forces to fight their enemies. Adding to the mix, the expanding coastal trade supplied increasingly deadly and sophisticated weapons of war from European manufacturers. By the eighteenth century, as more and more-lethal weapons became necessities for groups at war, acquiring goods to exchange for weapons—often captive humans—and keeping open supply routes toward the Atlantic were reasons in themselves for warfare.

Once the slave trade grew, powerful African men, who originally may have exchanged captives for tools or weapons, became so dependent on imported luxuries—cloth, spirits, tobacco—that they kept warriors steadily raiding and kidnapping for slaves to trade coastwise in order to satisfy their desires. Few resources other than gold could meet these needs. Warfare thus came to dominate many aspects of culture among societies so involved; it became a way of life. Historians continue to debate whether political or economic motives were the primary reasons for much of the warfare in eighteenth-century West Africa. Abd al-Rahman Ibrahima seemed to be a soldier in a state where one either raided and kept open paths to the coast for trade or else suffered being raided, captured, marched down those same paths, and sold. In such circumstances war was all around, and taking measures for protection, however futile some must have been, was on the minds of many people much of the time.

In the Americas, total war was less generalized, but no less transformative. In fact, eighteenth-century European conflicts regularly provoked border upheavals stretching from Argentina to Canada. Although New England produced little of the great wealth that imperialists cherished, it nonetheless had strategic value to Britain. People in the region also had their own reasons for entering conflicts begun across the ocean. One recruit noted that Protestant New Englanders were always eager to strike a blow against French "popery." Religious fervor and demographic and economic factors (large families, scarce arable land in proximity to kin, and long-lived parents who did not pass on family property to impatient sons) meant that "surplus" sons were always available for militia service. These New Englanders took part in campaigns alongside regular soldiers, although they generally provided support services. To pay for such engagements, New Englanders bore a high tax burden: during the Seven Years' War, Bostonians saw their taxes triple. But the experience of war was different for many other New Englanders because their places of settlement, like Number Four where the Johnsons lived, could be the actual targets of attack.

First the English and then the French targeted North American sites of civilian settlement in efforts to discourage rivals from inhabiting strategic places and to demoralize the enemy. From the 1680s to the 1760s, the French waged war Canadian style, encouraging Indian allies in Pennsylvania, New England, and New York to make raids on civilian homes. They had devised this strategy in response to the deadly raids visited on them by English-allied Iroquois, when the settlers of the St. Lawrence River valley found themselves experiencing total war. These raids made the simplest daily practice, from bringing cows in from pasture to cutting firewood, a potentially deadly ordeal. Such raids hindered settlement and left civilian populations in a state of chronic trepidation.

These French and French-allied Indian raiding parties followed clear patterns. As perfected over the course of the eighteenth century, the raids combined surprise attack with military discipline, the result being a formidable unit of destruction. Raiding parties usually consisted of a mixture of Indians, French soldiers, Canadian colonists, and *coureurs de bois* (fur traders). Here Indians were partners, not servants, and the French could only rely on the support of native participants if the latter perceived their own advantage in the arrangement. British, French, and Spanish alike had to learn to expect their Indian allies to withdraw if the war's costs grew too high or potential peace terms appeared too unpredictable or in any way unfavorable. European soldiers often wore Indian garb, including leather leggings and breechcloth, clothes better suited for freedom of motion in the northern woods, and a warm woolen coat and cap. In the lowland tropics of Central and South America, Brazilian and Spanish American militiamen adopted cotton armor, hammocks, canoes, and other accoutrements of indigenous-style campaigning. Flexibility and independent action were crucial, so regular soldiers had to be carefully retrained to reject the collective discipline to which they were accustomed. Raiders moved quickly and traveled lightly, carrying all of their supplies and hiding their goods in caches as they moved toward their target in order to sustain themselves on the way home.

Relying on the element of surprise, raiders generally attacked either homes or forts before dawn and planned on taking captives for use by French allies in prisoner exchanges or by the Indians for ritual purposes and ransom, the latter important when wars disrupted Indian economies. The French relied on their Indian allies for target selection, and for the Indians this reliance was always problematic. During the Seven Years' War, the Delaware helped the French determine which settlements to raid on the Pennsylvania frontier, but other members of the Delaware tribe lived within the colony and the English population grew suspicious of and hostile toward them in the aftermath of frontier raids. In any case, these raids were the subject of careful planning: Indian attackers in New England brought moccasins and snowshoes for their captives to wear on the long march north to Canada. The trail up the Connecticut River valley came to be called the "Captives Road," so regularly was it traveled by colonists. The raids frequently were devastating. In 1704, a French, Abenaki, and Mohawk force attacked the town of Deerfield in Massachusetts during the course of Queen Anne's War. Fifty-six people were killed in the initial attack (5 soldiers, 44 residents, and 7 men from nearby towns); 109 were taken captive. The damage can best be appreciated in the context of the community's modest size. Of Deerfield's 41 houses, 17 were destroyed. At the time of the Deerfield raid, so many captives lived among the French and their Indian allies that the raiding party brought with them and left hanging in a tree a bag of mail from captives seeking contact with their families. Altogether 1,641 people were taken captive from New England between 1675 and 1765. Colonists in New York, Pennsylvania, and Virginia were also vulnerable to raids in this period. While many captives eventually were repatriated, others settled in to new lives among their captors, Indian or French, often converting to Catholicism, a practice that made repatriation problematic. Women, particularly those with indigenous or French spouses and children, were more likely to remain in captivity than were men. Marie de l'Enfant Jesus, born Esther Wheelwright, was taken from her home in Wells, Maine, when she was a child in 1703. She was held first by the Abenaki, then ransomed by a Jesuit and placed with the Ursulines in Quebec. Refusing the pleas of her New England family to return home, she became an Ursuline herself and was elected the superior of the order in 1760.

The Regional Impact of Warfare

Around the Atlantic world, regions where rival powers lay in close proximity were vulnerable to protracted warfare. In places of regularly contested imperial power, indigenous and subordinate people were sometimes able to find opportunities to negotiate a status that otherwise might have been denied them. The mansa of Niumi, who collected tolls and marshaled traffic up the Gambia River from near its mouth, had an outpost of both England and

Lucy Terry Prince

One survivor of a Deerfield raid in 1746 was a sixteen-year-old African American slave named Lucy, whose story could stand as a symbol for life in the eighteenth-century Atlantic world. In her early life, Lucy knew little besides captivity: she was sold in West Africa to slave traders and brought in infancy to Rhode Island. Originally owned by the Terry family, Lucy was sold in 1735 to Ebenezer Wells of Deerfield, Massachusetts, who saw to it that she attended the local Puritan church. She remained with the Wells family until 1756, when she married a free African American, Abijah Prince, who may have had to buy her freedom. She eventually bore six children, one of whom, Cesar, fought for the Patriots in the Revolutionary War. She died in Vermont in 1821, at the age of ninety-one.

Lucy was a notable orator, storyteller, and poet. (She would argue a land case before the United States Supreme Court in the 1790s.) In 1746 she composed a poem about a raid near Deerfield that was passed down orally for more than a century. "Bar's Fight" is the title the poem appeared under when finally published in 1855. It reads:

Samuel Allen like a hero fout
And though he was so brave and bold
His face no more shall we behold.
Eleazer Hawks was killed outright
Before he had time to fight
Before he did the Indians see
Was shot and killed immediately.
Oliver Amsden he was slain
Which caused his friends much grief and pain
Samuel Amsden they found dead
Not many rods off from his head.
Adonijah Gillet we do hear
Did lose his life which was so dear.
John Saddler fled across the water
And so escaped the dreadful slaughter.
Eunice Allen see the Indians coming
And hoped to save herself by running
And had not her petticoats stopt her
The awful creatures had not cotched her
And tommyhawked her on the head
And left her on the ground for dead.
Young Samuel Allen, Oh! lack a-day
Was taken and carried to Canada.

Frontispiece and title page from "An affecting narrative of the captivity and sufferings of Mrs. Mary Smith" showing three Indian men, one with bow and arrow, facing three Euro-American men, two with rifles. Library of Congress, LC-DIG-ppmsca-02973.

France on his soil. When these European nations were at war with one another, or even when their representatives on the spot were wondering if they might be at war (which was much of the time), the mansa played one power against the other so skillfully that Machiavelli would have been proud. Likewise, the Fante of the Gold Coast found advantage in having forts at the waterside sponsored by England, France, Denmark, and the Netherlands. Local authorities grew wealthy from gifts the competing Europeans gave them merely to keep them sympathetic to one or another European cause.

Europeans rarely fought on African soil, either against Africans or among themselves, but in the American borderlands they were careful, when possible, to secure the loyalty, or at least the neutrality, of indigenous people whose alliance might easily tip the balance from defeat to victory. If Europeans needed Indian allies, Indians similarly needed European allies, especially along contested frontiers. To cement alliances, European diplomats in North America learned to adapt to woodland diplomacy, devoting the necessary time to negotiation rituals, even singing and dancing according to different customs. A common treaty protocol emerged as a result, stemming originally from Iroquois practice but by the early eighteenth century involving French, English, Spanish, and indigenous diplomats throughout eastern North America. The protocol took part in nine stages, starting with a formal invitation, accompanied by *wampum* (elaborately designed belts of wampum, small beads made of shells, were highly prized among Indians for decoration and religious and political purposes) and ending with a feast. Presentation of gifts was important throughout, as was willingness to devote several weeks to what could be protracted and time-consuming negotiations. With these rituals, Europeans sought to ensure neutrality or alliance from tribes in strategic regions—Indians of the Ohio River valley; the Iroquois and Abenaki in the north; and Cherokees, Creeks, and Choctaws to the south.

Enslaved people in the Americas similarly found openings when their masters embarked on wars. Rivals courted Africans and African Americans, and colonial inhabitants were aware both of the risks (for the slaveholders) and of the opportunities (for the slaves). When English investors in the Providence Island Company contemplated the growing number of slaves on this briefly held puritan outpost, located off the coast of Nicaragua, they wrote the governor to express their concern, "knowing how dangerous they may be if you should be assaulted with an enemy." Indeed, before the Spanish attacked the colony in 1640, they waited offshore, hoping to get information about the island's defenses from *renegades*, a term that included slaves as well as English servants, many of whom had previously escaped to the Spanish in canoes. The Dutch had tried similar tactics when seizing northeastern Brazil from the Portuguese in 1630, with mixed results. Finally, runaway slaves and renegades played a significant role in the chronic corsair and pirate raids of the seventeenth-century Caribbean.

In other instances, imperial rivalries provided opportunities for overt resistance. Enslaved Africans in English Carolina, who first slipped off alone or in small groups to sanctuary in Florida and then planned a revolt, did so against a backdrop of imperial rivalries. The Spanish government in nearby Florida even offered incentives to enslaved blacks to escape to their colony. With such promises of freedom and legal privileges to Carolina slaves, the Spanish hoped to weaken British power.

Geographic proximity was a crucial factor. The Carolina capital of Charles Town, settled in the 1670s by English planters from Barbados, was "but ten days journey" from the Spanish capital at St. Augustine. Once the English newcomers instituted chattel slavery and harsh regulatory codes that provided minimal protections for slaves and discouraged manumissions, the slaves were quick to learn the differences between the English and Spanish slave regimes and began running southward to Florida, appealing to the Spaniards for religious sanctuary. Responding in 1693, the Spanish king issued a decree "giving liberty to all [the] men as well as the women [so] that by their example and by my liberality others will do the same." Frustrated Carolina slave owners denounced Spain's provocative new policy and countered with more regulatory slave codes and patrols, but to no avail. Neither diplomatic negotiations nor military action stanched the southward flow of runaways. Adding insult to injury, Spanish governors armed the former slaves and sent them back to raid the very plantations they had fled. Thereafter, the freedmen formed an effective guerrilla force, protecting the Spanish settlement against English and Indian expeditions from Carolina and later, Georgia.

The Spanish crown periodically confirmed its sanctuary policy, and in 1733 wealthy Carolinians complained that the edict offering sanctuary had been proclaimed publicly, "by Beat of Drum round the Town of St. Augustine (where many Negroes belonging to English vessels that carried thither Supplies of provisions had the Opportunity of hearing it)." When four slaves and an Irish servant from Carolina escaped to Florida on stolen horses after reportedly killing one man and wounding another, landowners in Carolina angrily charged, "they were received" at St. Augustine "with great honours, one of them had a Commission given to him, and a Coat faced with Velvet."

As runaways continued to present themselves, the Spanish governor in 1738, following a legal precedent used earlier to pacify maroon populations in Panama, Mexico, Hispaniola, and Colombia, established the newly converted Catholics in a town of their own two miles north of St. Augustine, the aforementioned Gracia Real de Santa Teresa de Mose. Envoys from Carolina traveled to St. Augustine to press for the return of the runaways, but they made their trip in vain. Carolina's governor wrote that the planters were dissatisfied "to find their property now become so very precarious and uncertain" and feared that "Negroes which were their chief support may in little time become their Enemies, if not their Masters, and that this Government is unable to withstand or prevent it." Members of the South Carolina Commons offered bounties for runaways' scalps "with the two ears" to dissuade others from trying to escape, and for emphasis staged a public whipping and execution of two newly captured fugitives.

Events came to a head when on September 9, 1739, a group of Kongo slaves revolted near the Stono River in South Carolina, killing more than twenty whites and sacking and burning homes before heading for Florida. The *Charles Town South Carolina Gazette* had carried word, by way of Boston, that English privateers were outfitting to attack Spanish merchant ships, so the Africans knew that war was imminent. But when the rebels stopped along the road in hopes of attracting recruits from nearby plantations, Carolina troops struck back. Rebels who survived the first day's battle fought on for another week, moving southward toward St. Augustine, before a larger English force finally caught and killed most of them. All reports say that some of the rebels survived that battle as well, however, and if any of then made it to their destination, they would have been sheltered at Mose.

When European rivalries broke into war in tropical Africa or the Americas, local geography, power relations, and disease regimes affected greatly the course of the conflicts. Europeans were entirely dependent on Africans: to sustain trade along the Atlantic coast; to allow them to erect coastal forts and factories on soil that fell under the Africans' jurisdiction; and to supply those outposts and their ships with water and food. Because of this dependence, and because diseases in tropical Africa dealt death so indiscriminately to their agents and soldiers, Europeans played out imperial rivalries less frequently in tropical Africa. European wars might bring small engagements between vessels of one or another nation, or privateering in ports, or even destruction and plundering of one or another outpost, but engagements seldom broadened considerably or extended far inland. South Africa's Trekboers pressed in from the coastal base and brought violence to indigenous Africans as they went, of course, but the land into which they were moving was beyond the Tropic of Capricorn, so they tended not to be subject to malaria, yellow fever, and other killers of humans in regions nearer the equator.

This was not so for the Caribbean, however. As potential producers of enormous wealth from sugar production, the islands were tempting targets. Some larger islands also held as many as half a million slaves, an enormous capital resource in themselves and potential allies or booty for invaders. Beginning in the seventeenth century, European nations tossed islands back and forth in peace treaties. Trinidad, Tortuga, and Providence were successively Spanish and English; St. Kitts and St. Martin ended up shared between two powers, the former by France and England for eighty years, and the latter a joint French and Dutch possession. Frequently, rivals' islands were close to one another—French Guadeloupe being only forty miles from English Antigua, for instance—which made invasion a real threat during times of war.

But the Caribbean was more than a common place for warfare: it was a region where, out of necessity, combatants altered customary European practices of warfare. One important military strategy in Europe and elsewhere was the siege. In the seventeenth century, European powers upgraded their fortresses in the Americas to protect their wealth in the region. Stone bastions built in the European model were designed to hold out against attackers for six weeks, the theory being that within that time relief would arrive. (This almost never worked at forts as far away as India or Asia, incidentally, where relief never showed up in time, if at all, and defenders had to surrender before starving.) In the Atlantic tropics, siege warfare worked differently thanks to mosquitoes and other disease vectors. Major campaigns revealed the calamitous consequences of applying siege practices to tropical fortresses. Time and again, those laying siege succumbed to disease before they could penetrate the walls of a fort.

The War of Jenkins' Ear witnessed one such failure at Cartagena de Indias, Spanish America's main slave port in the Caribbean. The English admiral Edward Vernon tried to take the city in 1741 with an invasion force of almost 25,000 soldiers and mariners, the largest expedition ever assembled in the region. Vernon's men started to die, however, even as they waited in Jamaica for deployment in Cartagena. As the corpses of unlucky recruits from England and North America were flung overboard en route to the siege, sharks followed, prompting some to consider this an ill omen. In Cartagena harbor, still more men died as the keepers of the great fort of San Felipe de Barajas held out. The British forces inflicted heavy damage on Cartagena's city center, but the fort resisted bombardment and local citizens received fresh powder and supplies from the interior. The Cartagena campaign witnessed the death of 41 percent of the men under Vernon's charge. What caused the English and colonial recruits to die in such numbers? The historian John McNeill points to the differential mortality rates of European- and American-born participants in these campaigns: 77 percent of Vernon's men from Britain died, while slightly fewer of those born in the colonies did. Yellow fever killed most of these men, and it did so with such efficiency and reliability that defenders (if they were native born) needed to hold out for only for 3 to 6 weeks before attackers abandoned the effort.

Environmental transformations caused by urban development, cattle ranching, and sugar cultivation made Caribbean islands and the surrounding mainlands especially inviting for the *Aedes aegypti*, the species of mosquito that carries yellow fever. Cultivators cleared land to build houses, plant cane, or run cattle, all of which encouraged formation of mosquito-breeding puddles, pools, and swamps following heavy tropical downpours. Cities in this period were highly unsanitary to begin with, and areas where cattle congregated were likewise befouled. In addition, mosquito-killing frosts never occurred in this region. On plantations, large clay pots used for sugar refining also caught the rain. The availability of so much standing water and human blood in these warm, humid environments greatly facilitated mosquito colonization. Disease epidemics could break out, however, only when there were enough nonimmune people available for the pathogens to infect. People infected but not killed by yellow fever enjoy lifetime immunity from the disease. West Africans from regions where yellow fever was endemic carried such immunity, so slave populations were not themselves good incubators. Europeans, on the other hand, made perfect hosts. Therefore, when European armies arrived in such cities such as Cartagena and Veracruz, yellow-fever epidemics invariably followed, devastating ranks in predictable patterns and making the practice of siege warfare deadly.

War, Peace, and Geographic Ignorance

In the wake of war, the belligerent powers commonly sat down at a bargaining table and made peace. For most Africans, land transfers were rarely part of such discussions, in part because Africans tended not to look upon land ownership as others did. In nearly all of Africa, there was land in abundance; people were the scarce resource. Heads of states and empires therefore sought authority over people rather than land. We think otherwise because it was, and still is, a thoroughly European-derived tradition to map African empires, city-states, and alleged "tribes" with fixed lines around some chunk of territory as if it had inviolable boundaries. African rulers wanted people's loyalty, and often negotiated at war's end for various kinds of tribute payments that would signify dependence as much as bring in wealth.

But victorious Europeans wanted land, lots of land, especially land they perceived as strategically significant, and this meant that imperial holdings in the western Atlantic were frequently juggled in postwar negotiations. Not surprisingly, the pressing issues of concern to people in the Americas often were not resolved to their satisfaction in European peace treaties. For example, the 1748 Treaty of Aix-la-Chapelle, which ended the War of the Austrian Succession, failed to resolve boundary questions in the Ohio Valley. Treaties also provoked bitter feelings among those unable to participate in their negotiation who believed their interests were neglected. The return to France of the Nova Scotia fortress at Louisbourg in 1748, after New Englanders had taken it with heavy loss of life, caused a lingering animosity in the region that made its reacquisition crucial in the following war. But European diplomats distributed territory not only according to its potential fecundity or mineral wealth but also according to their (limited) geographic knowledge. The western boundaries of Virginia and other colonies, for example, remained unknown —and disputed—for a remarkably long time after colonization.

In fact, geographic misunderstandings of North America guided many European decisions about Atlantic warfare and peace negotiations in the eighteenth century. British and French cartographers did not understand the shape of the continent and had no idea where it ended and the waters of the Pacific began. About the western part of the continent, they tended not to trust the better-informed knowledge of the Spanish. So rumors circulated among the northern European countries that East Asians inhabited North America's west coast (which was not entirely untrue) and Thomas Jefferson theorized in 1787 that mammoths might still roam the American West. Even the Spanish lacked detailed knowledge of lands beyond their missions and presidios. So Europeans had to make decisions about the strategic value of their American holdings in the context of this ignorance.

Understanding what Europeans knew—or thought they knew—about North America explains why France and Britain fought so long for it. British exploration of Hudson Bay in the 1740s preoccupied the French. They suspected that the British were intent on taking Spanish American holdings and fretted that British exploration of the seemingly uninviting Hudson Bay pointed to the existence of a Northwest Passage through which the British might gain access to the Pacific. Combined with British activities in Central America, where they had logging camps in Honduras despite Spanish protest, and Cape Horn, at the southern tip of South America, Britain's plan seemed to the French unmistakable. In this mindset, rum-soaked logging camps of present-day Belize might serve as British bases for Pacific ventures. Although the French did not know if a Northwest Passage existed, the fact that the British sought one suggested that *they* knew it did. The Spanish shared French concerns. In this light, the British seemed to be pursuing the kind of aggressive imperialist expansion that the European powers had theoretically renounced in the peace that settled the War of the Spanish Succession in 1713, and their ultimate target, the French believed, was Spain's wealth in Peru and Mexico. Ironically, due to the much-disputed Bourbon succession in Spain, it was the French who possessed superior knowledge of Spanish America's wealth, potential, and vulnerabilities. French maritime activity in the Pacific was intense during the War of Spanish Succession, and not long afterwards, in 1739, Charles Marie de la Condamine and a team of French and Spanish scientists toured the Andes, fixed the location of the equator in South America, visited a number of mines and plantations, and navigated the Amazon River to reach the Atlantic. Another thing that Condamine explored upon his return to France was the commercial potential of natural rubber.

In this context of poor intelligence, in which geographic knowledge fused with perceptions of imperial aggression, the defense of the otherwise uninviting Ohio Valley—so important in the launching of the Seven Years' War in 1754— makes sense. The French were not as concerned with defending the limited resources of the valley as they were nervous about where Britain's conquest of the region might lead. Control of the Ohio Valley would give the British access, via rivers, to the Gulf of Mexico and thus the wealth of Spanish America. If the French could not hold the valley, Mexico might become Britain's. And so when George Washington, then a junior British army officer, accompanied by Indian allies, led a small number of soldiers into the Ohio Valley and foolishly attacked a French party there, events tumbled along toward the Atlantic world's greatest war to date.

The wars of the eighteenth century revealed the intimate and growing web of connections linking all parts of the Atlantic. Wars in Africa were more confined to the continent, but they generated the captives that fueled the steadily expanding Atlantic slave trade and brought the massive labor supply to the plantations and mines of the Americas. Wars over European succession—over who would govern Austria or sit on the throne of England or Spain—were fought both on the European continent and in distant commercial outlets and in remote colonial theatres. In the first half of the century, wars in the western Atlantic were spillovers of European battles, but by its middle decades, America became more important in war strategy. What England learned from King George's War in the 1740s, was that it could not defeat France and its allies in Europe. Instead, it would have to strike where France was weakest—and that was in North America. France recognized the peril of its American holdings when England first proposed this strategy in 1748. One French statesman insisted that New France be defended to the fullest, since, were it lost, England would be supreme not only in North America but also in Europe.

So the Seven Years' War, which began in North America as a small conflict on the Ohio frontier (prompted by geographic confusion and belligerence) spread like a brushfire around the globe. Naval power enabled England to disrupt France's supply lines and defeat the French at sea. The war was fought in North America, Europe, the Caribbean, the Mediterranean, India, and along the coast of Africa. At war's end, France was crushed, shed of its North American possessions and most of its territory in India. It clung to a few African outposts, its sugar colonies and—crucially, as it turned out—its fisheries. Revenge would come soon, during the American War for Independence and in the Napoleonic Wars that followed.

An Age of Imperial Reform

Impoverished after so much warfare, all three European empires with major American holdings stepped up imperial reform programs. One impetus for

The Cajuns

Some of the refugee populations produced by the Seven Years' War are well known in United States culture. The Cajuns of Louisiana, for example, derived from a population of French inhabitants in the province of Acadia (comprising modern Nova Scotia, New Brunswick, and Prince Edward Island) who were exiled from Canada in the wake of British conquests there. The Acadians refused to swear loyally to the British crown, and the British government eyed the region's arable land for British settlers. The British first dispersed and then expelled 7,000 of these Acadians in 1755. By the time the peace treaty was signed in 1763, some 10,000 Acadians languished across the Atlantic in France. Their migrations were not yet complete, however. Some refugees, prodded by the French government, attempted colonial settlement in Saint Domingue and Guyane before some survivors found their way to Louisiana. They settled west of New Orleans and the name Acadian shrank to "Cajun," the name by which their descendants are known.

Acadians driven into exile, 1755. Engraving by Albert Bobbett. Picture Collection, The Branch Libraries, The New York Public Library, Astor, Lenox and Tilden Foundations.

THE ACADIANS DRIVEN INTO EXILE.

these reforms was revenue: the wars left huge debts, and each empire seized the opportunity to enhance revenues through administrative reform in its overseas possessions. Once the reform process began, however, legislators typically moved beyond taxation and commercial regulation, initiating laws that reached into societies' mores and customs. Not surprisingly, all reforms sparked resistance from a wide range of imperial subjects, who drew on traditions of defiance and rebellion to express their displeasure.

Winner's regret is not restricted to lotteries and poker tournaments, and the irony of Britain's greatest territorial victory over France in the Seven Years' War could not have been more bitter. The French lost the least valuable part of their empire in their handover of Canada. Far more important, they kept their claim to the Atlantic fisheries, and the continued presence there of mariners and ships enabled the French to rebuild their navy—which, looking ahead, enabled their North American allies to beat the British at Yorktown in 1781. The governments of Spain and Portugal, for their part, launched vigorous centralizing projects that successfully drained the colonies of wealth in a period of economic expansion and population growth. While good for the Spanish and Portuguese crowns, these absolutist "reforms" sparked major rebellions from Mexico to Minas Gerais. The British reformed their empire, too, bringing forth such entrenched resistance in the North American mainland that they ended up losing half of their Atlantic colonies. The American Revolution would be only one of several unintended consequences of British victory in 1763.

Although the impetus for change was strong at war's end, initiation of many reforms predated the 1763 Treaty of Paris, and it is best to consider the age of Atlantic imperial reform as a long-term process that received a short-term boost with the end of the Seven Years' War. Attention to chronology is crucial because imperial reforms were embedded in larger intellectual and scientific currents customarily grouped under the term *Enlightenment*. Although difficult to summarize, the movement shared several basic themes. Scientists and writers began to reject religious explanations for such mysterious phenomena as flying fish and volcanic eruptions in favor of experimentation and direct observation. They called for a turn to rationalism and reason, in short, to a belief in human agency or the innate human capacity to know and change the world. The British physicist Isaac Newton was one such "enlightened" intellectual whose landmark *Principia* the Spanish monarch eventually ordered distributed in his colonies. Newton's alchemical musings were not as welcome, nor were his religious ideas. Intellectuals sought to apply scientific methods to all human affairs, and as one part of their effort to impose rationality and order on the world around them, they attacked what they regarded as arbitrary and artificial privileges. These intellectual trends had implications for imperial governance, as leaders sought to rationalize and regulate their holdings, which became a part of reform efforts already put in place by the major Atlantic powers.

The Spanish were the first to initiate Enlightenment-inspired reforms when a new, French-born monarch brought these intellectual currents to Spain. At this point, reform was particularly urgent for the Spanish Empire, which had fallen on hard times since its rapid expansion in the late sixteenth century. The financial strains of war, disease, and population decline at home and abroad, along with diminishing silver revenues from the Americas, all but crippled the once glorious empire. By the time the last Spanish Habsburg, Charles II (nicknamed "The Bewitched" for his mental and physical deficiencies), died without heir in 1700, the empire seemed on the verge of falling into French hands.

In the subsequent War of Spanish Succession, Spain had to buy French war materials with gold and silver bullion it needed to spend elsewhere. In the Peace of Utrecht that ended the war in 1713, Spain lost Naples, Sicily, Milan, and the Spanish Netherlands (roughly modern Belgium) and had to give England the *asiento*, or exclusive rights to sell African slaves in the key ports of Buenos Aires, Veracruz, Cartagena, and Havana. Spain had long held to mercantile policies that strictly limited foreign access to its ports, so this shift represented a major, and humiliating, change.

In exchange for these concessions, French-born Philip V's 1700 accession to the Spanish throne was allowed to stand. He quickly took charge, and some have argued that the English in fact lost out in the deal at Utrecht. This was certainly true in terms of the so-called European balance of power. Philip V was not the first Spanish monarch to seek to centralize the empire, but he would attempt to do so in a way distinct from that of his sixteenth-century predecessor and namesake, the Habsburg Philip II. Philip V's first challenge was to subdue the dissident kingdoms on Iberia's Mediterranean shores—Aragon, Catalonia, and Valencia—that were attempting to break away from the empire's decayed core. Of Spain's several autonomous ethnic groups, only the Basques in the northern mountains were able to retain some of their medieval privileges.

The homeland secured, Philip initiated conservative changes to the still medieval Spanish imperial system, modeling his administration after that of his grandfather, Louis XIV, and influenced by the Enlightenment's emphases on rationality, science, progress, and self-examination. To revive the ailing Spanish economy and boost imperial revenues, Philip and his Bourbon successors launched reforms emphasizing direct monarchical control, streamlining of bureaucracies, professionalization of defense, and new investment in agriculture, mining, and manufacturing. Philip curbed the *Mesta*, Spain's powerful sheep-herding corporation, and sponsored factories to produce fine wools, silks, tapestries, and porcelain—all luxuries Spain once imported (and paid for with American silver). New roads and bridges better integrated the economy and lowered transportation costs. In keeping with Enlightenment ideals, Spain's medieval universities placed new emphasis on the physical sciences, medicine, and engineering. The state imported new technologies and technicians as well as knowledge, largely in hopes of raising revenue in mining and other proven sectors. Groups under the *Sociedad de Amigos del País* (Society of Friends of the State) formed to read the latest literature and recommend change in almost every aspect of Spanish life. Admittedly, this was modernization with a touch of self-criticism. Yet, if there was a tendency to celebrate all things northern European and ignore past Spanish achievements in arts, letters, science, and exploration, the trends counteracted over a century of isolation and transformed Spain's character by the middle of the eighteenth century.

Shifting Atlantic empires also forced similar reforms in Portugal and its colonies beginning in the 1750s. Funded by Brazilian riches, these Portuguese reforms, guided by Dom José I's prime minister, eventually given the title Marquis de Pombal (1750–77), were meant to improve the imperial economy and create a more efficient administration. Pombal established a Board of Trade, a monopolistic whaling company, and new monopolies to control colonial commerce, particularly the slave trade: the Grão Pará and Maranhão Company imported enslaved Africans from Guinea, and the Pernambuco Company did the same from Angola. These companies were allowed to import slaves to Brazil duty free and traded them at cost for sugar, hides, and tobacco. Although this change had little effect on the number of captives taken from Portuguese-dominated ports on Africa's Atlantic coast and brought to Brazil, it did concentrate portions of the trade in the hands of fewer influential Lisbon merchants. Over the quarter century after 1761, the Pernambuco Company boarded more than 41,000 slaves at Luanda, which was perhaps one-quarter of all slaves moving through that Angolan port. In roughly the same period, about 20,000 slaves were taken to Brazil's far north from the Portuguese-dominated Guinean ports of Cacheu and Bissau. Pombal tried to enforce more effective mercantile controls on other trade, too, establishing separate fleets to Pernambuco, Bahia, and Rio. He also gave tax breaks to encourage industrial development in Portugal and reduce imports, as Spain had done, and he forbade colonial manufacturing while prodding the colonies to produce more primary materials with slave labor. It is interesting to note that although they were already well known, Brazil's vast iron ore deposits were consciously ignored so as not to distract from the production of gold and diamonds. Pombal also tried to diversify Brazil's economy in other ways, by encouraging production of cotton, rice, tobacco, and cacao, thereby reducing dependence on sugar. In one episode, he arranged for high-grade Virginian and Cuban tobacco strains popular among Europeans—strains of tobacco originally from northeast South America—to be brought to Brazil for experimentation. Until that project could mature, the Portuguese traded coarser, molasses-cured Brazilian tobacco to Africa and far north into Canada's fur-trade circuit. Like guns and rum, tobacco was one of only a few Atlantic commodities that proved highly lucrative in far-flung African, Native American, and European markets in the eighteenth century. Naturally, cash-starved imperial governments increasingly wanted to monopolize such things.

With the end of the inconclusive King George's War in 1748, the British commenced their own reform efforts when the Board of Trade set about improving imperial authority in the colonies. Among other things, the board ensured its members were routinely informed of colonial events and organized regular sailings between the colonies and home. In hindsight, one can recognize the midcentury dissolution of the Royal African Company, which the British crown had subsidized between 1730 and 1746, as an element of this reform. The company was a drain on taxpayers and its own investors. Better, thought Parliament, to take government out of the equation and let private investors assume full responsibility for the profits, or losses, of the African trade. By the middle of the eighteenth century, then, before the peace treaty of 1763, all three empires had begun to invest considerable resources, personnel, and imagination in governmental restructuring at home and abroad.

A massive impediment to reform in the Iberian empires was the wealthy and influential Catholic Church; in the cases of the Jesuit Order and the Inquisition, it resembled a state within a state. In Portugal, in efforts to reduce the power of the Inquisition and encourage investment in his various projects, the Marquis de Pombal prohibited persecution of and discrimination against New Christians (the descendants of those Jews whose families had converted to Christianity after 1492). When he brought Brazil under more direct crown control, Pombal already had been encroaching on the Church's claim to responsibility for indigenous populations. The prime minister soon came to see the Jesuits as the embodiment of many qualities he opposed: he disliked their power, wealth, independence, and control over education, and he was uncomfortable with their ties to Rome. Many Brazilian colonists had come to resent the Jesuits, too, since the latter were far and away Brazil's wealthiest land and slave owners. So it was with remarkable suddenness that, in 1759, Pombal expelled the Jesuits from all Portuguese territories. As the exiled padres sailed for Italy and other destinations, crown officials in Brazil confiscated and auctioned off their holdings in land, slaves, and livestock. The French emulated this policy, expelling Jesuits from French lands in 1764, and the Spanish crown followed suit in 1767. Aside from a few minor riots in Mexico, where many Jesuits were creoles, the expulsion of the Society of Jesus did not attract great criticism, least of all from such competing orders as the Franciscans and Dominicans.

With the Jesuits out of the way and the Catholic Church in a defensive mode, Spain and Portugal could join Britain in turning more complete attention to the task most urgent to all European powers following the Treaty of Paris: enhancing revenue. Some of the most aggressive imperial restructuring of the eighteenth century centered on extracting more money from colonial subjects and tropical commodities. Britain's enormous war debt made this agenda particularly pressing. At the time, the people of the British Isles were among the most heavily taxed in the world, whereas their colonial counterparts paid relatively little in taxes. It therefore seemed reasonable to Britons in Europe to expect the colonists to contribute their fair share for their own maintenance and protection. The activities of the crown and Parliament to change imperial policy for the simple sake of raising revenue lay at the heart of the buildup to the American Revolution. The 1764 Revenue (or Sugar) Act, the 1765 Stamp Act, and the 1767 Townshend Acts imposed a number of new taxes and fees that brought the grumbling of the mainland colonists to the pitch of a howl.

Spain's efforts to enhance revenue included reforms in trade, mining, and tribute collection. The Spanish needed first to bring trade under greater state control. It was in this spirit that the crown created the Viceroyalty of New Granada, admistered from Bogotá after 1739, and the Viceroyalty of La Plata, administered from Buenos Aires after 1776. Both these districts of the old Viceroyalty of Peru had become notorious for their high levels of contraband commerce. Bourbon monarchs rehabilitated the Spanish fleet system and rewarded merchants donating ships with titles of nobility. Intent on buttressing rather than replacing mercantilism, the crown relocated the House of Trade and Merchants Guild from Seville to the more accessible port of Cádiz in 1717 and created new, chartered companies in the 1720s to supply the colonies and monitor exports. Many of these changes were reversed beginning in the 1770s, however, when it was realized that taxing mining and commerce more efficiently—and lightly—could in fact enhance state revenues. For all their alleged innovation, then, the much-touted Bourbon commercial reforms mostly adhered to what the colonists and transatlantic merchants had already been doing. The state was legitimating a natural transformation well after the fact, and finally making some money from it.

Imperial officials needed accurate knowledge of overseas holdings in order to extract funds most efficiently. In the new spirit of scientific inquiry, Spain's American universities, the earliest dating to the 1550s, expanded their course offerings, updated their libraries, and opened schools of medicine and mining. The Bourbons also sponsored new learned societies, botanical gardens, and schools of art in the Americas to match those being created in Spain. Hoping to combine intellectual and economic benefits, Spain commissioned scientific expeditions through its American territories, and eventually a global one, led by Alejandro Malaspina, after the manner of England's James Cook. In the late 1730s, Antonio de Ulloa and Jorge Juan accompanied the French scientific expedition led by La Condamine to prove "that the Spaniards have not lost their appetite nor talent for great undertakings." These Spanish scientists related their travels in a five-volume work that described the cities of Cartagena, Portobello, Panama, Guayaquil, Quito, Lima, and Concepción. The wildly popular *A Voyage to South America*, soon translated into English, French, and German, was the first substantial new account of the Spanish Indies available in Europe since the sixteenth century. Ulloa and Juan also wrote a volume of *Secret Notices* for the king's eyes only, detailing corruption by priests and creole officials, who forced Indians to buy goods they did not need and entrapped them in permanent labor drafts. Ulloa went on in 1758 to become governor of the critical mercury-mining center of Huancavelica, in Peru. (Mercury, without which silver could not be processed, was a royal monopoly.) A popular saying was, "without Huancavelica, good-bye America." The mercury mines of Almadén, Spain, were also reorganized and staffed with hundreds of convicted criminals.

Specially charged visitors general toured New Spain and Peru, which boasted the largest concentrations of potential laborers and silver deposits. After a tour of New Spain in the mid-1760s, José de Gálvez ordered a reorganization of the colony's political economy. Shortage of labor and insufficient capital investment had closed many Mexican silver mines, whereas those still operating were crippled by taxes and so behind technologically that they were still using a mercury amalgamation process developed by a Mexican miner in the sixteenth century. In 1785, Spain commissioned the German-trained brothers Fausto and Juan José D'Elhuyar to organize scientific missions to the silver districts of Mexico, Peru, and New Granada, one eventual result of which was establishment of new schools of mines in Mexico City and Lima. Mexico's Visitor General Gálvez offered tax relief for mine owners, and soon the great Quebradilla mine in Zacatecas was back in operation and the incomparable Valenciana mine of Guanajuato boasted the deepest shaft and largest underground works in the world. Paid officials posted at the Mexican mint ensured that the crown collected its royalty on silver production (now 10 percent instead of 20) and enforced royal monopolies on mercury and gunpowder, while cutting their price in half. Silver production began to pick up throughout Mexico. Juan José D'Elhuyar's attempts to revive the less well-known silver mines of New Granada were not as successful, although the extensive gold mines of the region flourished with the increased availability and lower cost of African slaves. As in Brazil, the Spanish crown responded to miners' demands for cheaper labor by opening the way to importing more Africans.

Other profit-making commodities for the state were tobacco and distilled alcohol. Gálvez created new royal monopolies on both, establishing licensed factories and government-owned stores called *estancos*, a "reform" that ran counter to Britain's tendency away from monopolies. Not surprisingly, the estanco system produced violent rebellions as indigenous, mestizo, and mulatto growers, distillers, and retailers saw their livelihoods threatened. The royal visitor also substituted paid Spanish tax collectors for creole tax farmers and raised the *alcabala* (sales tax) from 4 to 6 percent. While effective in filling state coffers, these measures weighed most heavily on the poor, who received nothing tangible in return.

José Antonio Areche, who had served under Gálvez, instituted many of the same changes as visitor general of Peru. After conducting censuses, he created new tribute lists and then squeezed the Indians of the viceroyalty to pay an additional million pesos yearly. The dreaded mine mita was also revived, and applied to many other mines besides those of Potosí. Many indigenous tributaries had already fled their homelands to become a wandering underclass in the cities, and those remaining in communal villages faced added pressure to meet the new demands. Areche also attempted to collect tribute from mestizos and free blacks in certain districts, but these measures ultimately failed.

These enhanced revenues helped the Atlantic empires expand, exploit, and defend their frontiers, which would then, in circular fashion, provide more wealth still for the metropole. The British Proclamation Line of 1763 in North America is a good example of such an effort. Running north and south along the Appalachian crest, this line was designed to regulate colonizers' actions in the interior while securing the loyalty of indigenous people, most of whom had previously been allied to the French. Encroachment in the region by aggressive and expansion-minded English settlers put pressure on Indian lands, and regulating their movement was an expensive undertaking. The British resolved this problem by declaring lands west of the Appalachians an Indian reserve, allowing no English settlements on the frontier. Parliament designed this reform to be temporary, but it nonetheless infuriated influential land speculators in Virginia and Pennsylvania.

Government also encouraged colonization of frontier lands in order to secure them against invaders. For the British, the Peace of Paris in 1763 had obviated this concern, removing the French from Canada and Louisiana alike, but Portugal and Spain still had problems. Pombal perceived defense issues when he considered Brazil's frontiers, so he designed new polities to encourage settlement and strengthen state control of such a vast region as the Amazon basin. He removed such hard-to-manage intermediaries as parish clergy and mission villages, banned discrimination against Indians, and encouraged intermarriage between creoles and Indians. Spain branched out, too: its imperial policy had been geared toward expanding mining frontiers and exploiting indigenous economies and populations, but in the late eighteenth century, Spain turned to new regions where economies and mineral prospects were less promising. Spanish imperial officials encouraged Spaniards and colonial subjects to move into these lands. One of this scheme's great successes was the creation in 1776 of the Viceroyalty of La Plata (modern Bolivia, Argentina, Uruguay, and Paraguay) and development of the southeast South American lowlands' massive ranching economy. Another involved revitalization of Cuba's economy, where over the twenty-year period after 1763, sugar production tripled.

Of course, more populated and productive frontiers brought problems in themselves. As the Spanish and Portuguese had learned early, empires were mere shells if their frontiers could not be defended, and eighteenth-century warfare simply drew added attention to the most vulnerable regions. It was in response to this enhanced, or freshly recognized, vulnerability, for example, that the British augmented their fortifications in the West Indies, garrisoned their western lands in North America, and left a force of 10,000 regular soldiers on the continent. For its part, Spain could not act fast enough; Charles III (r. 1759–88) had barely settled into his throne than Havana fell to a surprise English attack in 1762. Havana boasted one of America's best natural harbors and had long been the gathering and provisioning point for Spain's outgoing, silver-laden transatlantic fleets. The victorious English immediately began to trade freely in Cuba: more than 700 ships sailed into Havana harbor within a year of the port's seizure, most of them packed with African slaves destined for Cuba's cane fields and sugar mills. Historians estimate that by the time Spain recovered Cuba in 1763, the English had transported more than 4,000 Africans to the island. Once English slavers put this machine in motion, slavery and the slave trade in Cuba expanded exponentially. By 1789, 100,000 Africans had been forcibly introduced, turning Cuba into a bona fide slave society, and almost 300,000 more arrived between 1790 and 1821.

Shaken by the loss, albeit temporary, of such a critical (and seemingly well-defended) port as Havana, Charles III began to overhaul defenses across the empire. If stationary forts and distant troops could not protect the colonies, a permanent and reorganized army would have to take up the job. After local officials conducted censuses to assess how many service-age men they could muster, the crown created new *fijos* (fixed military units) drawn from colonial populations and created new honors, titles, and privileges to encourage enlistments. The crown's reluctance to rely too heavily on creole soldiers and officers meant that the government tended to downplay the militias, but participation in these volunteer units was nonetheless a popular activity for imperial subjects of all colors. By the late eighteenth century, men of color made up one-fourth of Cuba's military. The militias of Veracruz, Cartagena, Buenos Aires, and many other port cities were similarly composed.

A related component of eighteenth-century reform, especially for the Iberian countries that had weakened the authority of the Church, was the rationalization of bureaucracy by bringing subjects and territories under more direct crown control. Of course, such centralization challenged local leaders' traditional authority. In the Spanish colonies, the Bourbon reforms sought to undo the typical Habsburg practice of farming out power to competing interest groups, the most powerful by this time being creole elites. Charles III quickened the pace of centralization when he brought into government a group of capable administrators (with an anti-English, and mostly pro-French bias), who launched governmental reforms across the Americas. Besides creating the new viceroyalties in South America, the imperial streamliners eliminated

Marriage as a Political Tool

If Spanish and English authorities considered using marriage to bring about political alliances or cement loyalty of people in distant locations, they may have come up with the idea from West Africans. In many African societies, marriage had a critical social and political function. Marriages tied together not only individuals or nuclear families, but also larger extended families and clans through related self-interest and obligations of reciprocity. One tended to help one's in-laws when they were attacked by enemies or when burdened by poor harvests, plagues of locusts, or epidemics. Patriarchs of clans carefully arranged for the marriage of clan daughters into wealthy and influential families, often ones some distance away and even speaking another language. Polygamy, with prominent men sometimes having a dozen or more wives, aided the establishment of such familial relationships. Ruling families of several dozen small states could form a kind of interlocking directorate. If you challenged one, they called in alliances through marriage and you soon were dealing with them all.

Europeans and Eurafricans residing on African soil, mixing business with pleasure, adopted African marriage customs. In 1715, David Francis, a Royal African Company agent in the Gambia River, complained to associates in London, "The French . . . at Albreda . . . are married to the Chief women of the country, who having canoes & boats up the river, prevent the merchants coming down with their trade." Over half a century later, Thomas Rutherford wrote from the same spot to the African Office in London, "The Castle Slaves [employed by the British at their fort on James Island] are so closely connected with the People of the Country by Marriages and other Social Ties, that an Attempt to remove any of the former would infallibly occasion very great Disturbances and Insurrections among the Natives, and render the Safety of the Forts and Settlements highly precarious, as their Defense more depends on the Attachment of the Slaves than on the feeble Force in Civil and Military Servants."

Using marriage to enhance frontier harmony was not an innovative strategy, and Pombal was not alone in his vision. In a pamphlet he published in the 1750s on the frontier problem, Archibald Kennedy, an English colonist in New York, proposed establishing forts, paying people to relocate there, and offering bounties for inter-marriage. The British government did not act on Kennedy's scheme, but it reflects the creative ways subjects and officials contemplated imperial reorganization and the continued political importance of marriage in the Atlantic world.

PRINCE MANGA BELL AND FAVORITE WIVES.

Prince Manga Bell and Favorite Wives from "Glimpses of Africa, West and Southwest Coast," by C.S. Smith, published 1895. Manuscripts, Archives and Rare Books Division, Schomburg Center for Research in Black Culture, The New York Public Library, Astor, Lenox and Tilden Foundations.

old regional units in favor of French-style intendancies, a process first tried in Cuba after the Seven Years' War and then exported to the mainland. Such captaincies-general as Venezuela further elaborated imperial control and demanded local accountability. Responses of creole elites to these innovations varied, but in some newly elevated regions this group benefited from enhanced levels of crown interest, and hence access to titles and other indicators of status. Thus, while La Plata gained its viceregal capital at Buenos Aires in 1776, with all its associated trappings and prestige, its merchant elite gained a modicum of control over the great Potosí silver mines.

But this was not the case in the territorially diminished viceroyalties of New Spain and Peru, where creole elite interests were more entrenched. Local resentment of the Bourbon project grew as Charles III also replaced creole officials at every level with *peninsulares* (Spanish-born men, from the Iberian Peninsula). The attitudes of these Spaniards, like those of the many scientists who came to revive mining and improve defense, were generally haughty and dismissive of local people and their customs. They reserved special disdain for local elites, whom they viewed as racially and culturally inferior. Following government directives to the letter, peninsular Spaniards occupied most important judicial positions in Peru by 1770, a near total reversal from the first decades of the century. The Bourbons also created new administrative posts, open only to Spanish men whom locals called "foreigners." Still, most hated by all classes were those peninsulares in charge of the alcohol and tobacco monopolies. Charles III hoped to secure more loyalty and obedience from his European-born officials than he believed could be secured from creoles, whose interests were invested in their local communities.

It did not take long for the rulers of the Iberian and British empires to learn that they could not reorganize the administration of their American colonies—bringing widespread change to long-standing government policies, reducing the authority of powerful and respected religious institutions, altering long-respected social customs, lowering the status of prominent families, and especially squeezing money out of their subjects—without breeding antipathy. Through the middle decades of the eighteenth century, across most classes and sectors of society in each of the Atlantic empires, as imperial reforms progressed, resentment grew from a steady simmer to, in places, a rolling boil. Through it all, what the historian David Brading notes as applying to Mexico seems to have been the case for all colonial locales in the Americas, from Boston to Buenos Aires: when faced with uprisings, the army remained the imperial government's "favored institution for securing the loyalty of its colonial subjects."

Resistance and Rebellion

The greatest challenge for "enlightened" Atlantic imperial reformers was to secure the cooperation of their colonial inhabitants. Even the most autocratic governments could not rule successfully or at length through force; like it or not, their authority ultimately depended on the consent and cooperation of the governed. The greatest obstacle to implementing reform was the creole elite class, those people of European descent customarily responsible for colonial administration and having interests rooted deeply in the soil. These creole leaders were targets of much Iberian reform, and so successful were Spain and Portugal in this regard that historians speak of these reforms cumulatively as the "Reconquest" of America. If the first conquest targeted indigenous populations, this eighteenth-century reconquest focused on creole populations with enough money and power (like the Jesuits) to challenge the state.

Throughout the eighteenth century, in all European empires in the Americas, subjects drew on customs of resistance and rebellion to defy unpopular government actions. Colonial uprisings were usually popular and spontaneous, rarely engaging broad political philosophies but seeking redress of specific grievances. Some resistance movements saw creole and casta populations cooperate; others were specific to an artisan class, ethnic group, rural community, or urban neighborhood. Most of these local rebellions had clear and limited goals, although uprisings could also generate new demands and bring to the surface latent desires. Crowds in Boston in 1734, 1737, and 1771, for example, destroyed bawdy houses to convey their objection to their presence in the city. In Philadelphia in 1727, a mob beset the house of Governor James Logan, who not only lived in ostentatious wealth at a time of economic depression, but insulted the impoverished by insisting that only "the Sot, the Rambler, the Spendthrift, and the Slip Season" were experiencing hard times. Poor Philadelphians, who blamed wealthy merchants for their poverty, moved on Logan's house, ripping off shutters and heaving bricks through the exposed windows.

The quick-tempered people of Boston engaged in yet another popular action in 1747, this a massive act of civil disobedience that involved rioting and attacking British sailors in response to impressment gangs (British sailors who coerced men to join the navy). When called out to bring order, Boston's local militia refused to respond. The crowd vented its collective rage by burning a barge. Building on the work of E. P. Thompson, historians sometimes talk of the "moral economy of the crowd," by which they mean that people imposed their own values within a community by acting in concert. They did not engage in acts of random violence, although one's perspective on the crowd clearly depends on one's relationship to it. A person whose house was ripped to shreds, as was Lieutenant Governor Thomas Hutchinson's in Boston, or who was tarred, feathered, and publicly humiliated, was likely to see a riot and a mob where others saw a logic-driven or morally centered crowd. But historians now emphasize that crowds worked not for personal interest but for the collective needs of the community. Crowds also had a surprising tendency to operate within rather than outside established social rules. In Boston, for instance, crowds (or mobs) observed the Sabbath. Throughout Spanish America, they hailed the King and Virgin Mary. In all of these actions, colonial crowds drew on European traditions of public collective action to redress communal grievances and perceived injustice.

The pressure of new taxation prompted those most affected by it—impoverished and wealthy alike—to respond in traditional ways to convey their opposition. Many of the poor on the western side of the Atlantic could not reasonably meet crown demands for more revenue, and they resented new regulations that curtailed their movement and modest recreation habits (which elites invariably labeled vices). Despite the modernizing efforts of Portugal's Pombal and of Spain's Bourbon reformers, great social inequality persisted in Latin America. A small class of elites made rich by gold, silver, sugar, and other exports lived lives of stunning opulence in full view of thousands of wretched plebeians of many subdivided colors and classes. Among these elites was Don Carlos Palacios y Blanco, owner of 160 slaves and guardian to his orphaned nephew, Simón Bolívar.

By the mid-eighteenth century, a fast-growing population of impoverished freed slaves, displaced Indians, orphaned mestizos, and other people of color came to form a diverse, largely miserable underclass in most Brazilian and Spanish American cities. These rootless and often kinless urban poor faced chronic unemployment and the opprobrium of crown and local authorities, who attempted to regulate criminality through censuses, curfews, patrols, raids on taverns and gaming places, and legislation that required the poor to carry proof of work contracts or patrons. Roundups of alleged vagabonds for hard labor drafts and military service became increasingly common, and hotly challenged. Help for the poor (such as it was) came from the Catholic Church and pious donors who supported hospitals, orphanages, and houses for "deposited" women whose virtue was in danger of being spoiled or who were escaping marital violence. Municipal authorities also made some attempt to stave off hunger and starvation by regulating food prices and maintaining public granaries, but periodic bread riots were an increasingly common feature of urban life, as were deteriorating infrastructures. Population pressures were felt everywhere. Mexico City, which once sparkled under Aztec maintenance, had become a polluted and unhealthy place to live by the mid-eighteenth century. If it was any consolation, other inhabitants of other Atlantic cities, especially ports, had it much worse.

Neither government paternalism nor the charity of the righteous was sufficient to address fully the misery of the masses. And the masses were not the only angry city dwellers at the time. As noted, colonial elites found their political power declining as European officials enhanced their control. The new Bourbon and Pombaline demands for taxes and tribute only exacerbated already existing tensions, making unrest endemic. Most of Brazil's eighteenth-century rebellions were concentrated in the rowdy gold and diamond zone of Minas Gerais, and some rebels became highly radicalized by the 1780s, when other Atlantic rebellions turned revolutionary. In the Spanish American Andes, historians have documented at least five uprisings sparked in the single decade of the 1740s, one of which lasted thirteen years. More than twice as many rebellions occurred in the 1750s, and twenty more took place in the 1760s.

The historians Anthony McFarlane and Kenneth Andrien have analyzed one of the most important of these uprisings—the 1765 Rebellion of the Barrios in Quito (modern Ecuador). Rude slogans had already been splashed upon city walls when the elite citizens of Quito organized a town meeting to protest the new royal monopolies and sales taxes. Before long, bells rang out and as many as 10,000 residents of the city's several parishes, or barrios—largely mestizos, Indians, and poor people of color—poured into the streets to attack the hated *estancos* (state monopoly outlets) and customs buildings. The rioters threw stones and vandalized a number of private and public structures until Jesuit priests (whom the Spanish did not expel until 1767) went into the street in an attempt to restore order with promises of a general pardon. As the region's main owners of the slave-staffed sugar estates that supplied the city with *aguardiente* (cane liquor), the Jesuits had more than a moral interest in containing the riot. When government officials later tried to arrest suspects, the riots began again, this time resulting in many fatalities—mostly among the rebels.

Farther south, in the coastal town of Lambayeque (modern Peru), Bourbon officials conducted a census, set up a new customs house, and instituted the royal monopoly on aguardiente, but when they tried to collect tribute from black militia officers, the men refused to pay. Instead, they drafted a petition reminding the viceroy in Lima that they were not a conquered people, but rather his loyal subjects with rights. Local officials complained that the men presented themselves "with an air of independence, their hats on their heads" and "threw the petition on the table and took seats without being asked." The black militiamen's lack of deference upset authorities as much as the lost revenues. Officials complained in New Granada, too, of what seemed to be a growing tendency among common folk, male and female, to speak to their social superiors with great "haughtiness and arrogance." Free-lance female gold panners openly confronted royal officials with rocks and sticks, running them out of town in fear for their lives. Full-scale regional rebellions soon followed.

The most serious of the Andean revolts came slightly later, in the three-year uprising (1781–83) led by José Gabriel Condorcanqui, an educated and wealthy mestizo who took the name Túpac Amaru II in honor of the last Inca ruler beheaded by Spanish conquerors in 1572. The name resonated throughout the Andes, but it proved unlucky. Although descended from Inca royalty, Condorcanqui lived like a Spanish noble; according to one witness, he typically wore "a long coat and knee britches of black velvet, a waistcoat of gold tissue worth seventy or eighty *duros*, embroidered linen, silk stockings, gold buckles at his knees and on his shoes, and a Spanish beaver hat valued at twenty-five *duros*. He kept his hair curled in ringlets that extended nearly to his waist." He lived, in short, like a neo-Inca nobleman.

Túpac's wealth derived from his large herds of mules that transported mercury and other goods to Potosí, so the new Bourbon taxes threatened his livelihood. As a *kuraka*, or indigenous leader responsible for collecting his subjects' tribute for the Spanish overlords, he was also aware of the growing misery of the people. In repeated petitions, the foppish rebel presented native demands: an end to the practice of forcing indigenous people to buy unwanted goods (called the *reparto*); removal of corrupt officials who ran the "company stores" that carried these goods; appointment of Indian provincial governors by popular assent; better conditions in mines and textile workshops; an end to labor drafts; and a new appeals court for Cuzco, the old Inca capital. In a desperate appeal to those on the bottom, he signed a "Proclamation of Liberty," the first manifesto in the Americas to declare slaves to be free.

Each of Túpac's legal efforts failed, including those sent to the new viceroyalty of La Plata, in Buenos Aires. Finally, in 1781, overtaxed Indians hanged a hated official, forcing panicked government agents from four nearby provinces to flee for their lives. Túpac quickly gathered a force of 40,000 native

Andeans and castas, which, although ill supplied and hampered by poor communications, defeated a royal army sent to capture him. Despite this initial victory, Túpac held back from attacking Cuzco, still hoping to rally disaffected creoles to his cause. But race trumped class in this revolt, and the creoles stayed home. Divisions within native ranks also undermined Túpac's power. Not all Inca nobles agreed on his course, while others, jealous of his prominence or fearful of a backlash, sided with the Spanish. Before long, documents surfaced allegedly proving that Túpac had planned to execute all Spaniards except clergymen and become king of Peru. In fact, he set up a rather effective government ruled by a junta of five, hardly the work of a megalomaniac. Subsequent uprisings in neighboring Bolivia made clear the depth and breadth of indigenous unhappiness with Spanish rule, with or without the leadership of a self-styled modern Inca. But the rebellion's brief success terrified Spanish officials, and when they finally captured Túpac, they behaved as had their sixteenth-century predecessors. Enlightened rationality was nowhere in sight when Túpac, his family, and his captains were tortured—their tongues cut out, their bodies quartered, their heads severed, and their body parts displayed in nearby provinces as warning of the gruesome fate that awaited a rebel.

Spanish troops finally restored peace in 1783, but only after the loss of 100,000 lives and destruction of much property. Túpac's revolt had failed, but Peru's shaken viceroy, Teodoro de Croix, implemented many indigenous demands: he ended the hated reparto, lightened *mita* (draft labor) burdens, and replaced a number of corrupt and abusive officials. He also established a new *audiencia* in Cuzco. But worried about the ethnic makeup of the city, he also disbanded Cuzco's provincial militia and replaced it with regular army units. To emphasize Spain's upper hand, the viceroy denied honors to creoles in Cuzco and lavished them on the Spanish in Peru's capital, Lima.

But rebellion was a monster with many heads, and revolts soon erupted in nearby New Granada. Unlike many earlier uprisings, the Comunero Revolt of 1781 in what is today Colombia was carefully organized. Participating towns elected a *común* (governing committee) that sent representatives to the town of Socorro, several days' journey north of the viceregal capital of Bogotá, to form a central commune in which all but black slaves voted. Creoles controlled leadership positions, but base support came from Indian and mestizo peasants. Rallying around the slogan, "Long live the king and death to bad government," 20,000 *comúneros*, as the rebels styled themselves, marched on Bogotá to present their demands, which included reduction of tribute and sales taxes, return of Indian lands, abolition of the new tobacco monopoly, a preference for creoles over Europeans in governmental appointments, free sacraments, the expulsion of the royal visitor, and the right to establish more grocery stores. Being a reaction against economic oppression, the demands were not aimed at overthrowing the king. In a play for time, the viceroy agreed to rebel demands, only to repudiate the agreement later on the grounds that it had been obtained by force. The rebels rose again, but when the last leader was betrayed and executed in 1782, the Comunero revolt ended.

As these examples illustrate, most eighteenth-century Latin American protest movements were not revolutionary. Instead, they were reactions against the heavy hand of royal reformers. Rebels usually represented themselves as loyal vassals of a just monarch, who asked only for relief from the excesses of colonial authorities.

The resistance movements of almost every Atlantic colony remained within this tradition of rebellion, but in one region of North America—one not even comprising all British colonies on the continent, much less accounting for the entirety of British holdings in the western Atlantic—tax resisters became revolutionaries. Like their counterparts in the colonies of Spain and Portugal, British subjects in some corners of America protested new taxes imposed on them by distant monarchies, and as the heavy imperial hand squeezed ever more tightly, people all over the colonies, on the mainland and in the Caribbean, began gathering in mass meetings, staging parades, lighting bonfires, and erecting liberty trees.

Why, then, did colonists in British mainland North America step out of this pattern of colonial resistance and become out-and-out revolutionaries? The answer lies in an unique confluence of factors, most of them an outgrowth of the devastating wars that followed 1689. Although revolts such as the one led by Túpac Amaru II shook the Andes, those uprisings ultimately lacked the destructive force of the conflicts that washed across northern seaport towns at midcentury. The Seven Years' War in particular disrupted shipping, paralyzed the trade that fueled coastal cities, caused inflation and postwar recession, accelerated class conflict, plunged people into poverty, allowed for slave rebellions, and elevated war profiteers to new positions of status and power. Perhaps this particular group was willing to risk the hardships of combat in the name of independence from powerful Britain precisely because they had lived with wars' privation, impoverishment, and terror since the dawn of the eighteenth century.

That resistance in this small region of the western Atlantic would become revolution, and how that revolution created a democratic republic that was to have an enormous impact on much of the Atlantic world, were both peculiar products of Atlantic cross currents, the ebb and flow of wars, ideas, commodities, and people. The revolution in British North America that emerged out of the ashes of the Seven Years' War, the most massive military and naval conflict of its time, began an Atlantic, and even a world, conflict that would drag on for more than three decades.

Selected Readings

Alford, Terry, *Prince Among Slaves, The True Story of an African Prince Sold into Slavery in the American South* (New York: Harcourt-Brace-Jovanovich, 1977).

Brading, David, *The First Americans: The Spanish Monarchy, Creole Patriots, and the Liberal State, 1492–1867* (Cambridge: Cambridge University Press, 1993).

Curtin, Philip D., *Economic Change in Precolonial Africa: Senegambia in the Era of the Slave Trade* (Madison: University of Wisconsin Press, 1975).

Demos, John P., *The Unredeemed Captive: A Family Story from Early America* (New York: Knopf, 1994).

Ferry, Robert, *The Colonial Elite of Early Caracas* (Berkeley: University of California Press, 1987).

Fisher, John, *Bourbon Peru, 1750–1824* (Liverpool: Liverpool University Press, 2003).

Fisher, Lillian Seward, *The Last Inca Revolt, 1780–1783* (Norman: University of Oklahoma Press, 1966).

Lang, James, *Conquest and Commerce: Spain and England in the Americas* (New York: Academic Press, 1975).

Lavrin, Asunción, *Sexuality and Marriage in Colonial Latin America* (Lincoln: University of Nebraska Press, 1989).

Lynch, John, *Spanish Colonial Administration: The Intendant System of the Viceroyalty of La Plata* (Westport: Greenwood, 1969).

Mapp, Paul W., "French Reactions to the British Search for a Northwest Passage from Hudson Bay and the Origins of the Seven Years' War," *Terrae Incognitae* 33 (2 vol.): 13–32.

Maxwell, Kenneth, *Conflicts and Conspiracies,* 2d ed. (New York: Routledge, 2004).

McNeill, J. R., "Yellow Jack and Geopolitics: Environment, Epidemics, and the Struggles for Empire in the American Tropics, 1650–1825," *OAH Magazine of History* 18, No. 3 (April, 2004): 9–13.

Phelan, John L., *The People and the King: The Comunero Revolution in Colombia* (Madison: University of Wisconsin Press, 1977).

Smaldone, Joseph P., *Warfare in the Sokoto Caliphate: Historical and Sociological Perspectives* (Cambridge: Cambridge University Press, 1977).

Socolow, Susan, *The Merchant Elite of Buenos Aires* (Cambridge, UK: Cambridge University Press, 1974).

Stein, Barbara, and Stanley Stein, *The Colonial Heritage of Latin America* (New York: Oxford University Press, 1970).

Terry, Robert, *The Colonial Elite of Early Caracas* (Berkeley: University of California Press, 1987).

Twinam, Ann, *Public Lives, Private Secrets: Gender, Honor, Sexuality, and Illegitimacy in Colonial Spanish America* (Stanford: Stanford University Press, 1999).

Representation du feu terrible a Nouvelle York (*The Burning of New York*). *1778 French propaganda print showing the west end of New York City in flames on the night of September 21, 1776. Hessian soldiers and black Loyalists are depicted as looters. Image courtesy Library of Congress, LC-USZ62-42.*

Chapter Ten

The First Imperial Rupture, 1754–1783

I have nothing more to offer than what General Washington would have had to offer, had he been taken by the British and put to trial. I have adventured my life in endeavoring to obtain the liberty of my countrymen, and am a willing sacrifice in their cause.
Enslaved revolutionary, Virginia

O ye that love mankind! . . . Every spot of the old world is over-run with oppression. Freedom hath been hunted round the globe. Asia, and Africa, have long expelled her. Europe regards her like a stranger, and England hath given a warning to depart. O! receive the fugitive, and prepare in time an asylum for mankind.
Thomas Paine, *Common Sense* (1776)

No exile penned a more plaintive and outraged account of his ordeal than Richard Cartwright of New York. Amid the ravages of war in the colony of New York (other residents might have called it a state, but Cartwright was a loyal subject of his king who would reject this turn of phrase and the treason it suggested), Cartwright found his home transformed into a place "where all Government was subverted, where Caprice was the only Rule and Measure of usurped Authority." He resolved to leave. But such a task was not so easily accomplished in these unsettled times. Cartwright had to secure permission from his local Committee of Safety, and with his pass securely in hand, he swallowed his regret at leaving his family and focused instead on his "sensible Pleasure to quit a Place where Discord reigned and all the miseries of Anarchy had long prevailed." His travels north took him through a land laid waste by the campaigns of war, a countryside once "agreeable and delightful" but now "a most shocking Picture of Havock and wild Desolation," populated by other refugees, many destitute and helpless. A British regiment stationed north of Fort George offered the sanctuary Cartwright longed for far from the "Outrage, Tumult, and Oppression" of the rebellious colonies. He took altogether a journey of only twelve days, but this short cross-country trek transported him from a scene of disorder and mayhem and capricious violence into a world still governed by his sovereign.

Just fifteen years earlier, Susanna Johnson had made a similar trek north, although she traveled as a captive of the Abenaki and journeyed to French Canada. Cartwright chose his exile, and he left a newly independent state for Canada, which was by then British. In between these journeys was the Peace of Paris of 1763, yet it was a peace on paper only. Complaints of violence, upheaval, disorder, and tyranny were recurring refrains of the turbulent years

COLONIAL MAINLAND
NORTH AMERICA

between 1754 and 1783. They came from all quarters, from slave and free, European and American, Indian and African, British and French, from the mainland and the West Indies, and even Africa. It was a time of almost endless war: even if the formal treaty of 1763 ushered in peace, resistance to imperial rule and conflicts on unsettled borders continued.

Locked in a seemingly endless competition for European hegemony, Britain and France first turned to the seas, as they sought to monopolize Atlantic commerce, before finally focusing on the Caribbean and the American mainland in a bid for control. The result was thirty years of nearly continuous warfare that reshaped the flow of emigrants to the Americas, redrew the map of the Western Hemisphere and West Africa, drained the treasuries of France and Spain, and laid the basis for another century of combat with Indian populations. Before this conflict for empire had ended, the Atlantic basin would witness a string of events that none could have foreseen or forestalled, as one major imperial system collapsed and with it the hierarchical, ideological framework for a class-based society. By the time the era ended, the political map of the North Atlantic world had been transformed.

It was a cataclysmic period. In 1763, Britain had emerged as the greatest European power within the Atlantic, dominant in North America and the North Atlantic alike; twenty years later, Britain ceded defeat to France on the European continent and lost part of its territory in mainland North America to revolutionaries. Colonies everywhere were transformed: thirteen joined together as a new nation, engaged in an ambitious republican experiment, but even those that remained loyal to Britain experienced their own transformations.

The Nine Years' War

The historian Fred Anderson has characterized the Seven Years' War as the war that made the United States. In any case, it certainly created a unique confluence of circumstances—localized economic hardship, clarified understanding of cultural differences between colonists and Britons, the removal of the French threat from the North American mainland and a commensurate cockiness in some North American colonists, lost opportunities for Native Americans to play rival empires off each other—that shaped the conflagration that followed. These peculiar local circumstances help explain why an age of war and imperial reform led to independence in parts of the British empire but to a continued loyal resistance to Spain in colonies to the south. But the American War for Independence had other transforming effects. This was the war that made Canada, the war that severed the Atlantic world's most powerful imperial entity, and the war that placed new pressures on the institution of slavery. If the Seven Years' War made America, the War for Independence remade the British Atlantic. These hemispheric changes commenced in a place of enormous strategic (if not economic) value, the Ohio River valley.

Among those who took a hand in this transformation was a buckskin-clad emissary to the French. Only twenty-one-years old, George Washington peered through the freezing rain at the fleur-de-lis flying over Fort LeBoeuf, just east of Lake Erie. It was December 4, 1753. Backed only by eleven militiamen and four Shawnee guides, Washington handed the letter he had carried from Williamsburg to the French commandant, Captain Jacques Legardeur de Saint-Pierre. The polite French offered wine and food but made no attempt to hide their intentions from the young deputy of Virginia governor Robert Dinwiddie, who, at six feet, three inches, towered over his hosts. "They told me it was their absolute design to take possession of the Ohio [River Valley]," Washington reported, "and by G[od] they would do it." Although badly outnumbered by Anglo-American settlers to the east, Legardeur laughed that English "motions were too slow & dilatory to prevent any undertakings of theirs" in the west.

Washington may have believed he was serving Virginia—or his own political ambitions, or even the economic interests of his family, since he and his kin were stockholders in the expansionist Ohio Company, a syndicate of colonial entrepreneurs and land speculators eager to open the region to settlement. But if his western adventures ultimately served all three and earned him fame and fortune beyond his wildest dreams, to a great extent he was but a pawn in a much larger Atlantic struggle that he scarcely could have understood.

At immediate issue was control of North Atlantic economies and the Ohio country, the trans-Appalachian region claimed by France and Britain, thanks to Virginia's never-surveyed sea-to-sea charter. Shortly after King George's War ended in 1748, the French monarch, Louis XV, ordered an armed force down the Ohio River with instructions to build fortifications from Fort Presqu'isle on Lake Erie to Duquesne in what the English regarded as western Pennsylvania (near present-day Pittsburgh). The third party in this struggle was the indigenous people of upper New York, southern Canada, and the Ohio Valley: members of the Iroquois Confederacy, the Shawnee, Delawares, and Hurons. Their concerns over the arrival of European forces abated when it became clear that the French forts were not agricultural settlements; most Indians in the region were more concerned with keeping English colonists on the eastern side of the Appalachians. But stockholders in the Ohio Company, including Dinwiddie and Washington, had precisely the opposite ambition.

Watching these events in London were King George II and his Privy Council, the thirty-odd courtiers and ministers who advised the monarch and staffed his principal offices. On August 21, the cabinet agreed to instruct all colonial governors "to prevent, by Force, These and any such attempts that may be made by the French," or their Indian allies. This vote, and instructions that followed, empowered the Virginia governor to send young Washington northwest to Fort LeBoeuf as his messenger.

In January 1754, Washington returned to Williamsburg and handed Legardeur's reply to Dinwiddie. Furious at the French refusal to "desist" and undoubtedly worried about his investments, Dinwiddie ordered now-Lieutenant Colonel Washington to return west and oversee the construction of an English fort at the forks of the Ohio River. The French already had begun construction on Fort Duquesne, and although Washington offered bounties of land for men who would march with him, few farmers were interested in dying for the cause of wealthy speculators. With a force of only forty-seven men, Washington returned west but soon encountered a French patrol. Ac-

What Happened at Fort William Henry?

James Fenimore Cooper, an American author of the early nineteenth century, drew on the story of the attack at Fort William Henry sixty years later in the writing of his often-filmed novel, The Last of the Mohicans (1826). Long characterized as a "massacre" in which uncontrolled and drunken French-allied indigenous warriors senselessly slaughtered British forces, the actual events of the day, as far as historians are able to reconstruct them, reveal complex ideas about war and the value of prisoners and point to the ways in which different cultures find meaning in warfare. When Europeans and Native Americans joined in alliance, as they did frequently during this long period of warfare, they did so because of common and often temporary interests, but not necessarily because they had common goals in war. The French general, Montcalm, offered the besieged English at the fort a "parole of honor," which permitted the men and women of the garrison to march to Fort Edward with all of their goods. But these terms, rooted as they were in European codes of military conduct, meant little to the Ottawa and Potawatomi warriors allied with the French, if, indeed, the terms of surrender were ever explained to them at all. The Indians went into war expecting a share of loot and of prisoners (who were valuable for religious and social and economic purposes), and the terms the French brokered thwarted both goals. As the British forces assembled to leave, Indians stripped them of their goods and seized Indians and blacks who had fought with the British. (The Indians regarded the blacks as property, so they fared better than did other prisoners.) Once the garrison began its march, the Indians (some 1,600 of them) attacked, killing as many as 50 people in the initial assault and seizing prisoners. French intervention reclaimed some prisoners; the others the Indians marched away in triumph. The Indians secured as many as 500 of the people paroled from Fort William Henry, either as prisoners or as scalps. The events are remembered in the histories written by Europeans and their descendants as a massacre because they violated European codes of warfare, but the timing of the attack and the seizure of property and the capture and occasional execution of prisoners were entirely consistent with indigenous codes.

Ian K. Steele, Betrayals: Fort William Henry and the "Massacre" (Oxford: Oxford University Press, 1990).

Depiction of Montcalm attempting to stop Native Americans from attacking British soldiers and civilians as they leave Fort William Henry. Library of Congress, LC-USZ62-120704.

cording to Private John Shaw, an Irishman who wrote of the events of May 28, both sides panicked and opened fire. Tanaghrisson, a Seneca guide also known as Half King, "took his Tomahawk and split the Head of the French Captain" in retaliation for allegations that the French wished him assassinated. What British colonists called the French and Indian War and European monarchs would christen the Seven Years' War had begun. It was to last nine years and become the third bloodiest conflict North Americans would ever fight in proportion to their population.

The war furthermore ushered in six decades of combat in the Americas and Europe, ending only with Napoleon's defeat at Waterloo and the treaty of 1815, which resolved major disputes in Europe and the Americas alike. Part of Britain's woes over this period stemmed from the capable but feckless King George II, who had come to power in 1727. But much of the difficulty grew out of the complicated European balance of power. Whatever the reason, the fighting in the western Atlantic between 1755 and 1757 was a near catastrophe for Britain. In central New York, French and Indian raiders seized Fort Bull in March of 1756—even before France formally declared war in May—and then turned north to burn Fort Oswego on Lake Ontario. Thirteen months later, eight thousand French soldiers, Canadian colonists, Indian allies, and Catholic priests under Louis-Joseph de Montcalm laid siege to Fort William Henry, a British outpost guarding the upper Hudson. Faced with a starving garrison, empty powder kegs, and cannon split from prolonged firing, Colonel George Monro surrendered the fort on August 9, 1757, and French-allied Indian warriors attacked the retreating men and women, turning what was originally just a humiliating defeat into a catastrophe.

British hopes, both in the kingdom and among American colonists, brightened in 1757. In that year, forty-nine-year-old William Pitt became prime minister of Great Britain. An expansionist whose ego matched his grandiose designs, Pitt announced: "I know that I can save this country, and that no one else can." Even more than his predecessors, he believed that Britain's greatness lay not in Europe but in a global empire. To that end, Pitt refocused the war effort on not merely obtaining the lands west of the Appalachians, but on completely driving France from mainland North America. The energetic minister dispatched another 2,000 soldiers to the northern colonies, assured the Americans he would raise 6,000 more, and urged them to muster 20,000 militiamen to support his regulars. By war's end, Pitt boasted of more than 50,000 armed men in the mainland colonies, a number that exceeded the entire population of New France.

Such plans, of course, required capital. Somewhat disingenuously, Pitt assured nervous colonial assemblies that this massive buildup would be "at His Majesty's expense," and briefly the minister tried just that: Pitt raised taxes on the overburdened home island and borrowed from banks in London and Amsterdam, doubling the English debt. Americans applauded this policy, but their fondness for Pitt was largely a result of the prosperity his policies brought to urban seaports. As British soldiers and British cash flooded the colonies, the coastal economies improved dramatically. Merchant princes along the eastern seaboard converted their small fleets and turned to privateering—the legalized pirating of enemy vessels licensed by colonial governments—and plundered French and Spanish ships. Typical was Thomas Hancock of Boston, uncle to the now-more-famous John Hancock, who used his wartime profits from such legalized thievery to construct a mansion atop Beacon Hill. Equally typical was the fate of his crew, the men who braved high waves and enemy cannon in hopes of bettering their lot. The mortality rate on privateers was wretched, due to perils of conflict and epidemics. But when the French ship *Soleil*, carrying a cargo valued at £30,000, was captured, the share of the prize granted to each seaman came to £78, more than four years normal wages. Urban artisans also enjoyed full employment in wartime as skilled craftsmen—from the tailors who stitched uniforms to the carpenters and sail makers who hammered together and fitted out the king's fleet—and supplied the arms and provisions required by militaries in an era that had no formal ordnance bureaus or distribution centers. Farmers who lived close enough to seaport towns planted extra crops and watched as their foodstuffs traded at high prices.

But as is always the case, the nine years of war brought devastation and heartache to workers on both sides of the Atlantic. Both colonists and taxpayers in Britain often found it impossible to put bread on the table while paying ever-increasing taxes on their already meager wages. The tax rate tripled over the course of three years in Virginia, while in Massachusetts it rose to £20 for each adult male, a staggering sum in a region where the average wealth was but £38 per capita. In Philadelphia, the conflict put those with the lowest wages out on the streets. "Many very poor people," one pamphleteer complained, were able to pay their property taxes only by "disposing of their huts and lots to others more wealthy than themselves."

As hard as that was, families counted themselves lucky if they lost nothing more than their homes. Especially in New England, close to the Canadian front, almost every young man saw combat at some point during the conflict. At war's end, Boston census takers found an equal number of males and females below the age of sixteen, but above that too-youthful line, women outnumbered men almost 7 to 5. In a time of limited and decentralized poor relief, the loss of a husband and father produced enormous hardship and led to what the historian Gary B. Nash has dubbed "the feminization of poverty" in British America.

Workers on both sides of the Atlantic conveyed their discontent in the time-honored tradition of collective bargaining by riot. In New York City, mariners who had no wish to exchange the high wages of an American privateer for likely death in the British navy rose in 1758 against an impressment gang. Even as the war began to turn in Britain's favor, those at the bottom of the Atlantic economic world saw little reason to impoverish themselves or widow their wives in the king's name. In London, disagreement over sailors' wages spread from town to town. English mariners rioted at Newcastle, Tinmouth, Sunderland, and Shields in hopes of obtaining a base pay of 35s. a month. Until this price was met, one sailor swore, "they would neither engage, nor suffer a ship to sail." Since the city's merchants and the government were little disposed to grant these concessions, "a great body of sailors," which some observers estimated as high as 15,000, marched to the Palace Yard to cheer their representatives' speeches. Faced with such resolve, several shippers, including the Hudson's Bay Company, reluctantly agreed to these "exorbitant" wages, and ships again moved down the Thames and out into the Atlantic.

In addition to financing his war through taxation, Pitt also chose to conciliate the western Indians. His envoys assured the Iroquois Confederation that London was willing to redress legitimate "grievances" in "respect to the lands which have been fraudulently taken from them." Most tribes saw the wisdom in playing the two European powers off each other, and by July 1758, when New England militiamen partly rebuilt Fort Oswego, numerous tribes were already renouncing the French cause. Several months later, hungry French soldiers abandoned Fort Duquesne to a larger British force, who renamed the site Fort Pitt (and later, Pittsburgh). By the spring of 1759, the last French fort along the New York frontier had fallen, opening the path for an invasion of French Canada that summer. In hopes of taking Canada before cold weather forced the British squadron south, General James Wolfe decided on an extremely risky attack on Quebec, a nearly impregnable city high above the river. During the night of September 12, Wolfe and his men scaled the 175-foot bluff, dragging two cannon after them. As dawn broke, the English fanned out across the Plains of Abraham behind the city. Inside the city walls were 16,000 French regulars, Canadian militiamen, Crees, and even thirty-five students from the Jesuit seminary. Yet the French general, Montcalm (of Fort William Henry fame), panicked. Instead of deploying his artillery against Wolfe's two guns, Montcalm marched his troops out onto the plain, and at ten o'clock that morning ordered them to advance into the heart of the British lines. Soldiers on both sides remembered the battle lasting from fifteen minutes to half an hour. Wolfe was among the first hit. Across the field, Montcalm's soldiers began to retreat after they saw their commander's belly and leg sliced apart by British grapeshot. With no officer left to replace Montcalm and the St. Lawrence clogged with British warships, Canadian officials had little choice but to surrender four days later. To the extent that Pitt had transformed the conflict into a war for global empire, the seizure of Canada marked a turning point in hostilities rather than its conclusion.

Not long after Wolfe's death, Britain lost yet another old soldier when George II tripped in his water closet, gashed his right temple against the corner of his bureau, and died. The new king, George III (r. 1760–1820), was his twenty-two-year-old grandson and scion of the notoriously dysfunctional Hanover family. The historian J. H. Plumb subsequently described King George III as profoundly "stupid," but in 1760 the handsome young monarch was immensely popular at home and in the western colonies. After having endured the Germanic manners of the early Hanovers, London society was thrilled to have at last a king born and bred in Britain. But when it became clear that the new king actually intended to play a leading role in government, the initial enthusiasm diminished. As George's initial speech was read to the Privy Council, Pitt was outraged to hear his nearly completed conflict described as "a bloody war." The minister rose to demand that the words "expensive but just and necessary" replace the term "bloody," but it was obvious to all present that the king would soon replace Pitt as his first minister.

Happily for Britain, the war was all but won, yet there was time for King George to plan a final campaign, one destined to be the only successful siege European powers pursued in the eighteenth century. Having captured several French sugar islands in the two years since the fall of Canada, he ordered seizure of Cuba, the possession of France's reluctant ally Spain, who had joined the conflict in 1761. To help Americans feel a part of the expanding empire, George emphasized that colonials should play a role in the invasion, so nearly 4,000 Americans joined 22,000 redcoats, slave traffickers, and aspiring merchants in the effort. Following a two-month siege during the summer of 1762, British forces took Havana. Most of the American volunteers were New York and New Jersey militiamen, who were unaccustomed to the mosquito-borne illnesses of the tropics. As had happened in Admiral Vernon's 1741 attack on Cartagena, the British force fell victim to something worse than bullets. Within six weeks of the August 13 surrender, 4,700 soldiers lay dead of yellow fever—*vómito negro* to the Spanish, since sufferers expired retching up their own partially digested blood. Another 1,800 men had died during the siege, 560 died shortly thereafter, and yet another 4,000 men were so sick they could not stand, let alone march on to Florida or eastern Mexico.

The Reshaping of the Americas

Although news of the sickness in Havana was only beginning to find its way to London by late September 1762, even early reports of the degree of the army's suffering prompted the British government to contact the French war minister about an exchange of envoys to negotiate a peace. Fearing that English control of Spanish Cuba would crumble before a determined King Charles III of Spain could retake it, Pitt's successor, the Earl of Bute, offered a favorable settlement. King Louis XV of France would accept the loss of his mainland possessions—in comparison to the profitable Caribbean, however, Canada had been a steady drain on the French treasury. Bute then offered to return to France the captured islands of Martinique, Guadeloupe, and St. Lucia. Britain claimed the cluster of Windward Islands referred to as the "ceded islands," including Grenada, St. Vincent, Dominica, and Tobago. Cuba was to be restored to Spain in exchange for Florida (the current state and what is now southern Alabama, Mississippi, and Louisiana east of the Mississippi River). As an incentive, Bute proposed to cede what had been French lands west of the Mississippi, including the valuable port of New Orleans, to Spain. Emissaries from Britain, France, and Spain inked the preliminary agreement, known as the Peace of Paris, on November 3, 1762.

But the conclusion of the momentous conflict did not so much resolve old imperial issues as to create new ones. Indeed, renewed fighting broke out almost immediately. From Spain's perspective, Britain's victory was but a prelude to assaults on Spain's Atlantic holdings. Spanish administrators in the Americas promptly set about strengthening their defenses and establishing new trade routes safe from British depredations. Assuming another Atlantic war, in 1770 a squadron from Buenos Aires destroyed a small British naval base on the Malvinas, or Falkland Islands—a small, windswept archipelago claimed by both countries since the 1590s—to guard Spanish ships and restrict foreign access to the Pacific via Cape Horn.

Even as Spanish subjects labored to protect their South Atlantic interests from the British, London's ministers worked to secure their newly won British holdings in North America. General James Murray, a participant in the battle of Quebec, was appointed governor of Canada and promptly set out to pacify his formerly French subjects. Although Murray ruled through a military government established under the Proclamation of 1763, he quickly came to like the Canadians. Hungry and weary of war, the Canadians proved docile, and Murray in turn governed with a light touch. Soon he was reporting that they constituted "the best race on the globe." If they could only be weaned of their Catholic faith, he wrote, they might "become the most faithful and useful set of men in this American empire." Murray's replacement, Guy Carleton, was even more accommodating. Although no more sympathetic to Catholicism than his predecessor, he regarded the colonists below the St. Lawrence as a contentious lot and suspected that the time would not be far off when London might need to arm its new holdings against Massachusetts. In 1766, without notifying Parliament, Carleton quietly allowed Quebec a Roman Catholic bishop, provided the majority faith promised religious toleration for the Protestant English emigrants already flooding into the colony. Equally vital were steps taken to integrate Canada's economic activities into Britain's Atlantic empire. Now British merchants, in the patterns of the French trappers and businessmen who had preceded them, insinuated themselves into alliances with local Indians as well as the major long-distance staple trades of fish and furs.

The handful of British merchants arriving in Quebec were only part of a flood of emigrants who sailed west after 1763, when the peace treaty at least made the high seas safer for passenger vessels. In the twelve years following the Treaty of Paris, 125,000 people departed the British Isles, many of whom settled outside previously settled areas. Nearly 11,000 German-speaking emigrants arrived from war-torn Europe, slavers brought 84,000 more Africans into the English mainland colonies, and another 33,000 Europeans settled in the Caribbean. So many farmers fled Britain that British landlords, vexed to see their tenants quit the estates, unsuccessfully lobbied Parliament to place limits on emigration. Put another way, nearly 10 percent of British North America's inhabitants in 1775 had arrived in the previous fifteen years. As always, the migration of Africans dwarfed the movement of Europeans, and, as always, the main destination of the former was the sugar colonies. In the years between 1751 and 1775, 634,950 captives were transported to the British Caribbean.

This rising tide of emigration had two consequences—one unexpected, the other more predictable—that shaped subsequent events. First, these new settlers tended to avoid the oldest mainland colonies, precisely the areas in which war-born animosities between Britons and colonials still rankled. During the late 1750s, British officers, many of them born into the gentry, made no secret of their disdain for American-born soldiers. Wolfe described them as "the dirtiest, most contemptible, cowardly dogs"; colonial veterans responded with the epithet "lobsterback." In Massachusetts, which had lost 1,700 young men to the war, anger dissipated slowly after 1763, if at all. The result is that most of the recent settlers, who had arrived in the Americas only after the fall of Quebec, were newcomers to this enmity, and it proved no accident that those colonies that received migrants at the highest rate were those least likely to agitate for independence after 1775. Especially in British Florida, where emigrants replaced the Spanish colonists who had relocated to Cuba—although offered the opportunity to remain in Florida, few were interested— or in Nova Scotia, whose population doubled by the mid-1770s, Loyalist sentiments ran high.

But the attachment of these older regions to the British Empire derived from more than the presence of newcomers. Economic orientation shaped relations to metropolitan culture as well. There were relatively few colonies from which the British derived considerable wealth: the sugar islands, the fisheries of Newfoundland, and the trading posts of Hudson Bay. In all of these colonies, there emerged a wealthy commercial elite that maintained close ties to Britain. In the case of the sugar colonies, the wealthiest planters were absentees, living in England. Joining the commercial elite in these places were imperial officials, and these colonies were likewise supported by garrisons, especially in the West Indies. The importance of the trades they fostered and the necessity of maritime conveyance and communication linked these regions tightly to Britain. They shared other important demographic features, including racially unbalanced populations, which made these regions resemble colonial settlements in Central and South America more fully than neighboring regions of New England and the Mid-Atlantic, and a dependence on European migration, with Africans the main resident population.

The thousands of migrants who poured into British America, and especially into Britain's newest holdings, also led to renewed conflict with indigenous people. At the onset of fighting between Britain and France, British diplomats made concerted efforts to woo the allegiance of tribes in the Ohio Valley. Aware that most of these tribes sided with their enemy, Parliament concluded that their policies should imitate those of the French. The king's new superintendent to the northern Indians, William Johnson, promised to remedy "monstrous Frauds and Abuses" and force Pennsylvanians to renounce the purchase of western lands they had made from the Iroquois in 1754. Johnson, himself an immigrant from Ireland who had carved an estate out of Mohawk land, even urged Parliament in 1758 to establish the "clear and fixed Boundaries between our Settlements and their Hunting Grounds."

As the war began to turn against the French, however, the tribes reassessed their own situations. Most embraced the position of the Delaware, who insisted that peace would only come when both European nations withdrew their soldiers and settlers from the Ohio Valley. Having never recognized the French as their overlords, they refused to agree to end hostilities merely because the British had replaced the French as the new power in the west. "Why don't you and the French fight in the old Country, and on the Sea," one Delaware asked. "Why do you come to fight on our Land?" Looking east from their territory, it was easy for Indians to conclude that the Europeans fought only for the right to steal their land.

When it became clear that Johnson could not make good on his promises, most western tribes realized that their war was far from over. During the spring of 1763, even as the Peace of Paris was being ratified in London and Paris, the Seneca sent out two red wampum war belts; one passed among the Shawnee and the Delaware of the Ohio, while the other was carried to the Detroit Indians. In May, the tribes simultaneously attacked British forts on the frontier, destroying Venango, Le Boeuf, and Presqu'isle. At Devil's Hole, just above Fort Niagara, five hundred Seneca surprised seventy-four English soldiers, only two of whom made it to the fort alive. But the confederacy ultimately failed to capture the forts at Pitt and Detroit, and reinforcements eventually arrived at Niagara. As Indian food supplies ran low, and as French hints of assistance failed to materialize—instead, French soldiers began preparations to turn New Orleans over to the Spanish—most of the tribes sought out Johnson and sued for peace.

Even before the assault, Parliament had planned to institute a policy they hoped would pacify their new holdings by containing European settlement. Historians tend to regard the Royal Proclamation of 1763, which drew a line along the Appalachian crest and set aside the lands west of that division as "Indian Country," a policy uniquely designed to address relations with Indians on the frontier. Paired as it was, however, with London's Canadian proclamation, which allowed French civil law in the Province of Quebec, the Proclamation of 1763 may be seen as part of a larger policy of pacification. The edict required specific authorization by Parliament for any further purchase of protected Indian territory, a stipulation that encouraged the tribes to lay down their muskets. But to the extent that it infuriated wealthy colonial speculators like Washington and his fellow investors in the Ohio Company, the Proclamation Line resolved one conflict even as it laid the basis for another.

The encroachment of colonial Europeans west was inexorable. In the same fifteen-year period after 1760, at least 2,000 settlers passed every year into Virginia's Shenandoah Valley. Blithely ignoring the Proclamation Line of 1763, farmers shoved the frontier westward, and with it, an expanded series of roads and general stores that tied the upcountry to the coastal plain in a network of internal trade. As Eric Hinderaker aptly noted, even the powerful British empire after 1763 was more the "creation of the people immediately engaged in colonization," or of those trying to repel it, "than of policy directives originating in London." The same could be said of Spanish, Portuguese, and French Atlantic colonization; the crown came in after the fact. So if 1763 marked a lull in the fighting in Europe, renewed emigration to the Americas merely increased the tensions that had existed along the frontier since Washington's excursion west in 1753.

British Imperial Reform and Anglo-American Political Culture

Efforts to curtail settlement and regulate new Canadian holdings were part of a larger strategy of imperial reform. Because Pitt had borrowed his way into victory, Britain now faced a staggering debt whose interest alone equaled roughly half of the government's entire peacetime budget. By the eighteenth century, politicians in Britain associated commercial power with geopolitical power, and thus expected that any economic weakness would cripple the kingdom's status. The British population was heavily burdened with taxes already, and so officials looked to North America for new sources of revenue. Faced with a much larger territory to govern in North America in the wake of the war, Britain tried to tighten metropolitan control in the style that had proved effective in the important staple regions of the West Indies, Hudson Bay, and Newfoundland. The viability of these territories hinged on naval power (to secure the seas) and garrisons (to monitor significant ports and passages). Halifax provided a prime base for the army and navy alike, while Quebec gave Britain an already-garrisoned town. But most of the mainland colonies were unaccustomed to this kind of intervention.

Compounding the problem for Britain was that existing taxes in the Americas were collected in such a haphazard fashion that the government was losing money on the effort. According to Prime Minister George Grenville's bookkeepers, the Molasses Act of 1733, which had set a duty of six pence per gallon, was controlled so inefficiently and ignored so widely that it cost Britain £8,000 to collect £2,000 in taxes. It was with this in mind that, within months of the Peace of Paris, Parliament passed the Sugar Act of 1764. Although the law reduced by half the duty on molasses, it required colonial shippers to file a new written log each time goods were loaded aboard a ship. Since Parliament correctly assumed that most merchants were seasoned smugglers, the act also mandated that shippers accused of violating the law be tried in a vice admiralty court in Halifax, Nova Scotia, where the burden of proof lay with the defendant and an appointed judge, rather than a friendly local jury, would hand down the verdict. To ensure that crown prosecutors were immune from damage suits, the act encouraged the judges to certify that "probable cause" for seizure had existed, even in cases in which a merchant won acquittal.

The problem became one of enforcement. The government could not enforce any measure without sufficient military power on the ground. With the Proclamation Line of 1763 enforced by soldiers, and the Sugar Act ably enforced by the navy, these two measures proved to be the most effective reforms the British government passed in this period. In contrast, the Stamp Act was not so easily enforced, and proved a dismal failure. This act required tax collection in major commercial centers, cities such as Philadelphia, New York, Charles Town, and Boston, none of which had significant garrisons in place (New York had one company in residence).

Popular opposition to these taxes was spontaneous, concerted, and violent, and tapped into concerns about liberty already pervasive in Anglo-American political culture. The case of the English journalist and politician John Wilkes illustrates the transatlantic context of political engagement and protest. An admittedly ugly man of enormous charm and wit—he regarded his powers of persuasion so highly that, he once remarked, it took him "only half an hour to talk away his face"—Wilkes assaulted king and cabinet in his newspaper, the *North Briton*, in 1763. Having all but called King George a liar in a speech before Parliament, Wilkes was arrested under a general warrant for seditious libel and clapped in the Tower of London. Released a week later, Wilkes fled to France and Italy; while he was abroad, the Court of King's Bench expelled him from Parliament and declared him an outlaw. Upon returning to England, Wilkes was incarcerated near St. George's Fields, where he was to serve two years for his alleged crimes. The government further damaged its reputation by shooting demonstrators who approached the prison in hopes of catching a glimpse of "the Patriot." With support from London radicals, Wilkes ran again for Parliament and was elected from his cell.

Following this story from British America were those who feared that the use of general warrants or seizure of personal papers might endanger their economic well being, which often meant their liberty to avoid English trade regulations. Toasts to "Wilkes and Liberty" echoed from Boston to Charles Town; in Massachusetts, an artisan named Nathaniel Barber was just one of many to name his son Wilkes. Wilkes-Barre, Pennsylvania, and Wilkesboro, North Carolina, also honor the great advocate of liberty. Planters from Virginia to Jamaica peppered the prisoner with gifts and letters and visits, for Wilkes appeared to champion both greater liberties and peaceful resistance to tyranny. When a crowd of protesters approached his cell wall with picks and axes, Wilkes leaned through the window and urged them to disperse. For nervous merchants who wished to achieve greater autonomy within the empire yet avoid further mob action, a popular leader who implored his followers "not to commit any violence" was a leader worth emulating.

Middle-class artisans, however, had another view of Wilkes, and they soon had an opportunity to show it. Despite the popular opposition to his policies on both sides of the Atlantic, Grenville pushed ahead with financial plans by announcing his intention to extend to the mainland and Caribbean colonies the same stamp revenue already paid by subjects on the home island. To appease the colonists, Grenville offered to grant the Americans one year either to tax themselves or propose alternatives. When the colonies offered no substitute, Grenville pronounced the Stamp Act in effect as of November 1765. The law required purchase of revenue stamps for every legal document, college diploma, pamphlet, newspaper (and advertisements in them), and almanac, as well as—clearly Grenville knew the Americans too well—liquor licenses, playing cards, and pairs of dice. (Spain had implemented similar "vice" taxes in its American colonies in the sixteenth century, and they remained a chronic source of discontent in the eighteenth).

Games of chance aside, the law fell hardest on the wealthiest and most influential elements of American society, but it was obnoxious to all. English ideas about property and the rights people held in land required men to go to court regularly to file deeds and wills: each such document required a stamp, bringing the lowliest farmer into contact with the policy. One prosperous Maryland attorney, Daniel Dulany, penned an influential treatise, *Considerations of the Propriety of Imposing Taxes*, asserting that since colonial assemblies formed separate political societies, a distant Parliament had no theoretical right to tax Americans. But the "lesser sort," from shopkeepers to artisans to

sailors, had no intention of paying another tax they could ill afford, especially given the economic dislocation that followed the end of the French and
Indian War. The ports that had bustled with the activity of war plunged into
depression afterward, and taxes had to be paid in hard currency, which many
lacked. Even before the new law took effect, Boston crowds had taken to the
streets. The stamp distributor Andrew Oliver, a wealthy merchant and brother-
in-law to Lieutenant Governor Thomas Hutchinson, awoke one morning to
find his effigy swinging from a large elm. When the sheriff attempted to cut it
down, a mob not only kept the effigy in place but leveled Oliver's new brick
office for good measure.

The working poor, of course, required no pamphleteer to remind them
of their distress. In late August, a Boston crowd composed of men and women
stormed Hutchinson's elegant home. As his family fled through the back door,
the mob chopped in the front door with axes then proceeded to dismantle
the interior and drink the contents of the lieutenant governor's well-stocked
wine cellar. The crowd left the shell standing, as a visible monument to their
determination. To the south, in Wilmington, North Carolina, a "furious Mobb
of Sailors &c." forced a stamp distributor to resign by threatening to do his
home a similar damage. As news of these small victories spread, mobs in
Antigua and St. Kitts "behaved like young Lions" and mobilized against the
Stamp Act. By the last days of 1765, stamp distributors from Nevis to Halifax
had either fled or quit their office, making it virtually impossible for London
to collect the tax. Colonial resistance succeeded in British North America, as
it had so often in Latin America

Faced with a threat of a colonial boycott, not to mention the virtual
nullification of the law at the hands of urban mobs, Parliament ignored
Grenville's plea to use the British army to collect the tax and instead repealed
it in March 1766. "Both England and America [are] governed by the mob,"
was Grenville's churlish rejoinder when told he was being replaced by the
inexperienced Charles Watson-Wentworth, the Second Marquis of Rocking-
ham. Americans celebrated, but the cheers came too soon. Far from giving
way on its right to control its empire, Parliament had simply beat an expedi-
ent retreat on this lone issue. As an act of bravado and stern warning to the
wayward colonists, on the same day that Parliament repealed the Stamp Act it
passed the Declaratory Act, which reasserted the government's right to legis-
late in behalf of the "subjects of the crown of Great Britain, in all cases whatsoever." Even William Pitt, who had favored repeal of the stamp duty, agreed
that "the authority of this kingdom over the colonies [was] sovereign and
supreme." The colonists could not say they had not been warned.

Although a brief interlude of peace followed the repeal of the Stamp Act,
two interlocking problems remained. Thanks to high interest rates, the debt
Great Britain carried continued to mushroom, and political instability in London inhibited any creative solution. Amid the turmoil, the Chancellor of the
Exchequer Charles Townshend proposed new import duties on a number of
commodities, including lead, glass, paint, and tea. Having carefully read Patrick
Henry's *Virginia Resolutions*, which denied Parliament the power to pass an
internal tax, Townshend hastened to assure the colonies that these 1767 mea-

When Does a War Begin?

Instructors often teach students of history to think in terms of precise dates. But as important as chronology often is in understanding the past, how do we explain larger trends that are so amorphous that they have no clear beginning or end? When, for example, did the American Revolution begin? For the British, the exact moment may have been August 23, 1775, when King George III and his Parliament declared the thirteen colonies to be in open rebellion. Yet the king's soldiers had already died at Lexington and Concord, and at Breed's Hill. Certainly those young men, as well as their families across the Atlantic, understood that war was on. In the same way, the Massachusetts militiamen who fought in those skirmishes believed themselves to be at war, but the Continental Congress had yet to adopt a "Declaration of the Causes and Necessities of Taking up Arms." Not until June 7, 1776, did Richard Henry Lee introduce into Congress a resolution for independence, debate over which consumed almost another full month.

Nor did all Americans perceive war to be necessary at the same moment. Wealthy Americans, justifiably nervous about confronting the military might of Great Britain, drafted the Olive Branch Petition at late as July 8, 1775, in hopes of reconciliation. Yet the five men shot in the so-called Boston Massacre of 1770, all of whom hailed from an economically and socially less powerful class, understood that Britain's imperial policies threatened their political liberties and monetary livelihood. As the mother of Samuel Maverick, a seventeen-year-old apprentice carpenter, gazed at the shattered body of her son, she may be forgiven for thinking that war was on.

Even participants in the event were hazy as to timing. "What do we mean by Revolution," John Adams famously wondered in later years. "The war? That was no part of the revolution. It was only the effect and consequence of it. The revolution was in the minds of the people, and this was effected from 1760 to 1775. In the course of 15 years this happened before a single drop of blood was shed at Lexington."

A sensationalized portrayal of "The Bloody Massacre perpetrated in King Street Boston on March 5th 1770," etching by Paul Revere. Signaled by Captain Thos. Preston, British soldiers fire on colonists. Behind the troops is a row of buildings including the Royal Custom House, bearing the sign "Butcher's Hall" (a sardonic comment). Also listed are the "unhappy Sufferers" Saml Gray, Saml Maverick, James Caldwell, Crispus Attucks, and Patrick Carr (killed) and it is noted that there were "Six wounded; two of them (Christr Monk & John Clark) Mortally." Library of Congress, Prints and Photographs Division. LC-USZ62-35522.

sures were imperial regulations only. But the subterfuge failed. In Philadelphia, the attorney John Dickinson, a correspondent of John Wilkes, responded with a series of essays, *Letters from a Farmer in Pennsylvania*, which scores of colonial newspapers reprinted. In them, Dickinson conceded that Parliament, as the center of an imperial web, enjoyed the right to impose tariffs on foreign products. But as Townshend's intent was to raise revenue in America, the minister's emphasis on an "external" tax was a distinction without a difference. Worse yet, some of the funds would pay the salaries of colonial officials, effectively destroying the one weapon colonial assemblies held over royal administrators in the Americas.

Once again, merchants responded with nonimportation agreements, celebrating their conviction with homespun and austerity. And once again, those who worked with their hands refused to follow the peaceful lead of those who worked with their ledgers. As growing numbers of soldiers filtered into coastal cities, local resentment at British authority grew. Especially contentious was the habit of British soldiers, themselves members of the working class who had been pressed into service, of accepting small jobs when off duty. In the early spring of 1770, one such soldier approached a group of rope makers in Boston. When told by the master that he might "clean the shithouse" if he wished, he left. Two days of street action culminated in events on March 5, in which a mob gathered at the Customs House and began to pelt a captain and eight soldiers with rocks and ice. Without warning, the terrified soldiers opened fire, killing five and wounding six more, two of whom died later. Known to colonists as the "Boston Massacre," the disorder ended only when now-Governor Hutchinson (he had been promoted recently) placated the crowd by moving troops out of the city and placing the soldiers in question under arrest. But for the "motley rabble of saucy boys, Negroes and molattoes, Irish teagues, and out landish Jack Tars"—to borrow John Adams's dismissive term for those shot down in the street—the American Revolution was on.

And yet, if the war was on for these Boston rioters, it was not underway for the majority of colonists. For several more years, colonists rose up in sporadic resistance to any perceived imperial intrusion. In the wake of the Tea Act (which actually lowered taxes on tea but which nonetheless offended the constitutional sensibilities of some) a tea ship mysteriously caught fire in Annapolis, Maryland, as did a New Jersey warehouse stuffed with tea. In Boston, Hutchinson had grown weary of the radicals' power, and in any case his two sons and a nephew were tea consignees who stood to lose money if tea was not landed and taxed. In hopes of forcing the governor to back down, brewer Samuel Adams called an extralegal town meeting, which 5,000 people —one-third of all Bostonians—attended. Still, Hutchinson refused. On the night of December 16, 1773, fifty men, wearing soot-blackened faces and blankets—either to resemble Indians to emphasize their Americanness or because they were inebriated, depending on whom one listened to—boarded the *Dartmouth* and two other tea ships docked in Boston harbor. While as many as eight thousand Bostonians shouted encouragement from the docks, the group chopped open 342 chests of tea and dumped the contents into the water. To demonstrate their respect for legitimate property, one raiding locksmith patiently repaired each broken lock after the tea had been dumped overboard. Estimated losses ranged from £9,000 to £18,000. Some 90,000 pounds of tea were dumped; the harbor's water remained brown and coated with tea for days, and bits of crate were found as far away as Dorchester.

The arsons, the destruction of taxable property, and the nearly fatal beating of a customs official in Maine all brought George III around to his minister's view that it was time to demonstrate his government's "authority in that country." When word of the Tea Party reached London in January 1774, Parliament responded with four Coercive Acts. Dubbed the Intolerable Acts by Massachusetts radicals, the laws included a new Quartering Act; a Justice Act, which removed the trial of a British official or soldier—such as those involved in the Boston Massacre—to Canada or even to Britain; and the Boston Port Act, which closed the harbor to trade until the East India Company was compensated for its losses. Most odious of all, the Massachusetts Government Act altered the colonial charter of 1691 to ban town meetings without the written approval of the governor. The law also mandated that the king choose the colonial Council (the upper house), rather than its members being elected by the lower house. Whereas earlier legislation had intended to pay off the war debt, the four new acts were designed to punish Massachusetts and restore imperial controls.

If the crown had devised the acts to isolate Massachusetts, they had the opposite effect. Merchants down the coast who had little use for Bostonians' tradition of street action saw in the government's behavior threats to their own rights. As if working to precipitate a crisis, his majesty's governors in other colonies unknowingly helped to support the view that Britain was conspiring to destroy American liberties. In Williamsburg, Governor John Murray, the Earl of Dunmore, dissolved the House of Burgesses for recommending a penitent day of fasting and reflection. Happier always to meet where rum flowed, the radicalized delegates simply adjourned to the Raleigh Tavern, where they agreed to a circular letter calling for an all-colonial conference. At the same time, the extralegal Massachusetts Provincial Congress issued a similar call for a meeting in Philadelphia.

This First Continental Congress, which began deliberations on September 5 in Carpenters' Hall, is often depicted as a major step toward imperial separation. For the few in attendance in 1774, however, that was far from clear. Samuel Adams, who in the Boston Tea Party had finally found a riot to his liking, represented the radical wing of the revolutionary movement, as did South Carolina's Christopher Gadsden. Like the Virginia delegates, Gadsden brought domestic slaves with him to Philadelphia—George Washington arrived with his personal slave, William Lee—a reminder that American cries of liberty were often more rhetorical than real. Attendees John Jay and John Dickinson, despite the earlier writing of the latter, denounced ideas of independence and instead advocated a policy of economic coercion to restore the old colonial patterns. Worse yet, despite Virginians' talk of solidarity among "sister colonies," distant Georgia sent no delegates. The 1774 Quebec Act had pacified French-speaking Catholics in the northern colonies, and as historian Michael Hart observes, Canada's newer residents simply lacked grievances "on the scale of that of the thirteen colonies" to their south.

Although the Jamaican assembly denounced the Coercive Acts, no Caribbean delegate came to Philadelphia. The threat of economic warfare terrified Jamaica's planters with thoughts of famine and slave unrest. West Indies planters, moreover, had their own direct access to lawmakers in London. Many of them, as mentioned, were absentees living in London, Bath, and Bristol, and a number of them held titles of nobility: there were 19 baronetcies in the West Indies, but only 3 in the 13 colonies. They also had their own agents (or lobbyists), and while changes in the British government left mainland colonists with their strongest ties to opposition leaders, West Indian planters maintained their connections to those who held power. Lord North, who served as prime minister during the revolutionary period, claimed of these West Indies planters "that they were the only masters he ever had." Planters themselves participated directly in British politics. In 1781, the agent for Jamaica claimed that 48 Members of the House of Commons had West Indies interests. These men had no need to make their way from the Caribbean or Britain in order to attend a meeting with their less-affluent and less-powerful counterparts in Philadelphia. In the end, the fifty-one men who met at Carpenters' Hall neither advocated independence nor even suggested a republican restructuring of their colonial assemblies.

The outbreak of fighting in Massachusetts in the spring of 1775 transformed the tone of debate in Philadelphia when the Second Continental Congress met on May 10. Now, radicals like Samuel Adams, driven by the will of their artisan constituents, were especially ready for hostilities, as was the young Virginian Thomas Jefferson, a new face in the Congress. "A frenzy of revenge," he observed, "seems to have seized all ranks of people." As colonial assemblies voted to transfer allegiance from their royal governors to the extralegal Continental Congress, delegates prepared to supplement the New England militias with six musket companies from the southern colonies. Having taken that step, Congress sent emissaries northward, hoping to convince "the oppressed inhabitants of Canada," to join in the struggle for "common liberty." The Canadians declined.

The War Widens

Far to the south, white residents of Britain's Caribbean colonies proved more sympathetic to the rebels, if not ultimately willing to pick up a musket. By the summer of 1775, as many as one-third of the roughly 13,000 whites in Jamaica favored the American cause, and in St. Kitts, toasts were raised to "Washington, [Arthur] Lee, and Independency to America." A small delegation from the Atlantic island of Bermuda even defied the Royal Navy and landed in Philadelphia, but such expressions of empathy had more to do with a desire to keep trade flowing than with any desire to join the revolutionary fray. As had been the case during the previous decade, Caribbean planters feared that chaos on the mainland, together with cession of the trade in foodstuffs, might lead to massive slave revolt in the islands. When black drivers on two estates in Hanover Parish, Jamaica, attempted just that, a conservative backlash to American chants of liberty quickly sprouted. Jamaica's creole slaves, according to the governor, "never were before engaged in Rebellion." Although such

confidence in contented slaves was a complete fiction, it was politically useful in the slave societies of the sugar islands. More realistic was the assembly's
fear that a withdrawal of British soldiers from the Caribbean to the mainland
was the opportunity upon which Jamaican slaves had "placed their strongest
hopes."

While their mainland counterparts chafed at the stepped-up presence of
British soldiers, West Indian planters delighted in the security they offered,
not only against foreign invasion but especially against the chronic threat
posed by slaves and maroons. They welcomed the garrisons, and requested
more, not *fewer*, troops. In 1770, the year of the Boston "massacre" which
sparked such outrage in Massachusetts, the St. Kitts assembly pleaded for 200
more troops, and three years later (in the memorable year of the continental
tea parties), the Jamaica assembly sought more troops to protect them from
the peril of "massacre and desolation from an internal Enemy."

Caribbean masters were right to be concerned. British critics of North
America's rebel elite were hardly alone in noticing that the vast majority of
them owned slaves. "How is it," wondered Samuel Johnson, the most celebrated writer in London, "that we hear the loudest yelps for liberty among
the drivers of Negroes?" In Williamsburg, Governor Dunmore put Johnson's
query to the test on November 7, 1775, when he announced the freedom of
any enslaved or indentured worker held by a rebel master. Among those who
made it to Dunmore's flotilla in the James River was young Ralph Henry, who
freed himself from slavery in the service of none other than Patrick Henry.
Other self-liberators included Ralph Reid and his sixteen-year-old wife; Ralph
Henry and James Reid served in the Royal Artillery, and Reid later became a
leader in the British colony of Sierra Leone. Word of the black regiment even
filtered across the Delaware River into New Jersey, where one Titus threw
down his hoe and headed for Virginia. By the time he approached Dunmore's
ships he had changed his name to Colonel Tye and announced himself a
"warrior" in the British forces.

Although the number of slaves who reached Dunmore by the end of
1775 may have numbered no more than three hundred—and revolutionary
forces at the Battle of Great Bridge promptly routed the irregular regiment of
black Loyalists in December—the psychological impact on both whites and
blacks was enormous. For Tidewater planters already concerned about the
prospect of the British navy shelling their estates, the prospect of also fighting
an internal enemy—who had access to them and every reason to hate them—
was particularly terrifying. For enslaved Virginians, the possibility of sudden
freedom prompted many of them to drop the mask of servility. So a
Williamsburg gentlewoman discovered when she berated a black man for
failing to yield the sidewalk and forcing her to step into the muddy street.
"Stay, you d[amne]d white bitch," he snapped, "till Lord Dunmore and his
black regiment come, and then we will see who is to take the wall."

The loss at Great Bridge meant that Dunmore's threat to "declare Freedom to the Slaves and reduce the City of Williamsburg to Ashes" came to
nothing. Dunmore and his followers soon abandoned Virginia for New York
City, which for most of the war remained the British headquarters in North
America. From there, the black Loyalists conducted raids into the country-

side, as well as across the river into New Jersey. The most successful ventures were led by guerilla leader, Tye, who in one extraordinary day captured eight militiamen, burned their barns and looted their farms, and dragged his captives and a handful of liberated slaves back into New York. Tye continued to harass revolutionary forces until taking a bullet in his wrist during a 1780 battle and dying of gangrene, although not before his men lynched his prize captive, Captain Josiah Huddy, infamous for his summary execution of Loyalists.

Declaring Independence and Building Republics

After eleven years of violent and passive resistance to British reforms and taxes, and after fourteen months of concerted fighting on colonial battlefields, thirteen mainland colonies did what no other imperial protesters in the western Atlantic had done before: they rejected the sovereignty of the king, they spurned imperial governance, and they declared independence. They did so in a document, signed in July of 1776 by members of the Continental Congress, which enumerated their perceived injuries at the hands of the king. In retrospect, the Declaration of Independence reads like an expression of collective madness and paranoia, with its litany of injuries and injustices, accusing the king of offenses such as inflicting the institution of slavery on the colonists, of fomenting civil war, of encouraging "the merciless Indian Savages" to attack colonial settlements. Yet it also articulated a specific political and ideological worldview. It asserted rights to self-government and the rule of law, both entirely consistent with the republican Anglo-American culture that produced it. And it also professed a universal doctrine of "unalienable" rights, one that transcended any particular place, any particular imperial unit, and based on the "Laws of Nature." It espoused glorious ideals of equality, of rights guaranteed to all men, and of the right of a people to reject a government that deprived them of those rights.

The Declaration owed much to radical politics in Britain and especially to Thomas Paine, a recent immigrant who had settled in Philadelphia in 1774. He embraced the urban political culture there, particularly the growing power of the city's artisans, many of whom became involved in politics for the first time through the boycotts, committees, and militia and crowd actions. Paine wrote *Common Sense*, a pamphlet that became a bestseller soon after its anonymous publication in January of 1776. Within three months, 100,000 copies were in circulation, and *Common Sense* went into twenty-five editions. Paine had the ability to put into clear, succinct prose sentiments that many Americans had been unable to articulate, and he persuaded many fence-sitters to embrace the cause of independence. Paine's argument was simple and direct. First, he attacked the English constitution, so revered by colonists, and all aristocratic institutions. Among these institutions was monarchy, which he loathed. He compiled evidence to show the power of the colonies and their ability to function independently of Britain. This was a universal, not particular cause. As Paine memorably put it, "The cause of America is in a great measure the cause of all mankind."

The political ideas within the Declaration of Independence called for a certain kind of government, one that created a model for the independence

Priscilla Mason's Address

In 1793, Priscilla Mason delivered the salutatory oration at the Young Ladies Academy of Philadelphia. This institution was established in the wake of the War for Independence by some of the city's most ardent revolutionaries. Mason wrestled in her address with the place of educated women within a republic. In a political system that called for the active engagement of all men, where, she asked, did women belong? She asserted that women's abilities were equal to those of men, and condemned those political rulers who first arbitrarily denied women access to education and then criticized them for being insufficiently educated. Assessing the changed world around her, Mason praised the opportunities then becoming available to women, but where, she asked, might women display the skills they had come to possess? "Man, despotic man," barred women from positions in the church, the government, or the legal profession, which she astutely recognized as the main avenues to power and prestige in her world. Mason's solution to this terrible predicament and injustice was deeply embedded in the political culture of the world around her. Like all good republicans of the period, including men who posed for portraits and sculptures donned in togas and designed public buildings in the architectural style of ancient Greece and Rome, Mason proposed a senate of women, such as the Roman emperor Heliogabalus had created. This senate would occupy itself with another crucial issue for the new nation: cultural independence. Almost all of American material and literary culture—books, culture, dress, housewares—derived from European models. How could the nation be independent if the arbiters of fashion lay in Europe? So Mason suggested that the Senate of Women take responsibility for an independent American fashion (of manners, behavior, ideas, education). This goal might seem modest and even silly to modern readers, but it reflected contemporary concerns about creating a new American culture, a preoccupation Noah Webster acted on in his dictionary and spelling book. Unlike Webster's innovative speller, however, Mason's belief that the Fashion Senate would be a proving ground for women who would then go on to "equal participation of honor and office" proved precocious.

Students of the Moravian Female Seminary in Bethlehem, ca. 1800. Seated in front of a stage, students await their Christmas pageant in this very rare interior depiction of the Seminary, which was comparable to the secular Young Ladies Academy of Philadelphia. Furniture, a tile stove, lamps, and the distinctive dress of academy girls of the period are shown. The drawing is attributed to Anna Rosina Kliest, a teacher at the school. The Moravian Archives, Bethlehem, PA.

movements in other parts of the Americas that followed. The new American states formed republics, thirteen of them, with each state creating its own model. While they varied in the amount of power afforded different constituent bodies, there were certain common features. All contained at least one representative body. All contained some sort of executive power, although this power might be very circumscribed. At its base, the republican form of government forged in America gave sovereignty to people, particularly men who held property of some sort (land or taxable wealth) that enabled them to be independent. *Independence* had a very special meaning in this context. Ideal republicans were selfless men who sacrificed their own good for that of the whole, always submerging self to public interest. Virtue was paramount. Citizenship was hard work and required those bestowed it to be educated, politically involved, always attentive to the malfeasance of unchecked power, and deeply engaged in the political process. In short, these republicans saw history as the constant struggle between power and liberty.

Republican imperatives sparked a range of social changes. New educational bodies—both academies and colleges—emerged in the wake of this new political sensibility. Educational opportunities expanded for girls on both sides of the Atlantic. In France, Olympe de Gouges, despite being a butcher's daughter, received an education that just a few years earlier would have been reserved for elite males, as did another future feminist author, Mary Wollstonecraft, the daughter of a failed British gentleman farmer. People at the time had difficulty imagining women acting with the independence political activity required—everything in English legal and social systems undermined the idea that women could act independently. Nonetheless, educated women enabled good republicans to create households of virtue, ones in which sons could be raised to assume the political responsibilities republics required.

As the hierarchical assumptions that had upheld monarchical rule were replaced with more egalitarian theories, the appropriation by one person of the body and labor of another person ran contrary to the view that just societies were based on the consent of the governed. As historian Rhys Isaac bluntly put it, virtually overnight for those who held human property "slavery became a problem." Unhappily, the ability of humans to live with their inconsistencies is legendary, and while slave-based states like Virginia passed legislation to allow for individual acts of manumission, planters like Jefferson were generally content to blame American slavery on the British crown. Only in those corners of the new republic where enslaved populations were small enough so that neither white paranoia nor property rights raised significant barriers were the egalitarian ideals of the Revolution actually put into practice. Vermont ratified a constitution in 1777 that read, "No male person ought to be holden by law to serve any person as a servant, slave, or apprentice after he arrives to the age of eighteen years." A Massachusetts court in 1783 ruled that the declaration in the state's constitution that "all men are born free and equal" applied, indeed, to all, and in the same year, New Hampshire's new constitution ended slavery in that state. The remaining northern states, beginning with Pennsylvania in 1780 and ending with New Jersey in 1804, passed laws abolishing slavery gradually, so gradually that the last slave in New Jersey was freed in 1865. In short, this was a great political and social experiment, but one with mixed results.

With their Declaration signed, white revolutionary leaders in Philadelphia gazed east across the Atlantic in search of foreign assistance. To lead its delegation seeking France's formal support, Congress had earlier dispatched to Paris seventy-year-old Benjamin Franklin, a man for whom the revolution was also a civil war: his son, William Franklin, was the governor of New Jersey and remained loyal to the crown. The two men remained estranged in the wake of this political division until their deaths. Leaving his wife and daughter, the elder Franklin set out for France, where he arrived on the coast in December 1776. Once on the continent, the popular Franklin, whose writings had already been translated into French, exchanged his powdered wig for a *Roussean* (Russian) fur cap. As the closest thing to a true American *philosophe*, a man with an international reputation for scientific experimentation, Franklin took Paris society by storm. But popularity in the salons did not translate into instant diplomatic success. Only with arrival of news that the British General John Burgoyne had been forced to surrender his entire force of 5,800 men to Horatio Gates and Benedict Arnold at Saratoga, New York, in early October 1777, was Franklin able to conclude a treaty with his hosts. Although the king remained concerned about entering into another conflict with Britain, the French foreign minister, the Comte de Vergennes, argued that the government had far more to fear from a Britain free to sail against the French Caribbean. Conversely, he reasoned, open support for American independence might not only win over the mainland's trade, but a French naval base in the southern colonies might permit France to move against the British sugar islands, the value of which would more than pay off any assistance to the Americans. Finally, Vergennes suggested that as another war with Britain was inevitable, it was far wiser to attack while the British army was preoccupied in the northern theater.

Unhappily for Vergennes, Louis XVI was not free to act. France's 1761 treaty with Bourbon Spain bound the governments to act in concert in matters of war. King Charles III, like the French monarch, sought revenge and hoped to recapture the Rock of Gibraltar, lost to Britain in 1704, but Spain saw little logic in assisting an aggressive republican nation that might either revolutionize its South American colonies and Caribbean holdings, or eventually invade westward into its largely undefended and thinly settled North American claims. Fearing that further delay would allow Britain to conciliate the Americans, Vergennes finally opted to ignore the 1761 agreement and signed two treaties with Franklin on February 6, 1778, one of commerce and one a permanent, defensive alliance that allowed for no separate peace with Britain. As expected, the treaties led to a British declaration of war against France four months later. Spain joined with France a year later. From the American perspective, the treaty contained two flaws: the Spanish Court declared itself only an ally of France and an enemy of Britain; the treaty was silent on American independence. Worse yet, the alliance called on France to fight until Gibraltar had been recaptured. Since the French had previously insisted that the American delegates make no separate peace, the latest treaty essentially obliged the colonies to fight on until the rock's recapture, even if their independence had already been assured.

At virtually the same moment that continental Europe began to unite against Britain, the tide began to turn as well on the North American mainland. American forces drove the British army out of Rhode Island, allowing the Comte de Rochambeau to land 5,000 French soldiers at Newport. Initially, General Rochambeau and General Washington planned to unite their forces against occupied New York City, but on August 14, 1781, word arrived that the French fleet, twenty-eight ships strong, was sailing for the Chesa-

The Great Smallpox Epidemic

The struggle by some North Americans for separation from Great Britain occurred during a smallpox epidemic that embraced the entire continent and killed at least 130,000 people. By comparison, the colonists endured only 25,000 deaths in the course of the American Revolution (many from smallpox). The epidemic began on the east coast and moved west along trade and communication routes, north from Mexico City, and southwest from Hudson Bay with missionaries, traders, hunters, refugees, and soldiers. Epidemics came regularly to North America, but this one hit in 1775, and thus became embedded in the colonial conflict. The British army had long-standing procedures for handling infected soldiers; the new American army under George Washington did not. Moreover, American-born soldiers (whichever side they fought for) had less exposure, and thus less immunity, to the disease than did European counterparts. So when the smallpox epidemic circulated, Washington sought to protect his troops from contamination, an ineffective and inefficient policy he finally abandoned in 1777 in favor of inoculation (a procedure in which live smallpox virus drawn from the pustules of sufferers was deliberately planted in a healthy person). Washington's commitment to inoculation saved his army to continue its fight. Others were not as fortunate, especially the militia and Loyalists (black and white), as the epidemic traveled south over the course of the conflict. Black slaves who fled to freedom in British alliance brought the disease with them. The British abandoned these men, finding them a hindrance in their poor health, and eyewitnesses reported the sight of dead bodies on the side of the road, "putrifying with the small pox." The war ended in 1783, and in the same decade the epidemic came to an end, leaving empty villages and piles of corpses in its wake. Native Americans were especially susceptible to the disease, and in the same way that smallpox shaped the pattern of conflict along the eastern seaboard, it dictated war and peace and new alliances in the rest of the continent.

Elizabeth A. Fenn, Pox Americana: The Great Smallpox Epidemic of 1775–82 (New York: Hill and Wang, 2001).

"Washington Taking Control of the American Army at Cambridge, Massachusetts, July 1775." Copy of a lithograph by Currier and Ives, 1876. Credit: National Archives and Records Administration.

peake under Admiral François Joseph de Grasse. Leaving but a skeleton force outside of New York as a decoy, Washington raced south in hopes of surrounding British general Charles Cornwallis at his camp at Yorktown.

From any perspective, the siege at Yorktown was hardly Britain's finest hour, but the army was plagued by disease. The British soldiers in the fort were sickened with malaria, an outbreak having visited the coastal regions of

the southeast—a recurring curse of the southern campaign to which American-born soldiers enjoyed a relative immunity. The black soldiers, meanwhile,
had contracted smallpox. As the garrison began to run short of provisions,
Cornwallis ordered the expulsion of the black soldiers and their dependents,
who had flocked to the British standard. "We had used them to good advantage," recorded one Hessian officer, "and set them free, and now, with fear
and trembling, they had to face the reward of their cruel masters." As his men
were slaughtered by the constant cannonade, Cornwallis retreated to the safety
of a dugout cave. By October 17, the English commander was ready to discuss
terms of surrender. At length, the ceremony was set for mid-afternoon, two
days hence. Since a petulant Cornwallis, claiming to be "indisposed," sent a
subordinate to tender his sword, Washington had a member of his staff accept it. As all 7,241 British soldiers moved forward to stack their weapons, an
English band, many of its members weeping, played the melancholy ballad
that George Washington had requested, "The World Turned Upside Down."

Loyalists: Red, White, and Black

Every war generates its refugees, and the American War for Independence produced several waves of them. These flows of people altered the social, demographic, economic, and political map of the British Atlantic world. The war
not only secured a new nation where previously thirteen separate colonies
existed, but those who fled it transformed British holdings in North America
and the Caribbean. Those exiles included free (black and white), enslaved,
and Native American allies of Great Britain. *Loyalism* is a broad term encompassing a range of people with diverse and often competing interests. In the
case of the American Revolution, Loyalists included those who professed an
attachment to their sovereign and a loathing of rebellion and treason as well
as men and women who found in the revolutionary upheaval a long-sought
opportunity for their own freedom through British alliance. Measured by their
share of white colonial populations, some colonies were Loyalist strongholds,
including Georgia, New York, and South Carolina, while in others (Virginia,
Maryland, and Delaware) Loyalists had a weaker presence. Massachusetts, a
bastion of revolutionary activity, was also a colony with a strong Loyalist presence. Conversely, colonies that remained loyal to the crown always contained
inhabitants whose sympathies lay with the revolutionaries.

Thousands of black Americans had run to British lines. Shortly after being notified of the preliminary peace treaty, Washington met with his latest
British counterpart, Sir Guy Carleton, in Orange Town, New York. The Virginian inquired about "obtaining the delivery of Negroes" as evidently required
by Article Seven of the Peace of Paris of 1783. Washington knew that British
forces evacuating the colonies had already carried away thousands of freed
people—as well as the slaves of Loyalists—with them. Embarkation lists from
Savannah for July and August 1782 show as many as six ships ferrying 1,568
blacks to Jamaica. By the following December, a slightly larger number of
Africans and their descendants were shipped to St. Augustine, Florida. In the
same month, the British evacuated Charleston, taking 5,327 blacks with them,
most destined also for Jamaica and Florida. Pressured by Washington, Carleton
now announced that he would return only those black refugees who had fled

to British lines since his recent arrival. The treaty, he insisted, did not cover freedmen promised their liberty by previous English officers. Carleton did agree, however, to provide Washington with a list of the 3,000 blacks who would soon embark for Nova Scotia, England, and several German kingdoms. Much to the Virginian's dismay, he noted the list included the name of forty-three-year-old Harry Washington, one of his own slaves who had fled Mount Vernon seven years ago.

Although Florida was temporarily "a commodious asylum" for white and black refugees, the agreement in Paris to return the peninsula to Spanish control meant that the Loyalists would have to move again if they wished to remain under British rule. The Spanish invited some, especially large planters, to stay, and many did. Approximately 10,000 emigrants, 6,540 of them black, sailed from St. Augustine in the summer of 1785; most of the blacks were slaves who were forced to relocate with their white masters. About half of that figure landed in Jamaica and the Bahamas. Most of the enslaved émigrés were sent into the fields, but a surprisingly large number, perhaps several thousand, became military slaves. Unable to spare soldiers for service in the Caribbean, where in any case the tropical climate amounted to a virtual death sentence for Englishmen, Britain had already experimented on a small scale with enslaved recruits. The Spanish and Portuguese were far ahead of the British in this regard: by the late eighteenth century they relied on thousands of free and enslaved militiamen of color from Buenos Aires to St. Augustine. But many of the refugees who landed in the British Caribbean after 1783 had already seen service on the mainland. On the advice of Archibald Campbell, governor of Jamaica and a veteran of the Seven Years' War and the Revolution, a battalion of "people of Color" was placed in defense of the island. Two hundred other recruits, mostly black South Carolinians, saw service in St. Lucia.

The three thousand freed blacks who sailed out of New York with Sir Guy Carleton fared little better. Most of these persons were field hands from the Chesapeake, but Britain settled them on rocky, thin soil in Nova Scotia. Unaccustomed to the harsh winters and hardly welcomed by the locals, the black Loyalists were soon reduced to working as sharecroppers on the farms of white Canadians. So many blacks gave up and sailed for England that by 1786 the government estimated twelve hundred impoverished African American refugees were begging in the streets of London. Yet another Atlantic migration, this one leading back to Africa, was soon in the works.

Alarmed by so many masterless people of color in their midst, the Lords of the Treasury endorsed a suggestion by the botanist Henry Smeathman that the black American refugees be transported to Sierra Leone, where they could build a settlement loyal to England. In the early summer of 1787, 377 settlers established Granville Town, named for the English abolitionist Granville Sharp, on the banks of the Sierra Leone River on the Guinea Coast. Within five years, more than a thousand more blacks arrived there from Nova Scotia. According to one account, one group of African American refugees waded ashore singing, "The day of jubilee is come, return ye ransomed sinners home." Africans saw the matter differently and regarded the settlers as invaders. The unhealthy tropical climate, together with persistent incursions by Africans and even an attack by a French naval squadron, devastated the settlement. Finally, in 1808, the British government would take over Sierra Leone and rule it as a crown colony.

If the decades of conflict translated into a difficult freedom and even a "return to Africa" for some African Americans, the removal of British and French forces from much of North America after 1783 threatened Indians' ability to protect their ancestral lands. For most North American tribes, the end of the Seven Years' War and the American War for Independence meant it was no longer possible to play one imperial power off another, a fact that precipitated a rapid decline in Indian autonomy. From the Abenakis of Canada to the Florida Seminoles, tribes pursued new strategies to maintain their independence. Those who resided on land abandoned by the British faced decades of combat with the victorious United States military.

Initially, most tribes were inclined to remain neutral in the American Revolution. The major combatants during the 1760s—the Iroquois, Delaware, and Shawnee—accepted the view of the Continental Congress that the war was a "family quarrel." As one Oneida lectured a British agent, "Let us Indians be of one mind, and live with one another and your white people settle your own disputes between yourselves." Ultimately, however, most tribes sided with Britain under the leadership of Mohawk warrior Thayendanegea, known to the English as Joseph Brant, and not merely because the invasion of Canada across Iroquois territory violated their understanding of neutrality. Since the United States was by definition a revolutionary nation fighting to overturn the status quo, its success inevitably spelled failure for Indian sovereignty. With the British defeated, the Proclamation Line would be erased, and members of Congress already spoke openly of selling off land between the Appalachians and the Mississippi River to defray defense expenditures and soldiers' salaries.

Although a handful of tribes remained neutral or fought on the American side—a reminder that for some tribes, as with white communities, the fighting was also a civil war—most Indians had little choice but to support the British. In retaliation, Congress ordered General John Sullivan into "the Heart of the Country of the six nations." Waging a sort of scorched-earth campaign, the army burned forty Iroquois towns, 160,000 bushels of corn, and "a vast quantity of vegetables of every kind." As some soldiers chopped down orchards, others desecrated burial grounds, in some cases skinning corpses for boots and razor strops. Even so, most tribes were still fighting when their British allies decided to cut their losses after Yorktown and transferred control of Indian lands they had never conquered to the newly formed United States. "We hope your [Indian] children will be remembered in the Treaty," one Wyandot urged a British soldier, but the agreement was silent concerning those in the west who continued to struggle for their independence.

Since the fledgling U.S. treasury was too depleted to finance a western assault in 1783, the second Peace of Paris brought a temporary lull in hostilities. But to borrow words from the historian Colin Calloway, the agreement that ended the war with Britain, France, and Spain was a "peace that brought

The Stockbridge Tribe

Most Indians sided with the British during the War for Independence, but there were a few exceptions, including the Oneida and Tuscarora. Among those groups who allied with the rebels were the Stockbridge Indians of Massachusetts. They were a composite tribe, one of many such groups configured out of the remnants of older entities, in this case formed from the Mahicans and Housatonics. They settled in Stockbridge, the last praying town to be established in the colony. Although it started as an Indian town, English settlers gradually encroached, owning land and holding offices alongside the Indian inhabitants. Even before war began, the Stockbridge Indians volunteered to serve in the militia. This pattern of service for the Americans continued throughout the war. They suffered especially hard losses at Kingsbridge in August of 1778, where an observer remarked on the hybrid nature of the fighters. They wore long white linen shirts, trousers, and moccasins; they fought with a musket and arrows and a battle-axe, and were adorned with jewelry and traditional hairstyles. At war's end, the Stockbridge soldiers found their tenure in Stockbridge weakened, as their land had been claimed by Anglo settlers. Displaced and cheated, the Stockbridge found haven with the Oneidas in New York, where they settled on a place they named New Stockbridge. From there, they continued to petition Congress for recognition of their military services and compensation for their losses. They received payment in 1795, but their struggles with the American nation were not over yet. Now their new land faced

continued pressure from acquisitive settlers, so the Stockbridges relocated west to Indiana in 1818, and finally to Wisconsin in 1822, where their reservation still exists. Apparently, the new United States had no room for its old allies, literally or metaphorically. The mixed world the Indians inhabited at Stockbridge before the war quickly gave way to separation and exile.

Stockbridge Indian, Drawing by Prussian officer Captain Johann Ewald, 1777. Captain Johann Ewald Diary, Volume II. Joseph P. Tustin Papers, Special Collections, Harvey A. Andruss Library, Bloomsburg, University of Pennsylvania.

no peace." Captain Pipe, a Delaware chief, anticipated British betrayal as early as 1781, so he told an English officer at Detroit. Captain Pipe suspected the British and French would make peace, even after they used the Indians as hunting dogs after their prey. If he looked back, he said, "I shall probably see my Father shaking hands with the Long Knives."

The ensuing decade saw regular conferences in which aggressive commissioners demanded lands from the Iroquois at Fort Stanwix in 1784, from the Delawares and Wyandots the following year at Fort McIntosh, and from the Shawnees at Fort Finney in 1786. During the early months of the Revolution, Congress had courted the Indians as if they were as sovereign a people as the Spanish, but during the 1780s negotiators adopted the blunt language of conquest. In the face of unrelenting pressure, some Indians followed other Loyalists and went into exile. Brant led his Mohawks into Ontario, where they built new communities on the Grand River. Traveling alongside Indian refugees was an even larger group of white Loyalists, known to the victors as *Tories*, the popular name for the conservative party in Britain. Along the North Atlantic coast, men and women had remained loyal to the crown for a variety of reasons. Some were wealthy social conservatives who had little use for egalitarian ideas of self-government. Others were Anglican clergymen or businessmen with ties to London merchants. Still others had more in common with the slaves who fled with Lord Dunmore, as they were impoverished minorities who had been persecuted by the lowcountry rebel elite, such as the Highland Scots of the Carolina backcountry. During the angriest days of the war, many states confiscated Loyalist property and doled it out to citizens deemed as deserving ; New York seized a home in New Rochelle and gave it to Tom Paine in payment for his rousing pamphlets and essays. In the uncertain months following war's end, a period the Loyalist David Colder characterized as "the most perplexing state of uncertainty," Loyalists in New York endured restrictions on their movement. In contrast to the safeguards provided by the treaty of 1783, local committees formed to monitor Loyalist movements. His nephew, like Colder included in an act of attainder that prevented his access to his estate, had gone to England. His niece fled with her husband and children to Nova Scotia. Another nephew had moved with his family to Quebec. Other family members were also in Canada or planning relocation in England. New York, Colder concluded was "a most horrid place to be in at present."

Sharing the sentiments of the Colder family, as many as 80,000 Loyalists fled the United States after 1783. Some, like Thomas Hutchinson of Massachusetts, sailed for England, but most found themselves in Canada or the Caribbean. The exodus of Loyalists into Canada had the result of altering, virtually overnight, the predominantly French and Catholic nature of the region. Some 40,000 to 50,000 Loyalists moved north to Canada, the majority of whom went to Nova Scotia. Their presence led to the creation of two new colonies, New Brunswick and Cape Breton Island (1784). Some 6,000 Loyalists settled in Quebec. This English enclave in western Quebec encouraged the subsequent division of the province in 1791 into two regions, Upper and Lower Canada.

New arrivals could have a disproportionate influence when they reached small settlements. Such was the case in the Bahamas, where 1,600 white planters, together with 5,700 free blacks and slaves, fled in the wake of the imperial schism. Their arrival tripled the population of the islands and changed the ratio of free and enslaved people. In the wake of this demographic shift, the governor urged the assembly in 1784 to pass stricter controls, and the assembly obliged with a more powerful militia. They also reenacted the colony's 1767 Act for the Governing of Negroes, Mulattoes, Mustees and Indians, this time with harsher restrictions not only for slaves, but also for freedmen. The newcomers placed new islands (including Grand Bahama, Abaco, and Turks and Caicos, covering an archipelago spanning some 600 miles) under cultivation and settlement. Moreover, they planted cotton, making the region one of the main sources of the crop for the British textile industry.

The numbers, however, tell only part of the story. Although French speakers still composed 60 percent of the population of Lower Canada by 1800, the arrival there of so many English refugees transformed the culture of the province. These new arrivals placed new land into cultivation, pushing settlement along the major waterways. They built new towns, introducing more urban centers to the region. The dominance of the Church of England in Canada weakened as well, as the tens of thousands of Loyalists brought their multiple denominational attachments with them. In the Bahamas, the refugees contributed to the rise of Nassau as a major trade center. They brought their attachment to Britain, but those Loyalists whose families had deep roots in North America also brought their expectations of the same political autonomy that had characterized colonial life elsewhere. The Loyalist exodus solidified and strengthened British power in the large regions of the western Atlantic still in its domain.

But if its colonies contained large cohorts of people loyal to the British empire, Britain itself contained people sympathetic to the colonial cause. The political and ideological issues that animated North American revolutionaries had emerged from an Anglo-American intellectual world. American ideas were derivative of British precursors, and Americans were deeply involved in the major debates of the period. Many Britons shared American concerns about corrupt officials and the pervasive stink of politics. Thus many in Britain supported the revolutionaries in their struggle. Some raised money to aid American prisoners of war; others showed their sympathy for the American cause by wearing the colonial colors, blue and buff. One of the more colorful displays came from the Duke of Richmond, who sailed his yacht with an American pennant among the ships of the British navy. The duke (after whom Richmond, Virginia, was named) was an advocate in England for the same causes that preoccupied Americans, although he went even further than the republicans in the United States, calling for universal manhood suffrage and annual parliaments. By 1779, a political reform movement had emerged in England, prompted by a range of concerns from the cost and waste of war, the weakness of Britain in its American struggle, and constitutional issues. The imperial schism was born in transatlantic political currents, and it continued to reverberate within the British political world.

More Atlantic Repercussions

Pride is the mother of exaggeration, and in that light one can be tolerant of the revolutionaries' remarkable claim that the rat-a-tat of weaponry that echoed perhaps half a mile from Lexington Green in 1775 was "the shot heard 'round the world." As we have seen, there had been rebels among western Atlantic settler populations since the time of the conquistadors, but now, for the first time, rebels had become revolutionaries and colonists had bucked European crown authority and won what proved to be a lasting independence. In a larger sense, the period of Atlantic imperial reform and subsequent rebellion and warfare that stretched from the 1760s to the 1780s affected lives far beyond North America. This was true even in Atlantic regions, such as western Africa, where continuities seemed the rule. Because the slave trade continued apace through the period—in fact, the 1780s witnessed a greater number of captive men, women, and children leaving Africa's Atlantic coasts for passage to the Americas than any other decade before or since—it is understandable why one would think that events in North America had minimal repercussions for Africa; that conclusion, however understandable, is dead wrong.

The American Revolution affected Africa in myriad and significant ways, resulting almost immediately in open hostilities among European countries whose nationals frequented the Guinea Coast. Not only did France become engaged in aiding the colonists at Britain's expense, but British actions on the high seas, contravening international law in boarding and searching foreign ships to prevent arms and supplies from reaching the rebellious colonials, brought the Dutch Republic to war with Great Britain between 1780 and 1784. The fighting among European nations stretched to their outposts in Africa. Around the forts and factories where European slave buyers met African sellers, the warfare, although centered mostly elsewhere, had a trickle-down effect on African populations that reached further than the trickle of any wealth the trade generated. The historian Ty Reese provides one example from the Gold Coast, where the American Revolution and ensuing European hostilities altered long-standing political relationships, changed the nature and volume of trade, and in some circumstances influenced people's notions of liberty and justice.

It was not unusual when, in 1775, Africans allied with the Dutch at two Gold Coast forts plundered longboats carrying goods belonging to British agents stationed at nearby Cape Coast. Such activity was normal, and maybe it was only because the British Governor of Cape Coast Castle, David Mill, was suspicious of anyone "selling arms or ammunition to any of His Majesty's rebellious subjects in America" that he arranged for a British cruiser, HMS *Pallas*, to force restitution with threats of bombardment and, in one instance, "a few shots at the town." More important was the disruption the American Revolution caused in the flow of commodities from the home island to its African outposts. Much British shipping was involved with taking troops and supplies to the areas in rebellion, which meant fewer vessels to bring trade goods and supplies to Britain's African enclaves. When in 1776 the regular British storeship was late in arriving, French vessels came swarming like mosquitoes and the Fante, long close commercial associates of the British, turned their attention to Annamaboe, down the coast, where the French were trading. "[The Fante's trading with the French] is not to be wondered, at such a time as this," lamented Mill, "when the country is full of slaves, scarce on provisions, and no English ships to take them off their hands." The lack of trade goods caused other problems, since the English kept local residents happy by giving them regular gifts—"dashes," they called them—and without their monthly dash, some of the notables who kept trade flowing toward the English establishments lost clout with Africans and grew angry over the situation.

Once at war with Great Britain, the Dutch were happy to apply additional pressure on English merchants at Cape Coast by denying them Brazilian tobacco, one of the most popular trade items and one that Dutch ship-pers largely controlled. When a renegade Portuguese captain bartered 200 rolls of tobacco to Cape Coast traders, the general in charge of Dutch Elmina summoned the captain to his ship, threw him overboard, and shot at him while he was in the water. From then on, the English governor at Cape Coast, fearing French, Dutch, and even Danish vessels roaming the coast and drop-ping off munitions at their respective forts, fretted more than usual over the sorry state of weapons in Cape Coast Castle, the tiny number of white sol-diers on hand (10), and the length of time it had been (2 years) since a Royal Navy vessel had visited.

More direct aspects of warfare in North America and Europe visited the Gold Coast in February 1781, when English privateers began hauling in Dutch prizes—eight of them within a few months—expecting the puny Cape Coast Castle garrison to house 150 Dutch prisoners. Then, when a gang of English privateers launched an unsuccessful attack on the Dutch fort at Commenda, the Dutch retaliated by dispatching a force of their African allies that cap-tured English Succondee and attacked the larger English post at Dixcove. All of this fighting, most of it conducted by Africans, grew problematic because of the lack of gunpowder, since all of that came via the Atlantic and both countries strove to interdict the other's line of supply. Not until 1782, when several Royal Navy vessels and two transport ships arrived, did the English have enough gunpowder to launch an attack and capture the Dutch forts.

The trailing off of hostilities in North America brought ships back to the Gold Coast, not only from the British Isles but from New England. The Ameri-can slavers came loaded with Rhode Island rum, an immensely popular com-modity among coastal Africans and one gravely missed during the war. De-spite their pursuit of captives, the U.S. crews arrived full of heady new ideas about liberty. A single vessel from Boston was the "cause of a great deal of disturbance," according to the British governor at Cape Coast in 1784, be-cause the Americans were giving free rum to Africans in an effort to "instill into them that spirit of republican freedom and independence" that resulted in "insolence" on the part of Britain's African allies and strained relationships around the trading forts. For their part, the Dutch in early 1786 encouraged Americans "to flood the coast with rum." U.S. traders had a great advantage in that the agents of the English Committee of Merchants Trading to Africa had for political reasons forbidden British slavers from dealing in American rum. This hurt Britain's African trade since, by the late 1780s, any European trader who did not have rum to offer was hard-pressed to acquire slaves.

The British recognized "insolence" most profoundly in dealings with their longtime allies, the Fetu around Cape Coast and the Fante more broadly along the Gold Coast. Just as the North Americans had rebelled when they considered themselves mistreated by their colonial masters, people living near Britain's Gold Coast forts pressed for fairer treatment. In 1782, Governor Miles noted, "the natives . . . are continually plaguing us to reimburse them their expenses in burying their dead, whom they have lost at different times in our service, since the commencement of the war, and to allow pensions to the maimed." In early 1786, when the commander of the HMS *Grampus* doled out goods to reimburse Africans for services to the British, some judged the quantity insufficient. In response, they blockaded Cape Coast Castle, "set upon" a gang of castle slaves "with bludgeons and stones, . . . ill used" some castle women, plundered the dwelling of a free trader in the town, and destroyed the castle's garden. When the governor demanded a meeting with Botty Caboceer, an influential Cape Coast merchant whom the British plied with gifts so he would further their interests with the local population, Miles learned that Caboceer "suffered from diminishing influence." Officers in Cape Coast Castle were astonished when, after they fired on the rebellious townspeople, the latter fired back.

As such "insolence" continued among the previously acquiescent Africans, British officials blamed it on the infusion of libertarian principles from the American Revolution. The Cape Coast governor and council in 1788 wrote to the committee's governing body in London that "your black servants, who as we can assure you, have so far imbibed the principles of liberty, so much the conversation now, as to be far above submitting to any restrictions we may communicate to them." Africans living near Annamaboe, the complaint continued, "say that their country belongs to them and they will trade with whom they please."

The situation around Britain's Gold Coast settlements remained tense into the early nineteenth century. In the end, the Africans who resided there relied too much on the trade the British brought them to want to exert fully their independent spirit, and they may have lacked the military power to expel the foreigners, anyway. But circumstances on the Gold Coast over the last quarter of the eighteenth century show the extent to which warfare in one sector of the Atlantic had repercussions in others as well as how ideas born of one Atlantic region swept across the ocean to influence the thinking of people in another. The American Revolution affected Atlantic commerce up and down the length of Africa's Atlantic coast, no doubt in some ways difficult to recognize after more than two centuries. British trade experienced a setback from the 1770s to the 1780s—so much so that they abandoned their outpost on James Island in the Gambia River in 1779, not to reestablish a presence in that river until 1816—and French, Dutch, Portuguese, and U.S. merchants filled the void. This shift in the European balance of power altered regional political alliances and may have served as an economic boost for slave traders from Brazil and Cuba to Dahomey and Angola, as well as those in Africa allied to them.

Repercussions of the American Revolution resounded elsewhere. In the same way that victory over France in 1763 compounded Britain's national debt, Spain's brief involvement in what amounted to a second Thirty Years' War led to financial hardship for Spain, and a need to squeeze more revenue from its American holdings. Before the signing of the second Peace of Paris in 1783, Spain raised much capital through Atlantic trade, leaving it to American viceroys to finance their own administrations. Buenos Aires had typically done so by collecting mining, sales, and customs revenues from the silver district of Potosí, which, following reforms, supplied 79 percent of the revenues for the Viceroyalty of La Plata. After 1783, however, King Charles III began to divert the bulk of Potosí's silver revenues to Madrid to service his debt. As a result, only 6 percent of the funds needed to maintain local administration, including officers' salaries and maintenance of the viceregal court, came from the silver mines. This not only made Buenos Aires more reliant on foreign trade—which is to say smuggling with Britain—but also forced crown administrators to levy new taxes on the interior. The result was a brief tax revolt that mirrored earlier protests in Quito, Arequipa, Boston, and other places and placed greater strains on the Spanish Empire. American colonists everywhere were getting tired of paying for mistakes made in Europe.

These three decades of Atlantic conflict and rebellion also created new problems in Paris and around what remained of the French Empire. With Cornwallis's defeat at Yorktown, most of the forces that had arrived on the mainland with Rochambeau sailed out of the Chesapeake in expectation of further action in the Caribbean. Several regiments remained stranded there, awaiting transport ships that never arrived. A few French officers, demonstrating more enterprise than prudence, shipped members of the enslaved Saint Domingue Legion back to the sugar colony; given these men's prolonged exposure to the rhetoric of equality, it was to be a fateful decision. Among those returned to the Caribbean's harshest slave regime was future Haitian rebel Henri Christophe, who had been wounded at the siege of Savannah. Other veterans of the U.S. independence wars found their way back to France, where they became angry reminders of the 35 million livres spent on the American cause. When told that many veterans were begging in the streets of Paris, King Louis XVI only replied: "I believe it, they are paid nothing." The Atlantic world had yet to be fully turned upside down.

Selected Readings

Anderson, Fred, *Crucible of War: The Seven Years' War and the Fate of Empire in British North America, 1754–1766* (New York: Alfred A. Knopf, 2000).

Bailyn, Bernard, *Voyagers to the West: A Passage in the Peopling of America on the Eve of the Revolution* (New York: Alfred A. Knopf, 1986).

Calloway, Colin G., *The American Revolution in Indian Country: Crisis and Diversity in Native American Communities* (Cambridge, UK: Cambridge University Press, 1995).

Craton, Michael, and Gail Saunders, *Islanders in the Stream: A History of the Bahamian People*, Vol. 1 (Athens: The University of Georgia Press, 1992).

Ferling, John, *The First of Men: A Life of George Washington* (Knoxville: University of Tennessee Press, 1988).

Frey, Sylvia, *Water From the Rock: Black Resistance in a Revolutionary Age* (Princeton: Princeton University Press, 1991).

Hart, Michael, *A Trading Nation: Canadian Trade Policy from Colonialism to Globalization* (Vancouver: UBC Press, 2002).

Hibbert, Christopher, *George III: A Personal History* (New York: Basic Books, 1999).

Hinderaker, Eric, *Elusive Empires: Constructing Colonialism in the Ohio Valley, 1673–1800* (Cambridge, UK: Cambridge University Press, 1997).

Hodges, Graham Russell, *The Black Loyalist Directory: African Americans in Exile after the American Revolution* (New York: Garland, 1995).

Hornsby, Stephen J., *British Atlantic, American Frontier: Spaces of Power in Early Modern British America* (Hanover: University Press of New England, 2005).

Meinig, D. W., *Atlantic America, 1492–1800* (New Haven: Yale University Press, 1986).

Merritt, Jane T., *At the Crossroads: Indians and Empires on a Mid-Atlantic Frontier, 1700–1763* (Chapel Hill: University of North Carolina Press, 2003).

Morgan, Edmund S., *Benjamin Franklin* (New Haven: Yale University Press, 2002).

———, and Helen M. Morgan, *The Stamp Act Crisis: Prologue to Revolution*, 2nd ed. (Chapel Hill: University of North Carolina Press, 1983).

Nash, Gary B., *The Urban Crucible: Social Change, Political Consciousness, and the Origins of the American Revolution* (Cambridge, MA: Harvard University Press, 1979).

O'Shaughnessy, Andrew Jackson, *An Empire Divided: The American Revolution and the British Caribbean* (Philadelphia: University of Pennsylvania Press, 2000).

Paine, Thomas, *Common Sense*, Ed., Isaac Kramnick (New York: Penguin, 1976).

Plumb, J. H., *The First Four Georges* (Boston: Little, Brown, 1975).

Reese, Ty M., "Liberty, Insolence, and Rum: Cape Coast and the American Revolution," *Hinerario: International Journal of the History of European Expansion and Global Interaction* 28:3 (Fall 2004), 18–37.

Rudé, George, *Hanoverian London, 1714–1808* (Berkeley: University of California Press, 1971).

Van Buskirk, Judith, *Generous Enemies: Patriots and Loyalists in Revolutionary New York* (Philadelphia: University of Pennsylvania Press, 2002).

Vinson, Ben, *Bearing Arms for His Majesty: The Free Colored Militia in Colonial Mexico* (Stanford: University of Stanford Press, 2001).

White, Richard, *The Middle Ground: Indians, Empires, and Republics in the Great Lakes Region, 1650–1815* (Cambridge, UK: Cambridge University Press, 1991).

Saint Domingue Revolt, 1802. Former slaves in the colony of Saint Domingue (now Haiti) battle French invasion forces led by General Charles Victor Leclerc. Contemporary engraving. Credit: Rue des Archives/The Granger Collection, New York.

Chapter Eleven

Revolutions and Counterrevolutions: The Season of Irony, 1789–1804

I have taken on the task of revenging you. I demand that freedom and equality reign on this entire island. It is the only goal that I want to attain. Come and join me, brothers, and fight on our side for the same cause.
Toussaint Louverture

What is that in your hand?
It is a branch.
Of What?
Of the Tree of Liberty.
Where did it first grow?
In America.
Where does it bloom?
In France.
Where did the seeds fall?
In Ireland.
Where are you going to plant it?
In the Crown of Great Britain.
A United Irishmen catechism from 1797

"**It** was the spring of hope, it was the winter of despair," as Charles Dickens so famously put it, and no writer has ever improved upon that assessment of the age of revolution in the Atlantic basin. He might have added that it was also the season of irony. Foolish monarchs lost their reason and sometimes their heads, men who spoke of terror and employed mass murder in the name of liberty championed black freedom in the Caribbean, while desperate Haitians cozied up to an antidemocratic administration that trod upon the most innocuous public criticism. Black Virginians who compared themselves to General Washington swung from the Richmond gibbet, hanged by men who flattered themselves "old revolutionaries," while a white Virginian, the author of one of the most egalitarian documents ever penned, conspired long distance with a Corsican, a self-professed "son of the revolution," to reestablish slavery in the Caribbean. Meanwhile, African potentates up and down the Guinea Coast continued enslaving enemies for shipment across the Atlantic, where these human beings were purchased by recent champions of liberty. It was an age of extremes—and irony—indeed.

The appropriate tone of irony was set as early as 1777. In that year, on August 9, King Louis XVI, even as he began seriously to consider aiding the

361

United States in its war for liberty, issued what would become the final, illiberal decree governing blacks living in France. (The *Code Noir* of 1685, promulgated by Louis XIV, covered only slavery in the French colonies.) Formally known as the *Police des Noirs* (the organizing of the blacks), the royal declaration was the first to employ skin color, rather than the condition of enslavement, as the legal basis for governing Africans and their descendants living in the French kingdom. (The term *esclave* was notably absent from the document.) The 1777 decree was also the first to be registered by the Parlement of Paris, the chief law court of the capital city, a move designed to prohibit slaves brought to the continent by their masters from suing for their freedom. If successful, observed Antoine Raimond de Sartine, the chief architect of the decree, such suits might teach blacks the erroneous lesson that they enjoyed the same privileges as "the superior beings they were destined to serve." Since French officers were returning from the United States with stories of how slavery was beginning to disappear in the northeastern states, Sartine and his sovereign worried about the legal rights of French colonists relocating to the continent with their enslaved servants in tow. As French warships prepared to swoop down on British sugar islands, the crown also pondered the continuing loyalty of French settlers in the Caribbean.

What is That in Your Hand?

In the end, the king and his advisors captured little more from the Treaty of Paris of 1783 than a massive war debt, which tripled between 1774 and 1789. Already bloated due to the wars and perverse taxation policies of Louis XIV, the debt grew so large that fully one-half of all incoming revenues went merely to service the interest charged by Parisian and Dutch bankers. The military consumed another 25 percent of the government's expenditures, while 6 percent more vanished into the lavish extravagance of the court at Versailles. In a situation that would try the wisdom of Solomon, the chronic financial difficulties of the government remained in the hands of Louis XVI, an affable but uncomplicated monarch more fond of hunting and gardening than governance; his penchant for tinkering with locks was just one of the many traits he shared with his cross-Channel rival, George III, an equally simple man who enjoyed tinkering with clocks. The most the French king could muster in the way of fiscal reform was to levy a uniform tax on all property without regard to class ranking, a fairly progressive idea in a time when French society was formally divided into three estates. But the Parlement of Paris promptly declared the new levy illegal on the sensible grounds that only the Estates General—which had not met since 1614—could pass such a sweeping revision.

Among those watching this drama unfold was Thomas Jefferson, the second American minister to Paris. After the Virginian's wife, Martha, died of childbirth complications in 1782, he fled abroad when offered the opportunity to replace the seventy-nine-year-old Benjamin Franklin. The new minister was in attendance at Versailles on May 5, 1789, at the dramatic opening ceremony of the Estates General. The vast majority of the 1,165 delegates present, the commoners of the Third Estate (who as wealthy attorneys, merchants, and *rentiers* [landlords], were anything *but* common), were forced to wait for hours while the king graciously welcomed the clergy and the nobles of the Second Estate, a group that included another hero of the American Revolution, the Marquis de Lafayette. Jefferson, as the principal author of the Declaration of Independence, had already begun collaborating with Lafayette and other reform-minded leaders on what should be included in a French statement of rights. But as he watched the opening procession into the palace, Jefferson doubted that real reform would come easily. Ordered to don black apparel from hat to toe, the delegates of the Third Estate appeared as dowdy and grim as those of the other two estates looked lustrous and triumphant.

Far more than costumes lay at issue. Since the national debt had occasioned the meeting, the Third Estate was justly concerned with creating a more equitable tax structure. In times long past, the Estates General had essentially met as three separate assemblies in three separate chambers. For any measure to become law, two orders and the monarch had to consent. Were that system of voting to continue, the commoners could expect to be outvoted on every bill, despite the fact that 97 percent of the French population fell within the Third Estate. Hoping to impose a compromise on the meeting, Louis XVI had already agreed to allow for the election of twice as many delegates for the Third Estate as for the first two. Even this modest gesture, which packed the great hall at Versailles with rich commoners but did nothing to alter the ancient voting arrangement, aroused the ire of the nobility, who regarded the principle of separate chambers as symbolic of their class prerogatives, and hence every bit as crucial as an actual vote on taxes.

For six weeks, both sides stubbornly refused to give way. On June 17, members of the Third Estate resolved to break the deadlock by announcing that they spoke for the public as the National Assembly, and they invited like-minded renegades from the first two chambers to join with them. Three days later, the commoners arrived at their chamber to find the door barred by armed guards. As the furious delegates milled about in the pouring rain, Joseph-Ignace Guillotin—a doctor and inventor who had recently devised a more efficient machine for removing the human head from the body—remembered a nearby tennis court. By comparison to their elegant chamber, the simple court, decorated only with a crude table borrowed from a tailor, gave an appropriately egalitarian flavor to the proceedings. There the members of the newly announced National Assembly swore an oath never to disband. Faced with defections from the clergy and nobility—and with a debt that literally grew worse by the day—the king relented. On June 27 he instructed the first two orders to meet with the third as a unified National Assembly, which promptly set about on its self-appointed task of devising France's first-ever constitution. The historic Estates General was no more.

Unhappily for events, the king was as temperamentally disinclined toward firmness as his wife, Marie Antoinette of Austria, was inclined toward inflexibility. The queen was a Habsburg, granddaughter to Emperor Charles VI and sister to Austrian King Leopold II, a staunch defender of aristocratic privilege and not above manipulating her ever-vacillating husband; several

Citizenship

No better illustration exists for the distinction between the promise and the political reality of the age of revolution than the often-enormous gulf between the egalitarian language of liberal declarations and the codification of citizenship in the northern Atlantic constitutions crafted in the years between 1787 and 1804. Although the fifty-five men who produced the United States Constitution included enough protections for slavery into their document to make it clear that black Americans were not citizens of the republic, it was not until the Fourteenth Amendment, ratified in 1868 to overturn parts of the Dred Scott decision of the U.S. Supreme Court, that citizenship was clearly bestowed upon "All persons born or naturalized in the United States."

In the same way, although the French Declaration of the Rights of Man incorporated the egalitarian rhetoric of the philosophes, the Constitution of 1791 backtracked on any promises of equality by creating two classes of citizens—active and passive—which effectively denied the vote to roughly one-third of the men, all of the women, and said nothing about the rights of mixed-race freemen or slaves in the French colonies. As was the case in the United States, many of the delegates who devised the French Constitution of 1791 were slaveholders whose demands for liberty were qualified along lines of race and gender.

As in many things, the Haitian example, although based in part on North American and European experiences, deviated from those practices in critical ways. The Haitian Constitution of 1801, for example, preceded the Haitian Declaration of Independence by two years. The Constitution's initial articles contained paraphrases from the Declaration of Rights of Man and the 1794 French abolition law, and so unlike the U.S. Constitution, the Haitian document "permanently abolished" slavery and granted citizenship to all residents, "no matter their color." Two years later, however, Louverture's dream of a biracial republic lay in ruins, and the Haitian Declaration, drafted by Louis Félix Boisrond-Tonnerre, restricted citizenship to people of color. The "difference between our color and theirs," he wrote, made clear to all that "they are not our brothers, [and] that they will never be."

days after the Tennis Court Oath, she arrived in the king's chamber with her two children, urging him to remain firm in their behalf. Having already sided with the bourgeoisie, Louis now began to listen to those who insisted that such leanings would undermine his authority and dignity. By the end of June he had brought nearly 18,000 soldiers from the provinces to Versailles. Almost certainly, Louis intended to dissolve the National Assembly by force.

In response, the Parisians formed a new militia, the National Guard, loyal to the Assembly. Requiring arms against the expected coup d'état, guardsmen on July 14 broke into an arsenal at the Invalides, an old military hospital. In search of still more armaments, the crowd next turned to the Bastille, a fourteenth-century fortress turned prison on the eastern edge of Paris. When Governor (warden) Bernard-René de Launay refused to turn over gunpowder recently moved to the prison from the Invalides, the crowd shoved into the courtyard, shouting, "Give us the Bastille." The few defending soldiers opened fire, killing eighty-three citizens. With the arrival of defecting soldiers from the king's army, several of whom were veterans of the American campaigns, the chaotic assault became an organized siege. At five o'clock that afternoon, the soldiers capitulated. Governor de Launay's head, sawed off with a pocket-knife, graced a tall sword that victorious guardsmen paraded through the streets. The king lay in bed, nearly asleep, when news of the attack reached Versailles. "Is it a revolt?" asked Louis. "No sire," came the reply. "It is a revolution."

Where Does It Bloom?

To better establish the new order, the National Assembly began work on a document designed to affirm the principles of the revolutionary state. According to Jefferson, almost everybody in Paris had tried their hand at a declaration since the previous January, and just before the assault on the Bastille, Lafayette sent his draft to the Virginian. Jefferson urged the Marquis to omit "property" as an imprescriptible right, just as in the American Declaration he had transformed Locke's explicit quest of "property" into the more encompassing "pursuit of happiness." Even so, Lafayette's handiwork betrayed more than a passing familiarity with the egalitarian ideas that had washed back and forth across the Atlantic. In the final version, passed on August 26, the Declaration of the Rights of Man and Citizen guaranteed freedom of thought and religion. "Men are born and remain," announced Article I, "free and equal in rights." Printed in countless pamphlets, letters, and volumes, the Declaration became the virtual catechism of revolutionary ideals. Yet, like its American counterpart, the document was a mere statement of principles; it had no legal standing as organic law. Perhaps for that reason, few wealthy bourgeois who toasted its adoption—many of whom had made their fortunes as absentee landlords in Saint Domingue —observed how its grand "ideas of an indeterminate liberty" contradicted both the colonial *Code Noir* and the continental *Police des Noirs*.

The Tricolor in Black and White

As Jefferson was to discover with his enslaved brother-in-law James Hemings, who accompanied his master to Paris to learn the art of French cooking but equally mastered the values of the two Declarations by demanding wages and his freedom before agreeing to return to the United States, those on the bottom typically failed to draw such fine political distinctions. Wealthy planters in the Caribbean might assure one another that their slaves, as property, could not be touched, but the few literate bondmen in Saint Domingue heard only the egalitarian promise of the revolution. Moreover, the propertied freedmen of mixed ancestry, the *gens de couleur*, met every criterion necessary under the Declaration to qualify for "active" citizenship under the new order. (Because they were partly white, they did not appear to be covered by the 1777 decree, which employed the terms *noirs* and *nègres*.) The issue only grew more pressing on September 20, when a delegation of prosperous freemen appeared before the National Assembly and demanded the same rights as whites. The Assembly sought to avoid the issue by referring the question to the Colonial Committee, where its chairman, Antoine Pierre Barnave, the brother of a wealthy planter, could be expected to bury the question. But in Saint Domingue, long regarded as the "powder keg" of the Americas, the twin issues of race and liberty were not so easily tabled.

Sporadic fighting between whites and gens de couleur in the French Caribbean began as early as April 1790. On Saint Domingue, several freemen murdered three whites near Port-au-Prince, the news of which prompted whites on the island of Martinique to slaughter two hundred free men of color without even the pretense of a trial. The violence threatened to escalate when the

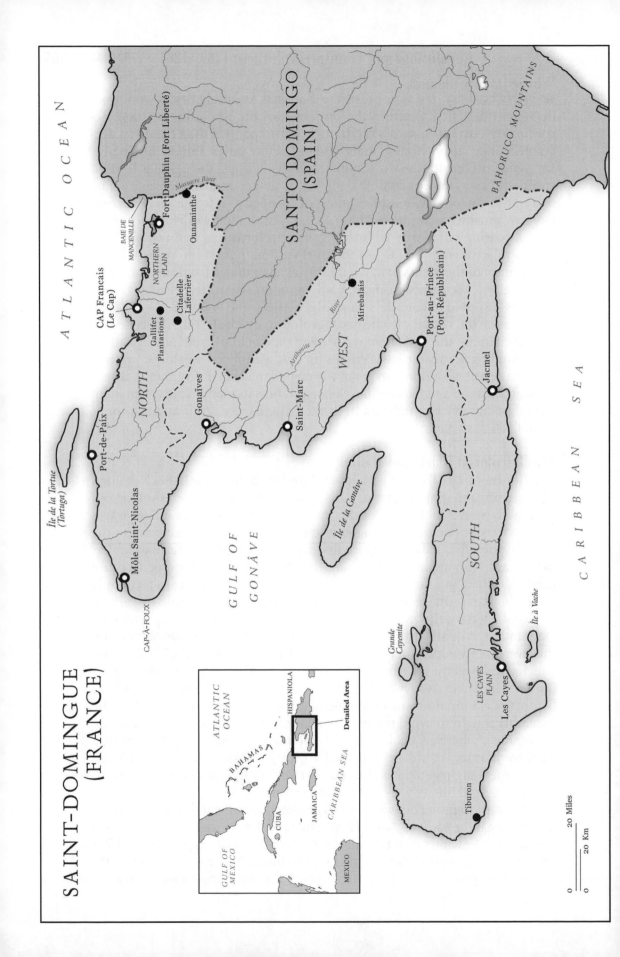

wealthy free man of color Vincent Ogé raised a force of nearly seven hundred men in Saint Domingue. Although his public pronouncements indicated that he had no desire to include "the Negro in slavery" in his revolutionary scheme, his private correspondence revealed that he secretly planned to lead slaves in a general insurrection in hopes of gaining mulatto equality. Armed with weapons purchased in Charleston, South Carolina, from Abraham Sasportas, a French weapons supplier, Ogé and his men moved on Le Cap François. After a bungled attack on the city, Ogé fell into the hands of vengeful whites. Following a two-month trial, he and two of his lieutenants were dragged to a public square (on the side opposite that reserved for the execution of white men), where they were broken on the wheel before being decapitated. The grisly executions satisfied white anger, but did nothing to satisfy the political demands of the gens de couleur.

The situation only grew worse when it became clear that the leading antislavery organization in France, the *Amis des Noirs*, regarded Ogé as a popular hero. Maximilien Robespierre, an earnest young lawyer, electrified the Assembly by threatening to abandon the Caribbean colonies "if the price" to be paid for the planters' "happiness, glory, and liberty" came at the cost of human rights. One Jacobin Club even began a circular letter that demanded full citizenship for free *and* propertied men of mixed ancestry. As such qualifiers empowered only seven hundred gens de couleur, the Assembly reluctantly agreed in its May 1791 Decree. Abbé Henri Grégoire hoped this was just the beginning, and he encouraged the freemen to lead the enslaved "progressively to liberty." Since many gens de couleur owned slaves themselves and had devised no less than sixty-four gradations of color, few had the slightest interest in manumission. But white delegates from Saint Domingue, Martinique, and Guadeloupe regarded the May Decree as the precipice of a very slippery slope and quit the Assembly in protest.

The delegates were at least half right. Of course, enslaved workers in no century required far-off white elites to inform them of their misery. What bondmen required instead was an opening, a division among the powerful. As historian Robin Blackburn has suggested, the French Revolution "furnish[ed] the conditions in which" the enslaved "could entrench the first forms of an antislavery power." Rumors—however badly mangled as they passed from port to plantation—that men of influence in Paris opposed their condition could only exacerbate the tense situation in Saint Domingue. On August 16, 1791, a *commandeur de plantation* (the equivalent of a slave driver) was caught torching a trash house. Under questioning, the slave confessed to being part of a far larger conspiracy to burn down a number of plantations. Authorities chose to regard the problem as local, since they doubted the ability of Africans to organize on a grand scale. Six days later, however, bondmen on the *Plaine du Nord* (North Plain) began what came to be known as the Night of Fire. Led by Boukman, a prominent slave and religious leader originally from Jamaica, bondmen set fire to the Noé plantation. Within days, as many as 100,000 slaves joined the revolt. As planters fled toward the safety of Le Cap François, slaves torched more than 300 plantations; refugees reported hearing roaring "fires and the explosions and whistling of cannon." Although

Saint Domingue would tenuously remain a French colony until 1803, the first phase of the Haitian Revolution had begun.

If events in France serve to explain the timing of the revolt, the early Haitian rebels demonstrated a uniquely African political sensibility. Some Kongolese slaves identified leaders, designated them as "kings" or "queens," and appointed them to rule in the plantation districts freed from white control. If instigators like Boukman were creoles, the leaders had to organize thousands of slaves, and they did so by organizing their armies along national lines. Utilizing military skills learned years before in Africa, Haitian rebels quickly developed armies that could best local militias, and as events would turn out, even professional soldiers sent from France. Yet even as early as 1791, crippling divisions began to emerge between the creole leadership and the African soldiers, who cared little for egalitarian theories and wished only to defend their newly won liberty, even if that meant turning their back on democracy.

As players in a transatlantic drama, the island's authorities were foolish to dismiss the early rumblings of revolt as a parochial affair. From its first moment, participants in the uprising understood themselves to be acting on a world stage. "The world has groaned at our fate," one rebel told the colony's governor as early as September 1791. The flood of white and mixed-race refugees into the greater Caribbean, with most exiles arriving in Kingston, Charleston, Norfolk, or New Orleans, served only to spread word of the revolt, as did the mariners who ferried emigrants away from Saint Domingue. In Spanish Town, Jamaica, white authorities rounded up a group of armed slaves who assembled to drink to abolitionist William Wilberforce's "health out of a cat's skull by way of a cup, and swearing secrecy to each other." Even the purest of motives served to backfire against the master class. In Charleston, the chandler Joseph Vesey formed a Benevolent Society to assist Domingan planters; details of the rebellion evidently made an impression on his domestic slave, then known as Telemaque but later to go by his free name of Denmark Vesey. To the north in Virginia, John Randolph overheard several slaves talking quietly below the window of his Richmond home. The "one who seemed to be the chief speaker said, you see how the blacks has killed the whites in the French Island and took it." Farther north yet, in Albany, New York, a bondman set a fire that nearly leveled the town in apparent imitation of the Night of Fire, while far to the south in the Brazilian city of Bahia, four men of color were hanged and quartered for the crime of promoting "the imaginary advantages of a Democratic Republic, in which all should be equal." Newspapers in Bogotá, Lima, and Mexico City reported similar rumblings, as did numerous planters and mine operators in their personal correspondence. Slave owners throughout the Atlantic world took notice.

To the extent that most earlier slave revolts across the Americas contained a restorationist or escapist quality, the tenor of black rebellion changed after 1791. Historian David Geggus has demonstrated that after that time, rebellious slaves around the Caribbean took some inspiration from Boukman and sought to overturn slave societies. The demographics of the circum-Caribbean explain why. With a largely African-descended population, Venezuela experienced many race-based revolts at places like Maracaibo, Puerto Cabello, Yare, and Minas de Burias. The population of Coro, a sugar-growing province on the western coast, stood at 26,000 persons, including 11,500 free people of color, almost as many slaves, and fewer than 4,000 whites. Many of those still enslaved operated on their free time as tenants, raising cattle and food crops, just like other residents of the province. The Bourbon reforms squeezed all alike, but unlike previous tumults, almost equal numbers of black slaves and free persons of color joined this rebellion. Smaller numbers of Indians also joined. Only the outnumbered whites sat it out. The Coro Rebellion featured sophisticated planning and a coherent platform whose primary goals were the abolition of slavery and the elimination of the sales taxes on slave-tenant produce. In their demands the free black leaders José Leonardo Chirino and José Caridad González cited the ideology of the French Revolution and referred to the slave revolt of Saint Domingue. They called for "the law of the French, the republic, the freedom of slaves and the suppression of the alcabala and other taxes." They also allegedly planned to kill whites and create a re-publican form of government based on social equality of the remaining popu-lation.

Like others, the Coro Rebellion was suppressed, but it worried Spanish elites in the capital of Caracas, who, on November 28, 1796, penned the following representation to the crown: "The establishment of militias led by officers of their own class has given the *pardos* [persons of color] a power which will be the ruin of America; incapable of resisting invasion led by a powerful enemy and outnumbering the whites in the task of controlling the slaves and maintaining internal order, they serve only to enhance the arro-gance of the pardos, giving them an organization, leaders, and arms, the more easily to prepare a revolution."

Around the Caribbean, the enslaved majority far outnumbered the heavily armed *blancs* and *gens de couleur*, who in any case adamantly refused to set aside their own political differences long enough to present the slaves with a united front. So when Boukman fell early in battle, there were others ready and willing to take his place. Certainly the most important new recruit was forty-eight-year-old Toussaint, one of the minority of Saint Dominguan slaves born on the island and not imported from Africa. Toussaint labored on the Bréda plantation as a coachman and took care of the livestock, but shortly after Toussaint reached the age of twenty, Bayon de Libertad, the manager of Bréda, gave him forty acres and thirteen slaves to supervise. At some point in the early 1770s, Toussaint became free, perhaps through self-purchase, and he rented a small coffee plantation, although not with great success. Even before that, Toussaint had learned the fundamentals of reading and writing under the tutelage of his godfather, the priest Simon Baptiste; one contempo-rary claimed Toussaint "spoke French poorly," however, and often resorted to the vernacular to express himself clearly. Only after it became clear that the Haitian Revolution stood a chance did the small man, regarded by most as unremarkable at first glance, cast his lot with the rebels. In the fall of 1791, after helping to spirit Libertad's family onto a ship sailing for the United States, Toussaint abandoned Bréda and rode for the camp of the insurgents.

Francisco de Miranda's Travels in the United States

Francisco de Miranda was thirty-three years old when he visited the new United States in 1783–84. Miranda was born and educated in Venezuela. When he was twenty-one, he set off for Spain and entered the army: he served in Africa in the 1770s. As a Spanish officer, he also fought against the British during the European conflicts that surrounded the American War for Independence. Ensnared in charges derived from his conduct at the end of the war, Miranda set out for Spain to clear his name and decided to visit the United States en route. Miranda's record of his travels conveys his diverse range of interests in the new American republic and its citizens. He faithfully assessed the physical attractions and social skills of local women, and marveled that some women of the Carolinas could "retain their beautiful coloring" despite the influence of malaria, which gives people a sallow appearance. He met all major political figures and military heroes, including George Washington, Alexander Hamilton, John Hancock, Samuel Adams (with whom he argued about the Massachusetts state constitution and the problem of ensuring a virtuous citizenry in a republic), the doctor Benjamin Rush, and the abolitionist Anthony Benezet. He toured fortifications and battlefields. He visited courthouses, and raved about the legal process he saw, writing, "Good God! What a contrast with the Spanish system!" There was much about this new republic that fascinated him. He attended

religious services in all faiths, sitting through a Quaker meeting in Philadelphia and enduring a "wearisome sermon" and a man's humiliating (to Miranda) public confession about premarital sex in New England; he visited public libraries; he admired the book collections, lectures, and scholars at Harvard and Yale. Miranda found much to praise, yet he was troubled by the "spirit of republicanism" he encountered in New England, where he was forced to dine with a coachman and only with difficulty was able to be sure that his own servant would eat separately. This was Miranda's first exposure to a political experiment centered around republican ideology: it would not be his last. After participating in the French Revolution as a field commander, Miranda settled in London and later took part in Venezuela's independence effort in 1810, where he promoted the colony's 1811 Declaration of Independence from Spain, an act which established (albeit unsuccessfully at the time) the region's first republic.

The New Democracy in America: Travels of Francisco de Miranda in the United States, 1783–84. Trans. Judson P. Wood and edited by John S. Ezell (Norman: University of Oklahoma Press, 1963).
Racine, Karen, Francisco de Miranda: A Transatlantic Life (Wilmington: Scholarly Resources, 2002).

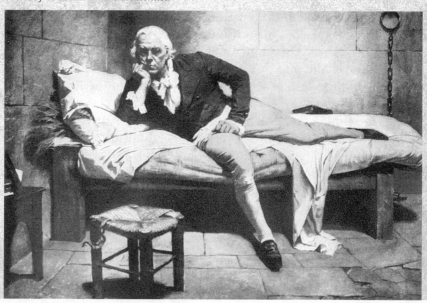

Venezuelan revolutionary Francisco de Miranda (1750?–1816). "Miranda in Prison," oil on canvas by Luis Montero. Credit: The Granger Collection, New York.

Even at this late hour, republicans in Paris continued to believe they could control events in Saint Domingue, and perhaps even use its black armies to revolutionize the slaves on British and Spanish islands in the Caribbean. To this end, in August 1792 the mayor of Paris, Jérome Pétion de Villeneuve, called upon the Venezuelan adventurer Francisco de Miranda. Trained as a Spanish officer, Miranda's tour of the United States during the 1780s had transformed him into a South American nationalist, and both his love of liberty and need of an army had brought him to France. For his part, Pétion hoped that the appointment of Miranda as governor of Saint Domingue would restore order (and hence profits) and lead to the conquest of other colonies. As one member of the National Assembly put it, "This Revolution must be made in Spain and Spanish America." Basing his plan on a convenient error that Miranda had served as a brigadier general in the American Revolution, journalist Jacques-Pierre Brissot had little doubt that the Venezuelan's name "will strike Spain with Fear and curse [William] Pitt [the Younger] with his dilatory Politics."

The French republicans finalized the bargain on August 25. Miranda was granted the title of field marshal and a salary of 25,000 livres. Following a brief period of service in the European war that France began against Austria and Prussia in 1792, Miranda would first be shipped to Saint Domingue and could then employ his troops in the cause of South American independence. Provided, Pétion wrote, that he did not mind leading "turbulent Whites" in battle while in Europe, he might later become the "Idol of the [free] people of Colour." How that was to be accomplished with Le Cap François in revolt was left unsaid by the mayor, who also declined to elaborate on the contradiction between fighting for the liberation of Spanish subjects while denying freedom to the enslaved majority on Saint Domingue. An enthusiastic Miranda took time only to write to his friend Alexander Hamilton that soon their old dream of a common "Country America [stretching] from the North to the South" would soon be realized before riding for the Belgian border to join French forces already under attack. The war against revolutionary France would continue around the Atlantic, with the exception of a brief respite from 1802 to 1804, for the next twenty-three years.

The Reign of Terror

At about the same time that Austria issued its declaration designed to assist Louis XVI, the king, never short on poor ideas, decided to flee the country. Departing at midnight on June 20, 1792, the royal family made an escape that took on aspects of a comic opera. Although the myth that the driver took a wrong turn and wandered about the Left Bank of the Seine is probably just that, one horse after another stumbled and fell, snapping the carriage harness and wasting two precious hours in its repair. After twenty-two hours of inconsistent travel, the party reached Varennes-en-Argonne, a dusty hamlet of only one hundred people. The driver needed fresh horses, the royal family food and wine. Louis awakened a restaurateur appropriately named Monsieur Sauce and demanded a full-course meal. According to one version of events, an unsuspecting Sauce recognized the king from the portrait on the money Louis used to pay the bill. A less dramatic but probably more accurate account is that Sauce, as a procurator of the local commune, knew all along who his guests were and served an elegant repast to delay the family while someone else summoned the National Guard. As the crowd that gathered consisted mostly of unarmed peasants, the king and his few bodyguards could have taken to the road without difficulty, but fearing for the safety of his children, Louis declined the sword that was offered him. As he "was a prisoner," a dejected Louis announced, he "had no orders to give."

The question was what to do with the royal family. "Let them go," was the advice of the Englishman Thomas Paine, now back in Europe as a member of the National Assembly. But for the city's radical Jacobins—who derived their name from the fact that they originally met in a former convent of the *Soeurs de Saint-Jacques*—the answer was simple, and engaged their desire to abolish the monarchy and set up a republic based upon the American model. Speaking through interpreters, since he spoke almost no French, Paine again urged that Louis be exiled to the United States, where he might be rehabilitated into a productive citizen, an idea seconded by Gouverneur Morris, the new American minister, and Edmond Charles Genet, who was preparing to depart for the United States, as the Assembly's minister there. But Jean-Paul Marat shouted that as a Quaker opposed to capital punishment, the Englishman could have no opinion on the matter. The date of execution was set for January 21, 1793.

Dr. Guillotin's machine, created as a reform designed to spare prisoners gratuitous pain, was constructed on the large square recently renamed the Place de la Révolution (it is today the Place de la Concorde). Louis rose at six o'clock and received communion, but due to the crowds and a damp fog, the coach did not arrive at the scaffold before ten. As many as twenty thousand spectators watched as the king mounted the platform and tried to speak. "I die innocent of all the crimes of which I have been charged," he shouted before a drum roll drowned out the remainder of his speech. Guards shoved the king onto a plank and strapped him down. Charles Sanson pulled the cord, and then, in keeping with tradition, lifted the dripping head from the basket to show it to the people. Ten months later, Marie Antoinette, better known simply as the "Widow Capet," followed her husband to the guillotine; the dauphin, ten-year-old Louis Charles, whom monarchists would later recognize as King Louis XVII, died of tuberculosis in June 1795 while in captivity. Revolutions, as the French revolutionary Georges Danton once dryly observed, could not be made with rosewater.

Washington's Dilemma

Britain's entrance into the Franco-Austrian conflict in 1795 gave pause to members of the Washington administration. The Franco-American military alliance of 1778 was a defensive one, and as the Convention—as the National Assembly had renamed itself—had declared war on England, the United States was not formally obliged to go to war. Paris might reasonably believe, however, that French privateers enjoyed the tacit right to tow their prizes into American ports, a privilege France allowed North American shippers before

1783. But in Philadelphia, Washington feared that preferential treatment for French warships would further strain already sour relations with London. On April 22, the president issued a proclamation warning American citizens not to become involved in the hostilities. Out of deference to Secretary of State Jefferson, who regarded France as a sister republic, the actual word *neutrality* did not appear in the document, but the intent of the administration could not be more clear.

Two weeks before, the first minister from the French republic, Edmond Charles Genet, arrived in Charleston. Aware that planters from the southern states favored Jefferson's Republican Party and were sympathetic to the French cause, the thirty-year-old Genet, already a seasoned veteran of the diplomatic corps, landed in South Carolina in hopes that a showy overland march for Pennsylvania would garner popular support and persuade Washington to side with France in the Atlantic wars. Shippers and artisans, wearing hats decorated with laurel branches, marched to the dock to escort the young *Girondin* (a member of the Republican party of France) to a reception at his hotel. Among them was Joseph Vesey, the same former slave trader who had helped raise funds for white Haitian refugees. Charlestonians offered toasts to the closer "union of the two Republics" and cheered the "speedy revolution of Great Britain and Ireland on Sans-Culotte Principles."

Yet even as Genet began his slow overland parade toward Philadelphia, white southerners started to turn against the brash diplomat, and not merely because he lacked balance and sound judgment. The Frenchman's enemies let it be known that Genet was a founding member of the *Société des Amis des Noirs*, the powerful Parisian antislavery society with ties to abolitionists in London and Philadelphia. Despite the fact that the policies pursued by the group were gradualist in nature, this affiliation served to discredit the minister in the eyes of white southerners. No sooner had the Jeffersonians realized that Genet, unlike their own political elite, actually believed in social revolution, than they began to abandon him. As one South Carolinian fretted, "Our French friends will do no good to our Blacks." Even Jefferson quickly abandoned the hapless Frenchman. On August 2 the cabinet unanimously agreed to demand Genet's recall. Rather than face disgrace and possible execution in France, Genet requested political asylum, married the daughter of Governor George Clinton, and settled into the life of a New York country gentleman.

Genet's preference for a bucolic retirement on Long Island is easy to appreciate. One month prior to his recall, Maximilien Robespierre, the austere and selfless young abolitionist, joined the Committee of Public Safety. The twelve-member group functioned as a kind of war cabinet, but was also instrumental in creating what Robespierre called a Republic of Virtue, a political atmosphere in which civic virtue rather than aristocratic corruption might flourish. "Terror is nothing but prompt, severe, inflexible justice," Robespierre explained to the Convention, "it is therefore an emanation of virtue." Since the new order could tolerate no remnants of the Old Regime, the Convention altered the calendar, de-emphasized traditional Christianity—even to the point of renaming the Cathedral of Notre Dame the Temple of Reason—and banned older forms of address in favor of "Citizen" and

On Names

The inability of residents of the United States, including too many historians, to spell correctly the names of foreign places and persons of importance says much about the way Americans see the world and their place in it. The nation that is now Haiti is a case in point. The indigenous Taínos of the island originally called it "Haiti," meaning mountainous. The Spanish renamed it "Hispaniola"— a word derived from "Hispania," a term the Romans gave to the Iberian Peninsula—and called the 1496 colony they established there Santo Domingo, in honor of Saint Dominic. French settlers wrestled the western side of the island, or Saint Domingue, away from Madrid's control, a loss Spain officially recognized in the 1697 Treaty of Ryswick. On November 29, 1803, Jean Jacque Dessalines and his generals met at Gonaives, where they chose the aboriginal name of "Haiti" for their now-independent republic.

Despite the fact that the island had been divided into French and Spanish colonies for nearly a century, American politicians in the 1790s linguistically fused the two together. Even before the 1795 Treaty of Basle temporarily united the island by ceding the Spanish half to France, Thomas Jefferson referred to the French colony as "St. Domingo," and historians have been confused ever since.

Similarly, Toussaint Louverture's name confounds modern scholars. As a slave, Toussaint lived at the Bréda plantation on the Plaine du Nord; like many slaves and freedmen, he often used his place of origin as a surname. As far as any extant document indicates, he first adopted the surname of Louverture in a proclamation dated August 29, 1793, after General Etienne Laveaux complained that the black leader "always manages to find an opening." His brother Paul and son Placide soon followed suit. Although literate, Louverture did not spell his name "L'Ouverture," either because his formal French was imperfect, or due to the Haitian

Toussaint Louverture from "Vie de Toussaint-L'Ouverture," by Saint-Remy of Hayti, Paris, 1850. Library of Congress, LC-YSZ62-7862.

tendency to slur words together and verbally eliminate accent stops.

Although most accounts of the 1790s spell diplomat Edmond Charles Genet's surname with a circumflex accent on the second "e," that is, "Genêt," the young Frenchman did not do so. The error evidently began with the publication of John Spencer Bassett's Federalist System, 1789–1801 (1906). Typical is David McCullough's Pulitzer Prize–winning John Adams (2001), which commits all three errors; one wonders how many awards the biography would have garnered if its author, along with the editors at Simon and Schuster, could not correctly spell "Britain" or "Monroe" or some other name that white scholars perceive as important.

"Citizenness," a fashion soon embraced by some Virginians, such as Jefferson's kinsman, the eccentric John Randolph of Roanoke. Before the Reign of Terror ended with Robespierre's own execution, as many as twenty thousand people— monarchists, devout Catholics, Girondins—had fallen victim to the national razor. Hoping to deny the crowd its pleasure, Augustine Robespierre, Maximilien's younger brother, threw himself from a window in the Hôtel de Ville, and Joseph Le Bas shot himself. Robespierre tried a similar act of suicide but succeeded only in shattering his jaw. The next morning, after strapping Robespierre to the plank, the executioner Sanson (the same who had presided over the death of the king) ripped the bandage from his victim's jaw to give the cutting edge an unobstructed fall. The screams ended only when the blade found its mark.

Few residents of the continent were sorry to see Robespierre fall. On the other hand, slaves in the French colonies did not share that view. As a member of the *Amis des Noirs*, the Apostle of Virtue had long called for an end to slavery in the Caribbean. Even before the Night of Fire, white planters in Saint Domingue and Guadeloupe began to collaborate with the English, whom they regarded as a more reliable defender of their crumbling plantation system. In London, Prime Minister William Pitt the Younger and Secretary of War Henry Dundas hoped to protect slavery in Jamaica and perhaps even capture Saint Domingue, which could either be retained or used as a valuable bargaining chip in any negotiated peace with Paris. To punish white "traitors" to the republic and cement an alliance with the emerging black leadership in the colony, on February 4, 1794, the Convention decreed, "slavery be abolished in all the territory of the Republic, including Saint Domingue," which had already been invaded by both the Spanish and British. Toussaint, who had adopted the surname of Louverture (meaning, "The Opening") a year before while fighting with the Spanish, promptly turned his coat and, in a public letter, tendered his services to the French nation. Together with André Rigaud, a mixed-race general, Louverture's forces shoved the Spanish eastward back into Santo Domingo, and the British west toward the Golfe de LaGonâve. Deciding they could no longer rely on the black hostages they had taken for safety, the British slaughtered more than one hundred captives, dumped their bodies into the sea, and made a hasty retreat south toward Port-au-Prince.

The Thermidorian Reaction

The debacle in the Caribbean was hardly the only British setback that year. The war with France, never popular among the English working poor who favored Parliamentary reform, dislocated the economy while removing young heads of households, who were impressed into the Royal Navy. Although a conservative tempering of the revolution in France, known as the Thermidorian Reaction (after the short-lived republican name for July), was well underway, Pitt cynically planned to use the emergency of war to stifle radical agitation at home. In a series of laws passed in 1794 and 1795, Parliament suspended habeas corpus and passed a new Treason Act as well as a Seditious Practices Act. Armed with these statutes, Pitt began a series of high-profile state trials, in which twelve leading members of the London Corresponding Society—a group of tradesmen and artisans who had been in communication with like-minded French reformers—were charged with treason.

Despite the government's prosecutions, London's radical community fought back. The Corresponding Society called for a mass demonstration at Copenhagen Fields near Islington, and as many as 150,000 protesters turned out. Three days later, on October 29, 1795, as King George traveled through the streets to open the new session of Parliament, a crowd pelted his carriage with rocks while shouting, "Down with Pitt" and "No War." Many of the protestors wore black crepe, a symbol that liberty was dead. A vender selling Paine's *The Rights of Man*, which defended the French Revolution from the attacks by the statesman and philosopher Edmund Burke, was seized by the royal guard but freed by the crowd, who then carried him triumphantly through the streets in a chair. Either a rock or a musket ball fractured the king's window. Upon reaching Parliament, the king stumbled inside, gasping, "My Lord, I, I, I've been shot at." On the following evening, so that the royal family might attend the theater, a small army of 100 infantry, 200 cavalrymen, and 500 constables cleared the roads of the king's subjects, whom one officer derided as "the worst and lowest sort."

For the war-weary English public, rumors that the British invasion of Saint Domingue had proved a spectacular failure and that a good number of young men would be returning home came as welcome news. As 1796 drew to a close, War Minister Henry Dundas calculated that his government had spent £4.4 million in its unsuccessful attempt to wrest the French Caribbean from the mercantilist grip of Paris, and to wring Saint Domingue from the hands of former Domingan slaves. Total casualties approached eighty thousand, of which forty thousand lay dead of yellow fever or wounds received in battle against now-General Louverture's soldiers. It remained only for the English commander, General Thomas Maitland, to salvage what he could from such an utter defeat and abandon the island. In what amounted to a document of surrender, Britain promised not to invade the colony again for "the entire duration of the present [European] war," provided that Louverture not allow France to use his "colonial troops" to attack Jamaica or Grenada during the same period.

For Britain, the one ray of hope was the election in the United States of John Adams at the head of a Federalist ticket in 1796. The election of the pro-British Adams as president threatened to lead to a diplomatic breach between France and the United States, which, even if it did not result in open war, might at least distract Paris from the war in Europe. Incensed at Genet's failure to secure access to mainland ports for French privateers, and enraged further by the profitable trade agreement John Jay obtained with Britain in 1794, the French Directory—the five-man executive body that governed France since the end of the Terror—in March of 1797 annulled the Franco-American commercial treaty of 1778 and allowed French warships to drag neutral (that is, United States) prizes into continental or colonial ports. Congress retaliated the following June by imposing an embargo on all shipping between the United States and France or its colonies. But because many American vessels sailed not for the war-torn continent but for the Caribbean, where they were easy prey for French privateers, insurance underwriters demanded special "war premiums" for those ships trading with British merchants in Jamaica or Barbados. Consequently, the emerging Quasi-War between France and the United States was largely waged in the Caribbean, and not in the North Atlantic.

Not wishing a complete breach with Paris, President Adams chose to send a special mission to France to resolve all outstanding issues. The delegation consisted of Charles Cotesworth Pinckney, John Marshall, and Adams's old friend Elbridge Gerry of Massachusetts. Upon arriving in Paris, the trio were met not by Charles Maurice de Talleyrand, the French foreign minister, but rather by four of his agents, who were later identified in the diplomatic correspondence as W, X, Y, and Z. As a woman, agent W, or Madame de Villette, the adopted daughter of the celebrated philosopher-poet Voltaire and reputedly his mistress as well, typically gets omitted from most modern accounts of the intrigue. (John Marshall, however, whose emotionally troubled wife remained in Virginia, regarded the seductive Villette as the most appealing part of his Paris adventure.) The agents informed the delegates that Talleyrand might meet with them at a later date, but only after they paid a cash bribe of $250,000 and helped to arrange for a loan from the United States of $12 million to the French government. A bribe was traditional enough in European diplomacy, but the loan, which was to be allocated to the French war effort, would trigger hostilities with Britain, as was no doubt intended. All but Gerry left Paris in frustration.

The Haitian Détente

Marshall's dispatches were not the only documents slowly sailing toward the United States capital of Philadelphia. On November 6, 1798, at about the same time that the delegates informed Adams of the failure of their mission, Toussaint Louverture took up his quill pen and began a long missive to President Adams. Having waged a bloody campaign against a British army that wished to re-enslave his soldiers, the shrewd Louverture recognized that English goodwill would last not a moment longer than the French threat in Europe. Yet neither could he turn to France for support. The current Directory had no intention of rescinding the decree of emancipation. But as the composition of the Directory changed each year, when a new member replaced a departing constituent, Paris rarely maintained a steady policy on any crucial matter. Louverture needed an ally, preferably one with provisions and warships. Affecting to understand nothing about the Quasi-War between the United States and the nation to which he allegedly remained loyal, Louverture did "not pretend to know" why American ships no longer filled his harbors. But he assured Adams "that Americans will find protection and security in the ports of Saint Domingue."

Given the growing estrangement between Philadelphia and Paris, military considerations—as well as trade, which was never far from any New Englander's mind—made it imperative to seduce Saint Domingue away from the French orbit. Not only had the Directory turned its Caribbean colonies into bases from which to attack American shipping, the French government even seriously considered sending a black army under General Theodore Hédouville, the infamous "Pacifier of the Vendée," to "invade both the Southern States of America and the Island of Jamaica" to "excite an insurrection among the negroes." Among those concerned about the very real possibility of a Franco-Domingan invasion force was George Washington, who had been called back into service to reorganize the recently enlarged U.S. Army. "If the

French should be so *mad*" as to invade the United States, he warned, "their operations will commence in the Southern quarter [as] there can be no doubt of their arming our own Negroes against us."

When Congress reconvened in January 1799, Harrison Gray Otis, chairman of the Committee on Defense, called upon the House to amend the June 1798 embargo with France to allow a resumption of trade with Saint Domingue. The thought that the Adams administration was prepared to recognize a government led by men of African ancestry infuriated even northern Republicans. Swiss-born congressman Albert Gallatin rose to complain that Louverture's army had only recently "been initiated to Liberty" through "rapine, pillage, and massacre." Ignoring all such warnings, the Federalist majority passed the bill, informally known as "Toussaint's clause," by a party-line vote. "We may expect therefore black crews, & supercargoes & missionaries" to pour "into the Southern States," fretted Jefferson.

To investigate the situation in the colony and represent American commercial interests, Adams appointed Dr. Edward Stevens as consul general to Saint Domingue. Stevens arrived in Le Cap François in mid-April. Philippe Roume, the agent of the Directory in Saint Domingue, greeted the consul. But Secretary Pickering had made it clear to the envoy that the "Negro general Toussaint now commands" the government in the colony, and Stevens requested an audience with the old soldier. Louverture arrived early the next morning and "received [Stevens] very favorably." The American diplomat emphasized that no trade could resume until all French privateers vacated the island, and on the following day, Louverture replied that he completely accepted "the Justice and Propriety of the President's Demands." Although the general's power was nominally confined to the colony's military administration, he and Stevens signed an agreement on April 25 consisting of nine articles. The accord banned French privateers from the ports under Louverture's control while opening his docks to "the Merchant Vessels and Ships of War of the United States." In this accord—a curious union forged out of military exigency—the Calvinist New Englander and the former slave racialized the age of revolution and advanced the possibility that political fraternity could look beyond color in the name of extending republican liberty to all.

It may seem baffling as to how a group of profoundly conservative Federalists might regard Louverture, to borrow Otis's words, as "a very able and influential character," while the liberal Jefferson could deride Haitian soldiers as "cannibals." But if Adams's statecraft knew neither color nor servitude, he was no champion of black social equality; he regarded Louverture as an African Burke, the sort of leader who might restore order to the region. As a social conservative and a spokesman for mercantile capitalism, Adams regarded slavery (as did many Federalist businessmen) as an anachronistic and inefficient way to organize labor. Unlike many white abolitionists in the northern Atlantic, who regarded slavery as an ethical affront to God, Adams simply saw no contradiction between believing in the moral superiority of free wage labor, while suggesting also, as John Jay once put it, that "those who own this country ought to govern it."

If Adams pursued a more enlightened diplomacy toward Haiti than did any other American administration prior to 1861, domestic affairs were quite another matter. In conscious imitation of the British government's gagging of free speech, in the summer of 1798 the Federalist majority in Congress passed a series of four laws, collectively known as the Alien and Sedition Acts, which explicitly responded to the radical ideas and the proponents thereof circulating in the northern Atlantic. The first three were directed at immigrants, Irish and French nationals whom the Federalists presumed to be insufficiently supportive of the Quasi-War. The fourth, the Sedition Act, meted out jail terms and fines of up to five years and $5,000 for persons who published or uttered "any false, scandalous and malicious writings against the government of the United States." Among those jailed was James Thomson Callender, who had fled England to escape Pitt's Sedition Act, and Luther Baldwin, a New Jersey inebriate who was luckless enough to be leaving a Newark dram shop as the president's carriage passed by on the way north to Quincy. When told that the cannon he heard were being fired in honor of Adams, Baldwin replied "that he did not care if they fired thro' his ass." Tried in a circuit court presided over by Bushrod Washington (the former president's nephew and an Associate Justice of the Supreme Court), Baldwin was fined $150 and committed to federal jail until the fine was paid.

Despite these successful assaults on dissenting voices, President Adams soon realized he was facing the threat of civil strife at home. The aged George Washington turned over active command of his forces to Hamilton. Long anxious for a full-scale war with France and openly demanding a naval alliance with Britain, Hamilton was again corresponding with Francisco de Miranda about the possibility of a joint Anglo-American invasion of Spanish New Orleans and East Florida. As Spain had forsaken the British coalition in 1796 and allied itself with the French Directory, the dream of an independent South America, which might grant commercial privileges to both London and Philadelphia, appeared to be within easy reach. "The command in this case," Hamilton informed Rufus King, then minister to Britain, "would very naturally fall upon me." This much Adams knew. What the president only suspected was that Hamilton's military ambitions encompassed far more than the Spanish colonies. Having once helped to lead an army into western Pennsylvania to crush the Whiskey Rebels, Hamilton now proposed to "put Virginia to the test" by marching an army through it.

Increasingly sensitive to Talleyrand's subtle hints that France would welcome another peace delegation, Adams decided to forestall Hamilton's intrigues. On February 18, 1799, without consulting his disloyal cabinet, the president notified the Senate of his decision to nominate yet another special envoy to Paris. Historians have traditionally applauded this "spectacularly courageous course," in seeking to end the Quasi-War. But by focusing only on domestic debates *within* the United States and not paying sufficient attention to events elsewhere in the Atlantic world, scholars have failed to note that by the fall of 1798, it appeared that Britain was about to lose its six-year-old conflict with France. And Adams had no desire to fight on without the protective umbrella of the Royal Navy, weak as it was at this time.

Indeed, the Royal Navy had virtually ceased to defend Britain, let alone the fledgling American military. The year before, in April 1797, naval mutinies erupted at Spithead and Nore, the anchorage beyond the mouth of the

Thames. The revolt began among the 1,600 men compressed into HMS *Sandwich*, a rotten carcass built decades before, during the Seven Years' War. No longer capable of navigating the high seas, the *Sandwich* was used as a harbor depot ship, a floating transfer station for young men culled from English prisons and poorhouses. When Admiral Lord Bridgeport inexplicably ordered the wreck into the Channel, the sailors aboard the *Sandwich* refused, and the mutiny quickly spread to every ship anchored at Spithead. The entire Channel Fleet, the force upon which Britain had relied for its very survival since the days of the Armada, refused their orders, put their officers ashore, and demanded better working conditions.

Although the revolt began due to the sad fact, as one mutineer complained, that no man in the Royal Navy "was looked on as a human being," the mutiny, in the words of historian E. P. Thompson, was no "parochial affair of ship's biscuits and arrears of pay," but rather a truly "revolutionary movement" designed to end the monarchy. Many of the sailors were aware that the French had transport ships waiting across the Channel at Calais, and with no fleet to stop them, their army could land at Dover within days. Other mariners had attended radical meetings—dubbed Jacobin Clubs, after their Paris and Philadelphia counterparts—in Chatham and Portsmouth, and members of the outlawed London Corresponding Society made contact with leaders of the mutiny, especially Richard Parker, whom delegates from mutinied vessels elected as their spokesman. One source placed a "gentleman in black," known only as Dr. Watson, at several seaboard meetings with Parker, and rumor had it that Watson was actively working for a French invasion.

Petitions sent directly to King George III were returned with an ultimatum that all sailors would be branded as rebels if they did not return their ships to duty. As thirst and hunger took their toll, two ships broke ranks and sailed for Portsmouth; Parker demanded that they be fired upon, but only a few guns blazed, and soon other ships quietly slipped away from the pack. Parker soon swung from the yardarm of the *Sandwich*, which was shortly afterward broken up as unnavigable.

Pitt's problems were far from over. Among the mutineers were hundreds of Irishmen impressed into naval service, Catholics who regarded a French alliance as the surest path to Irish independence. Fully aware that Ireland posed the greatest threat to England's war effort, Pitt offered several conciliatory reforms designed to encourage Irish pacifism. The proximity of Ireland to England's west coast presented an inviting staging ground for hostile troops, and Irish Catholics who chafed under British rule had for centuries demonstrated their willingness to seek alliances among England's most hated enemies. After 1793, a small number of Catholics were allowed to purchase land—prior to that date, Protestants alone owned all of the soil of Ireland—and the Relief Act of the same year allowed Irishmen to serve on juries and bear arms. But Catholics subjects of the British crown could not yet hold major office or be elected to Parliament, and Ireland remained a kingdom occupied by a foreign power.

By the 1790s, some of the aged animosities between Protestants and Catholics—the latter constituted three-quarters of the Irish population—had begun to fade, and more than a few Irish Protestants had come to believe that their interests lay elsewhere than London. The Catholic Committee, a benevolent society, fell into the hands of a radical leadership more taken with the ideals of the French Revolution than in refighting old sectarian battles. "What prevents you," one Catholic demanded of his followers, "from coalescing with your Protestant brethren? Nothing!" Soon the newly founded United Irish Club of Dublin boasted a membership of 130 Protestants and 140 Catholics. Until it was banned by the British government, a few Ulstermen formed "The Irish Jacobins of Belfast," a French term also embraced by militant artisans in Philadelphia and New York. Should the Irish truly unify, rebels to the west could pose a significant threat to war-weary Britain, as the population of Ireland equalled that of the United States, and half that of England.

Among those who remained dissatisfied with Pitt's pretense to reform was Theobald Wolfe Tone, a graduate of Trinity College, Dublin, who had studied law in London. One of the organizers of the Society of United Irishmen, Tone advocated cooperation between Catholics and his fellow Protestants in the name of independence. When he began to correspond with William Jackson, an agent for Robespierre's Committee of Public Safety, Parliament branded Tone a traitor. He fled first to the United States, and then to France, where he advocated an invasion of Britain by way of Ireland. Success of the venture relied on French support in precisely the same way that the American Revolution had hinged on a French alliance. Given the rank of adjutant general by the French government, Tone and General Lazare Hoche set sail with an impressive flotilla of forty-six ships in December 1796. A storm not unlike that visited upon the Spanish Armada 208 years earlier wrecked most of the ships. Tone waded ashore with a small expeditionary force, only to be captured by the English. Sentenced to swing, Tone cheated the hangman of his spectacle by cutting his throat in jail in November 1798.

The death of a single man rarely alters much, and that was hardly the end of the troubles. By the time of Tone's suicide, Irish anger at English rule had exploded into open revolt. Irish nationalists continued to look to France for aid, and at least one priest, Father O'Coigly, journeyed to Paris under the name of "Captain Jones." In London, R. T. Crossfield of the London Corresponding Society published "An Address to the Irish Nation," in which he voiced support for "two distinct republicks" and called on English soldiers to follow the example of the mutineers and refuse to act as "agents of enslaving Ireland." Determined to crush Jacobinism both at home and across the Irish Sea, Pitt set out on a course of brutal repression. Arrests and hangings ended any broader conspiracy to liberate Ireland and stage a coup d'état against the monarchy. Captured in London, Father O'Coigly was executed, and other radicals, such as Colonel Edmund Despard—veteran of the disastrous Mosquito Coast invasion of 1780—languished in prison. Although Protestants in much of Ireland banded together with Catholics in resisting English rule, in Ulster, where Protestants enjoyed a majority, it was not difficult for Pitt's agents to make their case against Irish-Franco cooperation. Now Ulster Protestants formed the Orange Society and burned Catholic homes and chapels. The British general in command of the city requested and received the right to declare martial law, but he used his reinforcements only against Catholic insurgents. By 1798 there were 140,000 British soldiers in Ireland. As the pile of corpses mounted, the rebellion collapsed.

But this rebellion ended just in time for another one to emerge, which served as an American incentive to peace. On the western shores of the Atlantic, President Adams's problems continued to mount, not least of which was the fact that Virginia slaves, not unlike the Irish poor, sought to take advantage of the chaos of the Quasi-War to free themselves. Among those talking revolution was a young blacksmith known only as Gabriel. Hired out to Richmond craftsmen for much of his adult life, Gabriel's vision of a more egalitarian society was shaped less by the tobacco plantation than by the democratic world of the urban artisans. As he explained it to his two brothers and other black artisans, Gabriel believed that the time had come for Chesapeake slaves to rise up for their freedom; his men also counted on assistance from "the poor white people" and "the most redoubtable republicans" in the state. In fact, Gabriel had the verbal support of two Frenchmen, soldiers with ties to Philadelphia who had first arrived in the region in the late 1770s with Rochambeau's army. Like those Haitian rebels who united behind Louverture, Gabriel's men sought not merely freedom, but full political and economic equality. As a Virginian born in 1776, Gabriel had been raised amidst the heady talk of liberty and natural rights, and as his former master was a close friend of Patrick Henry, it was no accident that Gabriel planned to march his army into Richmond beneath a flag reading "death or Liberty."

Exploiting their ability to hire out their time around the region, Gabriel's lieutenants recruited at least one hundred soldiers who agreed to meet just outside of Richmond. Understanding that a slave uprising, like any popular revolution, was more of a process than an event, Gabriel expected to raise another five hundred rebels as they marched toward the capital. But on the day appointed for the revolt, the skies opened and heavy rains washed away bridges and communications. In the midst of the downpour, several slaves lost their courage and informed their master of the plot. Gabriel briefly escaped downriver to Norfolk with a white, antislavery skipper, but dozens of slaves and free blacks were rounded up in the Richmond area and charged with "conspiracy and insurrection."

Eventually turned in by an enslaved mariner for the reward, Gabriel was returned to Richmond in chains. During his brief trial, one witness testified that no "Quakers, Methodists, [or] French people" were to be harmed, as they were the friends of equality. As a concerned Virginian worried, even on the gallows the black revolutionaries displayed a "sense of their [natural] rights, [and] a contempt of danger." Another rebel, upon being asked if he had anything to say upon sentence of death, boldly replied that he had "nothing more to offer than what General Washington would have had to offer, had he been taken by the British and put to trial" by King George. "I have adventured my life in endeavouring to obtain the liberty of my countrymen," he explained, "and am a willing sacrifice in their cause." In all, Gabriel and twenty-six others swung from the gibbet; another eight were transported to Spanish New Orleans, where they were most likely sold at auction.

In Philadelphia, President Adams read of all these events with growing trepidation. Although a staunchly antislavery man, he had no desire to see slave rebellions in the southern states. And if Ireland was the Achilles Heel of Britain's war effort, the Royal Navy was the United States' first line of defense. Although the French navy hardly rivaled its English counterpart, until its stunning defeat by the British navy off Cape Trafalgar in 1805, it remained a considerable threat to the unimpressive American military (Congress had created a Department of the Navy only in April 1798). Adams feared that King George's rumored descent into madness and Pitt's resulting fall from power might lead to an armistice between Britain and France, which would leave the United States to face alone the wrath of a victorious France. It was no small irony that, having once denounced King George as a tyrant and an enemy, Adams now relied upon the good will of that same monarch and the backing of an English prime minister for protection against the nation his fledgling country had turned to in 1778 for military support.

As far as the Federalist Party was concerned, the only cause for cheer in late 1798 and early 1799 was the success of Adams's détente with Louverture, which both aided in the recovery of American trade and weakened the French economy. The renewed commerce with the United States was particularly important to Louverture, as American merchants were willing to ship guns and ammunition, whereas French and British traders preferred to traffic in less lethal provisions. By March of 1799, Secretary of State Timothy Pickering "confidently" informed Rufus King in London that Louverture's appetite for American commerce, as well as his concerns over the growing conservative trend in Paris, was but a prelude to "the Independence" of Saint Domingue.

It is John Adams's fate, and perhaps his desserts, to be remembered as the president who signed the Sedition Act into law; yet it was this same commander-in-chief who dispatched American ships to crush both French power and the conservative gens de couleur who sided with General André Rigaud against Louverture. Consul General Stevens begged the administration to impose a naval blockade on the southern side of the colony so as to cut off "all Supplies of Provisions and Ammunition" to the ports under Rigaud's control. The frigates *Boston*, *Connecticut*, and *General Greene* cooperated with the Royal Navy along the southern coast of Saint Domingue, while the *Constitution* and the *Norfolk* attacked and captured a French vessel carrying instructions from Roume. With American and British warships acting the part of Louverture's navy by protecting his southern flank, the general made short work of Rigaud's attempts to keep the black army loyal to Paris. The "black Chiefs," as Stevens dubbed officers Jean Jacques Dessalines and Paul Louverture (Toussaint's brother), "now talk loudly and openly" in favor of autonomy. For his part, Toussaint Louverture wished to move slowly until forced to act by events in France. But his victory over Rigaud and Roume left the general with both military and civil authority on the entire island. "All connection with France will soon be broken off," Stevens informed Philadelphia in code.

So deeply invested was the Adams administration in Haitian liberty that Secretary of State Pickering even thought it worthwhile to advise Louverture on the shape of his emerging government. Having little experience in constitution building, the secretary naturally turned to one who did: Alexander Hamilton. The New Yorker's response indicated that Federalist confidence in the black general did not extend to his populace, but then Hamilton was never one to exhibit much faith in popular democracy. "The Government if independent must be military," he advised Pickering, "partaking of the feudal system." Echoing, ironically, Jefferson's doubts about the ability of former slaves to govern themselves, Hamilton preferred a monarchy for the island but recognized that such an idea was "impracticable." Instead, in words reminiscent of the position he had adopted at the Philadelphia constitutional convention in 1787, he recommended a "single Executive to hold his place for life." Land was to be divided among young men following obligatory military service. No extant evidence proves that Hamilton's missive ever reached Louverture's hands, but in a coincidence worthy of Dickens, shortly thereafter the general announced the first-ever constitution for Saint Domingue (which technically remained a French colony). According to the American consul, it "declared Genl. Toussaint Louverture Governor for life, with the power of naming his successor."

In an unfortunate way, Saint Domingue's constitution of 1801 mirrored the reactionary changes blowing about the Atlantic in the final moments of the eighteenth century. Just as the U.S. Constitution had retreated from the egalitarian promise of the Declaration of Independence, and as the governments of Britain and France had grown more repressive as the decade wore on, Louverture's handiwork revealed a shift toward order. Although the document renewed the French Assembly's 1794 ban on slavery and promised each "cultivator" a right to a portion of each plantation's revenues, workers were not allowed to leave the estates of their "fathers," the property owners. Undoubtedly, Louverture believed that a healthy agricultural economy was necessary for keeping his European enemies at bay, and that meant a forced return to the land, but the constitution also came at the cost of alienating now-Governor Louverture from the public he served. As one modern critic of the constitution has suggested, to "defend freedom," black workers "had to surrender their freedom to the new state."

Ultimately, however, what altered the course of Haitian history was the series of events in Paris and the new United States capital of Washington City. In France, the coup staged on November 9, 1799, by Napoleon Bonaparte and two members of the Directory, Emmanuel Sieyès and Roger Ducos, only strengthened Louverture's suspicions that much of the *ancien regime* would soon return. Bonaparte, perhaps influenced by his Martinique-born wife, Josephine, the owner of a plantation in Saint Domingue, immediately began to staff the colonial administration with men who had supported slavery during the early 1790s. To assuage Haitian concerns, Bonaparte issued a proclamation to the "Brave Blacks of St. Domingue," in which he insisted that the three consuls had no intention of revoking the emancipation decree of 1794. Privately, however, Bonaparte was enraged by Louverture's constitution. By declaring the Haitian people to be both "French" and "free," the black general had complicated Bonaparte's hopes of returning the island's freed people to an inferior status.

By then the international situation had rapidly changed. Bonaparte desired a quick end to American interference in the Caribbean, so that he might work to restore France's lost empire and focus his attention on the war he was waging in Europe, which gave signs of winding down following a failed Anglo-Russian invasion of northern Holland. After months of stalled negotiations, the American envoy agreed to drop the property claims in exchange for a release from the twenty-two-year-old treaties. The new arrangement, formally known as the Franco-American Convention, was signed in both languages on September 30, 1800, at Mortefontaine, Joseph Bonaparte's country estate eighteen miles north of Paris.

Although Adams insisted that administrative support for Louverture would continue, "as if no negotiation was going on," the end of the Quasi-War came as grim news in Cap François. Although Louverture had no way of knowing, worse yet was to come. Only one day later, on October 1, Louis-Alexandre Berthier, a French general and emissary, signed at San Ildefonso, the summer palace of Spain's King Charles IV, a secret treaty that restored the entire Louisiana region to French control. In exchange for the territory ceded to Spain in 1763, together with six warships, Berthier promised to obtain the northern Italian kingdom of Tuscany for the son-in-law of the Spanish king. Although many European diplomats believed that Charles was getting the better part of the bargain, Bonaparte correctly regarded Louisiana as a granary necessary to feed a re-enslaved Haitian population.

With his invasion of Holland a disaster and his navy continuously beset by mutinies, Pitt had little choice but to follow Adams's lead and quit the war. With his bellicose policy in tatters, Pitt resigned as prime minister on March 14, 1801. Seven months later, war-weary English delegates signed the preliminary Peace of Amiens, in which Britain pledged to turn over Malta. France, Holland, and Spain were to recover most of the colonies they had lost since fighting began in 1792. When Bonaparte's delegate reached London with the final documents, a joyful crowd unhitched his horses and pulled his carriage up to the doors of the Foreign Office, shouting: "*Vive la République française! Vive* Napoleon!"

The Revolutions of 1800 and 1804?

Until too recently, Jefferson's hagiographers have argued that under his leadership, the United States proved the exception to the "counter-revolutionary trends" sweeping much of the northern Atlantic world. Republican regimes and popular revolutions failed in France and Ireland, while governments in Britain and Haiti proved increasingly repressive. The biographer Dumas Malone suggested that Jefferson's victory over John Adams in the presidential election of 1800 resisted that drift, and undoubtedly radical journalists imprisoned under the Sedition Act would agree with that sentiment. Yet that simple picture of progress grows murkier when one examines subsequent events from the perspective of blacks in both the Caribbean and the southern parts of the United States. Nor was Jefferson's election a clear signal of ideological intent. Given the close margin of the Republican victory—Jefferson bested the fractured Federalist ticket by only eight electoral votes—there can be little doubt that had the nation learned earlier of the Peace of Mortefontaine, several crucial states would have cast their ballots for Adams. In fact, had three-fifths of the depoliticized slaves in the southern states not been counted for purposes of representation, Adams would have been reelected handily, with his support for politicized former slaves in the Caribbean uninterrupted.

Even less conjectural is the fact that a second term for Adams would have left European diplomacy in the staunchly anticolonial hands of men like young John Quincy Adams, then minister to Prussia. The younger Adams hoped to "protect [Haitian] independence" from French incursions with the American navy, while "leaving them as to their government totally to themselves." Instead, the Republican triumph returned James Monroe to his former ministerial post in France, and the Virginian was far less enamored of black liberty in the Caribbean. Writing in the wake of Gabriel's conspiracy, Monroe worried that the "occurrences in St. Doming[ue] for some years past were calculated and doubtless did excite some sensation among our Slaves" in Virginia.

The new president shared Monroe's fears of black rebellion, both at home and abroad. Despite Jefferson's tendency to refer to his election as "the revolution of 1800," it is hard not to conclude that for Americans of African descent, the Republican victory meant a diminution of liberty both in the Caribbean *and* on the western frontier. Although Adams and Pickering had long expressed concern about French designs on New Orleans, Jefferson was surprisingly slow to grasp Bonaparte's spectacular ambitions in the Americas. In July 1801, after only four months in office, Jefferson was approached by Louis André Pichon, the French chargé d'affaires, who wished to learn the president's opinion on a possible invasion of Saint Domingue. According to Pichon's report to his superiors, Jefferson assured him that "nothing would be more simple than to furnish your army and your fleet with everything and to starve out Toussaint."

Jefferson's failure to appreciate the connection between the Caribbean island and his western frontier has been shared by more than a few historians. But on this point, hindsight is the enemy of understanding; because today the American heartland serves as breadbasket to much of the world, while Haiti has collapsed into abject poverty, it is easy to assume that Louisiana was far more important in Bonaparte's mind. Yet before 1791, Saint Domingue accounted for roughly 40 percent of France's external trade. That level of productivity, Bonaparte concluded, could only be reestablished under slavery. He had intended to use the land west of the Mississippi River to supply the population of Saint Domingue with foodstuffs and beef, while the re-enslaved Haitian people furnished continental France with sugar and prosperity enough to challenge Britain's commercial hegemony. Had Bonaparte succeeded in recapturing the colony's African population, the First Consul would surely have refused to sell Louisiana. Notwithstanding his later public promises to wed his republic to the British fleet at the moment France actually took control of New Orleans, Jefferson and Monroe would have been forced to bargain with a powerful foe deeply entrenched in the Gulf Coast.

Word of Jefferson's support for a move against Louverture flew across the Atlantic. Talleyrand, continuing in the foreign office, counseled Bonaparte that American support was all he needed to subjugate Saint Domingue. "France ought to expect from the amity of the United States," he observed, "that they interdict every private adventure [that] may be destined to the ports of St. Doming[ue], occupied by the rebels." Jefferson had once been a rebel himself, but now he insisted that he "had no reason to be favorable" to anticolonial revolutionaries like Toussaint Louverture. When Tobias Lear, the new American consul, arrived in Le Cap François without so much as a perfunctory letter from the Virginian, Louverture "express[ed] his disappointment and disgust." His "Colour was the cause of his being neglected," he fumed, "and not thought worthy of the Usual attentions" once paid by President Adams.

The French invasion force of twenty-five-thousand men, led by General Charles Victor Leclerc, Bonaparte's brother-in-law, made landfall on January 29, 1802. His commanders included the recently exiled mixed-race general, André Rigaud, who was to organize the gens de couleur against the lower-class blacks. After French forces stormed Fort Liberté just east of Le Cap François and slaughtered the soldiers of the garrison as they tried to surrender, Henri Christophe, who had been wounded at the siege of Savannah years before, ordered the city put to the torch and retreated into the interior. When Leclerc marched through its gates on February 6, Cap François was but an empty, charred pile of rubble. Forcing himself to believe that Louverture was close to capitulation, Leclerc marched on Crête-à-Pierrot, a fortress that guarded the main pass into the Cahos Mountains. After several failed assaults, Leclerc settled into a siege operation. At night, during the pauses between French bombardments, blacks in the fort sang patriotic songs of the French Revolution. Many of the invading soldiers wept as they listened. The "airs generally produced a painful feeling," one veteran of the campaign remembered. "Our soldiers looked at each other questionably," as if to say, "have we become servile political instruments?"

Despite heavy French casualties, which in terms of the high incidence of death by yellow fever echoed earlier Anglo-American experiences in Cartagena and Havana, Louverture's officers, perhaps on his orders, began to surrender. Christophe capitulated in late April, and Louverture came to terms with Leclerc on May 1. According to the terms, which the black general surely did not believe would stand, Leclerc guaranteed black freedom, the acceptance of black officers into his army, and the safe retirement of Louverture and his staff to a plantation of his choosing. Since by the spring, many French officers had reported that they lacked fresh water and medical supplies, and that the uniforms had literally rotted off their soldiers, specialists continue to debate why Louverture chose to surrender. C. L. R. James, whose 1938 account of the episode remains a masterpiece, suspected it was but a tactical retreat, designed to keep his army intact for a few months while yellow fever diminished the French forces. More recently, the historian Thomas Ott argues that having learned of the final Treaty of Amiens, ratified on March 25, 1802, Louverture simply regarded black liberty as doomed and chose to kill no more of his men in a losing cause. Certainly the shrewd general was not much surprised when he was arrested at the Georges plantation near Gonaives on June 7 and hustled aboard the *Héros*, bound for France.

By then, word reached the Americas that on April 27, Bonaparte announced the restoration of slavery in Saint Domingue and Guadeloupe and the Atlantic trade in human bodies to French possessions reopened. When the news reached Le Cap François, three black regiments mutinied, and both Christophe and Jean Jacques Dessalines again turned their coats and rejoined the rebels. As his last act before dying of yellow fever, Leclerc ordered that several hundred still-loyal black soldiers, "together with their wives and children," be drowned in the harbor. Reinforcements from the continent failed to crush the revolt, and with forty thousand of his soldiers dead in Saint Domingue, the First Consul abandoned his plans for a western empire. With his dream of a re-enslaved island in ashes, Bonaparte decided that he no longer required mainland foodstuffs, and he instructed finance minister François de Barbé-Marbois to sell New Orleans to Robert Livingston and James Monroe, who had just arrived in Paris. As critic Alexander Hamilton archly observed, Jefferson's greatest achievement came not through adroit diplomacy or skillful negotiation, but because of "the courage and obstinate resistance made by black inhabitants" in Saint Domingue.

Louverture was imprisoned in an icy underground dungeon at Fort de Joux near the Swiss border. On the way there, his heavily guarded coach was stopped by officers of the Eighty-second Regiment, who before Leclerc's invasion had been garrisoned in Saint Domingue and served under Louverture's command. The twelve gendarmes who rode with the carriage feared an escape attempt, but the officers had come only to say their farewells. Several cried silently as they shook the hand of the general for the last time. Denied adequate food and clothing and abused by his jailors, Louverture died on the morning of April 7, 1803.

"Now they have felled the trunk of the Negroes' tree of liberty," Louverture had remarked when taken aboard the *Héros*. "However, new shoots will sprout because the roots are deep and many." He was right: seven months later, Dessalines and his officers met in Gonaives. The job of drafting a second Declaration of Independence—the first version, crafted by "an admirer of the work of Jefferson," was rejected as lacking in "heat and energy"—was given to the fiery young Louis Félix Boisrond-Tonnerre, whose prose style reflected the desire to use "the skin of a white man for parchment, his skull for an inkwell, [and] his blood for ink." The black generals chose the Taíno name of *Haiti* for their independent republic, the second in the Americas, and elected Dessalines governor for life, although he would soon, perhaps in imitation of Bonaparte, grant himself the title of emperor. For the Haitians, it was a costly victory. The total number of people who died on the island between 1791 and 1804 is estimated to be 350,000, or roughly nine times the number of people who died in France during the Reign of Terror and approximately two-thirds of the population of Saint Domingue in 1789. Elsewhere in the French Caribbean, slavery was restored. Unfree labor was reconstructed in Guadeloupe following the defeat of black insurgents there in May 1802.

Louverture's soldiers had once dubbed North Americans "the good whites," but that time had passed. In the fall of 1804, riding on a tidal wave of popularity due to the Louisiana Purchase treaty, which protected French and Spanish slave property in the region, Jefferson easily bested a demoralized Federalist ticket in a near landslide. One month later, on a cold and damp December 2, 1804, in a magnificent coronation at Notre Dame, Bonaparte dispensed with his latest title of Consul for Life in exchange for that of emperor. Pope Pius VII consecrated the emperor, but following Charlemagne's example, Napoleon lifted the golden crown from the cushion beside him, turned his back on the pope, and crowned himself. Ironically, having destroyed the republic, Bonaparte made the curiously republican gesture of submitting his new rank to the electorate. Even allowing for considerable pressure on the voters, the results were impressive: 3,572,329 citizens voted in favor of empire, while only 2,579 brave souls cast their lot with democracy—a statistical impossibility of 99.9993 percent. Thermidor was at last complete, and its heat had made the waters bubble and boil across four thousand miles of the Atlantic Ocean.

Selected Readings

Ammon, Harry, *The Genet Mission* (New York: Norton, 1973).

Blackburn, Robin, *The Overthrow of Colonial Slavery, 1776–1848* (New York: Verso, 1998).

DeConde, Alexander, *The Quasi-War: The Politics and Diplomacy of the Undeclared War With France, 1797–1801* (New York: Scribner's, 1966).

Dubois, Laurent, *Avengers of the New World: The Story of the Haitian Revolution* (Cambridge, MA: Harvard University Press, 2004).

Egerton, Douglas R., *Gabriel's Rebellion: The Virginia Slave Conspiracies of 1800 & 1802* (Chapel Hill: University of North Carolina Press, 1993).

Foner, Eric, *Tom Paine and Revolutionary America* (New York: Oxford University Press, 1976).

Fraser, Antonia, *Marie Antoinette: The Journey* (New York: Random House, 2001).

Gaspar, David Barry, and David P. Geggus, eds., *A Turbulent Time: The French Revolution and the Greater Caribbean* (Bloomington: Indiana University Press, 1997).

Geggus, David P., ed., *The Impact of the Haitian Revolution in the Atlantic World* (Columbia: University of South Carolina Press, 2001).

Horn, James, Jan Ellis Lewis, and Peter S. Onuf, eds., *The Revolution of 1800: Democracy, Race, and the New Republic* (Charlottesville: University of Virginia Press, 2003).

James, C. L. R., *The Black Jacobins: Toussaint Louverture and the Saint Domingue Revolution* (New York: Vintage Books, 1938, 1963).

Langley, Lester D., *The Americas in the Age of Revolution, 1750–1850* (New Haven: Yale University Press, 1996).

Malone, Dumas, *Jefferson and the Rights of Man* (Boston: Little, Brown, 1951).

Ott, Thomas O., *The Haitian Revolution, 1789–1804* (Knoxville: University of Tennessee Press, 1973).

Palmer, R. R., *The Age of the Democratic Revolution: The Struggle* (Princeton: Princeton University Press, 1964).

Peabody, Sue, *"There Are No Slaves in France": The Political Culture of Race and Slavery in the Ancien Regime* (New York: Oxford University Press, 1996).

Racine, Karen, *Francisco de Miranda: A Transatlantic Life* (Wilmington: Scholarly Resources, 2002).

Rudé, George, *The Crowd in the French Revolution* (New York: Oxford University Press, 1959).

Schama, Simon, *Citizens: A Chronicle of the French Revolution* (New York: Knopf, 1989).

Schom, Alan, *Napoleon Bonaparte* (New York: Harper Collins, 1997).

Thompson, E. P., *The Making of the English Working Class* (New York: Pantheon, 1963).

Simón Bolívar. Humanities and Social Sciences Library, Print Collection, Miriam & Ira D. Wallach Division of Art, Prints and Photographs, The New York Public Library, Astor, Lenox and Tilden Foundations.

Chapter Twelve

The Ebb and Flow of Empire, 1804–1830

It's destiny's joke. It seems we planted the ideal of independence so deep that now these countries are trying to win their independence from each other.
Field Marshal Antonio José de Sucre

"**An** invasion of armies can be resisted," wrote Victor Hugo, "but not an idea whose time has come." On that same gray December day of 1804, Pope Pius VII sat toward the front of Notre Dame Cathedral, resplendent in a cape of silver and gold, his tiara encrusted with 4,209 emeralds, rubies, and diamonds—one of the gifts Napoleon had offered to entice the reluctant pontiff to attend his coronation. Bonaparte himself arrived moments later in a carriage paneled in glass and bearing the emperor's coat of arms. As Napoleon turned his back to the pope and crowned himself, cannon exploded about the city and musicians played in the squares and on virtually every street corner. French police later estimated that 2 million guests had flooded into the city to witness the event. But in politics, perspective is everything. Among those watching the coronation was twenty-one-year-old Simón Bolívar. Although captivated by the cult of glory so critical to the regime of the French general, the young Venezuelan was already disgusted with what he regarded as Bonaparte's betrayal of republican ideals. "Since Napoleon crowned himself," Bolívar sneered, "his fame seems to me like the reflection of hell."

Some historians still claim that it was the Napoleonic wars, and in particular Bonaparte's seizure of Portugal and Spain, that touched off Latin America's independence movements. But to pose that argument, or to suggest that Haitian rebels were primarily inspired by the French Revolution, greatly diminishes American agency and implies that no long-simmering discontent existed in the colonies prior to the age of revolution. A more accurate formulation would be that Bonaparte's intervention in the Iberian Peninsula presented an opportunity to many colonists who had long wished to alter their relationship with their Iberian overlords. Still, despite growing discontent, the earliest attempts at self-governance between the years 1808 and 1814, with the single exception of Argentina, failed. It was in the post Napoleonic period, following the restoration of the Iberian kings and amid harsh attempts to reassert imperial authority, that Latin American independence was decisively won. Unforeseen events played a role as well, among them a thwarted British invasion in Argentina and the arrival of the Portuguese king and his court in Brazil. Independence in Spanish and Portuguese America, as in Haiti

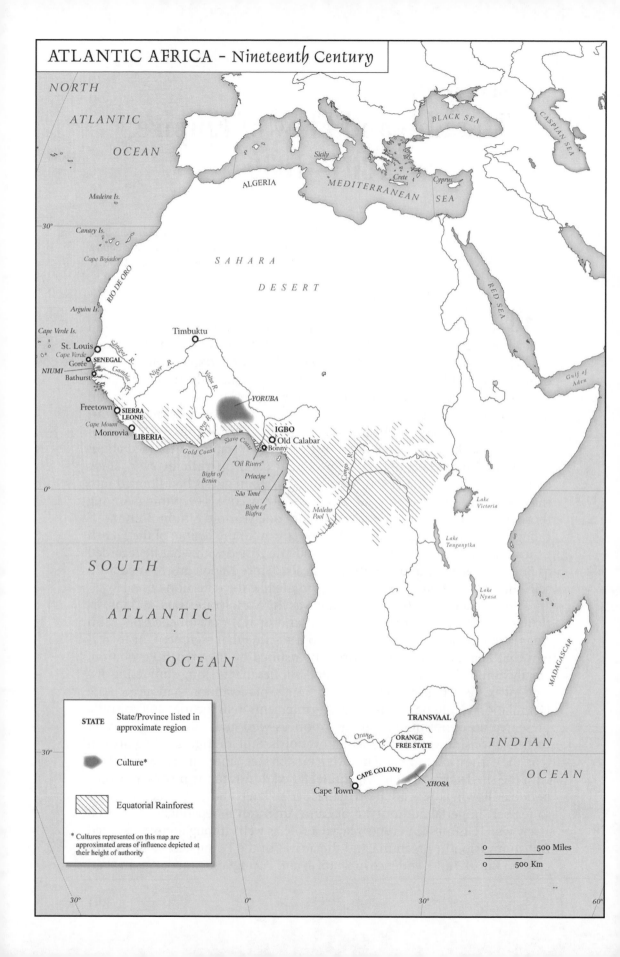

ATLANTIC AFRICA - Nineteenth Century

NORTH

ATLANTIC

OCEAN

BLACK SEA

CASPIAN SEA

Madeira Is.

30°

Canary Is.

Cape Bojador

ALGERIA

MEDITERRANEAN SEA

Sicily

Crete *Cyprus*

RIO DE ORO

SAHARA

DESERT

RED SEA

Arguim Is.

Cape Verde Is.

St. Louis
Cape Verde
Gorée
SENEGAL
NIUMI
Bathurst

Timbuktu

Senegal R.

Niger R.

Gambia R.

Volta R.

YORUBA

Gulf of Aden

Freetown **SIERRA LEONE**
Cape Mount
Monrovia **LIBERIA**

IGBO
Old Calabar
Bonny

Pra R.

Gold Coast

Slave Coast

"Oil Rivers"

Congo R.

Bight of Benin

Príncipe *

São Tomé

Bight of Biafra

0°

Malebo Pool

Lake Victoria

Lake Tanganyika

Lake Nyasa

SOUTH

ATLANTIC

OCEAN

MADAGASCAR

TRANSVAAL

Orange R.

ORANGE FREE STATE

INDIAN

OCEAN

30°

CAPE COLONY

XHOSA

Cape Town

Legend

STATE State/Province listed in approximate region

Culture*

Equatorial Rainforest

* Cultures represented on this map are approximated areas of influence depicted at their height of authority

0 — 500 Miles
0 — 500 Km

30°   0°   30°   60°

and British North America, emerged from a confluence of unpredictable circumstances. Other external factors, such as the military and commercial intervention of the powerful British Empire, would continue to play important roles long after independence. Still, creole leadership and interests ended up defining and directing the various independence struggles, and hence deserve most attention.

Although most independent Latin American nations adopted republican governments in the 1810s and 1820s, not all of them rejected monarchy. For various reasons, many, if not most, creole elites considered Napoleonic France and Great Britain more attractive models to emulate than the United States. The example of Haiti, imagined as a total upending of the old sociopolitical and economic order, was feared by all but the enslaved, some of whom threatened to emulate it. Unsurprisingly, popular sovereignty did not appeal to the upper classes, who had much to lose. How independence was won in Latin America differed considerably from country to country. Most former colonies gained independence through war, but others did so by secession and even royal decree. Brazil, for example, began its independent existence as an empire ruled by a member of the same dynasty that reigned in Portugal. Brazil was anomalous in other ways: its freedom was won almost without bloodshed; it held together as a nation after independence despite concerted regional challenges; and it was the only nation to achieve independence in this period with a predominantly enslaved population. Indeed, the enslaved fought vigorously for independence in much of Spanish South America, only to witness the survival of the institution for at least another generation in a number of places. As in the United States, mass slavery proved no barrier to independence—and even democratic republican government—as long as slaveholders could associate independence with furthering their own interests. Indeed, slavery's survival in the United States for nearly a century after independence, far longer than it lasted after independence anywhere in Latin America, should serve as a reminder of the malleability of republican ideals in the age of Atlantic revolutions. It was the enslaved who had to keep reminding their owners of the contradiction.

There were many other examples of persistent bondage amid what may seem like general Atlantic upheaval. Although the age of Bolívar was undoubtedly a time of independence, most Caribbean colonies remained parts of European empires. The several fledgling nations of the American mainland contained most of the hemisphere's population, but in terms of raw numbers, by 1830 far fewer new republics existed than extant colonies. This age of revolution left Dutch and Danish holdings in the Atlantic largely intact, and Britain still claimed Jamaica, Trinidad, British Honduras (Belize), Demerara, Bermuda, Barbados, numerous other Caribbean islands, and the enormous expanse of Canada. Spain's colonies had been reduced to Cuba and Puerto Rico, yet these were hardly trivial holdings from a wider Atlantic perspective; Cuba was rapidly transformed into Spain's version of French St. Domingue, a sugar empire built on slavery. Meanwhile, France clung to Guadeloupe, Martinique, and Guyane, all lucrative colonies despite their modest size. While colonists sought independence in some regions of the western Atlantic, in the eastern Atlantic, Europeans and other outsiders simultaneously deepened their political control over parts of Africa. They established new colonies such as Sierra Leone and strengthened their presence elsewhere. There were also new competitors, as North Americans and Brazilians vied for portions of the African trade. From an Atlantic perspective, then, while the age of independence movements weakened some empires and transformed others, a significant number of colonies remained embedded in imperial networks. Britain was by far strongest in this regard thanks to years of naval and commercial maritime development already linked with a burgeoning industrial sector. British actions and policies could not be ignored by anyone in the Atlantic basin. Thus, the dramatic accomplishments of Bolívar and like-minded Latin Americans pushed along one emerging pattern of revolutionary activity around the Atlantic even as an older pattern of imperialism and colonial subordination endured. The evermore pressing issues of slavery and the slave trade would in a sense get caught and spun between these two currents, yielding a broad range of outcomes all over the Atlantic.

The champions of Latin American independence drew on many historical and contemporary sources for inspiration and practical guidance in nation building. Many creole leaders had been educated in Europe and had witnessed and even participated in France's political upheaval. Venezuelans Bolívar and Francisco de Miranda had spent considerable time in France and England and had even traveled through the fledgling United States. Bolívar had also visited Haiti, whose leadership he greatly admired. Creole leaders were, in short, familiar with a variety of republican experiments. Other models were historical, embedded in the imperial past of Spain and Portugal. Most directly relevant to the leaders of independence movements in the Spanish colonies was the example set by the Netherlands. In the aftermath of the Bourbon reforms, as free trade became the refrain of the day, the financial success of the Dutch because of their commitment to free trade inspired intellectuals looking for their own path away from imperial regulation. When these colonial leaders chose to fight for independence, the Dutch example proved still more inspiring since the prosperous and united Netherlands had won their freedom from Spain. In 1813, one writer in Mexico joined these models. "Remember the United Provinces of the Netherlands; take a look at the United States: unite and consider both cases as a good precedent."

If the Spanish republics did not ultimately decide to emulate the Dutch government, revolutionaries did draw heavily on the model of Dutch heroism and resistance. In generating anti-Spanish propaganda, nineteenth-century revolutionaries in Mexico, Venezuela, and New Granada (Colombia) used stories of Spanish atrocities committed against the Dutch during their occupation in the sixteenth and seventeenth centuries.

The United States example, particularly its founding documents, proved similarly inspiring. Venezuelans closely modeled their Declaration of Independence after that of the United States, just as Gran Colombia—the federation of Venezuela, Colombia, Ecuador, and Panama—used the U.S. Constitution as its model. Not all creole leaders were so eager to copy the northern republic, however. Some objected to the U.S. model for its proposed egalitarianism, others for its separation of church and state. Anticlerical thinkers such as Bolívar simply considered the North American system's balance of powers unnecessarily cumbersome and complex. More important, perhaps, he doubted that ordinary Spanish Americans possessed the civic virtues necessary to succeed in republican government. Public education would thus become a central tenet of the liberal project, however delayed it was in particular cases. In part due to elite disagreements over the definition of active citizenship and the extent of the franchise, the century after independence proved tumultuous, with most Latin American nations groping their way towards a stable form of government. Exceptions in Brazil and Chile only seemed to prove the rule.

Independence: Northern South America

The Jamaican historian C. L. R. James once remarked, "Great men make history, but only such history as it is possible for them to make." James was writing about Haiti's Toussaint Louverture, but perhaps an even better example of that maxim was Spanish South America's so-called Liberator, Simón Bolívar. Born into a wealthy family in Caracas in 1783, Bolívar owned cacao plantations, cattle ranches, a few mines, and many slaves. Orphaned at a young age, he was heavily influenced by his early tutors: Andrés Bello, soon to be Chile's leading intellectual, and Simón Rodríguez. Both men steeped him in the ideas of the French Enlightenment. After Rodríguez was jailed for his part in a 1797 revolt that rocked Venezuela, Bolívar completed his education in Spain. In Europe he was greatly influenced by French Enlightenment ideas of natural law, utopianism, romantic liberalism, and Rousseau's social contract. He felt as though the scales were being lifted from his eyes. Once reconnected with Rodríguez, Bolívar traveled to Italy and France, where he witnessed the reversal of revolutionary ideals. An early admirer of Napoleon, Bolívar grew disillusioned after Napoleon's coronation. "From that day," he remarked, "I regarded him as a hypocritical tyrant."

In London, Bolívar joined the Masonic Lodge, to which his countryman Miranda belonged. Like the authors of U.S. and Haitian independence, most leaders of Latin American independence movements, such as Argentina's José de San Martín and Chile's Bernardo O'Higgins, were practicing masons. There were also masons among the independence agitators of Brazil. Freemasonry was in large part a British fad, and it was quickly criticized as simply a new means of perpetuating the clubby elitism of earlier times among an ascendant bourgeoisie. Yet its consequences were profound—both during and long after the independence struggles—in creating transatlantic ties among educated critics of absolutism and excessive power on the part of the Catholic Church. As in the early United States, freemasonry took on an increasingly local cast and shaped the careers of Latin American political leaders for generations to come. From the perspective of those on the outside, however, the lodges, with their vows of secrecy, simply fueled conspiracy theories and class resentment.

After touring Europe, Bolívar traveled to Boston, New York, Philadelphia, and Charles Town in the United States, returning to Venezuela on the heels of Miranda's failed invasion of 1808. Shortly thereafter, a French representative arrived in Caracas with the shocking news of Napoleon's invasion of Spain, the abdication of Charles IV, and the imprisonment of his son and successor, Ferdinand VII. The same news was being delivered around Spanish America and the common creole response was to form juntas to govern in Ferdinand's name until he was freed. Similar ad hoc governing bodies formed throughout Spain, joining in the southern city of Cádiz in 1810; the so-called Cádiz Cortes, though dominated by liberals interested in diminishing the power of the monarchy and promoting commerce, would eventually clash with the juntas and cabildos of the Americas.

In 1810 Venezuela's creole elites formed the Caracas Junta and called for free trade, opening ports (with preferential tariffs for Britain), and abolishing export duties, the traditional Spanish sales tax of the *alcabala*, and the slave trade. The latter decision was made less for altruistic reasons than out of fear of a local version of the Haitian Revolution. The great German naturalist and explorer Alexander von Humboldt, who had traveled through Venezuela in 1799, noted in his travels (which happened to be published in the midst of the Napoleonic crisis) that the Caracas aristocrats "would even prefer foreign domination to rule by Americans of a lower class." Put another way, they wanted "a new rider on the same mule."

Seeking aid for its independence, the Caracas Junta sent envoys, including Bolívar, to London. At the time, however, the British were fully occupied with Napoleon; the Duke of Wellington's armies were then fighting French troops in Spain. Bolívar nevertheless met Miranda and joined his masonic

Race and Citizenship

The first two republics of the western Atlantic, the United States and Haiti, each devised its own definition of citizenship. In the United States, citizenship was gendered, predicated on masculine attributes. To this day, when new citizens take their oath of citizenship, they pledge to take up arms in defense of the country, something that until recently women were barred from doing. Some Spanish American independence movements accommodated a wider range of colonial subjects, including mestizo, Indian, and pardo leaders, both in the course of fighting for independence and later in working out new constitutional configurations. Securing the support of enough of these different constituencies to gain independence proved an important challenge. In Venezuela, the first colony to declare independence in 1811, the white creole leaders were initially unable to secure the support of the mixed-race population, which found, as was often the case, greater tolerance and protection from the imperial government than from the colony's leaders. The

pardos supported the crown, which was able to regain control in 1814.

White creoles did not always remain in control of these new republics. Some new leaders were themselves of mixed ancestry, many of whom had emerged as leaders during the wars that produced independence. In contrast to the North American model, in which men of privilege retained political power, some Spanish American leaders experimented with social policies designed to reject the old racial hierarchies of the colonial world. In Paraguay, José Gaspar Rodríguez de Francia, who governed between 1816 and 1840, mandated a social revolution within the country even as he sought to isolate Paraguay from the rest of Latin America. He hoped to eliminate the upper class by requiring creoles to marry only Indians or people of mixed race. He also limited land ownership. Republics were experimental, even if they drew on other models, and there was no single path toward independence and citizenship.

lodge in London before returning with him to Caracas. There, Miranda became president of a new Patriotic Society; at its 1811 meeting, Bolívar urged and the Congress voted a Declaration of Venezuelan Independence. Society members wrote a constitution and set up the American Confederation of Venezuela, Spanish America's first independent republic. Although, like a similar government proclaimed in Bogotá about the same time, it did not survive, the first Venezuelan republic outlawed legal discrimination and the slave trade (a nod to Britain) and gave limited suffrage to property holders. It also responded to creoles' racial fears by setting up a national guard to apprehend fugitive slaves, patrol and search, capture and return, and enforce the law. Fearful too of the mobile and hence potentially dangerous *llaneros*, or mixed-race cowboys of the plains, it passed restrictive legislation tying the cattle to the land and requiring llaneros to carry passes. Like most such documents of the period, the Venezuelan constitution did not mention the rights of women.

While the creoles legislated, Spain dispatched a garrison from Puerto Rico to squelch the insolence. It was the alienated llaneros who secured Spanish victory, however. José Tomás Boves, an Austrian-born smuggler with a large llanero following, offered Venezuela's slaves freedom in the king's name and vowed to wage a war to the death on "whites and the rich." A wary Spanish captain-general warned, "zambos and mulattos are now fighting to destroy white creoles, their masters [and] it will not take long before they start to destroy white Europeans, who are also their masters." Miranda-led republican forces had also offered slaves freedom, but once taking power he ruled as a virtual dictator. When an earthquake destroyed Caracas in 1812, many took it as a sign of God's displeasure with Miranda and his ideas, and after the Spanish and llanero troops scored significant gains, Miranda had to surrender. Believing that Miranda had looted the republic's treasury, Bolívar arrested him and turned him over to the Spanish commander. Miranda ended his days in jail; Bolívar went to exile in Cartagena de Indias; and Venezuela's first republic was dead.

Reflecting on this failure, Bolívar, in a document known as the "Cartagena Manifesto," urged unity and centralization. Education and experiences in Spain, France, Britain, and the United States pushed Bolívar in a radical direction by the standards of the day, but he was at heart a creole and a member of the elite. On some issues he was socially and politically liberal, favoring abolition, freedom of religion, and laws to eliminate inequalities resulting from birth. But like Rousseau, Bolívar thought people needed preparation for democracy, which he considered the highest form of government and the most difficult to sustain. He admired the United States Constitution but thought it suitable only for "a republic of saints." Spanish America's class structure made him favor the tiered British parliamentary model, and he believed the continent needed a lifetime presidency and a hereditary senate. In addition to the three branches of government found in the United States, he advised a fourth branch to oversee morals by censure. Bolívar's seemingly contradictory views of freedom and civic virtue are reflected in the polarized views many observers have taken towards him since his own time. While some now regard Bolívar a champion of the underclass (inspiring radical political movements in Venezuela and Colombia), others see him as a dictator cut from the same cloth as Napoleon.

While in Colombia, Bolívar served in the Congress of New Granada and raised a small army in hopes of liberating neighboring Venezuela. After promising the llaneros return of their land, he won early victories, but elites feared his overtures to slaves and his hard line toward peninsular Spaniards—he vowed a war in which only the American born would be spared. In 1814 a Representative Assembly in Venezuela named Bolívar "all supreme" and established the Second Republic. As with the first republic, Boves's llanero royalists, whom he dubbed the "Legion of Hell," quickly undid this one, and once again Bolívar fled to Cartagena.

The same year, Ferdinand VII was returned to the Spanish throne, and he quickly abolished Spain's liberal Constitution of 1812, written by the Cortes in Cádiz while he was in exile in France. After restoring absolutism with a vengeance at home, Ferdinand turned his attention to doing the same in his American colonies. In 1815 he sent to America one of his ablest generals, Pablo Morillo, and the largest fleet yet to cross the Atlantic, nearly fifty ships and 10,000 troops, many of them veterans of the campaigns against Napoleon. The soldiers were not told where they would be fighting until they were well out to sea, since many had heard tales of war being waged with no quarter in Venezuela. Nonetheless, in short order Morillo, known by loyalist admirers as "The Pacifier" and by the rebels as "The Butcher," completed the Spanish reconquest of Venezuela and established key footholds in New Granada.

Due in part to royalist successes, Bolívar's efforts to unify Colombia continued to founder, and unable to settle the rivalry between Cartagena and Bogotá, he left in disgust for Jamaica. Despite the fact that he arrived nearly penniless and barely escaped assassination when a servant bribed with gold stabbed his hammock—he spent the night elsewhere on an amorous adventure—Bolívar remained confident of his eventual triumph. In his most famous essay written during this exile, the so-called Jamaica Letter of September 1815, he boldly restated his belief in independence and his conviction that success was virtually achieved. From Jamaica, Bolívar traveled to Haiti, where Alexander Pétion, leader of the hemisphere's first black republic (Haiti's national constitution declaring all of its citizens to be black), gave him money and supplies in return for Bolívar's promise to abolish slavery.

So with several thousand rifles, Bolívar returned to Venezuela, immediately freed his 800 slaves, and issued an emancipation decree. "Our unfortunate brothers who suffer enslavement are from this moment free," he announced. "The laws of nature and humanity, and the interest of the government proclaim their liberty. From now on there will be in Venezuela only one class of inhabitants: all will be citizens." Bolívar then joined the pardo, or "free brown," general, Manuel de Piar, who had been fighting royalist cowboys in the Orinoco hinterland. Bolívar's overtures to the llaneros and his emancipation decree encouraged many castas, enslaved and free, to join his ranks. In a pattern repeated throughout Spanish America, they formed the bulk of his armies and took the heaviest losses. Yet although philosophically as liberal as any Latin American leader of the time, Bolívar was as wary of what he termed a "pardocracy" as any Spanish general. Fearful that the talented Piar might achieve political autonomy by exploiting racial tensions, the Liberator ordered him executed for alleged complicity in a plot against the government. Thereafter, Bolívar drew support from the illiterate llanero José Antonio Páez, who would prove to be even less loyal.

After desperate battles against Morillo's Spanish troops in Venezuela, Bolívar staged a six-hundred-mile march back to New Granada. Crossing the plains of the Orinoco basin in the wet season, waist high in water, before moving up and over the Andes, he surprised the Spanish just north of Bogotá. The Battle of Boyacá, in August 1819, demoralized Spanish forces, forcing the viceroy to flee. Victorious, Bolívar returned to his base in eastern Venezuela in 1819, where a congress met in the riverside town of Angostura and adopted his republican ideas. Those in attendance created a hereditary senate, a lower house with elected representatives, and a president with almost kingly powers. To no one's surprise, the Congress elected Bolívar president of the new Republic of Gran Colombia, a vast and wealthy region encompassing the old Viceroyalty of New Granada.

Among the three thousand soldiers who started the trek across the Andes were several hundred British Legionnaires, mostly Irishmen who had nothing to return home to following Waterloo. Other volunteers came from the United States, German principalities, and France. Spanish Americans themselves were the principal fighters throughout, but Spanish American independence was, like the French Revolution, an Atlantic endeavor, supported tacitly or openly by Haiti, the United States, and Great Britain. Seasoned foreigners added legitimacy and esprit to the cause; the Irishman Daniel F. O'Leary became Bolívar's trusted confidante.

In 1820, dismayed by their losses and Ferdinand VII's revocation of the Liberal Constitution of 1812 and convinced there was no winning the American wars, Spanish troops mutinied in the so-called Riego Revolt. Denied reinforcements, General Morillo finally signed a truce after the Venezuelan battle of Carabobo in 1821. With all of Venezuela secured, Bolívar sent his lieutenant, Antonio José de Sucre, to liberate Ecuador, a task accomplished in May of 1822 at the Battle of Pichincha, near Quito. Shortly thereafter, Bolívar met in the port of Guayaquil with General José de San Martín, fresh from the liberation of Argentina and Chile, and convinced him to step aside. Bolívar and his lieutenant Sucre then proceeded to liberate Peru and Bolivia following the battles of Ayacucho and Junín. Although the Peruvians gave Bolívar dictatorial powers in 1824 and elected him president the following year under a new constitution, Bolívar warned Sucre, who at the same time became president of Bolivia, "in the final analysis, we suffer from the defect of being Venezuelans." Soon, jealous local elites would seize upon this "defect" and dash Bolívar's hopes for a united Spanish South America.

Independence: The Southern Cone

While Bolívar was liberating the northern half of the continent, creoles in the southern half waged their own battles. Race divided that region, too, as did the long-brewing hatred between creoles and peninsulars. Added to this conflict was a rivalry between the ports of Buenos Aires and Montevideo and a host of regional resentments. Like the merchants and ranchers of Montevideo, elites of the interior provinces of the Viceroyalty of La Plata resented the dominance of the new capital at Buenos Aires and the imposition of new taxes and trade restrictions. When Britain's war against Napoleon (and his unwilling ally, Spain) began, no one could have predicted that it would have consequences in Buenos Aires. Here was one of those momentous accidents of Atlantic history. In the summer of 1806 Sir Home Popham sailed northwest from the Cape of Good Hope and, without orders to do so, captured Buenos Aires. He also seized a shipment of silver, which aided his case back in Britain. To the disgust of creoles, La Plata's Viceroy, the Marquis of Sobremonte, fled. Although the British offered free trade and freedom of religion, the creole hero, Santiago Liniers, rallied the militia and his fellow porteños to drive out the British. As another angry creole, Manuel Belgrano, put it, "Either our old master or none at all."

Like Bolívar, Belgrano was a member of the local elite, born in Buenos Aires and educated there and in Spain. He was studying law in Spain when the French Revolution broke out, and it shaped his political ideology. Returning to Buenos Aires to take a position in the merchant's guild, Belgrano witnessed the Popham invasion and the subsequent capture of Montevideo, during which Sobremonte once again failed the test. Ashamed and angry at this peninsular incompetence and cowardice, the Audiencia of Buenos Aires took the unusual step of suspending the viceroy and replacing him with the creole hero Santiago Liniers. His luck soon proved little better. When the British returned to Buenos Aires in 1807, Liniers and the royal army failed in the defense. Fortunately for the porteños, a Spanish merchant, Martín de Alzaga, rallied militia forces to victory. The British finally withdrew, and the creole militias' defeat of a veteran European army was a boost to their self-confidence and sense of identity. (The British had only managed to reach and surround Buenos Aires with the aid of local gaucho guides, who had unwisely cast their lot with the foreigners.) Now creole Mariano Moreno wrote his "Representation of the Planters," a classic argument in support of free trade as proposed by Adam Smith. Peninsular merchants and Spanish monopolists, however, argued for reinstatement of old policies that would "protect domestic [i.e., Spanish] industries."

In 1810, after hearing that Spain's Central Junta had been dispersed, creole military officers in Buenos Aires staged a forum to discuss the events. When the new viceroy objected to local subjects seizing the political initiative, they arrested him and, still claiming to represent Ferdinand VII, established a three-member ruling body led by Bernardino Rivadavia. An Enlightenment-inspired liberal, Rivadavia drafted laws calling for a National Assembly and abolished the slave trade, the mita and encomienda systems, titles of nobility, and the Inquisition. The new constitution established civil liberties, a free press, and educational reforms modeled after those of the English philosopher Jeremy Bentham.

Despite Rivadavia's vision for a liberal republic in the southern Atlantic, revolutionary militants pushed to radicalize Buenos Aires's government. In 1811 this group established a Committee of Public Safety modeled on that of France and exiled the viceroy and other peninsular Spaniards. The radicalized junta also discriminated against Spaniards who stayed, confiscating their property and taxing them more heavily than creoles. Resistance led to executions. In its anti-Spanish zeal, the junta even ordered the execution of the creole military leader Santiago Liniers and the peninsular hero Martín de Alzaga, both once lauded for having saved the capital.

Coupled with failed military expeditions sent against what were still La Plata's subsidiary provinces of Bolivia and Paraguay, these killings disgraced the Buenos Aires radicals. A reaction against the violence restored provincial conservatives to the junta. Moreno died on a diplomatic mission abroad, and a short-lived republic, the United Provinces of La Plata, followed, but it was sharply divided between Buenos Aires centralists (mostly merchants) and those favoring provincial autonomy (mostly ranchers and others with local economic interests). By 1814 the triumvirate had failed and the country lay divided. Having set aside plans to take the silver-mining center of Potosí from local and royalist forces, the Constituent Assembly met in the interior town of San Miguel de Tucumán in 1816 to declare formally Argentine independence and authorize funds for an audacious expedition led by General San Martín. He planned to cross the Andes and liberate Chile, already in the midst of rebellion. The next stage was to attack the royalist stronghold of Lima from the Pacific.

In 1817, San Martín organized his Army of the Andes comprised of 5,500 volunteers, almost half of them freed slaves. But San Martín's army also included Chilean refugees like Bernardo O'Higgins, a radical creole elite of part Irish descent. In an unexpected move, San Martín sent forces across three different passes in the Andes, the highest 15,000 feet above sea level, surprising and defeating the Spanish army on the plains of Chacabuco. Santiago's grateful town council twice elected San Martín governor of Chile with unlimited power, but he refused, leaving O'Higgins as interim Supreme Director. As San Martín pushed northward in 1818, Chile declared its independence. O'Higgins ran Chilean affairs as quasi-dictator until 1823, when he was driven from power.

Viceregal Peru would challenge San Martín and his rebels, even with the aid, acquired in Valparaíso, Chile, of the British admiral and Napoleonic war veteran Lord Thomas Cochrane. An entrenched royalist and peninsular bureaucracy ruled in Peru's capital of Lima, where wealthy and landed creole elites were also concentrated. African slaves and Indian draft laborers produced grain, cotton, sugar, rum, wine, and brandy on large coastal plantations that supplied the capital and thriving silver mines in the neighboring highlands. Although additional Bourbon taxes, the loss of Potosí, and the shift of trade to Buenos Aires peeved wealthy Limeños, they worried more about the chronic indigenous unrest in the highland districts, and they were grateful for the presence of royal forces. When Napoleon's armies entered

Declaring Independence in the Atlantic World

The independence movements of the western Atlantic struck directly at the structure of imperial governments and introduced new political forms into old polities. Between 1776 and 1848, former colonies and kingdoms declared independence in the Americas, Africa (in Liberia in 1847), and Europe. During this period, declarations of self-determination generally emulated the American declaration of 1776, even as they drew on local conditions and regional political traditions. The 1789 French Declaration of Rights of Man and Citizen, written in quiet consultation with Jefferson, who was then in Paris, claimed an independence from the Old Order. Its drafters spoke of "imprescriptible rights" rather than "unalienable" ones, and revised Jefferson's list of natural liberties from "Life, Liberty, and the pursuit of Happiness" so that it accorded more with the original Lockean inventory of "liberty, property, security, and resistance to oppression." The Liberian declaration, drafted largely by a Virginia native, the former slave Hilary Teage, adopted a more bourgeois and practical tone by asserting the "inalienable rights [of] life, liberty, and the right to acquire, possess, enjoy, and defend property." But if Teage owed a rhetorical debt to Jefferson, the expatriate had a long memory of the racialized marginalization he had endured in North America: "We were made a separate and distinct class, and against us every avenue of improvement was effectively closed. Strangers from other lands, of a color different from ours, were preferred before us."

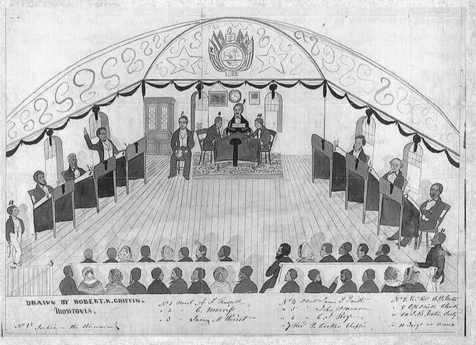

Robert K. Griffin's 1856 portrait of the Liberian senate. Image courtesy of the Library of Congress, Marian S. Carson Collection, Prints and Photographs Division, LC-USZC4-4908.

Spain, royalists in Peru staged public ceremonies to swear allegiance to Ferdinand VII and recognize Spain's Central Junta, which claimed to represent him. The following year they sent the rector of Peru's University of San Marcos to voice their grievances to the junta. Like other creoles in Spanish America, Peruvian elites wanted free trade, removal of peninsular officials called intendants, and equal access to public office. Despite these grievances, fear of renewed Indian unrest kept Peru's elites loyal to Spain.

When news of the 1820 Riego Revolt reached Peru, however, Spanish officers there also revolted against the ultraconservative viceroy and installed a more liberal replacement. At the same time, San Martín's fleet, commanded by Admiral Cochrane, sailed into Callao harbor to establish a blockade and force Spanish surrender. Unable to flee by water, the viceroy, the Spanish army, and peninsular merchants all left Lima and headed for shelter in the Bolivian highlands. Lima's town council welcomed San Martín in 1821, but dissension soon erupted between him and Cochrane. The Englishman took what silver there was in the local treasury as compensation for his services and sailed back around Cape Horn to the South Atlantic, where he would assist with Brazil's move to independence. Discouraged and ill, San Martín sailed to Guayaquil, where he handed the southern South America command over to Bolívar. All we know of this crucial meeting of Spanish South America's great liberators comes from the few notes taken by Bolívar's Irish secretary, Daniel O'Leary. San Martín returned to Argentina only to be rejected by the divided political factions of Buenos Aires. He sailed off to exile in Europe and died thirty years later on the outskirts of Paris, addicted to opium.

Chile, which on the map would appear a thoroughly Pacific nation rather than an Atlantic one, deserves closer examination. It should be noted that in both the colonial and early national periods, indeed up to at least the California gold rush of the mid-nineteenth century, Chile was largely oriented toward the Atlantic (a remnant of this is Chile's control of the Strait of Magellan and southern tip of the South American continent). Although quite active in the Pacific from an early date (Chile soon took Rapa Nui, or Easter Island, for example), this general Atlantic orientation held true in everything from trade to literary fashions. What makes Chile critical in the context of Atlantic revolutions was its atypical political stability following independence, comparable only with that of Brazil. Whereas nearly all the new Spanish American nations soon descended into internecine violence, chaos, and authoritar-ianism—and even the "model" United States lurched toward civil war—Chile forged a stable, democratic system only interrupted at the end of the nineteenth century.

Are there clues to Chilean exceptionalism in the years before Bernardo O'Higgins? Historians such as the late Simon Collier have unearthed some. First, Chile was a late bloomer as Spanish colonies went, gaining an appeals court, or *audiencia*, only in 1798 after a trade dispute with Peru. For most of the period after conquest, the 700-mile-long stretch of the colony that today makes up central Chile had been a destination for criminal exiles sent to fend off the indomitable Mapuche Indians of the south. By the mid-eighteenth century, the economy of this isolated "kingdom," as the Spanish called it, was based on a mix of subsistence agriculture, livestock raising, and precious metals mining. Wine production was still mostly for local consumption. The colony's fertile lands and mines were controlled by a small number of creole elite families, some of whom benefited from the 1767 expulsion of the Jesuits, known for their excellent vineyards. Unlike nearly all other Latin American countries, Chile did not rely on either enslaved African or coerced indigenous labor. Most workers were at least technically free mestizos, although a great many were held on farms, ranches, and in mines as debt-peons. Many of these so-called *inquilinos* were sharecroppers living at the margins of the vast and fertile Central Valley. African slaves were almost entirely limited to domestic service in the capital of Santiago and some port work at Valparaíso, whereas the Mapuche Indians remained outside state control. Chile's population around 1800, the Mapuche included, is estimated at about 1 million.

Despite its relative isolation and prosperity, all was not peace and happiness in late colonial, or even early republican, Chile. As in most of Spanish America, in Chile creole elites felt frustrated by their lack of access to high posts in both church and government, by the general underdevelopment and exploitation of their homeland, and by the lack of attention paid to education. As Collier has noted, these were the types of grievances that most creoles sought to redress, but through reform, not revolution. Devotion to the king ran deep, to the point of being unquestionable even in the midst of the Napoleonic invasion, and a series of able and enlightened governors, among them Bernardo O'Higgins's father, Ambrosio (in office 1788-96), in fact heightened rather than diminished most Chileans' respect for the crown. Still more frustrating for historians in search of roots, no evidence of secession-oriented plots or rebellions can be found to presage the truly revolutionary actions that were soon to come. But, something was clearly percolating, even if signs were scarce. A North American mariner who visited the small town of Talcahuano in 1802 noted in his diary that a prominent local officer had visited him and told him of the existence of a web of secret independence societies throughout Chile simply waiting for the proper moment to move. He was allegedly told: "Should the kingdom of Spain be invaded by a neighboring power, or should the security of the crown be threatened by the people, a revolution here would be the probable consequence."

Certainly only a tiny minority of Chileans was so inclined when news of Napoleon's sack of Madrid arrived in late 1808, but other circumstances conspired to push along the novel cause of independence. One was the rule of Chile's first unpopular royal governor in some time, Francisco Antonio García Carrasco (1808–10). One of García Carrasco's major missteps was to order the captain of an Anglo-American contraband trade vessel executed without trial. Suspicion of foreigners was the norm everywhere in Spanish America, particularly in wartime, but the ruthless killing of a known and trusted smuggler was apparently too much for the majority of free-trading Chileans to take. Members of the Chilean merchant elite requested and won García Carrasco's removal from office, and although a popular local figure was named to the post temporarily, creole elites began to think twice about whether they wanted a crown-appointed governor at all. Various notables soon entered the discussion, among them a well-traveled radical and native son named Bernardo Riquelme O'Higgins. During a stay in London, O'Higgins had met with Miranda and had become convinced of the wisdom of the Spanish American independence cause. His vision of a future Chilean state was of a liberal, if not quite fully fledged democratic, republic. There were setbacks along the way, like those faced by Bolívar and others, but O'Higgins was largely responsible for leading Chile to full independence by 1819.

This of course still does not explain Chile's post-independence stability. And in fact that stability requires some qualification. What happened in the years immediately following independence was not peace and cooperation, but rather a decade of bitter elite infighting not unlike that taking place elsewhere in the hemisphere. As in Bolívar's New Granada, there was quite a lot of coup plotting, and even a few assassinations. O'Higgins soon upset conservative enemies such as churchmen and hacienda owners with his liberal policies (the abolition of slavery in 1823 being the one exception), and he increasingly rankled supporters with his dictatorial style. O'Higgins was not, however, a cruel despot, and even in exile in Peru he was widely admired for his efforts to create one of the Americas' most open and modern republics. After O'Higgins's forced exit in 1823, Chilean politics entered a brief but uncertain period marked by constant quarrels between liberals, federalists, and conservatives. Liberals dominated the executive branch until 1829, but their chronic disarray and lack of leadership created an opening for the right, which seized power in 1830. Conservatives led by Diego Portales and his followers ruled Chile by election—of the gentlemanly, landowning kind—until 1861, when the Liberals (now as a party under that name) again took over and greatly expanded the franchise. Thus, Chile's early political trajectory was not perfectly smooth, by any means, but it was no more tumultuous than that of the antebellum United States. The key here was that most disputes were finally resolved by means of the ballot, not the bullet.

Chilean stability has been attributed to a number of factors, some of them structural, some serendipitous. The economy was not based on forced labor, and its population was more or less racially homogeneous. There was thus no fear, as in New Granada, for example, that the liberals would tap the resentments of a large and legally bound sector of the population. The fact that the Mapuche remained outside state control helped to heighten a sense of what it meant to be Chilean. The freeing of the nation's few thousand enslaved Africans within five years of independence had a similar unifying effect, as it played to a shared sense of Christian charity on the one hand, and to the novel discourse of liberty and justice on the other. Chile in the early national period was also compact, much smaller than the extensive, ribbon-like nation of today, and hence far from ungovernable or divided by intense regional loyalties. As the nation slowly expanded north and south, poor folks from the Central Valley were able to migrate in search of new opportunities as miners and homesteaders. Chile also lacked the pronounced highland-lowland split that divided northern Andeans, and its long isolation from neighbors enhanced a kind of independent spirit. Yet despite all of these seemingly special characteristics, Chile's path to nationhood was much like those all the new Atlantic nations trod, including the United States, in one sense: it was the decisions of creole elites to either resolve or inflame differences (by region, race, class, and so on) that proved most critical. Who is to say that Chile's early history, or that of New Granada, might not have gone another way?

Independence: New Spain

More than any of Spain's colonies, the independence struggle in New Spain (today's Mexico) revealed the social conservatism of Latin America's independence movements. As Spain's first viceroyalty and, after the decline of Potosí, its main source of silver, New Spain had always enjoyed special favor and status. But as in other parts of the empire, creoles in New Spain resented the Bourbon taxes, the expulsion of the Jesuits, and their own displacement by peninsular bureaucrats. The majority Indian population was suffering, too, although from other causes besides the Bourbon reforms. One advocate of indigenous rights, Bishop Manuel Abad y Queipo, decried the ineffectiveness of protective laws that were "an offensive weapon employed by the white class against the Indians, and never served to defend the latter." In practice, he argued, legal protections did them "little good and in most respects injure them greatly." As was increasingly the case to the north, in the United States, policies cloaked in paternalism confined indigenous people to a "narrow space [within] Indian towns, [where] they possess no individual property and are obliged to work communal lands." Although unintentionally, the bishop revealed that sympathy and understanding were not one and the same, for when Indians fought for communal holdings—to halt the expansion of haciendas—he assumed the individual ownership of land would serve them better. He also assumed that assimilation was the Indians' best course and criticized Spanish laws that "deprived [them] of the instruction and assistance that they should receive from contact with" the upper classes.

From his position the bishop could make such social critiques safely, but when loyal supporters took to the streets to protest the Jesuit-expulsion order in 1767, the Visitor General hanged eighty of them. News of the French Revolution also triggered easily squelched plots. But when Napoleon invaded Spain and placed his brother Joseph on the throne in place of the imprisoned Ferdinand, the crisis in legitimacy opened a fissure through which long pent-up indigenous resentments poured forth, and New Spain became a battle-ground.

Unlike the military men who drove the independence movements of Spanish South America, the leader of the indigenous uprising that sparked Mexican independence was a modestly wealthy creole and priest. Father Miguel Hidalgo y Costilla was raised on a hacienda in the mining region of Guanajuato, surrounded by indigenous laborers. He was a brilliant student at the Jesuit College of San Nicolás in Valladolid (now Morelia) and after that order was expelled he won fellowships to continue his studies (at what became a royal college). Hidalgo went on to earn a degree in theology from the University of Mexico. Following his ordination, Father Hidalgo returned to teach at San Nicolás and eventually become its rector. But the bright young priest fell afoul of the Inquisition. Enemies had charged that he kept mistresses, gambled, doubted the Virgin birth and papal infallibility, said fornication was not a sin, and called King Charles IV a tyrant and his wife worse. (Queen María was unpopular in Spain and abroad for openly taking Manuel Godoy as her lover and advancing him into the position of Foreign Minister.)

Hidalgo was released, however, and in 1803 became priest of the Indian parish of Dolores, a day's ride from Guanajuato, where he attempted to implement Enlightenment-inspired ideas. Trying to improve the lives and economic possibilities of his parishioners, he created cottage industries in tile making, tanning, carpentry, weaving, and beekeeping. But even in sleepy Dolores he found trouble. Like many late-colonial Latin American intellectuals, Hidalgo

Mexico's Virgin of Guadalupe

If separation of church and state was a fundamental principle of U.S. independence, such was hardly the case in Latin America. Even the most radical firebrands, such as Mexico's Miguel Hidalgo and José María Morelos, clung tenaciously to the colonial model of a single state religion, in this case Roman Catholicism. These men were, moreover, priests. In Spanish South America, Church power was deeply resented by liberal independence leaders such as Bolívar and O'Higgins, but even in this distinct political environment, theirs soon proved to be a minority view. Indeed, it appears that throughout Spanish America, and even in Portuguese Brazil, the independence struggle was substantially aided by widespread anger at enlightened, regalist attacks on the Church, not Church power itself. Thus, for conservative elites and indigenous peasants alike, the independence struggle was easily construed as a kind of millenarian restoration movement. In Mexico, the argument for independence in the midst of Napoleon's occupation of Spain meshed well with an old trend in creole religiosity. Since at least the 1640s, Mexican-born priests had argued that their piece of America, their native land, was unusually blessed. The Virgin Mary, they said in laudatory documents composed in Spanish, Náhuatl, and Latin, had appeared shortly after the Spaniards' arrival in the Valley of Mexico, and to a humble Indian to boot. The apparition that many hailed was a dark-skinned, perhaps native Mexican or mestiza, virgin (cleverly likened to an earlier and much-venerated apparition in the Spanish town of Guadalupe). By the turn of the nineteenth century, Mexican priests had successively reiterated the apparition's importance and finally all but enthroned the Virgin of Guadalupe. What the virgin meant for ordinary and elite Mexicans alike was protection, salvation, and most of all, legitimation. She cleansed them of the stain of being from the Indies, of being somehow inferior, incapable of self-rule. The virgin would thus become a perfect touchstone for Mexican nationalism once Miguel Hidalgo

let out his Grito de Dolores in September of 1810. As a call to arms, the perfect inverse of "Long live the Virgin of Guadalupe! Long live Mexico!" was "Death to the gachupines!" a derogatory reference to peninsula-born Spaniards, and hence all things Spanish; Catholicism was now thoroughly Mexican, Spaniards the antichrist, a race of hypocrites. The only thing missing was an attack on divine kingship which, interestingly, never came. The virulently anti-Spanish flavor of Mexican Catholic nationalism eventually faded, but the Guadalupe phenomenon continued to grow. Guadalupe has since become the patron saint of all the Americas.

Our Lady of Guadalupe, Basilica de Guadalupe in Mexico City. Juan Diego was said to have urged the construction of a shrine in 1531 after an apparition of the Virgin instructed him to do so. Her image appeared on his apron which has since been on display at the location of their meeting and is shown here. Photo, 2003, by Julio Cortez/ www.JulyThePhotoGuy.com

joined a literary club patterned on the French salon, where he discussed politics, including independence. A calling in of Church loans by the crown in 1804 led to confiscation of Hidalgo's modest landholdings, spurring him further toward antimonarchical sentiments. He found many sympathizers, but as in so many colonial-era plots, a traitor lay in his midst. Tipped off and fearing arrest, Hidalgo launched his revolution from a Dolores balcony on

September 16, 1810, calling on Indians and castas to free themselves, recover lands taken by Spaniards, and defend their religion. His famed *Grito* (cry) of Dolores, "Long live our Lady of Guadalupe! Death to bad government! Death to the *gachupines* [peninsular Spaniards]!", called on the mestiza Virgin and patron of Mexico, the Virgin of Guadalupe.

Soon thereafter, Hidalgo led an army of more than 60,000 angry farmers and ranch hands, most of them Indians, that captured nearby towns and gathered support from local militiamen and mine laborers. Hidalgo's recruits were untrained and hard to control; at the mining center of Guanajuato they forced 500 Spaniards and 2,000 of their Indian allies into a public granary and set it afire. Hidalgo's army went on to capture Zacatecas, San Luis Potosí, and Valladolid before heading for Mexico City. But low on supplies and fearful of what his army might do to the capital, Hidalgo ordered retreat. His decision to hold back proved fateful. A substitute attack on Guadalajara proved highly destructive of that city and its surrounding haciendas, but also greatly dissipated Hidalgo's forces. By 1811, the royalist armies were on the offensive, driving the rebels northward. Eventually catching up with them in Chihuahua, the army summarily executed hundreds of the remaining rebels. As a cleric, Hidalgo was tried by the Inquisition, found guilty of treason and heresy, defrocked, and executed by firing squad. As a warning to others, Spanish authorities placed the head of the rebel priest on a pike outside the burnt-out granary of Guanajuato.

But Mexican independence did not die with Hidalgo. Another radical priest, the mestizo José María Morelos y Pavón, took up the cause and, having learned from Hidalgo's mistakes, raised a small but effective army of one thousand men, mostly from the southern highlands, whom he trained in guerrilla tactics. Morelos knew not to count on the support of creole elites, who feared race war, and instead invoked the Mexica heroes Moctezuma and Cuautéhmoc. In 1813, Morelos, his troops menacing the outskirts of Mexico City, called a congress that produced the liberal Constitution of Chilpancingo. This document declared that sovereignty resided in the people and provided for universal male suffrage and abolition of slavery, racial labels, government monopolies, and judicial torture. It also declared Catholicism the state religion. Morelos was more of a military leader than was Hidalgo, but he could not withstand the full royal force directed against him. At length, he too was captured, tried for treason, defrocked, and executed. Thereafter, guerrilla bands fought on from the southern mountains, but there was no further unified resistance. By 1814, Napoleon was defeated, Ferdinand VII was back on the Spanish throne, Spain's Liberal Constitution of 1812 had been abrogated, and absolutism restored. When Morelos was executed in 1815, Spain's armies had largely regained control of the colonies.

Royal forces faced their strongest resistance from Guadalupe Victoria, a mestizo who led two thousand rebels near Puebla and the port of Veracruz, and Vicente Guerrero, a man of part African descent whose smaller band controlled Oaxaca. In 1819, Viceroy Juan Ruiz de Apodaca regained control of the central highlands and assigned an army of 2,500 men, led by Colonel Agustín de Iturbide, to go after Guerrero. Iturbide was the son of a wealthy and conservative rancher from Valladolid whose ruthlessness during the fight against Hidalgo had moved him up the ranks. But as Iturbide prepared to march on the rebels, he heard that Spanish troops had mutinied and refused to continue the war against fellow Mexicans. Recognizing Spain's weakness, and sensing the support of Mexico's creole elites, Iturbide changed his plans and offered to make peace with Guerrero. Together, Iturbide and Guerrero called for Mexican independence in the 1821 Plan of Iguala. Described in terms of its Three Guarantees, this plan was a far cry from the republic imagined by Hidalgo and Morelos. Mexico would be governed by a constitutional monarchy and Mexicans would offer the crown to Ferdinand. Should he refuse the honor (which was tacitly assumed), they would find another suitable monarch, and they guaranteed Catholicism as the state religion. The plan further declared the equality of creoles and peninsulars, as well as racial equality. This template for Mexican independence offered something for almost everyone, especially the wealthy, the army, and the Church, and it quickly won converts. The fact that Iturbide and Guerrero also carried the day on the battlefield earned them the support of conservative pragmatists. Seeing that the tide had turned, the viceroy resigned. In the chaos that followed, his successor had little choice but to sign an agreement with Iturbide accepting the Plan de Iguala, and in 1821 Iturbide marched into Mexico City at the head of his large army to be honored by the archbishop at a lavish reception. Momentarily, Iturbide became the president of a regency of strange bedfellows that included the viceroy and the head of the church. The army granted him a large salary and the title of Generalissimo of the Land and Sea. The provinces of Central America joined in the celebration, but soon plans emerged there to break from the long-resented dominance of Mexico City.

Mexico's independence had been won, but after eleven years of war the country of 6 million inhabitants lay devastated. Mines, crops, and animals had been destroyed; industries and families suffered when workers joined rebel or loyalist armies. Once those armies disbanded, the men, many of whom were disabled, found themselves unemployed. Commerce was disrupted and silver production had fallen drastically—from 26 million ounces in 1809 to less than 6 million ounces in 1821. Few of those with capital were inclined to invest in the ruined economy, and Iturbide's new government resorted to printing promissory notes and forcing loans. As expenses rose, the Congress tried to trim the size of the army and Iturbide's paid mobs protested, calling out "Viva Agustín I, Emperor of Mexico!" By 1821, the counterrevolution was accomplished, and Iturbide and fellow monarchists spent the next year refashioning Mexico in the Napoleonic model. Following his hero's lead, Iturbide made princes and princesses of his father, sisters, and children and named one son his heir apparent. In 1822 Iturbide was inaugurated emperor in a ceremony to rival that of Napoleon. The event was designed to remind Mexicans of their loyalty to a king, and to reinforce the role of the Church in state affairs. Nevertheless, violence and chaos would soon return, only to dominate Mexican history for the next hundred years. The revolution that would begin in 1910 was a stark reminder that the fight for independence had solved nothing.

Independence: Brazil

Of all the paths to independence taken in this period, the one Brazil took is perhaps the most revealing of the enduring power of transatlantic ties in a revolutionary age. It also amply demonstrates the growing contradictions of the Atlantic world at the dawn of the industrial era, particularly those surrounding the economics of slavery and the politics of freedom. At the most superficial level, the vast Atlantic offered an easy escape for the Portuguese crown prince when Napoleon's forces marched on Lisbon in 1807. Going back to the aftermath of the U.S., Haitian, and French revolutions, there had been political stirrings in several Brazilian cities inspired by these events and by radical Enlightenment books and ideas that had found their way ashore and well inland. On these occasions, elites and plebeians joined forces for the first time since the expulsion of the Dutch early in the seventeenth century, freely blending imported revolutionary ideas with homegrown resentments. Much more important in the long run, however, was Brazil's deep dependence on northern Atlantic markets for its many primary export products, among them sugar, cotton, coffee, rice, gold, diamonds, hides, and tobacco. One important Brazilian product was even taken from the South Atlantic itself and rendered on its shores: whale oil, in huge demand among European industrialists in need of fuel and lubricants. It is significant that *all* of these commodities were produced by enslaved Africans, a situation most Brazilians (with the exception of some rebellious and outspoken slaves) assumed to be both natural and inevitable. Indeed, it could be said that nowhere else in the Atlantic basin were the fortunes of Africa, America, and Europe so tightly bound together at this moment in history. And only with this in mind can one make sense of Brazil's strange path to independence.

The sequence of events was a long one and began on the Iberian Peninsula. Long a key ally of Great Britain against the Bourbons of Spain and France, Portugal had remained neutral until 1807, well into Napoleon's reign. If the French Revolution encouraged Portuguese isolation, a direct attack by Napoleon's forces called for retreat. In November 1807, Portugal's crown prince and effective ruler, Dom João, and his royal court fled Lisbon just two weeks before the French army reached the capital. The monarch and his entourage sailed with a British naval escort to Rio de Janeiro, where they reestablished the court. Almost unbelievably, and virtually overnight, Portugal had been reduced to the role of an outlying province in need of help from a powerful metropole on the other side of a vast ocean. Yet this sudden reversal of roles reflected not just practical need but also the changing dynamic between Portugal and its huge Atlantic colony. Brazil's export sector was booming as never before, even as Portugal's lay stagnant, even dying. While Haiti's sugar production plummeted in the wake of the 1791 revolution, for example, Brazilian planters enjoyed soaring world prices in the face of dwindling supply. So profitable was the sugar sector after 1791 that it grew faster than it had in the booming sixteenth century. At the same time, coffee emerged as a major export crop, one that would drive the next several phases of Brazilian history. Meanwhile, only Portuguese fortified wines remained profitable thanks to the reliable drinking habits of the British.

In boundless Brazil, on the other hand, the search was on for new products, among them tropical hardwoods, natural latex, rare minerals, and drugs. Traditional exports, like cotton and rice, found higher demand than ever before. European warfare was one major stimulus for Brazilian economic expansion, and rising consumerism in industrializing nations, as we have seen in previous chapters, was another. Strains of tobacco from Virginia and Cuba were planted and crossed with local varieties as demand for the aromatic leaf, long a staple of Brazil's export economy, soared in Europe, North America, Africa, and even the Middle East. Such colonial productivity generated prosperity for Portugal and made the small Iberian kingdom all the more dependent on the vast resources of its largest colony.

Despite the weakness of Portugal's internal economy, the court's political, economic, and cultural impact on Brazil was considerable. Rio de Janeiro changed most radically, a provincial capital suddenly remade as an imperial one. Schools and libraries proliferated, and by 1808 Brazil boasted its first printing press. The transition to metropolitan status was in fact so smooth that no one seriously doubted Brazil's potential as an independent nation. The government cultivated scientific and artistic visitors, the first in centuries to travel beyond the crowded Atlantic ports. The royal House of Bragança made itself right at home in Brazil's ruggedly beautiful southern tropics, so much so that by the end of the Napoleonic wars, with France expelled from Portugal in 1814, João decided to stay, transforming the colony into a kingdom equal in power to Portugal itself. The result was an experiment, ultimately unsuccessful, in dual monarchy. When Portugal's ailing and long-institutionalized Queen Maria died in 1816, João VI was crowned king of Portugal in Rio. Despite his obvious love of Brazil, however, King João was no longer as welcome as he had been in 1808. An antimonarchical revolt broke out in the northeastern region of Pernambuco in 1817, foreshadowing later episodes of anti-Portuguese unrest and, finally, independence.

Brazilian independence would come about, however, in the wake of further upheavals in Portugal. Liberals there formed a parliament, or Cortes, after an 1820 military revolt similar to the one that occurred in Spain. The Cortes pressured the monarch to return to Portugal and adopt a variant on the liberal Spanish constitution of 1812. In this new government, Brazil would be allocated seats in a representative assembly, but would be restored to subordinate, colonial status. Having enjoyed more than a small taste of equality in a world of aspiring and established Atlantic empires, Brazilians refused to accept the Cortes's demands. Most Brazilian opposition movements were by this time anticolonial, but not antimonarchical: Brazilian elites wished to keep their equal status and open trade. After João returned to Portugal, leaving his son Pedro as regent, Brazilians insisted that the son stay behind permanently, despite calls for him to return home, too. In late 1822, Pedro, who had spent most of his twenty-four years in the colony, was declared emperor of an independent Brazil. Pedro embraced his new role, and British naval forces under Admiral Thomas Cochrane, fresh from guaranteeing the independence of Peru and Chile, prevented any Portuguese attempt at reconquest. As one of the first acts of Brazil's new empire, Cochrane was named Marquis of Maranhão.

While this is how events shook out, one wonders whether there were deeper, more "Brazilian" roots of independence. Historian Emilia Viotti da Costa and other specialists of the period trace the roots of Brazilian separation to at least the early eighteenth century, when the Portuguese crown sought desperately to tap into and control the flow of gold and diamonds from the mining districts of the interior. Instead of encouraging the vibrant commerce and development that might have accompanied Brazil's first mining bonanza, the crown punished it, repeatedly and harshly. Vast iron deposits were intentionally ignored as a favor to Portuguese monopolists, who profited by selling Brazilians iron tools imported from as far away as Sweden. Creole merchants in port cities, meanwhile, felt perpetually harassed and overtaxed, a situation that only encouraged contraband trade and general defiance of royal authority. The monopoly system, though modified under the Marquis of Pombal and his successors to stimulate Brazilian growth, did little to promote the interests of local elites. Lisbon merchants and courtiers were the main beneficiaries. Long-festering resentment of Portuguese merchants and officials—especially those who looked down their noses at local customs and skin colors—would be fairly easily channeled into calls for independence when the time came. In this regard, Brazil was not so different from Spanish America or even, for that matter, parts of North America.

Many other ingredients besides creole alienation would be needed, however, to foment an independence movement. Ideological shifts were critical. The Miners' Revolt of Ouro Preto in 1789 drew direct inspiration from radical Enlightenment texts and the U.S. Constitution, and republican ideals of the French Revolution fueled a 1792 rebellion in the capital city of Rio and then the 1798 Tailors' Revolt in Pernambuco. Resentment of Portuguese merchants and officials grew right alongside discontent with slavery and race prejudice. This allowed for a phenomenon not witnessed before: cross-class, interracial alliances. As an example of their radicalism, several of these movements witnessed the erasure of honorific titles, with slaves for the first time addressing whites in the streets as "you" and "patriot" rather than the customary "your mercy." As we have seen, in 1798 in the northeastern city of Salvador, a group of artisans and soldiers and some educated white Brazilians tried to organize an uprising of slaves, free blacks, and pardos. They sought independence and a republican government but also called for liberty, equality, fraternity, emancipation, and an end to racial discrimination. "The happy day of Liberty is at hand" for all Bahians, one poster announced in August of 1798. Ideas derived from the French Revolution circulated by word of mouth among people with little formal education, and those who could read shared the printed word with their neighbors. With the image of Sainte Domingue's revolt vivid in their minds (half of the men arrested in Bahia were slaves or ex-slaves), the city's ruling class moved against this uprising and four of the leaders received the grisly punishment of the traitor: to be hanged, drawn, and quartered.

The Pernambuco rebellion of 1817 followed, with a much broader constituency (in part due to these rebels' disinterest in ending slavery, which as we have stressed, was deeply rooted throughout the colony). By this time the king was in Brazil, however, making it somewhat easier for royal forces to diffuse the situation through a mix of gruesome punishments and surprising concessions. Meanwhile, new tensions had arisen in and around the capital city of Rio, where once optimistic local elites, some of them phenomenally wealthy, found themselves reduced to second-rank courtiers. In the end, as in much of Spanish America, it was this breed of socially pretentious, conservative creoles that finally stepped in to take over and guide Brazil's accelerating separation movement; at some point around 1820 it became clear that the time had come to choose. The decision of the Cortes was just the last straw. Put another way, the landed elite's struggles for autonomy and respect at court just happened to coincide with the more basic struggles of their far more numerous subordinates—the true heroes and martyrs, as they are now termed in Brazilian historiography and urban statuary—of the independence movement. Given this counterrevolutionary triumph, it would take many more years of struggle for the aspirations of the likes of Tiradentes, the tooth-pulling leader of the 1789 mineral revolt, and the Pernambuco tailors to return to the fore.

It is still notable, especially in the context of the times, that Brazilian independence was accomplished without the violent upheavals and civil wars typical of nearly all the other American republics, and also without the splintering of old colonial districts into multiple, independent nations. Despite its enormous size and poorly developed communications and transportation infrastructure, Brazil remained intact, its small pockets of loyalist sentiment squelched. Where did this unity come from in the absence of a nationalist propaganda machine, what historian Benedict Anderson has termed "print capitalism"? Arguably, it was, as historian A. J. R. Russell-Wood has stressed, Brazil's deep-seated, almost universal addiction to slavery. Elites, north, south, and center, were making a killing exporting primary commodities into the vast and growing Atlantic market. Like their contemporaries in the U.S. South and much of the Caribbean, they simply could not imagine producing these commodities without relying utterly and totally on enslaved Africans and their descendants. Regional rebellions threatened the territorial integrity of the Brazilian Empire on a few occasions prior to the accession of Pedro II in 1840, but none of the fissures that prompted them compared with the growing gap between the U.S. North and South. Brazil would stay united in slavery until 1888 and in empire until 1889.

Aside from the great planters, ranchers, and mine owners, there were two other important constituencies that advocated independence, one of them proslavery, one—at least nominally—against. These were Brazil's city dwellers, whose numbers were rapidly growing, and the ever-formidable and persuasive British (who did more to further independence throughout the western Atlantic than any other nation, although primarily for their own economic reasons). As we have seen in the case of Rio, city dwellers at almost every social level were as fond of slavery as any sugar planter, and saw no reason to change things. And what of Britain's celebrated abolitionism in this, the Atlantic's most slavery-saturated society? Like some political leaders of the early United States, Dom Pedro was a free trade advocate deeply influenced by Scottish economists; he was initially hopeful about a quick end to slavery in Brazil in favor of free labor. The moral aspect of the question was apparently of little concern to him, at least publicly. The fact was, however, that British antislavery sentiments simply did not resonate with Brazilian creoles, whatever their class or regional affiliation. Faced with a multitude of challenges more acutely serious than this one, young Dom Pedro ceased calling for an end to slavery. Meanwhile, Britain's attempts to curtail the trade in captives between Angola and Brazil mostly failed, in good part for lack of trying; there was simply too much money to be made from Brazilian exports to intervene too heavy handedly in what was after all the distant South Atlantic. British merchants and mining engineers who set up shop in Brazil—and there were significant communities in Rio, Salvador, and parts of Minas Gerais within a few years of independence—mostly kept their mouths shut about slavery or embraced it themselves. Meanwhile, Britain's substantial loans to the fledgling empire were quietly repaid with the profits and taxes derived from slave-produced commodities, and the issues of slavery and the transatlantic trade only came up when the two nations were in disagreement over tariffs or other potentially costly matters. Slavery and the society built around it thus remained so entrenched in Brazil that many historians do not regard independence as a clear watershed in the history of the nation. By way of contrast, slavery was abolished at or within a generation of independence in nearly all of Spanish America. Of the free nations of the revolutionary Atlantic, then, it was the United States and Brazil that stood out most.

British Triangulation and Neoimperialism

If the Napoleonic era provided an opportunity for American independence movements to coalesce and grow, it also enabled European powers to exploit the upheaval and rivalries of wartime to make their own claims to greater power in the Atlantic and beyond. The British in particular pursued aggressive expansion, hoping to tap the resources and markets that American independence opened. Silver from Mexico and Peru and gold from Brazil were as attractive as ever to British merchants and investors, many of whom rushed into the mining districts with new equipment and technicians. Loans to these and the other fledgling nations of Latin America constituted another step toward making them dependent on Britain, but the new kind of imperialism also required a fresh strategic vision. For Britain, this vision was a triangular one, encompassing Latin America, Africa, and Iceland. Britain accomplished its first move to peg out one of the triangle's corners when it took the Cape Colony from the Dutch during the Napoleonic wars. Since the Dutch had allied with the French, the British seized the opportunity to take various Dutch colonies, including Guiana and the Cape. In the peace of 1815, the English retained the Cape Colony and part of Guiana.

Acquisition of the Cape was a strategic matter, but Britain intruded so vigorously on Latin American independence movements to pin down two other corners of the triangulation scheme for another reason: commerce. In the eighteenth century, Britain had penetrated Latin American markets through a mix of warfare and state-sanctioned contraband. With the end of Spanish and Portuguese monopolies at independence, that era had ended. British trade schemes were nevertheless more independent than is often assumed. Many were proposed by private figures inspired by old-fashioned heroic and utopian visions of personal glory through colonial conquest. When the Napoleonic wars temporarily severed the oceanic link between Spain and its colonies, British merchants eager to trade for—and to appropriate—goods previously inaccessible to them made their move. It was the lure of Potosí silver that brought merchant and visionary Home Popham to seize Buenos Aires in 1806 and prompted a larger British contingent in 1807 to seize Montevideo. The British would subsequently play a key role in guaranteeing the independence of the entire River Plate district, lending millions of pounds sterling to the founders of each new nation. They would also play important diplomatic roles in the region, and would ultimately broker the creation of an independent Uruguay in 1830. The Falkland Islands, or Malvinas, also played a role in Britain's emerging South Atlantic strategy.

Another series of British plans involved the annexation of Iceland, then a possession of Denmark. The mastermind of one such plan was a Scot named John Cochrane, who hoped to obtain access to Icelandic sulfur, required to process the coal on his family's estate in Scotland. Cochrane proposed a land swap with the Danish, Crab Island, or present-day Vieques in the West Indies, for Iceland. Crab Island could join three other Danish colonies in the Caribbean, and Britain could enjoy the material benefits of Iceland. Cochrane's plan went nowhere at the time, but like any visionary he was not discouraged. He tried again with Sir Joseph Banks, who had taken part in a scientific venture to Iceland. Although pessimistic about the natural resources of the island, he speculated that annexation might benefit the Icelandic people. Again, the proposal met with no favorable response from the government. The final opportunity came when Denmark joined Napoleon in alliance in 1807, making Denmark Britain's enemy. Now Britain quickly grabbed the Danish holdings in the West Indies, and when the Danish government failed to act on Banks's newest proposal—offering the people of Iceland "the splendid option of placing themselves voluntarily under the rule of Britain"—a British merchant named Samuel Phelps seized Iceland's government in 1809 and declared independence for the country, an event marked with revolutionary proclamations guaranteeing universal male suffrage. Yet, because Phelps had acted without authorization, the Royal Navy restored Danish rule within two months. The historian Anna Agnarsdottir suggests the British did so knowing they could acquire the markets they wanted in Iceland without resorting to invasion—a lesson, incidentally, that the British government would apply repeatedly around the world throughout the first three quarters of the nineteenth century. Free trade won the day without the expense of warfare and territorial administration. The British model of neoimperialism that emerged with Latin American independence combined the economic might of the world's first industrial nation with the latent threat of matchless Atlantic naval power. If all went as hoped, the British could carve out an Atlantic shadow empire on the cheap, all in the name of "free trade." Competition over Africa, however, would complicate this plan.

Atlantic Africa

With a few exceptions, Britain's early nineteenth-century expansion in the Atlantic boded ill for local populations involved in overseas trade. It was not evident at the time, but the nature of the Atlantic game for coastal Africans would shift radically from relative independence to absolute colonial subjugation. With the possible exception of Brazil, which maintained close trade ties to Angola long after independence, Britain alone was in a position to think about trade with Africa over the long run. Most scholarly attention relating to Britain and West Africa through midcentury traditionally focused on the efforts of the powerful Royal Navy to suppress the Atlantic slave trade (including that of Brazil with Angola) and the related colonial venture in Sierra Leone, but less visible events—at least to European eyes—were occurring along the coast that involved change in long-standing power relationships. These shifts probably boded greater ill for the long-term political and economic well being of African states than the forced suppression of Atlantic slaving or the planting of a small and none-too-significant colony on a coastal promontory in Upper Guinea.

In one form or another, Parliament had funded operation of a British outpost in the Gambia River, James Fort on James Island, since the 1660s. A small garrison there, for a while under the Royal African Company and later the Committee of Merchants Trading to Africa, did its best to keep happy (which meant, among other things, plied with alcohol) rulers of the river's trading states, who held the balance of economic, political, and strategic power in the region. Unhappy local rulers meant not only no access to trade or high taxes and tolls on whatever items one procured, enslaved people among other things, but possibly no food and fresh water for ships' crews and the fort's garrison. French merchants maintained an outpost at Albreda on the river bank, a couple of miles from James Fort, for the same purpose, allowing canny officials of local states to play against one another the agents of the two European countries. Ships from these nations and others paid dearly to trade up the Gambia, even when the agents on James Island and Albreda were on good terms with all. Europeans were under no illusion: free trade this was not.

Over much of the eighteenth century French and English naval vessels and privateers took turns bombarding and sacking the outposts of the other nation, particularly as manifestations of hostilities in Europe. To an African living along the lower Gambia, it must have appeared like a game of musical trading posts. When the French sacked James Fort, they would detonate explosives to destroy its stone walls, only to have the English garrison rebuild them when they reoccupied the fort. Then, following a final French assault in 1779, Britain decided to abandon the tiny island (blowing up the fort's walls itself this time, so the French could not occupy it), and the long period of American and European warfare that ensued kept Britain from having an outpost in the river for more than three decades. France kept its nationals at Albreda longer, but with export of slaves from the river falling to 150 per year by the start of the nineteenth century, France, with its hands full, abandoned Albreda as well in 1804. Britain, meanwhile, had taken Gorée Island off Cape Verde from France in 1800, much as it had taken Cape Town from the Dutch as an element of the hostilities of the Napoleonic Wars. At the Congress of Vienna (1814–15), marking the end of the wars, the British Crown agreed to return Gorée to France, and it removed its garrison, which included a number of African spouses of English men (called *signares*), their mixed-heritage children, and a host of coastal traders, skilled craftspeople, and hangers-on, to the Gambia. No longer satisfied with minuscule James Island, the British set up shop on Banjul, a larger, if low and sandy, island only eight miles from the mouth of the river. They named the new settlement Bathurst after the British colonial secretary, the Earl of Bathurst. The transplanted merchants believed there would be sufficient trade to justify expenditures at the new location, but Parliament threw in funds also because a presence at Bathurst could command the entrance to the river and stop slavers from entering it. Parliament had outlawed slave trading as of the beginning of 1808, and halting the now-illicit traffic had become an important political factor in the growing humanitarian climate of postwar Great Britain.

The British expedition that reconnoitered in 1815, prior to resettling the Gorée bunch, was in no position to force new terms on local rulers, so the leader of the expedition, Alexander Grant, assured the most powerful local ruler, Mansa Kolimanka Manneh of Niumi, across the river from Bathurst, that he could continue to levy the same duties and tolls that his predecessors had collected back through the many years of river trading, there remaining sufficient commerce in cowhides, beeswax, and gum for this to matter to the British. But it would not take long for the Bathurst merchants to chafe under the old rules, which added costs and slowed trade, nor would Britain fail to recognize how different their power relationship was with Niumi and others and to press their advantage. A vague charge of "misconduct on the part of the [mansa] and his people" in 1817 brought Grant to advise captains of vessels entering the Gambia to pay only half of Niumi's customary duties and fees. Three years later, Grant began having the Bathurst customs office collect the mansa's due and deliver it to him; then, in 1822, a new administrator simply began paying Niumi's ruler an amount deemed roughly equivalent to the traditional tolls, taking the sum out of revenue accumulating from Bathurst's import duties. Unhappy with the change, Niumi's ruling elite grew testy. "The King [of Niumi] has frequently crossed over and levied contributions on the Merchants," reads a government report, and in "one very disgraceful transaction," Manneh "went to Government House and told the Commandant that he would take the place and burn his house if he did not give him what he wanted."

Britain's response was measured at first, but then strong. The Royal Navy brought one of the cruisers of its antislavery squadron into the river, a show of force in 1826 that convinced Manneh's successor, Burungai Sonko, to cede his state's entire riverbank for a mile inland to the British in return for quarterly payments equivalent to £87. When the British began erecting guns and a fort on the "Ceded Mile," across from Bathurst on what was Niumi territory, Sonko—considered by the British "an insane drunkard, who . . . can only be restrained by fear"—became "frequently troublesome." Finally, in 1831, forces led by Niumi's ruling families drove off settlers on a nearby island, closed all trade paths, stopped canoes from bringing supplies to Bathurst, and engaged the garrison of the newly erected fort. In its reaction, Britain showed the rulers of the African state how it could summon resources from around the Atlantic world. British naval forces blockaded Niumi's riverbank; an African allied with Britain in trade convinced Niumi's neighboring state to isolate Niumi by land and threaten attack; troops, some originally from the West Indies, arrived in Bathurst from Sierra Leone; and the French (eager to reduce Niumi's power for the benefit of its own traders) joined in with troops from Senegal and a warship to bombard Sonko's village. This force—451 officers and men, backed by the cannon of two vessels—invaded Niumi on November 11 and for a month kept up daily fire and a blockade on Sonko's village. By the end of January 1832, one report read, the people of Niumi were "so reduced as to consent to any conditions." Sonko and seventeen other Niumi officials signed a humiliating treaty on January 5, expressing "their sorrow, for the outrages that have committed"; offering hostages to ensure their "promise never to offend again"; ratifying again the cession of the state's riverbank to Great Britain; and agreeing to indemnify those harmed in the hostilities, turn over all pieces of ordinance, seek the consent of Bathurst before selection of any new mansa, and "to hold peace and friendship with the subjects of His Majesty the King of Great Britain for ever." After centuries of sovereignty and control of river trade in the face of warfare, slave raiding, and threats from within and without, Niumi's ruling lineages had met their match.

Of course, the Gambia River was not all of Atlantic Africa, or even Atlantic West Africa, and elsewhere to the south and east, along the Gold and Slave Coasts, around the Niger River Delta, and at points beyond, the balance of power remained in African hands beyond 1830. But the Napoleonic Wars had considerably enhanced British strength, and the nation's mantra was "free trade," which called for the elimination of tariffs and monopolies. Recovering European neighbors, such as France, picked up on the idea of free trade, although without giving up the notion of a restored land empire in the Americas. In short, free trade seemed to suit the militarily powerful, commercially expansive, industrializing Europeans in the 1830s. It led them to respect the independence of former Iberian colonies in the Americas, and to continue to recognize the sovereignty of states and polities on the Atlantic coast of Africa so long as it was to their advantage to do so.

But later in the century, when competition over natural resources and markets grew among European nations, and the Industrial Revolution enabled Europeans to have better weapons, travel faster, and—perhaps most incredibly by the standards of the time—avoid contracting malaria in the tropics, they would return to the sort of land-grabbing imperialism first practiced in the Americas. As factories spewed greater amounts of smoke and ash on Manchester and Leeds, Lowell and Lawrence, and eventually Dusseldorf and Bremen, the handwriting was beginning to appear on the walls of the old trade factories and forts that dotted Africa's Atlantic coastline, a warning that the nineteenth century was going to bring more change in power relationships that would not be in Africans' favor.

The Monroe Doctrine

By comparison with these broad British initiatives to alter Atlantic geopolitics and economies, U.S. approaches to establishing hegemony in the Western Hemisphere were modest and halting. In Washington, the administration of James Monroe (1817–25) determined that with Ferdinand preoccupied with internal affairs, the time had at last arrived to recognize the independence of some of the new Spanish American republics. Commercial interests in New England had long clamored for such recognition, fearing that inactivity could result in renewed European efforts at conquest, which would mean the closing off of newly opened Latin American markets to American merchants and shippers. With the collapse of the Federalist Party following the War of 1812, Monroe shifted toward the right to encompass his nation's emerging industrial interests, a move symbolized by the choice of former Federalist John Quincy Adams as secretary of state. Responding to a House request for documents relative to the struggle against Madrid, on March 8, 1822, Monroe sent a special message to Congress. Chile, Gran Colombia, Peru, Mexico, and the United Provinces of La Plata had all proven themselves to be independent, he argued, and Spain's chances of reconquest were "most remote." Madrid should not regard recognition as a hostile act, Monroe insisted, but having recently purchased Florida and secured by treaty a southern border to the Louisiana Purchase, the president no longer needed to concern himself with Spain's petulance.

Within two months, an enthusiastic Congress appropriated $100,000 to finance any diplomatic missions to the new republics "as the president might deem proper." The House vote was 167 to 1, and, anticipating the move, even before the ballot Bolívar appointed Manuel Torres as chargé d'affaires to the United States. An emotional Monroe—who loved all revolutionaries provided they were not slaves in his own nation—greeted the aged Torres on June 19, 1822. In exchange, Monroe appointed Richard C. Anderson as minister to Gran Colombia.

News traveled slowly in the days of wooden ships, but Monroe was right to be concerned about European designs on the west. Four months after Torres sailed up the Chesapeake, delegates representing the great powers converged on Verona, Italy, for the third European conference following Napoleon's downfall. Although this meeting was to address mainly a Greek uprising against the Turks, Bolívar understood that the revolt against Ferdinand VII would receive its due. It was no secret that since 1818, Tsar Alexander I of Russia had been urging the United States to join his Holy Alliance and side with legitimist Europe against popular revolutions around the Atlantic, a peculiar request to make of Monroe, who fancied himself an old revolutionary and continued to wear the knee breeches and white-topped boots of an earlier day.

Monroe's interest in preserving Latin American independence was more than nostalgic, of course, but a first question to ask is why Tsar Alexander or anyone else cared what the U.S. position was, given its notorious weakness in the grand scheme of world politics? The answer has two parts: one, the Holy

Alliance's profound interest in Spanish and Portuguese affairs had the potential to upset the so-called balance of power, and two, such an intervention might lead to concerted attempts to retake the rebellious colonies of the Iberian nations, an untenable outcome for British and U.S. merchants already reaping the benefits of free trade. Big or small, the tsar wanted allies against Britain, and Britain wanted allies against France and the Holy Alliance. The transatlantic side of the concern was of course to head off a possible French intervention in Latin America, or worse, to witness the return of France as a bona fide colonial empire and naval power. These fears were by no means unfounded, as France soon backed Spanish reconquest efforts in 1829 and then launched its own expedition to Mexico in the so-called Pastry War of 1838. (Nineteenth-century French intervention in Latin America culminated in the successful invasion of Mexico in 1861, treated in the following chapter.)

But this was all a long way off in Monroe's heyday. In August 1823 Britain's Secretary Canning summoned to his office Richard Rush, the American minister to Britain, where he unveiled his grandiose plan for a joint Anglo-American declaration against further European adventurism in the Americas. "What do you think your Government would say to going hand in hand with England in such a policy," he inquired. Rush lacked the standing instructions to accept what was tantamount to an informal alliance with a nation his country had fought as recently as 1815, but the wary minister hinted that Monroe might find the proposal acceptable provided that Britain first grant formal recognition to the emerging republics, a step heretofore blocked by conservatives in Parliament.

As luck would have it, a shake-up in the Foreign Office had landed the new secretary's cousin, Stratford Canning, in Washington City. Even as Rush's dispatches made their way across the ocean, Secretary of State Adams was informing Stratford that England's repudiation of the Holy Alliance presented "a suitable occasion for the United States and Great Britain to compare their ideas and purposes together." Despite such assurances, when the large packet of letters from Rush arrived on October 9, Adams began to harbor reservations about a joint manifesto. As interested in foreign trade as any man in the administration, the New Englander feared that Canning and his prime minister, Lord Liverpool, as leaders of the most powerful nation in the Atlantic, would assume leadership of the pact and reap the commercial bounty promised by unrestricted trade with Latin America. Guessing also that Liverpool would send his navy, regardless of Monroe's response, to halt any Franco-Spanish intervention in the Americas, Adams saw no reason to limit future American expansion south or west by agreeing to freeze the status quo. Far better it was to stand alone and "avow our principle explicitly," he lectured Monroe, "than to come in as a cock-boat in the wake of the British man-of-war."

The notoriously shy Jefferson had begun the tradition of sending his messages to Congress, rather than reading them himself, which in any case was consistent with his idea of a proper separation of powers. And so it was a clerk who droned out Monroe's seventh annual address to both houses of Congress on December 2, 1823. Out of thirteen printed pages, the two widely separated passages that came to be known as the Monroe Doctrine each took less than a single page. The first comment, in a passage completely drafted by Adams, announced that the American continents, "by the free and independent condition which they have assumed and maintain, and henceforth not to be considered as subjects for future colonization by any European powers." Following seven pages of domestic matters, Monroe turned to the dangers posed by the Holy Alliance. In the name of "amicable relations," the president advised, the United States "should consider any attempt on their part to extend their system to any portion of this hemisphere as dangerous to our peace and safety." Although Monroe hinted that any further intervention in the Americas could only be regarded as "unfriendly," there was no explicit warning that his country would go to war to protect the emerging Latin republics. Nor, despite elementary lessons taught to virtually every schoolchild, did the president demand that the Europeans vacate colonies not then in a state of rebellion.

In Europe, the response was chilly. Increasingly accustomed to seizing whatever sections of the globe best suited their interests, the European powers found Monroe's "lecture" an affront to their authority. Neither did the implicit defense of the right of revolution sit well with monarchs only recently restored to their thrones. "Arrogant," "haughty," and "monstrous" were just a few epithets hurled at the United States. Since Monroe had sent his address to Congress, rather than to them, no continental nation bothered to draft a formal reply, but the position of France was typical. The "document in question," observed the aged Louis XVIII, "merits only the most profound contempt." Only Canning found merit in the pronouncement. Rightly assuming that his overtures to Rush lay behind the U.S. position, the foreign secretary believed that if Monroe's implied threat, modest though the U.S. Navy and Army were, delivered the "coup de grace" to France's thoughts of meddling in Latin American affairs, that was to the good. Since British banks, shippers, and manufacturers could easily outcompete their American rivals in any future Latin American trade, Canning was willing to endure moralizing from the upstart republic in North America.

Even so, Canning decided to take no chances. To make it clear that it was the powerful British fleet, rather than Monroe's evidently hollow doctrine, that was keeping the French army from any act of American intervention—which in any case he believed unlikely—in early 1824 Canning published a copy of the memorandum he had presented to Prince Jules de Polignac, the French ambassador in London, the previous October 9. Bolívar now knew what he had suspected all along. Two months *before* Monroe sent his message to Congress, Britain had warned France that "the junction of any Foreign Power in an enterprise of Spain against the Colonies" would force England to take action to defend its interests. In the polite language of international diplomacy, such blunt threats were not taken lightly.

Better to make his point, Lord Liverpool formally recognized Gran Colombia, Mexico, and the United Provinces of La Plata on December 31, 1824. Parliament was alerted to this momentous act in the King's Speech of February 7, 1825, though George IV did not read it. Regarding the Latin American revolts as the latest episode in a long, unfortunate series of assaults on the right of kings, George begged off on the grounds that he had misplaced his glasses and suffered from an attack of gout. And so it fell to the lord chancellor to read the speech, which he did with as much ill grace as possible. Refusing to allow the king to bury his achievement, Canning went down to the Commons to explain his policy. Using the first person singular to emphasize his role, Canning crowed, "that if France had Spain, it should not be Spain with the Indies. I called the New World into existence to redress the balance of the Old."

The Panama Congress

Bolívar surely thought that the people of the Viceroyalty of New Granada were more responsible for the "existence" of Gran Colombia than was an English foreign secretary, yet he understood the role the Royal Navy played in its maintenance, particularly in the delicate first years of nation building. On his earlier visit to the United States in 1807, the president had witnessed the way in which disparate colonies had united against a European threat, and Bolívar knew that he could not rely on Canning's support indefinitely. "From the very beginning of the revolution I understood that if we could once establish free nations in South America," he insisted, "a federation among them would be the strongest form of union." As a first step, Bolívar engineered a series of bilateral alliances between his country and Peru in 1822, and then with Mexico (technically a part of North America). The treaties, curiously, both upheld and eroded political independence and sovereignty, as they guaranteed current borders but offered reciprocal rights of citizenship. They also took a second step: each treaty pledged their governments to send plenipotentiaries to an "Amphyctionic Assembly" of emerging states to be held on the Isthmus of Panama to unite the new nations into a republican confederation.

Although the idea of a Latin American Congress along the lines of the European Congresses of Vienna or Verona did not originate with Bolívar, he quickly embraced the concept as a counterweight to European designs. (Miranda first proposed the idea years before, and suggested Panama City as the "Corinth of the New World.") Speaking in behalf of the three treaty nations, Bolívar issued a circular on December 7, 1824, inviting those independent states formerly part of the Spanish empire to convene in the Colombian province of Panama the following October. Initially, invitations were only sent to Mexico, Peru, Chile, and the United Provinces of La Plata. A western organization, based on republicanism, he argued, could effectively confront the Holy Alliance. "While in Europe everything is done for the sake of tyranny," Bolívar wrote, "in America everything is done for the sake of freedom."

What happened next is less clear. President Guadalupe Victoria of Mexico, evidently acting on his own, instructed his minister in Washington to encourage the United States to attend. In Gran Colombia's capital of Bogotá, Vice President Santander, who served as chief executive while Bolívar was away on a military campaign, instructed Don Pedro Gual, Minister of Foreign Affairs, to discover if Monroe might be willing to send a delegation. Santander and

Bolívar were never close (Bolívar being a Venezuelan), and the president almost certainly had no advance warning of these invitations. Bolívar had considered inviting Great Britain to send a plenipotentiary as a method of encouraging further English naval protection—the president even toyed with the idea of granting British businessmen South American citizenship—and thus it made sense not to invite their recent foe in the War of 1812. Moreover, the United States, a prescient Bolívar confided to the British chargé d'affaires in Bogotá, "seem destined by Providence to plague [the rest of] America with torments in the name of freedom." The British, who continued to control the mainland colony of Guiana as well as their Caribbean sugar islands, were interested in exacerbating the divisions between Europe and the Americas while keeping their North American trading rivals at bay.

The decision not to invite Haiti, the second independent nation in the Western Hemisphere, is less easily explained away. Hints that the island republic was not contiguous to the mainland, given Bolívar's flirtation with a British invitation, rang hollow; in any case, Colombian ships could make port in Le Cap François in half the time it took to reach Chile. Ironically, nobody had greater reason than Bolívar to be grateful to Haiti. Had it not been for Pétion's assistance in 1816, the Liberator might well have finished his days as had Miranda, dead in prison. But gratitude was hard to come by in a world of racial animus. Although Bolívar did not share the common diplomatic view of Haiti as an international menace, he understood that the countries he needed for his confederation, such as slaveholding Brazil, had no desire to treat with Haitian delegates. As the historian George Dangerfield so aptly put it: "Bolívar concealed a core of robust eighteenth-century realism beneath his panoply of romantic attributes." If the cost of protecting Gran Colombia from European recolonization was the continued isolation of the second republic of the western Atlantic, Bolívar was willing to pay it.

It was but a small group that assembled on June 22 in the Franciscan monastery in Panama City. Following a comedy of errors that almost seems typical of the period, the U.S. delegation never arrived. Bolívar may well have been quietly pleased, ambivalent as he was about U.S. intentions, but in other ways, the Panamanian Conference failed to fulfill his expectations. Despite the president's hints of material rewards, Britain sent only a single diplomat of a low rank, Edward J. Dawkins, carefully defined as an "observer." Slaveholding Brazil shared the fears of U.S. southerners like John Randolph and ultimately declined to attend, as did Argentina. The Peruvians arrived first, followed by the Colombians, and shortly thereafter, representatives from Mexico and Guatemala reached the city. Even Bolívar was absent; the excuse given was that the Liberator was off on another campaign in Lima, but a more likely reason was his sensitivity to charges that he wished to rule a united Latin world as a Napoleonic dictator. Even so, the failure of Bolívar, arguably the most prominent man in the Western Hemisphere in 1826, to attend a conference called by his own republic further served to diminish any standing it might have had.

The congress sat for three weeks and adjourned on July 15 after issuing a series of resolutions. The four nations present agreed to a defensive alliance, which was open to all American states for membership. This proposed federation would create a central army and navy entrusted with the defense of Latin American affairs. As was the case with the short-lived European congress system, the Panama Conference was to be the first of a series of biannual meetings, which in case of war would become yearly conferences. Aware of Panama's well-earned reputation as a malarial quagmire, the delegates proposed that future summits be moved to the Mexican city of Tacubaya. But Panama's rump session was the last.

As befitting a man whose life had been equal parts victory and heartache, Bolívar accepted the failure of his Panama venture with equanimity. "I considered the Congress of the Straits as a theatrical performance," he later sighed, called only "in order to create a sensation." With that, Bolívar abandoned as impractical any hopes of creating a grand confederation of all Latin republics in the Americas, and turned instead to uniting the nations liberated by him into one vast nation under his control, a Confederation of the Andes. In any case, by late 1826 the dangers of further European intervention had receded, thanks in part to the death of Louis XVIII in 1824.

The victim of provincial jealousies, internal rivalries, and fears that his military successes might evolve into a popular dictatorship, and badly shaken by several assassination attempts, Bolívar resigned the presidency of Gran Colombia at the end of April 1830, said a final farewell to Manuela Sáenz, his longtime mistress, and left Bogotá for the Atlantic coast.

Bolívar initially intended to quit Gran Colombia for a foreign nation, but neither his health nor the new government—which feared he would again return at the head of an invading army—allowed for that scenario. Diagnosed with advanced tuberculosis, Bolívar drafted a will and, recognizing the importance of the faith to his followers, accepted the last rites of the Catholic Church. Toward the end of his life, Bolívar grew resigned, both as to his fate and that of his nation. "He who serves a revolution," he lamented, "ploughs the seas." On December 17, 1830, Bolívar died at the age of forty-seven on a hacienda outside Santa Marta. His only shirt was torn, so General Silva sent the embalmers one of his, so that the Liberator would not be buried in rags.

Bolívar's Republic of Gran Colombia faced many of the same problems that plagued the early United States—an underdeveloped, colonial economy; a society divided along racial, class, and regional lines; and a landed gentry that spoke in the language of democracy but feared extending rights to those on the bottom. So what explains Gran Colombia's failure, when the United States seems to have succeeded? Some historians suggest that despite Bolívar's occasionally dictatorial tendencies, his central government was in fact too weak to forge an integrated political society. Others note that Spanish America's wars for independence, far more than that of the United States, were also civil wars, ones that mostly remained unresolved in the nineteenth century. In the North American struggle, loyalists fled, while those in Gran Colombia's (and other Latin American nations) remained close at hand to form a reactionary presence. This tendency toward elite factionalism was exacerbated by intense regional rivalries and aided by complex geography and difficulties of long-distance transport. Still other historians point to the rapid militarization of Spanish American politics, common to many countries, like Mexico, where

Iturbide was succeeded by a series of generals and dictators like Antonio López de Santa Anna. To the extent that many creole elites across the Americas made it clear that they wished to retain much of the social structure of the pre-independence world, their success depended on how effectively civil authorities used force to crush opponents of the state (including the lower classes), while drawing the majority of narrowly defined "citizens" into the political system. As we have seen, only Chile and Brazil stand out as genuine exceptions, the former a stable republic from independence to 1890, the latter a fairly peaceful monarchy until 1889. Independent Latin American nations were not impossible to govern, just difficult.

Bolívar's final message to his country urged its people to "work for the inestimable benefits of unity," but even as he lay dying, Gran Colombia was already disintegrating. Venezuela pulled free of Colombian control in 1829, and Ecuador followed in 1830. In 1903, ninety-nine years after Bolívar watched Bonaparte crown himself emperor in Paris, Panama too declared itself independent, aided by a United States whose growing power the Liberator had always feared.

Selected Readings

Adelman, Jeremy, *Republic of Capital: Buenos Aires and the Legal Transformation of the Atlantic World* (Stanford: Stanford University Press, 1999).

Barman, Roderick J., *Brazil: The Forging of a Nation, 1798–1852* (Stanford: Stanford University Press, 1988).

Bemis, Samuel Flagg, *John Quincy Adams and the Foundations of American Foreign Policy* (New York: Alfred A. Knopf, 1949).

Bethell, Leslie, ed., *The Independence of Latin America* (New York: Cambridge University Press, 1987).

Bushnell, David, *Simón Bolívar: Liberation and Disappointment* (New York: Pearson Longman, 2004).

Collier, Simon, *Chile: The Making of a Republic: 1830–1865* (Cambridge, UK: Cambridge University Press, 2003).

———, *Ideas and Politics of Chilean Independence, 1808–1833* (Cambridge, UK: Cambridge University Press, 1966).

Cunningham, Noble E., Jr., *The Presidency of James Monroe* (Lawrence: University Press of Kansas, 1996).

Dangerfield, George, *The Era of Good Feelings* (New York: Harcourt, Brace, 1952).

Kinsbruner, Jay, *Independence in Spanish America: Civil Wars, Revolutions, and Underdevelopment*, 3rd ed. (Albuquerque: University of New Mexico Press, 2004).

Lynch, John, *Simón Bolívar, A Life* (New Haven: Yale University Press, 2006).

Masur, Gerhard, *Simón Bolívar* (Albuquerque: University of New Mexico Press, 1948).

Parsons, Lynn Hudson, *John Quincy Adams* (Madison: Madison House Publishers, 1998).

Rodríguez, Jaime, *The Independence of Spanish America* (Cambridge, UK: Cambridge University Press, 1998).

Russell-Wood, A. J. R., ed., *From Colony to Nation: Essays on the Independence of Brazil* (Baltimore: The Johns Hopkins University Press, 1975).

Schultz, Kirsten, *Tropical Versailles: Empire, Monarchy, and the Portuguese Royal Court in Rio de Janeiro, 1808–1821* (New York: Routledge, 2001).

Van Young, Eric, *The Other Rebellion: Popular Violence, Ideology, and the Mexican Struggle for Independence, 1810–1821* (Stanford: Stanford University Press, 2001).

Viotti da Costa, Emilia, *The Brazilian Empire: Myths and Histories,* Revised ed. (Chapel Hill: University of North Carolina Press, 2000).

Wright, Donald R., *The World and a Very Small Place in Africa: A History of Globalization in Niumi, The Gambia,* 2nd ed. (Armonk, NY: M. E. Sharpe, 2004).

Boers visiting a Zulu kraal in South Africa. The Boer leader Pieter Retief and his men leaving their guns outside the kraal of King Dingaan before attending what they expected to be a dance in their honor. They were instead executed by armed Zulus. February 3, 1838. Credit: The Granger Collection, New York.

Chapter Thirteen

Industrialization and a New Imperialism, 1780–1850

Sir, This is to acquaint you that if your thrashing Machines are not destroyed by you directly, we shall commence our labours.
Signed on behalf of the whole
Captain Swing

In the year of Bolívar's death, a visitor to Massachusetts remarked on the housing around the Lowell textile mills. Young New England women, mostly farmers' daughters, resided within the company's paternalistic boardinghouses. Nearby stood "John Bull's Row" and the "Scots Block," corporate-owned cottages inhabited by skilled English and Scottish workers. Farther away, just beyond a canal, sat an acre known as "New Dublin," where "not far from 500 Irish" were confined to one hundred dilapidated cabins "built of slabs and rough boards." Segregated by their Catholicism more than by the artificial waterway, the Irish immigrants worked for the Proprietors of Locks and Canals, while the newly arrived Protestants toiled in a nearby carpet factory. The crossing of three thousand miles of ocean had failed to wash away old ethnic and religious divisions; the hand of industrial capitalism had simply transplanted them.

Mercantile Capitalism Transformed

Neither the transformation of mercantile capital into industrial capital nor the transportation of hundreds of thousands of impoverished men and women from the British Isles to the United States happened overnight. As early as 1740, the infant mortality rate in Great Britain declined markedly, perhaps due to improved midwifery, and with it came steady population growth. Between 1750 and 1800, the population of England and Wales alone leapt from 6 million to 10 million. For a tiny nation with limited farmland, this meant an expanding working class with diminishing options; this combined with ample capital, rising foreign markets and increased agricultural output laid the foundations for industrialization. Coupled with technological advances in shipping and communications, industrialization would shrink the Atlantic considerably by the mid-nineteenth century. Yet even toward the end of the nineteenth century, as discussed in the next and final chapter, far-flung Atlantic consumers of industrial products could still be mired in slavery, debt peonage, and other unfree labor conditions. Indeed, perhaps the greatest tension to arise in this last period of study was how rapid industrial development in Europe and New England was to coexist—or clash—with slavery and underdevelopment in parts south. On no shore of the vast Atlantic basin did industrialization bring freedom quickly to anyone.

Industry began with textiles. The spinning of yarn, as well as its weaving into cloth, had long been conducted under the domestic, or putting-out system, in which farmers' wives labored in behalf of merchants on their home wheels and looms. Typically, these women neither bought the cotton or wool they spun, nor did they market their finished product. Instead, they were paid by the piece (hence the term "piece-work"), or the spool, by merchants who marketed the thread. Consequently, in the eighteenth century, industrial development was decentralized and took place within a rural setting. The crude spinning wheels and handlooms that adorned every peasant's two-room cottage, rather than a factory, collectively made up the earliest manufacturing units.

The putting-out system had thrived in various parts of northwest Europe during boom cycles in the sixteenth and seventeenth centuries, but things changed drastically later in the eighteenth century. Britain's rising population yielded a larger work force and greater domestic demand for textile products. So did the rising populations throughout the Americas, and both placed strains on the rustic putting-out system. In response to this swelling demand, a number of early industrialists—most of them born into the lower middle class—came up with ingenious technical innovations. Although many of these inventions were modifications of earlier work, the sheer number of them, as well as their interlocking nature, served to advance industrial change exponentially. The names of the innovators—John Kay, Richard Arkwright, James Hargreaves, James Watt—have been a staple in history textbooks for decades, and undoubtedly they deserve their fame. But of greater moment from an Atlantic perspective is the effect that the "Industrial Revolution," a deceptively simple term, had on the millions of men and women who did not profit from the spinning jenny—laborers first residing in Britain, but soon workers all about the Atlantic basin, some in places the captains of industry scarcely knew existed—as the effects of industrialization spread from Lancashire to Lowell, Charleston to Caracas, and Bathurst to Boma.

Richard Arkwright began his working life as a barber, but he died a wealthy capitalist. Definitions are important, and perhaps no single word remains in greater need of clarification than *capitalism*. In its most basic form, capital was, and is, money, and in that sense, the term had been used in the western sections of Europe since the late Middle Ages. But it was not until the time of the English Civil War—and certainly this was no coincidence—that English speakers began thinking of capital in a broader sense of a surplus commodity used most wisely to invest, typically in mercantile enterprises. To the extent that Jacobean merchants poured their spare funds into such ventures as the Virginia Company, they qualified as petty capitalists. But those early ventures were characterized by scores of men who invested small sums in numerous companies, whereas the opposite was true a century later. By the time of the earliest known use of the word capitalism, in 1793, it was meant to describe a system in which a relatively small number of individuals owned and controlled the means of production. In his Cromford Mill, for example, Arkwright constructed the largest of all Lancashire cotton factories, which employed more than two thousand men, women, and children—*hands*, to use the term of the day.

Nonetheless, several factors impeded industrial growth, chief among them inadequate banking facilities. Many a shipper was ready to invest part of his profits in early industrial experiments, but the movement of mercantile capital into industrial capital proved slow, if steady, into the late eighteenth century. Even in the principal commercial regions of western Europe, large banks were concentrated in London, Amsterdam, and Paris. There were no country banks in Britain in the first part of the eighteenth century, so not only was investment capital geographically remote from many potential industrial towns, but even coins for payrolls were hard to find.

Even more serious an impediment was obtaining enough cotton, which did not grow in English latitudes, to feed the mills. One can measure the speed of early British industrial growth, as well as mark its shift from cottage industry to water-powered mills, by examining raw cotton imports. At midcentury, British ships brought in 2.5 million pounds of cotton, some from the Bahamas and lowcountry Georgia and South Carolina, but more from India. Most of this cotton was destined for looms belonging to farmers' wives. But only forty years later, in 1787, Britain was importing 22 million pounds of raw cotton, most of which went to large mechanical mills. Also by this time, English cloth could be found in all corners of the Atlantic basin, even in places where it was officially barred. African weavers, who in places had managed through the years of heightened Atlantic slaving to hold out against cloth imported from India, now began seeing their market opt for English imitations of Indian calicos, muslins, and chintz. Cheap, mass-produced British cloth also flooded both the legal and contraband markets of Latin America by the mid-eighteenth century, with dire consequences for local artisans. The traditional cotton textile industry of southern Ecuador, like that of parts of western Africa, was crippled. As cotton textiles became the single most important industrial venture in terms of capital investment, output, and employment, the only question facing men like Arkwright was where to find more raw materials. It is worth noting that the English government, steward of the world's most powerful navy, was increasingly on the side of the budding capitalists. Indeed, alongside labor, technology, raw materials, and money, the state was a crucial factor of production. It could also enable—or impede, as all the imperial nations did freely and often to great destructive effect in their colonies—distribution and consumption.

In terms of economic change, what in hindsight appears inevitable is often mere serendipity. It is evident that English, and later western European and U.S. industrial expansion, impoverished less-developed Atlantic economies. But the effects of this change differed even within some regional economies. One consequence of Britain's massive industrial demand for raw cotton was that it helped to sustain a noncapitalist, slave-based society in the southern United States. As had happened earlier with Iberian merchant capitalism, economic gains and improved living standards in one part of the Atlantic basin were reliant on the expansion and intensification of socially and economically retrogressive trends in another. Happy consumers, in short, did not make happy producers.

The Market Revolution and the American South

Cotton was hardly new to the U.S. South. Almost since the first settlement at Jamestown, farmers planted small amounts of cotton for domestic use. But neither of the two known varieties of cotton suited commercial production. The green-seed variety was hardy and grew in most soils, but its short fibers clung obstinately to the seed; it took an adult an entire working day to clean a pound of lint. A second type of cotton, known as black-seed, proved easier to clean, but it thrived only in wet, coastal Carolina and was susceptible to rot. In the wake of U.S. independence, however, Loyalist refugees returning to Charleston from the Bahamas brought with them a more rot-resistant variety of the green-seed type. Cleaned by means of a *charkha*, a roller devised centuries before in India, this variety led to the first cotton boom in the Carolina lowcountry, and between 1784 and 1791, British imports of cotton from its former mainland colonies increased by 216 percent.

The real breakthrough came in 1793. While visiting Mulberry Grove, a Georgia plantation, the Connecticut Yankee Eli Whitney hit upon an idea to modernize the charkha. The old device, which consisted of two parallel rollers that allowed the lint through but squeezed out the seeds, was ineffective on green-seed cotton. Whitney overheard planters grumbling about "the extreme difficulty" in cleaning cotton and thought to affix wire teeth to one roller, while adding a third roller, this one with small brushes, to separate the lint from the wire teeth. Using this device, a single worker could clean more than fifty pounds of cotton a day. Whitney's cotton engine, "gin" for short, together with the introduction of a still more rot-resistant cotton, allowed the upland regions of the U.S. South to compete with India for the British market. Within two decades, Georgia and South Carolina alone were producing 60 million pounds of cotton annually, most of which went to feed overseas factories. Other producers of plantation cotton such as Brazil and Egypt remained well behind in output, and did not undergo the same revolutionary changes.

Perhaps nothing better illustrates the increasingly interconnected nature of the Atlantic economy than the fact that a series of synergistic technological innovations in Britain and the United States ultimately resulted in the greatest surge yet of the importation of captive Africans into the United States, followed by the largest-ever forced internal migration within the latter. At the same time that Carolina planters were putting back into full production their rice and indigo plantations in the coastal lowcountry, cotton production was spreading inland. For this reason, South Carolina legislators overcame their worries about importing enslaved Africans who might be "infected with the disease of Haitian liberty" and in late 1803 voted to reopen the foreign traffic in slaves. Over the next four years, until the United States Congress finally banned the importation of Africans, as of January 1, 1808, wealthy Charlestonians grabbed the initiative. During that same period they fitted out more slaving vessels than such notorious ports as Newport and Bristol, Rhode Island, or Liverpool and Bristol, England, and played the major role in bringing 75,000 slaves to Sullivan's Island, a hellish counterpart of Ellis Island for Africans, just outside Charleston harbor. Most of these captive men, women, and children came from the Atlantic coast of Africa, but some came from Spanish Florida and British Martinique and Jamaica. "Gullah" Jack Pritchard—later a conspirator with Denmark Vesey—arrived from as far away as the East African island of Zanzibar.

But as the cotton boom expanded west, the Charleston entrepot proved inadequate, and planters in the Upper South quickly stepped into the void. In the decades after the Revolution, tobacco producers in the Chesapeake diversified their assets by planting cereal crops, which were far less labor intensive, and hence required fewer hands. But instead of manumitting their surplus slaves, financially strapped and profit-oriented Virginians sold them to professional slave traders. In scenes reminiscent of Luanda, Angola, and contemporary Rio de Janeiro, hundreds of slaves were gathered and held in pens in Washington and Richmond for shipment to New Orleans and Mobile. Young slaves living in exporting states—the Atlantic seaboard south from Delaware to South Carolina—faced dangerous odds, a one in three chance of being resold to the newly cleared cotton lands of the Lower South. In what the historian Steven Deyle calls the "irony of liberty," the closure of the external Atlantic slave trade merely gave rise to an internal traffic of extraordinary proportions. In the four decades prior to South Carolina's secession from the Union in 1860, 1 million slaves were uprooted for resale inland, nearly twice the sum of all Africans brought into English mainland North America before 1808. Even the Brazilian gold rush of the previous century did not result in such a massive relocation.

Just as ownership of British cotton factories was limited to a few wealthy entrepreneurs, those early-nineteenth-century U.S. citizens who owned slaves were an equally elite group. By the time Whitney died in 1825, only 36 percent of all white southerners owned even a single slave, and of that figure, just 1 percent owned more than fifty (a figure that increased only to 2.7 percent by 1860). Yet more than half of all slaves in the United States lived on plantations having a black population of at least twenty workers. Put another way, while the typical white southerner owned few or no slaves, the typical black southerner lived on a sizeable estate that produced staple export crops. As a result, enslaved men and women who planted and harvested cotton—or worked the steamboats or labored on the docks in New Orleans and Charleston—were actually more tied to the Atlantic market economy than were most southern yeomen. As one Carolina farmer bragged: "I never spent more than ten dollars a year, which was for salt, nails, and the like." Like most smallholders, he purchased "nothing to wear, or eat or drink," as his "farm provided all."

Large slaveholders in the nineteenth-century southern United States, as in Brazil and Cuba, adopted some of the language of industrial capitalism, and even argued for the rationality of this peculiarly cruel and inhumane mode of production. Meanwhile, despite their dependence on slave-produced commodities, inhabitants of the northern Atlantic, including those of Britain and the northern United States, came to regard slavery as economically backward and morally reprehensible. Slaveholders thus found themselves increasingly on the defensive, unable to square slavery with the dictates of modern capitalism as it came to be defined in industrialized regions. More than simply an economic investment, slave labor provided the foundation for societies that grew increasingly distinct from those of the northern Atlantic world. The need to discipline and defend unfree labor gave rise to rigidly hierarchical and racialized societies in the southern Atlantic and southern United States founded upon paternalism, an ideology that enlaced whites and blacks in a web of mutual responsibilities and obligations—a bloody and, in northern terms, premodern relationship.

The growing contradictions were not self-evident from the perspective of the southern elite. Carolina planters like John C. Calhoun sold their cotton to British factories, but that did not hinder them from lashing out at free-labor ideology. Insisting that European and free-state "wage slaves" enjoyed little more than the right to starve while searching for temporary employment, southern apologists contrasted their seigneurial community, which boasted "a place for everyone, and everyone in their place." One pamphleteer claimed that wage work constituted "the most intolerable slavery that men can suffer." Where black cotton producers possessed the love and protection of their white masters, cotton factory workers "were liable to have that employment [terminated] at any moment, either by caprice, ill health, or the state of trade." Far from being simply deceitful or hypocritical replies to northern free-labor advocates, such statements indicate the extent to which planters in the U.S. South believed in a neoclassical ideal of organic relations of dependency and mutuality. As in contemporary Cuba, Brazil, and New Granada, slave owners in the United States cast themselves in the role of Greek and Roman citizens and named their slaves accordingly. Others relied more heavily on religious scripture to support slavery, even as northern abolitionists used it to the opposite effect. More than insincere bluster, the anticapitalist sentiments of slavery-supporting politicians were the logical product of their society's relationship between the ownership and means of production, that is, between the master and the slave.

Patriarchal attitudes of a different kind could be found eight hundred miles to the north in Rhode Island and Massachusetts, destination of one-quarter of southern cotton. By comparison to British manufacturing, however, New England industry remained haphazard. Part of the difficulty was Britain's determination to safeguard its dominant position in the textile market. To protect its lead in industrialization, Parliament banned the export of textile machinery and architectural drawings. In this period, factories required water power to drive the gears that turned the spindles and moved the shuttles that spun yard and wove thread, which meant that even if American businessmen could obtain the highly guarded technology, the best places to build textile plants would probably not be near low-lying urban centers. Where else would one look for a pool of laborers? Perhaps the biggest problem was capital, however, not labor or access to technology. Most New England merchants preferred to remain in old trading patterns with Britain, and those lucky enough to acquire surplus capital typically chose to invest in land or more ships. This meant also that Boston's business elite, like southern U.S. planters, continued to champion free trade and low tariffs, neither of which benefited industrial development.

The first complication was resolved by the Englishman Samuel Slater, who had worked in Britain as an apprentice to one of Arkwright's partners. As an immigrant, Slater brought nothing with him to America but his extraordinary ability to retain information, and working from memory, he and his partners Moses Brown and William Almy, two Providence merchants, constructed the first spinning mill in America in 1790. Brown and Almy, his son-in-law, had made their fortunes in the Atlantic trades of iron, rum, and most of all, enslaved Africans. As investors in the slave trade to Charleston, they understood that the expansion of enslaved labor across the U.S. South boded well for mills like Slater's. By the end of the decade, Slater's mill, powered by the falls of Pawtucket, employed more than one hundred people. Without closing his original operation, Slater began construction of a second and larger mill. Within four years, imitators had financed two more mills, and by 1808— the same year the United States banned the importation of African slaves— the number of textile mills in New England had exploded to eighty-seven.

After technology came the problem of labor. Initially, Slater's relationship to labor followed the model he had learned in England. His first mill spun only cotton yarn, leaving it to nearby farm wives to weave into cloth on their home looms. But the burgeoning New England mills, like their Old English counterparts, quickly moved beyond the putting-out system. In Slatersville and elsewhere, industrialists turned to what they dubbed, euphemistically, the "family system," in which they constructed entire villages surrounded by company-owned farmland. Men and their sons worked the fields, while their wives and daughters operated looms within the factory. Even in construction, the Rhode Island and Massachusetts mills revealed their English ancestry; just as Slater carried Arkwright's design to North America, it was men from Slatersville who passed on the design to other industrialists. As one observer noted, "nearly all the cotton factories in this country from 1791 to 1805, were built under the direction of men who learned the art or skill of building machinery, in Mr. Slater's employ."

If anything marked the New England mills as unique, it was the curious variety of corporate paternalism that pervaded towns like Slatersville, and, later, Lowell, Massachusetts. Whether the attitude reflected pious New England's penchant for an ordered world or indicated an awkward transition from farm life to industrial capitalism, mill owners sought to avoid the "degradation" commonly associated with "the manufacturing cities of Europe." Most companies demanded their employees attend "public worship on the Sabbath" in the name of "the preservation of good order," and several refused to hire any hand who was "habitually absent" from village churches. One industrialist banned "every kind of ardent spirit" from his company town, while another established a 10:00 PM curfew in company housing. Like U.S. plantation overseers, mill agents and boardinghouse keepers were instructed to regard their workers as wayward children and "report all cases of intemperance, or of dissolute manners." Mill hands fired for immorality were denied discharge papers and had their names sent to nearby companies, which made finding employment in the region nearly impossible. In the U.S. North and South, industrial capitalism seemed to demand a cowed, obedient work force.

Thomas Jefferson: Unwitting Industrial Promoter

With such ambivalent attitudes, New England did not become an industrial colossus overnight. Few Bostonians expressed a desire to exchange the comfortable role of consumer and shipper for that of factory hand and manufacturer. In many such industries as shoe manufacturing, the putting-out system remained the norm. What altered this complacency, and virtually overnight in the United States, was the Embargo Act of December 1807. Passed by the dominant Republicans in response to continuing British seizures of American cargo and sailors, the act prohibited American vessels from sailing to foreign ports. Contrary to myth, the act did not immediately ban imports, but it did reverse the sequence of commercial warfare during the American Revolution, when the 1774 ban on imports preceded a 1775 prohibition of all commerce. Jefferson regarded the Embargo Act as the only alternative to war and was confident the United States would win recognition of its rights as a neutral carrier of goods and raw materials. Combating Britain's new imperialism required a new diplomacy schooled in the logic of economic warfare. Instead of favorable dispatches from London, however, Jefferson received petitions from New England towns and cities begging for the repeal of the embargo. Jefferson dutifully recorded the receipt of 199 petitions against commercial warfare; he responded personally to the first thirty-eight but finally gave up and thereafter instructed the State Department to print form letters of reply.

Economically, the embargo was a disaster. U.S. exports in 1807, the peak year in overseas sales, brought in $108 million, but by the end of 1808, that figure had plunged to $22 million. With farmers and planters unable to ship their crops to English consumers and cotton mills, Canadian farmers rushed to fill the void, and British shippers happily took over the carrying trade abandoned by New England merchants. Unemployment in American seaport towns, where virtually all labor was tied to the Atlantic—from seamen to ships' caulkers, carters to attorneys—hit a low mark not reached since the depression of the early 1780s. The embargo was eventually repealed and replaced with an ever-more convoluted series of restrictive trade acts, but until the end of the Napoleonic wars in 1815, the United States conducted virtually no business with the rest of the Atlantic world. In the meantime, if American consumers desired manufactured goods, it was up to them to produce them.

The agrarian Jefferson once famously suggested that his nation would be better off if "the workshops remained in Europe," yet it was almost as if his embargo was designed to drive mercantile capital into industrial ventures. As ships rotted at wharfs in New York and Philadelphia, some eastern merchants shifted their investments into land speculation. But a far greater number of enterprises poured their capital into transportation and manufacturing. Between 1809 and 1815, the number of mills in Providence alone increased from 41 to 169, while the total value of capital invested in New England factories in 1815 stood at $50 million. (To put this in perspective, Jefferson paid $15 million for the entire Louisiana Purchase territory.)

By the end of the War of 1812, Rhode Island had new competition. In 1810, Francis Cabot Lowell, a Boston entrepreneur, had visited a number of British mills while ostensibly on a holiday. While impressed by his polite interest, his English hosts had no idea he was an industrial spy. Every evening he drew detailed plans of all he had seen during the day. Upon returning to Massachusetts, Lowell became partners with a mechanic, Paul Moody, and together with mercantile capital began construction of a mill that went beyond anything Slater—or anyone in Britain, for that matter—had devised. By diverting water from the Merrimack River into canals, Lowell was able to power not only the machinery for spinning cotton, but also a series of power looms. In doing so, he created the world's first "vertically" integrated cotton mill, one that combined every aspect of production apart from growing the raw materials.

Faced with this unexpected competition, the same Parliament that ratified the Treaty of Ghent (which ended the War of 1812 between Britain and the United States) fought back. Prime Minister Lord Liverpool, who spoke for the gentry, not the new industrial elite, was nonetheless concerned enough to urge manufacturers to slash prices in hopes of driving the Americans out of business. The following year, 1816, Congress responded with its first industrial tariff. In another sign of times changed, none other than President James Madison, Jefferson's Virginia protégé, called on his Republican Party to protect Federalist mill owners by approving protective import tariffs of 20 percent. In an indication of how rapidly New England capital had shifted forms, Federalist congressmen supported the measure by a vote of 25 to 23. Massachusetts representatives, who just two years earlier at the Hartford Convention had demanded constitutional amendments to protect shipping and free trade, split 7 to 4 in favor of the tariff. South Carolinians (who, of course, did not wish the British to respond in kind to the cotton it exported to them) cast a slim majority against the measure, but enough endorsed the act to indicate a willingness to conduct business with New England as well as with Britain.

Having tried to aid his manufacturers, who in truth needed no assistance in marketing cottons around other parts of the Atlantic basin, Lord Liverpool hastened to lavish attention on his traditional constituents, the landed elite. Nearly a generation of war had brought an expansion of cultivated land in Britain, but with the navy being reduced in size and the continent returning to a peacetime economy, Parliament moved to soften the blow that peace appeared certain to give to agriculture. Unhappily, its solution was the Corn Law of 1815, designed to drive foreign foodstuffs out of the British market. (In England usage, *corn* means *grain*, and as wheat was the most important cereal grain, its price per quarter—or eight bushels—was the basis for the prohibitive duty.) English tenant farmers did not eat well as it was, but for urban workers cheap bread and oatmeal, together with such a variety of "inferior meats" as cow heel, sheep's trotters (the fleshless part of the leg), and pig's ear, marked the difference between survival and starvation. When news that the Corn Law was about to pass reached London's poor, crowds of laborers took to the streets, and the act came to a vote only after protective troops surrounded Parliament.

Beyond a blatant disregard for the welfare of laboring people, the Corn Laws mark a moment of transition in Parliament's economic policies. Reasonable lawmakers, even those from the countryside or port cities, might have recognized that such selective assistance for the landed gentry, like all legislation that established commercial monopolies, was untenable in an age of expanding international trade, industrialization, and heightened worker consciousness. If it was the eighteenth-century, wooden-ship mercantilist ideology that had forced the United States into the War of 1812, it was Britain's industrial capacity that lay behind the destruction of Bonaparte. In the peace that followed Waterloo, British industry required access to Atlantic markets, not domination of the North American shipping trade. Criticizing historical figures for not recognizing what appears obvious from a modern perspective admittedly constitutes an unfair historian's trick. But even a cursory tour of the emerging factory towns of Manchester or Preston (the model for Dickens' fictitious Coketown), or a glance at the London *Times* to read how fast cotton

Fast Times

The speed at which Britain's economy and society changed between the start of the conflict with France and the eventual peace agreements hammered out at Vienna and Ghent may be seen in the curious fact that one member of Lord Liverpool's cabinet had a highwayman rob him of his watch in 1786, while a second was run down by a steam locomotive in 1830.

George Stephenson's first steam engine "Locomotion Number One" (1825) operated on the opening day of the Stockton and Darlington Railway, the world's first public railway. Original is on display at the North Road Station Museum in Darlington. Collection of E. A. Reitan.

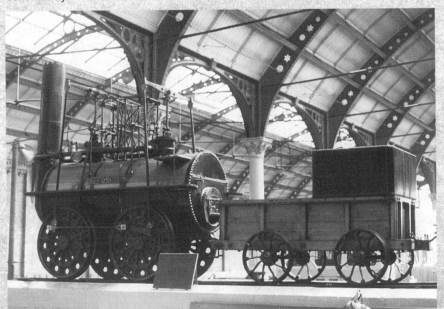

was driving enslaved labor across the U.S. South (Mississippi became a state in 1817, Alabama in 1819), should have alerted legislators to the increasingly interconnected nature of the Atlantic economy in the age of industry. More change was on the way. In the midst of northern Atlantic industrial expansion came Latin American independence, suddenly opening massive new markets for manufactured goods to be exchanged for bullion and raw materials. Forced labor would get a massive boost here, too.

So now it fell to those who worked the looms and yet failed to put enough food into their children's bowls to draw attention to how thoroughly the likes of Arkwright and Whitney had changed the Atlantic world. Among them was William Cobbett, a onetime anti-Jacobin essayist who during his brief time in Philadelphia had gone by the penname of Peter Porcupine; so Francophobic was he that when in 1801 a brief truce was arranged between Britain and Bonaparte, Cobbett had his London window smashed for refusing to light a candle of thanksgiving. But Cobbett had been born in the countryside, and like many an urban radical, his vocal hatred of the landed aristocrat echoed earlier rural insurgencies. Following a brief stay in Newgate Prison for the crime of suggesting that the royal family should pay taxes like everybody else, Cobbett began to publish a weekly journal in 1816, the *Political Register*. In an attempt to keep printed information a prerogative of the prosperous, Parliament levied a heavy tax on newspapers. (The *Times* cost seven pence, which made it an occasional luxury even for middle-class shopkeepers.) By publishing his paper as a pamphlet, Cobbett avoided the tax and had to pay only a small sum on the entire print run. He priced his paper at two pence, and soon the *Register* circulated throughout the nation, as it passed from hand to hand or was read aloud at taverns for the benefit of the illiterate. Impoverished mill hands hardly needed a Cobbett to remind them of their despair, but his angry words served to articulate their demands and brought about the first political indoctrination of the mass of urban workers.

The landed gentlemen sitting in Parliament, of course, saw things differently. Prime Minister Liverpool was part of that long tradition which held that those on the bottom were content with their lot provided that troublesome reformers did not tell them otherwise. The prime minister's determination to maintain labor peace through repression became clear in December 1816, when Arthur Thistlewood and Henry Hunt called for a mass meeting at Spa Fields in the north of London. Six to eight thousand people assembled to hear the fiery Hunt demand political reform and an end to the Corn Laws. What took place toward the end of the rally remains unclear. Some witnesses insisted that demonstrators broke into "bakers' and butchers' shops" that were charging too high a price. Others swore that Thistlewood led a group to nearby Clerkenwell, where they sacked a gunsmith's shop in hopes of obtaining weapons enough to seize the Tower of London and establish a Committee of Public Safety. What is beyond doubt is that Liverpool's government maintained a small army of spies and agent provocateurs, many of whom justified their wages by concocting the sort of disquieting stories the cabinet wished to hear.

One month later, in January 1817, tensions between government and the governed increased when an attack was allegedly made on the life of

George, Prince of Wales, who ruled as Regent. As had been the case with his father in 1795, the Regent's carriage was mobbed and its windows smashed, either by rocks, or, as the prince chose to believe, by pellets from an air gun. In response, Parliament appointed two secret committees to investigate. Within seven weeks, the committees reached their conclusions. Both the Spa meeting and the attacks on the prince were part of a treasonous conspiracy formed for "the purpose of overthrowing, by means of a general insurrection, the established government" so as to effect "a general plunder and division of property." Virtually without debate, Parliament suspended habeas corpus, renewed William Pitt's 1795 Sedition Act, and ordered the lords lieutenant to round up the "chief incendiary writers" responsible for "seditious and blasphemous material." Among those on the list was William Cobbett, who fled to the United States.

The historian E. P. Thompson writes about what would follow: "There is no term for it but class war." After England's poor harvest of 1818 drove the price of bread ever higher, aged veterans of the wars against Bonaparte began to organize military drills on open fields on the outskirts of London, sometimes with staves at their shoulders in place of muskets. But the majority of the sixty thousand men and women who converged on St Peter's Field in Manchester on the morning of August 16, 1819, demanded nothing more radical than expanded voting rights and a living wage. The organizers of the event were largely moderates, and Henry Hunt, the principal speaker, had denounced the military drills as "playing at soldiers." But when Hunt began to speak, Justices of the Peace decided to arrest him. Hoping not to anger the assembly by using regular troops, authorities instead ordered the Cheshire Yeomanry—mounted manufacturers and merchants—to wade toward the front and seize Hunt. When this ill-trained cavalry found itself surrounded by taunting people, the magistrates were forced to send in a troop of trained Hussars to clear the grounds. According to a witness, within ten minutes "the field was an open and almost deserted place." All that remained were "strewed caps, bonnets, hats, shawls, and shoes," all of them "trampled, torn, and bloody." The result was eleven people trampled or slashed to death, two of them women, and four hundred injured.

The battle of "Peterloo," as Hunt dubbed the massacre, quickly received the government's approbation. Addington and the Prince Regent thanked the magistrates "for their prompt, decisive, and efficient measures for the preservation of the public peace." The Lord Chancellor added his "clear opinion" that the rally "was an overt act of treason." A few brave voices called for a Parliamentary investigation, but without success. At length, state prosecutions commenced, but not against the cavalry or the two Hussars seen "cutting at the people." Instead, Manchester prosecutors singled out Hunt and charged him with high treason.

Not content merely to return Hunt to prison, Parliament set about to suppress permanently radical newspapers and public meetings. When government reconvened in late November, Addington introduced six laws designed to "animate the loyal and awe the disaffected." Of the Six Acts, two dealt with weapons and civilian musters. The Newspaper and Stamp Duties

Act raised taxes on printed materials, which now included pamphlets and periodicals as political matter. The Seditious Meetings Act banned gatherings of more than fifty persons without the consent of a local magistrate, and the Blasphemous and Seditious Libels fixed penalties for these crimes to fourteen years' transportation, that is, indentured servitude in the colonies.

Historians disagree as to the repressive impact of the Six Acts, but for such critics of government policy as Cobbett and Arthur Thistlewood, the results were quick and catastrophic. Fear of arrest impelled radicals and reformers out into the Atlantic world. While hiding in New York with his two sons, Cobbett read that his wife and younger children had been evicted from their home in Botley, his books sold to satisfy his creditors. (When he at last returned to Britain, he brought with him Tom Paine's bones, so that the English radical could finally rest in his native soil.) Thistlewood was charged with plotting to assassinate the entire cabinet, parade their severed heads through the streets of London, and proclaim a republic with himself as president. The fact that the supposedly deadly Thistlewood was captured while cowering in a grubby Cato Street attic, or that the wildly implausible conspiracy was revealed by paid informants, concerned the prosecutor not in the least, and Thistlewood swung from the gibbet in 1820. Like slavery, the new class war was a thoroughly transatlantic affair.

An Army of Redressers

Although the Six Acts drove journalists like Cobbett across the Atlantic, they forced more radical pamphleteers, along with the larger English labor movement, into extralegal and underground activities. Of note were attacks on industry and machines known as wrecking or Luddism, named for fictitious Ned Ludd, the Robin Hood "Redresser" or "Grand Executioner" who defended rights established "by Custom and Law." In part, wrecking was a reflex response to Liverpool's repressive tenure, but as political activity it also stood out as a rebuff to the laissez-faire, antipaternalistic thinking of the day. Popular reactions to the more alienating features of industrialization resonated back and forth across the Atlantic, even as the contradictions grew. Just as the rise of the cotton market led to the refastening of paternalism on the U.S. South, it helped to erode older patterns of munificence in the industrial centers of New and Old England.

Whether in the southern United States, England, Spain, or Brazil, paternalism, never based on a sense of benevolence, was a philosophy developed by elites, for elites. As the historian Eugene Genovese observes, "paternalism in any historical setting defines relations of superordination and subordination." Nevertheless, paternalism did assume, as outlined by such esteemed classical thinkers as Aristotle and Cicero, that working people had traditional rights, and that the government had a responsibility to ensure the economic well being of all subjects. As late as 1773 in England, the Spitalfield Act recognized a legal minimum wage for silk weavers. The trend of the early nineteenth century went in the other direction, however. One result of more than two decades of northern Atlantic warfare was the erosion of paternalistic protection for England's large class of artisans. Between the renewal of war with

France in 1803 and the entry of victorious forces into Paris in March 1814, Parliament repealed all regulation of the woolen trade, as well as apprenticeship laws protecting workers that dated back more than two centuries. New legislation also swept away statutes that empowered magistrates to enforce minimum wages, although lawmakers were careful to retain a clause that made it a crime to leave work unfinished. Removal of these protections, intended to speed development of a labor market, sparked strong reactions from the working class. According to traditional understandings of just prices for bread, meat, and a day's work, the advent of industrial capitalism and homage to the free market were not an improvement but a "foul imposition" on time-honored practices.

"Corporations have neither bodies to be kicked, nor souls to be damned," went a favorite aphorism in industrializing sections of the United States. But in Britain, if workers had no public forum or other means to challenge economic ideas, the machines that often maimed them became symbols of the emerging factory system. In the years after Peterloo, Luddites smashed any mechanical innovation that threatened their livelihood. Especially in areas where demobilization of nearly 250,000 soldiers and sailors swamped the labor market and depressed wages, workers wrecked looms and intimidated industrialists who hired child labor. As one threatening letter from "Ned Ludd" promised, "We will never lay down Arms [until] The House of Commons passes an Act to put down all Machinery hurtful to Commonality."

The wrecking of machines in Britain reached its peak during the fall of 1830—a year of revolution on the continent—when rioters in the southeast smashed threshing equipment and burned barns and homes belonging to overseers of the poor. This time the rioters rose in the name of the legendary folk hero Captain Swing, but many of their demands were the same as the Luddites. Several hundred laborers, armed with staves and flails, clogged the streets of Overton, chanting for higher wages and cheaper food. By November, riots had spread west. At Andover, mobs destroyed threshing machinery and demolished iron foundries. When magistrates apprehended one wrecker, a "huge multitude" broke open the gates of the jail, freed the prisoner, and paraded him triumphantly through the town. Among those on the scene was Henry Hunt, who told the jubilant mob: "Let the mayor and corporation, who have raised the storm, quell it." Order was restored only after a troop of Lancers invaded the town and took several wreckers prisoner.

As the so-called Swing riots spread across Britain, erupting in almost every county, patterns emerged. Large towns rather than small hamlets witnessed most of the disturbances, meaning that people in urban areas where economic change and laissez-faire policy were most advanced were more likely to wreck machinery. Not surprisingly, those who marched at the head of rioters were typically craftsmen, blacksmiths, and cobblers; many leaders were literate, as their threatening letters attest. Reminiscent of early eighteenth-century rural protests against land enclosure, working-class wreckers blackened their faces and operated in the dead of night. As time passed, protesters rioted by day, sometimes in a festive manner. Leaders donned white hats or mounted white horses, and wreckers blew horns to announce their approach.

One witness described the insurgents "as being in general very fine-looking young men, and particularly well dressed as if they had put on their best clo' for the occasion." As if the wrecking itself was not enough to alarm men of property, wreckers outside of London "hoisted the tricoloured flag" in honor of the July revolt in Paris that had toppled the reactionary King Charles X.

Because of the crisis in France, Parliament was reluctant to send forces too far north, and in any case, too many destitute veterans had cast their lot with the wreckers. But when the Duke of Richmond financed a mercenary force of shopkeepers and "respectable" yeomen in Sussex, the government quickly endorsed this plan as the model for other counties to follow. At the same time, Lord Melbourne, who had only taken his post in the Home Office the day before, issued a decree on November 23 to appeal to the most impoverished rioters. By offering £500 rewards for bringing rebels to justice, Melbourne encouraged rioters to turn and inform on the craftsmen who led them. Soon, country jails brimmed with more than 1,900 wreckers; to speed up the trials, and guard against the rural loyalties of local magistrates, the government formed a Special Commission to try the prisoners in five counties where crowd action had been most pronounced.

In all, the Commission heard 992 cases. Sixteen men were hanged for arson and three more for wrecking. Another 252 men were sent to prison, and 479 men and 2 women were sentenced to transportation to Australia. In some southern English counties, it took several generations for the gender ratio to fall again into balance. In most cases, transportation lasted seven years, but return costs were not provided, and as the 12,000-mile journey was expensive, few banished rioters ever returned to England. But if the wreckers failed to slow the steady march of industrialization, fears that the events of 1830 might erupt again prompted the government to maintain the wage concessions of that year. As one curate put it, "them there riots and burnings did the poor a terrible deal of good."

Migration in an Industrial Age

Toward the end of the Swing riots, an entire farm in Surrey burned to the ground. Although the conflagration began with the barn that housed the mechanized thresher, no one suspected wreckers as the probable arsonists. Gossip held that the incendiaries were Irish workers who took a lantern to the property of their Protestant employers, while old hands around town suspected that Protestant laborers had destroyed the farm as a warning not to hire Irishmen. Local magistrates never established which story reflected the truth, but the logic of the presumption was impeccable, since Irish emigration around the Atlantic world was on the rise. Other migrations would soon follow, transforming regions as far afield as the United States, Canada, South Africa, and Argentina.

As if high food prices caused by the Corn Laws were not tragedy enough, a potato blight hit the Irish countryside in 1845, blanketing acre upon acre of potatoes (a plant native to South America that had become the staple of the Irish diet by this time) with a black rot that rendered the tubers inedible. For tenant farmers, potatoes provided not only sustenance but the cash necessary to pay the rents to their Protestant English landlords. In desperation, starving peasants ate their rotting crops, and entire villages succumbed to typhus and cholera. And when unable to lay out their fees, hundreds of thousands of Irish farm families faced eviction. Refugees from the countryside crowded into disease-infested parish workhouses or stumbled toward Dublin in search of work. Within five years, more than 1 million people sailed from Ireland for New York, Boston, Norfolk, and other English-speaking ports. (Between starvation, sickness, and emigration, the population of Ireland shrank from 8.5 million to 6.5 million during the period.) The "coffin ships," as they came to be known, often lost a third of their passengers to disease and malnutrition, a percentage that rivaled African slavers of the previous century. Among those who staggered ashore in Massachusetts was twenty-six-year-old Patrick Kennedy, whose great grandson would defeat another son of Ireland for the U.S. presidency in 1960.

The Irish migration of the famine years constituted only a small segment of a larger migration of Europeans to the Americas during the industrial age. The Irish diaspora, however, was distinguished by the high percentage of its subjects who emigrated: no other country experienced such a dramatic depletion of its population so quickly, with an overall decline from a prefamine high of 8.5 million to 4.4 million in 1911. This migration was also focused on a single nation, the United States, which received 85 percent of the Irish migrants. Although exceptional in numbers, rate of migration, and common destination, the Irish migration reflected and anticipated major trends in the nineteenth century, a period when the pace of European migration rose dramatically. Through 1800 at least 2 million Europeans had traveled to the Americas. Napoleonic warfare interrupted transatlantic migration, and it did not recover until the 1820s; but when it recovered, it soared.

From 1821 to 1845, 1,376,100 Europeans migrated to the Americas. These were predominantly northern Europeans, Britons, Germans, and Irish journeying to North America. In the next seventy-five years, the number of European emigrants rose to 45,183,800, people who settled in every part of the Americas, but mostly in the United States, Brazil, Argentina, Cuba, Mexico, Canada, and Uruguay. The second transatlantic wave included many southern and central Europeans, mostly originating in Italy, Poland, Spain, and Portugal. These nations were experiencing extraordinary population growth as a result of improved healthcare and nutrition, but without commensurate industrial development to employ the surplus population. After 1880, European migration to Latin America surpassed that to the United States. Even by comparison to the Atlantic slave trade, this was an unprecedented exodus. In the cases of Brazil and Cuba, European migration was linked to the demise of slavery. By the 1870s, the Brazilian state, now cut off from the African slave trade, began subsidizing the migration and settlement of hundreds of thousands of Italian, Portuguese, and Spanish coffee-bean pickers. Recently freed slaves, meanwhile, were left to their own devices, a pattern repeated in most ex-slave societies. And in keeping with the racist doctrines of the era, what has come to be known as "scientific racism," Brazilian authorities openly touted European immigration as a means to "whitening" their nation's population.

This surge in transatlantic migration was also linked to technology. Innovations in transportation originating mostly in Britain made transatlantic travel quicker and cheaper. Steamboats replaced clipper ships after the 1860s. The spread of railroads, the growth of canals, and improvements in riverine transportation carried newcomers more easily and quickly into landlocked hinterlands, furthering displacement of indigenous people and accelerating environmental changes. Steamships aided transformation of the upper Amazon and Congo basins, for example, when natural rubber became a much-desired industrial commodity around 1870. Communications also leaped forward with the invention of the telegraph and the laying of transatlantic cables— those linking the British Isles and North America were fully functional by 1866. New advances in the production and distribution of gas and electricity for urban, domestic use created cities of light, but also extended work hours, making unprecedented "night shifts" possible. New York and Buenos Aires underwent the most noticeable changes: by 1914 these were the largest cities in the Western Hemisphere, each pushing toward a million inhabitants. Rio de Janeiro came in third, its migrant-driven population growth spurred on by large-scale public works projects and successful, government-sponsored mosquito eradication programs.

Although migration was linked to macroeconomic transformations— industrialization and improved transportation of bulk commodities, for instance—migrants did not travel aimlessly in search of opportunity; cultural considerations guided their economic decisions. As seen in Brazil, newly independent nations of the Americas could set their own policies concerning migration and naturalization, and many of them used migration policies to shape their future and character. In the eighteenth century, the British Empire had facilitated the migration of non-British subjects to North America by permitting such perceived aliens as migrants from the Holy Roman Empire to own land and secure legal privileges. Meanwhile, imperial policy intentionally hindered westward migration in order to protect the rights and lands of Britain's indigenous allies and tributaries. But with independence, the United States shed this concern about the rights of conquered indigenous people and threw open the frontier to settlement and exploitation by European immigrants. As the new nation was being created, private investors and companies of land speculators—who typically diversified their portfolios by investing also in industrial ventures—sought to populate their new holdings in order to profit from them. The displacement of the Cherokee, Shawnee, and many other Indian people, and their replacement by European and creole migrants, was one important theme of national self-definition. Similar processes emerged in Argentina, Brazil, Chile, and finally, southern Africa and Canada. Throughout the nineteenth-century Atlantic world, frontier settlement was tied to national ideologies of race.

As a means of clarifying citizenship, in 1790 the U.S. Congress drafted its first naturalization act. Under the law, "all free white persons" who migrated into the country with the intent to remain were "entitled to the rights of citizenship" after only a single year. Although a few members of Congress wondered aloud whether Jews or Catholics could claim to be "white," the

Canada's Move to Independence

Of the many settlement frontiers of the Greater Atlantic, that of interior Canada was one of the last to be transformed. Still, even in the late eighteenth century, a number of competing merchant interests vied to bring British North American primary goods to Atlantic shores for export, mostly to northern Europe. By 1800, Canada's fur trade linked indigenous groups, backwoods traders, and urban merchants in a chain of exchanges stretching from the Yukon to Edinburgh. Items such as Brazilian tobacco and mass-produced English guns were traded to indigenous beaver trappers thousands of miles beyond the Great Lakes. After the war of 1812, other commodities began to displace furs in importance, setting the stage for local capital accumulation and a desire for political independence from Great Britain. Canada's other great export industry, cod fishing on the Newfoundland Banks, continued to thrive, helping to define the interests of settlers in the Maritime provinces. Increasing attention was also paid to timber and grain, the former initially absorbed in shipbuilding and the latter sent to feed Britain's industrial workers. Mining, mostly for precious metals in the far west and along the margins of the Canadian Shield, drove the next

wave of territorial expansion and capital accumulation. Given its small population, vast natural resources, and close trade ties to Great Britain, it was only natural that Canada's industrialization lagged well behind that of the United States. Canadian independence in 1867 in fact came about as much due to external as internal factors. Canada's disparate provinces (then called "the Canadas"), such as Quebec, the Maritimes, and the newly created territory of British Columbia, had quite different interests, along with distinct cultural and political traditions. Native peoples, especially in the west, tended to see the British imperial government as a defense against white Canadians of all sorts. Thus it was the combination of the U.S. Civil War and a British desire to off-load the costs of imperial government that sparked formation of a national coalition in 1864. The threat of a U.S. invasion should the South win separation was considered quite serious, prompting Canadian provincial leaders to set aside their many differences and prepare a defense. Home rule was declared on July 1, 1867. Regional differences soon resurged, however, and to this day Canadian unity remains tenuous.

intent of such migration policy was to make acquisition of land easy for foreign immigrants. The U.S. Constitution provided mechanisms by which foreign-born people could become full citizens of the new nation, thus ensuring legal privileges enabling them to hold title to land and testify in courts. And the federal government actually subsidized migrants' land purchases. The United States thus attracted the vast majority of voluntary European migrants in the first half of the nineteenth century, but other population flows reveal the importance of migration policies in other new countries. Some migrant groups used state policies to create long-lasting ethnic enclaves.

In Brazil until 1850, the majority of new colonists were German-speaking. Most settled in southern Brazil, a region beyond the tropics that supported European-style agriculture and livestock raising. Dom Pedro II's government perceived the migrants as ideal colonists; government agents and private colonies joined in recruiting them. Germans established dozens of settlements in Santa Catarina and Rio Grande do Sul between 1824 and 1873. Like some German-migrant-homesteader enclaves of the early United States, these were isolated, rural communities where families were given plots of land on which they were required to erect dwellings and clear land for cultivation. Some adopted local crops, but most sought to recreate their traditional foodstuffs in their new environment—beer making, for example. But if nearly all of them took Brazilian citizenship, the German colonists, replenished by regular waves of German-speaking newcomers, clung to German culture, embodied in language, press, associational life, and recreational pursuits. These and some other South American ethnic enclaves still survive. Even refugees from the U.S. Civil War, the *Confederados*, found a home in Brazil, and independence benefited religious refugees. In 1822 official persecution of Jews in Brazil came to an end, and Jews migrated to Rio de Janeiro, Salvador, and other cities. Later in the nineteenth century, some Jews settled in the Amazon boomtowns of Manaus and Iquitos, while a much more substantial Jewish community formed in Buenos Aires.

The new Spanish American republics also linked migration policy to nationalist, elite-driven goals. Like Brazil, several Spanish American nations courted Europeans in an effort to "whiten" heavily African-descended or indigenous populations. Peru launched aggressive if unsuccessful recruitment campaigns, offering free land, transportation, and temporary lodging to willing Europeans. In part due to its isolation and political instability, Peru got few takers. So the state, run by elites with interests in sugar production and mining, turned to the Pacific, first China, then Japan, for laboring migrants. Cuba, Brazil, Mexico, and the United States would do the same. In such nations as Colombia, Paraguay, and Mexico that were embroiled in internal and foreign wars, European migration remained limited before 1880. Where there was peace, in flowed migrants. Still within the Spanish empire, Cuba received more Spanish migrants than did Argentina in the period before the island nation won independence in 1886.

Although "America," north or south, was by far the most popular destination for European migrants, parts of Africa appealed to them as well. In some cases the appeal was to poor farmers, hoping to start a better life, but many imperialist governments were also eager to establish a colonial foothold in Africa while simultaneously ridding themselves of their disgruntled poor. With migration as one strategy of domination, this new imperialism would reach full flower in Africa in the late nineteenth century. Before 1850, when quinine gained wide use as a malarial suppressant, nearly all of sub-Saharan Africa remained out of bounds to European migrants. Death rates among Europeans forced to visit Africa's Atlantic coast during or soon after a rainy season, when puddles, pools, and other standing water served as breeding grounds for mosquitos, were astonishing. Among British military personnel serving in Sierra Leone and the Gold Coast between 1817 and 1836, death rates from disease were 483 and 668 per 1,000 respectively. (Experienced African armies knew that when engaged by European soldiers, the most efficacious tactics were stalling, negotiation, and retreat.) It is telling that a portion of The Gambia's capital, Banjul, a British outpost since 1816, is still known as "Half Die."

The *anopheles* mosquito, now known to be the vector of the deadly falciparum variety of malaria—rather than something inhaled in vapors given off by Africa's swamps, hence malaria's name, "bad air"—does not breed outside the tropics, which meant that locations on the northern and southern extremes of the continent attracted European settlers. Proximity and high-handedness brought about French involvement. France invaded Algeria in

1830 largely in hope of using military success across the Mediterranean to divert attention from misgovernment at home. Though it would take French forces scores of years to gain control of resisters in Algeria's mountainous regions, its armies more quickly removed indigenous people from the fertile coastal plains, opening this prime land to French settlers, 100,000 by 1847, 350,000 by 1880. Nearly all of these migrants were poor, many of them from the south of France where disease in vineyards had ruined the livelihood of small-time winemakers.

Africa's opposite end appealed to British migrants even earlier. As part of the warfare against Napoleon and his allies, Great Britain had taken the Cape Colony from the Dutch in 1806. Thirteen years later, in search of a safety valve for the social unrest caused by postwar economic collapse and massive unemployment, Parliament approved £50,000 to support transporting 4,000 men, women, and children, selected from 90,000 applicants from the lower-middle classes of England, Wales, Scotland, and Ireland, to lands in the eastern Cape claimed by indigenous Xhosa speakers but coveted by the colony's expanding Trekboer population. One thousand more beyond the 4,000 selectees paid their own way, and all set out on twenty-one ships between December 1819 and January 1820, gleefully unaware they were participating in what one of the operation's chroniclers, the journalist Noël Mostert, labels "probably the most callous act of mass settlement in the entire history of empire."

Though most of these migrants had been urban artisans, tradesmen, and mechanics in the United Kingdom, the government settled them in 100-acre plots of poor land, hoping they would take up agriculture. Great minds in Britain's Colonial Office expected the settlers to mix with the Trekboers and, over time, bring the largely Dutch-descended folk around to English (which in their thinking meant "more civilized") ways of thinking and living, while somehow simultaneously finding ways to live in harmony with the Xhosa, the land's original possessors. Neither worked. The new migrants did not take to farming; more than half of them moved within a few years to villages and towns—and moving was not easy, since, as Mostert puts it, "[t]here were no roads, other than well-worn wagon tracks, many of which had been engineered by the elephants"—and all regarded the Trekboers, who remained tenders of cattle on huge tracts, as ignorant and backward people better left to marry within their own and go about their business. About the only point where the British settlers agreed with the Trekboers was in their view of the indigenous population, for both recognized the value of Africans as cheap labor but felt the basic insecurity of individuals inhabiting land claimed by a vastly larger population. Through midcentury, the settlers became involved in warfare with the Xhosa, sometimes on the defensive and sometimes on the offensive. These experiences heightened racism ingrained in British thinking and became part of the cultural foundation for South Africa's sad twentieth-century history.

In much of this nineteenth-century Atlantic migration, circular patterns and return migration continued as the norm. Some people who left Europe for other parts, particularly men, would return within a few years. During their time away, such people remained embedded in their old lives in what they still considered home. Rates of return migration everywhere were high, with local variations that are not always easy to explain: Brazil had higher return rates than the United States, for example, but lower rates than Argentina.

Perhaps typical of nineteenth-century Atlantic travelers was John Christian Zimmermann, the son of a merchant born in Echenhagen in Berg in 1786. At the age of fifteen, following the death of his father, Zimmermann traveled first to Amsterdam and then to North America. His journey as a young, single man fit larger migration patterns. He worked for a New York commercial firm and journeyed for them on business to Cuba and England. Like most migrants, Zimmermann was vulnerable to vagaries of commerce, upheavals of international warfare, and the merciless volatility of global economic cycles well beyond his control and likely beyond his understanding. Undeterred by failures in the northern Atlantic, Zimmermann pursued other opportunities, which took him ultimately to Buenos Aires, where he established himself and his family in 1817. He remained in the southern cone but moved to Montevideo, Uruguay, and even contemplated migration to the Chilean capital, Santiago. His Protestant religion, language, and origin were no barrier to Zimmermann's expansive perception of South America as his land of opportunity.

Zimmermann proved a cosmopolitan settler: his first wife was German; one business partner was an American based in Philadelphia; he served as a consul for different German cities; and he moved within a diplomatic and commercial community of Argentines and foreigners, clinging to his Protestant faith in a Catholic nation yet immersing himself in his new Latin American home. Taciturn and disapproving references to political upheavals and revolutions intrude on his personal narrative, leading as they often did to economic reversals. But Zimmermann was tenacious. Only during the long siege of Montevideo that began in 1843 and ultimately launched a nine-year war did he leave, migrating one more time to the United States with his wife and four of his children. Although he traveled to Europe, Zimmermann never returned to South America. He died in New York in 1857.

Economic Neo-Colonialism

As Zimmermann's travels and business ventures indicate, the United States and the nations of Latin America, despite their recent independence, followed different paths of economic development. Even as some northern Atlantic nations began to industrialize, most of Latin America retained colonial patterns of production, as exporters of agricultural staples, livestock products, minerals, and other raw materials. Brazil, a monarchy until 1889, embodied this tendency toward post-independence continuity. This vast and geographically diverse South American nation, roughly the size of the United States, boasted a range of resources, from gold mines to prairies to rubber trees. Powerful Brazilian elites shared the vision of Thomas Jefferson and the French Physiocrats in linking their nation's future to its seemingly boundless agricultural potential. They drafted legislation aimed at thorough exploitation, inviting British mining interests to revive the gold district of Minas Gerais, and later opening the Amazon rainforest to those interested in rubber, cacao, quinine, and other forest products. Before long it was coffee, however, an im-

ported African crop in demand among the armies of sleepy industrial workers in the northern Atlantic, that sustained Brazil through the nineteenth and
early twentieth centuries. As had happened with cotton in the United States,
industrial demands in the north for warm-weather agricultural products helped
sustain slavery in the south. Only after Brazil abolished slavery in 1888 and
the creation of the first Brazilian Republic in 1889 would capital accumulated in coffee production be invested in industrial development. This would
give rise to Brazil's manufacturing and mining metropolises of São Paulo and
Belo Horizonte. In this case, industrialization occurred, but only after a long
period of export-led growth.

Unlike Brazil, which experienced a peaceful transition to nationhood,
the former Spanish colonies endured the same agonies of independence that
the English colonies on the northern mainland faced several decades earlier—the occupation of major urban areas, a brutal civil conflict between loyalists and rebels, and a soaring national debt. Unlike the United States, however, the Spanish American republics did not shift toward economic self-sufficiency or industrialization. Instead, by emerging into independence just when
parts of Britain and the United States were beginning to industrialize, nearly
all Latin American economies became, if anything, ever more controlled by
the appetites of northern Atlantic industrial capitalism. Mexico's and Bolivia's
silver industries were revived; Peru and Chile became increasingly dependent
on exports of guano and other mineral salts used as fertilizer in Europe and
North America; Argentina depended on European purchases of beef, hides,
and grain, and Colombia on exports of gold and later coffee. Nearly all of
these republics were born in debt to British bankers, and dependency on northern Atlantic technologies would only deepen over the course of the nineteenth century.

The path the United States took towards Atlantic domination in industry and finance was not smooth or bloodless, either. Its regional differences
amounted to a mix between Latin American and British modes of production, and such internal contradictions would result by the 1860s in Americas'
deadliest and most destructive civil war. Whereas residents of antebellum
Pennsylvania and New York enjoyed widespread property ownership and did
not rely on forced labor, the opposite was true of Mississippi and Alabama.
Even in relatively stable regions of Latin America, meanwhile, where slavery
was already a thing of the past, distribution of wealth remained grossly unequal. As Chilean writer José de Cos Iriberri complained, "who would imagine that in the midst of the lavishness and splendor of nature the population
would be so scanty and that most of it would be groaning under the oppressive yoke of poverty?" Echoing Kentucky politician Henry Clay, who attributed his state's underdeveloped economic condition to slavery, Iriberri blamed
Chile's unimproved social condition on the unequal distribution of land, in
which a few wealthy planters dominated a large population of underpaid,
landless peasants. The United States South, Cuba, and Brazil remained agrarian societies in which slaves labored to produce raw materials for northern
Atlantic factories and consumers. In a hemispheric perspective, the divergent
development of the northeastern United States toward industrialization, wage

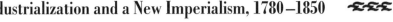

labor, and a more-equal distribution of wealth was an anomaly, one that citizens of the United States would come to define in terms of moral superiority. With regard to U.S. policy in Latin America, that legacy endures.

The increasing intensity of internal conflict over labor, land, and the future economic role of newly settled western territories kept U.S. intervention in Latin American political and economic affairs at a minimum until the late nineteenth century. In the meantime, Britain's vocal support for the principles of the Monroe Doctrine and Latin American political sovereignty had never disguised a new type of imperialistic desires. "Spanish America is free," Foreign Secretary Canning asserted in 1824, "and if we do not mismanage our affairs sadly, she is English." English merchants did not wait to see the outcome of colonial struggles; as soon as Bonaparte invaded Spain, British shippers set up trading houses in South American cities. By 1810, 120 English businessmen resided in Buenos Aires, and in 1824 the city's British population reached 3,000. Little wonder that neither Spain nor France challenged Monroe's toothless doctrine, since English, rather than American, warships patrolled South American and Caribbean waters, ostensibly to protect its merchant fleet, but in reality to keep the humbled Spanish at bay.

The nature and size of English investments in Latin America illustrated the importance of Latin American goods to industrial Europe and the way in which British bankers and diplomats securely fashioned the chains of neocolonial control. In 1822, even before Parliament recognized the independence of the emerging republics, London banks floated four substantial loans to Latin America, mostly tied to British-negotiated indemnity settlements with Spain and Portugal. In other words, the Latin American republics had to borrow millions of pounds sterling that they then paid to the former mother country in exchange for a promise not to re-invade. Still more loans refilled the local treasuries that fleeing officials emptied. By 1824, the number of loans had risen to nine, and in 1825 the Bank of London approved an additional five. Typical was the pattern Parliament followed with Brazil. Britain formally recognized Pedro I's government in 1825, but the price of international respect came high. Brazil had to consent to grant England a tariff rate lower than that given any other nation, which in any case could not exceed 15 percent. Consequently, the treaty not only guaranteed English exporters domination of Brazilian markets, it diminished any Brazilian incentive to industrialize by flooding the nation with inexpensive manufactured goods. So quickly did England supplant Portugal in Brazil's economic life that by the time Brazilian slaveholders voted not to attend the Panama Conference, British exports into the nation amounted to half of those sent to the United States and equaled those shipped to the rest of Latin America combined.

Again, technology facilitated this shift of economic power, since steamships enabled cheaper transport of goods and people. As in the United States after Robert Fulton pushed up the Hudson River in a vessel powered by steam-driven paddle wheels in 1807, steamships in South America first worked the inland and coastal trades. When the *Guapiassú* smoked its way 900 miles up the Amazon River in nine days, it cut two months off the standard travel time. In the 1840s, Britain and the United States initiated steamship service to Central and South America, and again, Latin American entrepreneurs found themselves serving northern Atlantic economies. The Royal Mail Steam Packet Company stopped twice monthly at every important Caribbean island and its ships docked at every mainland port city from Buenos Aires to Veracruz. The increased speed of steam navigation even enhanced existing enterprises; in the wake of the potato blight, England imported steers from Argentinean cattle barons. True to the pattern, the European desire for American crops and foodstuffs enriched a few landed gentlemen and served to reharness American suppliers to a dependence on old commercial networks and socially regressive forms of labor.

That industrialization in Britain and parts of the United States posed a mixed blessing for the rest of the Atlantic world is evident in the rate of Latin American economic growth. Historians enamored of the increasingly interdependent nature of the Atlantic economies point to the expansion of trade, and expand it did. Between 1829 and 1855, the value of Argentina's exports tripled, from $5.2 million to $15.2 million. Still, most of the increased sales came from the export of raw materials—in this case hides and salt beef—that entailed little addition of value by means of technology or skilled labor and thus meant continuing low wages for farmers, *gauchos* (cowboys), tanners, and meatpackers. Although not enslaved, these workers had only limited potential as consumers. This would only change with the industrialization of Argentina's meatpacking sector in the early twentieth century. Nor was the rate of increase in nineteenth-century Latin American exports impressive by comparison to that of industrializing countries. General international trade increased fivefold during that same period, while U.S. exports improved by a factor of eight. Harder to quantify or compare were the social and environmental costs of U.S. and northern European economic growth. England's coal miners lived and worked in deplorable conditions, and the factories of Manchester, Sheffield, and other industrial cities belched thick black smoke that shortened the lives of all who lived in their shadow. In the case of the southern United States, slavery was not only reinforced by northern industrialization but lasted longer there than anywhere in Latin America besides Brazil, Cuba, and Puerto Rico.

Many factors limited Latin American economic growth in the nineteenth century, prime among them dependence on northern Atlantic markets, capital, and technology. U.S. exporters had the advantages in trading with Europe of a shorter Atlantic crossing and access to local technical innovations. In the United States, free-state farmers seized a disproportionately large share of European markets for foodstuffs by taking advantage of the reduction in ocean transport costs and mechanization on the farm. By 1830, an efficient if expensive grain cradle became the standard tool for harvesting wheat, and within a decade, even this hand tool, advanced by southern or Latin American standards, was replaced by Cyrus McCormick's mass-produced reaper. Patented in 1834, the horse-drawn reaper could harvest twelve acres of wheat a day, by comparison to the three acres cut by scythe. In turn, cash raised through commercial agriculture helped to finance roads and canals, on which midwestern wheat was taken to eastern cities, stops on the way to blighted Europe. Industry and export agriculture in most of Latin America did not operate in such a synergistic way. Latin America's advantages remained limited mostly to special access to minerals or an ability to produce large quantities of tropical agricultural products. Railroads and canals built by British, French, or U.S. investors went directly from the Atlantic coast to these resource enclaves, providing no service to neighboring cities and towns.

A shift toward free trade among Europe's industrial powers also aided northern Atlantic hegemony of the Atlantic economies. Faced with starvation in Ireland and the need to secure North American wheat, Britain repealed the last of its Corn Laws in 1846 and set off on a course of tariff reduction (and even elimination); Belgium, France, and many German states followed suit. Latin American politicians expressed doubts about theories advanced by British publicists, but when faced with pressure from British diplomats—who made clear that further loans for railroads and other internal improvements necessary to carry inland goods to port cities rested in the balance—few were inclined to refuse British demands for "free trade." Of all the newly independent American nations, only the United States, whose tariffs inched higher over the decades (with one brief detour toward free trade during the administration of cotton planter James K. Polk), was able to develop an industrial sector while simultaneously exporting great quantities of raw materials.

Although a lack of capital and banking facilities, together with what historians Stanley and Barbara Stein characterize as "massive imports of British manufactures," simply "crushed" Latin American attempts to industrialize, the wars of independence and subsequent internal strife also left the emerging republics with a host of problems not visited upon the United States by its earlier revolution. While 80,000 Loyalists abandoned the United States for Britain, Canada, and the British Caribbean, the Latin American colonies received immigrants fleeing Bonaparte's invasion of the Iberian Peninsula. Among those who arrived on Latin American shores were officers, merchants, absentee landlords, and bureaucrats—many of whom formed the core of opposition to independence. In economic terms, most of the new arrivals reflected fondly on the past. The new merchant class wished only to sell cheap European imports, not to improve their fellow Americans' standard of living. To the north, U.S. citizens spent much of the early national era in disputes over financial policies, from Alexander Hamilton's establishment of the National Bank to Andrew Jackson's war on it. It is important to remember that the future course of U.S. history was not fixed, and these were not trifling matters. Nonetheless, fiscal issues lay at the heart of these debates, while in most of the emerging Spanish American republics national energies (and treasuries) were frequently spent in violent and destructive regional and, to a lesser extent, ideological power struggles. Out of these struggles emerged powerful and usually conservative military dictators, called *caudillos*, among them Mexico's Santa Anna and Argentina's Juan Manuel de Rosas. Their visions for the future tended to be rooted in the colonial past.

In the same way Carolina planters following the Revolution sought not to build a new society but to rebuild a seigneurial past, Latin American landlords tried to recapture the eighteenth century through the accumulation of vast estates. In Mexico, José Miguel Sánchez Navarro not only held onto his considerable holdings during the late colonial era, but he and his sons acquired more haciendas, until by 1848 the family owned 16 million acres, the largest *latifundio* (landed estate) ever to exist in Mexico, an area the size of the state of West Virginia. In Argentina, wealthy Buenos Aires merchant Tomás Manuel de Anchorenas bought 1.6 million acres of land confiscated from Indians and the Catholic Church; by 1830, 500 Argentinians owned 21 million acres, the vast majority of which remained undeveloped. By comparison, Virginia planter and land speculator George Washington owned only 63,000 acres in trans-Appalachia (and the unethical methods he used to obtain land bounties from common soldiers is not a nice story), but his intent was to develop and sell the land to farmers who would ship their foodstuffs east in exchange for Slater's manufactured wares. English readers of *Hard Times* may have wondered if the changes wrought by Arkwright and Hargreaves were in any way beneficial to the majority of English workers, but they would be hard put not to notice the rapid transformation of their island. Like the slaves of the U.S. South, the majority of Latin American peasants, domestic servants, stevedores, artisans, and cowboys witnessed only an intensification of colonial-style work regimes. Under the new Atlantic imperialism, driven by northern industrialization, the past and future seemed locked in interregional struggle.

Atlantic Africa: New Exports, Cheap Imports, Heightened Dependence

The same struggle would play out even more dramatically in Atlantic Africa. Most Africans along the Atlantic rim would have no colonial masters until late in the nineteenth century, but they would experience economic and social change earlier as a result of forces unleashed by the Industrial Revolution and the British-led attack on the slave trade. New, better, and cheaper manufactured goods began arriving in Africa not long after Napoleon's defeat; demand grew, if slowly, in Europe and America for African products; Atlantic slaving slowly declined; and these occurrences combined in places to change the loci of wealth and power. Viewed most simply, at the height of the Atlantic slave trade in the 1780s, African elites were in control of their own people and the trade that passed through and along the borders of their realms, but by the 1880s, the slave trade had ended, some old-guard elites had been replaced, and many Africans found themselves tied to an economy geared toward providing primary products needed by European factories in exchange for manufactured goods those factories produced. Late in the nineteenth century, as they witnessed political authority passing to Europeans, Africans may have understood that the controlling factor in their lives was no longer some visible local potentate, or even some swaggering colonial official, but, instead, the hidden hand of an economic system centered in the industrialized nations on both sides of the North Atlantic.

As with Latin America, important in tying African economies to the industrializing nations were the new forms of technology; the steamship headed the list into the second half of the nineteenth century. Before then, African primary products passed to Europe in wooden sailing ships. Steamers with iron hulls existed before midcentury: the Liverpool trader Macgregor Laird took two small steamers on an 1832 expedition seeking ivory and indigo in the Niger. But technological problems hampered their use, not the least being a reluctance to raise steam pressure high enough for sufficient power. (When asked in 1834 why he recommended limiting steam pressure to ten pounds per inch when "American vessels [are] working as high as thirty," Laird replied it was because in America "they kill about a thousand people every year.") Shortly after midcentury, enough technological innovations—not only high-pressure boilers but wider use of iron hulls and propellers rather then exposed paddle-wheels—were incorporated into steamships so as to make them efficient and cost effective. Thus steamships quickly gained acceptance by private traders, who recognized their advantage faster than did the decision makers for the tradition-bound European navies. The African Steam Ship Company, formed in England in 1851, and French and German lines joined the competition (or engaged in price-fixing to avoid cutthroat competition) some years later.

Long before steamships came into play, however, African initiatives began reshaping West Africans' relationship to the Atlantic economy. At the very time Francis Lowell and Paul Moody were building textile mills in Massachusetts, King Opobu of Bonny, on the eastern side of the Niger Delta, was pondering how his people might benefit from a growing Atlantic demand for tropical products. Perceiving that the work of British abolitionists boded ill for his slave-trading city-state, "Opobu the Great," as he is remembered, took the initiative to open palm-oil markets around his neighborhood on the Bight of Biafra. Prices that British traders were paying for palm oil, extracted from the fruit of the oil palm that grew semiwild in the vicinity, had been rising. Initially, the main use for the oil in Europe was to lubricate the machines clanking away in industrial centers or as an ingredient in candles that illuminated factories and houses. As the nineteenth century progressed and cleanliness took its place alongside godliness in European thinking, however, palm oil became a popular ingredient in soap. (The mixture of palm oil and olive oil was washing away grime long before an American firm marketed "Palmolive" soap.) So Opobu's vision of his region's economic future turned out to be—literally—on the money.

The transatlantic slave trade disappeared quickly in some West African locales and more slowly in others. As slaving waned, into the 1850s, some Africans—though not always the ones involved in slave trading—were able to substitute production of what contemporaries called "legitimate" (nonslave) commodities for the lost commerce in humans. So dependent were many coastal societies on the products they were obtaining in exchange for slaves that, as the slave trade declined, elites in those societies faced what historians speak of as a "crisis of adaptation." Those who would come up with legitimate products in demand somewhere around the Atlantic might retain their authority. Those who could not found their grip on power and prestige increasingly tenuous.

Of course, the trade from Africa's west coast always comprised more than slaves. The nature of slave production, with people capable of carrying goods being marched to delivery points along the coast, lent itself to supplying markets around the Atlantic with various products. At different times and places, gum (for use in confectioneries and processing cloth), hides, ivory, beeswax (for candles), timber, dyewoods, gold, kola nuts, pepper, and provisions for slaving vessels were products exported from Africa's Atlantic ports. Once the Industrial Revolution took hold and spread, demand increased for some of these commodities and for new ones, especially oils derived from palm trees and peanuts. Onward from the 1770s, the idea of developing an African trade in products other than slaves appealed to opponents of slave trading. Along with more farsighted industrialists, opponents of the slave trade believed that since Europe's industries needed tropical raw materials, it would serve both God and mammon to stop trading slaves across the Atlantic and allow persons who might otherwise have been traded as slaves to work as free laborers producing the raw materials. King Opobu did not necessarily share a glorification of free labor, but he knew that he and other middlemen were dependent on imports, which, though growing less expensive as industrialization spread in Europe, could be obtained only by having an export commodity in demand to exchange for them. If that commodity would not be slaves, as European humanitarians hoped, then Opobu ventured it might be palm oil.

Traders around the Niger Delta had been producing and trading palm oil for a long time: it was the reason Europeans called the streams flowing into the Bights of Benin and Biafra the "Oil Rivers." Once industrial demand for palm oil grew, its price rose and exports increased. From the Bight of Biafra alone, palm oil exports grew from 150 tons per year in the 1790s to 3,000 tons in 1819, and then to 8,000 tons in 1829 and 25,000 tons in 1855. Steamships were important in this growth, but so was the fact that palm-oil trading was compatible with slave trading: units of exchange, credit systems (including use of pawns as security), and agreements on commissions worked for both. Even slaves' capture, movement, and sale were compatible with palm oil production, for it was mostly dependent labor that harvested, processed, and transported the oil to the coast. Thus, as the Atlantic market for slaves declined, local commodity production stepped in and partly made up for the loss by its need for cheap labor. Making this trade more profitable for producers were falling prices of European manufactures, especially cotton cloth. Between 1820 and 1850, the price of British textiles fell by as much as 75 percent, and the quantity of British cotton goods exported to West Africa increased thirty fold. The first half of the nineteenth century was simply a good time to be a palm-oil exporter. Of course, this meant that others outside of the Niger Delta (where Britain was obtaining 90 percent of its palm oil in the 1820s) would get in on the business. By the 1840s, men and women inland from the Bight of Benin, the Slave Coast, and even the Gold Coast were entering the palm-oil trade.

Two thousand miles up the coast from the Niger Delta, where savannas rather than forests meet the shoreline and thus where oil palms do not grow in abundance, rulers, chiefs, and lineage heads began early to feel the pinch brought on by the decline in revenue from slaving. As described in the last chapter, after the Congress of Vienna in 1815, Britain returned Goreé Island off Cape Verde and St. Louis at the mouth of the Senegal River to France and built its own new settlement, Bathurst, on a sandspit in the Gambia River. By making use of these headquarters, the European nations shut down most of the flow of slaves into the Atlantic from Senegambia. This meant that rulers of the regional states, who for ages had lived off taxes and tolls on Atlantic-bound trade, faced a cut in revenues. Along the Senegal River valley, growing European demand for gum in the 1830s and 1840s brought about a "gum boom," which induced Moorish masters to use slaves to gather gum from acacia trees for shipment down the river toward St. Louis. But for areas to the south, with no noticeable spike in the market for hides or beeswax, what were people to do?

Fortunately for them, European traders were asking the same question, and they had allies in government-funded institutes whose scientists were conducting tests on tropical products that might have uses in Europe's industrial economy. In the early 1830s, researchers began experimenting with peanuts, which Portuguese sailors had brought to Africa from Brazil in the sixteenth century but which had been important to Africans only when drought or locusts ruined their grain harvest, forcing them to eat the legumes to survive. But these were different times. Already, French cooks were judging peanut oil a good and inexpensive substitute for olive oil, and a taste for roasted peanuts was spreading in the United States, where one could find them sold on the streets of New York City and at traveling circuses and shows. Then, as with palm oil, a breakthrough occurred when peanut oil became a popular ingredient in soap. Marseilles soap makers found they could make a peanut-oil-based "blue-marble" soap that appealed to finicky French bathers, who disliked all yellow (which denoted palm-oil-based) soaps. Hence, by the 1840s, a rush to buy peanuts was on. Marseilles imported one ton of peanuts in 1841, 205 tons in 1845, and 5,500 tons in 1854. Out of the Gambia River alone, where nary a peanut was exported before 1830, came over 10,000 tons of peanuts (valued at more than £130,000) per year in the 1850s. Since peanuts were difficult to transport over land without wheeled vehicles, thousands of male peasants (with slaves or clients in tow) began migrating seasonally to areas close to the Atlantic or the Senegal and Gambia Rivers where they could grow and ship their produce. Village heads would designate land where these "strange farmers" (called *navetanes* by the French in Senegal) could set up and make a crop, with a portion of the revenue from its sale going to the locals. Such seasonal migrations increased production in places abundant in land yet lacking a sizeable labor force.

The transition from slave trading to legitimate trading was smoother in some regions than in others. In Opobu's eastern Niger Delta, the small, competitive city-states under control of grand trading families were suited for production and marketing of palm oil as well as slaves. In some places, former slaves found ways in the new commercial system to rise to prominence, but they did so with the support of a patronage system controlled by their old masters rather than in competition with them. In some zones of palm-oil production, however, the transition to legitimate trade brought into existence societies of an entirely different nature. In Yorubaland, astute and ambitious men and women gravitated to new production centers like Ibadan or Abeokuta,

The Raft of the Medusa

The ship that the French government sent to convey the new governor and his staff to St. Louis in 1816, La Méduse, did not fare well. Its captain, so designated because of his political ties to French royalty rather than his skill at navigating vessels at sea, wrecked the ship off the west coast of Africa. As the vessel broke up, captain and crew took command of a lifeboat and threw a line to a makeshift raft from the ship's hull carrying 149 surviving passengers. Before long, however, the raft slowed the boat's progress toward safety, so the captain cut it loose, leaving those on board the raft to drift at sea, without provisions, for twelve days. By the time they were spotted, only fifteen remained alive. French artist Theodore Gericault depicted the tragedy in what would become one of his best-known works, The Raft of the Medusa, a painting of dying humanity, hoping, praying, imploring, signaling for help, their plight made more desperate by the tropical heat and the swells of the green-brown ocean threatening to engulf them.

"The Raft of the Medusa." Oil on Canvas by Theodore Gericault, 1818. Credit: The Granger Collection, New York.

where they joined with like-minded people willing to take advantage of such political or economic opportunities that came along. Through the mid-nineteenth century, opportunity involved slaving more than anything else, as slaves continued to flow through Lagos and the lagoons lining the Bight of Benin. But after 1850, when the British began shutting down even that slave trade, the new class of entrepreneurs and their clients moved into palm-oil production.

In Senegambia, transition to peanut production had equally serious consequences. Through the slave-trading era, elite lineages held control in several dozen states. By the nineteenth century, with Atlantic demand for slaves waning, this old guard clung precariously to authority. Slave soldiers attached to these rulers spun out of control, raiding peasants and creating disorder. It was amid this chaos that, after 1840, aggrieved peasants took advantage of the opportunity to grow and sell peanuts, thus gaining income and using it to obtain weapons for fighting against their oppressive rulers. Across the region in the 1860s, armed peasants, led by Muslim merchant-clerics, waged wars to overthrow traditional authority. Only European intervention in some places to prop up the old guard kept the revolution from succeeding completely.

An ironic aspect of the transition from slave to legitimate trade along Africa's Atlantic rim was a spreading of slavery within Africa. It largely was unfree labor that harvested the palm fruit, extracted the oil, and transported it to coastal stations, just as slaves gathered and hauled the gum and planted, harvested, and moved much of the peanuts. It is hard to know how much slavery was a part of earlier West African societies, but by the twentieth century, slavery was essential to production in most regions. The historian Martin Klein estimates that between one-third and one-half of the early-twentieth-century population of French West Africa was enslaved. So, whereas European colonizers used the abolition of slavery to justify their takeover of Africa after 1880, most of them learned quickly that abolition would bring many African economies to a grinding halt. Decades would pass before formal, legal slavery ended in these societies.

Another aspect of the transition, only recently considered, has to do with its effect on women, which, too, was mixed. Among the Yoruba, women seemed able to organize palm-oil production and trade on their own and thus to have gained access to wealth, status, and independence from men in ways not before possible. But this may have been the exception rather than the rule. Among the Ibo, although women were the main palm-oil producers prior to the nineteenth-century boom, once the market grew, men took over production, leading, according to the historian Robin Law, "to greater expropriation of women's labour rather than to their enrichment." The same was true among peanut growers in Senegambia. Women were the major agricultural producers prior to the region's mid-nineteenth-century "peanut revolution," but once peanuts could be sold for cash, they constituted a man's crop, with women relegated to production of rice for family consumption. As time passed, men enhanced their positions as controllers of money, and as economies moved away from subsistence production, with greater reliance on cash crops and importation of foodstuffs for families to purchase, women lost economic power.

In the end, perhaps the most far-reaching effect of the Industrial Revolution on Africans was to alter their relationship with the Atlantic market. As was occurring in Latin America, after the mid-nineteenth century more Africans were becoming dependent on European and North American demand for their agricultural products. Eventually, this would move beyond gum, peanuts, and palm oil. At Africa's southern tip, discovery of diamonds and gold between the late-1860s and mid-1880s would bring new levels of production of these minerals for purchase by the industrial nations. This, in turn, would change life for nearly all southern Africans, from pastoral or agrarian production to migration in search of subsistence-level work in mines or related industries. Closer to the Equator, along the Congo River, when latex, the raw material for rubber, came into demand for use in making pneumatic tires, local residents tapped trees to enhance the accounts of their new master, the greedy, deceptive, careless, and exploitative King Leopold II of the Belgians. It was not coincidence that indigenous people straight across the Atlantic, in the Amazon basin, were at the same time turning their productive capacities toward the same enterprise (to line the pockets of the same investors in European and North American rubber companies). Industrialization in the north was tied intimately to the new imperialism in the south.

How did these changes in the Atlantic economy feel to those who experienced them? People today tend instinctively to characterize technological change as progress, and to an extent they are right in doing so. New England farm families said good things about the putting-out system, as it enabled wives and daughters to combine domestic labor with the larger market and use their earnings to buy mass-produced goods. The Indiana farmers who flocked to purchase McCormick's reaper saw the machine as a tangible symbol of progress: it rendered farms more profitable and workdays shorter. But for every James Watt who grew rich from technology, there were numerous slaves whose bodies were sold into the newly cleared lands of the U.S. cotton South. For every northern Atlantic resident who experienced the thrill of a bicycle ride, there were hundreds of Congolese youths and Amazonian Indians forced to tap rubber deep in the forest in appalling conditions. For every Tomás Manuel de Anchorena who bought hundreds of thousands of acres with the capital he acquired by importing cheap European goods, there were hundreds of thousands more "cuicos," or "monkeys," as he called the poor, who remained landless and destitute. The vast majority of people around the Atlantic basin never saw England's "dark, satanic mills," to borrow the words of the poet William Blake, but they felt their impact.

Selected Readings

Baily, Samuel L., and Eduardo Jose Miguez, eds., *Mass Migration to Modern Latin America* (Wilmington: Scholarly Resources, 2003).

Bulmer-Thomas, Victor, *The Economic History of Latin America Since Independence* (Cambridge, UK: Cambridge University Press, 2003).

Curtin, Philip D., *Death by Migration: Europe's Encounter with the Tropical World in the Nineteenth Century* (Cambridge, UK: Cambridge University Press, 1989).

David, Saul, *The Prince of Pleasure: The Prince of Wales and the Making of the Regency* (New York: Atlantic Monthly Press, 1999).

Deyle, Steven, *Carry Me Back: The Domestic Slave Trade in American Life* (New York: Oxford University Press, 2005).

Dublin, Thomas, *Women at Work: The Transformation of Work and Community in Lowell, Massachusetts, 1826–1860* (New York: Columbia University Press, 1979).

Durey, Michael, *Transatlantic Radicals and the Early American Republic* (Lawrence: University Press of Kansas, 1997).

Franko, Patrice, *The Puzzle of Latin American Economic Development* (Lanham: Rowman and Littlefield, 2003).

Gilje, Paul, ed., *Wages of Independence: Capitalism in the Early American Republic* (Madison: Madison House Publishers, 1997).

Halperin-Donghi, Tulio, *The Aftermath of Revolution in Latin America* (New York: Harper, 1973).

Hobsbawm, Eric, and George Rudé, *Captain Swing: A Social History of the Great English Agricultural Uprising of 1830* (London: Lawrence and Wishart, 1970).

Hochschild, Adam, *King Leopold's Ghost: A Story of Greed, Terror, and Heroicism in Colonial Africa* (Boston: Houghton Mifflin, 1998).

Hoerder, Dirk, *Cultures in Contact: World Migrations in the Second Millennium* (Durham: Duke University Press, 2002).

Klein, Martin A., *Slavery and Colonial Rule in French West Africa* (Cambridge, UK: Cambridge University Press, 1998).

Law, Robin, ed., *From Slave Trade to 'Legitimate' Commerce: The Commercial Transition in Nineteenth-Century West Africa* (Cambridge, UK: Cambridge University Press, 1995).

Laxton, Edward, *The Famine Ships: The Irish Exodus to America* (New York: Henry Holt, 1997).

Mostert, Noël, *Frontiers: The Epic of South Africa's Creation and the Tragedy of the Xhosa People* (New York: Alfred A. Knopf, 1992).

Stein, Stanley J., and Barbara H. Stein, *The Colonial Heritage of Latin America: Essays on Economic Dependence in Perspective* (New York: Oxford University Press, 1970).

Thompson, E. P., *The Making of the English Working Class* (New York: Pantheon, 1963).

ISAAC and ROSA, Emancipated Slave Children,
From the Free Schools of Louisiana,
Photographed by KIMBALL, 477 Broadway. N.Y.
Entered according to Act of Congress, in the year 1863 by GEO. H.
HANKS. in the Clerk's Office of the U. S. for the Sou. Dist. of N.Y.

Freedmen School, 1863. Souvenir carte-de-visite photograph, 1863, sold in the northern states for the benefit of the Freedmen Schools of Louisiana. Credit: The Granger Collection, New York.

Chapter Fourteen

Abolishing Slavery in the Western Atlantic, 1750–1888

I remember, in the vessel in which I was brought over, in the men's apartment, there were several brothers, who, in the sale, were sold in different lots; and it was very moving on this occasion, to see and hear their cries at parting. O, ye nominal Christians! might not an African ask you, "Learned you this from your God, who says unto you, Do unto all men as you would men should do unto you?" Is it not enough that we are torn from our country and friends, to toil for your luxury and lust of gain?
Olaudah Equiano
The Interesting Narrative, 1789

William Littleton was aware of the circumstances as he walked into Parliament's meeting place in London's Palace of Westminster to testify before a Committee of the Whole House on June 18, 1789. Over the previous two years, petitions demanding abolition or curbs on the slave trade cluttered desks occupied by members of Britain's legislative body, and a year earlier, the House of Commons dealt with its first ever anti–slave trade motion. (It had been soundly defeated.) Now the committee was receiving testimony to "consider further of the Circumstances of the Slave Trade." Who would know better the workings of the trade than an "old coaster," an Englishman who had sailed Africa's coast and Atlantic waters on a slaving vessel? Littleton was such a man.

From a 1762 start as a mate on an English slaver, Littleton had spent eleven years trading in Guinea before advancing to ship's captain. Half a dozen times he had crossed the Atlantic, ferrying African slaves to South Carolina or the West Indies. Now he was to speak from this experience. Like boxers starting a match, Littleton and the committee danced around one another, the captain saying nothing more than he had to. But eventually Littleton offered pointed testimony—about how Africans obtained slaves, death rates on transatlantic slaving voyages, living conditions of enslaved Africans on board ships, and Africa's commercial possibilities beyond the trade in captive laborers. Throughout his testimony, Littleton insisted that he and his crew accommodated the slaves "in the best manner we possibly can, to render their situation as comfortable as possible." In his way of thinking, slaves died along the way as a result of their being "very meagre" when first received on board, "owing to the great scarcity of provisions in the country from which they came";

cleanliness of the slave decks was "one of the first objects we attend to"; and the crew's "principal employment in the Middle passage" was in keeping up "the health and spirits of the Slaves." When asked, "In all those voyages, were the Slaves treated with humanity and tenderness?" Littleton answered, "Always."

In matter-of-fact form, the questioning continued: How much air do slaves get below decks? How much room is there for each? Do the chains gall slaves' limbs? Was there food enough? Littleton, fearing nothing from a Parliament comprised solely of exceedingly wealthy males, discussed the "comfort" of a slave ship and insisted that he provided Africans with "plenty of Food, Victuals and Drink, and the best lodgings we can."

Then, like the clang of a ship's bell: "Are the circumstances of being chained two and two, of not having room to lay on their backs, of sea sickness, excoriation, shackles, rings reeved through the chains, kiln-dried Horsebeans for food, confinement between decks, lying crouded together in a close hold in a tropical climate, confining them all night in a fetid atmosphere, and keeping them there all day when the weather is bad, articles of comfort?"

The rhetorical question brought Littleton's objection and direction for him to withdraw. It must have been bewildering for the old Africa hand. Had not slaves been crossing the Atlantic for centuries? Was it not slave trafficking that had brought wealth to Bristol and Liverpool? Were not African slaves the backbone of American plantation production that fueled the English economy? And would the committee not soon be breaking for tea and lacing their drink with sugar, a commodity produced by the labor of slaves?

The end of the transatlantic slave trade, and of slavery in the Western Hemisphere, did not come about overnight. Abolition was instead a protracted process shaped by the actions of abolitionists, black and white, and perhaps most important of enslaved people themselves, working sometimes in tandem, more often pursuing separate strategies for personal and collective freedom. Enslaved peoples' resistance to their condition was constant and manifold from the beginning, and in the end impossible to quantify. A quest for freedom and dignity shaped most discussions. Many of those who pressed for legal abolition in the northern Atlantic were often middle- and upper-class Europeans or their descendants, persons with little or no direct connection either to slavery or the slave trade. Many of these abolitionists were driven by religious concerns, others by ethical or philosophical ones. Some white reformers embraced gradual emancipation and were at best antislavery sympathizers, while others wrote, spoke, and voted for an immediate end to unfree labor. Some advocated peaceful activism and "moral suasion," while white and black militants sharpened a sword or picked up a rifle in the name of black liberty. Across the Atlantic world, slavery ended by law, by fiat, and through violence, in revolution, civil war, and waves of rebellions.

Abolition: The Early Years

The Englishmen who assailed Littleton were not the first to question the morality of the slave trade and slavery, but they were on the leading edge of a movement growing in strength on both sides of the Atlantic in the second half of the eighteenth century. Spanish, Portuguese, and Dutch jurists and theologians had grappled with the moral and legal underpinnings of slavery and the slave trade, but by the 1600s all had come down in favor of the trans-atlantic trade in Africans, provided the slaves were made Christians. Among the English, early arguments against slavery came from members of religious sects, especially the Society of Friends, or from philosophers in Europe's Enlightenment. The Friends (or Quakers), following an alternative form of Christianity that emerged in the mid-seventeenth century, paid heed to an inner light, the divine essence that they believed existed in all people, which advocated equality and pacifism—both incompatible with slavery. In a way reminiscent of Jesuits in Latin America at the time, Quakers were involved in slave owning and slave trading on both sides of the Atlantic. As time wore on, some Friends, who increasingly saw a duty to confront evil, denounced those among them who engaged in immoral business, in part defined by its relationship to violence. Through the 1740s, one New Jersey Quaker, John Woolman, called on his flock to emancipate their slaves, and with the assistance of Anthony Benezet, who ran a school for Africans and African Americans in Philadelphia, persuaded the assembly at the Society's 1758 annual meeting to condemn the holding of enslaved persons and trafficking in them.

Among Enlightenment philosophers, only a few spoke out against slavery, but some of these scribes carried influence beyond their numbers. The Scottish philosopher Francis Hutcheson, author of the 1738 *A System of Moral Philosophy*, wrote, "Nature makes none masters, none slaves." A decade later from Bordeaux, Baron de Montesquieu argued in *On the Spirit of Laws* that slavery "is bad of its own nature," bad for the master as well as the slave "because he contracts all manner of bad habits with his slaves; he accustoms himself insensibly to the want of all moral virtues; he grows fierce, hasty, severe, choleric, voluptuous, and cruel." The Seven Years' War brought together these sentiments. Outspoken Quakers called for nonparticipation in any aspect of Atlantic slaving. John Locke's idea that a state of slavery might exist alongside the inalienable rights of natural liberty ceased to be logical in the minds of such philosophers as Adam Smith. Though the latter would argue against slavery on economic grounds in his *Wealth of Nations* (1776), the Scotsman, once Hutcheson's student in Glasgow, wrote in his *Theory of Moral Sentiments* (1759) of the cruelty involved in reducing people "into the vilest of all states, that of domestic slavery, and to sell them, man, woman, and child, like so many herds of cattle, to the highest bidder in the world."

Enslaved Africans and their free relatives had of course known all this and more since the Atlantic slave trade began in the fifteenth century, but Europeans systematically silenced their protests. Even those whites who openly doubted the morality of the slave system almost never bothered to ponder, much less record, black peoples' thoughts. The Haitian Revolution, as the historian Michel-Rolph Trouillot has reminded us, was the clearest cry for abolition ever made in the Atlantic world, yet white elites immediately painted it as something else, a harbinger of anarchy and race war. Black abolitionists were thus never absent, but they only started to gain public recognition as individuals at the very end of the eighteenth century, when white crusaders

Capitalism and Slavery

A broad consensus that abolition was largely a morally inspired, humanitarian effort was challenged in 1944 when the historian Eric Williams, in Capitalism and Slavery, argued that abolition's strength came from the new class of British industrialists, who regarded slave labor as an outdated mode of production (as evidenced by declining profits from West Indian plantations), better ended so as not to become a drag on Britain's growing industrial economy. "Mercantilism" lay behind the rise of the Atlantic slave system, Williams argued; "mature capitalism" caused its fall. He also argued that profits from colonial slave production provided the capital for the beginning of Britain's Industrial Revolution. While many scholars agreed with Williams, others did not. Eventually, historian Seymour Drescher marshaled data, published in Econocide: British Slavery and the Era of Abolition (1977), showing that plantation profits were not declining before

abolition; in fact, they were as high as ever. It was, he concluded, the ending of slavery that triggered a precipitous drop in profit of enterprises based on slave production.

But Williams's arguments endure. More historians today, while emphasizing the humanitarian spirit and systematic direction of public sentiment to bring pressure on Parliament, recognize the necessity of placing the abolition movement in its economic and political setting. Could it have been coincidence that the weak and often singular voices found ears at the very time that English industries were establishing their solid footing with a basis in free labor? Like so many issues, the abolition movement had a basis in the Atlantic world's economic and political culture, as well as a foundation in the intellectual ferment stimulated by Europe's Enlightenment. It is best examined in the context of the whole, which turned out to be greater than the sum of its parts.

The interior of a weaving workroom located in Spitalfields, the center of London's thriving silk industry, from the series of drawings "Industry and Idleness," by William Hogarth (London, 1747). Depicted here is Francis Goodchild applying his skills as a deft weaver, and Tom Idle asleep, having drunk a copious amount of beer. © The Trustees of the British Museum.

solicited their aid. One of the first and most widely read black abolitionists was Olaudah Equiano, also known as Gustavus Vassa, who lived in London. Many would follow in his footsteps.

Both religious and philosophical antislavery views gained tacit support from a more general sympathy growing in western European and American intellectual circles, at least momentarily, for people from foreign, and especially "exotic," cultures. These early abolitionists were thoroughly and openly racist, but for many of them, Africans' cultural differences stopped being negative factors and even took on positive connotations: John Wesley, a leader in the Methodist movement, considered Africans lesser sorts of humans, yet still innocent children of nature, true "noble savages" whose cultures manifested virtue and creative potential. The "noble savage" image was "little more than a literary convention," writes the historian David Brion Davis, but it served at a critical time "to counteract the many fears and prejudices that had long cut the African off from the normal mechanisms of sympathy and identification." In 1788, when one of pottery maker Josiah Wedgwood's craftsmen came up with a design—made initially for a stamp for wax used in closing envelopes— portraying an African in chains, hands clasped in supplication, asking, "Am I not a man and a brother?" The logo gained instant popularity. It showed up on leaflets and adorned cufflinks and hatpins worn by influential men and women around the English-speaking Atlantic world, having an impact, according to Benjamin Franklin, "equal to that of the best written Pamphlet."

The quest for abolition in England also had an economic underpinning among members of the earliest generation to experience the Industrial Revolution. Increasing numbers of people in the British Isles were beginning to think of free labor as a marker that a society had advanced beyond its feudal past and was truly modern. The new, late-eighteenth-century industrialists in British cities were convinced of this, but so were the growing hordes of workers, caught up in an early manifestation of free-market capitalism, who recognized unfair competition to their wage-driven existence. One need not harbor concern for Africans or slaves to consider slavery, even if it existed thousands of miles away, across the ocean, a threat to one's well being. Ultimately, of course, it matters little if the men in Parliament who spoke against the slave trade represented the rising industrial elite or the landed gentry. The early antislavery movement reflected values and attitudes of the emerging capitalist order: for Adam Smith and his disciples, unwaged labor was every bit as irrational as mercantilist controls over wages and prices.

As these religious and intellectual waves were breaking on Atlantic shores—at the very time when the British crown was looking to rebuild its war-depleted treasury with colonial revenues, and residents of the colonies were growing edgy over mercantile restrictions—a British subject purchased a slave in colonial Virginia and thereby set in motion events that would bring slavery's place in English law before the highest court in the land. Long overshadowed in historians' minds by events building toward the revolutionary break of the North American colonies from Britain, the case of *Somerset v. Stewart*, heard in 1772, was the London media event of its time. It placed antislavery arguments before the English public and effectively ended slavery in the homeland of some of the Atlantic world's wealthiest slave traders and plantation owners.

Charles Stewart foresaw none of this, of course, when in August 1769 he bought a slave in Virginia. Soon after the purchase, Stewart found he had business in London, so he crossed the Atlantic in the fall, taking along his newly acquired slave to serve him on the venture. Records indicate that in London, Stewart had his slave baptized, giving him the name James Somerset, and that Somerset served his master for twenty-three months, apparently without incident, as Stewart conducted his business from a residence in

Marylebone. But the lure of freedom in the big city eventually got the better of Somerset, who, in October 1771 fled and ventured forth to try his luck on his own. That luck did not take him far, for seven weeks later agents of Stewart found the runaway, and, on his master's orders, placed him in the custody of the captain of the Jamaica-bound packet *Ann and Mary*, with orders to sell Somerset once he arrived at his destination.

Here, friends of London's enslaved population intervened and, before the *Ann and Mary* could weigh anchor, placed a writ of habeas corpus before the King's Bench, forcing production of Somerset before the court, where he argued he was being detained without cause and sued for restoration of his freedom. Aware of the implications of the case, several young lawyers, perhaps as keen to make a reputation for themselves as they were in accord with antislavery sentiment, agreed to argue Somerset's case pro bono. Although Somerset's argument rested on his having been detained without due process, the case broadened. Soon court proceedings involved discussion of slavery's legality in history, enumeration of the institution's "destructive consequences," and the body of English law authorizing slavery. (Of this last, it turns out, there was none.) Such a case could not have been presented in these terms in Iberia or Latin America precisely because a vast body of laws circumscribing slavery had been building since the Middle Ages. In the end, before a Westminster Hall gallery packed with slave owners, reporters, and black Londoners eager, in the words of one London newspaper correspondent, "to hear the event of a cause so interesting to their tribe," Lord Chief Justice William Mansfield ruled, "The state of slavery . . . is so odious that nothing can be suffered to support it, but positive law. Whatever inconveniences, therefore, may follow from the decision, I cannot say this case is allowed or approved by the law of England; and therefore the black must be discharged."

Concerned with "setting 14,000 or 15,000 people at once loose by a solemn opinion," Mansfield made his ruling narrow, so his decree freed Somerset alone. Thus, slavery did not end in England in 1772, and masters continued to sell their slaves and send them from the nation. But the case quickly took on its own reality. The *Morning Chronicle and London Advertiser* reported that upon hearing the decision, blacks in the audience "bowed with profound respect to the Judges, and shaking each other by the hand, congratulated themselves upon their recovery of the rights of human nature, and their happy lot that permitted them to breathe the free air of England." Here was but a hint of that deep reservoir of black protest so rarely recorded by fearful and knowing whites. Three weeks later, John Riddell of Bristol complained to Somerset's now-former master, Stewart, about one of his own slaves, who "told the [other] servants that he had rec'd a letter from his Uncle Somerset acquainting him that Lord Mansfield had given them their freedom & he was determined to leave me as soon as I returned from London which he did without even speaking to me." Riddle added that his slaves had carried off none of his master's less moveable property. He "only carried off all his own cloths which I don't know whether he had any right so to do. I believe I shall not give my self any trouble to look after the ungrateful villain." As word from "Uncle Somerset" spread, as more slaves absconded, and as more masters refused to trouble themselves to look after their runaways, the *Somerset* case came to serve as the beginning of the end of slavery in England and Ireland, with Scotland joining the group in 1778.

But slavery had not ended in the British Empire, or in the holdings of any other European country in the Atlantic world. Shortly before his fall from power in 1777, the Marquis de Pombal had outlawed importation of slaves to Portugal, where they were likely to serve in elite households, so that no able hands would be spared from Brazil's plantations and mines. And Spanish planters, with English help, were turning Cuba into a sugar-based slave society. Indeed, through the decades that followed Somerset's suit, enslaved Africans continued to produce staples in the Americas for a mostly European market, and, more than ever, European shippers transported captive humans westward; by the mid-1770s, the transatlantic slave system was booming and would soon reach its peak.

This world of slave production was the backdrop for U.S. independence, an effort that would heighten the moral focus on slavery. During the Seven Years' War, Quaker efforts toward abolition in these colonies were, in the words of the historian Donald L. Robinson, "like fireflies in the night." But in the years thereafter, antislavery arguments were more like bonfires. The ideology supporting the colonies' break with the mother country, grounded in Enlightenment thinking on man's creative intelligence and rational, benevolent behavior, argued against oppression by religious zealots or tyrannous monarchs and called for a new order that would allow all persons freedom to seek happiness and unleash their talents on their natural circumstances, to the benefit of all. That slavery had no place in such arguments is evident in the early documents justifying the break with England. Though a slaveholder and a person who later enslaved his own offspring (from the long-standing union with his enslaved sister-in-law, Sally Hemings), Thomas Jefferson wrote a passage (later excised by the Continental Congress) in his draft of the Declaration of Independence: "[The English monarch] has waged cruel war against human nature itself, violating its most sacred rights of life and liberty, in the persons of a distant people who never offended him, captivating and carrying them into slavery in another hemisphere, or to incur miserable death in their transportation thither. Determined to keep open a market where MEN should be bought and sold, he has prostituted his negative for suppressing most every legislative attempt to prohibit or to restrain this execrable commerce."

But the Treaty of Paris that ended the Revolutionary War in 1783 reopened the Atlantic slave trade to North America, and the revival of plantation production in the southern United States generated unprecedented demand for slaves. The invention of the cotton gin assisted in this growth, even, ironically, as American cotton helped to generate the capitalist mentality that undermined support for unfree labor in Britain. Still, many more slaves were sent to Cuba, Brazil, Saint Domingue, New Granada, and dozens of other plantation and mining regions. Popular demand in industrialized regions for sugar and coffee, along with increased Atlantic shipping capacities, stoked the slave system to a level not witnessed in the previous 350 years. Beginning in the 1780s, more enslaved Africans would reach the Americas than ever, and the extent of the traffic in humans would refocus the attention of religious and moral crusaders—not in the Americas and centers of slave production, but in Europe. As one might expect, slave owners from Buenos Aires to Baltimore were highly reluctant to abolish the labor system that sustained them.

Abolition by Law

If the *Somerset* case brought more British subjects on both sides of the Atlantic to consider the evils of slavery, it also made them aware of the difficulties they would face in trying to end the institution outside the British Isles. Among other things, *Somerset* had caught the attention of planters in the British Caribbean, and they marshaled their forces for what might be a greater battle. It was clear that the so-called Sugar Lobby had much more clout in Parliament than did a handful—and in the 1770s, their numbers were truly few—of Quakers, evangelicals, and moral philosophers who believed that slavery neither fit into God's plan nor conformed to the proper conduct of civil society. No practical reformer could have regarded the time as ripe for taking on chattel slavery throughout the European colonial Atlantic, but some began thinking differently about attacking the most obviously brutal element in the Atlantic system: the *trafficking* of slaves.

The Atlantic slave trade commanded reformers' attention in part because of its scale. People might be inclined to ignore tweaks to their conscience over the transatlantic transport of human captives, in chains and exposed to the elements, sleeping on raw planks, so long as they could tell themselves that the number of such victims was relatively low. But during each year of the 1780s an average of 80,000 enslaved Africans—roughly the population of a large Atlantic city of the time—was forcibly taken across the ocean to the Americas. Like the modern drug trade, the slave trade was so lucrative, so internationally connected, and so large in scale that it could not flourish unnoticed, even where no one felt its immediate effects. The port cities linked to the slave trade formed a kind of intermediate zone, where the nature of the business was less easily hidden. In Liverpool, London, or Bristol—just as in Nantes, La Rochelle, or Le Havre—everyone knew where the big ships with all the chains, casks, and planking were heading, and for what purpose.

What needed to be made more widely known, reformers believed, was how horrid the middle passage was, and into this task stepped two men noticeable at the time for their youth. Thomas Clarkson was a Church of England deacon and graduate of Cambridge University who could feel, he said, "a fire of indignation kindling within me" after visiting a slave vessel on the Thames. He felt his "blood boil" when reading about a massacre of slaves by British traders near the Niger River. In 1787, Clarkson joined nine Quakers and two evangelicals to form the Society for the Abolition of the Slave Trade, and as the society spawned similar groups in other cities, Clarkson rode off to gather information in England's biggest slaving ports. While Clarkson labored on the society's behalf from outside the political system, a young Parliament member, William Wilberforce, took the responsibility within the Commons.

Not a Quaker—Quakers, deemed eccentric dissenters, would not be allowed to serve in England's legislative body for another half century—but the son of a wealthy family from Hull, Wilberforce, who used family money to gain election to the House of Commons at the age of twenty in 1779, converted to evangelical Christianity in 1784 and thereafter followed a path toward social reform. Clarkson and Wilberforce joined a handful of others to organize the British campaign against the slave trade.

The effort leaped forward with new tactics. To humanize the issue, which had heretofore been debated with statistical calculations, committee members turned to London's free black community, which had risen to nearly ten thousand since British evacuation of the United States. Some of the "loyal blacks," as Englishmen dubbed them, had helped Somerset finance his case, while others circulated petitions to Parliament against slavery itself. Perhaps the most influential black speaker was Olaudah Equiano, billed as "A NATIVE OF AFRICA, many years a Slave in the West-Indies." Equiano's autobiography was soon published, and despite disagreement over his birthplace, his narrative still stands as one of the most remarkable documents in Atlantic history. As a survivor and witness of slavery and the slave trade at their cruelest height, Equiano brought the truth home in a way no white abolitionist could. His matter-of-fact relation of horrific events, combined with an almost forgiving, plaintive tone, made his personal plea for black freedom all the more compelling. Britain's white abolitionists knew they needed just such a witness at this juncture, just as Equiano acknowledged that he, along with millions of enslaved Africans, needed them, despite their racism and general misunderstanding of the black experience, to effect change. Society members stayed informed with newsletters and organized petition drives. As quickly as 1788, such activity netted 60,000 signatures on petitions asking Parliament to act against the trade. In time, concerned citizens joined a movement to boycott the sugar that slave labor produced. By the early 1790s, Clarkson estimated that "no fewer than three hundred thousand persons had abandoned the use of sugar."

Sugar and slaving interests countered by distributing proslavery literature, sponsoring a London musical entitled *The Benevolent Planters*, and developing their own code of conduct for slave treatment in hopes of heading off government interference. One slavery supporter in 1789 suggested they could solve the problem by ceasing to use the word *slaves*, calling captive laborers instead "Assistant-Planters." Then came the Parliamentary hearings, with men like Littleton testifying about slave trading. (Littleton was hardly the most outrageous apologist. "If the Weather is sultry, and there appears the least Perspiration upon their Skins, when they come upon Deck, there are Two Men attending with Cloths to rub them perfectly dry, and another to give them a little Cordial," testified former captain James Penny. "They are then supplied with Pipes and Tobacco [and] are amused with Instruments of Music peculiar to their own country" and "when tired of Music and Dancing, they then go to Games of Chance.") The 1791 slave rebellion on Saint Domingue, though stunning to slaveholders everywhere, encouraged most planters not to consider alternative labor forms, but to develop more effec-

Who Was Olaudah Equiano?

In 1789, a member of London's free black community published The Interesting Narrative of the Life of Olaudah Equiano, or Gustavus Vassa, the African. *A gripping account on many levels, the book was intended in large part to promote the campaign against the transatlantic slave trade. It was one of the first abolitionist texts written by a former slave. In it, Equiano related his remarkable and heart-rending odyssey, beginning with his capture as a child in the region of West Africa's lower Niger River. He was subsequently traded within Africa before being sold to overseas merchants. Equiano's experience as a slave took him next to the western Atlantic. He lived briefly in Virginia, but was soon purchased, around the age of ten, by an officer in the Royal Navy. From Virginia, he sailed around the Atlantic, where he saw slavery in its many different forms, including the brutal punishments of plantation slaves. The Seven Years' War took him to Canada, a quite different world from the Caribbean or southern mainland colonies. In 1766, Equiano purchased his freedom from his last master, a shipowner, and subsequently participated in several expeditions, including one to the Arctic, before settling in England. A brief stint as a plantation manager on the Mosquito Coast of Nicaragua, then controlled by Britain, convinced him that slavery could not be ameliorated. Now he returned to England to join the abolitionist cause. After writing his personal narrative, which he published only after convincing a number of subscribers, Equiano went on campaign throughout Europe to promote his work. He married Susanna Cullen in 1792 in England and helped raise two daughters before his death in 1797.*

Although still one of the most thorough indictments of slavery ever written, one portion of Equiano's narrative has recently been challenged by new evidence. The scholar Vincent Carretta determined in the course of preparing a new edition of Equiano's writings that Equiano defined himself twice, in a British naval record and a baptismal record, as born in Carolina rather than Nigeria. Specialists in early modern Africa and the slave trade have mostly interpreted these documentary claims as deriving from an adolescent slave's need to hide an African past, as this would only weaken any future claim to freedom. The baptismal document in question does not date to Equiano's birth, but rather to a church register from about the age of fourteen, recorded in England. Scholars continue to disagree on Equiano's birthplace, but no one challenges the fact that he wrote from experience, and in a style that was effective even with readers disinclined to agree with him. His narrative went through nine editions within five years of first publication in London, Dublin, Edinburgh, Norwich, and New York, and it continues to be reprinted today.

GUSTAVUS VASSA.

Gustavus Vassa (Olaudah Equiano) from "Men of Mark: Eminent, Progressive and Rising," by William J. Simmons, published 1887. General Research & Reference Division, Schomburg Center for Research in Black Culture, The New York Public Library, Astor, Lenox and Tilden Foundations.

tive means of heading off or punishing slave unrest. The political efforts of these planters and the merchants who financed them and provided them slaves were continued and effective.

A 1792 petition campaign brought a Parliamentary resolution that the slave trade should be abolished, but British fear of radicalism, fueled by the French Revolution and reaction to popular movements generally, helped kill the effort. Abolitionists had to be satisfied with laws attempting to mitigate the worst horrors of the slave trade—like a 1799 bill establishing limits on the manner of carrying slaves and setting space requirements on British ships. Denmark's outlawing of slave trading in 1803 set a hopeful precedent, however, and British acquisition through war of other West Indian islands, which meant competition for the established planters, brought nervous sugar growers to cease their opposition to halting the trade in Africans. Bills limiting the English trade in 1805 (abolishing it to conquered territories) and 1806 (to foreign colonies) passed both houses of Parliament, and these were encompassed in March 1807 in the final act to abolish all British slave trading, which became effective on January 1, 1808. This was, coincidentally, the earliest date allowable in the U.S. Constitution for legislation affecting the slave trade, and, as the nation had absorbed 170,000 African captives over the previous twenty-five years, the U.S. Congress proved willing to enact a law preventing its countrymen from participating in the slave trade at exactly the same time. Thus, in 1808, two of the most significant slave-trading nations opted out of the trade, at least formally. Smugglers continued to operate for another half century.

Britain and the United States differed, however, in their concern over actions of other slave-trading nations. The much weaker United States, largely headed by slaveholding presidents, devoted little attention to the continuance of slaving operations of France, Spain, or Portugal. It was even unwilling to investigate, much less stop, the slave-trading activities of its own citizens. But in Britain, where, once the trade was banned, colonial interests joined humanitarians on the issue—because the country's West Indian colonies faced competition from rivals who could still import slaves—the government prepared to devote its diplomatic strength and naval power to end slave trading all around the Atlantic. Killing the immoral transoceanic traffic in captive Africans would turn out to be a greater task than anyone imagined.

The early laws forbidding slave trading came at the height of the Napoleonic Wars, which disrupted Atlantic commerce and enforcement of international law, so not until those conflicts neared an end, in the 1810s, did reformers refocus attention on the issue. The ban on slaving was well timed, some say cynically so, as it facilitated search and seizure of commercial vessels flying enemy colors. But popular support for abolition had swelled in Britain. As the Congress of Vienna was meeting in 1814, 700 petitions carrying nearly 1 million signatures strengthened Foreign Secretary Lord Castlereagh's call for universal abolition. Eventually, at Castlereagh's insistence, the Act of Vienna contained a declaration condemning the slave trade as "repugnant to the principles of humanity and universal morality." While this did not render the trade illegal, it expressed a general acceptance of it as an international evil that should be ended. Under continuing British pressure, and with its own abolition movement making noise at home, France agreed in 1815 to limit slave trading to its colonies and end the traffic altogether by 1820. In separate treaties with Portugal (with whom Britain had leverage as its supporter in continental matters and as a protected market for its wine), Spain (which needed cash for its efforts to suppress independence

Abolition in South African History

Britain's outlawing of slavery in all its territories had an immediate effect in the Cape Colony at the southern tip of Africa. Britain had taken the colony from the Netherlands in 1806 and found settled there the primarily Dutch-descended cattle ranchers, or Trekboers, a self-reliant, Calvinist bunch who considered themselves among God's chosen. The Trekboers dominated African populations in their midst, exploited native people with apprenticeship and slavery so they could manage large herds on grand holdings, and were adamant about maintaining their way of life. They chafed under new laws of a liberal British government, but for many of them, abolition of slavery was the last straw. Beginning in the mid-1830s, many Trekboer families loaded their worldly goods into wagons and, with slaves and apprentices in tow, headed north and east in search of land away from British influence where they could re-establish

their independent living. For two decades, this "Great Trek" continued, until the Trekboers, having overcome African resistance, were left inhabiting South Africa's high plains on either side of the Vaal River in the Orange Free State and the Republic of South Africa (or Transvaal). The Trekboers maintained their independence in these republics for several decades, but discovery of gold in the Transvaal in 1886 heightened British interests and, following the Anglo-Boer War of 1899–1902, the two former republics came under British control. In 1910, they were amalgamated with the Cape Colony and British Natal to form the Union of South Africa. Slave labor they would have no more, but Trekboers and British settlers proceeded to join hands in systematically exploiting African labor, the precursor of the apartheid system that plagued South African history through most of the second half of the twentieth century.

Boers returning from hunting. Illustration by Samuel Daniell, 1804. © The British Library. Record: c5568-05, Shelf-mark: 458.h.14 part 1, Page Folio: 11.

rebellions in the Americas), and Brazil (independent of Portugal from 1822), Britain eventually achieved its goal of having the slave trade declared illegal in all of America's Atlantic ports. Brazil was last to agree, in 1830.

It was partly the British government's inability to bring about quick agreement on ending the slave trade—that, and ideas circulating that abolition of the British slave trade had done nothing to improve circumstances on plantations in the Caribbean—that brought British abolitionists to turn their attention toward slavery itself. In 1823, several aging crusaders created the Anti-Slavery Society to push for better plantation conditions and gradual emancipation. In an 1824 pamphlet, the Quaker Elizabeth Heyrick sounded the first argument for *Immediate not Gradual Emancipation*, and that idea spread among more radical abolitionists on both sides of the Atlantic. In 1831, a faction of mostly younger British abolitionists split off into the Agency Anti-Slavery Society, devoting themselves to immediate, unconditional abolition. Britain's Reform Act of 1832 brought a host of new voters, many with abolitionist leanings, and in August 1833 Parliament passed a law abolishing slavery in all British possessions.

On the heels of action against the slave trade by every major nation involved, passage of the act to end slavery in the British Empire was an enormous moral victory in which generations of British abolitionists could take pride. But slave-based production was still thriving, and in fact in many areas in the Americas was growing. As we have seen, shifts in international demand for slave-produced commodities could suddenly fuel massive internal slave trades, along with promoting contraband. Outlawing the slave trade was not enough to end slavery, and even enforcing the laws so enthusiastically passed during the Napoleonic wars would prove difficult for the next half century.

Stopping the Slave Trade

Enforcement of anti–slave-trading laws required naval patrols of Atlantic waters, and only one nation, Great Britain, had a navy adequate for the job. But could even the Royal Navy make a dent in the tens of thousands of slaves still crossing the ocean, given the enormity of the setting and the prickliness of nations in a period when international law was barely developed? It was along 3,000 miles of African coast that slavers sought captives, and out of hundreds of inlets, bays, creeks, and rivers that swift slaving vessels shot at nightfall so as to be well on their way in the vast ocean by morning, when patrollers might spot them. Standing in close to known African slave markets, where agents could keep a close eye on comings and goings, was ill advised in this prequinine era, when malaria could fell a ship's crew. On the other side of the ocean, a stubborn Brazil and a weak Spain (which still possessed Cuba and Puerto Rico) were unwilling and unable to arrest slave traders. And in between lay the sticky wickets of maritime law and national honor. Under normal circumstances, British naval vessels did not have the right to stop, search, and detain ships flying the flags of other nations, nor could they bring in vessels suspected of being slavers solely because they carried chains, water casks for hundreds, or planking for extra decks. The British government eventually was able to negotiate "right-of-search" treaties and "equipment clauses" with several nations. But there were holdouts, most notably the United States, where merchants complained about the Royal Navy's illegal practices and politicians remembered the "impressment" issue that was one factor leading to the War of 1812. Illegal slavers soon figured out that they could fly the stars and stripes and not worry about apprehension by any of the patrolling British cruisers. Thus, according to the American Consul in Rio de Janeiro in 1840, the United States was "a byword among nations" for its participation in illegal slave trading. Seven years later, the U.S. minister to Brazil admitted that 45,000 slaves had entered that country the preceding year, most of whom were "carried in vessels built by the United States and under the flag of our country."

Great Britain wanted the United States to police the African coast for slavers flying American colors, or, failing that, to patrol jointly with British cruisers to skirt the right-of-search issue, but a government aware of its small navy and still testy with its former mother country held out until 1842. In that year, in Article VIII of the Webster-Ashburton Treaty, the United States agreed to station a naval force of eighty guns along Africa's Atlantic coast for the avowed purpose of interdicting the slave trade. It was heady language—both nations agreed to "give such orders to the officers commanding their respective forces, as shall enable them most effectually to act in concert and cooperation"—that amounted to little. The American force turned out to be more inclined to protect and push legitimate American trade in African waters than to work with the Royal Navy to seek out illegal slavers. During its eighteen years of operation, the U.S. African squadron captured only 24 ships, liberating 4,945 slaves, with half the captures made during the last two years of the squadron, when a resourceful commander changed methods of operation. By contrast, the British African Squadron, which averaged 19 ships and 148 guns on patrol (versus 5 ships and 76 guns for the Americans), captured 595 ships and liberated 45,612 slaves from them. By the late 1850s, the combined squadrons may have been apprehending only 5 percent of all vessels making illegal attempts to carry slaves across the Atlantic.

Finding itself unable to halt illegal slave trading through the 1840s, Britain turned its attention to the remaining markets for captive Africans in the Americas, the biggest of which was Brazil. This country had long been the largest single importer of slaves, to produce sugar and mine gold. In the nineteenth century, as they were transforming the countryside to plant coffee farther south, primarily around São Paulo, Brazilian planters wanted even greater access to cheap labor. Soaring demand for coffee in the industrial north fueled a revival of enslaved labor in the south. Although avid consumers and shippers of slave-produced gold, coffee, cotton, and tobacco, in the 1840s the British sought to curb Brazil's appetite for enslaved African laborers. Diplomats applied pressure on Brazil's imperial government (the Anglophile emperors Pedro I and II were in fact opposed to slavery, but bowed to local elites with regard to the trade and the institution) while working to change public opinion in the nation. These efforts yielded few results given the long-established ties between merchants in Rio de Janeiro and those of Luanda, Angola, so beginning in 1849, the Royal Navy blockaded Brazilian ports and entered harbors to battle Brazilian ships and even soldiers. Though this was in violation of international law, the cause was widely deemed just, and no nation would come to Brazil's defense. Brazilians were thus forced, in September 1850, to halt slave importing. In one fell swoop, Britain cut the volume of the remaining trade by more than half.

This meant that by the early 1850s, only Spanish Cuba and Puerto Rico continued to import a significant number of Africans, and Cuba was no Brazil. One commonality, however, was the link between growing demand in the industrialized north for tropical products, in this case sugar. But in terms of

Matthew Perry
and the African Squadron

Matthew C. Perry, "Old Bruin" to those who served under the gruff commodore in the United States Navy, is best known for steaming into Tokyo Bay in 1853 and forcing Japan to open its doors to American trade and influence—one of many factors in a process that broadened an integrated Atlantic economic system into a global one. Less well known is his twenty-month service, in 1843–45, as the first commander of the U.S. African Squadron, sent to patrol Africa's Atlantic coastline for illegal slavers. As later on Asian shores, Perry's over-riding interest in Africa was in fostering American trade. He was quick to shoot up African villages when American merchants complained of ill treatment. On one occasion, he sent a vessel up an African river to protect Portuguese traders under attack from Africans, because the threatened merchants owed $40,000 to Americans. This venture, in 1844, cost sixteen sailors their lives

to malaria and brought such illness to the remaining crew that the vessel was never again effective to the squadron's larger mission. Yet, through all of this, Perry was blind to illegal American slaving in African waters (writing to the Secretary of the Navy, "I cannot hear of any American vessels being engaged in the transportation of slaves; nor do I believe there has been one so engaged for several years prior to 1841") and unwilling to establish procedures for patrol that would open the eyes of his officers. Under Perry's command, the squadron apprehended only one slave vessel. More serious for the long run, subsequent commanders adopted Perry's patrolling policies. Not until these changed, in the last two years of its existence in the late 1850s, was the U.S. African Squadron an effective force for combating the illegal slave trade conducted in American vessels.

U.S. ship patrolling Basua Harbor, Liberia. Watercolor by Robert K. Griffin, ca. 1856. Image courtesy Library of Congress, LC-USZC4-2570.

diplomacy, whereas Brazil had been openly defiant of Britain's (and much of the rest of the Atlantic world's) will to abolish the slave trade, and thus became vulnerable to British intervention, Spain played a double game, promising to stop the slave trade but taking no action against it. And the British were more reluctant to intervene in Cuba for another reason: fear of antagonizing southern planters in the United States, who supplied the empire with cotton and kept a hopeful eye on Cuba as a place for American annexation. Once the Civil War broke out in the United States, removing Southern voices from consideration and putting the U.S. government in a position of needing to speak against slavery to keep Britain from supporting the slave-holding Confederacy, the Lincoln administration agreed to give the Royal Navy the right to search American vessels and to cooperate in the struggle against the slave trade. In this circumstance, slavers heading for Cuba stood little chance. Realizing this, Spain passed in 1866 an effective Anti-Slave Trade Act, leaving the traffic with no open ports in the Americas. What is said to be the last ship crossing the Atlantic with slaves from Africa landed its cargo secretly in Cuba in 1867. After more than four centuries, the forced transportation across the ocean of nearly 12 million captives, the Atlantic slave trade, had finally ended.

When considering the full set of tragedies associated with the Atlantic slave trade, one need realize that its volume remained high following the 1807 laws. Nearly 2.5 million slaves were carried across the Atlantic and sold in the Americas *after* 1808, a sum amounting to about one-quarter of all the Africans uprooted and sold across the span of four centuries. And the slaves brought to the Americas in the nineteenth century were critical to the expansion of sugar production on selected Caribbean islands, Cuba in particular, and coffee production in central and southern Brazil. When the traffic in African slaves did finally stop, planters turned to Europe and Asia in search of indentured laborers. In the British case, this was something like a return to the beginning.

The End of Slavery in Europe and the Americas

While the transatlantic trade in enslaved Africans declined in the 1850s, slavery itself lingered in the United States, Brazil, and Cuba, as well as in much of Africa. Notably, by this time slavery had been abolished virtually throughout independent Spanish America, a region that some regarded as backward, uneducated, and politically illiberal. Mexico and Chile were pioneers, ending slavery soon after independence; only those countries with significant plantations and mines—Colombia, Venezuela, Peru—hesitated. By the mid-nineteenth century, the number of persons living on one of the continents bordering the Atlantic who were thoroughly opposed to human bondage was growing steadily. National and international abolition movements added supporters and marshaled forces for the final push to eradicate slavery from North and South America. In Africa, where slavery was more culturally varied and less closely linked to Atlantic capitalism, the issue would wait.

Through this protracted period of antislavery activity, free (white and black) and enslaved abolitionists shaped slavery's end. Events in the British Empire between 1816 and 1831 show a conjunction of legal and violent activities. In the wake of abolition of the transatlantic trade, British antislavery activists turned to improve the conditions of slaves. Men and women lobbied Parliament to pass laws that offered slaves legal protections and some rights, laws that island planters commonly refused to enforce. Enslaved workers added their own pressure in the face of planters' recalcitrance: three rebellions in British colonies prodded abolitionists to push harder in London and forced planters, in spite of their repeated avowals of the system's humanity, to confront anew the brutality required to maintain slavery.

The wave of uprisings that gave the lie to planters' claims also prodded abolitionists toward an immediate solution to the problem of slavery. Slaves were aware of abolitionists' activity: on Barbados, slave Nancy Grigg read newspapers and passed along word of Wilberforce and others. Thus, slavery's immediate hardship and the broader milieu of transatlantic abolitionist activity established the context for resistance. In 1816, Barbados slaves rose in a short-lived rebellion. Although led by an African, most of the rebels were Barbadians, as was 92 percent of the enslaved population. The rebels destroyed considerable property; the complacent planters were shocked.

In succession came uprisings in British Demerara in 1823 and Jamaica in 1831, both instigated by the plantation's slave elite. (The Demerara revolt began on the plantation of John Gladstone, father of the future prime minister of Britain.) Enslaved rebels also plotted for freedom in Spanish Puerto Rico in 1812 and Cuba in 1825—some of those involved had been sold away from Charleston following Denmark Vesey's conspiracy—and again in 1844. It was clear to imperial administrators and planters that sustaining slavery required a cost that neither constituency was willing to pay. It was also clear that slaves were participants in their own emancipation, even where it was accomplished by law, not force. Although students today assume that the term *abolitionist* denotes wealthy white evangelicals, it was enslaved rebels who typically forced the hand of western governments. Had slaves in Demerara and Jamaica not made the cost of running a slave society in the Caribbean far too high, white reformers in Britain could never have made headway against politically entrenched sugar lobbyists.

The situation in the United States differed from that in Britain and France in one critical aspect. Caribbean investors rarely resided for long, if at all, on the sugar plantations that made them rich, whereas North American masters were rarely absentee landlords. Planters like Andrew Jackson spent much of the year on their estates; their unwaged workers were not figures in a ledger book but humans whose names they knew. As they struggled to articulate a paternalistic justification for their ownership of humans, masters in South Carolina or Mississippi developed the sort of personal stake in the system generally lacking in European absentee investors. As a result, antislavery activism in the United States was largely an internal matter, though abolitionists received assistance from like-minded men and women in England and France after the 1820s, while slave owners knew they had tacit support from New England and foreign industrialists who liked the quality and price of the cotton they supplied. Slavery was by no means dying out when the nation achieved independence, but it surged with the rising demand for raw cotton in British industries; the U.S. acquisition of new, semitropical land (largely through treaties with Spain or France and the subsequent killing or removing of its native population) ideal for growing cotton, mainly in states bordering the Gulf of Mexico; the rapid natural increase of the nation's existing slave population and movement of slaves from the old plantation regions of the Upper South to the newer sites in the Lower South; and the willingness of politicians in free states to accept slavery as the price for national unity. The quandary of many was in how to deal with a social evil while continuing to respect the rights of private property, so carefully protected by the United States Constitution. The more profitable slavery became, the more property rights trumped social evils, the more slavery expanded, and the more vigorous became the racist justifications for holding men and women of African descent in bondage. The Atlantic economy seemed more than ever to be stuck with slavery, even as blacks and whites joined as never before to call for its abolition.

In its earliest moments, organized antislavery in the United States took a gradualist, even racist form. As northern states passed legislation for gradual emancipation, many black northerners and white elites from the border South, assuming that former slaves could never live in harmony beside their ex-masters, began to consider plans for the repatriation of African Americans to the land of their ancestors. Although Jefferson had urged colonization in his 1785 *Notes on the State of Virginia*, insisting that "deep rooted prejudices entertained by whites," and "then thousand recollections, by the blacks, of the injuries they have sustained" rendered peaceful coexistence impossible, it was Paul Cuffe, a Massachusetts-born, free-black entrepreneur, who gave the idea new life around the time of the War of 1812. Cuffe wanted to "uplift" indigenous Africans by bringing moral, religious, and propertied African Americans to live among them, and he took fifty-eight American blacks to settle in Sierra Leone after the war ended.

Before Cuffe could follow with more, wealthy whites in Virginia revived the push for the colonization of free blacks. Fearing that blacks not in slavery would form a permanent "banditti," an "idle, and vicious population, who sally forth from their coverts [to] plunder the rich proprietors in the valleys," Charles Fenton Mercer argued in the Virginia legislature for African colonization in 1816. Before the year was out, Mercer and Presbyterian clergyman Robert Finley marshaled support in the United States Congress for an American Society for Colonizing the Free People of Color. Finley's argument was blunt: "We would be cleared of them." The society was headed by Supreme Court Justice Bushrod Washington and listed as members Henry Clay, Francis Scott Key, and John Marshall. With such political clout behind the movement, President James Monroe authorized the United States Navy to select and procure a site for colonization. Monrovia, on Cape Mesurado, was so designated, and under sponsorship of the American Colonization Society, free African Americans began arriving. By 1847, more than 10,000 such persons had taken up residence. In that year Monrovia became the capital of a new, independent Republic of Liberia.

Although some former slaves from the southern states, despairing that the United States would ever recognize their political rights, relocated to Liberia, blacks in Philadelphia and Boston resolutely resisted both colonization and gradualism. In the North, many activists adopted the mass-action propaganda tactics of European antislavery societies. From Massachusetts, David Walker published an *Appeal to the Colored Citizens of the World* (1829), declaring African Americans "the most wretched, degraded and abject set of beings that ever lived since the world began." Although born free in North Carolina, Walker likely resided in Charleston during the Vesey conspiracy, and he urged fellow blacks to "Kill or be killed" unless slavery was ended immediately. Two years later, Virginia slave Nathaniel Turner did just that, leading an insurrection that took the lives of sixty whites—and eventually his own, two dozen accomplices, and one hundred or more other slaves and free blacks—and frightened not only slave owners but most whites living in America's slave societies. The actions of Harriet Tubman in helping spirit slaves to freedom in Canada and the writings of black abolitionist Frederick Douglass added heroism and poignancy to the cause. Soon, the nation's powerful slave interests, feeling under siege, withdrew psychologically and turned the American South into what the historian Stephen B. Oates describes as "a closed, martial society, determined to preserve and perpetuate its slave-based civilization come what may." In hindsight it is possible to see that once this occurred, nothing short of war was likely to dislodge the southerners from their ideology and their grasp of what had become a "peculiar institution."

To the extent that Douglass and Tubman were former slaves, while other black abolitionists, like Walker, had lived in the Carolinas, African American activists were the most likely to countenance violence as a legitimate means to end unfree labor. At a time when many white evangelicals in the northern states hoped to persuade slaveholders of the error in their ways and literally prayed for a more Godly republic, black speakers swore that enslaved Americans enjoyed a moral right to resist in any way possible. Douglass, who as a slave had wrestled a celebrated "slave breaker" into subservience, had little use for the genteel racism of his more cautious allies. "We want Nat Turner—not speeches," he shouted on one occasion, "Denmark Vesey—not resolutions." Nor were black activists unaware that northern whites shared many of the cultural biases of their planter enemies. After all, slavery lingered on in New York State until 1827, and in New Jersey until 1865.

It was not the existence of slavery so much as efforts to extend it into new territories, however, that led to the United States Civil War that brought slavery to judgment. The United States was continually acquiring new territory as part of its self-proclaimed "Manifest Destiny" to absorb lands stretching to the Pacific Ocean. In a nation almost equally divided between states where slavery could exist and states where it could not—and a government that reflected this sectional dispute, with neither side wanting to become subordinate to the other—the question of slavery's status in territories soon to become states loomed large. Political compromises had settled the matter in 1820 and 1850, but after that, as tensions over slavery rose to a new pitch, parties took up arms and in one territory far removed from Atlantic shores, Kansas, murdered one another over the issue. Now slave owners and their supporters threatened to pull their states out of the Union under certain circumstances, one of which being the election as president of Abraham Lincoln, whose new Republican Party had roots in antislavery political efforts of the 1840s. Although Lincoln promised not to move against slavery where it already existed legally, his descriptions of unfree labor as evil and immoral, together with his determination to restrict slavery from the western territories were enough for southern elites, so his election in 1860 triggered the secession of seven (and eventually eleven) southern states to form the Confederate States of America, where slavery remained. Upon taking office in 1861, Lincoln declared secession illegal and vowed to enforce federal law in the seceded states. When troops in South Carolina fired on a federal fort in Charleston's harbor, Lincoln called for volunteers "to bring the [south] into a state of submission," and the American Civil War had begun.

What began as a war to bring the southern states back into the Union turned, after two years of intense fighting, into a war that would end slavery in the United States. A catalyst for this change was African Americans' desire for freedom. Soon after the start of the conflict, and continuing through its duration, whenever U.S. armies approached, slaves fled to sanctuary and freedom behind the lines of the blue-suited military forces. Deciding how legally to deal with these fugitives brought the United States Congress initially to declare them as "contraband of war," and thus usable for the war effort, and then as virtually free. Meanwhile, as death tolls mounted and pressures grew on the president to rally Union sentiment and give the war greater cause, Lincoln issued an Emancipation Proclamation, effective January 1, 1863. Though some incorrectly argue that this decree technically freed no one at the time, it transformed the war into one to rid the nation of slavery. The proclamation also allowed for the enlistment into the U.S. Army of African American soldiers, and by the war's end, nearly 200,000 had done so. Late in 1863, more than a year before the South finally surrendered, Lincoln commemorated the fallen in an address at the Gettysburg, Pennsylvania, battlefield with a vow "that this nation under God shall have a new birth of freedom." By then, everyone hearing or reading his words knew to what group that freedom was to extend. As the war neared completion, early in 1865, Congress amended the Constitution, stipulating that "Neither slavery nor involuntary servitude . . . shall exist within the United States, or any place subject to their jurisdiction." The Civil War had cost 618,000 lives, but the institution that had existed on the North American mainland for more than a quarter of a millennium was no more.

Even as the brutal conflict raged in the United States, in the Spanish colonies of Cuba and Puerto Rico more than half a million slaves labored daily to produce sugar for northern Atlantic consumers. The British, long makers of the loudest arguments against slavery and the slave trade, had been the instigators of a slave-based economy on these islands a century earlier, importing thousands of Africans after the Seven Years' War. The change in attitude was as difficult for Cuban and Puerto Rican planters to accept as it was to those of Brazil or the U.S. South. Like their British counterparts in Jamaica and elsewhere, back at the turn of the nineteenth century Spanish entrepreneurs on these islands took advantage of the destruction that revolutionary warfare brought to sugar production on Saint Domingue and began importing increasing numbers of African slaves. With more than 160,000 enslaved Africans imported in the 1810s alone, and another 200,000 over the following four decades, Cuba moved steadily toward becoming the world's major producer of sugar. British capital and machinery, including steam-driven cane presses, railroads, and ships, advanced the project. Spain had outlawed slavery in 1811 and the slave trade in 1820, both products of the liberal Cortes that gained power in the Napoleonic era, but Cuban and Puerto Rican landowners defied both laws, and Spain's conservative monarchs showed neither inclination nor ability to enforce them. As in the case of Brazil, the satisfaction of powerful planters and the wealth their economic growth provided shaped royal policy with regard to slavery, and for a time they were determined for unfree labor to continue.

Resentment and protest grew along the way, however, and they took a toll. On both islands, abolition efforts became enmeshed with a fight against Spanish rule. Rebellion was more easily suppressed in Puerto Rico, but a long-active abolition movement there, aided by that in Spain, finally succeeded: an 1873 royal edict ended slavery in Puerto Rico. Cuba held out longer, although gradual steps toward abolition began after the end of the slave trade in 1867. The Ten Years' War, after 1868, united Cuba's poor farmers with wealthy planters on the eastern part of the island, and their struggle against the Spanish army united Cubans across lines of race and class. Slaves had always fought to end their bondage, but a broader dissatisfaction with slavery surfaced after the war—in which more than 200,000 Spanish soldiers and 50,000 Cubans had lost their lives—ended in a protracted truce in 1878. Even some wealthy Cuban planters switched sides once they realized they could hire inexpensive day laborers at times of peak demand. The Spanish government also sought to fill the labor void with indentured Chinese immigrants as well as Maya Indians from the neighboring Yucatan Peninsula of Mexico. Thus, Spain moved to abolish Cuban slavery, first in 1870 with a law guaranteeing freedom to those born after that year, and then in 1880 with provision for an eight-year "apprenticeship," a euphemism first used by the British in the Caribbean for continued enslavement of able-bodied youths in their prime productive years. A royal decree abolishing slavery once and for all in Cuba came only in 1886, by which time only 30,000 men, women, and children remained in bondage on the island.

In all the Western Hemisphere, only Brazil clung to slavery. This was the one place where wars of independence played no major role in slave liberation. Indeed, slave conspiracies in Brazil were more common in the era of Dom Pedro I than in the 1880s. Yet with the disruption of the Atlantic slave trade after 1807, Brazil's enslaved population began declining—it was at a rate of 1 to 2 percent per year by midcentury—and the number of unfree laborers was insufficient to operate the nation's farms, ranches, and plantations. Unlike the United States, this was a tropical environment in which slave health and reproductive needs were barely considered. Playing on the natural decline of the slave population once cut off from Africa, Brazil's abolitionists, headed by the lawyer Joaquim Nabuco, had made emancipation the central issue of the country's politics by the late 1860s. In response, the imperial government ordered emancipation of children of slaves (with "apprenticeships" to age twenty-one) in 1871 and elderly slaves in 1885. But slavery would not die quietly until replacement labor was found. Like their counterparts in Cuba, some Brazilian planters were slowly coming to realize that paying wage workers would cost less than what they spent on the upkeep of slaves. Aiding this realization was rapid population growth in parts of Europe and Asia, as well as lowered costs and improved security of steamship transport for immigrants. Amid the varying pressures and options, in May

1888, Princess Regent Isabel, the daughter of Brazil's absent emperor, signed the so-called Golden Law, emancipating the remaining half million slaves in the country. With slavery died the Brazilian Empire, replaced in 1889 with a democratic republic.

More than a century after the demise of slavery in Europe and the Americas, historians continue to disagree as to the motives behind abolition. Was there a deep moral and religious foundation to the endeavor that spanned generations, or was the critical issue that slavery was becoming less necessary in a world dominated by the free market (in labor as well as exchange of goods) and industrial enterprise? Or was it the slaves themselves who played the key but least acknowledged role by consistently exposing slavery's evils, proving by the very fact of their survival, creation of family and community, maintenance of dignity in the face of hatred and discrimination, and sometimes violent resistance the insuppressible nature of the human spirit and hence the fundamental injustice of the institution? "Regardless of the final importance of contending interests," the historian David Brion Davis points out, "it was the inherent contradiction of chattel slavery—the impossible effort to bestialize human beings—that provided substance for a revolution in moral perception, a recognition that slaves could become masters or masters slaves, and that we are therefore not required to resign ourselves to the world that has always been."

Abolition and Africa

On three of the continents bordering the Atlantic, the substance was sufficient for the revolution in moral perception to rid societies of human slavery, but on the fourth, Africa, the story was different. In the original homeland of all those millions of American slaves, any potential for progress on social fronts that had been evident early in the nineteenth century was blunted and then seemingly reversed as the century wore on—not that no one expressed sympathy for those enslaved in Africa. When Parliament ended slavery in the British Empire, abolitionists continued meeting so they could marshal evidence for a Parliamentary Select Committee on Aborigines, and in 1839 they formed a separate Aborigines Protection Committee to bring the exploitation and unfortunate circumstances of Britain's subject peoples before a caring populace. But as the century drew to an end, and especially following the last gasps of the slave trade, the focus of the populace shifted to its own place in a rapidly industrializing world and less on the welfare of foreign others, particularly those of a darker hue.

While growing numbers of Europeans and Americas were condemning the slave trade and slavery, even noting the pain the trade was inflicting on Africans, they made scant reference to slavery in Africa, partly because they knew little about the people living there. One of the ironies of abolition is that the effort to bring about the end of the slave trade led Europeans and Americans to garner *greater* knowledge of, and have more influence on, African societies, rather than less. And the more they learned about Africa, the more they realized that slavery was not a problem unique to American plantation agriculture. Ending slavery in Africa, where foreign observers supposed it had been part of the social makeup since time began, would be difficult, but Europeans would see that effort as a part of their larger mission to bring "civilization" to African people. As the Atlantic slave trade was winding down, the sense, especially among Europe's evangelical Christians, that Africa was a continent in need of God and civilization was filling the void left by diminishing concern over the slave trade.

Humanitarians had pressed for abolition at a time when England was industrializing and its government's strongest supporters had markets and raw materials on their minds. The settlement of Bathurst after 1816 soon ended Atlantic-directed slave trading in the Gambia River and stimulated legitimate trade there. At other places along Africa's Atlantic coast, control spread more slowly. In 1840, Britain landed a force near Cape Mount, 400 miles south of the Gambia, to liberate captives held in pens and awaiting sale. Offers of annual payments, made with gunboats sitting offshore, prompted African sovereigns of coastal entities to sign treaties permitting British intervention to stop slave trading. Along the eastern section of the Gold Coast in the 1850s, Britain began acquiring the forts of other European nations and imposing customs duties to pay the costs of occupation and patrolling, and in 1851 it supported a claimant to power in Lagos, on the Slave Coast, on his promise to end the slave trade—an action that led to Britain's proclaiming of Lagos as a colony ten years later. Not to be outdone, France appointed Louis Faidherbe as governor of Senegal in 1854, and he began ten years of conquest along the lower Senegal River valley.

But this gradual expansion of European control at individual sites along Atlantic West Africa—though stimulating European interest later in the century—had less immediate effects on West African cultural and intellectual history than what was occurring at a single spot on the Upper-Guinea Coast: Freetown, Sierra Leone. This British colony was an outgrowth of Atlantic slaving as well as the American Revolution, and the abolition and evangelical Christian movements helped shape its culture.

As with abolition generally, British leaders involved with Sierra Leone kept one eye on helping those in need and the other on the extension of capitalist enterprise. (Sierra Leone involved "humanitarianism plus six per cent," noted one commentator.) By the time that the British government took over the struggling colony in January 1808, the experiment was no longer merely a dumping ground for London paupers and black American Loyalists. Given its new determination to outlaw Atlantic slave trading, Britain needed a place to serve as a base for its operations against the illegal traffic, and Sierra Leone became that place. It would also play the role of principal dumping ground for unwanted refugees. Under the terms of the 1807 act abolishing the slave trade, Britain set up at Freetown a vice-admiralty court to try slavers and dispose of ships and cargo. In this fashion, Sierra Leone became the point of liberation of men, women, and children from several thousand miles of West Africa's Atlantic coastline, whom the patrols "recaptured" from illegal slavers in the transatlantic crossing. Between 1808 and 1864, more than 50,000 "Liberated Africans" were released from captured vessels, and these persons took up residence around Freetown.

The earliest of the recaptives—and there were more than 6,000 in the first decade of anti–slave-trade patrols—were fortunate to have been released from slavery, but less so in terms of living circumstances. The historian Lamin Sanneh writes that the early recaptives were "crowded into ramshackle mountain districts of the colony, unexpected, untaught, unchurched, and unled." Once this misery gained the crown's attention, however, it began encouraging missionaries to set up shop in Sierra Leone with the goal of helping meet the recaptives' immediate needs and then of preparing them for better lives through education and instruction in Christianity. This was occurring at the start of a great age of evangelical Christianity in Anglo America and parts of northern Europe, and English-speaking missionaries were eager to lead the movement in Africa. The Church of England's Church Missionary Society, formed in London in 1799 "to endeavor to propagate the knowledge of the Gospel among the heathen," sent missionaries to Sierra Leone as early as 1804 and took on the betterment of all settlers there as Liberated Africans began pouring in. Methodist missionaries soon followed. The missions constructed schools for basic instruction in the English language and survival skills for the new environment. In 1827, the Church Missionary Society started Fourah Bay College to train Africans as catechists, clergymen, and teachers.

Initially, the Nova Scotians and maroons, familiar with English customs and norms, held contempt for the Liberated Africans, who soon outnumbered the earlier settlers and their descendants by three or four to one. In time, however, education, religion, and common circumstances, which included being different from a much larger indigenous population, brought the immigrants together. By midcentury, in and around Freetown, lived an identifiable, educated, Christian population that took on an identity as "Creoles," their language Krio, an English-based patois. This group, especially those among it known as "Aku," originally from Yorubaland in Nigeria, who still possessed cultural knowledge of their homeland, would be well placed to begin spreading European habits and Christianity in other regions of coastal West Africa in the last half of the nineteenth century.

Proselytize they did. Aligned with Europe's missionary movement, the Sierra Leoneans saw it as their duty to venture forth in an effort to end slavery among indigenous Africans. By the 1840s, most Protestant denominations had mission stations along the Gold and Slave Coasts, all the way to eastern Nigeria, and Roman Catholics were joining the effort. A Niger expedition in 1841, instigated by recaptive Yoruba in Sierra Leone and joined by the Church Missionary Society and the British government, was intended to bring Christianity to the region and use it as a tool to end slave trading and slavery. One could regard this—occurring just as twenty-seven-year-old Dr. David Livingstone was arriving in South Africa to work on behalf of the London Missionary Society—as the beginning of a long effort by Africans familiar with European customs, missionaries, and European humanitarians to bring pressure on their governments to end slavery in Africa. By the 1880s, a full century after Captain Littleton testified about the humane treatment captives received on the middle passage to the Americas, most people living in Europe and the Americas believed slavery to be immoral and intolerable. In Africa, where their national governments were scrambling to take over the 90 percent of the continent not already in their hands, Europeans used as a principal justification for their land grabbing a desire to wipe out all lingering manifestations of the evil institution.

Two ironies remained. One is that in many situations, Africa's European conquerors found slavery to be even more prevalent, and more important to local economies, than they had known. "[Slaves] are our hands and feet," one African family head confessed to a new British administrator, prompting the officer to report that "proclaiming freedom would paralyze all trade and cultivation." Since trade and cultivation were to bring money to Africans, which colonial officials could in turn tax to pay the costs of administration, as well as to help provide raw materials for Europe's hungry industries, abolition of slavery in Africa could bring bad news on several levels.

The other irony is that while Africa's European conquerors were products of a long effort to abolish the slave trade and end human bondage, they also were products of a society that over several centuries had altered its own economic foundation. Commercial capitalism had been the economic basis of eighteenth-century European societies; industrial capitalism was their economic engine by the end of the nineteenth century. This new economic circumstance had brought rapid social and material change, to the point that European masters of industrial production believed their societies more "advanced" and more "civilized" than those of people living in nonindustrial lands. In the minds of many Europeans and Americans who were championing the new body of knowledge they called "social science," the obvious reason behind this difference, which they claimed to have established through careful inquiry and observation, was race. In fact, when the owners of these minds applied Charles Darwin's revolutionary ideas about natural selection and survival of the fittest to human society (as Darwin never intended), they could argue that the world's darker people were less well equipped to survive than whites. Thus, in some popular thinking of the time, among such "backward and brutish" folk one might need to tolerate such a backward and brutish institution as slavery, at least until the societies could be uplifted through proper European tutelage. In this economic and intellectual milieu of Africa's colonizers, although abolished around the rest of the Atlantic world, slavery would continue in Africa into the early decades of the twentieth century.

Labor in the Post-Emancipation Period

In most places where slaves were emancipated, planters and other employers created a buffer system called "apprenticeship." Apprenticeship bound ex-slaves to masters for finite periods, usually the most productive years of the ex-slaves' lives, under state supervision. This was a legal extension of slavery meant to subsidize the planter class until the transition to some other form of labor was effected. The system, which had nothing to do with imparting useful skills that would aid former slaves in freedom, lasted five years in the British colonies, ten years with the Dutch. Ex-slaves saw the system for what it was and resisted it. When apprenticeship periods ended by law, planters and employers faced a precipitous decline in their labor supply because, once liberated, agricultural workers rejected plantation agriculture. From Jamaica to South Carolina, former slaves wished, as one visitor to Cuba put it, to "cultivate small patches of ground for themselves," tendencies one conservative Cuban newspaper derided as "vicious, vagrant habits."

The free or partially free labor that gradual emancipation produced caused problems for most slave-based societies. In the British Caribbean, worker unrest arose in the 1830s in the wake of emancipation. Freedpeople who remained on plantations found that planters' attitudes had changed but little; the same racism, resentment, physical coercion, and social ostracism were still in place. Perhaps expecting as much, many other freedpeople left the plantations immediately to establish themselves in the hills above the sugar fields and engage in subsistence agriculture. They created not only small subsistence farms but a new peasantry with an aversion to plantation labor. Sweet sugar carried bitter memories.

Similar patterns emerged following emancipation in Spanish America, although freedpeople's experiences varied by region and work regime. In western Colombia's gold mining district, freedmen were active in local and regional politics even before abolition in 1850, helping propel the Liberal Party to power. Other freedpeople retreated to the interior to mine gold through cooperative, extended family networks. Indigenous people, meanwhile, tended to favor the Conservative Party, since it guaranteed maintenance of colonial-style, communal landholdings. Similar splits between indigenous and African-descended populations emerged in other nations. Former slaves and their descendants in many Spanish American countries continued to work in mines, on plantations, and in cities and port facilities. Women often carried on in domestic service, much as in slavery, although some advanced socially through market activity. Some men found means to social and political advancement in the military, a trend dating to late colonial times. Throughout Spanish America, despite nationalist and liberationist rhetoric to the contrary, racism continued to limit opportunities for people of color to enter the upper social and political echelons. The black and mulatto populations of Bolivia, Ecuador, Chile, and Argentina remained entirely marginalized. Still, Spanish America was notable for its absence of segregationist legislation from the time of independence forward, and for its mixed-heritage presidents and other political leaders. Mexico was perhaps most open in this regard. People of color, including slaves, had always been guaranteed certain legal rights under Spanish law, and marriage and legitimate birth remained central to honor and respectability.

Freedom changed family and gender roles even more radically in the British colonies. With new legal protection of marriage and rights to their children—men and women, able now to implement family strategies apart from the perils of family separation, sexual assault, or death—reconfigured households. Women, who before emancipation in such places as Jamaica comprised the majority of field laborers, withdrew from agricultural work, preferring domestic employment. Children worked less, as parents sent them to new missionary schools. British missionaries and abolitionists who journeyed to the colonies encouraged these new gender roles, seeking in the utopian moment of emancipation a chance to begin the world anew. Ex-slaves, missionaries such as William Knibb believed, should not emulate their former masters, but should assimilate idealized white British middle-class mores. For men, this "black Victorian" sensibility meant Christianity, diligence, and independence; for women it involved a life within the domestic sphere. Former slaves sought their own variation on these goals: independence, distance from ex-masters, and freedom—finally—to order their households as they wished.

This universal rejection of plantation labor occurred as sugar planters faced new competition from an expanding world supply (the continued slave regimes of Cuba and Brazil taking up much of the slack as the British Caribbean declined). As prices dropped, prompting planters to reduce labor costs, they turned to new forms of coerced labor, drawing on imperial networks to resupply their cane fields with cheap workers and prodding governments to assist in confining ex-slaves to plantations. Governments moved quickly to price land out of the reach of poor farmers, which forced them into share-cropping and ensured their continued subordination to the planter class. West Indian planters recruited aggressively among European laborers and free blacks from the United States, of whom some one thousand migrated to Trinidad. But this supply was inadequate to meet the planters' needs, and by 1841 the sugar producing regions were in a state of labor crisis.

The French and British governments, the first imperial powers to abolish slavery, moved to redress the need for labor their imperial systems had created by drawing on their subject people from around the world. Empire was an essential part of new labor migrations, and nineteenth-century labor patterns point to the tenacity of imperial powers in the Atlantic. To be sure, Atlantic empires had endured pressures and losses in the late eighteenth and early nineteenth centuries. Spain, France, and Britain found their holdings greatly diminished by the end of the age of revolution and independence. But all three nonetheless retained global holdings: the losses and reshufflings in the wake of wars in 1763, 1783, and 1815, and in the independence movements in Spanish America, diminished these empires' Atlantic focus and highlighted their global character. If Britain lost thirteen colonies in mainland North America, it kept the British Caribbean, Guyana, Canada, Sierra Leone, and the Cape Colony, to name major holdings in the Atlantic, and it claimed dominion over much of India and new territories in the South Pacific. France lost Saint Domingue, but it retained Martinique, Guadeloupe, and French Guiana in the Caribbean, with enclaves in India and holdings in Africa (Algeria and Senegal) and the Pacific (Reunion). The imperial networks that encompassed these remote places facilitated reallocation of labor, one of the most important imperial resources.

And older transatlantic labor streams kept flowing: migrants continued to come out of Africa, for instance. Although the slave trade had officially ended, as indeed had slavery itself in places under British control, these workers resembled slaves in many ways, particularly in the mechanisms of their acquisition in Africa. Few of these people migrated voluntarily, but were obtained through violence, fraud, and purchase. The historian David Northrup has determined that less than 10 percent of some 60,000 indentured Africans in the western Atlantic between 1824 and 1867 were voluntary laborers. Some of these African laborers were "recaptives" whose sale to America had been interrupted by British antislavery patrols between 1810 and 1864. Few of these people were repatriated, and not all were taken to Freetown, Sierra Leone: a good number ended up transported to other British jurisdictions, especially Jamaica, Trinidad, and Guiana, where courts heard their cases. They often found themselves indentured in these new settings.

The British also recruited from Sierra Leone, offering promises to entice people to cultivate sugar in the West Indies. It was not easy to persuade Sierra Leoneans to try their fortune outside the colony, which itself offered opportunities to recaptives and migrants from the West Indies and North America. Many recognized the relative advantages of staying in Sierra Leone: "Their wants are so few," remarked the English resident Elizabeth Callender Melville, "that each man, if careful, can yearly raise upon his halfrood of allotted ground" enough food to sustain himself, with a surplus to sell. Recruiters found women even more reluctant than men to consider migration, and thus a law that required that one-third of all migrants be female could not be enforced. Extravagant claims accompanied the recruiting posters ambitious agents put up in Sierra Leone. One recruiter promised laborers their own house, rum, and a wage of $5 per day in Trinidad. One Guiana agent labeled Sierra Leone "not a state in which you can repose confidence for a continuation of emigration." Only 8,000 Sierra Leoneans found such offers enticing, and only 2,000 of them reached Jamaica. In the pattern of labor migration at the time, they envisioned their migration as temporary, a return to the homeland imminent.

The French recruited Africans, too, beginning in 1854 for French Guiana, followed by Martinique and Guadeloupe in 1857. The experiments were brief—the last worker reached Martinique in 1862—and brought only 20,000 Africans, mainly from Senegal, Lagos, Luanda, and Loango, to the French Caribbean. These efforts were simultaneous with French attempts to secure laborers for the island of Reunion in the Indian Ocean, and tapped into the same sources. In terms of mechanisms of purchase and capture, the lot of the laborers closely resembled that of slaves. Contract workers were actually slaves purchased or redeemed after they had allegedly consented to being indentured. The system outraged the British, who accused the French of promoting the slave trade in Africa through their policy of slave redemption. In 1858, one British observer described African traders dragging slaves "in twos and threes . . . secured by ropes to the forked end of a wooden pole encircling their necks, their hands strongly bound," prodded by a shepherd with a whip. But one chief at Old Calabar near the mouth of the Niger River remarked on an 1850 British redemption scheme, "It be all same as old slave-trade."

The most truly voluntary African laborers who went to French colonies were the Kru of coastal Liberia, who had a long tradition of involvement with European trade and traders in Africa, especially as crewmen on European vessels. In the economic stagnation that accompanied the slave trade's demise, many Kru were casting about for new opportunities. In the 1840s and 1850s, Kru people migrated agreeably when guaranteed a fixed term of labor and repatriation; when repatriation did not happen, the supply of labor quickly dried up. Once in French and British Guiana, the Kru were assertive in protecting their rights and contracts.

But for all of these efforts, African labor after the abolition of slavery posed problems: the number of migrants was inadequate, and humanitarian concerns about their acquisition made officials uncomfortable. In this milieu, two new regions emerged as sources for Atlantic labor, India and East Asia. The historian Walton Look Lai characterizes Chinese migration to the Americas as a broadening of existing patterns, and the Indian migration as an overflow.

By 1815, the British Empire claimed 40 million South Asian subjects, the vast majority of them poor. Many already migrated within a regional labor market, so imperial officials redirected some of that migration to benefit sugar planters elsewhere. As in the age of revolution, ideology and action contradicted one another through the period of emancipation. The imperial government would have been unable to implement a system of indenture without the approval of British abolitionists. In their effort to ensure the demise of slavery, many abolitionists, who were advocates of free (wage) labor in addition to their humanitarian, religious, and philosophical objections to slavery, found themselves supporting schemes for contract labor, ensuring the continuation of dependent, nonwage labor, albeit not enslaved. They justified the continued practice of unfree labor with assurances (to themselves) of benefits to these laborers and to India once the contract workers returned home. Aggressive recruitment by European agents attracted a wide range of people: urban, rural, Muslim, Hindu, Sikh, male, female, skilled and unskilled. The only thing most South Asian immigrants to the Caribbean plantations had in common was relative youth. As ever, migration decisions were embedded in personal circumstances and broader economic and political developments. Some women fled bad marriages; some men left behind failed revolutionary schemes. It was no accident that South Asian migration peaked in 1858, a year after the eruption of the so-called Sepoy (Indian) Mutiny against the British overlords.

Poor young men from British India traveled as indentured servants to other places within the empire, including South Africa, Jamaica, Trinidad, Tobago, and Guyana. They journeyed with formal contracts, and often enjoyed living conditions that were an improvement on those experienced by indentured laborers in previous centuries. They had access to modest medical care, and their employers covered room and board. Field laborers earned wages tied not to the number of hours worked, but to the completion of the task. On Jamaica, indentured South Asians were offered a nine-hour day and their own garden plot. Despite these measures, few of these migrants adapted well to the harsh demands of sugar production, and Hindus, because of their religious beliefs, could not be forced to work as cattle drivers. As the slaves had, many South Asians fell sick amid the rigors of their labor in a new disease environment. After their contracts expired, some renewed for another term simply to win a promise of passage home upon completion. Many others did not renew, however, and instead settled in the Americas, contributing to the cultural heterogeneity of tropical life. In all, half a million South Asians traveled to other, mostly Caribbean, colonies.

Imperial networks facilitated these interoceanic migrations, but migrants crossed imperial borders as well: almost 35,000 Indians worked in Dutch Suriname, and by 1850, 70,000 Indians labored in French colonies. Some Indians came from French enclaves, but the supply proved inadequate. So the French pressed for access to others, pointing out that if the British wished them to stop "redeeming" slaves in Africa for American labor, they needed to help find an alternate source. In 1860 and 1861, the French secured such recruiting privileges in India, in return for complying with the same recruiting laws that guided British agents, and in 1862, the French stopped entrapping workers in Africa.

Contract workers also traveled to the Atlantic from East Asia. Like their Indian counterparts, these East Asian (primarily Chinese) laborers were already accustomed to regional labor migration. Chinese workers went to some of the same places as Indians, but their numbers were relatively few, only 27,000 making their way to the Caribbean. Chinese migration to the Caribbean ended almost completely in the 1860s, largely because the cost of transporting South Asians to British American plantations was far cheaper. In contrast, 290,000 Chinese workers went to non-British plantation societies, including Cuba, Peru, and Hawaii. A few East Asian migrants trickled to Brazil and the U.S. South, but neither place was supportive of Chinese migration. In the latter locale, once slavery ended in 1865 white planters and merchants quickly took advantage of the former slaves' lack of resources to institute a system of sharecropping and debt peonage that would keep the African American laboring population poor, dependent, and tied to the land long into the next century. In Peru until the 1880s, laborers from China comprised the majority of the plantation, railroad, and in some places mining work force. Of all Chinese immigrants working in the Americas in this period, most were not indentured; however, those who went to the Atlantic world of the plantations disproportionately were.

The 125,000 indentured Chinese sent to Cuba between 1847 and 1874 did not—at least in theory—replace slaves: they traveled to an island where slavery was still legal during a time of economic boom and worked alongside slaves. (Of course, the outlawing of the slave trade was an obvious impetus for their recruitment). Also in contrast to prevailing nineteenth-century patterns of labor recruitment and supply, transport and contracting in this case were left to private individuals, with minimal government involvement. In these respects, the Cuban example was reminiscent of indentured migration in the seventeenth and eighteenth centuries, when European indentured labor was a private enterprise and in places servants worked alongside slaves. Slavery and indenture were thus not stages in some evolutionary or progressive Atlantic scheme, but adaptations to a set of political, demographic, and economic conditions.

How free were former slaves and contract laborers in the post-emancipation Atlantic world? Although emancipation entailed freedom from sale and forced settlement, in many places government policies, particularly those that priced land out of their reach, trapped ex-slaves in a continued dependence on employers, often their former masters. Indentured laborers served finite periods after which they, too, secured a kind of freedom, but during their indenture were subject to the whim of masters and authorities as to whether or not provisions of their contracts would be upheld. The movements and actions of all such "free" people were closely monitored, and punishment for infractions harsh.

In sum, the end of the nineteenth century marked the end of slavery in the western Atlantic, but it did not simultaneously usher in an era of freedom for all. Even those protected by contracts confronted lingering inequities. In the French Caribbean, for example, Africans served six-year terms, Indians five. Both served the same contract year of 312 workdays, but wages differed: Indian men received more than African men, and both were paid more than Indian women. Indians were guaranteed free repatriation after 1861, but Africans had to pay their way home. Indians returned home in higher proportions than did Africans, in part because of the paucity of Indian women in the colonies.

Rules governing the treatment of indentured laborers resembled slavery in some places. Cuban laws from 1849 permitted corporal punishment of Chinese servants, and laborers could be placed in irons and stocks for as long as two months for refusing to work and four months for running away the first time; repeat offenses secured a longer term. An 1873 government inquiry revealed conditions for Cuba's Chinese laborers that were akin to slavery. Slave catchers chased down indentured servants who fled from the brutality on sugar plantations. Shrewdly assessing the best prospect of freedom, these servants also behaved like slaves during the first War of Independence: they fought for the Cuban rebels in exchanges for promises of freedom. Laws governing treatment of laborers in British dominions were more humane, but depended on government oversight and enforcement. Workers complained about being cheated out of their wages, and laws confining them to a two-mile radius of the workplace hindered their free movement. This was not slavery, but it was not freedom, either, and in places it created new, semi-privileged groups in already racially divided societies. Whether in the age of emancipation or the era of first contact, slavery and freedom in the Atlantic world were simply two extreme points on a broad spectrum, and many people fell somewhere in the middle. Yet everywhere, people of African descent faced the most substantial hurdles in gaining status, economic opportunity, and enfranchisement.

Reconfiguring the Global Process

The new migration patterns of the nineteenth century illustrate the extent to which the Atlantic world was becoming more emphatically a part of the greater global system. As always, the Atlantic was but a slice—for a long time a distinct one, as we have argued here—of a much larger pie. The so-called Columbian exchange discussed in earlier chapters illustrated this balance between regional and global networks from the first return trips across the Atlantic Ocean. The diseases that mariners and invaders introduced to the

Americas were diseases of the "old world" landmass of Europe, Africa, and Asia. The unique American commodities that crossed the ocean transformed diets not only in Europe and Africa but in Asia as well. Silver from American mines traveled to Europe, but it moved in equal amounts west across the Pacific, into Asian economies. Europeans who occupied and profited from territory in the Americas were similarly, and often more fully, engaged in commercial and extractive enterprises around the globe. But when measured in terms of the cumulative flow of people, commodities, political power, and religious ideas, the Atlantic constituted a coherent region for nearly four hundred years.

Like the earlier Mediterranean and Indian Ocean worlds, however, this coherence eventually gave way, and by the middle of the nineteenth century the greater Atlantic region was being drawn more fully into a world system, one increasingly linked by communication, commerce, ideology, and war. In some areas, there was substantial lagging and overlap. Slavery and abolition, so fundamental to Atlantic history as presented here, carried on as core concerns around the world. Atlantic-style European imperialism also blossomed in the late nineteenth century, and with it increasing interest in accumulating subject peoples and primary commodities. Industrialization eventually expanded beyond its northern Atlantic nucleus, generating new demands and desires. The case of sugar is illustrative of all these trends. The plant's journey from Southeast Asia to the Mediterranean via India and the Arabian Peninsula had taken millennia, but then on tiny islands such as Chios, about the time of Columbus, sugar was combined with slave labor and new technologies of milling and overseas transport. Once sugar was taken into the Atlantic, the plantation system took root wherever these factors could be combined, virtually defining the period covered by this book. But sugar did not stop there. Even before abolition in Cuba and Brazil, the plantation model—modified to accommodate free labor, steamships, and industrial-scale mills complete with railroads to the fields—was carried back around the world, into the Indian and Pacific Oceans.

In the same period, as Atlantic producers, laborers, and consumers confronted more emphatically the vagaries of world markets, the region's asymmetrical power relations shifted. European traders and diplomats had generally confronted Africa from a position of weakness, but in the nineteenth century we begin to see the transformation of that power dynamic. Europeans began to establish more settlements in Africa, and before the end of the century embarked on full-fledged conquests and occupations, claiming dominion over vast territories where they had once ventured only with the consent of local rulers. They were greatly helped by revolutions in life-saving and life-taking technologies. This new dynamic redirected Europe's imperial energies, once deployed west across the Atlantic to govern the Americas. Still, those old ties were not completely severed. In the wake of political realignments, Europeans tightened economic relations, particularly in Latin America. The difference was that the impetus came from Britain, not from the Iberian kingdoms that once ruled the region. The United States would eventually replace Britain as the dominant economic and political power in the Atlantic, then the world. Always fluid, the Atlantic world was redefined after the end of slavery by new imperial dynamics and new economic ties, even as its myriad peoples became more fully embedded in and shaped by global processes.

Selected Readings

Andrews, George Reid, *Afro-Latin America, 1800–2000* (New York: Oxford University Press, 2004).

Beckles, Hilary, *Black Rebellion in Barbados: The Struggle Against Slavery, 1627–1838* (Bridgetown: Antilles Publications, 1984).

Blackburn, Robin, *The Overthrow of Colonial Slavery, 1776–1848* (London: Verso, 1988).

Carretta, Vincent, *Equiano, the African: Biography of a Self-Made Man* (Athens: The University of Georgia Press, 2005).

Eltis, David, *Economic Growth and the Ending of the Transatlantic Slave Trade* (Oxford: Oxford University Press, 1987).

Emmer, P. C., *Colonialism and Migration: Indentured Labour Before and After Slavery* (Dordrecht: Martinus Nijhoff Publishers, 1986).

Hochschild, Adam, *Bury the Chains: Prophets and Rebels in the Fight to Free an Empire's Slaves* (Boston: Houghton Mifflin, 2005).

Holt, Thomas, *The Problem of Freedom: Race, Labor, and Politics in Jamaica and Britain, 1832–1939* (Baltimore: Johns Hopkins University Press, 1992).

Kale, Madhavi, *Fragments of Empire: Capital, Slavery, and Indian Indentured Labor Migration to the British Caribbean* (Philadelphia: University of Pennsylvania Press, 1998).

Miers, Suzanne, *Britain and the Ending of the Slave Trade* (New York: Africana Publishing Company, 1975).

Northrup, David, *Indentured Labor in the Age of Imperialism, 1834–1922* (New York: Cambridge University Press, 1995).

Oldfield, James, *Popular Politics and British Anti-Slavery: The Mobilisation of Public Opinion against the Slave Trade* (Manchester: Manchester University Press, 1995).

Sanneh, Lamin, *Abolitionists Abroad: American Blacks and the Making of Modern West Africa* (Cambridge: Harvard University Press, 2001).

Scott, Rebecca J., *Slave Emancipation in Cuba: The Transition to Free Labor, 1860–1899* (Princeton: Princeton University Press, 1985).

Temperley, Howard, ed., *After Slavery: Emancipation and Its Discontents* (London: Frank Cass, 2000).

Toplin, Robert Brent, *The Abolition of Slavery in Brazil* (New York: Atheneum, 1972).

Viotti da Costa, Emilia, *Crowns of Glory, Tears of Blood: The Demerara Slave Rebellion of 1823* (New York: Oxford University Press, 1994).

Walvin, James, *Making the Black Atlantic: Britain and the African Diaspora* (London: Blackwell, 2000).

Index

The Atlantic World: A History, 1400–1888
Developmental editor and copy editor: Andrew J. Davidson
Production editor: Lucy Herz
Proofreader: Claudia Siler
Photo editor: Linda Gaio
Cartographer: Jason Casanova, Pegleg Graphics
Indexer: Carol Roberts
Cover designer: Christopher Calvetti, c2it graphics
Printer: McNaughton & Gunn, Inc.